D1597452

Childhood in the Past Monograph Series: Volume 1

Childhood and Violence in the Western Tradition

Edited by

Laurence Brockliss
and
Heather Montgomery

Oxbow Books
Oxford and Oakville

Childhood in the Past Monograph Series

Volume 1: Childhood and Violence in the Western Tradition
           edited by Laurence Brockliss and Heather Montgomery

To Samuel James Chamberlain, born 12 January 2010
and
Antonio Seurat Montgomery, born 27 June 2009

May they never experience the violence that this world contains

Published by
Oxbow Books, Oxford

© Oxbow Books and the individual authors, 2010

ISBN 978-1-84217-978-9

This book is available direct from

Oxbow Books
Phone: 01865-241249; Fax: 01865-794449

and

The David Brown Book Company
PO Box 511, Oakville, CT 06779, USA
Phone: 860-945-9329; Fax: 860-945-9468

or from our website

www.oxbowbooks.com

A CIP record is available for this book from the British Library

Library of Congress Cataloging-in-Publication Data

Childhood and violence in the Western tradition / edited by Laurence Brockliss and Heather
Montgomery.
    p. cm. -- (Childhood in the past monograph series ; v. 1)
  Includes bibliographical references and index.
  ISBN 978-1-84217-978-9
 1. Children--History. 2. Child abuse--History. 3. Children--Violence against--History. 4. Child
rearing--History. 5. Children--Social conditions. 6. Civilization, Western--History. I. Brockliss,
L. W. B. II. Montgomery, Heather.
  HQ767.87.C4765 2010
  306.87409182'1--dc22
                        2010032838

Printed in Great Britain by
Short Run Press, Exeter

Contents

Preface

In early twenty-first century Britain the use of all forms of force, but especially physical violence, to bend another human being to one's will is generally deplored and increasingly deemed illegal. Adults are not supposed to strike one another and are permitted to use only minimal force in correcting children or defending themselves from attack. Children on the other hand are not expected to lash out at adults and certainly discouraged from hitting each other. The only arena where the use of violence, within limits, is still legitimate is on the sports field. We live then in the kind of state envisaged and promoted in the mid-seventeenth century by Thomas Hobbes in his *Leviathan* (1651). In theory, if not of course in fact, the use of violence is a state monopoly. Indeed, the analogy with the commonwealth of the *Leviathan* is all the more apt in that the Hobbesian utopia outlawed the private use of violence (except to save one's own life) within the state, but assumed that force would continue to be the normal way that states would settle their disputes with one another. It is a paradox of our modern world that the British and other western governments are intolerant of violent behaviour perpetrated by their own citizens, yet are ready to use, and seem relatively untroubled in using, physical force to impose their will on certain regimes around the globe that they feel are in some way a threat or simply behaving brutally and unjustly.

The state of the *Leviathan*, however, is a recent creation. It has admittedly been the case that in this country there has been a persistent commitment to restraining and reducing inter-personal violence since the creation of the English monarchy by the kings of Wessex. But until the modern era the state was primarily interested in outlawing and punishing its worst excesses: private armies, gang rapes, murder. Recourse to brawling and fisticuffs in response to slights or more material grievances were winked at as long as fighting did not degenerate into riot. Moreover, community norms were not enforced by agents of the state or even the instruments of local government but until the seventeenth century were at least partly upheld by self-appointed vigilantes. Above all, the use of physical force to police inferiors – children, wives, dependents, workers, common soldiers and sailors, and so on – was expected and completely approved of. In particular, the writ of the state seldom penetrated within the domestic interior. It is only in the second half of the twentieth century that the British state has taken a strong interest in battered wives and children who are physically abused in the home, and only in recent decades that the concept of violent behaviour has been extended to embrace mental as well as physical cruelty. In our modern culture of well-being and entitlement, violence can be done to an individual simply by deliberately withholding or removing an expectation.

What has happened over the last half century is that the boundary between the legitimate and illegitimate use of force has been significantly shifted. As a result, it appears as if our ancestors were extremely violent and vicious. Yet it must always be remembered that while they were in our terms they were not in their own. Just as much as we do, they differentiated between the legitimate and illegitimate use of force but they drew the boundary in different places. Wife-murder was unacceptable and therefore an act of violence; wife-beating was not. Just like us, too, our ancestors had a rationale for drawing the boundary where they did. It was not simply that the state was much smaller before the modern era and unable to police violence effectively. Its physical reach was certainly limited; it could never have begun to intrude into every corner of our lives, as it does today. But it did not want to. Both ruler and ruled shared a common conviction that the private use of physical force as an instrument of a social control was not just legitimate but essential, given the nature of human beings, as their world understood it. All men were corrupt and born to sin, but children, women, the lower orders and the destitute poor were more wilful and less rational, so had to be licked into shape. Our modern boundary line reflects a radically different, and to modern eyes, a more scientific, sensitive and positive way of thinking about humankind. It may be that people in the past were more prone to acts of violence than today: changes in standards of living, health and diet must have some role in how we behave. It is also the case that in a society where physical force is an acceptable form of chastisement and correction, there is a greater possibility of the boundary between the acceptable and the unacceptable being breached. But even if it can be shown that the murder rate in particular was higher in the pre-modern than in the modern world, this does not explain where the boundary was placed. What is deemed a legitimate or illegitimate use of physical force or how we define violence more broadly is principally generated by the way we explain the human condition: it cannot be divorced from contemporary theories of human purpose, physiology, psychology, and age and gender distinctions, for instance.

This present book is a contribution to our understanding of the cultural construction of violence in the particular context of adult-child relations. It is principally a study of things that parents and those *in loco parentis* have done to or demanded of infants and children in the past that most people in the West today would consider wrong or harmful and an abuse of adult power. It attempts both to make sense of these practices and to show how our own very different views of permissible behaviour arose. The emphasis throughout is on the existence of boundaries that were known to both adults and children. The book also shows how children have been given some sort of role in policing these boundaries, have been entrusted with using physical force themselves, and have found various violent and non-violent ways of finding solace when the codes were transgressed or their normal world destroyed through war, social upheaval, familial breakdown, or simply going to work outside the home. Thereby it aims to show that in the past, as in the present, children have not simply been victims but have been active and sometimes destructive agents. The book is specifically a study of child-rearing practices and ideas about childhood that were once deeply embedded in western civilisation but that the West has now turned its back on. It only deals in passing with child-rearing practices in other cultures. It covers some three millennia, extending in time from the pre-classical Mediterranean world to the present. It makes no claim to be a detailed and complete survey, but nor is it an overview. Rather, it is a pointillist survey, a series of period specific vignettes written by experts and knitted together into a coherent narrative by the two editors, a historian and an anthropologist. It is hoped that the result is a book that is scholarly and informative but also entertaining.

In preparing the book, the editors have incurred many debts. By far the most important is to the 34 contributors who made it possible. The book began as the first in a five-part cross-disciplinary seminar series run by the Oxford Centre for the

History of Childhood devoted to the historical exploration of aspects of childhood that are of particular interest and concern to present day policy makers, educationalists, paediatricians and child welfare professionals. Given the widespread impression conveyed by the media that Britain is awash with both violent parents and carers and feral children, childhood and violence seemed an obvious theme to explore. It was the success of the seminar that gave the editors the idea of creating a new type of book that was not simply a set of essays. Our thanks are owed first to the speakers who contributed to the original seminar and the subsequent one-day colloquium for without them the book would never have taken shape. However, only a dozen or so people were involved in the project in its initial stage. To produce the book as it stands, it was necessary to persuade many others to join the enterprise. To them is due special thanks. On our approaching them, they agreed willingly to take part in a somewhat bizarre literary experiment, wrote their short contribution in good time, and have borne with us patiently while we linked the different essays together, often playing about with their text in the process.

Secondly, we would like to thank the large number of libraries, museums, art galleries, societies, organisations and schools who have allowed us to publish images of paintings, artefacts, engravings, photographs and book illustrations in their collections. Thanks in particular go to the Bodleian Library, the British Museum, the National Gallery of Ireland, the Uffizi Museum Florence, the Musée Calvet Avignon, the Musée des Ursulines Mâcon, the Foundling Museum London, the National Maritime Museum London, the Museum of English Rural Life at the University of Reading (especially to Ollie Douglas and Guy Baxter), Bolton Libraries, Oldham Local Studies and Archives, the Adoption History Project at the University of Oregon, Marie Stopes International, the Staatsbibliothek Berlin, the Staatliche Graphische Sammlung Munich and the Art Gallery of Ontario Toronto. Thanks too go to Thames and Hudson for permission to reproduce images from *Hogarth. The Complete Engravings*, and to Andrew Chapman for allowing us to photograph illustrations from his copy of the third edition of *Oliver Twist*. Our thanks also go to John Drysdale, Julie Vatain, Catriona Kelly, Chrysanthi Gallou, Ellen Herman and Jane Eagan for the use of their personal photographs. We are further grateful to the governors and head teacher of Kingsmead School London for allowing us to publish a poem by one of their pupils. We are grateful in addition to Magdalen College Oxford and the Open University for supporting part of the cost of obtaining and publishing the illustrations.

Finally, we owe a real debt of gratitude to Clare Litt, Julie Gardiner, Tara Evans and the publications team at Oxbow Books. It required a leap of faith on their part to take on this book. We are extremely grateful for the enthusiasm that they have always evinced for the project; we acknowledge the great help they have given in putting this book together; we thank them warmly for the beautiful book they have produced; and hope fervently that *Childhood and Violence* will live up to the great commitment they have made.

Laurence Brockliss and Heather Montgomery
28 January 2010

Note

In order to distinguish between the words of the editors and those of the contributors we have used two different fonts. The editors' prose appears in Palatino Linotype while that of the contributors appears in Stone Serif.

List of Illustrations

Front Cover: George Cruikshank, '*Oliver plucks up spirit*', 1837, engraving. From Charles Dickens, *Oliver Twist*. Photograph by Jane Eagan. With kind permission of Andrew Chapman. In Dickens's novel *Oliver Twist*, the eponymous hero fresh from the workhouse is apprenticed to an undertaker. Noah Claypole, an older boy in the service of the undertaker, proceeds to make Oliver's life a misery. When Claypole casts aspersions on Oliver's parentage, Oliver responds in time-honoured fashion: he thrashes his tormentor.

Back Cover: Orazio Gentileschi, *David and Goliath*, c. 1600. David's defeat of Goliath reminds us that children have never just been victims; they have frequently been powerful and aggressive actors. David is the prototype of the boy soldier who wins the applause of his elders for his performance on the battlefield: by using a childish skill, he defeats a powerful and wicked adult. He is also an innocent shepherd boy who prefigures Christ in overcoming evil. Gentileschi (1563-1639) was a friend and follower of Caravaggio.

List of Contributors

SAUL BECKER
School of Sociology and Social Policy
University of Nottingham (Social Policy)

LAURENCE BROCKLISS
Magdalen College and Faculty of History
Oxford University (History)

JOHN CARDWELL
Curator, Royal Commonwealth Society
    Collections
University Library
Cambridge University (History)

SALLY CRAWFORD
Institute of Archaeology
Oxford University (Archaeology)

STEPHEN CRETNEY
All Souls College and Faculty of Law
Oxford University (Law)

ELISABETH DUTTON
Worcester College and Faculty of English
Oxford University (English)

HEATHER ELLIS
Centre for British Studies
Humboldt University
Berlin (History)

JULIANE FÜRST
Department of History
University of Bristol (History)

ADRIAN GREGORY
Pembroke College and Faculty of History
Oxford University (History)

THE REVD CANON DR JAMES FRANCIS
Cranmer Hall, St John's College
Durham (Theology)

CHRYSANTHI GALLOU
Department of Archaeology
University of Nottingham (Archaeology)

JANE HUMPHRIES
All Souls College and Faculty of History
Oxford University (History)

CATRIONA KELLY
New College and Faculty of Modern
    Languages
Oxford University (Russian)

NIGEL KENNELL
formerly American School of Classical
    Studies at Athens (Classics)

MARTIN INGRAM
Brasenose College and Faculty of History
Oxford University (History)

ELLIE LEE
School of Social Policy, Sociology and Social
    Research
Kent University (Social Policy)

ALYSA LEVENE
Department of History
Oxford Brookes University (History)

HENRIETTA LEYSER
St Peter's College and Faculty of History
Oxford University (History)

PAWEL MACIEJKO
Interdisciplinary Research Center in Jewish
    Studies
The Hebrew University of Jerusalem (History)

DAVID MASKELL
Oriel College and Faculty of Modern
    Languages
Oxford University (French)

JOSEPHINE MCDONAGH
Department of English
King's College, University of London (English)

HEATHER MONTGOMERY
Faculty of Education and Language Studies
The Open University (Social Anthropology)

ANJA MÜLLER
Department of English
Otto-Friedrich-Universität Bamberg (English)

ROSEMARY PEACOCKE
Early Years Education Consultant (Education)

LYNDAL ROPER
Balliol College and Faculty of History
Oxford University (History)

ALAN ROSS
University of Göttingen (History)

GEORGE ROUSSEAU
Centre for the History of Childhood
Oxford University (English)

KIERON SHEEHY
Faculty of Education and Language Studies
The Open University (Psychology)

NICOLA SHELDON
Institute of Historical Research
University of London (History)

ALEXANDRA SHEPARD
Department of History
University of Glasgow (History)

HEATHER SHORE
School of Cultural Studies
Leeds Metropolitan University (History)

NICHOLAS STARGARDT
Magdalen College and Faculty of History
Oxford University (History)

FRANCESCA STAVRAKOPOULOU
Department of Theology and Religion
University of Exeter (Theology)

ABIGAIL WILLS
formerly Brasenose College and Faculty of
    History
Oxford University (History)

Introduction

Laurence Brockliss and Heather Montgomery

Purpose and Range

At the beginning of the twenty-first century the media and the different agencies of central and local government who look after the welfare and safety of children would have us believe that modern British society is awash with irresponsible, cruel and homicidal parents and carers. Unmarried mothers go off on holiday and leave their children to fend for themselves; married middle-class mothers stifle their babies in their cots; fathers from all sections of society beat their sons and sexually abuse their daughters; children in care are assaulted and purportedly killed by people entrusted by the state and charities to look after them; while guardians and relatives in immigrant communities starve and maltreat their charges to free them from the clutches of the devil.[1] Although there may be disagreement as to the true extent of violence and neglect, there appears to be a consensus that a problem exists and a tendency for police, social workers, doctors and teachers to suspect the worst.[2] At the same time, due to some horrific cases of abuse, ignored or mishandled by the social services, there is a concurrent distrust by parents of state agencies and those who work in them.

It would be unjust to the thousands of childcare professionals in this country and elsewhere who dedicate their lives to the welfare of the young to dismiss the present obsession with the bad parent as the inevitable result of the ever-increasing intrusion of the state and the law into the family home in the twenty-first century. There are clearly appalling acts of neglect and brutality committed by some parents and carers, as the cases of Victoria Climbié and, more recently, Baby 'P' have revealed.[3] It would be fair to say, however, that the growing belief that parenting is a skill which needs to be taught and that bad parenting is closely associated with social deprivation has created a visible pool of inadequate parents and carers who need to be closely watched by the child services, all

---

[1] Virtually every day instances of cruelty and neglect are reported in the British press. According to *The Times* four children a week die as a result of the way they are treated at home (19 Oct. 2008, p. 1.)

[2] In 2008, 29,820 children in England were judged to be at risk from their home environment and placed on the child protection register. In Scotland the figures were 2,437, in Northern Ireland 2,071 and in Wales, 2,320. Figures from http://www.nspcc.org.uk/Inform/factsandfigures/statistics/child_protection_register_statistics_wda48723.html (accessed 28 Aug. 2009).

[3] Victoria Climbié from the Ivory Coast, aged eight, died in Haringay, London, in 2000, from neglect and abuse by her guardians, who were her great-aunt and her great-aunt's partner. The abuse had been ignored and misdiagnosed by the local child protection and welfare agencies: http://www.victoria-climbie inquiry.org.uk (accessed 22 May 2009). Despite the author of this report, Lord Laming, calling for improved safeguards and more integrated services, the case of Peter Connelly, 'Baby P', who, aged seventeen months and living in the same borough as Victoria, was abused and killed by his mother, her partner and his brother in 2007, revealed further shortcomings in the care provided to children. This case occasioned a further report from Lord Laming, *The Protection of Children in England: A Progress Report* (London: HMSO, 2009).

the more that the archetype of the bad parent was developed at the very time it apparently became much easier to detect physical and sexual abuse.[4] It would also be fair to say that childcare professionals have taken little interest in the history of parent-child violence and neglect, except to assume that bad parenting, like the poor, has been always with us, that it began to be exposed by late Victorian philanthropy, and that it has now finally been made visible through the grace of state paternalism.[5]

This book is an attempt to historicise our contemporary understanding of abusive parenting by examining the distance between our own conceptions of normative parenting and those of the past. Moving from the Judaic and Graeco-Roman origins of European civilisation to the present, it examines historically attitudes to a number of parenting practices which today would be considered beyond or near the edge of the pale. Thereby, it aims to clarify what, as Europeans, are our core and long-term cultural assumptions of improper parental behaviour and what are much more recent constructs. It is a work of history, but it is also a contribution to today's debate about parenting. To the extent it moves outside the family, it does so only in regard to individuals and institutions placed *in loco parentis* when children, either permanently or on a daily basis, were removed from their home environment to live, work or learn.

Violence, like childhood, is a loaded term, and to couple them is to invite a strong emotional reaction. However it is the belief of the editors that by examining the ways in which peoples in the past have understood childhood and consequently how they have treated children, it becomes easier to see the changing relationship between violence and children, as well as the links between parents, the state and the child. These are not natural phenomena but social, historical and cultural constructs that have not always had the attention paid to them that they deserve. Once our contemporary concern about abusive parenting is placed in an historical perspective, the dimensions of the problem will be better understood. Because at present the worst is always suspected on the grounds that everything is possible and must be continually expected, the best intentioned can easily misread ambiguous signs, spread panic and encourage witch-hunts, as appears to have happened in the recent spate of cases of mothers accused of harming their babies to bring attention upon themselves.[6] The study of a phenomenon over time will, at the very least, identify whether certain types of behaviour deemed deviant today have been cultural commonplaces in European civilisation over the long term. If such behaviour has been historically exceptional, then either it is unlikely to be widespread in the present, or, if it is, then it can only be the result of peculiar contemporary circumstances. Either way, historical knowledge should help childcare professionals to assess and deal with the problem.

---

[4] A sure diagnosis of physical abuse was described for the first time in C. H. Kempe, F. N. Silverman, B. F. Steele, W. Droegemueller and H. K. Silver, 'The Battered Child Syndrome', *Journal of the American Medical Association*, 181:1 (1962), 17–24. See also C. H. Kempe and R. E. Helfer *The Battered Child*, 3rd edn (Chicago: University of Chicago Press, 1980). Identifying sexual abuse remains more problematic as the question marks raised against the diagnoses of Dr Marietta Higgs in Cleveland, based on the anal dilation reflex test in the early 1990s demonstrate: see D. P. H. Jones, *Communicating with Vulnerable Children. A Guide to Practitioners* (London: Gaskell, 2003), ch. 3. The Cleveland case is put in historical perspective in H. Hendrick, *Child Welfare: Historical Dimensions, Contemporary Debates* (Bristol: The Policy Press, 2003), pp. 194–96.
[5] Cf. the lecture given at Dartington Hall by the Children's Commissioner for England, paediatrician, Professor Albert Aynsley-Green, *Do ye hear the children weeping, O my brothers, Ere the sorrow comes with years* (Nottingham, 2003).
[6] So-called Munchausen's Syndrome by Proxy. Paediatricians in the late 1990s, notably Dr Roy Meadow in Birmingham, became convinced that this syndrome was common among new mothers and several women whose babies had died unexpectedly were found guilty of murder. Since then a number of judgements have been overturned and other cases are still being contested. A useful introduction to the campaign is B. Beech and J. Robinson, 'Child Protection: Consumer Voices', unpublished paper, 2004, prepared on behalf of the Association for the Improvement in the Maternity Services (AIMS).

The book is specifically a study of what we would today deem to be violence, neglect or exploitation. Although we use the term child abuse as a short-hand throughout the book, it is these three categories to which we are referring, and its aim is to show how historically subjective and contested these terms are. The book does not discuss child sexual abuse. While the physical and sexual abuse of children are frequently lumped together, and it is easy with our modern categories to associate violence with sex and vice versa, the two have very different histories. As the book will show, and try to explain, many parenting practices that we today would consider cruel and counter-productive were accepted as normal until the very recent past. On the other hand, the sexual abuse of children, if very much brushed under the carpet before the late-twentieth century and not treated, as is the case today, as the ultimate betrayal, has never ever been condoned in the Christian era by the authorities.[7]

The range and content of the book will be explored more fully in the following pages. First, our use of the terms childhood and child abuse will be carefully defined. Not only are these slippery, for the boundaries of both are culture specific – they would resonate differently in the ears of a European and a non-European – but even within the west their meaning is not stable but has evolved considerably over the last 50 years. The idea of child abuse in particular is highly elastic and needs to be clarified at the outset. Secondly, the focus of the book will be related to the broader historiography. The history of childhood has mushroomed into a recognisable sub-discipline since the 1960s but surprisingly little attention has been paid to the theme of violence and neglect in parent-child relations. The book's legitimacy as a historical work stems from the fact that this is an under-studied area of the history of childhood. Thirdly, the structure of the book is explained. This, it will be seen, is a novel work in its organisation as much as in its content. In order to produce a book which makes a genuine attempt to explore the theme of violence, neglect and exploitation across two and a half millennia, it has been necessary to knit together the knowledge of a large number of scholars. It is not a multi-authored work, nor a series of discrete essays, but more a series of connected readings.

What is a child?

It would be possible to spend an entire book dealing with the vexed questions of what, or who, is a child? To define a child by a contemporary definition, that the term refers to anyone under the age of eighteen, is clearly inadequate when discussing childhoods across such a vast time frame.[8] One of the insights that historical studies (as well as those from anthropology and sociology) have brought to understandings of childhood is the impossibility of defining childhood simply by age.[9] To decide that childhood runs from

---

[7] Child-adult sexual relations in their various physical and non-physical manifestations through the ages are dealt with in G. Rousseau (ed.), *Children and Sexuality: From the Greeks to the Great War* (Basingstoke: Palgrave-Macmillan, 2007).

[8] A child is anyone under eighteen in most current international and national law and is enshrined in the United Nations Convention on the Rights of the Child, article 1: http://www.unhchr.ch/html/menu3/b/k2crc. htm (accessed 20 Nov. 2008).

[9] Not only is the cut off point of eighteen highly problematic but so is the starting point. When childhood begins, as well as when it ends, is always a matter of social construction and negotiation and is not consistent within, let alone across, societies. The UNCRC fudges the issues. The preamble states that 'the child needs special safeguards and care, including appropriate legal protection, before as well as after birth' but it does not enshrine this as a legal right in the Convention as it would be unacceptable to those states that allow abortion. Indeed on signing the Convention the UK explicitly stated that it 'interprets the Convention as applicable only following a live birth'. J. Fortin, *Children's Rights and the Developing Law* (Cambridge: Cambridge University Press, 2003), p. 38, fn. 50. The UK government takes the position that childhood starts at birth and only at this point does a child has full legal protection and rights. Other states, and indeed individuals within the

nought to eighteen is to impose a modern, western straightjacket on studying children which denies the realities of many children's lives, both past and present, where young people have married, become parents, run their own households, and worked for several years before they turned eighteen. Such a definition also ignores historical realities where children or young people were still considered minors well after the age of eighteen. Under Roman law, for instance, childhood may have formally ended when the toga was assumed at puberty, but a father was still allowed (and expected) to punish his children until the age of 25 and his son was not considered formally emancipated until his father had died.[10] In contemporary society, many parents continue to fund their children well into their twenties or even thirties, paying for their university education, allowing them to live rent-free at home after university and helping them buy their first homes. This has allowed newspapers to coin a new phrase, 'the boomerang generation' to describe those young people who repeatedly leave home but return for monetary reasons and who remain, therefore, financially and socially dependent on their parents well into adulthood.[11]

This problem is further compounded by the fact that there are at least two meanings of the word 'child'. Firstly it can refer to anyone legally designated as a child: that is anyone under the age of eighteen. Secondly it refers to a relationship so that someone, no matter how old, is the 'child of' someone else. It is possible to be an adult-child, both in the sense (as in Roman law) of a legal minor and as a statement of relationship. Often however the word child is ambiguous and must be qualified with further adjectives such as 'young' child, 'nursery' child or 'school' child. One of the most difficult issues in editing this book was drawing meaningful boundaries which encompass the entire age range of childhood without anachronistically claiming some groups as children when neither they nor their contemporaries would have seen them as so. Referring to a seventeen-year-old apprentice in eighteenth-century France as a child is clearly problematic – although he could not be called an adult in any meaningful sense either.[12] The contributors to his volume therefore have generally used the term children to refer to young children and the word adolescent when discussing the experiences of children past puberty or around the ages of twelve or thirteen. There are no hard and fast rules, however, and we are careful not to offer any definitive categorisations or to draw the boundaries too tightly or too arbitrarily.

In this we are following the theorisation coming out of Childhood Studies which argues that, while the idea of a childhood bounded by chronology is a useful shorthand for policy makers, who must draw the line somewhere, childhood is best analysed as a social, cultural and temporal construct which cannot be understood as a universal given or a fixed entity.[13] In 1955, Margaret Mead and her colleague Martha Wolfenstein could write confidently that children 'walk in a world where adults are taller, much taller than they, pygmies among giants, ignorant among the knowledgeable, wordless among the articulate ... And to the adults, children everywhere represent something weak and helpless, in need of protection, supervision, training, models, skills, beliefs, "character"'.[14] By the beginning of the twenty-first century, such a universal, biologically based view of childhood seems completely outdated, both in its understanding of children as weak, dependent and passive and also in its view that all children can be understood within a single framework which takes no

UK, disagree very strongly.
[10] P. Stein, *Roman Law in European History* (Cambridge: Cambridge University Press, 1999), p. 7.
[11] See for instance, A. Akwagyiram, 'Bit of a Crowd in the Empty Nest', *The Guardian*, 20 Jan. 2004.
[12] Cf. what is said below about the childhood and adolescence of an eighteenth-century Parisian French glazier, called Jacques-Louis Ménétra: Ch. 3, pp. 122–27; Ch. 5, pp. 219 and 225.
[13] H. Montgomery, 'Childhood in Time and Place', in M. Woodhead and H. Montgomery (eds), *Understanding Childhood: An Interdisciplinary Approach* (Chichester: John Wiley, 2003).
[14] M. Mead and M. Wolfenstein (eds), *Childhood in Contemporary Cultures* (Chicago: University of Chicago Press, 1955), pp. 6–7.

account of the historical, social, political, economic or cultural circumstances in which they live. Furthermore, the idea of childhood as a homogeneous category is problematic; studies of children's lives have shown very distinctly that girls have very different childhoods to boys, first born children to third born, poor children to rich ones, and so on.[15]

Rather than setting fixed chronological or biological boundaries between childhood, adolescence and adulthood, this book understands these categories as stages in life characterised by biological growth and imposed social immaturity and by social and familial powerlessness. This is not to imply that children are socially incompetent or have not acted as independent agents in their lives: much recent literature within Childhood Studies shows the very real degree of control that children exercise over their own lives and their importance in shaping their families and societies.[16] In Europe's past too, it is clear that older children have had the capacity to display an impressive degree of independence, even in hierarchical and conformist societies.[17] It is impossible to talk about violence or abuse, however, without acknowledging the large power differentials between adults and children and the ways in which parents, and those *in loco parentis*, deploy that power.[18] In this regard an interesting fissure has opened up between childhood studies and gender studies. When second wave feminists such as Shulamith Firestone first turned their attention to children, they viewed them as a burden on women's time and a threat to women's autonomy, the 'heart of women's oppression is her childbearing and childrearing role'.[19] Children were women's problem, never their allies, even though they were symbolically and practically linked and, in terms of access to power and influence, in 'the same lousy boat'.[20] As scholars began to look more closely at children's lives, however, this emphasis shifted so that the division was not between men and women (and their children) but between adults and children. The battle was not one of gender but of generation.[21] Women and children were seen as occupying very different social positions and, perhaps more importantly, women were understood as being as likely to oppress or exploit children as men.[22]

---

[15] See, for example, B. Mayall (ed.), *Children's Childhoods: Observed and Experienced* (London: The Falmer Press, 1994); F. Waksler, 'Studying Children: Phenomenological Insights', in F. Waksler (ed.), *Studying the Social Worlds of Children: Sociological Readings* (London: The Falmer Press, 1991); A. James and A. Prout, *Constructing and Reconstructing Childhood*, 2nd edn (Basingstoke: Falmer Press, 1998).

[16] A. West, 'Power Relationships and Adult Resistance to Children's Participation', *Children Youth and Environment*, 17:1 (2007), 123–35.

[17] The most obvious example is their role in the Children's Crusade of 1212. Although historians today reject the traditional view that the bands of pilgrims who left northern Germany to take ship for the Holy Land and the huge flock of people who descended on Paris in the same year were solely comprised of children, it is clear that there were many teenage boys and girls, as well as young unmarried men in their midst. The leader of the Paris band was a twelve-year-old shepherd boy called Stephen of Cloyes. Moved by the church's propaganda and unnerved by the failure of the elite to recapture Jerusalem, young peasants seem to have taken it upon themselves to perform the task. For an introduction, see C. Tyerman, *God's War. A New History of the Crusades* (London: Penguin, 2007), pp. 607–11.

[18] S. Firestone, *The Dialectic of Sex* (London: Jonathan Cape, 1971), p. 79.

[19] *Ibid.*, p. 102.

[20] J. E. Korbin (ed.), *Child Abuse and Neglect. Cross Cultural Perspectives* (Berkeley: University of California Press, 1981), ch. 1.

[21] A. Oakley, 'Women and Children First and Last: Parallels and Differences between Children's and Women's Studies', in B. Mayall (ed.), *Children's Childhoods: Observed and Experienced* (London: Falmer Press, 1994).

[22] The field is now a large one but some of the early pioneers were C. Hardman, 'Can There be an Anthropology of Children?', *Journal of the Anthropological Society of Oxford*, 4:2 (1973), 85–99; M. Bluebond-Langer, *The Private Worlds of Dying Children* (Princeton: Princeton University Press, 1978); J. La Fontaine (ed.), *Sex and Age as Principles of Social Differentiation* (London: Athlone Press, 1978); J. La Fontaine, 'An Anthropological Perspective on Children in Social Worlds', in M. Richards and P. Light (eds), *Children of Social Worlds* (Cambridge: Polity Press, 1986); A. James, *Childhood Identities: Self and Social Relationship in the Experience of the Child* (Edinburgh: Edinburgh University Press, 1993).

Another way of understanding childhood is by examining the processes by which social personhood is conferred. In many instances, childhood is a time whereby the young gradually become fully part of society and are socialised and integrated into it. Childhood is the time of learning to become a full social person and, while children need not be seen as incomplete or incompetent adults, they are rarely granted the same status as adult members of the same society. One of the few generalisations that can be safely made is that all societies, both historical and contemporary ones, acknowledge that there are differences between adults and children. However, it is the social meanings that are given to these differences which need to be examined and which provide the focus of historical, anthropological and sociological research. The transfer from childhood to adulthood, it must be emphasised, is always stadial. Even in modern British society, the idea of childhood ending suddenly at the age of eighteen is a bureaucratic fiction when young people can marry, be held legally responsible, own property and so on from an earlier age.

Inspired by the 1989 United Nations Convention on the Rights of the Child (UNCRC), the novel idea of a child as an autonomous, rights-bearing citizen has begun to emerge. This global child, with legally enshrined rights to protection, provision and participation is held up as a universal model for all childhoods, regardless of circumstances. Yet this idealised vision of what childhood should be like has also been heavily contested, most notably by the USA which is the only country in the world (other than Somalia) to refuse to ratify the Convention, arguing that children's rights are best protected within, and by, their families. Even those countries which have ratified the Convention (and it remains the most widely ratified convention in history) have often been less than vigilant in ensuring that children's rights are actually enforced.

Within the social sciences this new vision of childhood has caused a noticeable shift in studies of childhood, especially in the use of children as informants and as the central participants in research. By the 1990s children's lived experiences, as described by children themselves, had become the focus of many studies. This way of examining childhood and children's lives was seen as a corrective to the previous neglect; supporting the notion that a child's perspectives and understandings should be taken seriously and rejecting the idea that children were in any way incomplete or incompetent. This new perspective entailed changing the emphasis within studies of childhood from socialisation, and how parents raised their children, to how children themselves perceived their lives, surroundings, parents and upbringing.[23] Taking children themselves as a starting point meant that they could no longer be seen as a homogenous group with views and priorities that depended only on their physical advancement. This form of child-centred research firmly rejected the idea that because children's roles were impermanent, they were also unimportant. Furthermore it reflected a recognition that children possessed agency and that they could, and did, influence their own lives, the lives of their peers and that of the wider community around them.[24]

What is violence, neglect or exploitation?

The abuse of children cannot be separated from issues of power and the relative vulnerability of children. Indeed, one of the threads running through this book is that violence is usually

---

[23] In this, of course, anthropologists maintain one great advantage over historians in their sources. They may worry over the best ways of researching children or conveying an authentic child voice, but at least they can interview them, discuss their findings with them and reflect their own observations about their lives. The true voice of the child in history remains frustratingly oblique.

[24] Waksler, 'Studying Children'; V. Morrow, 'Invisible Children? Toward a Re-conceptualisation of Childhood Dependency and Responsibility', *Sociological Studies of Children*, 7 (1995), 207–30.

inflicted by the powerful on the weak, be they midshipmen, apprentices or children. As children begin to be envisaged as equals, or rights-bearers, and family relationships are idealised less in terms of hierarchies, so the issue of child abuse, and the question of appropriate and inappropriate use of force, becomes more problematic. It is a subject that generates much controversy with some claiming that fears of child abuse are actually out of proportion to the risks faced by children,[25] others claiming that it is under-reported and still shrouded in secrecy.[26] Actual definitions of child abuse are also contested, so that, in some instances, emotional abuse, or exposure to cigarette smoke, are also claimed as forms of abuse.[27] Nevertheless, there can be no doubt that in the present day uncovering child abuse has become a primary western concern, and one that has been exported to other parts of the world as they become increasingly westernised.[28] James, Jenks and Prout sum this up succinctly:

> The phenomenon of child abuse has emerged as a malign and exponential growth towards the conclusion of the twentieth century not because of any significant alteration in the pattern of behavior towards children but because of the changing patterns of personal, political and moral control in social life more generally. These have, in turn, affected our vision of childhood. Whereas an antique vision of the child rendered abuse unseen or unintelligible, modernity has illuminated mistreatment and highlighted the necessity of care.[29]

In order to examine the childcare practices of the past without either demonising parents on the one hand, or taking a position of extreme cultural, or historical, relativism on the other, it is important to use a structure which differentiates between forms of violence so that what is acceptable or not can be understood within its context. While various forms of harsh treatment may be seen as totally unacceptable to a modern audience it is hard to label them as abusive *per se* if they were judged fair and reasonable within the society within which they occurred. Anthropologist Jill Korbin has provided such a framework which differentiates between three types of practices which need to be untangled in discussions of violence and abuse. The first category she examines is that of cultural practices such as initiation or beatings which may seem harsh, unnecessary and even abusive to outsiders, but which are deemed culturally necessary and have the full approval of the community. Her second category is the idiosyncratic or individual maltreatment of a child, carried out against cultural norms and almost always condemned. The third type of abuse she identifies is the social or structural abuse of children, where children as a group are targeted, or when they suffer distinctive consequences as a result of poverty, ill health or social neglect.[30]

The first type of practice Korbin identifies is that which is frowned upon or condemned in one culture, or at one period of time, but not in another. It is not difficult to find examples from both historical and ethnographic accounts of what appear to be extremely painful and physically and mentally harmful practices inflicted on children, such as elongating babies' heads, scarification, neck stretching, foot binding, tattooing, ear piercing or other bodily

---

[25] J. Best, *Threatened Children: Rhetoric and Concern about Child Victims* (Chicago: Chicago University Press, 1990).

[26] W. Stainton Rogers, D. Hevey and E. Ash, *Child Abuse and Neglect* (London: Batsford, 1989).

[27] The NSPCC for instance, defines emotional abuse as 'when a parent or carer behaves in a way that is likely to seriously affect their child's emotional development. It can range from constant rejection and denial of affection, through to continual severe criticism, deliberate humiliation and other ways of verbally "terrorising" a child'. http://www.nspcc.org.uk/HelpAndAdvice/WhatChildAbuse/EmotionalAbuse/emotionalabuse_wda36358.html (accessed 22 May 2009).

[28] R. Goodman, *Children of the Japanese State* (Oxford: Oxford University Press, 2000).

[29] A. James, C. Jenks and A. Prout, *Theorizing Childhood*, (Cambridge: Polity Press, 1998), pp. 152–53.

[30] J. E. Korbin, 'Anthropological Contributions to the Study of Child Abuse', *Child Abuse and Neglect: The International Journal*, 1:1 (1977), 7–24.

modifications. One of the most emotive examples of these is female circumcision (called by some female genital mutilation as a way of emphasising its abusive nature). Often carried out on very young girls, it is immensely painful and, it is claimed, can affect a woman's later sexual health.[31] Yet, although painful and sometimes having life long effects, it is hard to argue that these body modifications constitute abuse. They are carried out, not to inflict injury or harm, but to mark out membership of a community and culture and within that setting they are culturally sanctioned.[32]

The second type of abuse concerns behaviours that are outside the range of acceptable practices within cultures and socially acknowledged as such. Abuse, in this second category, is carried out on an individual and idiosyncratic basis and is likely to cause a child serious harm. In modern Britain sexual abuse or severe beatings would fall into this category, although whether or not other practices can also be defined as abuse is heavily contested, as the issue of physical discipline shows. It is still permissible to hit a child in England, based on an 1860 law which allowed parents to discipline their children using 'reasonable chastisement'. What was reasonable was never accurately defined, however, and remains the subject of much debate in national, and more recently, European courts of law. As of 2005, any punishment which causes visible bruising, grazes, scratches, minor swellings or cuts is outlawed, although smacking, if it does not leave a mark, is not.[33] Nevertheless, there is an understanding that while some forms of hitting may be considered acceptable to some, others, such as beating a child unconscious, or hitting with an implement, or indeed, hitting the very young is unacceptable and abusive. The important point, however, is not the moment at which the pain is too great, or the beating too severe, but the deviation from the cultural norm.

The third kind of abuse in Korbin's typology is that caused by social or structural factors rather than by individuals. This is the social and economic form of child abuse, typified by poverty, hunger, social inequality, poor health, war and by governmental policy. It is rarely referred to as child abuse and in affluent western countries there is a much greater emphasis placed on the behaviour of individual parents, or more sensationally, on the dangers posed by strangers and outsiders, than on the collective responsibility that a wealthy society has to its youngest members. Many studies point to the special vulnerabilities of children in the face of poverty or violence. Others discuss the disproportionate affect that social problems such as racism, violent neighbourhoods, environmental pollution or nuclear testing have on children. All of these studies acknowledge that while individual pathology plays a part in the mistreatment and abuse of children, it is the wider social forces which can have the most devastating impact on children's lives.[34]

---

[31] N. Sa'dawii, *The Hidden Face of Eve: Women in the Arab World* (London: Zed Books, 1989). For a discussion of the impacts of this practice see F. S. Ahmadu and R. A. Shweder, 'Disputing the Myth of the Sexual Dysfunction of Circumcised Women: An interview with Fuambai S. Ahmadu by Richard A. Shweder', *Anthropology Today*, 25:6 (2009), 14–17.

[32] It should be borne in mind too that historians of medicine have begun to realise that pain itself is a relative concept, so that initiation practices may not be as burdensome to the initiates as outsiders suppose: see R. Rey, *The History of Pain* (English trans.; Cambridge: Harvard University Press, 1993).

[33] In May 2009, a devout Christian father of three was sentenced to 27 months in prison for using a horsewhip on his children aged between seven and twelve. He defended himself by declaring that he was trying to be a good father by disciplining the children in order to teach them the difference between right and wrong. The judge however jailed him for assault and cruelty. *The Daily Telegraph*, 18 May 2009. http://www. telegraph.co.uk/news/newstopics/politics/lawandorder/5343126/Father-jailed-for-horsewhipping-children. html (accessed 22 May 2009).

[34] 'The "choice" of child abuse as a master social problem of our times, also includes a strong "choice" for only certain forms of child abuse – battering and sexual abuse – and a selective inattention to other forms – specifically poverty-related neglect. This selective inattention is a consequence of the need to deny the role of our punitive public policies in contributing to the "feminization of poverty", and to the problem of childhood mortality in our inner-city, minority neighbourhoods.' N. Scheper-Hughes and H. Stein, 'Child

Historiography

The modern history of western childhood begins with Philippe Ariès's publication of *L'enfant et la vie familiale sous l'ancien régime* in 1960.[35] In this work Ariès (1914–84) argued that a concept of childhood had been largely lacking in the middle ages. Although medieval texts distinguished between infancy (nought to seven), childhood (seven to fourteen) and adolescence (fourteen to 21 or older), these divisions had little meaning in practice: once an infant could walk and talk, it immediately entered the world of adults. It was only from about 1500, he believed, that a modern understanding of childhood began to develop, as adults slowly started to value children for their own sake and sought to give them a separate identity. Modern childhood was the construction of the period 1400–1700, the era of the Renaissance and Reformation, in which a new view of human dignity, civility and self-control was forged and Roman Christendom was split into two warring camps. Relying on a rich mixture of visual sources, advice books and memoirs, Ariès concluded that the key century was the seventeenth. This century, he insisted, saw the emergence of a specific costume for the under-sevens, specific children's games and toys, and the promotion of the belief that the young should be sheltered from adult sexuality. At the same time, Protestant and Catholic moralists were increasingly insistent that all over-sevens should not be immediately thrust into the adult world of work but sent to school where they would be turned into disciplined servants of Christ.

For Ariès the valorisation of universal schooling was the most important milestone on the road to the creation of the modern child. Pre-1500 schools and universities had primarily been the training-ground of the clergy and had not been age-specific: if and when an opportunity arose for entering the church, then and only then would the neophyte engage in institutionalised study. By the eighteenth century, however, it was widely held that the laity as well as the clergy, and the poor as well as the rich, should have had some form of education. It was belief thereafter increasingly taken up by the state for its own less spiritual ends, and in the modern industrial era the number of years that were to be spent in school steadily lengthened. By the time Ariès was writing, few children in western Europe could enter the adult world before they were fifteen, and in most countries complete immersion for young men was only possible after they had completed a period of national (usually military) service in the years following their eighteenth birthday.[36]

Ariès maintained that the creation and diffusion of the modern idea of childhood went hand in hand with the development of two other significant social developments. The first was the invention of the modern family. There may have been affection in the medieval family but the institution was not organised in a manner likely to encourage the close supervision of the young. Family life was community life: there was little distinction between public and private, and children, boys and girls, were commonly (so he asserted) sent away from the family home at a young age (seven to nine) to live and work with relatives or neighbours. The Renaissance and Reformations eras, however, saw the emergence of a new idea of the nuclear family where parents and children took a delight in each other's company and steadily cut themselves off from the outside world. In the modern age, the very public Twelfth Night festivities were finally replaced by the family Christmas. The second development was the rise of the bourgeoisie. Ariès believed that the modern concepts of

---

Abuse and the Unconscious', in N. Scheper-Hughes (ed.), *Child Survival. Anthropological Perspectives on the Treatment and Maltreatment of Children* (Dordrecht: D. Reidel, 1987), p. 353.
[35] P. Ariès, *L'enfant et la vie familiale sous l'ancien régime* (Paris: Plon, 1960); translated into English as *Centuries of Childhood* (Harmondsworth: Penguin, 1962).
[36] The establishment of systems of universal mass education in Europe and many other parts of the world on the eve of the First World War is the subject of L. W. B. Brockliss and N. Sheldon (eds), *Mass Education and the Limits of State Building*, c. *1870–1930* (Basingstoke: Palgrave Macmillan, forthcoming).

childhood and the family initially took root among the urban well-to-do. In the early modern world, the mercantile and professional classes alone had the wealth and the kind of value-system that was needed for these ideas to flourish. The growing power of the bourgeoisie in the centuries before the French Revolution, therefore, and its eventual dominance in the industrial era guaranteed that the new concepts would become the norm.

In this regard, then, Ariès might seem typical of the *marxisant* historians who dominated French early modern historiography in the two decades following the Second World War and who saw the middle-classes as the motor of modernity. But in other respects, he was very different. In many ways, he was an amateur historian. Although trained as a historian at the Sorbonne in the 1930s, he never held an academic post until near the end of his life, when he joined the École des Hautes Études in 1978, the prestigious Parisian research institute. In addition, he was on the right rather than the left, having supported Action Française as a student and having held a teaching post under the Vichy Regime.[37] Understandably, as a result, he wore his historical materialism lightly. One of the least satisfactory elements of the book is the absence of a carefully articulated explanation for the changes he describes. His emphasis on the seventeenth century would suggest that he believed that the most important influence on the creation of a new idea of childhood and the family in France (the primary centre of his interest) was the Counter-Reformation. On the other hand, since he finds the first signs of change as early as the twelfth century, he presumably locates the genesis of the development in a much earlier period of cultural renewal.[38] At no point, though, are the vectors of change made clear. It seems that they lie in the church and the bourgeoisie is merely a conduit for their eventual realisation, but this is never certain. Indeed, but for his evident commitment to the Braudelian *longue durée* – that new ideas take centuries to become fully manifest – Ariès would seem to have more in common with the cultural historian, Michel Foucault (1926–84), than the *Annales*. [39]

Whatever the deficiencies of the work, *L'Enfant et la vie familiale* has set the parameters for the study of the history of childhood in Europe and the west for the last 50 years. Virtually all later historians have been inspired by his initial research and directly or indirectly engaged with his argument. Yet, as our knowledge of what had been hitherto a virtual *terra incognita* has thickened over the years, so the criticisms have grown.[40] Some have found Ariès's methodology open to question. Although he was undoubtedly a pioneer in the use of visual evidence as a source, art historians have tended to feel that he used

[37] For Ariès's life as a French historian, see P. Hutton, *Philippe Ariès and the Politics of French Cultural History* (Amherst: University of Massachusetts Press, 2004).
[38] The century of the birth of the university saw a renewed interest in the classical inheritance as well as a novel enthusiasm for Christ as man and child. See the classic C. H. Haskins, *The Renaissance of the Twelfth Century* (Cambridge: Harvard University Press, 1927).
[39] Michel Foucault's first works on cultural history also appeared in the early 1960s. Along with his belief that Europe's past can be divided into a series of discrete cultural epochs identified by a common epistemology, he also maintained that the change from one to another was rapid. The generation of the Annales School who began research after the Second World War, and whose doctoral theses were published in the course of the 1960s, figures such as Pierre Goubert and Emmanuel Le Roi Ladurie, were principally interested at this stage of their lives in man as a socio-economic animal. Fernand Braudel (1902–85), their inspiration if not their mentor (this was Ernest Labrousse, 1895–1988), evinced a greater interest in the autonomy of the cultural domain but still gave it only a subordinate importance in his pioneering *La Méditérranée et le monde méditerranéan à l'époque de Philippe II* (Paris: Colin, 1949). They were all men of the left, close to or members of the French Communist Party: Le Roi Ladurie was a Stalinist. For an introduction to the school, see T. Stoianovich, *French Historical Method. The 'Annales' Paradigm* (Ithaca: Cornell University Press, 1976).
[40] For a short but useful overview of the literature, see B. Roberts, 'History of Childhood: Europe', in P. Fass (ed.), *Encyclopedia of Children and Childhood: In History and Society* (3 vols; Indianapolis: Macmillan USA, 2004), ii, pp. 422–26.

material cavalierly and was too ready to treat the represented as the real.[41] Others have taken issue with his timeline. Several early modern historians – notably Alan Macfarlane and Linda Pollock – have argued that modern parental love and concern is not an invention of the seventeenth century but was already well-established two centuries before, long before the Renaissance and Reformation affected the culture of this country. Louis Haas came to the same conclusion in his study of wet-nursing in late medieval Florence, as did Steven Ozment in his recent work on Germany: out of sight did not mean out of mind.[42] Conversely, other historians have accepted Ariès's contention that our present-day view of childhood is a relatively recent construction but have wanted to push the crucial period of change into the eighteenth century. Ariès gave no role to the European Enlightenment in the creation of a new concept of childhood, making no mention of John Locke (1632–1704) and ignoring Jean-Jacques Rousseau (1712–78) almost completely. For historians of England and France such as Lawrence Stone and Georges Snyders, this was perverse. In their view, child-rearing and child well-being, just like affective marriage, first became an obsession in the eighteenth century and were closely related to a growing scepticism of original sin and more optimistic notions of human potential. This new concern about children was only partly connected with developments in the era of confessionalism.[43]

Historians of the modern era have equally found Ariès's chronology wanting. For the French historian, Jean-Louis Flandrin, and the American Edward Shorter, both writing in the 1970s, the modern concept of the family was born out of Romanticism and industrialisation and had no place in a traditional society. The modern concept of childhood was part of the wider phenomenon of *embourgeoisement* and the division of labour which placed women in the 'Dolls' House' and encouraged children to be enthroned as innocent pets.[44] Hugh Cunningham, in his overview of the history of childhood in the west largely agrees, but argues that 'it is in the twentieth century that there has been most rapid change in conceptualisation and experience of childhood'.[45] This is not because parents in the last hundred years have showered affection on children as never before: levels of parental love, he believes, are impossible to measure in any epoch. It is rather that in the twentieth century

---

[41] For the problems of taking art as the measure of reality in the study of children in the past, see K. Retford, *The Art of Domestic Life: Family Portraiture in Eighteenth-Century England* (London: Yale University Press, 2006), ch. 1.

[42] L. Pollock, *Forgotten Children: Parent – Child Relations from 1500 to 1900* (Cambridge: Cambridge University Press, 1983); A. Macfarlane, *Marriage and Love in England 1300–1840: Modes of Reproduction* (Oxford: Blackwell, 1986); L. Haas, *The Renaissance Man and His Children: Childbirth and Early Childhood in Florence, 1300–1600* (Basingstoke: Macmillan, 1998); S. Ozment, *Ancestors. The Loving Family in Old Europe* (Cambridge: Harvard University Press, 2001). For an overview of the literature, see L. Pollock, 'Parent-Child Relations', in D. I. Kertzer and M. Barbagli (eds), *Family Life in Early Modern Times 1500–1789* (London: Yale University Press, 2001), ch. 7.

[43] L. Stone, *The Family, Sex and Marriage in England 1500–1800* (London: Weidenfeld and Nicholson, 1977); G. Snyders, *La pédagogie en France aux XVIIe et XVIIIe siècles* (Paris: Presses Universitaires de France, 1965), pp. 271–345. See also the important article by J. H. Plumb, 'The New World of Children in Eighteenth-Century England', *Past and Present*, 67:1 (1975), 64–93.

[44] E. Shorter, *The Making of the Modern Family* (London: Collins, 1976); J.-L. Flandrin, *Families in Former Times: Kinship, Household and Sexuality*, English trans. (Cambridge: Cambridge University Press, 1979); original French edn, 1976. See also E. Badinter, *The Myth of Motherhood: An Historical View of the Maternal Instinct*, English trans. (London: Souvenir Press, 1981).

[45] H. Cunningham, *Children and Childhood in Western Society since 1500* (Harlow: Longman, 1995), p. 202. The twentieth century is also privileged in C. Heywood, *A History of Childhood: Children and Childhood in the West from Medieval to Modern Times* (Cambridge: Polity Press, 2001). Cunningham's overview of the specifically English experience, *The Invention of Childhood* (London: BBC Books, 2006), takes much the same line, though in this second book he is more ready to accept that there were significant moments of change before the twentieth century.

the state became fully committed to the agenda originally developed by Locke and Rousseau that children were not fallen souls to be saved but innocent fledglings to be nurtured and allowed to grow naturally by enjoying a life of their own. Moreover, writing from the vantage point of the turn of the twenty-first century, Cunningham wonders whether the question that first inspired Ariès – the history of the emergence of the modern concept of childhood – has now lost much of its edge. Children in recent decades, he suggests, have begun to break free from the web of dependency and infantilisation created over previous centuries and started to demand that they be treated as equals. At the same time, the readiness of the state to acknowledge that children have rights would once again seem to be eliding the division between adult and child.[46]

To a large extent, then, Ariès's narrative is discredited today but it has stood the test of time better than another attempt in the recent past to write a total history of childhood. In 1974 American psychoanalyst Lloyd deMause published a long introduction to a book of essays entitled *The History of Childhood*, where he plotted the child's experience of childhood from the Babylonians to the present.[47] Essentially, until the recent past, he argued, this has been a story of universal pain and misery, the result, he believed, of adult failure to empathise with children and see the world from a child's eyes. For most of recorded history children were either the victims of projections of the adult unconscious or treated as substitutes for people whom adults had depended upon in their own early years. As a result, in the ancient world children were both routinely beaten and killed to expiate adult sins and routinely abused to provide parents with the unconditional physical love and affection they craved. The situation began to improve from the fourth century CE as the sexual abuse of children gradually declined, but it was only in the eighteenth century that children ceased to be considered sinful vessels which had to be literally whipped into an ideal shape. Even then, the emphasis continued to be on forming or socialising the child in a manner approved of by adults, albeit by training and guidance rather than force. It was the mid-twentieth century before parents really began to engage with children on their own terms, becoming facilitators rather than tyrants, and adopting what deMause called a 'helping' child-rearing mode:

> The helping mode involves the proposition that the child knows better than the parent what it needs at each stage of its life and fully involves both parents in the child's life as they work to empathize with and fulfill its expanding and particular needs. There is no attempt at all to discipline or form 'habits'. Children are neither struck nor scolded, and are apologized to if yelled at under stress.[48]

Like Ariès, deMause was not an academic. But nor was he a trained historian, and unlike Ariès his approach was unashamedly Whiggish.[49] He made no attempt to stand back from his narrative but made his preference for, and commitment to, the 'helping mode' abundantly clear from his opening sentence: 'The history of childhood is a nightmare from which we have only recently begun to awaken. The further back in history one goes, the lower the level of child care, and the more likely children are to be killed, abandoned, beaten, terrorized, and

---

[46] Cunningham, *Children and Childhood*, esp. conclusion. He says nothing about the purported breakdown in family life. Arguably, the most revisionist account of the history of English childhood in the recent past is A. Fletcher, *Growing Up in England: The Experience of Childhood, 1600–1914* (London: Yale University Press, 2008). According to him there was no significant change in the culture of child-rearing during this period; Ariès is not even mentioned.

[47] L. deMause, 'The Evolution of Childhood', in L. deMause (ed.), *The History of Childhood* (New York: Psychohistory Press, 1974), pp. 1–74.

[48] *Ibid.*, p. 52.

[49] deMause (p. 5) argues that Ariès preferred the 'world we have lost' to the one we slowly gained from *c.* 1400, but nostalgia for an age before childhood was 'invented' is not obvious in the Frenchman's text.

sexually abused'.[50] Inevitably, his argument received, and still receives, scant applause from the historical community.[51] From the outset, it was dismissed as psycho-babble in that the narrative was based on interpreting parent-child relations across the ages in terms of three different reactions of twentieth-century adults to other human beings (projective, reversal and empathic) and had no regard for the economic, social and cultural context. Advance came through 'psychogenic' change in the human personality and 'originated in the adult's need to regress and in the child's striving for relationship',[52] but no explanation was given as to how this could come about. It was all decidedly un-Rankean. More importantly, over the years his argument has been undermined empirically, not just by historians such as Pollock who believe that parental love and concern were already alive and well in the late middle ages, but more especially in the last fifteen years by classical and medieval scholars. At best deMause has been accused of using evidence selectively, at worst of misreading it and of showing no understanding of societies or cultures being unique. In consequence, in the light of the recent sensitive explorations of the plethora of archaeological and visual sources now available, it is hard to believe that the fate of children before 1400, let alone 1800, was as relentlessly dismal as deMause claimed. Moreover, as Beryl Rawson's study of four centuries of the Roman world shows, parent-child relations are never written in stone in earlier ages but continually influenced by regime-change, war and peace, and general levels of wealth.[53]

In consequence, deMause's stock at the present day seems to be universally low.[54] He continues to exert an influence on the history of childhood through his journal, the *History of Childhood Quarterly* (which quickly became the *Journal of Psychohistory*), but his argument has long since ceased to engage historians.[55] Yet deMause should not be dismissed too quickly. If his overarching narrative is impossible to accept, it did focus attention, from a modern perspective, on the significant and continual part played by violence, neglect and exploitation in adult-child relations. Perhaps in part because deMause gave it such a prominent place in the history of childhood, it is not an aspect that recent historians have particularly dwelt on. If anything, abusive parenting practices in the European past have been downplayed. On the one hand, the worst kinds of child abuse, such as infanticide, are said to have only rarely occurred. On the other, currently unacceptable practices such as corporal punishment and child labour are admitted to have been common but deemed to be perfectly consistent with broader cultural values and not usually damaging. Nor was such treatment inconsistent with a caring parent-child relationship. According to Pollock, even the frequent recourse among the lower orders in early modern Europe to child abandonment was not an act of cruelty and indifference but the hard result of economic reality. 'For many women the decision to relinquish a wanted child was heart-rending. With respect to the London foundlings, the babies were left in well-frequented places so that they would be found quickly, and

---

[50] *Ibid.*, p. 1.

[51] See, for example, the review by J. F. Kett in *American Historical Review*, 80:5 (1975), 1296.

[52] deMause, 'Evolution', p. 3.

[53] B. Rawson, *Children and Childhood in Roman Italy* (Oxford: Oxford University Press, 2003), Intro. Two other seminal studies are M. Golden, *Children and Childhood in Classical Athens* (London: Johns Hopkins University Press, 1990) and N. Orme, *Medieval Children* (London: Yale University Press, 2001). Orme is Britain's leading historian of medieval childhood and has recently suggested that there were two crucial moments of transition towards a more child-conscious if not a more child-centred society in the middle ages, the twelfth century and 1370 1430: see N. Orme, 'Medieval Childhood: Challenge, Change and Achievement', *Childhood in the Past: An International Journal*, 1 (2008), 106–19.

[54] Unlike Ariès, he did not merit a separate article in the three volume 2004 *Encyclopedia of Children and Childhood*, although he did receive a paragraph in the article 'Theories of Childhood'.

[55] The journal began in 1973 and became the *Journal of Psychohistory* three years later. Tellingly, Oxford University ceased to subscribe after the first three volumes.

many had been well-cared for until the time they were left'.[56] Real physical child abuse was therefore the work of the pathological few and was never condoned.

All this may be true, but downplaying the level of parental abuse in child-rearing in Europe in the past only provides a corrective to deMause's paranoia: it does not remove abuse from the childcare equation. deMause is surely right to believe that until the second half of the twentieth century most children in the western world have been subject to levels of violence, neglect and exploitation which seem shocking today. His critics are equally right to argue that most parents in the past would not have found corporal punishment in particular offensive or demeaning and that they would have recognised clear boundaries between the acceptable and unacceptable: they too would have rated some forms of behaviour cruel and wrong. Children were not routinely thrashed or worked to an inch of their life. However, by remaining content to debunk deMause, modern historians of childhood have passed too quickly over the significant questions the historicisation of adult violence towards children throws up. If the difference between past and present attitudes about cruelty to children is a consequence of drawing the existing limits of the permissible ever more tightly over the past 50 years, then we need to know much more about the boundaries in earlier periods. Where was the line between right and wrong behaviour drawn historically? How was this demarcation explained and policed? How has this line moved across recorded time? Has the line been drawn ever more tightly (as deMause's linear argument would have us believe) or has it moved in and out in different socio-cultural contexts? What are the connections between alterations to the boundaries of acceptable parental behaviour and changing attitudes towards abusive behaviour more generally in society?

These are the main questions that this present book attempts to address. In so doing, the volume aims to get away from the stale debate over whether parents in the past loved their children or beat them black and blue and left them to starve in the cold. Rather, by exploring historically the changing boundary between the permissible and the impermissible, it seeks to distinguish more clearly the constant from the inconstant features in the western tradition of normative parenting. This in turn should bring practical benefit to today's social policy makers. It would be very wrong to argue that the present media hysteria about the abuse of children has no basis in fact, but it is difficult not to believe it is partly fuelled by the belief that historically cruelty has been a commonplace. deMause makes sense to the childcare professional, if he is out of favour with the historian. As in all revolutions, the forgers of our new child-rearing world – paediatricians, social workers, teachers, politicians and so on - fear that they have not taken the people with them. Once it becomes understood, however, that there have always been boundaries and rules, and that parents in the past, even though their behaviour may seem to cruel, have never been culturally free to do what they like with their offspring, the childcare professional should no longer feel he or she lives in a Hobbesian world, where through constantly expecting the worst, the worst is always found. Moreover, by understanding the historical reality, it will become easier to devise effective ways of ensuring widespread support on the ground for the new policies of zero tolerance. Success is much more likely if educators work with rather than against existing prejudices.[57]

Structure

To date there is no historical overview of violence, neglect and exploitation in the European family beyond deMause's linear musings. This, though, does not mean the subject is virgin

---

[56] Pollock, 'Parent-Child Relations', p. 217.

[57] This fear needs to be swiftly assuaged all the more that history suggests that suspicion of the people 'out there' can easily lead to acts of injustice and, at worst, establishment terror: see F. Furet, 'Auguste Cochin: La Théorie du Jacobinisme', in F. Furet, *Penser la Révolution Française* (Paris: Gallimard, 1978), pp. 212–59.

terrain. Many scholars – historians, anthropologists, theologians, sociologists, psychologists and literary critics – have developed an expertise in some aspect or other of the subject in the course of working in their particular periods or fields of interest. This then is not an uncharted continent but an archipelago of discrete, well-tilled islands which have not yet been formed into one economy. The book endeavours to bring the fruits of this rich harvest together for the first time. This is not done by synthesising the welter of available material. This was a possible option which the editors considered but put to one side. It was feared that a general overview written by two or three scholars with their own limited areas of expertise in the subject would produce a work which was dry and unbalanced. Instead, the decision was taken to let the experts speak for themselves. In consequence, the book consists of contributions from 34 scholars in a wide variety of disciplines, which the editors have knitted together into an argument under a series of thematic heads. Initially, the reader may find the resultant text disconcerting. Unlike a single or multi-authored volume, most of the book is written by scholars whose names do not appear on the cover. Unlike a collection of essays, on the other hand, the contributions do not stand alone but have been fitted into a narrative that their authors have been allowed to comment on but not ultimately control. It is hoped, however, that the reader will find the approach novel and stimulating. As much as possible, an attempt has been made to create a seamless web by constructing a text with a clear organisation and argument and an even tone but without implying a deMausean teleology. But equally there has been no attempt to hide the fact that this is a work of cross-disciplinary collaboration and that the contributors write from different viewpoints and have different methodological allegiances. No one, therefore, can come away from the book feeling that he or she has been presented with a definitive, cut-and-dried statement about the historical role of violence, neglect and exploitation in parent-child relations in the West. Rather, it will be clear that this book is not intended to be a synthesis but an invitation to an on-going conversation.

The volume proper consists of six thematic chapters that explore aspects of parent-child violence and neglect in the western tradition. The first four deal with different types of adult behaviour which the modern liberal western establishment would consider to be pernicious and unacceptable. The first, child sacrifice or the deliberate killing of a child who is loved and wanted in order to appease or thank a higher power, has always been deemed beyond the pale in the Judaic, Graeco-Roman and Christian world. The second – the murder, casting-out or aborting of unwanted children – has equally always been an anathema in Jewish and Christian culture, although Christians from the Renaissance have found ways of legitimising and organising abandonment, and the personhood of the neonate has always been a matter of debate. The third and fourth chapters, on the other hand, deal with forms of adult behaviour where the boundaries between the acceptable and unacceptable have been historically fluid. Beating children, the principal subject of the third chapter, is universally condemned in the modern west, but until very recently corporal punishment, in many different forms, as a way of disciplining the disobedient, inattentive or slow-to-learn child, was not thought to be cruel or illegitimate. In past periods, the debate has primarily turned around the age of the child who could be subjected to such punishment and its form. Similarly, the subject of the fourth chapter, the belief that children should not be expected or forced to labour, inside or outside the home, is a singularly modern shibboleth. Until the last century, it was a commonplace for children to contribute to the family economy and the debate still rages, as it has done since the late-eighteenth century, as to where the line between socialisation and exploitation exactly falls. Today there remains a respectable body of opinion that believes that children should be allowed to work if they want to, provided it does not harm their physical and intellectual development.[58]

---

[58] For a fuller discussion of these issues see J. Boyden, B. Ling and W. Myers, *What Works for Working Children*

In each of these four chapters, an attempt is made to trace the theme from the beginnings of western civilisation to the present. There is no pretence at blanket coverage, however. Rather, significant moments in the narrative are illustrated wherever possible by representative anecdotes, which are intended to bring the text to life. Readers who seek a fuller understanding are directed to the substantial secondary material cited in the footnotes. Nor are the chapters intended to convey a linear argument. The boundaries between acceptable and unacceptable behaviour may have changed over the two and a half millennia, especially in the last 50 years, but that does not mean that normative modern parenting is necessarily non-violent or non-exploitative. There are many features of contemporary society that our ancestors would have considered cruel or stupid. Sacrificing babies is wrong but not, apparently, sacrificing teenagers over the age of eighteen in godly wars. Infanticide is forbidden but not abortion. Again, beating and starving have been outlawed but punishment through humiliation and other forms of denial remain perfectly acceptable, if the antics of TV's 'Supernanny' are anything to go by.[59] Similarly, a child who works is thought by many to be the victim of exploitation, but few modern liberals think it tyranny to keep the less intellectually able at their studies until they are sixteen (and even eighteen in Britain from 2013) or to make all children do homework.[60] There is nothing Whiggish about the book, therefore. Throughout the four chapters runs a contrapuntal voice, whispering that the boundaries have been merely changed and the definition of what is violent, thoughtless or exploitative behaviour simply refined.

The last two chapters move the attention from boundaries and boundary-breaking to how children in the West have coped with abuse. The first explores the range of aggressive or intimidating responses. The emphasis here is on criminal and violent behaviour directed towards both children and adults. The second examines various less confrontational ways children have found of dealing with the pressure they have found themselves under – seeking protection from other adults, running-away, acting out their fears in games, or simply self-harming, the bane of our modern age. Throughout the two chapters the illustrative material principally relates to children who were, or felt that they had been, treated badly by adults in terms of the boundaries of their own day. There must have been many children, however, who were brought up perfectly reasonably by the tenets of their contemporary world, but who still felt and acted as if abused without being able to conceptualise their ennui or sense of alienation. It is quite possible that many parents in the past adapted their behaviour accordingly when dealing with sick, disturbed or just plain sensitive children, but it can be assumed that many, equally, did not.

These two chapters are alive, too, to the fact that the gamut of responses available to brutalised and neglected children has not always been the same. In different eras some possibilities are closed while others open. Before 1700, for instance, society offered much more opportunity for legitimate violence than it does today. In a much more vertically organised and self-policing community, it was youth who were given the duty of upholding the honour of the village, municipality or corporation. The abused did not have to wait long before they could vent their frustration and get their revenge on outsiders. Today, just as the range of adult behaviour deemed unacceptable has grown much wider, so the victims of boundary-breaking arguably have fewer physical outlets for their angst. Traditional expressions of violence by children – teasing, bullying, plain fighting, even simulated fighting – have all been increasingly outlawed in the last 50 years.[61] We have waged war on

(Stockholm: Rädda Barnen, 1998).
[59] 'Supernanny' starring nanny Jo Frost was first shown on Channel 4 in Britain in the autumn of 2004. The first series drew five million viewers. The programme format has since been imitated around Europe and in the United States. See http://en.wikipedia.org/wiki/Supernanny (accessed 21 Nov. 2008).
[60] A point made in Cunningham, *Invention of Childhood*, pp. 237–39 and 245.
[61] The outlaw of gun-play, for instance, has been consistently promoted in British nursery and primary schools

expressions of child violence with the same intensity as we have waged war on adult cruelty to children, so that children who murder today are treated with much less understanding than they were in the mid-nineteenth century.[62] Perhaps this is why self-harm has become such a modern disease: it is the one form of violence left to the abused or lonely child who accepts all of the contemporary world's prohibitions on harming others. Self-harm, especially child suicide, seems to have occurred less frequently in earlier eras. Its frequency today is the most graphic reminder that we still live in a country where many children are frightened and desperate, despite all attempts by the state to police family behaviour ever more closely. As a poignant reminder of this fact, the last chapter closes by publishing the suicide note of a fourteen-year-old boy, who felt he could no longer live in modern Britain.

This suicide note alerts us to a paradox that lies at the heart of contemporary social policy concerning children; today there are more initiatives and legislation than ever about how best to improve children's lives and yet children seem uniquely unhappy. Maybe we now know more about children than we ever did and so we have a greater insight into their feelings or maybe all the anxiety adults have generated about children's welfare has been counter productive and created the very conditions we fear most. The UK regularly comes near the bottom of UNICEF's child well-being league,[63] while children's concerns over bullying seem to dominate their lives.[64] It is quite possible that historians of the future will be as critical of our ways of raising and socialising children as we are today of the factory owners of the industrial revolution. Already some sociologists and professionals working with children are talking of the damage inflicted on children who are over-protected and made miserable by parents' continual worries and attempts to safeguard them.[65]

Looked at in this way there is rather less on which to congratulate ourselves – we may have legislated certain forms of violence out of existence, but have been wilfully blind to others. The third type of violence identified by Jill Korbin – that of structural violence – remains under-acknowledged. Yet the gap between rich and poor and between minority and majority communities remains as entrenched as ever and seems to be getting worse. Social mobility in the UK is one of the lowest in Europe and has fallen since the 1950s and the opportunities, as well as expectations, for many children in poverty remain dire.[66] The Labour government's promise to halve child poverty by 2010 and to end it by 2020 appears, at the time of writing, to be wildly unrealistic and poverty remains a toxic form of violence in many children's lives.

There are other forms of violence also which are deliberately ignored but can cause great damage. Psychological violence has been given very limited attention and yet, with the levels of children's unhappiness seemingly at epidemic proportions, must be taken seriously and

---

since the 1950s. The orthodoxy is now being challenged: see P. Holland, *We Don't Play With Guns Here: War, Weapons and Superhero Play in the Early Years* (Buckingham: Open University Press, 2003).

[62] In an unpublished paper given at Oxford in autumn 2002, shortly before he died, the distinguished English children's lawyer, Allan Levy QC, compared the paranoia unleashed by the murder in 1993 of the two-year-old James Bulger by two ten-year-old boys with the much more balanced response to a similar case in mid-Victorian England. See also Cunningham, *Invention of Childhood*, p. 243.

[63] In 2007, the UK ranked bottom out of 21 countries in UNICEF's table of children's well-being based on factors such as material well-being, family and peer relationships, health and safety, behaviour and risks, and children's own sense of their educational and subjective well-being: see www.unicef-irc.org/publications/pdf/rc7_eng.pdf (accessed 18 Aug. 2009).

[64] See A. Aynsley-Green's comments on children's concerns about bullying at http://news.bbc.co.uk/cbbcnews/hi/newsid_4440000/newsid_4441900/4441962.stm

[65] F. Furedi, *Paranoid Parenting: Abandon your Anxieties and be a Good Parent* (London: Allen Lane, 2001); S. Palmer, *Toxic Childhood: How the Modern World is Damaging our Children and What We Can Do About it* (London: Orion, 2007); K. Ecclestone and D. Hayes, *The Dangerous Rise of Therapeutic Education* (London: Routledge, 2009).

[66] J. Blanden, P. Gregg and S. Machin, *Intergenerational Mobility in Europe and North America* (London: Centre for Economic Performance at the London School of Economics, 2005).

acknowledged as real. The expectations placed on children, which push them beyond their academic, physical or social capacities cause great stress and have more to do with parents' needs and wants than children's. The continual assessment of children in schools puts many under great strain and finds others wanting, and can lead not only to social division among peers but to individual misery. This very modern culture of violence is further exacerbated when normal childish behaviour is pathologised and even medicated so that a child who might once have been seen as boisterous is now labelled as aggressive or suffering from ADHD (Attention-Deficit Hyperactivity Disorder). As the range of normal and acceptable children's behaviour has narrowed, those children who do not conform are increasingly marginalised and stigmatised.

In other arenas too, the psychological and social violence against children is becoming more visible. While both boys and girls are exploited by the media and turned as soon as possible into consumers, girls' sexuality has been a particular focus for advertisers who tap into their desire to look attractive.[67] The consequent eroticisation of girls and the expectations placed on them to be both innocent and sexual at the same time leads again to both social and individual anxiety. It is surely not too wild a prediction to say that any sociologist or historian in the future looking back at the early twenty-first century will be amazed to see fears over paedophilia expressed at the same time as models in magazines, and young people in the media more generally, are getting younger and dressed more provocatively so that girls aged ten wearing make-up and high heels have become the norm rather than the exception.

Finally, there is the form of psychological violence that Steven Mintz has described as 'perhaps the most unsettling of all: the objectification of childhood'.[68] He goes on to describe this phenomenon in American society but his commentary has resonance throughout the modern west.

> This involves viewing children as objects to be shaped and moulded for their own good. Compared to its predecessors, contemporary American society is much more controlling in an institutional and ideological sense. We expect children to conform to standards that few adults could meet. Meanwhile, as the baby boom generation ages, we inhabit an increasingly adult-oriented society, a society that has fewer "free" spaces for the young, a society that values youth primarily as service workers and consumers and gawks at them as sex objects.

There is no conclusion at the end of this book therefore as putting one in place would imply an end point rather than a continuing debate. The history of abusive, neglectful or simply incompetent parent-child relationships has not come to an end. The problem is simply changing shape and remains an ongoing source of argument and worry for childcare professionals, governmental agencies and parents themselves. What is new is that the voices of children themselves have entered the debate: discussions of the treatment of children in the past have shown how parents and educators treated children and, in some cases, how children responded, but we have rarely heard from children themselves. With the benefit of hindsight it will be fascinating to know whether today's children see themselves as the most cosseted, cherished and protected generation in history or if they look back in anger on their childhood selves as the victims of oppressive, and even abusive, control, masquerading as concern.

---

[67] D. Buckingham and S. Bragg, 'Children and Consumer Culture', in H. Montgomery and M. Kellett (eds), *Children and Young People's Worlds: Developing Frameworks for Integrated Practice* (Bristol: The Policy Press, 2009).

[68] S. Mintz, 'The Changing State of Childhood: American Childhood as a Social and Cultural Construct', unpublished paper, 2009.

1. Child Sacrifice

Francesca Stavrakopoulou, James Francis, Elisabeth Dutton,
David Maskell, Pawel Maciejko and Adrian Gregory

Then Herod, when he saw that he was mocked of the wise men, was exceeding wroth, and sent forth, and slew all the children that were in Bethlehem, and in all the coasts thereof, from two years old and under, according to the time which he had diligently enquired of the wise men. Then was fulfilled that which was spoken by Jeremy the prophet, saying, In Rama was there a voice heard, lamentation, and weeping, and great mourning, Rachel weeping for her children, and would not be comforted, because they are not.

St Matth. ii. 16–18

Then shall the Priest say, Hear what comfortable words our Saviour Christ saith unto all that truly turn to him.

Come unto me all that travail and are heavy laden, and I will refresh you. *St Matth. xi. 28*

So God loved the world, that he gave his only-begotten Son, to the end that all that believe in him should not perish, but have everlasting life. *St John iii. 16*

Hear also what Saint Paul saith: This is a true saying, and worthy of all men to be received, That Christ Jesus came into the world to save sinners. *1 Tim. i. 15*

Hear also what Saint John saith: If any man sin, we have an Advocate with the Father, Jesus Christ the righteous; and he is the propitiation for our sins. *1 St John ii. 1*

The Book of Common Prayer

> Then Abram bound the youth with belts and straps.
> And builded parapets and trenches there,
> And stretched forth the knife to slay his son.
> When lo! an angel called him out of heaven,
> Saying, Lay not thy hand upon the lad,
> Neither do anything to him. Behold,
> A ram, caught in a thicket by its horns;
> Offer the Ram of Pride instead of him.
> But the old man would not so, but slew his son,
> And half the seed of Europe, one by one.

Wilfred Owen, *The Parable of the Old Man and the Young*

The extent to which human sacrifice has been practised by any civilisation in the past remains a matter of contention. The present consensus seems to be that it did occur but was never as widespread as westerners once thought. What can be said with certain is that the gradual colonisation of the world by Christian Europeans from the late fifteenth century onwards put an end to the practice in places such as central America where it was definitely extant. That human sacrifice was one practice that European colonisers would not tolerate is scarcely surprising. If there is one taboo that has been a consistent feature of Judaic, Christian and Islamic civilisation over the last three millennia, it is ritual human sacrifice. God demands that we worship him and obey his moral law, even to the extent of laying down our life rather than embrace false beliefs, but he does not expect us to offer up another human being to better win his favour.[1]

While the offering up of any human life to the divine is deemed abhorrent within Judaism, Christianity and Islam, the offering up of a child, especially by his or her parent, is considered a particular abomination.[2] Through the graphic Genesis story of Abraham and Isaac, Jews, Christians and Muslims learn that this is one sacrifice God certainly does not expect us to make. Yet, if child sacrifice is an abomination, it is a practice with which Christians have had a complex relationship. By the very fact that God is understood to have offered up his own son on the cross in order to redeem humankind, Christians are constantly reminded that child sacrifice can be the most life-enhancing act imaginable: it is the ultimate evidence of love, re-enacted in the Roman Catholic church whenever mass is celebrated.[3] In consequence, if a parent cannot literally sacrifice his own child, it is perfectly possible for a parent to give his or her blessing to a decision made by a grown-up child that might end in that child's death, if the aim is good and the child, like Christ, has consented.[4]

At the same time, and doubtless as a result of the special significance of Christ's death as a filial sacrifice, European Christians through the centuries have frequently suspected non-Christian groups in their midst, or simply the ungodly, or marginal, class or national enemies, of imitating God's ultimate act of love, be it out of mockery or for some deeper nefarious purpose. There is never hard evidence for such a belief, but it is one that has continued through to the present day in different forms, sometimes with horrific consequences. At times, the accusations are specific and centre on a supposed ritual involving the shedding of blood of babies or children; often, especially in the recent past, the paranoia has taken a more general form: those who wage war unjustly do not have God on their side and must therefore be guilty of deliberately killing babies as positive proof of their stereotypical godlessness.[5]

This chapter explores the various ways in which the Christian obsession with child sacrifice has manifested itself over the centuries in Europe, particularly in its negative form. It is not a chapter about a practice which we would today deem child abuse or neglect but that up to the recent past was seen as normal and uncontroversial. As far we know, Christian parents (apart from a handful of very disturbed individuals) have never wilfully

---

[1] For opinions about human sacrifice in different cultures, see J. N. Bremmer (ed.), *The Strange World of Human Sacrifice* (Leuven: Peeters, 2007); see also K. Finsterbusch, A. Lange and K. F. Diethard Romheld (eds), *Human Sacrifice in Jewish and Christian Tradition* (Leiden: Brill, 2006) and the literature noted below, fn. 14.

[2] Child sacrifice appears to have been practised by several pre-conquest American indigenous peoples, such as the Maya: see the works cited in fn. 100 below.

[3] See J. D. Levenson, *The Death and Resurrection of the Beloved Son: The Transformation of Child Sacrifice in Judaism and Christianity* (New Haven: Yale University Press, 1993), chs 15–16.

[4] All Christians must be ready to be martyrs. The tradition of martyrdom of course is equally strong in the Jewish and Muslim tradition. In the Jewish case this too is linked to the Abraham and Isaac story: see below, pp. 22–26.

[5] The theory of the just war outlines the situations in which a Christian government can be permitted to take up arms and lays down the rules under which that war can be conducted. For its development, see F. H. Russell, *The Just War in the Middle Ages* (Cambridge: Cambridge University Press, 1977).

sacrificed their children as a divine offering.[6] Indeed, literal child sacrifice was equally anathema to the classical Greeks and Romans, as well as the Jews. The Christian disavowal was built on a long-standing Mediterranean tradition. The chapter then is about a belief and its consequences, principally the fear that many Christian parents had until the nineteenth century that their children might be whisked away for ritual slaughter.

On the other hand, there is reason to believe that pre-classical civilisations in the Mediterranean and so-called pagan peoples in northern Europe did practise child sacrifice, if the evidence remains disputed. Arguably, then, child sacrifice for the greater good of the family or the community was once a part of our distant past, perhaps even a very significant one in the Mediterranean world. But just because the practice belongs to a world our ancestors forsook a very long time ago, it does not mean it should be swept under the carpet or neglected in any long-term study of violence to children. Moreover, for those who follow Ginsburg in looking for the origin of Europe's most tenacious 'irrational' beliefs, such as witchcraft, in the uncultivable permafrost of prehistory, then the European fascination with child sacrifice may well have much deeper roots than the paradox of the Cross.[7] Significantly and disturbingly, too, this putative practice of our prehistorical ancestors even appears to be given some sort of valorisation in certain Old Testament texts, suggesting that the early Hebrews themselves were proponents. If this were the case – and not all Biblical scholars would go down this path – then the peculiarity of the ancient Israelites – the ancestors of the early Jewish people – lies not in the claim that they were always culturally distinguished from surrounding peoples by their abhorrence of the practice of child sacrifice, but rather in their forceful abandonment of it.

The chapter begins with an account of the textual evidence for concluding that the early Hebrews practised child sacrifice, then briefly explores the death of Christ on the cross as a filial sacrifice. The middle portion of the chapter examines Christian Europe's readiness to believe that marginal groups in its midst, especially the Jews, sacrificed infants. One contribution looks at dramatic presentations of the 'blood libel', the completely unfounded accusation of ritual killing of infants that Christians levelled against Jews in the late middle ages. Succeeding sections reveal first how Europe's elite continued to be fascinated by depictions of child sacrifice throughout the Renaissance and beyond, and next how tenacious the blood libel remained in eastern Europe, where it was continually invoked in the purported Age of Enlightenment. The last part of the chapter takes us on to the twentieth century and switches the emphasis back to the theme of filial sacrifice. The last contribution looks at the way the language of Christian offering and sacrifice was attached to the slaughter of the First World War. The chapter ends with a coda pointing out how much that language became and remains a commonplace when describing the death of soldiers in the twentieth and early twenty-first century, while also reminding us that even today some evangelical Christians and an uncritical media are still willing to believe in the existence of real ritual killings of children.

---

[6] For general parental violence and neglect, see Ch. 3 below.
[7] C. Ginzburg, *Ecstacies. Deciphering the Witches' Sabbath*, English trans. (London: Penguin, 1991).

Child Sacrifice in the Ancient World:
Blessings for the Beloved

Francesca Stavrakopoulou

Responding to divine command, Abraham takes Isaac, his 'beloved' and 'only-begotten' son, to a high mountain, to sacrifice him to God. Just as the ritual slaughter is about to occur, a divine messenger intervenes, supplying him with a ram as a substitute for Isaac, and bestowing upon Abraham a blessing from God, which promises him a multitude of descendants in reward for his obedience to the divine instruction. (See Figure 1).

Abraham's obedience is central to the theological presentation of this well-known biblical story in Genesis 22, traditionally called the *Akedah* ('binding'). From the outset, the near-sacrifice of Isaac is described as a divine test (22:1), designed to challenge Abraham's love of God. Indeed, this is the common perception of the ancient story, and Abraham continues to be venerated today in three world religions as the model of faithfulness to God. Yet an attentive reading of the biblical story reveals that the divine command to sacrifice Isaac appears *not* to prove testing for Abraham. Despite the striking and repeated emphasis upon Isaac as Abraham's 'beloved' and 'only-begotten' son (vv. 2, 12, 16),[8] the choice with which Abraham is confronted – his son, or his God – is not a difficult one. The assumed dilemma is simply not represented in the story, for Abraham's emotional response to the divine command is not described, nor is there any indication that the prospect of sacrificing his son is spiritually challenging to him.[9] Rather, without question or hesitation, Abraham obeys God's command, and attempts to sacrifice his son as a burnt offering. Even the intervention of a divine messenger and the appearance of a ram as a substitute elicit no thankful response from Abraham.

This stands in contrast to the biblical story of Jephthah's sacrifice of his daughter in chapter 11 of the book of Judges. In this text, the mighty warrior and chosen leader of the Israelite tribes vows to God that he will sacrifice to him the first person to greet him at home, if only God will grant him victory over the hated Ammonites. Accordingly, God delivers up the Ammonites to Jephthah, and upon his jubilant return home, Jephthah is distressed to find his daughter, described as his 'only-begotten child' (v. 34), coming out of the house to greet him. Despite his emotional turmoil and demonstrated grief (symbolised in verse 35 by the common biblical motif of the tearing of clothes), father and daughter agree to abide by the vow in fulfilling its requirements. And so it is that Jephthah sacrifices his daughter to God as a burnt offering (vv. 31, 39). Like that of the *Akedah*, a key theme of this story is obedience: the obedience of a father to sacrifice his 'only-begotten' child to God. This theme is often eclipsed in both scholarly and religious discussions by an emphasis upon the supposed rashness of Jephthah's vow – the assumed 'moral' of the story warning that a hasty decision can lead to unexpected disaster.[10] Yet this is to misunderstand the narrator's intentions, for the complicity of God is heavily implied at the beginning of the story, when the 'spirit of YHWH'[11] is

---

[8] Note also the frequent designation of Isaac as 'his son', and that of Abraham as 'his father' throughout the story.

[9] This appears to jar with Abraham's compassionate objection to the divine annihilation of the inhabitants of Sodom and Gomorrah in his appeals to God's righteousness (Gen. 18:16–33).

[10] See further D. M. Gunn, *Judges* (Blackwell Bible Commentary; Oxford: Blackwell, 2005), pp. 142–46.

[11] The designation YHWH is a transliteration of the biblical Hebrew name of God, which is itself an approximate representation of the proper name of an ancient deity worshipped in and around ancient Syro-

said to fall upon Jephthah, prompting his vow (v. 29). Moreover, despite his grief at his ordeal (to say, much like the narrator, nothing of that of his daughter), Jephthah makes no attempt to negotiate a substitution offering, or to avert the impending death of his daughter.[12] Indeed, God appears unmoved by Jephthah's distress, for neither a divine messenger nor a substitute animal appears in order to prevent the girl's death.

Whilst these biblical stories have generated centuries of uneasy theological debate, they remain discomforting to modern sensibilities – whether religiously-felt or not – for the biblical traditions have played a formative role in the shaping of modern western societies and their moral and ethical parameters. As such, the biblical portrayals of the apparently acceptable face of child sacrifice are, for many, distinctly unsettling. Accordingly, it is tempting to read these biblical stories as powerful polemics directed against the practice of child sacrifice in particular, and human sacrifice more generally. However, in neither story is God presented as an unwilling or reluctant recipient of this type of offering. An alternative approach might confront head-on the religious reality of child sacrifice in ancient civilisations, but lessen its impact by casting the practice as a 'primitive' form of population control or socio-economic prudence, in which the sacrifice of Jephthah's daughter and the non-sacrifice of Abraham's son vividly illustrate the preferential status of male children over female children. But this would be equally misconstrued, for both stories and their wider biblical contexts emphasise the valued and cherished status of the children destined for sacrifice.[13]

Indeed, it is precisely the high socio-religious value of Isaac and Jephthah's daughter as 'only-begotten' and 'beloved' children that mark them out as potential sacrificial offerings. This is clearly demonstrated in biblical material legislating for the sacrifice of the firstborn of both humans and animals to God: unblemished, perfect firstborns, which are God's by right of a return on his continued blessing of fertility. Though several texts allow for the redemption or 'rescue' of the human firstborn – by means of a substitute animal or a financial donation to the local sanctuary – the unqualified law commanding the sacrifice of the human and animal firstborn alike is made plain in Exod. 13:1–2 and 22:29–30 (Hebrew version 22:28–29). In chapter 6 of the book of the prophet Micah, the human firstborn is placed at the climax of a list of increasingly valuable and acceptable sacrifices offered to God (vv. 6–7). And yet elsewhere, child sacrifice is outlawed as an unacceptable ritual, and in the book of Jeremiah, God denies that he had ever commanded the sacrifice of children (7:31; 19:5; 32:35). This tension in the biblical material is felt most strongly in chapter 20 of the book of Ezekiel, in which God claims he deliberately commanded the sacrifice of all the firstborn not to bring life (as suggested in Exod. 13:1–2; 22:29–30), but in order to defile and to devastate his people, the Israelites (Ezek. 20:25–26).

In portraying God as a willing recipient of child sacrifice, these texts offer a faint reflection of the prominent role of the practice in the religious heritage of the biblical writers. Ancient Israelite religion, which, to a certain and notable degree, is to be distinguished from its later biblical imaging, was constructed upon a complex belief-system which focused upon the interrelation of birth and death, ancestors and descendents. As a component of this belief-system, child sacrifice played an essential role, for it appears to have functioned as a sophisticated and specialised fertility ritual. Whilst ancient literary traditions, along with inscriptional, iconographic and other

Palestine, and revered as the national god of the Iron Age kingdoms of Israel and Judah.

[12] Though the girl's immediate sacrifice is delayed, it is at her own request, rather than at the suggestion of her father (vv. 37–39).

[13] Isaac is the valued son, divinely-promised and miraculously born to the barren Sarah and the aged Abraham (Gen. 16:1–6; 17:15–22; 18:1–15; 21:1–14); the high social status of Jephthah's daughter is demonstrated in the annual ritual of lament performed in her honour by the women of Israel (Judg. 11:39–40).

archaeological material, suggest that various forms of human sacrifice were known in classical antiquity and ancient Europe,[14] it would appear that the specific practice of child sacrifice played a role in the religious expressions of ancient Syro-Palestinian societies, including the kingdoms of Israel and Judah. Archaeological evidence from sites in ancient Israel's northern territories and in neighbouring Phoenicia attest to the burning of babies and the careful collection of their remains in urns, which were buried beneath decorated monuments, some of which are inscribed with dedications to the goddess Tanit.[15] The sacrificial nature of these material remains is confirmed by parallel evidence from Phoenicia's Punic colonies in North Africa and throughout the Mediterranean. At several sites,[16] sacred precincts dedicated to the god Baal Hammon and his consort Tanit are filled with the burned and buried remains of babies and young animals, predominantly lambs. Highly decorative stelae, erected above the remains of each child, bear the symbols of Baal Hammon and Tanit; many also depict swaddled babies, or lambs. One notable example, from the sacred precinct at Carthage, depicts a priest, carrying a baby in the crook of his arm.[17] The stelae are also inscribed with dedications by the parents, describing the sacrifices in technical, cultic terminology as *mlk* offerings, a term probably derived from the common Semitic root *mlk*, 'royal'. The inscriptions indicate that the *mlk* sacrifices are offered in fulfilment of a vow, and in response to a divine blessing. Though these dedications tend not to be specific, they frequently refer to a 'scion' or 'sprout' – terminology loaded with dynastic connotations. One inscription indicates that the divine blessing was a pregnancy, and that the vow fulfilled refers to the burned remains of a newborn baby buried beneath the memorial.[18]

This archaeological material finds a striking and significant parallel in biblical descriptions of a sacrifice in which children are 'burned' or, more euphemistically, 'passed over' in the fire as *mlk* ('royal') offerings.[19] Despite ancient scribal attempts to disguise or to reinterpret and revocalise the biblical Hebrew term *mlk* as the name of a fictitious foreign god called 'Molek',[20] it is increasingly accepted that the biblical word *mlk* is cognate with the Phoenician-Punic term *mlk*.[21] As such, the biblical texts would

---

[14] On child sacrifice in classical antiquity, see M. Halm-Tisserant, *Cannibalisme et immortalité: l'enfant dans le chaudron en Grèce ancienne* (Paris: Belles Lettres, 1993). On human sacrifice more generally, see D. D. Hughes, *Human Sacrifice in Ancient Greece* (London: Routledge, 1991); M. A. Green, *Dying for the Gods: Human Sacrifice in Iron Age and Roman Europe* (Stroud: Tempus, 2001).

[15] H. Sader, 'Phoenician Stelae from Tyre', *Berytus*, 39 (1991), 101–26; H. Seeden, 'A *tophet* in Tyre?', *Berytus*, 39 (1991), 39–82.

[16] Sites include those at Carthage and Sousse in North Africa, Motya in Sicily, Nora Sulcis, Monte Sirai and Tharros in Sardinia, and possibly Amathus in Cyprus.

[17] See further S. Brown, *Late Carthaginian Child Sacrifice and Sacrificial Monuments in their Mediterranean Context* (JSOT/ASORMS 3; Sheffield: JSOT Press, 1991).

[18] Recent attempts to identify these burial precincts as children's cemeteries, or as a socially acceptable mechanism for the disposal of unwanted children, are unpersuasive (not least in view of the identical, ritual treatment of both human and animal infants in this religious context). For a detailed discussion of this archaeological material, see F. Stavrakopoulou, *King Manasseh and Child Sacrifice: Biblical Distortions of Historical Realities* (Berlin/New York: Walter de Gruyter, 2004), pp. 215–39, plus the literature cited there.

[19] Deut. 12:31; 18:10; 2 Kgs 16:3; 17:17, 31; 21:6; 23:10; 2 Chr. 28:3; 33:6; Jer. 7:31; 19:5; 32:35. Other references to child sacrifice include Lev. 18:21; 20:2–5; Josh. 6:26; 1 Kgs 16:34; 2 Kgs 3:27; Ps. 106:37–38; Isa. 57:5; Ezek. 16:20–21; 20:26, 31; 23:37, 39; Mic. 6:7.

[20] Lev. 18:21; 20:2–5; 2 Kgs 23:10; Jer. 32:35; cf. 1 Kgs 11:7.

[21] As originally suggested by O. Eissfeldt, *Molk als Opferbegriff im Punischen und Hebräischen und das Ende des Gottes Moloch* (Halle: Niemeyer, 1935). See also K. A. D. Smelik, 'Moloch, Molekh or Molk-Sacrifice? A Reassessment of the Evidence Concerning the Hebrew Term Molekh', *Scandinavian Journal of the Old Testament*, 9 (1995), 133–42; Stavrakopoulou, *King Manasseh and Child Sacrifice*, pp. 240–61.

appear to reflect – albeit somewhat reluctantly – a sacrificial practice similar to that evidenced in the sacred precincts of the Phoenician and Punic worlds.

Further research has constructed a plausible case for the *mlk* sacrifice in ancient Israel, Phoenicia and her Punic colonies as an originally royal sacrifice, of a royal child, offered to a royal god. This appears to have been a specialisation of a cult of child sacrifice focused upon firstborn or 'only-begotten' children. Indeed, an ancient Phoenician myth recounted in Philo of Byblos's *Phoenician History* (cited in Eusebius's *Praeparatio evangelica*) describes the god El (identified here with Kronos) as a divine king, who arrays his son in royal robes and sacrifices him as a burnt offering.[22] This myth exhibits striking analogies with biblical stories of child sacrifice. El's sacrificed, divine son is described as an 'only-begotten' child. His Semitic name is given in two parallel texts: in one, he is called *Iedoud*; in another, he is called *Ieoud*. The latter is to be related to the Semitic word *yādîd*, meaning 'beloved', whilst the former is to be identified with the Semitic term *yāh[îd*, meaning 'only-begotten'. In the light of the archaeological and philological similarities between the Phoenician-Punic cult of child sacrifice and the practices described in the biblical texts, it is no coincidence that these same designations, *yādîd* ('beloved') and *yāh[îd* ('only-begotten'), are applied to Isaac and to Jephthah's daughter in the Hebrew Bible (Old Testament) and its Greek variants.[23]

A further and notable parallel between the Phoenician myth concerning child sacrifice and the biblical stories is the detail in the former that, before sacrificing his son, the god El circumcises himself; a feature which is mirrored in the biblical narrative in the account of Abraham's circumcision in the chapters preceding the stories of Isaac's conception, birth and near-sacrifice (Gen. 17–22). This narrative sequence of events strikes an important theological chord, for elsewhere in the biblical texts circumcision is likened to the pruning of a fruit tree, enabling it to produce an increased yield.[24] It is thus notable that Abraham's circumcision precipitates both the divine endorsement of his name, meaning 'Father/Ancestor of Many', and the bestowal of God's blessing of perpetual fertility for his descendants, actualised and symbolised in the figure of his new son Isaac, through whom the nation of Israel is destined to emerge.[25]

There is yet another ancient tradition of child sacrifice underlying the story of Abraham and Isaac. In the biblical narrative, God is repeatedly called '*šadday*' or '*El šadday*'. These divine designations are to be related to that occurring in inscriptions from an ancient Israelite sanctuary at Deir 'Alla, on the east bank of the river Jordan. The inscriptions appear to tell of the sacrifice of a child, described as a 'scion' or 'sprout'; the sacrifice is offered to the '*šadday*-gods' in response to a divine threat of communal and agricultural infertility.[26] The shared context of child sacrifice, set alongside its apparent

---

[22] Euseb. *Praep. ev.* 1.10.33, 44.

[23] Gen. 22:2, 12, 16; Judg. 11:34.

[24] Lev. 19:23–25. See further H. Eilberg-Schwartz, *The Savage in Judaism: An Anthropology of Israelite Religion and Ancient Judaism* (Bloomington: Indiana University Press, 1990), p. 152.

[25] The biblical association of circumcision with child sacrifice is also evident in Exod. 4:24–26. Although there are difficulties in understanding and translating these verses, this text appears to tell a story in which, upon 'encountering' God one night, Moses suddenly attempts to kill his son. The death of the child is averted by Moses's wife Zipporah, who cuts off her son's foreskin, and daubs the bloodied skin on Moses' own genitalia, apparently reaffirming his paternity of the child in her designating her husband as 'a bridegroom of blood by circumcision'. This is a play on the Semitic word for circumcision, *h[atan*, which means both 'bridegroom' and 'protect'. Here, the circumcision of the child appears to protect him from his father's attempt to kill him. Again, the complicity of God is inferred in his 'encountering' Moses, apparently initiating Moses' actions (v. 24).

[26] J.-A. Hackett, *The Balaam Text from Deir 'Alla* (Chico: Scholars Press, 1984).

association with fertility, and coupled with the use of the divine designation *šadday* in the biblical and inscriptional texts, is remarkable. Yet the commonalities between the traditions resonate with a deeper significance in view of another biblical text, Psalm 106. In verses 37–38, child sacrifice is portrayed as an abhorrent and alien practice, which is performed in honour of deities erroneously described as 'demons' in most translations. This misnomer is based upon an ancient scribal misvocalisation of the consonantal biblical Hebrew term *šdym*, for the deities are not 'demons' (*šēdîm*), but a group of gods called '*šaddayyim*' or '*šadday*-gods', a designation etymologically related to both that of the *šadday*-gods in the Deir 'Alla inscriptions and the divine epithets *šadday* and *El šadday* in the biblical narratives.[27]

In drawing this material together, a fragmentary picture emerges of a practice in which children were sacrificed to God. This sacrifice appears to have functioned as a fertility ritual, in which the firstborn, the 'only-begotten' and 'beloved' child, might be returned to God in recognition of his blessing of fertility, and in the hope of procuring more children. The sacrifice of the child thus revolved around its high, socio-religious value as both symbol and agent of the perpetuation of the generations. Despite attempts by biblical writers and editors to portray child sacrifice as an abhorrent practice, performed in honour of foreign gods, and alien to legitimate forms of worship, the texts offer distant – if distorted – reflections of this practice, testifying to its ancient role in the religious heritage of the biblical writers. As such, the story of Abraham's near-sacrifice of Isaac resonates with the fertility function of the sacrifice of the 'only-begotten' and 'beloved' child. Though he is not Abraham's firstborn, he is the 'only-begotten' child of Sarah, whose barrenness is miraculously reversed in the conception and birth of Isaac, a child promised by God following Abraham's circumcision. And so it is that Abraham, the ideological ancestor of Israel, attempts to sacrifice this child at the explicit and willing command of God. But the emphasis of the story falls not upon the *non*-sacrifice of Isaac, but upon the divine blessing of fertility upon Abraham in response to his *willingness* to sacrifice his 'only-begotten' and 'beloved' son to his God.

The willingness of God to command and to receive the sacrifice, coupled with the willingness of Abraham to offer up his son, jars theologically and ethically with the ignorance of the child as the sacrificial victim, pointedly demonstrated by the narrator with Isaac's question, 'Father ... the fire and the wood are here, but where is the lamb for the burnt offering?' (Gen. 22:7). Whilst Isaac's ignorance contributes to the dramatic tension of the story, it might also be read in representative terms as a symbol of the exclusion of the child from the sacrificial pact between a father and his god in pre-classical Mediterranean cultures. The archaeological material surveyed above suggests that most sacrificed children were babies, and thus unaware of their religious fate, let alone able to comprehend or comply with it. Equally, some of the biblical material images the children to be sacrificed as newborns (for example, Exod. 22:29–30). And yet, Jephthah's daughter, like Isaac also a grown child, does seemingly agree to her own death (Judg. 11:34, 36–37). This seems intended to ease some of the ethical and theological tensions, but it makes the story less easy to resolve in terms of what is known of child-sacrifice around the Mediterranean. Text and context point in the same direction but they cannot totally be brought into line.

[27] Stavrakopoulou, *King Manasseh and Child Sacrifice*, pp. 261–82.

Whether or not the ancient Israelites had practised child sacrifice, by the time of the compilation of the books of the Hebrew Bible (Old Testament), some time in the sixth to second centuries BCE, the custom was firmly opposed by the Jews. By the middle of the first millennium BCE, moreover, they were not the only people in the pre-Christian Mediterranean world to abhor child sacrifice. The classical Greeks and the Romans were also appalled by the practice, which they located in an older age that they, like the Jews, had left behind. Classical Greece of the fifth and fourth century BCE had its own Abraham and Isaac story, the sacrifice of Iphigenia, daughter of Agamemnon. In the dramatisation of this myth by Euripides (*c.* 484–407 BCE) and Aeschylus (*c.* 525–456 BCE), Agamemnon displeases the gods when he mistakenly kills a deity masquerading as a stag in a hunt. The gods then punish the king by becalming his fleet and preventing it from setting out to Troy. When the high priest, Calchas, suggests that the gods can be appeased by the sacrifice of his daughter, Agamemnon reluctantly obeys and places Iphigenia on the funeral pyre. Artemis, however, takes pity on the victim and whisks Iphigenia away to safety, replacing her body with a deer's. Agamemnon, on the other hand, is not forgiven for his temerity, and his future woes and murder by the hand of his wife are his punishment for his readiness to offer up his daughter.

The Iphigenia story was widely disseminated in the Graeco-Roman world. A Greek vase in the British Museum depicts the moment that Iphigenia is replaced by a stag, and there is particularly graphic illustration of her being carried to the pyre on a fresco at Pompeii. (See Figure 2).[28] Still, before the sixteenth century and the European-wide renewal of interest in classical culture, few Christians can have encountered the Iphigenia story. It was the Biblical accounts of the attempted sacrifice of Isaac which the Christians of the middle ages imbibed. As Christians, however, they understood it very differently from their Jewish and Muslim cousins, and in a way that could only heighten interest and unease in the practice of child sacrifice. In the Christian tradition the story of Abraham and Isaac prefigures Christ's death in the New Testament. The Father who has forbidden child sacrifice lets his own son be sacrificed so that the world may be redeemed. At the same time, Christians were taught that the Son, the sacrificial victim, placed peculiar emphasis during his mission on earth on the innocence and holiness of children. The portrayal of Jesus as both a knowing adult and a valued child (who is childlike in his sinlessness) is crucial to the Christian theological presentation of his death as a sacrifice. Jesus is not an uncomprehending victim; unlike Isaac, Jesus is not unaware of his fate.[29] Instead, like Jephthah's daughter and Iphigenia, he is a sacrificial offering who is a willing participant. Viewed from the theological perspective of the New Testament, the motif of child sacrifice takes on a second dimension as it is conflated with another motif familiar from its Jewish cultural heritage: that of self-sacrifice.[30]

[28] http://lilt.ilstu.edu/drjclassics/syllabi/greekreligion/iphigenia2.htm (24 Sept. 2005). The myth was also known to the Etruscans. There is a terracotta slab bearing a painting of Iphigenia being dragged to the altar in the Louvre.
[29] It is interesting to note that later Jewish, Christian, and Islamic interpretations of the story frequently depict Abraham's son as a knowing and enthusiastic offering; on this and the possible interrelation of these varying religious traditions, see further M. E. Kessler, *Bound by the Bible: Jews, Christians and the Sacrifice of Isaac* (Cambridge: Cambridge University Press, 2004), esp. pp. 100–18; R. Firestone, 'Merit, Mimesis, and Martyrdom: Aspects of Shi'ite Meta-historical Exegesis on Abraham's Sacrifice in Light of Jewish, Christian, and Sunni Muslim Tradition', *Journal of the American Academy of Religion*, 66 (1998), 93–116; F. Manns (ed.), *The Sacrifice of Isaac in the Three Monotheistic Religions* (Jerusalem: Franciscan Printing Press, 1995).
[30] There are numerous scholarly discussions of self-sacrifice and martyrdom. For a sampling of views, see further A. J. Droge and J. D. Tabor (eds), *A Noble Death: Suicide and Martyrdom among Christians and Jews in Antiquity* (San Francisco: Harper, 1991); J. W. van Henten and F. Aremarie (eds), *Martyrdom and Noble Death: Selected Texts from Graeco-Roman, Jewish and Christian Antiquity* (London: Routledge, 2002).

Childhood, Sacrifice and Redemption

James Francis

Whatever is to be said about child sacrifice in some ancient traditions in the Hebrew Scriptures, the early church inherited the normative Jewish idea of the abhorrence of the practice. More generally Judaism and Christianity were known in the ancient world for not following the custom of the exposure of unwanted children. Children, including the unborn, were within God's covenant.[31] Nevertheless violence against children could be a fact of political life (Matt. 2.13ff), and children could suffer the consequences of a sudden parental change of fortune (Matt. 18.25). The early Christian church shared the Jewish view of children as a gift from God (cf. Matt. 7.9ff), with barrenness and childlessness viewed as a great misfortune (Gen. 15.1; Gen. 30.1). This attitude would certainly have been reinforced by Jesus's own explicit welcome of children, including babes in arms, and his modelling of entry to and discipleship in the Kingdom of God through child imagery. Generally speaking, the social world of the New Testament was one in which children continued to signify stability and perpetuity.[32] So in Mark 12.18–23 (Matt. 22.23–28 and Luke 20.27–33) the Sadducees' test question about the Resurrection acknowledges the importance of children as heirs;[33] the parable of the friend at midnight (Luke 11.7) reflects the common pattern of a family in a single-roomed house ('my children are with me in bed and I cannot get up...'); and the mention of children almost in passing in many places in the gospels suggests that they were simply part of everyday life, whether playing in the street (Matt. 11.16ff; Luke 7.31ff) or growing up in the home (Luke 2.40, 52; Ephes. 6.1–4; Col. 3.20–21; 1 Tim. 5.4; Titus 2.4).

Nevertheless, whilst the idea of child sacrifice was abhorrent, the Christological significance of Jesus as son or child of God, metaphorically speaking, contributed to the understanding of Jesus's death as a sacrifice and as an act of divine redemption. This is rooted in the way in which Jesus's ministry culminating in his death is imaged as the obedience of Jesus as God's son, or child or servant (the word *pais* in encompassing the last two descriptions is ambiguous). And this death is considered to be an offering/ sacrifice, drawing upon an interpretation of the *Akedah* (lit. 'binding') of Isaac tradition of Genesis 22.[34] Central to this, as the corollary to the obedience of Jesus as son/child and servant, is the righteousness of Jesus (or his sinlessness) in his offering, supported by belief in the Resurrection, namely that God would never raise to life someone justly put to death, and therefore a sinner. Consequently the church came to believe that the offering of Jesus was not only an offering to God for the sins of the world but a fulfilment of a divine intention that was at work throughout his ministry and indeed within his very person. Moreover in the imagery there is the echo from Gen. 22 of

---

[31] See Psalm 139.13ff; Psalm 131; cf. the early second century CE Epistle of Barnabas 19 '... thou shalt not murder a child by abortion, nor again shalt thou kill it when it is born'. The murder of the orphan was also a heinous act: Psalm 94.6; cf. Job 24.9. On exposure and abortion in the classical era, see Ch. 2, pp. 59–64.

[32] For a range of perspectives on children and the family in Biblical, historical and contemporary contexts see S. C. Barton (ed.), *The Family in Theological Perspective* (Edinburgh: T. and T. Clark, 1996).

[33] In fulfilment of Deut. 25.5.

[34] For a detailed study see N.A. Dahl, 'The Atonement – An Adequate Reward for the Akedah?', in E. E. Ellis and M. Wilcox, *Neotestamentica et Semitica (Studies in Honour of M. Black)* (Edinburgh: T. and T. Clark, 1969), pp. 15–29. See also M. Moskowitz, 'Towards a Rehumanization of the Akedah and Other Sacrifices', *Judaism*, 37 (1988), 288–94.

Isaac specifically as the only child, *i.e.*, dear or precious, in that Jesus is also thought of as God's own dear child or son (in John's Gospel as 'only begotten'). This, therefore, makes the sacrifice of Jesus (together with belief in the resurrection of the son of God) of particular redemptive significance for Christian belief as the foundation of a new creation, or (in Johannine language) a new beginning.

In the Jewish Midrashic[35] tradition the *Akedah* symbolises devotion to God rather than God's requirement for a sacrifice of Abraham's son. The purpose for Judaism of the *Akedah* is that God might remember his people. In the prayer of one who sounds the shofar (ram's horn) at Ro'sh ha-Shanah (the Jewish New Year), it is said: 'gaze upon the ashes of Isaac our father, heaped upon the altar, and deal with your people, Israel, according to the attribute of mercy'. So God when he hears the sound will recall the *Akedah* and remember the distress (alliteratively, *''akta'*) of his people.[36] In this the role of Isaac may come to be seen as important as that of Abraham, and indeed Isaac could become a model for martyrs (cf. 4 Macc. 7.14, 13.12, 16.20). (In some elaborations of tradition Isaac is actually slain and burnt and returns to life when his ashes are touched with the dew of resurrection.) Nevertheless, for Judaism human sacrifice is not sanctioned by God. It is by allowing Isaac to live that God shows his love. Moreover, as a wider principle, faith remains subject to the commandments of the Torah.[37]

Christianity, on the other hand, in wrestling with the death of Jesus followed a different path. It theologised Jesus's death as a sacrifice not only as a form of martyrdom (Mark 10.45), but also as the demonstration of God's love in the offering of the only son (John 3.16; Heb. 1.10), an act that matches the intended offering by Abraham of Isaac as his only son. It is easy to see how this grew out of, and also contributed to, a complex of metaphorical allusions concerning obedience and sonship associated with Israel and Jesus. Any person deemed righteous could be called a son or child of God, and indeed Israel itself could be so described. Christians also began to call themselves children or sons of God, and martyrdom (including the veneration of child martyrs) became part of the endorsement of its heroes of faith (though there is no mention of children in the catalogue of martyrs in Hebrews 11).[38] It is also readily seen how, much later on, the culturally imbedded Christian association of son/child imagery, obedience and sacrifice (in the appropriation of John 15.13) would come to express the death of a nation's sons (and daughters) as a noble ideal in the cause of freedom.[39]

· ·

---

[35] Early interpretations and commentaries on Biblical texts.

[36] Targum Neofiti (Aramaic version of the Pentateuch) Gen. 22.14. Equally in the Jewish New Year liturgy when the ram's horn is sounded the words of Hosea 6.6 are called to mind: 'For I desire steadfast love and not sacrifice, the knowledge of God rather than burnt offerings'. See also Dahl 'The Atonement', pp. 20–22.

[37] In *Fear and Trembling* (1843) the Danish philosopher Søren Kierkegaard contrasts Abraham with the other patriarchs in that his faith transcends the claims of ethics. But this misunderstands the centrality of the moral law for Judaism which is not to be set aside. Judaism will recognise Abraham's merit in being willing to go to such lengths in the demonstration of faith, but that does not mean that God would be pleased with such an offering.

[38] In the church of the third century CE a connection is made between the innocents murdered in Matt. 2.16ff and a sacrificial ideal of ascetic 'martyrdom'. This is derived from an association of ideas between childhood and innocence (a prevalent theme in early church and Gnostic type thinking). So the Massacre of the Innocents becomes identified with the martyrs of the Book of Revelation, with those who had not become defiled by women (Rev. 14.4). The (holy) innocents in Matthew's gospel were male babies, and in so far as it was infants whom Jesus had received and declared to be recipients of the kingdom (Matt. 18.3; cf. Mark 10.15), to be a child or to become as a little child is construed as a male who embraces the kingdom in sexual ascetic innocence.

[39] See below, pp. 50–52.

In the early years of the second century CE pagan Romans who misunderstood the mystery of the sacrifice of the mass accused Christians of the ritual murder of infants. Purportedly, they sacrificed children and then consumed their bodies in a communal meal. Christians were attacked on occasion and even killed as a result.[40] In denying these practices, early Christians were not only concerned to counter the accusations, but to use the denials to set themselves apart from other religious groups in the Ancient Middle East where the biblical texts appear to show that sacrifice of children was part of rituals of fertility. The Christian church later accused religious enemies of the same heinous crime. Thus, according to the Latin Father, Augustine of Hippo (354–430), the Manichees (the followers of the Persian Mani, d. c. 276) indulged in wild nocturnal orgies and then baked the ashes of children born of them into bread for use as a sacrament.[41] It was only in the twelfth century, however, that Christians began to attack groups in their midst whom they suspected of child-killing, when they attached their fears to Europe's Jews who were to suffer persecution as a result until after the Second World War.

By then many European Christians would have inherited or encountered tales of an independent tradition of child sacrifice that had no connection with the pre-classical Mediterranean world and was part of Viking culture. It appears to have been the custom of pagan Scandinavians to sacrifice a healthy child when a community was struck by an epidemic. The child would be buried alive or burnt as a propitiatory offering. Little is known about the custom but it was still alive in the folk memory of nineteenth-century Scandinavians. Indeed, the practice seems to have survived the region's conversion to Christianity, for as late as 1604 a court case in Denmark concerned a ritual sacrifice of this kind (the child was thought to be a carrier of the plague).[42] Whether the custom was limited to Viking Scandinavia or had been current among the Germanic peoples generally at the time of the Anglo-Saxon invasions of Roman Britain is impossible to say, but a variation certainly circulated in Württemberg as late as the end of the eighteenth century. When the village of Beutelsbach was struck by an animal epidemic in 1796, the community attempted to get rid of the disease by burying alive a healthy bull at the village cross-roads.[43]

The accusations levelled against the Jews in the late middle ages, however, owe nothing specifically to the Viking tradition. Rather they bear a close resemblance to the charges laid at the Manichees' door. The classic Jewish blood libel, as outlined in numerous books and pamphlets across time, asserts a secret Jewish ritual in which a Christian child is tortured and killed, often in a manner perceived to imitate Christ's passion, and its blood collected, usually for baking in the unleavened bread eaten at Passover. In fact, these were two different accusations which became conflated in the literature. The first appearance of the libel in England and France in the twelfth and thirteenth centuries involved a full-fledged re-enacting of the passion of Jesus, in which Jews were accused of tormenting, flogging, and eventually crucifying a child victim. At this stage blood magic did not seem to play any significant role in the accusations and the charges did not mention the Passover observances: the Jews were accused of a cruel mockery of Christian rites rather than of using blood in

---

[40] N. Cohn, *Europe's Inner Demons* (London: Pimlico, 1976), p. 3.

[41] Guibert of Nogent, *Autobiographie: texte et traduction*, ed. E. R. Labande (Paris: Belles-Lettres, 1981), pp. iii, xvii, 428–34; R. I. Moore, *The Origins of European Dissent* (London: Allen Lane, 1977), pp. 67–68, 166–67. The Manichees embraced an uncompromising dualism where control of the world was divided between a good and evil principle.

[42] H.-E. Hauge, *Levande Begravd eller Bränd i Nordisk Folkmedicin. En Studie I Offer och Magi* (Acta Universitatis Stockholmiensis. Stockholm Studies in Comparative Religion 6; Stockholm: Almquist and Wiksell, 1965). The editors are indebted to Grete Lillehammer of the Stavanger Museum of Archaeology for providing us with a summary of the contents of the book.

[43] D. W. Sabean, *Power in the Blood. Popular Culture and Village Discourse in Early Modern Germany* (Cambridge: Cambridge University Press, 1984), ch. 6.

their own rituals. For the accusers, the supposed ritual murders were transformed into a form of *imitatio Christi*, 'in which the representations of the boy victims and the child Jesus became fused and ritual murderers came to be associated with Host desecrations'.[44] In later centuries another form of the libel developed in continental Europe, especially in the German-speaking lands, which did emphasise the use of the victim's blood, albeit a totally implausible idea to anyone conversant with Jewish belief.[45] The accusations reached their peak towards the end of the fifteenth century, and it was around that time that the vast majority of cases achieved a consistent and standardised pattern. The victim would be a prepubescent boy, who would disappear around Easter. The unburied body would be discovered dumped in a river or in a forest. Autopsy would reveal numerous wounds inflicted with needles or daggers. Although the corpse would be completely drained of blood, it would supposedly start bleeding when approached by a Jew, thus miraculously revealing the murderer.[46] Images of the crime itself would be conflated with the eucharist; the motive of the 'murder' would be the need of the Jews to obtain Christian blood, which was supposed to possess salvific and magic powers.[47]

The appearance and widespread promotion of these charges has been associated with a wider network of libels and accusations by which princes and prelates, and the literati in their employ, achieved a new level of control over Europe's peoples in the late middle ages. The blood libel, it is argued, was an integral part of 'the formation of a persecuting society', that is a society where persecution became central to the exercise of bureaucratic power, the power by which the Christian literati gained ascendancy. In an era when Europe's Christian intelligentsia was still thin on the ground after the Dark Ages – the first universities were founded only at the turn of the twelfth century – the Jews with their 'truly formidable social and intellectual coherence', were potential rival claimants to such power, and had to be debased 'by legend' to a position below common humanity. Jews were thus portrayed as filthy, perverted, and menacing to Christian society by the power of the satanic forces with which they were in league.[48]

This, though, can only be part of the answer. The appearance and popularity of the myth of the Jewish blood sacrifice must also be connected in some way with changing theological sensibilities. Christ had traditionally been seen as the distant, unapproachable Son of God, but during the eleventh century a novel interest in his humanity and suffering, both as child and man, took root in northern European monasteries. In the following century, this new idea that Christians should empathise with the life of the Redeemer was popularised by the Cistercians, whose founder Bernard of Clairvaux (1090–1153) had particularly developed a cult of the infant Jesus. In the twelfth century, too, a new emphasis was given to the life

---

[44] R. Po-chia Hsia, *The Myth of Ritual Murder: Jews and Magic in Reformation Germany* (New Haven: Yale University Press, 1988), p. 55.

[45] Joseph Jacobs is one of many scholars to point out, on religious grounds, 'how impossible it is for Jews to use human blood' in their rituals, and that contact with a corpse 'renders a Jew impure … and incapable of performing any religious rite'. He argues furthermore that there are no traces of any Jewish sects deviating from this, and concludes: 'That some Jews may have been murderers of little children during the long course of Jewish history, no one for a moment would deny; but that they did so for any religious reason, there is absolutely not a vestige of evidence to show'. See his 'Little St. Hugh of Lincoln: Researches in History, Archaeology, and Legend', in J. Jacobs, *Jewish Ideals and Other Essays* (New York: Macmillan, 1896), pp. 198–99.

[46] A. Dundas (ed.), *The Blood Libel Legend: A Casebook of Anti-Semitic Folk Lore* (Madison: University of Wisconsin Press, 1991).

[47] Jacobs, 'Little St Hugh', p. 204.

[48] R. I. Moore, *The Formation of a Persecuting Society: Power and Deviance in Western Europe 950–1250* (Oxford: Blackwell, 1987), p. 152. The Jewish intellectual powerhouse was Spain, a part of Europe long divided between Muslims and Christians and the conduit whereby the Graeco-Roman literary and philosophical inheritance was once again made available to northern Europe in the course of the eleventh and twelfth centuries.

and holiness of the Virgin Mary, epitomised by the first appearance of a collection of her miracles, and sculptors began to portray mother and child naturalistically rather than as icons.[49] Whatever the reason for this shift, it cannot but have encouraged a popular belief that Christ on the cross was in some way a sacrificial lamb, a slaughtered babe. This association can only have been heightened after the Lateran Council of 1215, where the Church decided that the mass was an actual sacrifice in which the death of Christ was literally re-enacted and where the body and blood of Christ were actually consumed, even if the host was seen only as a wafer and the wine-turned-blood remained invisible in the chalice. In such circumstances, it is not surprising that from the thirteenth century reports multiplied of people seeing visions of a bleeding child in the host, and the child on the altar became a frequent subject of iconographic illustration.[50] Nor is it surprising that anti-Semitic Christian propagandists played with this new conception of the mass as an actual sacrifice in creating the blood libel. It struck a chord to argue that the Jews who lived in Europe must also use blood in their rituals and, having no Christian priests to work miracles for them, must murder children to get it.

The consequence of the blood sacrifice paranoia was that the Jews were eventually expelled from a number of western European states in the succeeding centuries. At the end of the thirteenth century, in the reign of Edward I (r. 1272–1307), they were ejected from England; in 1492, those who refused to convert were finally removed from the kingdoms of Castile and Aragon, the one part of western Europe where they had been present in large number; and in 1615 they were formally expelled from France. The removal of the Jews, however, did not mean that the blood-libel disappeared from popular consciousness in these countries. On the contrary, it remained alive and well in England and the myth became a popular literary trope for instance. Throughout the late middle ages anti-Semitism was an integral feature of early English poetry and drama, and the myth was thus absorbed by courtier and townsman alike.

The Blood Libel – Literary Representations of Ritual Child murder in Medieval England

Elisabeth Dutton

The first blood libel in England related to events in 1144, when the body of a twelve-year-old boy, William, was found in a wood outside Norwich on Easter Sunday.[51] Thomas of Monmouth's Latin *Life and Miracles of St William of Norwich*, written about 1173, records the gradual 'discovery' of the Jews' guilt in William's 'martyrdom': Gavin Langmuir has demonstrated that Thomas's investigations were probably responsible

---

[49] R. W. Southern, *The Making of the Middle Ages* (London: Hutchinson, 1967), pp. 221–44; C. Bynum, *Jesus as Mother: Studies in the Spirituality of the High Middle Ages* (Berkeley: University of California Press, 1982).

[50] This image of the bleeding child in the host is discussed, with many helpful illustrative plates, in M. Rubin, *Gentile Tales: The Narrative Assault on Late Medieval Jews* (New Haven: Yale University Press, 1999). For the importance of the eucharist in the middle ages, see her *Corpus Christi: The Eucharist in Late Medieval Culture* (Cambridge: Cambridge University Press, 1991). Interestingly, it is to unbelievers – especially Jews – that the vision of the host as bleeding body is generally given; its revelation of the theological 'truth' of the real presence at once horrifies unbelievers and converts them to Christian orthodoxy.

[51] This is usually taken to be the first documented case of the blood libel. But see I. Yuval, *Shene goyim be-vitnekh: Yehudim ve-Notsrim, dumuyim hadadiyim* (Tel Aviv: 'Alma / 'Am 'Oved, 2000), pp. 184–88.

for creating as well as recording this blood libel.[52] In particular, Langmuir attributes to Thomas the creation of the 'fantasy' that Jews ritually murdered Christians by crucifixion: 'the only person at Norwich up to 1150 who had explicitly asserted that the Jews had crucified the boy was Thomas himself'.[53] Thomas was not motivated by unusual hatred of the Jews, although he used the witness of others who apparently were – William's family, who accused them of murder, and a converted Jew named Theobold who introduced the idea of an annual Jewish sacrifice – to his own ends. Those ends were the beatification of William and the creation of his cult: with this purpose Thomas weaves his story as that of an innocent boy crucified by Jews during Passover and in Easter week, *in imitatione Christi*.

Following the case of William of Norwich, Jews were accused of the murder of the child Harold of Gloucester in 1168, and of the young boy Robert of Bury-St-Edmunds in 1181. Robert was celebrated as a martyr, but more renowned was the 'martyr' Hugh of Lincoln, reputedly victim of Jewish child murder in 1255. The story was immortalised in the ballad of 'Sir Hugh, or, the Jew's Daughter',[54] and lies behind Chaucer's blood libel narrative, *The Prioress's Tale*: these literary treatments have ensured its celebrity, but it was earlier recorded in the annals of the abbey of Burton-on-Trent, and with some variation and elaboration, in the chronicles of Matthew Paris (d. 1259).[55] Paris echoes the language of Christ's passion as he describes the scourging, piercing and crucifixion of eight-year-old Hugh in insult to Jesus Christ. Hugh's body is discovered by his mother in the well of a Jew, Copin. Copin is interrogated and confesses that the Jews annually crucify a boy in this way: he implicates all the Jewry of England as complicit with the crime. King Henry III (r. 1216–72) investigates the charges and large numbers of Jews are imprisoned in the Tower of London and condemned, but some are rescued by the intercessions of the Franciscans (or the Dominicans, in the version of the abbey annals).

Though even Matthew Paris condemns Copin's efforts to implicate all the nation's Jews as 'ravings' (*deliramenta*), the account demonstrates that the blood libel's ripples spread alarmingly from the local to the national as more Jews, religious orders, and even the King were brought into the narrative. Paris also, perhaps innocently, suggests the power of the blood libel myth to pervert justice, for the only real evidence his account offers of Jewish guilt is the confession of Copin, which, he makes clear, is extracted under threat. But when a body is found in a Jewish well, John of Lexington, who, we are told, is a learned man, is able to apply 'knowledge' of the blood ritual myth and declare: 'We have heard sometimes that the Jews have dared to attempt such things in insult to our crucified Lord Jesus Christ'.[56] By 1255, it seems, the blood libel was a fiction which was fashioning fact.

The blood libel continued, in the thirteenth century, to be primarily a tool for persecution of the Jews by the authorities, not the grounds for widespread popular anti-Jewish sentiment. Edward I finally expelled the Jews from England in 1290 because of financial exigency: the Jews' status as financiers to the crown ensured their royal protection but also made them vulnerable to this 'single and arbitrary act of spoliation'.[57]

---

[52] G. I. Langmuir, 'Thomas of Monmouth: Detector of Ritual Murder', *Speculum*, 59 (1984), 820–46.

[53] *Ibid.*, p. 842.

[54] The ballad is number 155 in F. J. Child, *English and Scottish Popular Ballads* (5 vols; London: Houghton, Miflin and Co., 1882–98), and is a frequently-used source for scholars. See for example Jacobs, 'Little St. Hugh of Lincoln', and G. I. Langmuir, 'The Knight's Tale of Young Hugh of Lincoln', *Speculum*, 47 (1972), 459–82.

[55] See Jacobs, 'Little St Hugh', for a comparison of the abbey annals' account and that of Matthew Paris.

[56] Cited in Jacobs, 'Little St Hugh', p. 201.

[57] Moore, *Formation of a Persecuting Society*, p. 44. The political and economic motivations behind the expulsion of Jews from England are dramatised in Steven Berkoff's play, *Ritual in Blood*, which appears in his *Collected*

R. I. Moore reads the story of the English Jews as one of royal persecution without the endorsement of popular hostility. None the less, he notes that 'the apparatus for the persecution of Jews in Europe was fully worked out during the thirteenth century' – the persecutors' image of the Jew is established and drawings begin to depict Jews as physically distinctive, with long, hooked noses.[58]

Since, like the image of the hooked-nose Jew, the Jewish blood libel is a fiction, it is perhaps less peculiar than it might at first seem that the blood libel should have a vibrant afterlife as a literary phenomenon in England long after the Jewish expulsion. *The Prioress's Tale* is written late in the fourteenth century; into the fifteenth and sixteenth centuries anti-Semitic stereotypes[59] are central to the staging of the mystery cycles.[60] The English miracle play, *The Croxton Play of the Sacrament*, tells a story related to the blood libel – that of Jewish host desecration, in which Jews stab the consecrated host which then miraculously bleeds. *Croxton*'s Jews, who swear by Mohammed, are clearly fiction unrelated to fact: their mockery of the Christian belief in 'God in a cake' relates to supposed Jewish literal-mindedness but their determination to test the belief implies potential faith and, when the host is transformed into a vision of the bleeding Christ, *Croxton*'s Jews have the 'happy ending' of conversion.[61]

When Christ miraculously appeared in the host in *The Croxton Play of the Sacrament*, we are told that he appears bleeding and in the form of a child.[62] (See Figure 3). Numerous host desecration narratives across Europe relate the apparition of a bleeding child: numerous medieval visual representations of this vision survive.[63] While the

---

Plays, vol. 3 (London: Faber, 2000).

[58] *Ibid.*, p. 45, and B. Blumenkranz, *Le Juif médiéval au miroir de l'art chrétien* (Paris: Etudes Augustiniennes, 1966), pp. 15–32.

[59] The term 'anti-Semitic', as distinct from 'anti-Jewish', is itself controversial among scholars. The terms may be differentiated thus: 'To be "anti-Jewish" is to attack the real faith and culture of Judaism and those who identify as Jews. Conversely, antisemitism is constituted by imaginative and imaginary slanders forced on to those identified as Jews; antisemitism can flourish without "real" Jews as it is not concerned with reporting material reality': see A. Bale, 'Fictions of Judaism in England before 1290', in P. Skinner (ed.), *Jews in Medieval Britain* (Woodbridge: Boydell Press, 2003), pp. 129–44 (at p. 129). But Elisa Narin van Court considers this distinction unhelpful in the medieval period: 'the argument that anti-Judaism becomes anti-Semitism when it becomes irrationally predicated on and enacted in irrational charges against the Jews (ritual murder, host desecration) assigns a particular date, that of the first ritual murder charge in England (1150) to this transformation from anti-Judaism to anti-Semitism. But this does not account for earlier irrational responses to the Jews, such as that of John Chrysostom in fourth-century Antioch, and it does not account for the anachronism inherent in the term anti-Semitism which is a creation of nineteenth-century racial theory': E. Narin van Court, 'Socially Marginal, Culturally Central: Representing Jews in Late Medieval English Literature', *Exemplaria*, 12:2 (2000), 293–326, at p. 293, fn. 1.

[60] Michael Jones finds an inherent theatricality in medieval representations of the Jew: see M. Jones, '"The Place of the Jews": Anti-Judaism and Theatricality in Medieval Culture', *Exemplaria*, 12:2 (2000), 327–57. Of course the Jew is also a vital figure in much renaissance theatre – most notably in Marlowe's *Jew of Malta* and Shakespeare's *Merchant of Venice*: see J. Shapiro, *Shakespeare and the Jews* (New York: Columbia University Press, 1996).

[61] On *Croxton* see L. Lampert, *Gender and Jewish Difference from Paul to Shakespeare* (Philadelphia: University of Pennsylvania Press, 2004), pp. 108–22. For the text of the play see *The Play of the Sacrament*, in *Medieval Drama: An Anthology*, ed. G. Walker (Oxford: Blackwell, 2000), pp. 212–33.

[62] 'Here … must … an image appere out with woundys bledyng', *The Play of the Sacrament*, line 228.

[63] See the two works by M. Rubin cited in fn. 50 above. Rubin's focus, in *Gentile Tales*, is on the Jew rather than the child, but she does note that 'child-like innocence paralleled the child-like persona of Christ, the innocence of Christ, and raised the level of compassion and drama in the narrative: the host itself could turn into a child… Children were agents of discovery, and symbolic victims as abused hosts turned into child-like figures' (p. 77). The story which Rubin discusses (pp. 5–39) of the little Jewish boy who receives the sacrament and is thrown as punishment into an oven by his father, but is preserved miraculously by the Virgin and

persistent and destructive levelling of both ritual murder and host desecration charges against the Jews has rightly led historians to discuss both libels in the context of Jewish persecution, the persistent presence, in both ritual murder and host desecration accounts, of a crucified child victim has not generally led historians to discuss the libels as moments in the history of childhood.[64]

There are of course good reasons for this. In the case of the blood libel, it is known that Jews were charged with and executed for the ritual crucifixion of children, but it is not known that a single child was ever actually crucified; in the case of host desecration charges, the crucified child is always, clearly, a substitutionary image for Christ's presence in the host: in both cases the child is an imaged, projected victim, literary rather than literal.[65] When the blood libel becomes entirely literary Chaucer, in *The Prioress's Tale*, offers a narrative distanced not only by its remote setting in Asia but also by its almost sentimentally fictionalised tone. The child or 'little clergeon' who is murdered by Jews for singing the *Alma redemptoris* is seven years old and repeatedly described as 'small', 'little, 'young and tender of age', but he is idealised not for the Marian devotion which moves his song but for his virginity. As a 'martyr', 'united to virginity', he will follow the celestial lamb with others that 'never knew women in the flesh'.[66] The worrying possibility of sexualisation of the child is actually asserted by its unnecessary denial – a seven-year-old's virginity should be unremarkable. At one level, however, the focus on virginity makes sense in the context of the identification with the child of the Prioress herself, for whom bodily chastity is a powerful ideal:[67] the Prioress also associates herself with the child in her lack of education, for the *Tale* links the unschooled praise of God by suckling infants, by the little boy who does not understand the Latin of the *Alma Redemptoris* he sings, and by the Prioress whose praise of the Virgin is as ignorant, she claims, as that of a child less than a year old.[68] The Prioress through her *Tale* asserts the validity of a devotion which 'feels the call of the spirit without comprehension of the letter'.[69] There is furthermore a critical, even subversive irony to the story. As Lisa Lampert notes, it is 'the Jews who understand both the literal meaning of the *Alma* and its spiritual impact, which they do not accept, yet comprehend well enough to kill the boy'.[70] Furthermore, the Jews are here curiously

---

converts his mother to Christianity, seems to combine the roles of child witness and child victim: that the image of Christ which appears in *The Play of the Sacrament* bursts from an oven in which the host has been thrown perhaps furthers the iconographic connection with this story. There is also a practical consideration for the staging of this play – that is it easier to fit a child actor than an adult into a stage-prop oven.

[64] A notable exception is Magdalene Schultz, who writes that the motif of the child victim is 'closely connected with how the majority of the population – and the [Jewish] minority within it – treated their own children': M. Schultz, 'The Blood Libel: A Motif in the History of Childhood', *Journal of Psychohistory*, 14 (1986), 1–24, at p. 1. While her arguments are not compelling, and suffer by her own admission from a paucity of historical data, her suggestion that the blood libel should be considered as a motif in the history of childhood is challenging, if only because it urges reflection on the constructed nature of the child victim.

[65] See James Francis's comment, above p. 28, on the suggestive ambiguity of the application to the crucified Christ of the word *pais*, which can mean God's son, child or servant.

[66] *The Prioress's Tale* in *The Riverside Chaucer*, ed. L. D. Benson (Oxford: Oxford University Press, 1988), pp. 209–12, lines 579–85.

[67] On the connection between the body of the little boy and the ideal of chastity for a nun such as the Prioress, see S. Spector, 'Empathy and Enmity in the *Prioress's Tale*', in R. R. Edwards and S. Spector (eds), *The Olde Daunce: Love, Friendship and Marriage in the Medieval World* (Albany: State University of New York Press, 1991), p. 222. See also fn. 38 above on the interpretation of Christ's words that children shall inherit the kingdom as referring to sexual ascetic innocence.

[68] *The Prioress's Tale*, lines 453–59, 516–35, 481–87.

[69] Lampert, *Gender and Jewish Difference*, p. 82.

[70] *Ibid.*

aligned with the male ecclesiastical institution where the 'clergeon' risks being beaten three times in an hour for learning the *Alma* at the expense of his regular lessons.[71]

The Prioress's tale of child murder retains the associations of murderous Jews with usury, filth and accursedness which earlier persecutors of the Jews developed.[72] It appears, however, to have moved a long way from the impulse which R. I. Moore has argued lies behind the legend's creation – the need to protect the interests of Christian literati by the denigration of rival Jewish cultural achievement.[73] This shift was doubtless made possible by the expulsion of the Jews from England in 1290 who might otherwise have challenged their literary construction. Yet if the expulsion facilitated shifts in the position of the constructed Jew, children were always present in these later anti-Semitic stories, and there seems a continuity in the role of the child victim. In literary and pictorial representations, the Christian viewer is 'not simply drawn into the scene of ritual murder voyeuristically, but he or she is also called upon to identify with this suffering child, to feel him- or herself equally vulnerable to such evil and protected only by faith'.[74] Arguably, the reason for this lies in the uncertainty of life in the late middle ages both before and after the expulsion. As Langmuir comments in his analysis of Thomas of Monmouth's account of the persecution of William of Norwich, the child victimised *in imitatione Christi* 'would seem a representative of all those who felt defenceless as a child against the little-understood forces that menaced their existence, and who turned for comfort to their faith that Christ might intervene'.[75] The construction of the child victim then is not so much a moment in the history of childhood, but principally a projection of the Christian adult's own fear of persecution in a precarious pre-modern world.

· ·

Despite the frequency, in the Holy Roman Empire in particular, with which Jews in the late middle ages were accused of 'sacrificing' Christian children, the blood libel quickly disappeared from the court rooms of Europe west of the Elbe in the century following the Reformation. Thereafter in a western Europe now split into two mutually hostile Christian camps, it seldom reared its head in any form, except in learned theological tomes, especially once the papacy made clear it would have no truck with the belief. Even if Jews were forced to live in ghettos in countries where their presence was still tolerated, they were largely left to their own devices. Indeed, there was something of a shift in official attitudes. The majority of Europe's university educated elite remained anti-Semitic way into the nineteenth century, if not beyond, but a growing number of intellectuals, both inside and outside the confessional churches of the post-Reformation world began to take a new and positive interest in the Hebrew language and Jewish culture. As a result, from the mid-seventeenth century, Jews were once more able to establish themselves without undue difficulty in England, and on

---

[71] See R. Hanning, 'From *Eva* and *Ave* to Eglentyne and Alisoun: Chaucer's Insight into the Roles Women Play', *Signs*, 2 (1977), 580–99, at p. 590.

[72] See, *e.g.*, *The Prioress's Tale*, lines 490–92, 567–78. The *Tale* is not precisely that of Hugh of Lincoln but it echoes it in many ways, and closes with an invocation to Hugh (lines 684–87):

> O yonge Hugh of Lyncoln, slayn also
> With cursed Jewes, as it is notable,
> For it is but a litel while ago,
> Preye eek for us…

[73] See above, p. 31.

[74] Lampert, *Gender and Jewish Difference*, p. 96

[75] Langmuir, 'Thomas of Monmouth', p. 845.

the eve of the French Revolution, in a state such as the Austrian empire where they were numerous, they had been given the right to worship openly.[76]

Admittedly, the Jewish blood libel was not entirely forgotten and courts on occasion could still display the blind prejudice of earlier centuries. In 1669 a young boy went missing near Metz, a city in France that had formerly been part of the Holy Roman Empire and had a sizeable Jewish population.[77] Reports circulated of a man carrying a boy on his horse. Witnesses identified the horseman as Raphaël Lévy, a Jewish butcher from nearby Boulay. He was accused of abducting the boy for sacrificial purposes. Raphaël voluntarily gave himself up, confident of his innocence. The mangled remains of the child were found, apparently eaten by wild animals. But the Parlement of Metz found Raphaël guilty and sentenced him to be tortured and then burned at the stake. The verdict was probably influenced by Christian merchants, jealous of their Jewish competitors. It was followed by measures to expel the Jews from Metz. In January 1670 the citizens of Metz watched the smoke drift heavenwards from the roasting flesh of Raphaël Lévy, expiating a crime of which he was innocent. What is significant about this case, however, is that the behaviour of the Metz judges was soon disowned by royal authority. When King Louis XIV (r. 1642–1715) personally took charge of the case six months later, he censured the magistrates of Metz and vindicated the Jewish community.[78]

Yet if the Jews in western Europe were only infrequently accused of ritual killing in the sixteenth and seventeenth centuries, other targets took their place. The period 1550–1650 was the great age of witch-hunting in pre-modern Europe, a novel phenomenon whose advent and eventual disappearance is still a matter of vibrant historical debate.[79] Undoubtedly, the panic was fostered by theologians, both before and after the Reformation, who laid out an elaborate ideology of satanism and witchcraft for the first time and encouraged Europe's rulers to eradicate the devil from their midst. But it is also evident that ordinary Christians living in the countryside were both frightened and seduced by the purported power of witches to control and manipulate nature through secret brews and potions and could be easily persuaded to provide the judicial authorities with victims. Just like the Jews, witches were thought to sacrifice babies in their rituals. In a number of cases in Germany, for instance, they were accused of making a diabolic soup out of the bodies of unbaptised children which they would cook, then use the stock to raise storms.[80] In part the accusation reflected current medical orthodoxy. Many learned doctors believed in the peculiar therapeutic virtues of human blood and bone, so judges and accusers understandably suspected witches of using

---

[76] Anti-Semitic views continued to be propounded by many of Europe's most 'enlightened' intellectuals in the eighteenth century, notably Voltaire: see A. Hertzberg, *The French Enlightenment and the Jews* (New York: Columbia University Press, 1968). For Hebrew studies and philosemitism at Oxford and in England generally in the seventeenth century, see D. Katz, *Philo-Semitism and the Readmission of the Jews to England* (Oxford: Clarendon Press, 1992); M. Feingold, 'Oriental Studies', in N. Tyacke (ed.), *History of the University of Oxford, vol. iv, The Seventeenth Century* (Oxford: Oxford University Press, 1997), pp. 450–75; E. Glaser, *Judaism without Jews: Philosemitism and Christian Polemic in Early Modern England* (Basingstoke: Palgrave, 2007).

[77] Theoretically, as discussed above, there were no Jews in France. But as the border moved eastwards in the sixteenth and seventeenth centuries with territorial gains at the expense of the Habsburgs, the kingdom inherited several Jewish colonies and no attempt was made to displace them.

[78] P. Birnbaum, *Un récit du 'meurtre rituel' au grand siècle: l'affaire Raphaël Levy. Metz 1669* (Paris: Fayard, 2008). Levy or Lévy's cause was taken up by the Catholic Biblical critic, Richard Simon (1638–1712). Joseph Reinach, *Une erreur judiciaire sous Louis XIV: Raphaël Lévy* (Paris: Delagrave, 1888), gives the key documents, including Simon's pamphlet (pp. 119–35) and a translation into French of a diary of the case written in Yiddish by an anonymous Jew of Metz (pp. 137–94).

[79] The literature on witchcraft is now extensive. A good starting-point is R. Briggs, *Witches and Neighbours: The Social and Cultural Context of European Witchcraft* (London: HarperCollins, 1996).

[80] The editors are indebted to Lyndal Roper for this information.

bodies, especially the succulent bodies of children in their spells.[81] But the accusation equally indicated the ease with which the deep-rooted cultural suspicion about child sacrifice could be transferred from one marginal group to another, in this case one that was even more worrying to the good Christian because it was not segregated from the host community.[82]

Throughout the sixteenth and seventeenth centuries, furthermore, the western European elite was clearly fascinated with the theme of child sacrifice and child slaughter *tout court*, even if the Jewish blood libel quickly lost its allure. In Catholic Europe in particular, where there was an apparently insatiable appetite for religious art and drama, popular Bible stories were constantly re-imagined by artists and writers. The fact that the stories concerning child murder were among the most frequently reworked suggests that they had a particular resonance in the elite's imagination. It can be assumed that this imagination was only stirred further by the news brought back to Europe by the Spanish *conquistadores* of child sacrifice in parts of the Americas, which led to an attempt by some charitable commentators to make sense of the practice.[83] Biblical stories, moreover, were not the only source of artistic inspiration. The Italian Renaissance of the fifteenth century had seen the rehabilitation of Graeco-Roman culture and the rediscovery of many lost classical texts. In the course of the sixteenth and the first half of the seventeenth centuries, exposure to these classical sources steadily increased with the institutionalisation of this revivified Graeco-Roman culture in the schoolroom and the rapid dissemination of the novel belief that laymen as well as clerics should be given an education in Latin and Greek.[84] The emphasis on teaching pupils to be good public speakers also encouraged schoolmasters to pen suitable dramas for their charges to perform, and child sacrifice was understandably a popular theme.[85]

Child Sacrifice in Early Modern Europe:
Text, Image and Fantasy

David Maskell

Child sacrifice exercised hearts and minds in early modern Europe. Two sources powerfully encouraged this – the Bible and the writings of Greece and Rome. From the Bible the two most celebrated stories of child sacrifice are those of Abraham and Jephthah; from classical antiquity, Agamemnon's sacrifice of Iphigenia. The common element to all three is a father sacrificing a child to win favour from a deity. Most people found this idea repugnant, but theologians had to wrestle with the two biblical episodes, especially Jephthah, who actually sacrifices his daughter. Repugnance, however, did not prevent artists and dramatists being fascinated. By far the most popular of the three

---

[81] Epilepsy could supposedly be treated with powders and potions concocted from a human skull, human bones, and semen collected under a waning moon: see L. W. B. Brockliss and C. Jones, *The Medical World of Early Modern France* (Oxford: Oxford University Press, 1997), p. 136.

[82] People accused of witchcraft tended to be old women without support in the community, but it was never suggested that this was a 'mark' of being a witch. Witches were 'hidden' until exposed by their 'nefarious' acts and their own confession.

[83] See below, pp. 41–42.

[84] The establishment of colleges and grammar schools teaching the Latin and Greek humanities is discussed in Ch. 3, p. 124.

[85] From the end of the sixteenth century, especially in colleges run by the Jesuits, it was commonplace to stage an end-of-year play in Latin which was attended by the pupils' parents and local municipal and landed grandees: see E. Boysse, *Le Théâtre des Jésuites*, reprint edn (Geneva: Slatkin, 1970).

subjects was Abraham's sacrifice, which generated at least 25 paintings by major artists between 1400 and 1700, including Caravaggio, Rubens and Rembrandt, and numerous works by lesser figures, such as Felice Ficherelli (1605–1660). (See Figure 4). The stories of Jephthah and Iphigenia, in contrast, only inspired half a dozen each, mostly by minor painters. Important dramatisations were Théodore de Bèze's *Abraham sacrifiant* (1550), George Buchanan's *Jephthes* (1554) and Racine's *Iphigénie* (1675).[86]

Child sacrifice for religious reasons should not be seen in isolation, but in the broader context of children being killed for other motives. Examples in the Bible are the stories of Athaliah, Zedechiah or Herod; in Greek myth, Atreus, Hecuba, or Medea. Inspired by these narratives, the visual and dramatic arts of early modern Europe are littered with the corpses of children. The multiplicity of data invites classification. Is the purpose propitiatory sacrifice, or revenge, or the elimination of dynastic rivals? Does the sacrificial victim resist or acquiesce? Is the killer a parent, a relative or a third party? Is the emphasis on childhood (infants or adolescents), or on the parent-offspring relationship? Do the children die? Are they spared? Is a substitute found? Or does the diversity of data invalidate attempts to classify? The answers are complex. Only one point can be made here. The expiatory dimension of child sacrifice may permeate the killing of children even when the motive is politics or revenge. Herod massacres the babies of Judea to rid himself of rivals to the throne. (See Figure 5). Yet the Christian tradition, exemplified by Heinsius' tragedy *Herodes infanticida* (1632), often suggested that the martyrdom of the Holy Innocents cleansed them of original sin. Medea slaughters her two children primarily for revenge upon Jason, their unfaithful father. Yet in the act, Medea also thinks to placate the spirit of her brother whom she herself murdered. This expiatory dimension is found in the *Medea* of both Euripides and Seneca as well as in the versions of two Christian dramatists, Jean Bastier de La Péruse (1553) and Pierre Corneille (1635).[87]

It is not surprising that Renaissance dramatists, recreating ancient tragedy in their own languages, should have been intrigued by child killing. It looms large in extant Greek tragedy, and even more so in the influential Latin dramas of Seneca, four of whose nine tragedies include child killing, all with sacrificial overtones (*Medea, Thyestes, Troades, Hercules Furens*).[88] However, it was through the Christian religion that the concept of human sacrifice exerted its most profound influence. Stavrakopoulou claims that 'the variety of "afterlives" of child sacrifice within the biblical and post-biblical traditions suggests that the practice was impossible to erase from the religious and cultural memories of the inheritors of the Judahite deity worship'.[89] It is a paradox that Christianity, so opposed to the sacrifice of humans and animals, should generate so many images, both direct and oblique of the sacrifice of human children.

In Genesis 22 God commands Abraham to sacrifice his son Isaac. The father has to cut his son's throat and burn the body on the altar. Without hesitation Abraham obeys, but an angel stays his hand, and Abraham sacrifices a ram instead. Jewish and Christian exegesis emphasise the lessons of obedience or deliverance contained in the

---

[86] Théodore de Bèze (1519–1605) was Calvin's successor at Geneva; George Buchanan (1506–82) was a Scottish humanist and Protestant who taught on the continent before returning home in 1562 to tutor Mary Queen of Scots.

[87] Seneca, *Medea*, lines 967–77; Jean Bastier de La Péruse, *Médée*, Act 5, lines 1175–83; Pierre Corneille, *Médée*, Act 5, scenes 4–5, lines 1561–74. For the various versions of the Medea story and its depiction in art, see C. O. Pache, *Baby and Child Heroes in Ancient Greece* (Chicago: University of Illinois Press, 2004), ch. 1. La Péruse (1529–54) was a Paris educated poet and dramatist taught by Buchanan.

[88] Calchas requires that Polyxena and Astynanax be sacrificed to the gods (*Troades* lines 360–70, 1099–1103); Atreus sacrifices his brother's children (*Thyestes* lines 682–88, 1057–65); Hercules treats the killing of his own children as a sacrifice (*Hercules Furens*, lines 991–1041); for *Medea*, see previous fn.

[89] Stavrakopoulou, *King Manasseh and Child Sacrifice*, p. 321.

story. Obedience is the key theme in *Abraham sacrifiant* (1550) by Théodore de Bèze, leader of the French protestants. But whilst *Genesis* 22 portrays Abraham obeying God's command with disquieting promptness, implying that there was nothing unusual in God commanding child sacrifice, Bèze gives Abraham an anguished speech, wondering what evil he can have done to deserve such a punishment. This illustrates the repugnance that child sacrifice inspired in the sixteenth century, but Bèze's text does not suggest that Abraham (or his wife) judge it to be an alien practice, just a test of obedience and faith.[90]

Whilst Jews and Christians stress Abraham's obedience, it was Christian tradition, not Jewish, which kept alive the concept that human sacrifice could be pleasing to God. Christians interpreted Abraham's near-sacrifice of Isaac as a prefiguration of God sending his beloved son to die on the cross to atone for the sins of mankind. This typological link between the Old and New Testament narratives was enthusiastically exploited in word and image from the earliest Christian centuries down to the early modern period and beyond.[91]

On its own the parallel between the boy Isaac and the adult Christ might not have perpetuated the concept of child sacrifice, for it is the adult Christ who was crucified. So how does the child re-emerge? As was noted earlier in the chapter, the Lateran Council of 1215, by insisting that in the eucharist the bread and wine were turned into the body and blood of Christ, gave impetus to two parallel developments. Child sacrifice became domesticated within the Christian tradition through an iconographic system linking the infant Jesus to the adult crucified Christ. On the other hand, the practice of child sacrifice was projected on to Jews by accusations that they were engaged in the ritual murder of male Christian children.[92]

Although Christian teaching insisted that the Mass was a commemoration and its sacrifice unbloody, from the thirteenth century reports multiplied of people seeing visions in the host. This led to the boy child on the altar becoming a frequent subject of iconographic illustration. Miri Rubin lists many examples and concludes: 'The transgression involved in contemplating, viewing and representing scenes of infanticide within the Eucharistic discourse provided sites for fantasy which could hardly have been tolerated in other reaches of the same culture'.[93] Such fantasies were also fed by woodcuts and prints depicting grisly images of Christian boys sacrificed by Jews, who were further accused of purloining consecrated hosts to desecrate them. These images drew inspiration from the Christian belief that the Jewish people were responsible for Christ's crucifixion and that they continued to re-enact the deicide.[94]

Meanwhile within the Christian tradition further evocations of child sacrifice developed. The gospel account of the presentation of the infant Jesus in the Temple (Luke 2.22–38) was a vehicle for gathering into a single image Jewish and Christian concepts of sacrifice and redemption. Jesus was brought by his parents to the Temple to satisfy the law: 'Every first-born male shall be designated as holy to the Lord' (v. 23).

---

[90] Théodore de Bèze, *Abraham Sacrifiant*, lines 705–938, in *Four Renaissance Tragedies*, ed. D. Stone Jr (Cambridge: Harvard University Press, 1966).

[91] See R. M. Jensen, *Understanding Early Christian Art* (London and New York: Routledge, 2000), pp. 143–48.

[92] Above, pp. 32–36. Regulations were promulgated requiring the church altar to be furnished with a crucifix and two candles: see J. Gardner, 'Altars and Art History: Legislation and Usage', in E. Borsook and F. S. Gioffredi (eds), *Italian Altarpieces 1250–1500: Function and Design* (Oxford: Oxford University Press, 1994), pp. 6–9.

[93] Rubin, *Corpus Christi*, p. 139.

[94] H. Schreckenberg, *The Jews in Christian Art: An Illustrated History* (New York: Continuum, 1996); 'Profanation of the Host' (pp. 264–73); 'Charges Relating to Blood: The Accusation of Ritual Murder' (pp. 273–91).

This refers back to God's command to the Israelites 'Consecrate to me all the firstborn' (*Exodus* 13.2). Whether this and similar passages were commands to sacrifice the firstborn male child as a burnt offering, or simply to dedicate its life to the service of God, makes little difference in the case of Jesus, since he was sent by his father to be a redemptive sacrifice. This is made clear in the prophecy of Anna which concludes Luke's account: 'She spoke about the child to all who were looking for the redemption of Jerusalem' (v. 38).

Many Christian representations of the Presentation in the Temple show the child on an altar. The infant Jesus is subsumed into the sacrificial death of the adult Christ.[95] Many a Gothic and Renaissance altarpiece showed a Virgin and Child in the centre panel, thus placing the image of a child on the altar where the sacrifice of the Mass was celebrated.[96] Ubiquitous Madonnas as altarpieces or for private devotion often included symbolic allusions to Christ's passion – a sacrificial lamb or a cross. John the Baptist may be in attendance, pointing to the infant Jesus, whilst holding a scroll inscribed with '*Ecce Agnus Dei*' referring to the words 'Here is the Lamb of God who takes away the sins of the world' (John 1:29). The wider context of child sacrifice invites fresh appraisal of many familiar paintings of the Renaissance. Barbarity can be glimpsed beneath the urbanity. The sleeping Christ child has the sleep of death in the *Madonna of the Meadow* (c. 1500) by Giovanni Bellini (c. 1430–1516). The Christ child in the *Heaven and Earthly Trinities* (1680s) by Murillo (c. 1617–82) stands on stones evoking an altar.[97] Christian devotion and Christian polemic may mirror each other. Woodcuts circulated showing Jews binding and nailing the boy William of Norwich to a cross (1493).[98] The Bolognese artist, Giacomo Francia (1487–1557) in the 1540s and Murillo in the 1680s created devotional images showing the baby Jesus lying on the wooden cross of the crucifixion.[99]

Even as Renaissance artists were devising oblique evocations of child sacrifice, Spanish soldiers were crossing the Atlantic and discovering real child sacrifice among the American Indians.[100] Claiming a moral obligation to prevent such atrocities, the Spaniards slaughtered the Indians in their thousands. Horrified at the massacres, the Spanish monk Bartolomé de Las Casas (1474–1566) opposed the conquistadors' murderous logic. In his *Defence of the Indians* (c. 1552) he takes an ethnographic line, arguing that human sacrifice exists in many cultures and represents a praiseworthy offering to God of what is most precious, namely human life. Christianity of course condemns human sacrifice, but Las Casas argued that when the American Indians practise it, they are only following natural law in a misguided manner. They merit colonisation and correction, not extermination.[101]

[95] A. Henry, *Biblia Pauperum* [*c.* 1460]: *A Facsimile and Edition* (Aldershot: Scolar Press, 1987); H. J. Hornick and M. C. Parsons, *Illuminating Luke: The Infancy Narrative in Italian Renaissance Painting* (Harrisburg, London, New York: Trinity Press, 2003), pp. 123–49, on Ambrogio Lorenzetti's *Presentation in the Temple* (1342).

[96] C. Limentani Verdis and M. Pietrogiovanna, *Gothic and Renaissance Altarpieces* (London: Thames and Hudson, 2002), *passim*.

[97] For these and other examples, see G. Finaldi *et al.*, *The Images of Christ: The Catalogue of the Exhibition of 'Seeing Salvation'* (London: National Gallery Company, 2000), pp. 44–73.

[98] Schreckenberg, *The Jews in Christian Art*, p. 274.

[99] Finaldi, *The Image of Christ*, pp. 64–65.

[100] For child sacrifice among American Indians, see M. P. Winter, *The Aztecs, Maya and their Predecessors: Archaeology of MesoAmerica*, 3rd edn (San Diego, New York and Boston: American Press, 1993), pp. 208–09, citing archaeological evidence and the sixteenth-century accounts of Diego Durán and Bernadino de Sahaguin. Also T. Ardren and S. R. Hutson, *The Social Experience of Childhood in Ancient MesoAmerica* (Boulder: University Press of Colorado, 2006), pp. 269–70.

[101] Bartolomé de Las Casas, *In Defence of the Indians*, trans. by S. Poole (De Kalb: Northern Illinois Press, 1974), pp. 221–43; see D. K. Shuger, *The Renaissance Bible: Scholarship, Sacrifice and Subjectivity* (Berkeley, Los Angeles

Las Casas was concerned with the evils of Spanish imperialism, not with theology. However, in his view, 'it can be persuasively argued, from the fact that God commanded Abraham to sacrifice to him his only son Isaac, that it is not altogether detestable to sacrifice human beings to God'.[102] The Dutch jurist Hugo Grotius (1583–1645) went a stage further, bringing ethnographic arguments to bear on the central mystery of the Christian religion. In his *De satisfactione Christi* (1617) he sought to place the Christian doctrine of Atonement on a rational basis, explaining in juridical terms why God the father required the bloody sacrifice of his beloved son. In his final chapter he turns from jurisprudence to ethnography, listing examples of human sacrifice, including children, to show that the practice was widely accepted in many cultures as an effective way of placating angry deities. His list starts with the most alien (Canaanite sacrifices to Moloch), then progresses from the exotic to European cultures close to home.[103] Grotius locates the Crucifixion in the broad cultural context of blood expiation. But he is not attacking Christianity. He is defending it on rational grounds. The rituals of blood sacrifice are ordained by God – *ritus a Deo traditos* – and were sanctioned by God's command to Abraham.[104]

At the end of the seventeenth century a French classical drama provides a remarkable synthesis of many of these issues. Racine's last tragedy *Athalie* (1691), recounts the triumph of God over the worshippers of Baal, building on the account in 2 Kings 8.16–11.16. Racine's protagonist, Queen Athaliah, a Baal worshipper, has usurped the throne of Judah, having slaughtered her own grandchildren in order to exterminate the family of King David to which her husband had belonged.[105] The only Davidic heir to survive this massacre is the child Joash, who was hidden in the Temple. At the climax of Racine's play Joash is proclaimed the rightful king of Judah. However, just before this proclamation, his adoptive mother places a diadem on his head. Joash is terrified and asks 'Am I to be offered as a holocaust to appease the anger of God, as Jephthah's daughter once was?'[106] The boy's role was written to be performed by a girl, thus blurring genders. The question which Racine puts in Joash's mouth is puzzling because it misrepresents the story of Jephthah in *Judges 11*, who sacrificed his daughter, not to appease God's anger, but to fulfil a vow of thanksgiving for victory. However, it is likely that Racine intended both Joash and Jephthah's daughter to be seen as prefigurations of Christ. Louis Cappel (1585–1658), a Protestant contemporary of Racine, links the story of Jephthah's sacrifice with God's sacrifice of his son: 'In the deed of Jephthah's daughter we find a type of Christ, who was consecrated to death by his Father for our salvation'.[107] Cappel provides the link from Christ to Jephthah's daughter. Racine emphasises the links between Joash and Christ – both were of Davidic ancestry; both escaped a massacre; both were called king of the Jews. Through the anxious questioning which Racine has invented for the boy Joash the theme of child sacrifice links the

---

and London: University of California Press, 1994), pp. 80–83, for analysis of Las Casas's argument.

[102] Las Casas, *Defence*, p. 239.

[103] Hugo Grotius, *Defensio Fidei Catholicae de Satisfactione Christi Adversus Faustum Socinum*, ed. E. Rabbie, trans. H. Mulder (Maastricht: Van Gorcum, 1990), ch. 10, pp. 247–77; the argument is analysed in Shuger, *Renaissance Bible*, pp. 54–55, 82–87.

[104] Grotius, *Defensio*, pp. 256 and 266.

[105] Athaliah is thought to have ruled Judah from 841 to 835 BCE. Another source for the story is Josephus, *Antiquitates Judaicae*, viii–ix.

[106] 'Est-ce qu'en holocauste aujourd'hui presenté / Je dois, comme autrefois la fille du Jephté, / Du Seigneur par ma mort apaiser la colère?' (*Athalie*, Act 4, sc. 1, lines 1259–61).

[107] 'In Jephtae autem facto Christi a Patre pro salute nostro devoti et facti katara [Greek] … typum habemus'; see Louis Cappel, 'De Voto Jephtae', in *id., Critici Sacri* (London: J. Flescher, 1670), vol. 2, p. 2075, col. 2, para. 85); see also Shuger, *Renaissance Bible*, pp. 148–49.

worlds of the Old and New Testament. We may also note that in Racine's play Joash's question implies that child sacrifice was acceptable among Jews at the time of Queen Athaliah. To imply that child sacrifice was a Jewish custom in biblical times could have lent weight to the allegations that the Jews of Europe continued to sacrifice Christian children. This, though, can hardly have been Racine's intention, since his few direct comments on Judaism and Jews are positive.

Christians have always abhorred human sacrifice. Yet the central mystery of their faith was God's sacrifice of his beloved son. In early modern western Europe, child sacrifice provoked learned debate in theology, law and ethnography. Vibrant images of child sacrifice fed Christian imaginations through drama, paintings, engravings and woodcuts. Moreover, there was still a darker side that connected the world of the Renaissance and the Baroque with the middle ages. Intolerant rapacity and murderous fantasy, fuelled by horror of child sacrifice, caused the massacre of American Indians who did practise it, and from time to time, as the case of Raphaël Lévy reminds us, the burning alive of Jews who did not. In such manifold ways child sacrifice continued to impinge upon the consciousness of western Europe long after 1500.

· ·

From the second half of the seventeenth century, the witch-craze quickly died down, as the civil authorities virtually everywhere in western Europe came under the influence of the sceptical ideology of the Scientific Revolution and refused any longer to endorse the reality of witchcraft or acknowledge that a witch could be positively identified. At the same time, too, artistic renderings of child sacrifice or slaughter appear to have lost much of their appeal. Racine was at the end of a tradition.[108] On the other hand, the belief that children were being sought and killed for their blood or sacrificed in black masses appears to have retained a firm hold on the popular imagination, especially in Ancien Régime Paris.

Towards the middle of the seventeenth century, a rumour circulated that a number of abandoned children (who were carted off to the city orphanage, called the *Couche*) were being 'sold to people with a mad passion for life, who disembowelled them in order to plunge themselves in blood baths, imagining … an infallible remedy for all their ills'.[109] Later on in the century, in 1675, a similar rumour swept through the French capital that children were being abducted and killed on the orders of a noble woman stricken with leprosy who wanted to bathe in their blood. It was followed a few years later by the revelation, in the course of a legal investigation into claims that female courtiers were poisoning their rivals, that necromancers in the capital were sacrificing babies to the devil.[110] The scare in this case was largely manufactured from above and was the result of political in-fighting around Louis XIV. Yet a fourth panic in 1749–50 was evidence of growing class tension in the city and an early sign that the crown and aristocracy were no longer respected. In that year a fresh rumour swept the capital that the children of artisans were being abducted and murdered so that a decrepit, usually leprous, prince or princess or even the king himself might bathe in their sacrificed blood.[111]

---

[108] Admittedly, Handel wrote two oratorios on the subject, *Athaliah* (1733) and *Jephtha* (1752).

[109] Régis de Chantelauze, *Saint Vincent de Paul et les Gondis* (Paris: E. Plon, 1882), p. 260 fn. The *Couche* was paid for by the Paris parishes and the care received by the abandoned children was notoriously poor. For abandoned children and their fate in early modern Europe, see Ch. 2, pp. 73–79 and Ch. 3, p. 120.

[110] A. Somerset, *The Affair of the Poisons: Murder, Infanticide and Satanism at the Court of Louis XIV* (London: Weidenfeld and Nicolson, 2003), pp. 244–45, 248–50 and 326–27.

[111] A. Farge and J. Revel, *The Ruler of Rebellion: Child Abduction in Paris in 1750*, English trans. (Cambridge: Cambridge University Press, 1991), pp. 104–13. The truth of the matter was that the city authorities were rounding up street children in a heavy-handed manner as part of a crack down on disorder. The belief

To western Europe's educated elite in the eighteenth century such beliefs were evidence of popular superstition that needed to be eradicated with all the other manifestations of the people's 'irrationality' by their 'enlightened' betters.[112] This, though, was not the view in the eastern part of Europe. Just as in so many other ways, it is possible to divide western and eastern Europe in the early modern period, so their histories differed profoundly in this regard too.[113] Above all, this was true in the case of the Jewish blood libel. Whereas there were few practising Jews in Europe west of the Rhine after 1500, they remained a significant proportion of the population east of the Elbe. In the large state of Poland (that in the seventeenth century stretched from the Baltic to the Black Sea) Jews probably formed about ten per cent of the inhabitants. Yet in the later middle ages the blood libel had remained a western European phenomenon. It only properly took hold in Poland at the moment the accusation seems to have disappeared from the west for good. In Poland, too, the blood libel seems to have been 'intellectualised' to a much greater extent than ever before.

The Blood Libel against the Jews in Poland

Pawel Maciejko[114]

Shortly after the consolidation of the ritual murder discourse in late medieval Germany, the coherent paradigm began to fall apart. Already in the sixteenth century, deviations from the ideal type became more common: victims came to include people of all ages, both men and women, the identification of the sacrificial children and the eucharist would disappear from the trials, and the belief in the magical potency of Christian blood would be played down or completely abandoned.[115] The disintegration of the magical and religious discourse of ritual murder was paralleled by the decline of the number of trials in the German lands. Scholars have attributed these developments to the spread of the Reformation with its rejection of the Catholic doctrine of transubstantiation and the general 'disenchantment of the world'. However, the waning of the trials did not mean that the blood libel vanished completely: the belief that the Jews murder Christian children persisted in popular discourse and in collective memory, and 'passed from the realm of the functional – where beliefs and actual accusations could lead to inquests, trials, sentencing, or dismissal – into that nebulous region of myth (...) thus creating a knowledge to be transmitted under the guise of history'.[116] While the trials

---

that leprosy could be cured by drinking blood is a key part of the story of the conversion of the Emperor Constantine (*c.* 274–337). Constantine refused to heed God's call and was struck down with leprosy, a mark of sin. He was about to have children sacrificed for their blood, when he saw the light and was converted to Christianity. No one in 1750 thought the king of France had leprosy, but according to Farge and Revel he and his decadent court were seen as moral lepers.

[112] Cf. the views of the enlightened circle centred on the Avignon *érudit*, Esprit Calvet (1728–1810): L. W. B. Brockliss, *Calvet's Web. Enlightenment and the Republic of Letters in Eighteenth-Century France* (Oxford: Oxford University Press, 2002), pp. 398–99 and 401.

[113] It has been customary to divide Europe east and west of the Elbe in the early modern period. The east became a serf society just as the west ceased to be one.

[114] The following contribution is based, in part, on a chapter of my book *The Mixed Multitude: Jacob Frank and the Frankist Movement 1755–1816* (Philadelphia: University of Pennsylvania Press, forthcoming).

[115] Hsai, *Myth of Ritual Murder*, p. 204.

[116] *Ibid.*, p. 208.

gradually disappeared, the past accusations achieved the status of 'facts' attested by chronicles, histories, places of pilgrimage, paintings and sculptures. In western Europe, the blood libel moved from courtrooms to books.

The rumours about ritual murder did not reach Poland until the fifteenth century,[117] and the first documented trial took place in Rawa Mazowiecka in 1547.[118] It was the end of the seventeenth and the beginning of the eighteenth century when the Polish-Lithuanian Commonwealth witnessed what the historian Simon Dubnow termed 'a frenzy of blood accusations'.[119] And particularly violent and lethal outbursts of Church-backed anti-Semitism continued throughout the eighteenth century. In 1753, for instance, 31 Jews were arrested in Żytomierz on the orders of the suffragan bishop of Kiev, Kajetan Sołtyk (1715–88) after the body of a three-and-a-half year old boy was found on Easter Monday. The district court found them guilty of ritual murder and sentenced six of them to be flayed alive, then quartered; and a further six to be simply quartered. The sentences were carried out, although those who agreed to be baptised were merely beheaded.[120]

In Poland, the blood libel developed in inverse ratio to western Europe: very few cases occurred during the time the phenomenon reached its apogee in the German lands, while in the eighteenth century, when the trials virtually came to an end in the west of Europe, they rapidly increased in number in Poland-Lithuania.[121] In this regard, Poland resembled the lands of the Bohemian crown and Hungary. The most important consequence of this time lag between east-central and western Europe was that the blood libel discourse in Eastern Europe did not develop independently during the trials, but was absorbed in the process of cultural transmission. Those who authored works advocating blood libel treated past cases as historically established facts, often quoting earlier 'scholarly' literature on the subject. Accordingly, the accusation in Poland was linked with the development of anti-Jewish literature more closely than was the case in western Europe. Although the German lands saw many more ritual murder court cases than Poland, it seems that the amount of accusatory literature produced in Poland well surpasses anything ever published in Germany, or, for that matter, anywhere else prior to the nineteenth and twentieth centuries. Until 1800 not less than 96 works devoted solely to ritual murders were published; reprints, newspaper reports, remarks scattered in works on other subjects, memoirs, and almanacs go into hundreds. In particular, the 1750s and 60s saw a rapid increase in publishing activity; some of the books and pamphlets published during this time achieved the status of bestsellers and went through many editions.

Moreover, Polish eighteenth-century works propounding blood libel were much more extensive and detailed than their earlier west European counterparts. Several writers provided long lists of ritual murders in different countries or discussed various arcane aspects of the blood rite attributed to the Jews. The historian Ronnie Po-chia Hsia described Johannes Eck's *Ains Judenbüchlins Verlegung* (1541) as 'the summa of learned

---

[117] Hanna Węgrzynek, *"Czarna legenda" Żydów. Procesy o rzekome mordy rytualne w dawnej Polsce* (Warsaw: Bellona, 1995), p. 9.

[118] *Ibid.*, p. 8.

[119] S. Dubnow, *History of the Jews in Russia and Poland. From the Earliest Times until the Present Day*, trans. I. Friedlander (Philadelphia: Jewish Publication Society of America, 1946), vol. 1, p. 172.

[120] P. Majiecko, 'The Frankist Movement in Poland, the Czech Lands, and Germany (1755–1816)', D.Phil., University of Oxford 2004, pp. 28–34.

[121] Z. Guldon and J. Wijaczka *Procesy o mordy rytualne w Polsce w XVI–XVIII wieku* (Kielce: DCF, 1995) have established that in Poland between 1547 and 1787 there were 81 cases of ritual murder accusations. It is generally accepted that the existing lists of ritual murder accusations are incomplete.

discourse on ritual murder' produced by the wave of accusations in Germany.[122] It is illustrative to compare the German sixteenth-century 'summa' to its Polish eighteenth-century counterpart, Gaudenty Pikulski's *Złość żydowska* [Jewish wrath]. Pikulski's work was first published in 1758, it had four expanded editions within three years from the first publication, and the excerpts from it are being reprinted by various anti-Semitic groups to this day.[123]

Eck's book has 191 pages; the most expanded version of Pikulski's book is almost 1,000 pages long. More important than the sheer volume of the work is its ambition. For Eck, Jewish ritual murders constitute a barbarous custom, not a theological principle. His account of Jewish customs and rituals was superficial, at best. He gave no references to the Talmudic material, and relatively few references to the works written by Jewish converts to Christianity or Christian Hebraists. In contrast, Pikulski's work drew heavily on Christian Hebraists, especially on Johann Reuchlin (1455–1522) and Pietro Colonna Galatino (d. after 1539), and gave long quotations from the Talmud and other rabbinic works. Pikulski's account of the Jewish history during the Second Temple period was for the most part accurate and went beyond run-of-the-mill quotations of the first century CE Jewish historian, Josephus. Some sections, such as his discussion of regional varieties in the pronunciation of Hebrew in liturgy are in fact very interesting, attest to substantial linguistic knowledge and sensibility, and bring a lot of information not available elsewhere.

Without risking too broad a generalisation, we may say that in early modern western Europe, the blood libel discourse was associated with practical attacks on Judaism, not with theological polemic. The issue did not appear during the most infamous medieval Jewish-Christian disputations. Those who advocated blood libel seldom attacked the Talmud or theological tenets of Judaism. And vice versa: Pope Gregory IX, who issued the ban on the Talmud after the Paris disputation of 1240, also issued an anti-blood libel bull. For the most part, early modern anti-Jewish literature produced by intellectual elites in western Europe does not contain the blood libel accusation. The majority of Christian theologians attacking various aspects of Jewish rites and belief denied the truth of the libel.[124] The same is true, albeit with some exceptions, about converts from Judaism who authored tracts against their former religion and community.[125] The closest analogy for Pikulski's work is the most learned work of early modern anti-Semitism, Johann Andreas Eisenmenger's *Entdecktes Judenthums* (1700). In a few cases, both works argue the same points on the basis of the same sources: both Pikulski and Eisenmenger were convinced that the Jews are commanded by their religion to abuse what is sacred to other religions, notably to Christianity, and believed that robbery, deceit, and murder are allowed or even encouraged by Jewish law. Further, both Pikulski and Eisenmenger, based their arguments on the premise that the absolutely unethical behaviour of the

---

[122] Hsia, *Myth of Ritual Murder*, p. 124. Eck (1486–1543) was one of the leading opponents of Luther. His book was published in response to a pamphlet by the Lutheran, Andreas Osiander (1498–1552), which defended the Jews against the blood libel. It contained an authoritative 'exposition' of demonic Jewish blood magic, as well as 'history' of ritual murder cases.

[123] A copy I was able to buy in Warsaw was printed in the late 1990s.

[124] See Johann Christian Wagenseil, *Der denen Juden fälschlich beygemessene Gebrauch des Christen-Bluts* in his *Benachrichtigungen wegen einiger die Judenschaft angehenden wichtigen Sachen* (Leipzig: Johann Heiniches Wittwe, 1705), part 1, pp. 126–206; Johann Christian Wagenseil, *Hoffnung der Erlösung Israels* (Nuremberg and Altdorf: publisher unknown, 1707).

[125] For examples see H. L. Strack, *Der Blutaberglaube bei Christen und Juden*, (München: Hermann Leberecht, 1891), pp. 239–50; the most notable exception is Paul Christian Kirchner, *Jüdisches Ceremoniel (sic!) oder Beschreibung derjenigen Gebräucher, welche die Juden sowol inn – als ausser dem Tempel, bey allen und jeden Fest-Tagen, im Gebet, bey der Beschneidung (...), in acht zu nehmen pflegen* (Nürnberg: Verlegts Peter Conrad Monath, 1724; photoffset Leipzig 1999), pp. 150–52.

Jews derives from their sacred literature, and that all derogatory or discriminatory motifs of this literature refer – explicitly or implicitly – to Christians. Still, the blood libel does not play an important part in Eisenmenger's narrative, and *Entdecktes Judentums* does not link the alleged cases of ritual murders with talmudic principles. After giving a list of ritual murder trials, Eisenmenger concluded: 'not everything [I adduced here] is bound to be untrue, but I will leave the matter undecided'.[126] For Pikulski, in contrast, human sacrifice was a crucial element of Jewish tradition, and blood rituals were described and advocated in a veiled way in the Talmud.

In early modern western Europe, even the most virulent proponents of the libel stopped short of claiming that the use of Christian blood or human sacrifice were intrinsic parts of the Jewish religion. The elite theological discourse directed against the Talmud, and the popular discourse advocating blood libel seldom, if ever, overlapped. In the words of Jonathan Frankel, 'the perfect fit between the upper-level demonology and the folk belief in black magic, maleficium, which fuelled the witch-craze of the sixteenth and seventeenth centuries was never fully achieved with regard to the ritual murder accusation'.[127] Pikulski's work and some other works published around the same period attest, however, that this perfect fit *was* achieved in eighteenth-century Poland. That said, the official view of the Catholic Church and the pope was that the accusation was false and ludicrous.[128] In eighteenth-century Poland, therefore, there were many cases in which the blood libel was used as a political tool by people who were not motivated by any religious reasons and who clearly knew that the accusations were untrue. Magical and theological discourse merged with, or in some cases was entirely replaced by, the language of politics and power struggle.

· ·

It might have been thought that the Jewish blood libel would have died out once and for all in Europe in the nineteenth century. After all, the French revolution and the triumph of French arms in the subsequent revolutionary wars led to the dismantling of the confessional state virtually all over Europe, while as the century progressed a growing section of the elite distanced themselves from traditional Christianity altogether, especially after Darwin published his *Origin of the Species* in 1859. But the nineteenth century was also an age of aggressive nationalism, which could be a doctrinaire religious as well as a secular ideology. In the Russian empire in particular the nationalism fostered by the state was totally associated with the Russian orthodox church. It is not surprising then that the economic, social and cultural dislocation brought about by industrialisation and the growth of state power towards the end of the century led to outbreaks of vicious anti-Semitism in parts of Europe with a large Jewish population. At the turn of the twentieth century Jews became the target once more of the blood libel accusation in Russia and Poland, and even as far west as the German Rhineland. In 1913 a Ukrainian Jew, Menaham Mendel Beilis (1874–1934) was actually put on trial for the ritual murder of a thirteen-year-old child.[129] Europe west

---

[126] J. A. Eisenmenger, *Entdecktes Judenthum* (Frankfurt, 1700), vol. ii, pp. 220–27.

[127] J. Frankel, *The Damascus Affair: "Ritual Murder", Politics, and the Jews in 1840* (Cambridge: Cambridge University Press, 1997), p. 45.

[128] For a collection of official pronouncements by the papacy on the blood libel, see C. Roth, *The Ritual Murder Libel and the Jews* (London: Woburn Press, 1934). Of particular significance in this case was Pope Clement XIII's condemnation of the blood ritual accusations as slander in 1760 following an investigation into the Polish trials by Cardinal Ganganelli (later Clement XIV).

[129] M. Samuel, *Blood Accusation: The Strange History of the Beilis Case* (New York: Knopf, 1966); H. W. Smith, *The Butcher's Tale: Murder and Anti-Semitism in a German Town* (London: W. W. Norton, 2002). Beilis was acquitted.

of the Rhine was also not immune. In France the right-wing nationalism that developed in opposition to the secular republicanism of the third French Republic was viscerally Roman Catholic and anti-Jewish, and was the leading factor fanning the flames of the Dreyfus affair in the second half of the 1890s.[130] Here, too, the blood libel resurfaced at the end of the nineteenth century, with the Catholic magazine, *Le Pèlerin*, reprinting in 1892 an early German woodcut of a purported ritual killing of 134.[131]

Broader fascination with child sacrifice and child murder equally did not disappear completely in the nineteenth century. Artists once more found the subject engrossing. The French illustrator, Gustav Doré (1832–83) engraved an *Abraham and Isaac* that emphasises Abraham's pain as his son carries the wood for the pyre, while the pre-Raphaelites were obsessed by the story of Iphigenia. An Abraham-Isaac theme can also be identified in Ibsen's *Brand* (1866), which tells the story of a doctrinaire Lutheran pastor sacrificing his family (his son Ulf dies from neglect) rather than abandon the mission that God has given him to bring light to an isolated village. And the Nordic tradition of sacrificing children in times of disease was placed squarely in the public domain by the folklorists of Scandinavia.[132] Most famously, the practice of pubescent sacrifice among the Scythians, the ancient inhabitants of Russia, who supposedly performed a fertility ritual each year where a maiden was offered to the gods, was brought to life by Stravinsky in his 1913 ballet, *Rite of Spring*.

There again, it seems unlikely that there were many Europeans by the turn of the twentieth century, outside the peasant world of eastern Europe, who really believed that children were deliberately murdered and used in rituals. The undermining of traditional village culture that came in the wake of nineteenth-century economic and social change and the specific campaign waged against popular superstitions by the state with new weapons, such as mass education, must have largely laid to rest the age-old cultural unease. Certainly, the states of central and western Europe had no desire to reinvigorate the traditional fears, if they were happy to let them survive as fairy-tales. Their elites, too, did not want to be reminded too graphically of the world they had lost either, if the initial reception of Stravinsky's ballet is any indication. As conceived by the composer and choreographed by Nijinsky, it was intended to recreate the Scythians' ritual dance. When premiered in Paris, the music and dancing touched a nerve and the audience rioted.[133]

Yet if the establishment was nervous about rekindling old superstitions, this did not stop the British press in particular from manipulating more general cultural fears of the child-killing 'other' during the First World War. The idea that ideological enemies were child-killers was deeply rooted in Christian culture through the account of Herod's massacre of the innocents. In the early modern era it was a topos which had been frequently deployed by Protestant and Catholic apologists to blacken their opponents during the era of religious war. In the Thirty Years War of the seventeenth century, for instance, soldiers were accused of almost every atrocity imaginable against children, including in the case of the Croats

---

[130] Alfred Dreyfus (1859–1935) was a Jewish army officer wrongly convicted of treason. The case became a political football after his conviction, with the French right playing the anti-Semitic card.

[131] R. Harris, *Lourdes: Body and Spirit in a Secular Age* (Harmondsworth: Penguin, 1999), pp. 277–78. Anti-Semitism was also strong in early twentieth-century Britain where sections of the elite were unsettled by Jewish immigration from eastern Europe; for a particularly lurid example, see L. W. B. Brockliss (ed.), *Magdalen College: A History* (Oxford: Magdalen College, 2008), p. 474. At a much earlier date, in the late 1830s, Dickens indirectly used the blood libel in a complex and subversive way in *Oliver Twist*. Fagin 'abducts' street children to exploit their innocence and agility to become a rich man (metaphorically sucking their blood), but he also provides the homeless with food and shelter.

[132] Scandinavian folklorists found the memory of the old tradition was alive in the villages they visited. The stories they recorded were the chief source for Hauge's reconstruction of the Nordic pagan past in the work cited in fn. 42 above.

[133] O. Figes, *Natasha's Dance. A Cultural History of Russia* (London: Penguin, 2002), pp. 279–82. Whether or not the Scythians did practise human sacrifice remains undecided.

fighting for the Holy Roman emperor, killing babies for food.[134] For several centuries, such accusations were largely laid to rest, partly because armies became better disciplined and were less predatory. The Great War saw them deployed again. The First World War was seen in both Britain and France as an ideological, apocalyptic struggle between the forces of good and evil, civilisation and barbarism, and so on. It was not long before the Germans were also targeted for massacring the innocent. Admittedly, the extent to which they were accused by the British press of baby-killing as they marched into Belgium and France must not be exaggerated. The accusation was really only developed and used to maximum effect a little later in the war. None the less, there can be no doubt that once this particular chord was struck, it resonated deeply in the public mind.

The First World War, however, was not only significant for the way the story of Herod was given a contemporary gloss. It also gave new emphasis to the historic complexity of Christianity's relationship with child sacrifice and child-killing. Throughout the Christian era, as was pointed out at the beginning of the chapter, there had always been a sense in which sacrificing a child to God could be a work of piety rather than an abomination. Thus, throughout the middle ages children had been continually placed in monasteries and convents ostensibly as a gift or an *ex voto* oblation, even if there were often less elevated reasons behind the decision. And the practice still continued in a later era. Towards the end of the seventeenth century Madame de Sévigné's little granddaughter was packed off to an Aix convent at the age of nine as a parental 'burnt-offering' for the birth of a son. The daughter, the first-born, had been unwanted, and her mother had wished to thank God for his goodness in now giving her an heir.[135] On the other hand, there was never any hint – nor could there have been – that God would have been pleased by a literal sacrifice. Children might volunteer knowingly for martyrdom – and indeed could be celebrated by later generations for their steadfast faith.[136] But no pre-modern theologian would have suggested that parents should knowingly hand over their children to be killed, or even run the risk of being so. The idea first appeared during the French Revolution, when two boy soldiers who had died in action against the Republic's internal enemies in 1793, Joseph Bara, aged thirteen, and Agricole Viala, one year older, were deliberately celebrated as innocent martyrs for liberty and raised to the ranks of revolutionary heroes by the Jacobin government.[137] (See Figure 6). But the rhetoric of sacrifice was developed by politicians and militants who largely prided themselves in having broken with their Christian inheritance and drew on the Rousseauvian idea of the citizen.[138] This was not the case in the First World War. When

---

[134] P. Vincent, *The Lamentations of Germany. Wherein, as in a Glasse, we may Behold her Miserable Condition, and Reade the Woefulle Effects of Sin* ... (London: E. G. for I. Rothwell, 1638), pp. 26 and 44. We wish to thank Alan Ross for this reference. On the use of violence as a topos in the Thirty Years War, see Ch. 5, pp. 241–46.

[135] E. W. Marwick, 'Nature versus Nurture: Patterns and Trends in Seventeenth-Century French Child Rearing', in L. deMause (ed.), *The History of Childhood* (New York: Psychohistory Press, 1974), p. 283. Marie de Rabutin-Chantal, Marquise de Sévigné (1626–96) has left in her letters one of the fullest accounts of a mother-daughter relationship in the pre-modern era. On children as oblates, see Ch. 2, pp. 63–64.

[136] Medieval Europe was awash with child saints. For an introduction, see P. H. Wasyliw, *Martyrdom, Murder and Magic: Child Saints and their Cults in Medieval Europe* (New York: P. Lang, 2008).

[137] It was intended that their ashes would be placed in the Panthéon with the other heroes of the revolution but Robespierre fell the day before the ceremony. In the 1880s, Bara, described in an 1870 poem as 'l'enfant sublime', was presented in the classroom of the Third Republic as the model to which all young citizens should aspire. See M.-P. Foissy-Aufrère *et al.*, *La Mort de Bara. De l'évenèment au mythe. Autour du tableau de Jacques-Louis David* (Avignon: Musée Calvet, 1989).

[138] Rousseau argued in *The Social Contract* (1762) that every citizen must bear arms in defence of the right-ordered state when called upon to do so and be ready to lay down his life in return for the civil rights that such a state would establish and uphold. In the state of the Social Contract, 'life is no longer a mere bounty of nature, but a gift made conditionally by the state'. *The Social Contract and Discourses*, trans. G. D. H. Cole (London: Dent, 1923), p. 27 (Bk. 1, ch. 5).

young men, not yet adults in law, were called upon to join up and marched off to slaughter in their millions, parents, especially mothers, were encouraged to hand over their sons to the new Moloch of the nation state, and accept their loss as a Christian sacrifice which God would approve of and reward. Young soldiers were expected to be Christ-like and obey their country's requirement that they put their life on the line for a greater end. Christianity was built on the peculiar and perfect sacrifice of God's son; the new religion of Christian patriotism demanded the potential sacrifice of everyman's son. The culturally embedded Christian association of son/child imagery with obedience and sacrifice was appropriated to express the death of a nation's sons (and daughters in some cases) as a noble ideal in the cause of freedom.

The First World War and Child Sacrifice

Adrian Gregory

The widespread image of the British press in the First World War as obsessed with the murder of Belgian babies by German soldiers requires serious qualification. The image of a Belgian baby pierced by a German bayonet and held aloft certainly existed, it was published in the *Daily Chronicle* in 1915, but in the first months of the war the specific allegation of baby killing was intermittent in the British press. Even in the avowedly Germanophopic *Daily Mail* there were comparatively few lurid stories about child murder, compared with the much more voluminous coverage of mass shootings of adults and the destruction of historic buildings.[139]

The image of Germans specifically as 'baby killers' had a much more precise origin, the bombardment of the east coast towns, the Hartlepools and the seaside resort of Scarborough on 16 December 1914. The press reporting of these attacks dwarfs any incident in Belgium in terms of column inches dedicated. There was also a circulation spike for newspaper sales and the stories generated had a much greater impact on readers of the press. The diary of Ethel Bilsborough, deposited in the Imperial War Museum, includes a substantial number of clippings about the attack. Under one of them she wrote the comment 'House in Scarborough where dead babies were found'.[140] Stories of child killing in Belgium had circulated widely in oral form, but the deaths of children in the Hartlepools and Scarborough were verifiable and backed up with hard evidence. The *Daily Mail* published family photographs of children killed, all of the press reported at length the coroners' inquests on all the victims, which concluded that they had been 'unlawfully killed'. Even the most hardened sceptic could not dismiss this incident as either rumour or invented propaganda. It was a clear matter of public record, easily checked, that, for example, three out of six children in the Dixon household of Hartlepool had been killed by a German shell. It was this verifiability that empowered the First Lord of the Admiralty, Winston Churchill, to stand up in the House of Commons and denounce the German Navy as the 'Baby killers of Scarborough', the first clear British ministerial endorsement of the accusation of atrocities committed by Germany.

---

[139] For a rare case where such a story does achieve prominence, complete with a rather dubious photograph of a burned child's foot, see *Daily Mail*, 18 Sept. 1914. The nature of 1914 atrocity propaganda is discussed in A. Gregory, *The Last Great War* (Cambridge: Cambridge University Press, 2009).

[140] Entry 19 Dec. 1914, E. M. Bilsborough Diary, Con shelf. Imperial War Museum, London.

The outrage over this incident would be eclipsed by a much more massive case of 'baby killing' by the German Navy. The sinking of the *Lusitania* in May 1915 resulted in the deaths of 94 children. Of the 39 passengers under the age of one, 35 died. The shocking photograph of the recovered corpses of babies in the morgue in Queenstown Ireland published in the *Daily Mail* is, even today, gut wrenching; its impact in 1915 must have been extraordinary. Facts and images such as these paved the way for the infamous Bryce Report on the German Atrocities in Belgium, which did contain gruesome and generally dubious accounts of atrocities committed against children by the German Army. But by that time the basic plausibility of the Germans as baby killers had been established in the British mind by the actions of the German Navy.

The propaganda usefulness of baby killing as a way of dehumanising the enemy other cannot be doubted. Immediately after the *Lusitania* sinking the popular illustrated magazine, *The Passing Show*, published a cartoon of a fanged ape in a spiked German helmet carrying away a child. But the obvious propaganda usefulness of accusations of child killing in constructing an inhuman and unnatural enemy other cannot be taken, as it frequently is, as automatic disproof the fact of child killing.[141] Indeed in this case, the plausibility and indeed verifiability of specific cases was precisely what made this such effective propaganda. What the German Navy had verifiably done, the German Army might plausibly have done. Baby killing had become a transferable generic characteristic of the 'German Race'.[142]

At the very moment when the killing of children was being used as an indictment of the enemy, the immemorial concept of parents sacrificing their children for the general good was taking on new and more literal force. During the period of voluntary recruitment, the willingness of parents to allow their children to enlist and die on behalf of the country was remarkable. Famously in *Goodbye to All That* (1929), Robert Graves (1895–1985) lambasts a 'little mother' who had supposedly written to the press celebrating the death of her son in battle and talking of women's role being to produce 'human ammunition' for the country.[143] Although Graves has a satirical and hostile view of this performance of the traditional 'Spartan Mother' role, the expectation was widespread that parents would be willing and honoured to give up their adult male children for the national cause. 'Better a son's life lost for his country than a coward saved at the expense of his honour and manhood'.[144]

In practice this performance could still cause unease, the London journalist Michael Macdonagh wrote of an encounter with such a mother:

> I have met with a Spartan mother who grieves not for her son killed in the war but glories in his fate. Calling on her today to give my condolences on the loss of her son, aged 18, who has fallen in battle, she told me she felt no grief, only pride that a boy of hers should have died for his country and I could see the pride was all the more intense for the deep love that she bore him. I wonder are there many more mothers like her. Her deep stoicism seems unnatural.[145]

---

[141] As is the case, of course, of accusations about deliberate or ritual child-killing through history. See J. M. Read, *Atrocity Propaganda 1914–1919* (New Haven: Yale University Press, 1941).

[142] For a more detailed discussion of these issues, see A. Gregory, 'A Clash of Cultures: The British Press and the Opening of the Great War', in T. Paddock (ed.) *A Call to Arms: Propaganda, Public Opinion and Newspapers in the Great War* (London: Praeger, 2005), pp. 15–49, specifically pp. 25–39.

[143] R. Graves, *Good-bye to All That: An Autobiography* (Oxford: Berghahn, 1995), p. 204.

[144] N. Gulace, *The Blood of Our Sons: Men, Women and the Renegotiation of Citizenship during the Great War* (New York: Palgrave Macmillan, 2002). p. 67.

[145] Diary entry for 22 Apr. 1915 in M. Macdonagh, *In London During the Great War; the Diary of a Journalist* (London: Eyre and Spottiswoode, 1935), p. 60.

But Macdonagh in seeing the performance as unnatural fails to perceive its essentially Christian character. This was not a 'Spartan mother' but a parent (in the role of God the Father or the Madonna) who had sacrificed her child for the redemption of humanity.[146] Edwardian Britain was saturated with Christian imagery and the central idea of Christian sacrifice was entirely familiar. Furthermore this was a war being fought from the outset for millennial ends, the term 'War to End All Wars' was coined by H. G. Wells in August 1914. Christian clergymen speculated openly in 1914 whether the war might in some way usher in a new age of Christian fellowship, a genuine kingdom of heaven, although they were generally very careful not to specifically and heretically equate the sacrifice of soldiers with Christ's sacrifice. Nevertheless, it is clear that a popular patri-passionism was widespread during the war. In these circumstances a mother or father giving up a child was clearly perceived as a metaphysical sacrifice and in fact the perception of this sacrifice on the part of mothers played a major role in creating an ideological atmosphere favourable to the admission of older women to full citizenship in the Representation of the People Act of 1918.[147]

The deep historical resonances of the idea of child sacrifice were still at work in Britain in 1914–18 but had bifurcated in an interesting way. The physical act of killing young children remained a sign of barbarism or even the unnatural; it was one way of demonising the enemy. At the same time the voluntary sacrifice of adult children by their parents was afforded the highest moral value, even if occasionally perceived by astute observers as also partaking of the unnatural. And once established, the idea that death in a just conflict was a form of sacrifice would be rehearsed time and again thereafter, not only in the Second World War with some cause, but in the many other conflicts that western European powers have been involved in since 1945, not least the present 'peace keeping' operation in Afghanistan.

• •

The idea that the dead of the First and Second World Wars had made a sacrifice of their young lives for the greater good became part of the permanent rhetoric of the victors, which was etched on cenotaphs and war memorials, collective and individual. They were lost youths who, in the words of the famous poem, *The Fallen*, by Laurence Binyon (1869–1943), would 'not grow old, as we that are left grow old'.[148] At the end of the 1939–45 conflict the awfulness and precariousness of the gift was spelt out with particular poignancy on the memorial to the British and Indian dead of the Forgotten Army at Kohima. 'For your tomorrow, we gave our today'.[149]

The idea, moreover, that the dead were children not adults, and as such, involuntary but obedient victims to fatherly authority, was given lasting visual embodiment in the village war memorials in France. There was a longstanding political rhetoric in France whereby

---

[146] The idea of the 'Spartan mother' in the First World War has been analysed by the feminist social thinker J. B. Elshtain, *Women and War*, 2nd edn (Chicago: University of Chicago Press, 1995), pp. 106–08, 211–14.

[147] Summary of material and arguments to be found in Gulace, *The Blood of Our Sons*.

[148] It also became part of the rhetoric of Irish nationalism. The young Irishmen who had died in the Easter Rising of 1916 had made the blood sacrifice that was need for Ireland to be free. The idea was celebrated and shaped by Yeats's *Easter 1916*, although Yeats was not totally convinced that the 'terrible beauty' the Rising had given birth to was completely positive: 'Too long a sacrifice/can make a stone of the heart'. The first Irish writer to question the value of the nationalists' blood sacrifice was Sean O'Casey (1880–1964). His pacifist play, *The Plough and the Stars*, caused a riot when first staged at the Abbey Theatre, Dublin, in 1926.

[149] The Battle of Kohima was fought from April to June 1944 on the border between India and Burma. For the British and Indian forces it was the turning point in the land war against Japan.

Frenchmen and eventually women were accustomed to see themselves as children under the watchful eye of the state. At the time of the Revolution, they moved from being 'enfants du roi' to 'enfants de la patrie' and the concept, enshrined in the blood-curdling lyrics of the Marseillaise, came to carry a much more active resonance. Frenchmen were citizens not subjects who were expected to defend their homeland with their lives, as a good and obedient child would defend its father and mother. The two million French dead of the First World War were therefore described on the country's war memorials as 'enfants morts pour la France', and the representative soldier displayed on the monument receiving the martyr's or victor's crown was not a grizzled veteran but a boyish, beardless young man. (See Figure 7).

It is only in the last few decades that the positive rhetoric of the child-soldier has begun to seem incongruous. With the establishment from the late 1960s of eighteen, rather than 21 or later as the end of childhood in European states (a development made a universal constant by the United Nations Convention on the Rights of the Child 1989), and the rigorous enforcement of a longstanding military rule that no one younger than eighteen should be put in the front line (even if they might join at an earlier age), none of the fighting soldiers in European armies is any longer legally a child. In recent decades, too, European public opinion has been confronted head-on with the reality of the child-soldier, young boys not even in their teens, caught up in the myriad inter-tribal and inter-regional conflicts that have flared up in sub-Saharan Africa in the wake of the ending of colonisation.[150] There is nothing innocent about a twelve-year-old with a machine gun or a machete murdering unarmed civilians, whatever the initial horror that may have led such a child to be recruited. At the beginning of the twenty-first century the concept of the soldier as child seems at best a nonsense, at worst transgressive, and an offence against childhood.

It is not surprising then that Britain's First World War poets are more appreciated today than they ever were in the 1920s and 30s, for they too refused to see the child-soldiers of their own day as heroic willing martyrs.[151] Rather, they were the victims of evil, irresponsible men, so many lambs slaughtered in a purposeless cause. Wilfred Owen in his poem '*The Parable of the Old Man and the Young*', quoted at the beginning of this chapter, envisaged the war as an inverted version of the Abraham and Isaac story. In prosecuting the conflict, fathers had turned their back on God's mercy and sacrificed their sons against His express command.

The second-half of the twentieth century has also seen the sedulously cultivated myth of the 1914–45 era, that in a just war the unjust deliberately and callously 'sacrifice' innocent children, develop in a way that the victors of the two world wars cannot have expected. The belief has proved a double-edged sword for western democracies involved in conflicts post-1945, where public opinion has been seldom unanimously behind the government. This was particularly true in the case of the Vietnamese war of the second half of the 1960s and early 1970s. The American propaganda machine during the war tried to demonise the Vietcong as indiscriminate killers, but it was the American armed forces themselves who

---

[150] The legal position is fully explored in I. Cohen and G. Goodwin-Gill, *Child Soldiers: The Role of Children in Armed Conflict* (Oxford: Clarendon Press, 1994). For a recent study of the phenomenon in several parts of the world, see D. M. Rosen, *Armies of the Young: Child Soldiers in War and Terrorism* (New Brunswick: Rutgers University Press, 2005). See also Ch. 5, pp. 241–46.

[151] In this regard they were very different from their French counterparts who subscribed wholeheartedly to the myth of sacrifice (doubtless because France was so nearly overrun). See I. Higgins (ed.), *Anthology of First World War French Poetry* (Glasgow: University of Glasgow French and German Publications, 1997). The possibility of the young being sanctified through suffering was a perpetual theme of the Catholic writer, Paul Claudel (1868–1955) throughout the first third of the twentieth century, culminating in his 1935 opera, *Jeanne au Bûcher*, about France's most famous soldier-saint, beatified in 1909 and canonised in 1920. Joan of Arc was probably nineteen when she was burnt in 1431. We are indebted to Toby Garfitt for this information.

were specifically labelled by opponents of the war throughout the western world as 'baby-killers'. When protestors marched, their favourite chant immediately placed the American military, supposed defenders of democracy, on the side of the barbarians: 'Hey, Hey, LBJ! How many kids did you kill today?'[152] Admittedly, as in the allied propaganda of the two wars there was no suggestion that the B-47 bombers were involved in ritual killings with their napalm strikes. It was the arbitrary slaughter and maiming of the very young in modern warfare which came to exercise the western conscience in the second half of the twentieth century.[153]

In the First World War, media propaganda ensured that it was dead children 'on our side' who were the sole focus of concern. Today, now that modern technology allows virtual instant access to the horrors of war and public opinion is unnerved by ill-treatment meted out to any child, the unease is unbounded. This, of course, only demonstrates how strongly rooted the taboo against child-killing is, whatever a state or community's reasons for resorting to it might be. Indeed, from being a sign of an enemy's depravity in war time, it has now become a *casus belli* in its own right. When the extremist Hutus began to massacre the Tutsis in Rwanda in 1994, they started with the children, hacking off their limbs and genitals and throwing them at their terrified parents. This, more than anything, made the failure of the United States and the states of the European Union to intervene and halt the genocide appear culpable in the eyes of many of their citizens.[154]

The Hutu massacres, of course, could also be read as ritual killings, which only accentuated the horror, for the European fascination with child sacrifice has still not been completely scotched. Until very recently, there had been little sign since the Second World War that the secular, post-Christian European seriously entertained the view that children were being ritually murdered in his or her midst. The last time the Jewish blood libel raised its ugly end on the continent was in a pogrom in central Poland in 1946. There again, the myth of child sacrifice continues to resonate in covert and less lethal ways in horror films and popular children's fiction. In the singularly successful *Harry Potter* books of J. K. Rowling (b. 1965), the villainous wizard, Voldemort, is kept alive by drinking unicorn's blood.[155] The sacrifice of Iphigenia, too, if not the Abraham and Isaac story, continues to fascinate artists. Rothko (1903–70) painted a very disturbing and ambiguous *Sacrifice of Iphigenia* in 1942, while Euripedes's tragedy has continued to be part of the contemporary theatre's repertoire, and the story has been used to comment on contemporary events.[156] In a recent production at the National Theatre in London (2004), Agamemnon's readiness to surrender his daughter was given an interesting pacifist slant: politicians will do anything to promote a war.[157]

In consequence, the longstanding unease about child sacrifice remains a partly closed wound, one that is frequently scratched in various ways by storytellers and artists so that it never completely heals. Indeed, had it done so, then the peculiar panic about ritual

---

[152] LBJ: the initials of the President of the United States, 1963–68, Lyndon Baines Johnson.

[153] The myth is still being used in a creative way by the British in the conflict in Afghanistan. When in December 2008 a number of British soldiers were killed by a child suicide bomber, Prime Minister Gordon Brown insisted that this was proof positive that the Taliban were cowardly barbarians: only evil men would sacrifice the life of a child in this way: http://www.guardian.co.uk/world/2008/dec/13/afghanistan-gordon-brown-troop-numbers (accessed 22 Dec. 2008).

[154] R. Dallaire, *Shake Hands with the Devil: The Failure of Humanity in Rwanda* (Toronto: Random House, 2003).

[155] J. K. Rowling (b. 1965) has been a publishing sensation since her first novel, *Harry Potter and the Philosopher's Stone* first appeared in 1997. In 2008 her books had been translated into 65 languages and several made into highly successful films.

[156] There was also an important film made of the play in 1977 by the Greek director, Michael Cacoganis. Rothko's work can be seen on http://www.nga.gov/feature/rothko/myths2.shtm (accessed 22 Dec. 2008).

[157] Directed by Katie Mitchell. The contemporary event alluded to was the use of the British government's 'dodgy dossier' to justify the invasion of Iraq in 2003: for details, see http://en.wikipedia.org/wiki/Dodgy_Dossier (accessed 30 Dec. 2009).

child-killing that gripped the London media, police and politicians in the first years of the present century would have been incomprehensible. The panic spread from the United States, where some fundamentalist Christians continue to believe not only that satan is active in the world but that he is served by an untold coterie of worshippers who use children's blood in their rituals. It began in Britain in the 1990s, when a number of police forces claimed to have uncovered home-grown satanists involved in child abuse among the majority white population.[158] However, given the absence of any evidence that children had been actually ritually killed, there appears to have been no real concern that child sacrifice had come to Britain, despite the growing number of fundamentalist Christians on this side of the Atlantic who also believe that satan is among us.[159] This changed in 2001. In that year a headless torso of a black boy was found in the Thames. In the subsequent, never completed investigation, the suggestion was mooted that the child, christened Adam, was the victim of ritual murder, indeed that his death was only the tip of the iceberg.[160] The finger of blame was levelled not at white satanists, but African immigrants who had supposedly introduced pagan witchcraft cults into the country. Lurid stories began to circulate in the press that children were being imported from a part of Nigeria close to the old kingdom of Benin (a centre of human sacrifice before the British arrived) to feed the blood lust, and that black children were mysteriously disappearing from school rolls.[161] The rumours were taken so seriously by the authorities that the Metropolitan police commissioned a report to take soundings among the black community. Published in July 2005, the report seemed to confirm the media's worst fears. 'Members of the workshop stated that for a spell to be powerful it required a sacrifice involving a male child unblemished by circumcision. They allege that boy children are being trafficked into the UK for this purpose'.[162]

No evidence, however, was ever found to support the rumours, and they quietly disappeared amidst ongoing concern about broader child abuse and neglect among both the black and white communities.[163] The rumours remain, though, a graphic witness to the

---

[158] Some credibility was given to this belief with the discovery of a number of religious cults around the world which did seem to have abused the children of members in different ways. When the FBI moved against the most famous of these – the Branch Davidian cult at Waco, Texas – the suspicion that children might still be sacrificed on the pyre even in the late twentieth century was apparently poignantly affirmed. When the headquarters of the cult were stormed in early 1993, 25 (some sources give 21) children (seventeen under ten) were killed in the fires that appear to have been started on the orders of the cult leader. For the sect and its beliefs, especially the belief that the millennium would begin with the immolation of the elect and their rising from the ashes, see K. G. C. Newport, *The Branch Davidians of Waco: The History and Beliefs of an Apocalyptic Sect* (Oxford: Oxford University Press, 2006), esp. chs 14 and 15.

[159] Whereas in the first half of the century exorcism might have been regarded as a rare and outworn practice, by the end of the century every British diocese had appointed an exorcist.

[160] See the discussion in the BBC television documentary 'Black Britain: Nobody's Child' (broadcast in the UK on 2 Apr. 2002).

[161] According to government statistics several thousand black children disappear from school rolls each year, although the reasons for this continue to be debated. See H. Montgomery, 'Children and Family in an International Context: The Case of Transnational Fostering', in H. Montgomery and M. Kellett (eds), *Children and Young People's Worlds: Developing Frameworks for Integrated Practice* (Bristol: The Policy Press, 2009).

[162] 'Boys used for human sacrifice'at http://news.bbc.co.uk/2/hi/uk_news/4098172.stm (accessed 28 Jun. 2005).

[163] See Ch. 3, pp. 155–58. The anthropologist, Jean La Fontaine, believes that the panic can only be understood in this wider historical context. 'The stories followed a long period in which the ill treatment of children by their parents and other adults and proven stories of incest and murder, had been exposed. These crimes had horrified the nation and the accused were found guilty at trial not just on the strength of confessions but from solid forensic science. When believers in the new threat argued that satanic abuse was merely a further dimension of what had already been established they were readily believed, even if there were those who realised that unlike established crimes there was no independent evidence to support allegations of satanic abuse'. Furthermore, La Fontaine points out that in the United States in particular the panic occurred in an environment where not only fundamental Christianity was flourishing but where there had been 'a mushroom

power that an age-old and apparently long-since discredited superstition still retains, and how easily and quickly that power can be reactivated if the ground is sufficiently fertile. In contemporary Britain, residual racism and widespread fears about immigration, which successive governments have done little to allay, provided the perfect soil. Given the right environment, it would seem, post-modern Londoners proved little different from pre-modern Parisians. The Paris panic of 1750, however, was evidence of the continuing popular unease; what has been most alarming and salutary about the recent outbreak of hysteria in London has been the degree to which it was media-created, media-led and backed by the police.

---

growth of non-Christian and anti-Christian religions', some avowedly satanist. Add to this the fact that there was no shortage of adults, some well-educated, willing to claim 'they had been victims of satanic abuse' and no shortage either of childcare professionals ready to entertain their stories on the less than solid grounds that children do not lie about such matters, then the panic becomes readily comprehensible. Jean La Fontaine, unpublished communication to the editors. The editors would like to thank Professor La Fontaine for her help in putting together the last paragraphs of this chapter. See also J. S. La Fontaine. *Speak of the Devil: Tales of Satanic Abuse in Contemporary Britain* (Cambridge: Cambridge University Press, 1998).

2. Infanticide, Abandonment and Abortion

Sally Crawford, Martin Ingram, Alysa Levene, Heather Montgomery, Kieron Sheehy, Ellie Lee

A typical case [of neo-naticide] is a 20-year-old single woman who has successfully concealed her pregnancy... this women was able to convince not only her workmates, whom she lived with, but also her immediate family whom she saw regularly ... and even a man with whom she had a sexual relationship in the seventh month of the pregnancy, that she was not pregnant. She "knew" she was pregnant and yet when labor pains started (at term) she thought the pains were caused by something she had eaten. She was alone at the time and the infant was born into the toilet and subsequently died of neglect. The morning of the infant's delivery she returned to work complaining of a heavy period.

> M. Marks, 'Parents at risk of Filicide', in G.-F. Pinard and L. Pagani (eds),
> *Clinical Assessment of Dangerousness: Empirical Contributions*
> (Cambridge: Cambridge University Press, 2001), p. 164.

Many State legislatures have enacted legislation to address infant abandonment and infanticide in response to a reported increase in the abandonment of infants. Beginning in Texas in 1999, "Baby Moses laws" or infant safe haven laws have been enacted as an incentive for mothers in crisis to safely relinquish their babies to designated locations where the babies are protected and provided with medical care until a permanent home is found. Safe haven laws generally allow the parent, or an agent of the parent, to remain anonymous and to be shielded from prosecution for abandonment or neglect in exchange for surrendering the baby to a safe haven. To date, approximately 47 States and Puerto Rico have enacted safe haven legislation. The focus of these laws is protecting newborns. In approximately 15 States, infants who are 72 hours old or younger may be relinquished to a designated safe haven. Approximately 14 States and Puerto Rico accept infants up to 1 month old. Other States specify varying age limits in their statutes.

> http://www.childwelfare.gov/systemwide/laws_policies/statutes/safehaven.cfm
> (accessed 16 Dec. 16 2009)

[One] point appears to be common to all plausible accounts of what it is that makes something a person: an entity cannot be a person unless it possesses, or has previously possessed, the capacity for thought. And the psychological and neurophysiological evidence makes it most unlikely that humans, in the first few weeks after birth, possess this capacity.

> M. Tooley, *Abortion and Infanticide* (Oxford: Oxford University Press, 1983), p. 421.

While western civilisation has since at least the fifth century BCE outlawed the sacrifice of healthy and loved children, it has been less consistent in its attitude towards killing or disposing of unwanted or imperfect offspring. Before the Christian era, it seems to have been perfectly acceptable to expose malformed babies, although the extent and purpose of the practice remains a subject of great debate.[1] Christianity in theory put an end to getting rid of unwanted children. But infanticide and abandonment have continued to be a feature of western society until the present day and were the common response of the young, unprotected unmarried mother in the past. Abortion, too, was outlawed by Christianity, but abortions have always occurred and grounds have always been found to justify them. In the second half of the twentieth century, the goal posts were significantly moved with the acceptance in virtually all western societies of the legality of medical abortion, but this immediately raised the question of when a human baby changes from being a non-person to a partial person and sets out on the road to full personhood. This is not a new question for western civilisation but one that is proving extremely difficult to answer in the light of advancing technology that allows ever-younger pre-term babies to survive. The advent of a vocal children's rights lobby further complicates matters, and the conflict between understandings of the child's right to life and women's reproductive rights has proved particularly intractable. The difference between abortion and infanticide is still the topic of great debate and the ending of potential life remains a supremely emotive topic.

In both historical and contemporary societies the problem of children, or potential children, who are unwanted, a strain on resources, or who will bring shame and social ostracism on their parents is one that has been dealt with through infanticide, abandonment and abortion. There is an enormous overlap between such terms and very difficult problems of definition mean that these words can be deployed and manipulated depending on circumstances.[2] Infanticide can range from the active killing of a child through smothering to the passive withholding of food or attention (a distinction that may still be made in the contemporary medical treatment of premature babies).[3] There are also many instances in the historical records of several children in one family being 'overlaid' and being suffocated in their sleep, which may be seen as carelessness or murder, depending on viewpoint.[4] It can be argued that abandonment is very different from infanticide because there is no active intention to kill, although abandoning a child may well prove a death sentence. Exposure too can be analysed as both a deliberate form of infanticide and as a loving act, done in the hope of the child being found and rescued. Abortion is the most contested, being seen as

---

[1] W. Langer, 'Infanticide: A Historical Survey', *History of Childhood Quarterly*, 1:3 (1974), 353–65; J. Boswell, *The Kindness of Strangers: The Abandonment of Children in Western Europe from Late Antiquity to the Renaissance* (New York: Pantheon Books, 1988).

[2] Langer defines infanticide as 'the wilful destruction of newborn babes through exposure, starvation, strangulation, smothering, poisoning, or through the use of some lethal weapon', Langer, 'Infanticide', p. 355. In current law in English and Wales the term infanticide refers to a specific legal offence, not the 'murder' of a child in general but to cases 'Where a woman by any wilful act or omission causes the death of her child under the age of twelve months, but at the time of the act or omission the balance of her mind was disturbed by reason of her not having fully recovered from the effect of giving birth to the child or by reason of the effect of lactation'. The Infanticide Act 1938 C. 36. Available online at http://www.opsi.gov.uk/RevisedStatutes/Acts/ukpga/1938/cukpga_19380036_en_1 (accessed 17 May 2009). Under this law, infanticide refers to child killing by the mother; there is no such defence for fathers. T. Ward, 'Legislating for Human Nature: Legal Responses to Infanticide, 1860–1938', in M. Jackson (ed.), *Historical Perspectives on Child Murder and Concealment, 1550–2000* (Aldershot: Ashgate, 2002).

[3] P. Alderson, J. Hawthorne and M. Killen, 'Are Premature Babies Citizens with Rights? Provision Rights and the Edges of Citizenship', *Journal of Social Sciences*, 9 (2005), 71–81.

[4] Bishop Bartholomew of Exeter (d. 1184) argued that those who fatally 'oppressed' children in bed should do penance and in later centuries the overlying of children remained a concern for the church. By the end of the fifteenth century, women suspected of such deaths were called before church courts although it is unclear if this was a punishment or a warning. See N. Orme, *Medieval Childhood* (New Haven: Yale University Press, 2001), p. 78.

either the killing of the unborn, or the removal of a non-viable foetus, and debates, especially in the UK, revolve around the question of at how many weeks gestation a foetus can be regarded as a feasible human being.

The chapter will inevitably raise more questions than it answers and perhaps the best that can be done is to take a dispassionate look at the ways in which various European societies have dealt with the problem of unwanted children. It focuses in particular on neonatal children and parents' attempts to relieve themselves of such children before or shortly after birth. Children of all ages have been abandoned,[5] and killed, but the disposal of the newly born, or unborn, has usually been regarded as conceptually different. Infanticide, abandonment and abortion all occur during a liminal period of life in which personhood and human status are most heavily contested and also when children are at their most vulnerable and dependent and, when without care and attention, they will die. The underlying link between all of the following pieces is the changing boundaries of personhood in the western tradition, which can make exposure/infanticide acceptable in the classical world but not in the Christian era, and abortion but not infanticide acceptable in the modern secular world. By examining these practices across millennia, a picture will emerge as to why individuals at different times have transgressed these boundaries and/or availed themselves of legitimate ways of ridding themselves of unwanted children. The scene is set in the first contribution, which looks at what archaeology and physical remains can tell us about infanticide, abandonment and abortion from pre-history, through the Graeco-Roman world, and into the middle ages.

Infanticide, Abandonment and Abortion in the Graeco-Roman and Early Medieval World: Archaeological Perspectives

Sally Crawford

At different times in the past, babies were unwanted, and ways were sought in which to get rid of them. Getting rid of babies, however, is not the normative approach to children in any human society. Social reactions to the idea of babies being unwanted, and to the disposal of such babies, offer insight into political, social and domestic structures in the past. As the following brief overview of the archaeological and historical evidence for the past in parts of Europe up to the medieval period will make clear, the decision to get rid of a baby, which babies were considered unwanted and why, and the methods used to carry out the act, varied widely, as did the extent to which the disposal of an unwanted infant was embedded in legal or social practices, or were considered entirely non-normative, private and secret acts of social deviance.[6]

---

[5] In recent years many US states have brought in legislation that allows parents to leave young children at hospitals without fear of prosecution but the 2008 legislation in Nebraska allowed parents to abandon children up to the age of nineteen. This rapidly became a source of great concern when, in September 2008 alone, at least fifteen children were abandoned (*The Guardian*, 4 Oct. 2008).

[6] The incidence of infanticide and abortion have been discussed for the Greek, Roman and medieval worlds in, for example, S. Pomeroy, 'Infanticide in Hellenistic Greece', in A. Cameron and A. Kuhrt (eds), *Images of Women in Antiquity* (London: Croom Helm, 1983); B. Rawson, *Children and Childhood in Roman Italy* (Oxford: Oxford University Press, 2003); B. A. Kellum, 'Infanticide in England in the Later Middle Ages', *History of*

There are three principle methods of getting rid of an unwanted baby: abandonment, infanticide, and abortion. Of these three, there is least evidence for abortion in the past. Abortion carried a significant threat, until very recent times, to the life of the mother as well as the child, and techniques for aborting a foetus carried a high probability of failure. Abortion was a desperate and potentially suicidal act for a woman to undertake. Abortion is necessarily invisible in the archaeological evidence: two foetuses, one perhaps nine months in utero, the other too fragmentary to age closely, have been found in an eighth-century midden pit in Southampton, England, but the disposal of such foetuses, even in places socially inappropriate for human remains, cannot necessarily be assumed to be the result of an abortion.[7] Textual evidence for abortions is also, perhaps not unexpectedly, relatively infrequent, though the possibility of the act was recognised. Early medieval Irish law codes allowed a husband to divorce a wife for inducing an abortion,[8] and late Anglo-Saxon vernacular medical texts, drawing on Graeco-Roman medical exemplars, carried remedies to provoke menstruation or to draw out a baby.[9]

If the aim was to destroy the life of an unwanted child, infanticide offered a far safer and more certain remedy than abortion. The extent to which infanticide was ever condoned as an acceptable method of removing unwanted babies from the population pool in the pre- and proto-historic past – either because the child was considered disabled, or the wrong gender, or because the presence of a new baby would affect the chances of survival of existing children, or because the mother or other carers were unable to rear the child, is much debated. There are a number of problems in interpreting the archaeological evidence.[10] The presence of infant burials in significant numbers, or in places outside the normal disposal areas for human remains, might be taken as evidence for the practice of infanticide. This is particularly noticeable for the Roman period in Britain: examples include the first century BCE site at Owlesbury, Hampshire, where 60 per cent of burials were of infants; fourteen burials were found under a domestic floor at the Romano-British settlement at Springhead, Essex; and, most well-known, 97 infants were found in the yard of a Romano-British building complex at Hambledon, Buckinghamshire. Similar examples of infant clusters in association with Roman villas have been excavated elsewhere in Europe.[11] The presence of many infant skeletons, or of babies in non-normative locations, however, need not necessarily be interpreted as evidence for infanticide. Where clusters of burials have been found, this could be evidence of socially-constructed strategies for population control, but equally may be evidence that infants dying from natural causes were normally given segregated or different burial. This is certainly the case for the Roman period, where the dead were by law buried away from settlements, with the exception of infants: the collections of infant bodies associated with settlements and villas across the Roman world are plausibly explained as normative locations for infant burial.

Childhood Quarterly, 1:3 (1974), 367–88.

[7] A. Morton (ed.), *Excavations at Hamwic, vol. 1: Excavations 1946–83, Excluding Six Dials and Melbourne Street* (York: Council for British Archaeology, 1992) p. 84; P. Andrews (ed.), *Excavations at Hamwic, vol. 2* (York: Council for British Archaeology, 1997), pp. 109–204.

[8] F. Kelly, *A Guide to Early Irish Law* (Dublin: Institute for Advanced Studies, 1988), p. 75.

[9] O. Cockayne, *Leechdoms, Wortcunning, and Starcraft of Early England: Being a Collection of Documents, for the Most Part Never Before Printed, Illustrating the History of Science in this Country Before the Norman Conquest*, 3 vols (London, 1864–6); Sally Crawford, *Childhood in Anglo-Saxon England* (Stroud: Sutton, 1999), pp. 63–64.

[10] See E. Scott, *The Archaeology of Infancy and Infant Death* (Oxford: Archaeopress, 1999), esp. ch. 6 for a full overview of the archaeological evidence for infanticide.

[11] For summaries of these sites, see D. and N. Soren, *A Roman Villa and a late Roman Infant Cemetery: Excavation at Poggio Gramignano, Lugnano in Teverina* (Rome: l'Erma di Bretschneider, 1999), p. 479.

Isolated infant bodies in non-normative locations, in pits, wells, building foundations and ditches, might be considered as more convincing evidence of the casual disposal of dead babies, and perhaps of infanticide, but making a distinction between 'casual disposal' and sacrificial or votive deposition is not straightforward. The infant bodies found in Bronze Age ditch and pit contexts in Britain, for example, are part of a stratified, seasonal deposit of human, material and animal remains, whose purpose is more ritual than casual. The finds of infant bodies in post-pits, even where treated with an apparent lack of emotion, can still not be asserted to be examples of infanticide. Four babies were inserted into four post-pits at the time of the construction of a Roman temple at Springhead; two were decapitated. Here, however, even an interpretation of infant sacrifice may be going too far. Compare these burials with the single burial of an infant in the tenth-century church at Raunds, Northamptonshire. The burial, the only intra-mural inhumation, was contemporary with a rebuilding and remodelling of the church. It cannot, given the Christian context of the burial, represent a 'sacrifice'; rather the rebuilding occurred after a child had died naturally and been buried in the churchyard.[12]

From the tenth century in England, burial in the churchyard was mandatory, though canon law forbade the burial of unbaptised infants in Christian cemeteries, as elsewhere in medieval Europe.[13] It was not until the end of the medieval period that it was permissible for lay people, particularly midwives, to perform emergency baptisms in a crisis, even before the baby had exited the womb, thereby enabling stillborn children to be buried in consecrated ground.[14] Under these circumstances, the discovery of infant bodies in non-churchyard locations might appear to predicate infanticide, but might also represent late abortion, stillbirth, or the premature death of a baby before baptism. Special sites apparently dedicated to infant burial are particularly evident in Ireland, where they are typically located at prominent places in the landscape, such as prehistoric monuments, or in and around derelict castles or abandoned churches.[15] Known as 'cíllín' sites, medieval examples of non-churchyard infant burial sites are also known from Wales, northern Britain, Scotland and Scandinavia. Though the earliest cíllíni are prehistoric in date, the practice continued into the medieval and post-medieval period.[16] Some of the bodies found at these sites may have been victims of infanticide, but the majority were more likely to be examples of stillbirth or death by natural causes. It is possible that there may have been an economic motive to the choice of cíllín burial: burial in the church yard was costly, and for some poorer parents, it is possible that obligations to living children may have been even more powerful than the need to conform to Christian burial practice.[17]

Economic imperatives may also have driven the occasional finds of infant bodies in medieval settlement sites in England, where no infants should have been. At the longhouse complex at Upton, Gloucestershire, for example, the thirteenth-century burial of a three- to six-month-old baby took place in the south-east corner of a room. The baby was buried with a spindle whorl and a large whelk shell, and a floor slab

---

[12] A. Boddington, *Raunds Furnells: The Anglo-Saxon Church and Churchyard* (London: English Heritage Archaeological Report 7, 1996).
[13] J. Blair, *The Church in Anglo-Saxon Society* (Oxford: Oxford University Press, 2005), p. 464; M. Lauwers, *Naissance du cimetière: lieux sacrés et terre des morts dans l'occident mediéval* (Paris: Éditions Flammarion, 2005).
[14] B. Spinks, *Early and Medieval Rituals and Theologies of Baptism: From the New Testament to the Council of Trent* (Farnham: Ashgate, 2006), p. 150.
[15] N. Finlay, 'Outside of Life: Traditions of Infant Burial in Ireland from Cíllín to Cist', *World Archaeology*, 3:33 (2000), 407–22.
[16] *Ibid*.
[17] Scott, *The Archaeology of Infancy*, p. 122.

covered the grave. Again, this may be posited as a case of infanticide, but the care with which the child was buried, and the artefacts deposited with the body, suggest that this was not a case of the casual disposal of an unwanted baby, even though the burial vehemently contradicted normal mortuary practice for the time.[18]

A theory that the deliberate murder of girl babies may have been practised in prehistoric times – arguably based more on anthropological parallels with modern societies than on any clear evidence – has been tested by attempting to assess the comparative numbers of adult males to females in the mortuary record. Skewing of a normal gender balance has been identified in Romano-British cemetery populations, for example, in favour of males, but this is not sufficient proof of female infanticide, since it assumes retrieval of all social and gender groups from the archaeological record, and the accurate sexing of skeletal remains. A recent study of 31 perinatal Romano-British infants using DNA analysis to try to test the sex and demonstrate female infanticide proved inconclusive: only thirteen infants could be sexed, of which nine were males and four females.[19]

None the less, the evidence from some periods does show startling variation in gender balance, which may be explicable in terms of infanticide. Simon Mays notes an imbalance in favour of men in adult burials for the medieval period, but notes that his sample is biased by religious cemeteries and by documentary evidence of female migration to towns: most of his cemeteries are rural.[20] However, he suggests that documentary evidence supports continuing unsanctioned infanticide in the medieval period, and argues that excavated infant burials do not show the expected peak at full term because infants killed by infanticide were placed in rivers or otherwise disposed of in a non-archaeologically visible way. Scandinavian Viking-period cemeteries also have populations skewed in favour of males, which has been interpreted as evidence for female infanticide.[21]

Recently, more careful assessment of the age at death of infants has offered firmer grounds on which to assert infanticide. Comparative analysis of Roman and medieval mortuary populations in England indicates that there was death by natural causes in medieval times, but infanticide in the Roman period. The main strand of evidence is the contrast in age mortality patterns in the sampled Romano-British cemeteries compared with contemporary patterns of natural infant death. The abnormal peak of deaths at full term in Romano-British infants corroborates the picture of infanticide.[22] Infants in both the adult cemeteries and in the infant cemeteries associated with settlements exhibited this pattern, arguing for public compliance in, and acceptance of, the practice.

There is documentary evidence to support the idea that some, at least, of the infants recovered from the burial evidence were victims of infanticide, and that in

[18] P. Rahtz, 'Upton, Gloucestershire, 1964–1968, Second Report', *Transactions of the Bristol and Gloucestershire Archaeological Society*, 88 (1969), 74–124.
[19] Scott, *The Archaeology of Infancy*, pp. 67–68; S. Mays and M. Faerman, 'Sex Identification in some Putative Infanticide Victims from Roman Britain using Ancient DNA', *Journal of Archaeological Science*, 28:5 (2001), 555–59.
[20] S. Mays, 'Killing the Unwanted Child' *British Archaeology*, 2 (1995), 8–9.
[21] Scott, *The Archaeology of Infancy*, pp. 76–77; N. Wicker, 'Selective Female Infanticide as Partial Explanation for the Dearth of Women in Viking Age Scandinavia', in G. Halsall (ed.), *Violence and Society in the Early Medieval West. Private, Public and Ritual*, (Woodbridge: The Boydell Press, 1998), pp. 205–22. See also C. Clover, 'The Politics of Scarcity: Notes on the Sex Ratio in Early Scandinavia', *Scandinavian Studies*, 60 (1988), 147–88, in which she argues that female infanticide led to a shortage of women in Scandinavia, and encouraged the Viking expansion. This thesis has been recently questioned by E. Christiansen, *Norsemen in the Viking Age* (Oxford: Blackwell, 2002), p. 40.
[22] Mays, 'Killing the Unwanted Child'.

these cases, their deaths were part of an acknowledged, public strategy of controlling paternal obligation. Viking sources, for example, indicate that a husband who did not acknowledge paternity of the child doomed the newborn to death.[23] The link between unacknowledged paternity and infanticide may be explicit and condoned in Viking sources, but in all sources, women making similar choices had to implement their wishes against social norms and as a private act: early medieval Irish literary sources have a consistent motif of step-mothers encouraging the deaths of their step-children, and the introduction of Christianity to Scandinavia similarly turned an act which had been a paternal privilege into a female crime; Christianity guaranteed the child the right to live.[24]

The few instances where infanticide is thought to have been regularly and openly practised, such as ancient Sparta, are highly unusual. In a famous, if unreliable passage, Plutarch gives a description of the formalised exposure of physically imperfect infants among the Spartans:

> Nor was it in the power of the father to dispose of the child as he thought fit; he was obliged to carry it before certain triers at a place called Lesche; these were some of the elders of the tribe to which the child belonged; their business it was carefully to view the infant, and, if they found it stout and well made, they gave order for its rearing, and allotted to it one of the nine thousand shares of land above mentioned for its maintenance, but, if they found it puny and ill-shaped, ordered it to be taken to what was called the Apothetae, a sort of chasm under Taygetus; as thinking it neither for the good of the child itself, nor for the public interest, that it should be brought up, if it did not, from the very outset, appear made to be healthy and vigorous.[25]

This account of the mechanism of infanticide offers some possibility that a strategy for the apparent disposal of an infant was not necessarily intended to be fatal for the child. The children were to be killed by exposure at a site dedicated to that purpose. By exposing their child, parents publicly rejected their offspring, and the child effectively 'died' for the parents in practical and social terms. However, the hope that the child might be rescued and reared by other adults (or even, in the case of the legend of Romulus and Remus, by animals) might have played a significant part in enabling the mother at least to carry out this act.[26] This possibility was well recognised and exploited in the plots of Hellenistic and Roman literature, for example, as it continued to be in the early modern era in more complex story lines.[27] (See Figure 8). In the medieval period, unwanted children were regularly left at the church door – dead to the parents, maybe, but with a reasonable expectation that either the church or a passer-by would find a home for the child. Abandonment of a baby in a public place may have offered a more bearable option for the mother of the unwanted child, as well as allowing babies to be raised free from any later claims by its biological relations.[28]

Writers, of course, recognised the potential perils of abandonment – when an abandoned child grew to adulthood, there was potential for unwitting incest. The church side-stepped this possibility through the stratagem of infant oblation. This allowed the public and acknowledged 'abandonment' of an infant to the church. Child

---

[23] J. Jochens, *Women in Old Norse Society* (New York: Cornell University Press, 1998), pp. 82, 85–86.
[24] L. Bitel, *Land of Women: Tales of Sex and Gender from Early Ireland* (New York: Cornell University Press, 1996), p. 95; Jochens, *Women in Old Norse Society*, p. 82.
[25] Internet Classics Archive at the MIT webpage http://classics.mit.edu/Plutarch/lycurgus.html (accessed 28 Jan. 2010).
[26] Boswell, *The Kindness of Strangers*, p. 25; M. Golden, 'Demography and the Exposure of Girls at Athens', *Phoenix*, 35:4 (1981), 330–31.
[27] Rawson, *Roman Italy*, p. 118.
[28] *Ibid.*; Boswell, *The Kindness of Strangers*.

oblation was not simply evidence for the charitable disposal of unwanted children, however; for some parents, dedicating their children to the church from birth was a devotional act, and documentary evidence shows concerned fathers and mothers taking an active interest in the subsequent careers of their children.[29]

· ·

Given the limited archaeological evidence for infanticide, it is worth looking at anthropological accounts of the practice in contemporary societies.[30] It is, of course, problematic to project uncritically the findings of contemporary ethnographic accounts onto societies in the past, and some of the evidence is contradictory, but nevertheless anthropological accounts do suggest that certain children are particularly at risk and make some reasonable suppositions about why infanticide occurs. In a cross-cultural study Laila Williamson claims that 'Infanticide has been practiced on every continent and by people on every level of cultural complexity, from hunters and gatherers to high civilisation, including our own ancestors. Rather than being an exception, then, it has been the rule'.[31] It has certainly been a topic much debated and discussed by anthropologists who have argued variously that infanticide is carried out in particular economic conditions, as a way of balancing family size or structure, or as the best way of disposing of sickly or deformed infants who would otherwise impose an intolerable strain on the community.[32] Perhaps the most common reason of all is that infanticide is the safest and most effective form of birth control in the absence of modern contraceptives and medical abortion.[33] As Williamson argues, abortion techniques

> such as the use of magic, may be harmless though ineffective; or they may be crude, mechanical methods, such as stomping on the abdomen or inserting foreign objects into the uterus. The latter may injure the women seriously, even fatally. Infanticide is a safer method for the woman, who is a more valuable member of society than a newborn infant, and it has the additional advantage of allowing the family or society to select infants of one sex or other.[34]

There is also anthropological evidence that particular kinds of children are most in danger, particularly twins or any other child whose birth deviates from accepted norms, such as breech births, or babies born with a caul.[35] The literature on twins focuses on their ambiguous nature, whether they have one soul or two, whether they are children or spirits, monsters or people but this analysis holds true for any children who are not perceived as 'normal'. Newborn children are thus particularly vulnerable, not just physically, but because infancy is also the time when personhood is negotiated and contested most explicitly. It is the

---

[29] M. de Jong, *In Samuel's Image: Child Oblation in the Early Medieval West* (Leiden: Brill, 1996).

[30] The following refers to small-scale, traditional communities. There is also strong evidence of female infanticide in contemporary China and India, where preferences for sons means that parents are ready to kill unwanted daughters The increasing use of technology in prenatal testing has also meant that decisions are being taken about a child's chance of life before she is born: G. Aravamudan, *Disappearing Daughters: The Tragedy of Female Foeticide* (London: Penguin Books, 2007).

[31] L. Williamson, 'Infanticide: An Anthropological Analysis', in M. Kohl (ed.), *Infanticide and the Value of Life* (New York: Prometheus Books, 1978).

[32] H. Montgomery, *An Introduction to Childhood: Anthropological Perspectives on Children's Lives* (Oxford: Wiley-Blackwell, 2008), ch. 3.

[33] L. Minturn and J. Stashak, 'Infanticide as a Terminal Abortion Procedure', *Cross-Cultural Research*, 17:1–2 (1982), 70–90.

[34] Williamson, 'Infanticide', p. 63.

[35] Montgomery, *An Introduction to Childhood*, p. 98.

time when whether or not these children are considered human dramatically affects their life chances. Any children born in ways that are considered unacceptable or deviant may arouse suspicions that they are in some way evil or possessed of a non-human nature.[36] Most anomalous, and vulnerable, of all are children born with obvious birth defects or physical deformities.

> Whereas stigma may consign the spurned adult to a life of exclusion and marginality, the stigmatization of a hopelessly dependent neonate is inevitably a death sentence. The sickly, wasted, or congenitally deformed infant challenges the tentative and fragile symbolic boundaries between human and nonhuman, natural and supernatural, normal and abominable. Such infants may fall out of category, and they can be viewed with caution or with revulsion as a source of pollution, disorder, and danger.[37]

It can be argued that such children are a drain on their families, and on the wider community, and therefore the denial of personhood is a way of protecting the community from the time-consuming work that looking after them would entail. As William Langer claims, 'Infanticide has, from time immemorial, been the accepted procedure for disposing not only of the sickly infant, but of all newborns who might strain the resources of the individual family or the larger community'.[38]

Building on these insights from anthropology, there is now a growing body of literature from within history on infanticide, particularly in the early modern period where historians can find evidence from church courts and other sources. Earlier studies of infanticide focused on several key themes, such as the shame and stigma of unmarried motherhood, poverty, and the lack of emotional involvement with newly born children. Others have seen infanticide as a form of population control, while others have seen it as a symptom of maternal psychosis.[39] More recent work has pointed to a more nuanced picture in which social norms, prevailing attitudes and crucially, religious beliefs, have to be understood as well as the criminal intent, or not, of the mother.[40] Several scholars, challenging Philippe Ariès's view that children under seven were largely disregarded before the seventeenth century, have stressed the strong social opprobrium for child murder and the fact that other women often informed on women suspected of infanticide and performed the tests that confirmed or disproved pregnancy. Recent studies have revealed several key continuities, 'such as the fact that young single women were the main culprits; that there was a high proportion of domestic servants charged with concealing their pregnancy [and] giving birth in secret and killing the infant almost immediately after delivery'. (See Figure 9). They have

---

[36] Parkin, in his study of the Giriama of Kenya, has found historical evidence that children born feet first or whose top teeth came through before the bottom ones were seen as deviant and that such children might be drowned by non-family members worried about bringing evil into the community. D. Parkin, *Sacred Void: Spatial Images of Work and Ritual among the Giriama of Kenya* (Cambridge: Cambridge University Press, 1991), p. 213. In other cases, children's behaviour as they grow arouses suspicion that they are not what they seem. Among the Beng of west Africa some children are labelled 'snake children' and are thought to be born after a snake invades their mother's womb and dislodges the foetus. When the child is born it fails to thrive and shows signs of snake-like behaviour. Diviners are called in and offer the child snake food which, if it rejects, is a sign of its humanity, while if it likes the food, it is revealed as a snake. Often, however, these children are allowed to live, and while they cannot marry, they are tolerated and enabled to grow up. A. Gottlieb, *The Afterlife is Where We Come From: The Culture of Infancy in West Africa* (Chicago: Chicago University Press, 2004).

[37] N. Scheper-Hughes, *Death Without Weeping: The Violence of Everyday Life in Brazil* (Berkeley: University of California Press, 1992), p. 375.

[38] Langer, 'Infanticide', p. 355.

[39] M. Piers, *Infanticide, Past and Present* (New York: W. W. Norton, 1978).

[40] For an overview of this literature see A.-M. Kilday and K. Watson, 'Infanticide, Religion and Community in the British Isles, 1720–1920', *Family and Community History*, 11:2 (2008), 84–99.

also noted that there was clear evidence of a growing degree of toleration for the offence during the eighteenth and nineteenth centuries'.[41]

In addition, there has been agreement that, on the whole, methods of infanticide were not especially brutal, relying heavily on asphyxiation and smothering.[42] As one of the early scholars of infanticide, Samuel Radbill puts it ,'The methods in infanticide have not changed much throughout history. Blood is rarely shed'.[43] This has been supported by studies of seventeenth- and eighteenth-century Ireland and England.[44] One notable exception to this, however, is Scotland. In her book on women's violence in Scotland, Anne-Marie Kilday claims that 63 per cent of the cases that she investigated (out of 140) involved incidents where blood was shed and the method of killing children was brutal. To give but two examples: in 1805, Jean Allison was brought before the West Circuit Court, where it was claimed she 'barbarously, wickedly and inhumanely cutt [cut] the child's throat from ear to ear with a razor in a gret [great] effusion of blood, with such force as causing the windpipe thereof to sever in two'. Eight years previously at the same court, Catherine MacDonald was charged with using a spade to attack her child in which its 'left leg above the knee was torn off...its right leg was disjointed and its nose flatted [flattened]'. The child's remains were then fed to a dog.[45] Women in Scotland, like women elsewhere may well have been motivated by shame and fear of economic ruin, but they differed noticeably in their methods of killing

---

[41] *Ibid.*, p. 88.

[42] Drawing parallels with contemporary anthropological accounts, it is also important to distinguish between active and passive infanticide. Scrimshaw has examined patterns of infant mortality and fertility in both historical and contemporary contexts and argues that there are many forms of infanticide, ranging from the overt to the passive in which children are given 'lower biological and emotional support'. S. Scrimshaw, 'Infanticide in Human Populations. Societal and Individual Concerns', in G. Hausfater and S. B. Hrdy, (eds), *Infanticide: Comparative and Evolutionary Perspectives* (New York: Aldine, 1984), p. 449. She gives several reasons for this, including population control, maximising reproductive success and cultural attitudes that require 'a "waiting" period after birth before full membership in society is bestowed on an individual' (p. 461). In another article she claims that when children are unwanted, or there is an acceptance of high levels of infant mortality, then there is likely to be parental 'underinvestment' in children, emotionally, physically, and in response to their illnesses, which will inevitably lead to their deaths. S. Scrimshaw, 'Infant Mortality and Behavior in the Regulation of Family Size', *Population and Development Review*, 4:3 (1978), 383–403. This insight was carried forward by Scheper-Hughes, *Death Without Weeping* (p. 413) whose account of infant death and child neglect in the *favelas* of north-eastern Brazil details, with much sympathy, the same phenomenon of underinvestment in the very young which she refers to as 'delayed anthropomorphization'. She identifies great ambivalence about infants among such poor mothers, noting that they do not 'trust' these children to survive, and therefore invest little emotional energy in them. Mothers in the *favelas* do not recognise or acknowledge individual personhood, reusing the same name several times over for successive siblings and rarely mourning openly for infants. There is little personalisation of the very young and it is only when children show signs of being active, or having the will to survive, that mothers acknowledge them as more fully human. Until this happens, mothers tend, so Scheper-Hughes claims, to neglect young children who seem passive or sickly. They feel that some children are not meant to survive and they do not fight to keep them alive, do not give them medicine (and usually cannot afford to) and treat their deaths with indifference and resignation. More actively, some mothers make the decision to withhold food from one child in order to give it to a more favoured one.

[43] S. Radbill, 'A History of Child Abuse and Infanticide', in R. E. Helfer and Ruth S. Kempe (eds), *The Battered Child* (Chicago: University of Chicago Press, 1968).

[44] J. Kelly, 'Infanticide in Eighteenth-Century Ireland', *Irish Economic and Social History*, 19 (1992), 5–26; L. Gowing, 'Secret Births and Infanticide in Seventeenth-Century England', *Past and Present*, 156:1 (1997), 87–115; K. Wrightson, 'Infanticide in Earlier Seventeenth-Century England', *Local Population Studies*, 15 (1975), 10–22; R. W. Malcolmson. 'Infanticide in the Eighteenth Century', in J. S. Cockburn (ed.), *Crime in England 1550–1800* (London: Methuen, 1977).

[45] A.-M. Kilday, *Women and Violent Crime in Enlightenment Scotland* (Woodbridge: Royal Historical Society, 2007), p. 69.

unwanted children,[46] leading Kilday to conclude that 'The reasons why Scottish lowland women behaved so aggressively in the perpetuation of infanticide remain partially opaque, but their actions shatter traditional conceptions of infanticidal women as pitiable, desperate 'victims' who killed with a conscience'.[47]

One final point concerns the status of the dead child. It might be assumed that part of the horror occasioned by the death of a newborn child is the idea of its vulnerability and its innocence. Yet often in infanticide cases in the early modern period the child was simply evidence against the mother and the greater crime was the concealment of pregnancy and of this pregnancy occurring outside marriage. Infanticide may well have been a form of violence against children but prosecution for the act was more concerned with punishing the mother than with justice for the child. Even in the contemporary era, the positioning of infanticide as a specific (and lesser) offence to murder might be taken as a sign that infants are not seen as fully human, with the same rights as older children and adults. Their deaths, while regrettable, are not important. The following contribution looks more closely at the attitudes towards the practice in early modern England.

Infanticide in Late Medieval and Early Modern England

Martin Ingram

In 1517 there appeared before the bishop of Lincoln's commissary general

> Alice Ridyng singlewoman daughter of John Ridyng of Eton [Buckinghamshire] ... and confessed that she was gotten with a male child by Sir Thomas Denys then chaplain of Master Geoffrey Wren and gave birth to the same in her father's house at Eton aforesaid a month last Sunday; and ... within a quarter of an hour after she had brought forth the child she killed the same by putting her hand in the infant's mouth and thus stifled it and ... buried it in a dunghill in her father's garden. She said also that she had no midwife at the time of her delivery nor was it ever certainly known to any that she was pregnant; however certain women of Windsor and Eton suspected and declared that she was with child, but the same Alice always denied it saying that she had other diseases in her belly. However on the Tuesday next after the birth of her child the women and honest wives of Windsor and Eton took her and searched her breasts and belly by which they knew for certain that she had given birth and then she confessed all to them and showed them the place where she had laid the child. She said also that neither her father nor her mother knew that she was with child because she always denied the same ... Further examined she says by virtue of the oath that she then took on the holy gospels that she was never carnally known by any man save the said Thomas and that neither he ... nor any other was of counsel or consenting to the death of the child. She said also that the child was begotten on the day of the Purification of the Blessed Virgin Mary last past in the time of high mass in the house of Master Geoffrey Wren at Spytell [a leper hospital near Windsor] where Master Geoffrey was then farmer.[48]

---

[46] Some contemporary cases of infanticide also involve extreme violence. In 1999 a fifteen-year-old girl pleaded guilty to infanticide after she admitted stabbing her newly born baby to death after giving birth secretly in her home. 'Girl, 15, stabbed her baby to death after secret birth', *The Guardian*, 12 Nov. 1999. Available online at http://www.guardian.co.uk/uk/1999/nov/12/audreygillan (accessed 10 Jan. 2010).

[47] Kilday, *Women and Violent Crime*, p. 79.

[48] Translated from M. Bowker (ed.), *An Episcopal Court Book for the Diocese of Lincoln, 1514–1520* (Lincoln: Lincoln Record Society, 61, 1967), p. 53.

Nearly 250 years later, in 1756, the *Northampton Mercury* reported the committal to prison of

> Mary Light, for that too common and most unnatural crime of murdering her own illegitimate infant. She is about 21 years of age, and lived as servant to one farmer Kerswell at a village near Modbury ... [Devon], where, she says, a young fellow, servant also in the same house, courted her, to whose importunities she yielded, and became pregnant by him. Her condition was suspected by her mother, who charged her strictly with it, but she still denied it, concealing it also from all except her seducer, who, on her acquainting him with it, left her and his service. About five weeks ago she was in bed seized with great pains, and was delivered of a living female child, without the knowledge of two girls who lay in the same room. She gathered up her infant, and got again into bed, wrapping the babe in one corner of the rug, and rising at her wonted hour, went about her household work. Her mistress going into her chamber, found the child stifled.[49]

The second case is more typical in that the woman supposed to have killed her child was a household servant, unlike the Eton girl who was living with her parents. Together they illustrate the key features of the great majority of cases of infanticide that are known from late medieval and early modern England. The child was illegitimate; the pregnancy was concealed; and the woman, usually quite young and of humble status, gave birth alone. The actions of neighbours, and the reports of such cases in court records and other accounts, do not suggest that the killing of babies was either readily condoned or really as 'common' as the *Northampton Mercury* suggested. However, concern for the infant was only one of the grounds for these attitudes; others, perhaps more important, were the conviction that for a mother to kill her baby was an 'unnatural' act and, more broadly, condemnation of the moral, social and economic consequences of illicit sexual activity. Yet such condemnation was never absolute, even at the peak of concern about sexual transgression and illegitimacy in the late sixteenth and early seventeenth centuries. It was mitigated by pragmatism and, within limits, by compassion for the infanticidal mother, to the extent that by 1800 the difficulty of securing convictions prompted a reform of the law.[50]

How had the legal situation developed? Whether or not infanticide was actually 'the prevailing and stubborn vice of antiquity' imagined by Gibbon,[51] the fathers of the early Christian Church set their faces firmly against the practice. The central texts of canon law and later provincial constitutions and canons therefore proscribed not merely the killing of infants but acts of commission and omission that might lead to their accidental death. Accordingly, the late medieval English church courts did not confine themselves to the kind of case quoted earlier. They were concerned to ensure the maintenance of illegitimate children who might otherwise be neglected, and they also prosecuted mothers (and sometimes fathers) who irresponsibly rather than deliberately suffocated their offspring by 'overlaying' them in bed. In situations where a child had been killed, intentionally or otherwise, the church imposed some form of penance, its severity depending on the circumstances.[52] The fact that Alice Ridyng's child had been begotten by a supposedly celibate priest on a high feast of the Virgin, and further that she had deprived the child of the sacrament of baptism and so prevented him from joining the Christian community, were regarded as aggravating factors and her

---

[49] Quoted in Malcolmson, 'Infanticide in the Eighteenth Century', p. 187.

[50] This discussion is based mainly on cases from legal records. For literary representations, which present a rather different picture, see F. E. Dolan, *Dangerous Familiars: Representations of Domestic Crime in England, 1550–1700* (Ithaca: Cornell University Press, 1994), ch. 4.

[51] Quoted in Langer, 'Infanticide', p. 355. The broader context is surveyed also by K. Wrightson, 'Infanticide in European History', *Criminal Justice History*, 3 (1982), 1–20.

[52] R. H. Helmholz, 'Infanticide in the Province of Canterbury during the Fifteenth Century', *History of Childhood Quarterly*, 2:3 (1975), 379–90.

punishment was correspondingly severe. On the three Sundays next coming she was to perform public penance in the parish church of Eton, going bare-headed, barefoot and bare-legged in procession dressed only in her smock and carrying a lighted candle, and to perform a similar penance on one further Sunday in the church of Windsor. On the following Ash Wednesday (the beginning of the penitential season of Lent), and again on 1 April, she was to perform public penance in Lincoln Cathedral. She was also to do penance on a Wednesday before the image of the Blessed Virgin Mary of Windsor, pausing at Eton to say the Pater Noster, the Hail Mary and the Apostles' Creed. Every day throughout her life before she ate or drank she was to say three Pater Nosters, three Ave Marias and one Creed. One day every week she was to fast on bread and water. Finally she was bound not to commit any such act again so long as she lived and always to advise women against similar behaviour.[53]

The ecclesiastical judge was careful to note that that these penances were enjoined for offences subject to his correction. Homicide, including the killing of infants, was within the jurisdiction of the king. In practice prosecutions at common law in the late middle ages were exceedingly rare. This was perhaps because the ordinary punishment for intentional homicide, death by hanging, was considered disproportionate for the killing of an infant, most likely the illegitimate child of a poor woman. Perhaps also the evidential problems were felt to be so great, and the procedures for bringing indictments so cumbersome, that jurors were inclined to take no action and to leave matters to the church courts. Occasionally married women were indicted for killing offspring who had survived for twelve months or more to develop into toddlers or young children. Such crimes were thought to spring not from malice but from 'distraction' or 'frenzy', in other words insanity, and the women were almost invariably pardoned.[54]

Throughout the sixteenth century it was by no means easy to bring a successful prosecution for killing a newborn child because the crown had to demonstrate that the baby had been born alive. None the less cases were brought and in some convictions, usually leading to a death sentence, were secured, often on the basis of palpable signs of violence on the baby's body. The trend was towards greater severity. Richard Crompton's 1583 enlargement of Anthony Fitzherbert's *L'Office et Auctorite de Iustices de Peace* drew attention to a 1560 Cheshire case in which a woman, described as *feme putayne* (in contemporary parlance a whore), had abandoned her newly delivered child in an orchard, covered in leaves. The infant had actually been killed by a kite, but the woman was convicted of murder on the grounds that she had intended its death.[55] A statute of 1624 further hardened the law in respect of women who gave birth to bastard children. Noting that 'many lewd women … to avoid their shame, and to escape punishment, do secretly bury or conceal the death' of such offspring, the act laid down that such concealment made the mother liable to the death penalty as in case of murder unless she could prove by at least one witness that the child was actually born dead.[56] Thereafter cases were brought regularly and led to a substantial number of convictions.[57] For example, at the Essex assizes in the period 1620–80 a total of 83 women were accused of killing their newborn children, and at least 30 were convicted and sentenced to hang.[58]

---

[53] Bowker (ed.), *Episcopal Court Book*, p. 54.

[54] Kellum, 'Infanticide in the Later Middle Ages', pp. 367–88.

[55] P. Hoffer and N. E. H. Hull, *Murdering Mothers: Infanticide in England and New England, 1558–1803* (New York: New York University Press, 1981), pp. 3–22.

[56] 21 James I c. 27.

[57] Hoffer and Hull, *Murdering Mothers*, pp. 19–27; M. Jackson, *New-born Child Murder: Women, Illegitimacy and the Courts in Eighteenth-Century England* (Manchester: Manchester University Press, 1996), ch. 2; Wrightson, 'Infanticide in Earlier Seventeenth-Century England', pp. 10–22.

[58] J. A. Sharpe, *Crime in Seventeenth-Century England: A County Study* (Cambridge: Cambridge University Press and Editions de la Maison des Sciences de l'Homme, 1983), pp. 135–37. For a different perspective see

Contemporaries, whether clerical and legal commentators or neighbours of the accused, commonly described infanticide as 'unnatural', sometimes as 'wicked' or 'barbarous'. Condemnation was often framed in religious terms even by local people. In Cuckfield (Sussex) in 1578, the midwife told Mercy Gould that 'hanging is too good for thee', and met her abject pleas for mercy with the injunction to 'arise up, for we are no gods ... Cry to God for mercy, and repent'.[59] As in this and the earlier case of Alice Ridyng, local women were often assiduous in cornering a woman suspected of killing her baby and pressurising her to tell the truth. They minutely examined both her body and her bedding or other surroundings for signs of recent childbirth; 'drawing' the breasts to see if they contained milk was a common procedure. Local menfolk were active in searching for a body, if one was thought to exist. Often they included constables and overseers of the poor – important figures in their communities, concerned not only with maintaining order and morality but also with administering the poor law and making sure that the poor rates contributed by local inhabitants were not wasted. In the minds of the inhabitants of these local communities, economic concerns and moral issues were a seamless web that cannot in retrospect be distinguished. Together they created a climate of condemnation of infanticidal acts that ensured that cases, once identified, were very likely to be pursued in the courts.[60]

Attitudes were not unmixed, however – an issue that needs to be approached from more than one angle. Part of the background was a society in which knowledge of abortifacients, particularly infusions of the herb savin but including other 'powders' and 'potions', was evidently quite widespread, and undoubtedly they were put to use – how commonly cannot be known – to forestall unwanted pregnancies.[61] Some of these brews were potent and could be dangerous. Mercy Gould was supposed to have taken what she described as 'a cruel hot drink', while in 1504 a Nottinghamshire woman was said to have died after drinking a poisonous draught intended to destroy the child in her womb.[62] Infanticide may be seen as another means of achieving much the same end. On this basis, some historians have assumed that prosecuted cases of infanticide, along with occasional coroners' inquests on the corpses of unidentified infants, represented merely the visible part of a much larger social phenomenon. The fact that some infanticidal mothers had accomplices, commonly their mother or other female relative, occasionally the child's father, is sometimes cited in support of this proposition; but it is surely hazardous to infer wider social attitudes from the fact that close family members were on occasion willing to lend aid in what must often have been a desperate situation.[63] Clear-cut statements of tolerant attitudes towards infanticide are uncommon. In Colchester (Essex) around 1635, a maidservant assured the bearer of a bastard child that 'tush, it was not the first that she had made away', but the mother herself, Lydia Downes, protested that she 'was not so hard hearted' as to kill the baby. The context was one of extreme brutality. Her lover, Richard Skeete,

---

G. Walker, *Crime, Gender and Social Order in Early Modern England* (Cambridge: Cambridge University Press, 2003), pp. 149–51, who cautions against exaggerating the impact of the 1624 act.

[59] Quoted in D. Cressy, *Travesties and Transgressions in Tudor and Stuart England: Tales of Discord and Dissension* (Oxford: Oxford University Press, 2000), p. 53.

[60] Gowing, 'Secret Births', pp. 41–42, 45–51, 60–73.

[61] A. McLaren, *Reproductive Rituals: The Perception of Fertility in England from the Sixteenth to the Nineteenth Century* (London: Methuen, 1984), pp. 102–06.

[62] Cressy, *Travesties and Transgressions*, p. 53; R. F. Hunnisett (ed.), *Calendar of Nottinghamshire Coroners' Inquests, 1485–1558* (Nottingham: Thoroton Society, Record Series, 25, 1969), pp. 8–9.

[63] Sharpe, *Crime in Seventeenth-Century England*, pp. 136–37; J. R. Dickinson and J. A. Sharpe, 'Infanticide in Early Modern England: the Court of Great Sessions at Chester, 1650–1800', in Jackson, *Infanticide*, pp. 42–44, 47.

a local doctor or 'cunning man', went on to kill several more of her children, on one occasion threatening her 'that if she would not consent ... she should never go home again to tell tales'. He was also accused of poisoning another woman and likewise murdering his wife. Both Skeete and Downes were hanged in 1639.[64]

Another approach is to assume that, far from being taken for granted, cases of suspected infanticide were thought to require considerable explanation and investigation. The incidence of illegitimacy was never extremely high in early modern England but, especially at its peak around 1600, bastardy was hardly an uncommon phenomenon.[65] It is true that, as the 1624 act implied, unmarried mothers risked shame and even social ostracism; they were often dismissed from service or suffered other economic penalties; they were usually reported to the ecclesiastical courts, and had to perform public penance in church or suffer excommunication; while some of them were also dealt with by the secular magistrates and, under an act of 1576, might suffer a whipping or, from 1610, be sent to the House of Correction for as long as a year.[66] On the other hand, the combined provisions of the bastardy and poor relief statutes, which became fully operational in virtually all areas in the course of the seventeenth century, did ensure that unmarried women and their babies received at least a minimum of maintenance.[67] In any event it is plain that only a tiny proportion of unmarried mothers can have resorted to infanticide, even if it is assumed – as many historians seem to without much warrant – that most of those accused in the courts had actually committed the crime.[68]

Contemporaries were more circumspect. While the act of 1624 in some ways tipped the balance against the accused, its terms did ensure that the circumstances of untoward infant deaths, at least in the case of illegitimate (or supposedly illegitimate) children, were carefully sifted. No mercy could be expected if the facts indicated brutality or simply plain violence[69] – if the child's throat had been cut or its head smashed, for instance, if it had been mercilessly strangled, or (as in a Sussex case in 1575) suffocated by having nettles thrust into its mouth.[70] But some cases of smothering – more commonly the cause of death – evoked equivocal responses, because they could have been accidental. Throwing an infant's body down a well or privy, or into a ditch, pond, stream, or river did not necessarily lead to legal condemnation (as opposed to moral disapproval), because it was often an issue whether the foetus had come to term or the child had been born dead. Women often insisted that the baby was stillborn and sometimes claimed that what they had brought forth 'had not the form of a child' or was a mere 'gristle'.[71] If inquest juries thought that a child was plainly dead at birth they might return a verdict accordingly, and their willingness so to do increased as time

[64] Cressy, *Travesties and Transgressions*, ch. 5 (quotations at pp. 78, 80); Sharpe, *Crime in Seventeenth-Century England*, p. 137.

[65] P. Laslett, K. Oosterveen and R. M. Smith (eds), *Bastardy and its Comparative History* (London: Edward Arnold, 1980), part 1.

[66] M. Ingram, *Church Courts, Sex and Marriage in England, 1570–1640* (Cambridge: Cambridge University Press, 1987), pp. 152, 259–81, 334–40, 353–55.

[67] Walker, *Crime, Gender and Social Order*, pp. 227–37; more generally see S. Hindle, *On the Parish? The Micro-Politics of Poor Relief in Rural England, c. 1550–1750* (Oxford: Clarendon Press, 2004).

[68] Hoffer and Hull, *Murdering Mothers*, p. 145; Jackson, *New-Born Child Murder*, p. 11.

[69] E.g., R. F. Hunnisett (ed.), *Sussex Coroners' Inquests, 1558–1603* (Kew: PRO Publications, 1996), pp. 91–92; R F Hunnisett (ed.), *Sussex Coroners' Inquests, 1603–1688* (Kew: PRO Publications, 1998), pp. 28–29, 81, 87–88; cf. Dickinson and Sharpe, 'Infanticide in Early Modern England', p. 39; Walker, *Crime, Gender and Social Order*, pp. 152–53.

[70] Hunnisett (ed.), *Sussex Coroners' Inquests, 1558–1603*, p. 33.

[71] Jackson, *New-Born Child Murder*, pp. 74–76; Gowing, 'Secret Births and Infanticide', p. 98.

went on. In cases that proceeded to indictment, considerable attention was likewise paid to the possibility of premature parturition or stillbirth. The size of the body and the presence or otherwise of hair and nails were taken as important indicators, but there were many expressions of uncertainty by the midwives and, increasingly as time went on, medical practitioners who were brought in to give evidence.[72] Just as clear marks of violence strongly predisposed jurors to convict, so the absence of 'any squat or bruise, whereby the said child should come to his death' generated doubts which might lead to acquittal.[73] In the eighteenth century a common procedure conducted by medical witnesses was to immerse the baby's lungs in water to see if they floated, supposedly indicating that it had actually inhaled. But the reliability of this test was eventually discredited.[74]

Proof not merely of concealment but of intent to conceal was required by the 1624 act, and this opened up important lines of defence. Failure to inform others of a pregnancy or to call on the midwife or other women for aid in delivery was *prima facie* an incriminating factor, but the probing of this issue could reveal mitigating circumstances. There were many instances where – as the carefully collected evidence in well documented cases shows – the mother was plainly ill, distracted, or in desperate straits. Inexperienced young women who had concealed their pregnancies, or simply been too bewildered or scared to acknowledge their condition – in some cases even to themselves – were often uncertain when they had conceived and hence when they were due to give birth. A young woman lodging with a Southampton widow in 1628 claimed that she was 'sick with the stone colic' but, on retiring, she immediately gave birth to a child, which she said was stillborn. When the body was discovered in her bed and she was asked about her pregnancy, she replied, according to a witness, 'How can that be when I never did know what man was?' Her later statements might be taken to imply that this response was deliberately disingenuous. But it is hard to be sure, and there are other indications in the evidence that at the time of the birth she was in a state of mental dissociation if not acute denial. Plainly contemporaries would not have thought in such terms, but it is striking that evidence on such matters was faithfully recorded and, it may be presumed, carefully evaluated.[75] Married women, it should be noted, were still assumed to have no obvious motive for infanticide and in their case contemporaries looked more readily to mental disturbance for an explanation. A Buckinghamshire case of 1668, discussed in detail by Sir Matthew Hale, established that even a temporary 'phrenzy' – in this instance brought on by 'having not slept many nights' – could serve as exculpation. It is possible that this development encouraged a more understanding attitude even in the case of unmarried women.[76]

By the late seventeenth century one particular kind of evidence was assuming special importance in deciding the issue of intent. If the child's mother had prepared baby clothes or such like it was thought less likely that she had intended to conceal the death of the child. 'Benefit of linen' became a stock feature of trials, to the indignation of sceptics like Daniel Defoe who scoffed at 'the stale pretence of a scrap or two of

[72] Jackson, *New-Born Child Murder*, pp. 84–93.
[73] R. C. Anderson (ed.), *The Book of Examinations and Depositions, AD 1622–1644*, 4 vols (Southampton: Southampton Record Society, vols 29, 31, 34, 36, 1929–36), ii. 15; Walker, *Crime, Gender and Social Order*, p. 153.
[74] Jackson, *New-Born Child Murder*, pp. 93–100.
[75] Anderson, *Book of Examinations and Depositions*, ii. 14–16; Gowing, 'Secret Births and Infanticide', pp. 106–08. See also M. MacDonald, *Mystical Bedlam: Madness, Anxiety, and Healing in Seventeenth-Century England* (Cambridge: Cambridge University Press, 1981), p. 83.
[76] Sir Matthew Hale, *Historia Placitorum Coronae. The History of the Pleas of the Crown*, ed. S. Emlyn, 2 vols (London: printed by E. and R. Nutt and R. Gosling for F. Gyles, 1736), i. 36.

child-bed linen being found in the murderer's box, *etc.*'[77] In any case the framework of attitudes gradually shifted in the late seventeenth and, more decisively, the eighteenth century. Attitudes to women changed, not least as a result of an altered view of the female constitution based in new ideas about the nervous system and the emotions. This led to an increased tendency to view infanticidal mothers in particular, and bastard-bearers in general, as the deluded victims of male seducers rather than simply wicked. More broadly a less harsh vision of Christian morality softened the social climate somewhat. The results were both a declining incidence of prosecutions in many areas and a growing rate of acquittal. At the same time, the 1624 act was gradually undermined by accumulating legal doubts on the justice of convicting women on evidence of concealment alone, and as the measure came to be seen as redolent of outdated values and concerns. By the late eighteenth century, proponents of reform claimed that the severity of the existing law worked against the interests of justice, since judges and jurors alike were disinclined to convict. Efforts in the 1770s to repeal the 1624 act were unsuccessful, but in 1803 this object was finally achieved.[78] A new statute returned the trials of women accused of infanticide to common law rules of evidence. However, in cases where murder was not proven, juries could return an alternative verdict of 'concealment of birth' carrying a maximum penalty of two years in prison: the 1624 act left a powerful legacy.[79]

. . . .

Abandonment has a long history in the western world, and in many stories it is a mark of someone special, favoured by the gods or by fate, who fulfils a great destiny despite their humble start. From Moses being cast adrift in his basket, through to Oedipus and Romulus and Remus, the trope of abandonment, followed by greatness, occurs frequently. In literature, Shakespeare's Perdita is abandoned, as are Edmund Spencer's Pastorella, Henry Fielding's Tom Jones and George Bernard Shaw's Mr Upshaft. Even Walt Disney's Snow White is abandoned by a servant in defiance of orders to put her to death. In all these cases the abandoned child is rescued and matures safely to adulthood having been saved by other people. Indeed there is usually a circularity in such tales which mean that, through a variety of coincidences, children are eventually reunited with their birth parents, unhappily for Oedipus but less so for Perdita.

While there is evidence and discussion about the extent of exposure and abandonment in the ancient world, much less is known about the practice in recent history and modern societies.[80] Much better documented are the institutionalised measures used to care for unwanted children, particularly the use of foundling homes which have a long history of caring for unwanted infants, and offering parents the opportunity to abandon their children safely. The foundling hospital was the late medieval church's answer to the perennial problem of abandonment. It is claimed that Pope Innocent III set up the first foundling hospital in 1198 in Rome having been horrified by the number of dead babies being found in the Tiber.[81] By the fourteenth century, the practice was becoming more formalised (and,

---

[77] Quoted in Malcolmson, 'Infanticide in the Eighteenth Century', p. 199. See also J. M. Beattie, *Crime and the Courts in England, 1660–1800* (Oxford: Clarendon Press, 1986), pp. 113–24.

[78] Jackson, *New-Born Child Murder*, ch. 7.

[79] 43 George III *c.* 58; M. Jackson, 'The Trial of Harriet Vooght: Continuity and Change in the History of Infanticide', in Jackson, *Infanticide*, pp. 6–7.

[80] C. Panter-Brick, 'Nobody's Children? A Reconsideration of Child Abandonment', in C. Panter-Brick and M. Smith (eds), *Abandoned Children* (Cambridge: Cambridge University Press, 2000).

[81] D. Kertzer, 'The Lives of Foundlings in Nineteenth-Century Italy', in Panter-Brick and Smith, *Abandoned Children*.

arguably, normalised) through the foundation of foundling hospitals in parts of southern Europe. Babies could now be abandoned at a designated place where care would be assured, and the element of chance in whether a foundling was picked up was removed. A particularly dense network of such institutions grew up in Italy and Spain, where there was a strong emphasis on saving the souls of foundling babies through baptism. In northern Europe the development took hold more slowly, although other mechanisms were in place for dealing with abandoned children.[82] The institution of foundling hospitals received a second boost in the eighteenth century in England and Germany. At this time, Enlightenment and commercial ideals provided a new justification for preserving foundlings: the benefits to the nation of saving infants who had done no wrong so that they could become future workers, soldiers and parents.[83] Both Napolean Buonaparte and Catherine the Great explicitly tied the saving of foundling children to the strengthening of their states, although high mortality rates and the poor physical condition of many survivors thwarted their ambitions.[84] To encourage compliance by facilitating anonymity, children were often admitted to these hospitals and refuges through the now iconic wheels, placed in baskets in the walls.[85] Re-christened baby hatches, these wheels are currently being revived in some parts of the western world.[86] (See Figure 10.)

This history of such institutions, and the local differences between them, has been well documented,[87] and what is evident from some of these detailed studies is the very high rate of child mortality.[88] How to analyse these places therefore has become a matter of some debate. Some have argued that foundling homes must be seen in terms of 'the circulation of children', recycling children from poor homes into the service of the state, so that foundlings were simply 'a stock of children at society's disposal. The state could redistribute the mass of children without families according to its needs'.[89] In this respect, it has been

---

[82] Under the English Poor Law, local communities were charged with looking after unwanted infants. In France, the Paris Foundling Hospital dates from 1670 but in other parts of the country abandoned children were taken to all-purpose poor hospitals (*Hôtels-Dieu*) or general hospitals: see O. Hufton, *The Poor of Eighteenth-Century France, 1750–1789* (Oxford: Clarendon Press, 1974), p. 335.

[83] O. Ulbricht, 'The Debate about Foundling Hospitals in Enlightenment Germany: Infanticide, Illegitimacy and Infant Mortality Rates', *Central European History*, 18:3–4 (1985), 211–56, at p. 211.

[84] J.-P. Bardet, 'La Société et l'abandon', in *Enfance abandonée et société en Europe XIVe–XXe siècle* (Rome: Ecole Française de Rome, 1991), p. 14; D. L. Ransel, *Mothers of Misery: Child Abandonment in Russia* (Princeton: Princeton University Press, 1988), pp. 31–38.

[85] Baskets allowed children to be taken into the hospital unseen by placing them in one side of the wheel, which was then rotated through the wall. Wheels were often thought to confer a blessing on a child – there are cases in Italy of children being stuffed into the wheel so that they could be blessed, even at the cost of broken limbs: see G. Da Molin, *Nati e Abbandonati: Aspetti Demografici e Sociali dell'Infanzia Abbandonata in Italia nell'eta Moderna* (Bari: Cacucci, 1993).

[86] Germany's first new 'baby hatch' was opened in 1999 in Hamburg. It was located in a hospital wall and a sign over it read 'We'll take your child when no one else will. Without asking your name, without asking questions…' Some paediatricians estimated that 40 to 50 babies were being abandoned every year in Germany and that over half were dying. The baby hatches were set up to help mothers abandon their children in a place of safety. 'Germany Still Divided over the Idea of Baby Hatches', *Deutsche Welle*, 21 Dec. 2002. Available online at http://www.dw-world.de/dw/article/0,,718631,00.html (accessed 10 Jan. 2010). In 2006 the Jikei Hospital in Kumamoto Prefecture, Japan, also set up 'storks' cradles' to reduce the number of abandoned babies, see http://en.wikipedia.org/wiki/Baby_hatch (accessed 11 Sept. 2009).

[87] See, for example, the contributors in Panter-Brick and Smith, *Abandoned Children*.

[88] In her account of life for the poor in eighteenth-century France, Hufton notes that the hospitals taking in infants in Rennes and the Auvergne 'claimed an annual mortality rate of 60 per cent, 50 per cent in a good year. Indeed this would appear an average figure for foundling hospitals [i.e. *hotels-dieu* and *hôpitaux généraux*] throughout France', *The Poor of Eighteenth-Century France*, p. 342.

[89] I. dos Guimarães Sa, 'Circulation of Children in Eighteenth-Century Portugal', in Panter-Brick and Smith

argued, foundling hospitals were simply the extension of other patterns of child-rearing in which children were circulated into different households as apprentices or domestic workers.[90] Others have commented that placing children in institutions or orphanages was not abandonment, simply 'delegated motherhood',[91] defraying the costs of raising a child onto others. From this perspective, the assumption that abandonment involved children who were unwanted becomes a questionable one: many parents believed that they were offering their child a better chance in life by giving them up. This relatively benign view of the purpose of foundling institutions is countered, however, by those who point to the high levels of mortality within these places, suggesting that rather then being 'delegated motherhood', a more accurate description might be 'delegated infanticide'. What these debates suggest is that to portray abandonment as a straightforward or homogenous practice is to underestimate the variety of reasons parents and guardians might abandon their child. The following article sets out the scale of infant and child abandonment in the eighteenth and early nineteenth centuries when the problem appears to have been particularly acute, and explores some of the reasons that prompted parents to give up their offspring.

Infant Abandonment in Europe 1700–1850

Alysa Levene

By the early modern period infant abandonment was carried out on a large scale, and in many European countries there was an extensive network of institutions to receive these children. As already noted, several more institutions were founded during the eighteenth century, in response to Enlightenment ideals of saving the innocent. Most European foundling hospitals accepted all babies offered to them, although some specified family background. In Bologna in northern Italy, for example, the foundling hospital was intended for the use of unmarried mothers only, while other institutions used the rotating 'wheel' set into the wall of the hospital, alluded to above, to restrict the size of babies given up.[92] A more restrictive policy was used at the London Foundling Hospital, one of the eighteenth-century foundations (established in 1739), which took in only small groups of healthy infants for most of its history. (See Figure 11). Although this hospital was extremely oversubscribed, the necessity for a foundling institution was arguably lessened in England by the existence since the sixteenth century of a nationwide system of poor relief which gave financial and material support to the needy in their parish of settlement. The poor laws provided welfare support for foundlings, unmarried mothers or parents overburdened with children, and was, generally speaking, tolerant of unmarried mothers raising their children themselves. This was not the case in other parts of Europe, where notions of sexual and family honour played a much larger role, and where women were not allowed to keep illegitimate babies. This

---

(eds), *Abandoned Children*, p. 29.

[90] J. Goody and E. Goody, 'The Circulation of Women and Children in Northern Ghana' *Man*, 2:2 (1967), 226–48; see also Ch. 4, below.

[91] S. B. Hardy, 'Fitness Tradeoffs in the History and Evolution of Delegated Mothering with Special Reference to Wet-Nursing, Abandonment, and Infanticide', *Ethology and Sociobiology*, 13:5–6 (1992), 409–44.

[92] In Florence, a grill was added to the wheel in 1699 to prevent the abandonment of older infants. D. Kertzer, *Sacrificed for Honor. Italian Infant Abandonment and the Politics of Reproductive Control* (Boston: Beacon Press, 1993), pp. 84–88.

difference is offered as a reason why rates of abandonment differed from place to place: in parts of Italy, for example, unmarried mothers were forced to give their babies up to a foundling hospital immediately after the birth.[93] Despite the greater tolerance for unmarried motherhood in England, however, the anonymity offered by the London Foundling Hospital made it an attractive prospect for many, especially when for a short period in the 1750s, it exercised a policy of open admissions.

The existence of so many places to abandon babies, the apparent lack of tolerance for unmarried motherhood in parts of Europe, a rapid increase in population from 1740 and a rise in illegitimacy, all resulted in extremely high and rising levels of infant abandonment across the eighteenth and first half of the nineteenth centuries.[94] Poor economic conditions also forced parents to give up babies.[95] Volker Hunecke estimates that by the mid-nineteenth century, around 120,000 infants were being abandoned annually in Europe, with nearly 35,000 of these in Italy, more than 30,000 in France, 15,000 in Spain, and 15,000 in Portugal.[96] Admissions to the Milan foundling hospital grew six-fold between the 1770s and the 1850s, and there was similar growth at most other European foundling institutions.[97] For England equivalent figures are harder to reach, in the absence of a foundling hospital exercising open admissions until 1756. Valerie Fildes, however, finds a rise in foundling baptisms in several early modern London parishes from 1740 which was beyond the scope of population expansion alone.[98] Almost all of the children studied by Fildes were left in places where they were likely to be found, such as house entries and churches, although some may have been infanticide attempts. Many were left with notes, also suggesting that the parents hoped that someone would care for the child.

The fact that foundlings were increasingly abandoned into a formal care structure makes the relationship with infanticide difficult to determine. Parents may have used abandonment as a legal form of disposing of their infant, but with the same motivations. It is possible that as abandonment became more common, infanticide was seen as a particularly brutal alternative. On the other hand, evidence from crime records suggests that a more sympathetic attitude towards the desperation of infanticidal mothers developed in the eighteenth century, which may have run in tandem with the desire to assist vulnerable and unwanted infants.[99] Certainly the evidence from foundling hospitals shows that there were a variety of reasons why a baby might be

---

[93] Kertzer, *Sacrificed for Honor, passim.*

[94] For example, see Da Molin, *Nati e Abbandonati*, p. 178. M. Livi Bacci, *The Population of Europe: A History* (Oxford: Blackwell, 2000), pp. 150–51, sees the eighteenth-century rise in abandonment in Europe as a response to (among other factors) the higher absolute and relative cost of children. After a century of stagnation Europe's population (including that of Russia) virtually doubled across the second half of the eighteenth century, then kept on rising rapidly. The reasons for growing illegitimacy are contested. French historians relate the trend to de-Christianisation: see Hufton, *The Poor of Eighteenth-Century France*, p. 320, who gives illegitimacy rates in France on the eve of the Revolution as twelve to seventeen per cent.

[95] For example, see Da Molin, *Nati e Abbandonati*, pp. 63, 178, 191. Even in industrialising Britain real wages did not grow appreciably until the second quarter of the nineteenth century: see below, fn. 118.

[96] V. Hunecke, 'Intensità e Fluttuazioni degli Abbandoni dal XV al XIX Secolo', in Bardet (ed.), *Enfance abandonée*, pp. 36–38.

[97] Da Molin, *Nati e Abbandonati*, pp. 34–53.

[98] V. Fildes, 'Maternal Feelings Re-assessed: Child Abandonment and Neglect in London and Westminster, 1550–1800', in V. Fildes (ed.), *Women as Mothers in Pre-Industrial England* (London: Routledge, 1990), pp. 140–68.

[99] Above, p. 73. See also, M. Jackson, 'Suspicious Infant Deaths: The Statute of 1624 and Medical Evidence at Coroners' Inquests', in M. Clark and C. Crawford (eds), *Legal Medicine in History* (Cambridge: Cambridge University Press, 1994); for similar developments in Scotland, see D. Symonds, *Weep Not for Me: Women, Ballads and Infanticide in Early Modern Scotland* (University Park.: Pennsylvania State University Press, 1997).

abandoned, and that they were not all unwanted burdens who might otherwise have been at risk of infanticide. These were almost certainly mediated through both personal circumstances and local traditions of abandonment and welfare support. Several stories taken from foundling hospital records illustrate this variety.

On 1 May 1757, a five-week-old baby was taken to the London Foundling Hospital by her parents from her Essex home. In the note they left with her (a practice encouraged by the hospital in order to facilitate any future application to reclaim children), they stated that:

> The parents of this Female Infant do not expose & desert it, from any Want of Humanity or Virtue: but as their present Situation in Life must forbid their owning it, & having ye Inspection of its Infancy, thought it could be plac'd no where safer, than under y^t wise & good Government to which it is now committed....Va mon Enfant, prend ta Fortune – AB.[100]

This exceptionally poignant (and lucid) note indicates clearly that the parents felt that their child would get a better chance in life at the hospital than they could currently provide for it. Their baby was entered in the hospital's registers as child number 4,338 and christened Margaret Hall. Sadly, the parents' hopes of having their child back foundered somewhere along the way, and Margaret died under the hospital's care in 1763.

Quite a different set of circumstances may be discerned in the abandonment in Florence of a baby girl named Maria, born in the city and delivered on the day of her birth on 4 January 1777 to the Innocenti foundling hospital by a midwife from Via della Pergola. She died the same day. Another baby girl, Cammilla, was brought to the Innocenti from the Orbatello lying-in hospital on 13 January 1777, the day she was born, and died a week later.[101] These infants were probably illegitimate, and abandoned according to external pressures of family, church and lay officials. Midwives were frequently central to what Kertzer has identified as a network of surveillance of unmarried women, discovering pregnancies, and carrying babies straight to the nearest foundling hospital after the birth. These brief vignettes – we have scarcely enough details to call them stories – are representative of many babies left at foundling hospitals, but especially where abandonment was part of a system of policing sexual behaviour.

This is not to imply that parents in England were more attached to their infants than those in Florence, or that foundlings were more likely to be legitimate there.[102] There were undoubtedly many reasons for giving up a child in all geographical contexts, and our view is directed partly by the fact that the London Hospital asked for and preserved notes left with its charges. Indifferent parents were perhaps far less likely either to leave a note with their baby, or to apply to reclaim them, and there are many babies in the London hospital records who make only a brief and unmourned appearance. Occasionally, the evidence allows us to see more unusual cases, like the woman who petitioned the London Foundling Hospital for the admission of her baby in October 1772, citing the common scenario of abandonment by her partner and unemployment to explain her actions. The hospital officials were suspicious and noted that she 'appears

---

[100] London Metropolitan Archive (hereafter LMA), Foundling Hospital billets, A/FH/A09/1/53.

[101] Archive of the Spedale degli Innocenti, Florence, Italy (hereafter AOIF), *Balie e Bambini Registers*, 1777, *Serie* XVI.

[102] In fact, rates of legitimacy were frequently higher at Italian foundling hospitals than in London, although up to a third of admissions might have been born in wedlock there too. A. Levene, 'The Origins of the Children of the London Foundling Hospital, 1741–60: A Reconsideration', *Continuity and Change*, 18:2 (2003), 201–35; Kertzer, *Sacrificed for Honor*, pp. 71–102.

to be a woman of the town'.[103] She was, none the less, allowed to continue along the
admissions process. It is impossible to know how many foundlings were the offspring
of prostitutes (the implication in this case was that the woman had originally been
a domestic servant). These stories, however, serve to illustrate some of the reasons a
baby might be abandoned, as well as introducing certain local differences. As already
noted, unmarried mothers in Florence may have had little choice in abandoning their
new-born babies, but married parents also had a longer history there of being able to
rely on abandonment (and subsequent reclamation after the period of nursing) in times
of hardship. In England, abandonment to the parish was always an option, but it was
harder to do it secretly, and asking for help meant the public telling of the individual
or family's circumstances, and perhaps, admission to a workhouse. The English poor
law did, none the less, provide support for the needy without recourse to abandoning
a child. These local differences almost certainly had an impact on why babies were
abandoned.

   We may also speculate on how abandoning parents understood their actions. Many
were unmarried mothers who could not afford to keep their babies, either because of
financial reasons or because of the damage they represented to their future chances of
employment and marriage. Necessity forced these women to abandon, and in many
cases we can only speculate on how they felt about it. Many parents hoped that their
child would have better prospects by growing up at the hospital: foundling institutions
were often grand buildings patronised by the wealthy. This hope was voiced by Margaret
Hall's parents in their note, quoted above. They may not have known how high the
mortality rates were of the babies abandoned to almost all foundling hospitals in
this period: at least half of all foundlings died under the care of the hospitals, and
sometimes 80 per cent or higher.[104] Hospitals generally aimed to place their charges
with rural wet nurses, and the majority of deaths often took place in places far from
the city where the babies were abandoned. Other parents used foundling hospitals as a
means to keep their family at a size they could maintain. Again, this did not necessarily
indicate indifference, and some may have intended to reclaim their babies when times
improved. Others gave up their infants through the nursing period, and reclaimed them
when they would no longer tie their mother to the home instead of work.[105] Another
group of parents may have hoped simply that their dying infants would get a better
Christian burial if they were abandoned, or may have wanted to escape the costs of
such a burial. A set of 'Regulations for managing the [London Foundling] hospital...' of
1796 note this motivation for abandonment during the period of open admissions:

> The scite of the Hospital was in many instances converted into a burying ground; and
> parental care, though perhaps it would not have deserted an healthy or hopeful child,
> carried, the diseased and expiring infant, in some instances almost stripped of its cloathing,
> to take the chance of a change of air and situation, and of the efforts of medical skill and
> care: and, failing those, to receive the certainty of a decent interment.[106]

There was thus probably considerable variation in the way that parents used and
regarded infant abandonment in this period. The question of whether they saw their
baby as an ensouled person is an interesting one to consider as a corollary of this
variation, and has implications for the way they may have regarded their actions. Some

---

[103] LMA, Petitions to admit children, A/FH/A8/1/1/3.

[104] See A. Levene, 'The Estimation of Mortality at the London Foundling Hospital, 1741–99', *Population Studies*,
59:1 (2005), 89–99, and references.

[105] This was sometimes formally sanctioned, see Kertzer, *Sacrificed for Honor*, pp. 79 and 83.

[106] 'Regulations for Managing the Hospital for the Maintenance and Education of Exposed and Deserted
Young Children' (1796), LMA, A/FH/A1/6/1, p. 28.

parents may have felt that their baby was not yet a proper person, and were thus able to dispose of it without remorse or regret. The number who left notes with their babies at the London hospital, however, suggests that in many cases, a bond had already been made. While some notes are brief and factual, others are grief-stricken, such as one 'to Remember my Garle for Ever'.[107] Others were accompanied by embroidered ribbons and tokens, which implies a degree of care and bonding, and many had been breast-fed before being given up. A large proportion of infants given up to the London Foundling Hospital had been baptised prior to abandonment (64 per cent), a process which was not necessary for entry, and which cost the parent(s) money. There may have been a degree of concern for the baby's soul if it died unbaptised, but this was not the imperative as it was under Catholic belief. Baptism may, therefore, be an indicator of care and bonding, although we should be cautious in placing too much weight on it. None the less, the evidence suggests that many parents at the London Foundling Hospital had bonded with their baby, and that they regarded him or her as a person with hopes for a future. One of the most commonly articulated wishes in notes left with babies was that they be cared for so that the parent(s) might be able to return to reclaim them. On the other hand, many other parents left no note and the quality of the bond they had made with their infant, if any, can only be speculated upon. Isabel dos Guimarães Sa concludes from the evidence of notes left with babies at the foundling hospital in Porto that a loving bond had rarely been made, and that parents instead saw abandonment as a customary right.[108] Parents' motives for using the growing and growing number of foundling hospitals in the long eighteenth century varied, and as these examples have shown, their use was heavily influenced by local conditions and circumstances.

. . . .

A key problem for many foundling hospitals was the provision of basic sustenance for the children. In eighteenth-century France, Olwen Hufton writes of the care for the *enfants trouvés* consisting of authorities pushing these infants 'into a draughty attic with others of their kind, and still[ing] their cries with a rag soaked in milk and water, fairly confident their days were numbered'.[109] Feeding these foundlings relied heavily on a system of wet nurses who were prepared to take in such children, a situation that was ripe for abuse. Many studies of both infanticide and abandonment look at the question of wet-nurses, a common resort of the poor as well as the rich in pre-modern Europe, and suggest a very strong link between wet nursing and infant death.[110] Keith Wrightson, writing about England coined the term 'infanticidal wet-nursing', to describe a situation where a child was put out to nurse with the clear intention that it would be neglected to such an extent it died. He discusses a case from seventeenth-century Lancashire, unusual in that it was actually brought to trial, although the outcome of the case is unknown. The father of an illegitimate child gave the child, six shillings and a coverlet to a woman and told her to return in two weeks with the child when he had found a better nurse. This woman, Isabel Smith, was described as a 'traveller who had no certen place of abode'. She called herself a poor woman who made her living as a nurse and who had borne three bastard children already although she admitted 'that shee never gave any sucke to any child in all her lyef'. Smith took in two other children at

[107] Note left with child 3734, abandoned 12 Mar. 1757, died 6 Apr. 1765. A/FH/A/9/1/46.
[108] I. dos Guimarães Sa, 'The Circulation of Children in Eighteenth-Century Southern Europe: The Case of the Foundling Hospital of Porto' European University Institute, Florence: PhD thesis, 1992, pp. 244–77.
[109] Hufton, *The Poor of Eighteenth-Century France*, p. 337.
[110] See Ch. 3, fns 71 and 130.

the same time, claimed to have fed them with a pennyworth of milk and butter but by the next day all were dead. Clearly the court suspected that the children had been deliberately neglected and it was dealing with a case of infanticide.[111]

In France, a century later, there were similar instances of poor parents sending their children out to women who either had no milk or were unlikely to feed the child. For a few *livres* a mother could send her child to what Hufton calls a 'baby farm' where there was almost no expectation of survival. 'For a mother it was a way of killing the child vicariously; for the women who ran the baby farm it was a sordid means of making a living in a harsh world'.[112] Admission into French foundling hospitals was not automatic – they demanded proof that both mother and father were destitute and required a donation before the child could be admitted (70–80 *livres* compared to the five to ten asked by baby farms). The question of whether women knew that wet-nurses and baby farm proprietoresses were simply 'professional murderesses' can be answered therefore by understanding the lack of any other choices for such mothers. 'A mother suffering from malnutrition often found it impossible to feed her child and when her milk dried up the infant was supplied with a rag dipped in water, neither of which was necessarily clean, and in any case the expedient would not keep it long alive... The baby was not allowed to assume priority. Why should it, or, more pertinently, how could it?'[113]

The foundling hospitals offered an alternative to over-stretched or incapable parents but this did not guarantee that children would be well looked after or would thrive in such institutions. Furthermore, as ideas about proper infant care and the value of children began to change from the turn of the nineteenth century, the utility of these institutions was called into question. The Victorian cult of the child may only have been a reality for the middle-class few but the idea of the innocent and vulnerable child, dear to God, and in need of protection became widespread, spawning a flurry of legislative and charitable efforts to help the children of the poor.[114] By the middle of the nineteenth century concern over the mortality rates in the foundling hospitals was so high that the head of Milan's hospital claimed that such institutions were 'killing children at public expense'. Phrases such as slaughterhouses, tombs and legal infanticide were used to describe these institutions, while wet nurses themselves were described as 'angel makers'.[115] By then it was widely understood that institutions were places where disease spread quickly and were usually fatal to babies. Increasingly the bond between mother and child was emphasised and one of the criticisms levelled at the London Foundling Hospital by the 1860s was that it broke this bond.[116] Although the problem of unwanted babies had not gone away, wider social attitudes towards the 'innocent' infant were changing all over Europe.[117] In Britain, fears about infanticidal wet-nursing were the subject of an 1841 Parliamentary enquiry and baby farms came to be perceived as a serious social problem. By the end of the nineteenth century European foundling homes were in decline and other ways of dealing with unwanted children came to the fore.

---

[111] Wrightson, 'Infanticide in Earlier Seventeenth-Century England', pp.16–17.

[112] Hufton, *The Poor of Eighteenth-Century France*, p. 326.

[113] *Ibid.*, pp. 327, 331.

[114] H. Cunningham, *The Children of the Poor: Representations of Childhood since the Seventeenth Century* (Oxford: Blackwell, 1991); H. Hendrick, *Children, Childhood and English Society 1880–1990* (Cambridge: Cambridge University Press, 1997); H. Hendrick, *Child Welfare: England 1872–1989* (London: Routledge, 1994).

[115] D. Kertzer and M. White, 'Cheating the Angel-Makers: Surviving Infant Abandonment in Nineteenth-Century Italy', *Continuity and Change*, 9:3 (1994), 450–80, at p. 452.

[116] www.foundlingmuseum.org.uk (accessed 15 May 2009).

[117] For developments in France where 30,000–50,000 infants were abandoned each year in the nineteenth century see R. Fuchs, *Abandoned Children: Foundlings and Child Welfare in Nineteenth-Century France* (Albany: State University of New York Press, 1984). For Germany, see E. R. Dickinson, *The Politics of German Child Welfare from the Empire to the Federal Republic* (Cambridge: Harvard University Press, 1996).

As has been clear throughout this chapter, one of the root causes of abandonment has been poverty, and institutionalisation is likely to have been the recourse of the poor and of those for whom an extra child placed an enormous strain on their families. Until the mid-nineteenth century, wages were low, poor relief patchy and inefficient and unwanted children an intolerable burden. Although there are debates about when standards of living began to rise, by the 1860s in England there had been visible improvement, as measured by indicators such as health, life expectancy and the amount of leisure time.[118] Coupled with the new ideas about childhood and the responsibilities that adults had to children, this encouraged an unprecedented sense of the possible which was reflected both in terms of state policy and philanthropic provision.[119] Dr. Barnardo (1845–1905) and his homes for orphaned and indigent children may well be the most famous example of this trend, but other charitable agencies and private donors were also setting up homes to care for older children who had been forced from the family hearth by poverty or who had run away.[120] Some institutions specialised in particular groups of children. London, for instance, had orphanages for the children of sailors (The Sailors' Orphan Girls' School and Home at Hampstead) and for the children of servicemen killed in the Crimean War (The Royal Victoria Patriotic Asylum). Children were increasingly seen as a general social responsibility rather than a personal or parental one, although self-interest also played a part and the response to orphan children, while sometimes motivated by disinterested concern and pity, was also mixed with social fears about delinquency and the creation of an underclass. In 1870 journalist Thomas Archer wrote,

> I am every day more strongly convinced that our only hope of dealing effectually with the difficulties that daunt, and the dangers that threaten, us on the side [of] want, ignorance, and crime, must be founded on a liberal and intelligent recognition that we are to accept the orphans of society as our own, and hold ourselves responsible for their being trained to a life of usefulness and honour.[121]

---

[118] Nardinelli argues that while there are debates about when standards of living started to rise, there is good evidence to show that real wages grew slowly between 1781 and 1819 but that after 1819 they grew rapidly for all workers and doubled between 1819 and 1851. C. Nardinelli, 'Industrial Revolution and the Standard of Living', in D. R. Henderson (ed.), *The Concise Encyclopaedia of Economics*. Available online at http://www.econlib.org/library/Enc/IndustrialRevolutionandtheStandardofLiving.html (accessed 6 Aug. 2009). Others insisted there was little gain before the middle decades of the nineteenth century: see below Ch. 3, fn. 142.

[119] State provision for children had become a concern by the 1880s when the relationship between families and state was changing and the various responsibilities of each were undergoing a reformation. In the UK debates over school meals and who should provide food for poor children became highly emotive so that by the turn of the twentieth century some commentators were arguing that a central role of parenthood was the provision of food and that the state should not take the place of parents. In contrast others claimed that if parents could not provide, the state should. Similar issues were raised about medical care, see Cunningham, *The Children of the Poor*, pp. 201–17. Alongside this there was much greater state involvement in family life, shown for instance by the 1889 Prevention of Cruelty to, and Protection of, Children Act which allowed the state to step in to prosecute parents who were abusing their children or the 1899 Poor Law Act which allowed for the removal of a child from parents who were deemed mentally or morally incapable of looking after that child. M. Flegel, *Conceptualizing Cruelty to Children in Nineteenth-Century England. Literature, Representation and the NSPCC* (Farnham: Ashgate, 2009). In 1908 various different laws relating to child welfare, provision for children and juvenile justice were brought together under the 1908 Children Act, which allowed (among other things) for the prosecution of parents for neglect as well as abuse. It allowed the state to take on 'a general supervisory role involving the right to police the quality and behaviour of parents'. J. Stewart, 'Children, Parents and the State: The Children Act, 1908', *Children and Society*, 9:1 (1995), 90–99, at p. 96.

[120] L. Murdoch, *Imagined Orphans: Poor Families, Child Welfare, and Contested Citizenship in London* (New Brunswick.: Rutgers University Press, 2006).

[121] T. Archer, *The Terrible Sights of London and Labours of Love in the Midst of Them* (London: Stanley Rivers and Co, 1870), p. 1.

Archer reckoned there were over sixty institutions in London alone set up to care for orphan children (although he classifies orphans and destitute children together so it is hard to know how many children had actually lost parents). Unlike the abandoned infants of the London Foundling Hospital, these new institutions catered for older children and were designed to train children for a useful future. They were based on a belief that not only were children saveable but that adult philanthropists should step in to provide this redemption when parents could not.

For infants, and there were still plenty whose parents could not or did not want to care for them, other options were sought. Homes for abandoned or orphaned infants were set up, such as the Infant Orphan Asylum at Dalston in east London or the Infant Orphan Asylum, Wanstead, both of which looked after boys and girls between the ages of three months and seven years. However, it was well known that large institutions were disastrous for very young children and that children did much better in smaller settings which most closely resembled families. The child savers of the late Victorian era, backed by their belief in the innate goodness and potential for salvation in the innocent child, campaigned not only for children to be protected within the home but to be removed if parents could not fulfil their duty. They further recommended that such children be placed in family-like situations and fostered wherever possible. If this was not possible they demanded that institutions should become 'cottage-style': *i.e.* smaller, more intimate and with a mother and father figure running them.[122] Archer's saccharine description of the Alexandra Orphanage in Holloway suggests something of this ideal, although probably nothing of the reality. He describes the orphanage as being situated in:

> A quiet house and a quiet neighbourhood – a house, though, with a large allowance of bedrooms, each of which has quite a row of little iron cribs, some of them looking almost like dolls' bedsteads, covered with their clean white counterpanes....

> Forty-five little ones, whose angels do continually stand before the Father, are now standing before you: the eldest not quite eight, the youngest a little tot of perhaps two years old. Fifty future men and women, taken from who knows what of misery, want, and shame, to be sent upon a new and hopeful career, blessing, let us hope, and to be blessed.

> The Alexandra Orphanage for Infants. These little creatures have a sweet godmother. Her tender royal face is up there on the wall; and now that she has children of her own, she may well think sometimes of these. For these are children, and there is great comfort in that: I mean, they are not poor little depressed men and women, under the rigid rule which will dwarf a child's soul and crush its heart. See, some of them have got hold of your hand already; and those behind (such little chaps, that you hardly know girls from boys) are eager to clasp each a finger, and cry out 'Me! me!' to secure their share of petting.[123]

Of course this ideal did not always protect children and, despite the good intentions, this form of care was open to serious abuses. However, it represented a change in emphasis and by the early twentieth century there had been a noticeable shift from providing family-like care to children to supporting the creation of families into which children could be adopted. Not only did this provide homes for 'unwanted' children but it also gave couples who could not have children of their own the chance to raise families. In Britain throughout the nineteenth century, the middle-classes occasionally took in unwanted children who had crossed their path by chance – fictionalised, for example, in the adoption of Heathcliff in *Wuthering Heights* (1848) – and many orphaned paupers must have found shelter among their penurious neighbours.

---

[122] L. Curran, 'Foster Care', in P. Fass (ed.), *Encyclopedia of Children and Childhood. In History and Society* (3 vols; Indianapolis: Macmillan USA, 2004), ii, pp. 363–65.

[123] Archer, *The Terrible Sights of London*, pp. 111–12.

By the end of the century, on the other hand, as Claudia Nelson has recently emphasised, it was becoming a commonplace for people wanting to adopt children to seek them out actively by placing advertisements in national journals and newspapers. Some appear to have wanted a pet, such as 'a lady of position' in Staffordshire who wanted to adopt an 'attractive three year old'. For other parents adoption had a more utilitarian aspect and bringing in adopted children into the household was a means of fulfilling their need for domestic help. One family, for example, requested 'an orphan girl to be one of the family for general domestic work'. Nelson concludes that 'In an era of high infant mortality and unreliable baby food, would-be parents whose desire for an adopted child was rooted in emotion often specified that they wanted a toddler, as children of two or three were considered young enough to bond readily with their new family but old enough to be past the stage of greatest danger.' Older children were more likely to be 'adopted' as servants'.[124]

In the late Victorian era, however, this form of adoption was still unofficial. In many cases it was little different from the age-old custom of populating England's, then Britain's, colonies with indentured servants, a custom that continued to be vigorously pursued at the turn of the twentieth century. Between 1864 and 1924, 80,000 children of thirteen or under were sent by Poor Law guardians and the home missionary societies, especially Barnardo's, to help work Canadian farms. The aim was to give pauper children a new start in a rural family setting, but the reality was sometimes harsh and the children exploited.[125] But this was fostering out rather than adoption, as we would understand it. As the next contribution will discuss, it was only in the early twentieth century that adoption as something more than taking in a waif and stray, often for personal profit, was strenuously promoted and formally legalised.

Unwanted Children and Adoption in England

Heather Montgomery

To write about adoption in a series of pieces about infanticide, abortion and other forms of violence, seems at first rather odd. While the others can certainly be seen as forms of violence against children, adoption would appear to be the opposite.[126] Adoption is about wanting children, about bringing them into families and about mitigating potential violence against them rather than perpetrating it.[127] Yet adoption is also a

---

[124] C. Nelson, *Family Ties in Victorian England* (Westport.: Praeger Publishers, 2007), pp. 160–61.

[125] J. Parr, *Labouring Children. British Immigrant Apprentices to Canada 1864–1924* (London: Croom Helm, 1980). The same purpose lay behind the work of Charles Long Bruce who sent 86,000 New York children to farms in the American mid-west between 1854 and 1891: see M. Z. Langsam, *Children West: A History of the Placing Out System of the New York Children's Society 1852–90* (Madison: State Historical Society of Wisconsin, 1964). As early as 1619 the London Common Council sent out 100 vagrant children to the settlement of Jamestown, Virginia: see H. Cunningham, *Invention of Childhood* (London: BBC Books, 2006), p. 199.

[126] Goody defines the three purposes of adoption in western Europe as, firstly 'to provide homes for orphans, bastards, foundlings and the children of impaired families', secondly, 'to provide childless couples with social progeny' and finally 'to provide an individual or couple with an heir to their property'. J. Goody, 'Adoption in Cross-Cultural Perspective', *Comparative Studies in Society and History*, 11:1 (1969), 55–78, at p. 56.

[127] The specific case of England is under discussion here. In other contexts, there are certainly instances when adoption can be seen as a direct form of violence against children. Notorious cases include Australia's 'Stolen Generation' – the thousands of Aboriginal children who were removed from their parents by the Australian state, through coercion and trickery, between the 1940s and the 1970s. Commonwealth of Australia,

way of caring for the unwanted and can be seen therefore as a bridge between the abandonment of children in the eighteenth and nineteenth centuries and the rise of abortion at the end of the twentieth. A brief history of adoption places it in a period in which ideas about childhood, the nature of relationships between parents and children, and also between people, the church and state changed radically and in which the competing demands of the parent/child relationship were foregrounded.[128]

There is, of course, a long history of children being brought up outside their natal families or by people they might regard as strangers. From informal guardianships within the extended family, to the foundling hospitals of medieval Europe, to the work-houses and orphanages of Victorian England, children who could not be cared for by their families have been taken in by others, looked after and brought up in institutions other than the nuclear family. Some of these situations were benevolent and loving, replicating a family's care, others harsher and deliberately punitive, or simply incapable of providing adequate care to children. What distinguishes these forms of care from adoption, however, is that there was no attempt to replace family ties and there was no change of legal identity. Until the beginning of the twentieth century, the Anglican Church and its Roman predecessor had forbidden adoption for almost 1,500 years, acknowledging kinship only on the grounds of shared blood (consanguinity) and marriage.[129] The established church maintained this position and even if the parents were dead, their child was still legally and socially theirs and there was no confusion about their parentage, even if they were brought up from infancy in another family. Understandings of kinship were predicated on this notion of shared blood and legal adoption was impossible as it would challenge such a position by recognising that social ties could be of equal importance. Guardianship or wardship might have come with legally enforceable responsibilities, and might involve life long bonds of affection and care, but it was quite distinct from adoption.[130] If the biological parents were still alive, their rights remained absolute and they could, at any time, reclaim their children.[131] Formal adoption which transferred all legal, social and moral ties to the adopted parents and severed all connections with the birth parents was therefore impossible.[132] This is

---

The Report of the National Inquiry into the Separation of Aboriginal and Torres Strait Islander Children from their Families (Sydney: Human Rights and Equal Opportunity Commission, 1997).

[128] See fns 114 and 119 above.

[129] J. Goody, *The Development of the Family and Marriage in Europe* (Cambridge: Cambridge University Press, 1983), p. 101.

[130] Furthermore, the proceedings that enabled formal wardship and guardianship were extremely expensive and available only to the rich under English law.

[131] On the other hand, under Roman law, if a person was adopted as an adult, they renounced entirely their natal family and in some circumstances the worship of their natal family gods. J. A. Crook, *Law and Life of Rome* (London: Thames and Hudson, 1967).

[132] Cretney describes the situation at the beginning of the twentieth century as follows: 'the term "adoption" in relation to children was used in three different senses. First, it was used to describe the situation in which a child was taken into the home of a person other than the child's parent, and brought up to a greater or lesser extent as the child of the adopter. Examples of this practice are to be found in fictional classics, and there seems no reason to doubt that this kind of "adoption" had been and remained a familiar social institution in all classes of society. Secondly, there was the situation in which "adoption" was simulated: an unmarried pregnant women would arrange for her child to be delivered in a private lying-in house, the owner of which would be paid a lump sum in exchange for arranging the child's "adoption". The child would then be removed to "the worst class of baby-farming house" where it would usually be neglected and die. Thirdly, there was the so-called Poor Law Adoption in which the Poor Law Guardians assumed by resolution all the child's parents' rights and powers in respect of the child's upbringing; and would arrange for the child to be adopted'. S. Cretney, *Family Law in the Twentieth Century. A History* (Oxford: Oxford University Press, 2003), p. 596.

not to claim that children were not unofficially adopted, or did not take their adopters' name, or even inherit from them.[133] Legally, however, formal adoption which involves 'the transfer of an individual from one filial relationship to another, from a "natural" relationship to a "fictional" one, but one which is in most respects legally equivalent' was not permitted.[134]

Debates about allowing formal adoption took place in the context of profound changes about the nature of family relationships and about who controlled them. For many years, most family law was settled in ecclesiastical courts which operated outside the civil and criminal legal system. Marriage rules, both in terms of who could marry and who could not, and how marriages could be dissolved, were in the hands of the church. It was not until the nineteenth century that family law began to be seen as a civil rather than a religious matter and it was only from 1857 that matters relating to marriage and divorce were dealt with by civil rather than religious law.[135] As the family became increasingly seen as a secular institution issues such as adoption became less a matter for spiritual concern, and more about the practicalities of dealing with unwanted or abused children and solving the problem by creating families for childless couples.[136] (See Figure 12).

By the late nineteenth century it was increasingly understood that children might be in danger at home and that biological ties did not necessarily protect them from abuse, neglect and abandonment. This notion was made explicit by the formation of societies such as the National Society for the Prevention of Cruelty to Children (NSPCC). In 1881, Lord Shaftesbury (1801–85) was asked by a Liverpool clergyman to introduce a bill into Parliament to prevent parental cruelty towards their children. At first, he refused arguing that the matter was 'so private, internal and domestic a character as to be beyond the reach of legislation' but he later supported the bill, which came into force in 1889 as the Prevention of Cruelty to, and Protection of, Children Act.[137] It made the ill-treatment and neglect of children illegal and created a new offence of causing suffering to children. It also enabled police and magistrates to remove children from their parents if cruelty was suspected. Within five years, 5,400 parents had been convicted of cruelty to children in England.

The concern over unwanted children was further fuelled by the unease over the practice of baby farming, which achieved particular notoriety at the end of the nineteenth century. Baby farming involved a parent, usually an unmarried mother, paying a lump sum to a baby farmer who would take the child off her hands in order to enable the mother to go back to work. It was often done with the implicit assumption that the baby would be disposed of, either through placing the child in another family, or that it would die through neglect or, occasionally, murder. In 1871, eleven infants were found in a state of total neglect in a house in Brixton, five of whom subsequently died. The case, reported extremely sensationally, caused particular outrage; one of the women involved was hanged and, in consequence, the Protection of Infant Life Act

---

[133] Adopted children are a common motif in the nineteenth-century novel, for example, in Charles Dickens's *Bleak House* and *Oliver Twist,* George Eliot's *Silas Marner* and Jane Austen's *Sense and Sensibility.*

[134] Goody, 'Adoption in Cross-Cultural Perspective', p. 58.

[135] S. Wolfram, *In-Laws and Outlaws. Kinship and Marriage in England* (London: Croom Helm, 1987).

[136] The first modern adoption act was the Massachusetts Adoption of Children Act, passed in 1851. According to The Adoption History Project: 'Observers have frequently attributed the acceptance of adoption in the United States to its compatibility with cherished national traditions, from immigration to democracy. According to this way of thinking, solidarities achieved on purpose are more powerful – and more quintessentially American – than solidarities ascribed to blood'. Available online at http://darkwing. uoregon.edu/~adoption/ (accessed 2 Jun. 2009).

[137] Hendrick, *Children, Childhood and English Society,* p. 45.

was passed in 1872. Alongside this, new regulations were brought in compelling all those who looked after children for money to register with the local council and to limit the number of children they fostered. Even so, cases of baby farming continued to be reported up to 1919, when nine foster children were found starving in Walton-on-Thames, two of whom later died.[138]

The issue of adoption was raised again after the end of the First World War with the emergence of private adoption agencies, such as the National Children's Adoption Association, which sought to find new families for children left fatherless because of the war. The work expanded and in 1919 the Association set up a house in which babies waiting to be adopted would temporarily live. Between April 1919 and October 1920, 448 adoptions were completed, 2,310 children were passed as suitable for adoption (588 being rejected) and 1,653 adopters were approved. Although the numbers of children being adopted was increasing, adoption still had no formal status and two parliamentary commissions were set up to look at changing the law, under pressure from the adoption agencies for the adoptions they had already organised to be legalised. The first was set up in 1920 and the second four years later, purportedly to look at the issue of baby farming, although by this time the issue, while still emotive, was of less pressing concern. Of greater worry was the knowledge that illegitimacy rates had risen sharply during the war. Although much of the discussion about adoption focused on war orphans and foundlings, 75 per cent of children given up for unofficial adoption just after the war were illegitimate.[139] Yet despite this problem of illegitimacy there was limited enthusiasm for pressurising unmarried mothers into giving up their babies and many felt that women should be encouraged to keep their children. Although there were many different adoption societies, with different aims and agendas, groups as diverse as the National Council for the Unmarried Mother and her Child, the Jewish Association for the Protection of Girls and Women and the Salvation Army, all argued that, whenever possible, adoption should be a last resort, and that it was usually best to keep mother and child together. Other organisations, such as the NSPCC and Barnardo's, supported adoption only reluctantly, being very aware of the number of cases of child cruelty that occurred in foster families.

In 1926, formal, legalised adoption was allowed for the first time in England and, in 1949, the Adoption of Children Act accepted in law that an adopted child would have the same status as a child born into the family and that adoption would stand alongside blood as a marker of kinship.[140] Such a move was controversial for many reasons. It allowed parents to bring up children that were not born to them and were not biologically related to them and regarded these families, in law, in exactly the same way as ones in which parentage was based on blood. All rights and responsibilities between birth mother and child were broken and once the adoption was complete, it was final, with no changes of mind allowed. Furthermore, in order to preserve the unity of the adoptive family all contact between natural parents and the children they offered for adoption was strictly forbidden. In the vast majority of cases, names were changed and neither adoptive parent nor child was given information about the birth parents. The new family was protected from any claims by the biological parents. Such a system existed for the next 50 years, with unmarried women put under increasing pressure to give up their children, in the best interests of the child, as well as themselves. Many were told to forget they had given birth and to get on with their lives as if nothing had

---

[138] J. Keating, 'Struggle for Identity: Issues Underlying the Enactment of the 1926 Adoption of Children Act', *University of Sussex Journal of Contemporary History*, 3 (2001), 1–9.

[139] *Ibid.*, p. 3. Keating claims that 6.3 per cent of live births in 1918 were illegitimate and that the mortality rate of these children during their first year of life was more than double that of legitimate births.

[140] Cretney, *Family Law in the Twentieth Century*, ch. 17.

happened. Adoption was linked to social mobility, of giving the child a better chance and allowing it to be adopted into a materially or socially superior situation.

The late 1960s and early 1970s saw further shifts in thinking about adoption in the UK.[141] By this point, fewer adoptions were taking place, as a consequence of the availability of contraception, the introduction of legal abortion in 1967 and a greater tolerance of, and support for, single mothers raising their own children. As adoptive children grew up, many began to demand information about the circumstances surrounding their birth and adoption.[142] They felt that the lack of information about their biological origins meant that something very fundamental was missing from their sense of identity.[143] Recognising these people's need to know their social and biological origins, and thus re-stating the primary emphasis that English kinship had always placed on blood ties, a new Adoption Act was introduced in 1976 which allowed children to trace their biological parents.[144] The right to trace a parent was a retrospective one, so that any child adopted since 1926 could find their birth parents. Women who gave up their children for adoption over this 50-year period had been told that their records would remain sealed and that the child they had given birth to would never have any contact with them. Suddenly these women could be traced by their children although they were given no equivalent right to search for the children they had given up.[145]

Adoptions in the UK are now relatively rare, and tend to involve older children, groups of siblings or hard-to-place children. Very few children are adopted as infants and they tend to be closely matched with parents of similar ethnicity, circumstances and social background. Today keeping biological families together is seen as the best way of caring for children and the British state generally attempts to support and help parents (and mothers in particular) keep and care for their own children. The importance of the mother/child bond and the influence of theories of attachment pioneered by John Bowlby (1907–90) have become extremely influential, making adoption an increasingly unpopular choice in terms of child welfare.[146] Furthermore there is a deep-seated belief that biology and identity are closely intertwined and that carers should ideally share biological or genetic relatedness to the children they raise. It is only in rare circumstances that children, especially young children, are now given up for adoption rather than for short-term fostering in other families. Social networks and support mechanisms mean that young or unmarried women very rarely feel the need to have a child adopted, and the relative ease of abortion in the UK, further reduces the numbers of children given up. In the US, in contrast, stricter abortion laws mean a greater number of children are put up for adoption.[147]

---

[141] The numbers of children adopted in England and Wales peaked in 1968 when 24,831 children were adopted (compared to 14,109 in 1959). The majority of these children were under one. F. Bowie (ed.), *Cross-Cultural Approaches to Adoption* (London: Routledge, 2004), ch. 1. In 2007–2008, 120 children under one were adopted; British Association for Adoption and Fostering (www.baaf.co.uk).

[142] J. Triseliotis, *In Search of Origins. The Experiences of Adopted People* (London: Routledge, 1973).

[143] Similar issues have also been raised about children born as the result of sperm donation, and since 2005 these children have the right to find out information about their genetic parents.

[144] Such a view remains contested. In the US, for example, where many more adoptions take place than in Britain, some states still seal adoption records for 99 years, believing that preserving the integrity of the social family overrides a person's right to know their biological parentage. Others allow limited medical information but deny adopted children contact details; others allow open adoption when the child is free to contact his or her biological parents.

[145] In the UK, the 2002 Adoption and Children Act gave parents new rights to seek information about the children they previously gave up for adoption.

[146] J. Bowlby, *Child Care and the Growth of Love* (Harmondsworth: Penguin, 1953).

[147] J. Modell, *Kinship With Strangers: Adoption and Interpretations of Kinship in American Culture* (Berkeley: University of California Press, 1994); J. Berebitsky, *Like Our Very Own: Adoption and the Changing Culture of*

The needs of the child in Britain today are seen as paramount and adoption is rarely seen as a way of completing families. Yet the issue of adoption remains a difficult one because it touches directly on the issue of who are 'real' parents. It is also controversial because the state intervenes so directly in family life and adoptive parents are subject to a scrutiny and bureaucracy that natural parents are not. Biological parents are assumed to be able to look after their children and only when things go disastrously wrong does the state intervene. Potential adoptive parents have to prove to the state that they are suitable and the process is long and gruelling. Furthermore, it is difficult in that it has left children adopted in the past unsure of their origins and many claiming now that adoption is a form of psychic violence against them, stripping them of their identity and causing life-long damage.[148] Adoption has a complex and chequered history in England; it has been seen as a way of dealing with the problem of unwanted, illegitimate, or socially awkward children but also as a means of social mobility and offering children born in difficult circumstances a different chance in life.

· ·

For all its shortcomings, adoption proved a popular and humane solution to the problem of unwanted children in Britain and other European countries for 50 years. It never completely replaced institutionalisation, however, and in the United Kingdom homes run by voluntary children's societies and local government still exist in the early twenty-first century. There are still orphans left with no family, and if few children are literally abandoned anymore, there remain a large number whom the state takes into care on the grounds that they have been abandoned in all but name by inadequate and abusive parents.[149] Even so, two-thirds of the children in local authority care are in foster homes rather than institutions; proof that it is considered better for children to live with a non-biological family than with no family at all, especially given the evidence of systematic sexual and physical abuse uncovered in a number of institutions in the 1980s and 1990s.[150]

There is, and always has been, however, one particular group of children who are especially vulnerable to infanticide and institutionalisation and for whom adoption has rarely been possible – those classified as mentally or physically defective. Not only do these children require intensive long-term care that many parents simply cannot afford in terms of money or time but they also challenge symbolic categories of what it means to be human.[151] Although there is very limited evidence as to such children's fate historically, it is likely that they would have been left to die, or been killed, soon after birth. The fate of sickly and physically defective newborns has always been precarious and it must be assumed that those with obvious mental defects, especially those with concurrent physical discrepancies associated with syndromes such as Down's, would have been equally vulnerable.[152] Even today, these children are more likely to be given up for adoption, or aborted, than almost

---

Motherhood, 1851–1950 (Lawrence: University Press of Kansas, 2000); E. W. Carp, *Adoption in America: Historical Perspectives* (Ann Arbor: University of Michigan Press, 2002).

[148] Triseliotis, *In Search of Origins*.

[149] Approximately 8,000 children leave care homes every year, usually with very limited prospects: see H. Montgomery, 'Moving', in M.-J. Kehily (ed.), *Youth: Perspectives, Identities and Practices* (London: Sage, 2006).

[150] The data coming out of studies of children abandoned in the Romanian orphanages of the 1980s suggests quite how devastating such treatment can be to the very young: see M. Rutter and the English and Romanian Adoptees (ERA) Study Team, 'Developmental Catch-up, and Deficit, Following Adoption after Severe Global Early Privation', *Journal of Child Psychology and Psychiatry*, 39:4 (1998), 465–76.

[151] See fn. 36, above.

[152] Down's Syndrome is the historical term – today the preferred term is Down Syndrome.

any other.[153] Yet while such babies are easy to identify at birth or very soon afterwards, in other cases, cognitive impairments do not become apparent for many years, long after the child has been socially recognised as a person. As this chapter has emphasised, the neonatal child exists as a special category for whom 'personhood is imminent but not assured'[154] and infanticide is usually classified very differently to murder. Once a child is older however, no matter how 'defective' they may be, killing them is impossible, and before the twentieth century has rarely been justified or condoned. Those children, which we now term as having mental deficiencies, may well have been institutionalised and left to exist in places which actively or passively shortened their lives, but their murder was unthinkable.

Some reformers from the late eighteenth century set about finding ways to help these children once born, either through institutions or pushing for state help for their parents.[155] By the mid-Victorian era, however, others viewed the problem as being less about what to do with such children once born but how to prevent them from being born in the first place. Not only were the lives of these children individually worthless but they represented a stain on society, which could not improve and go forward with the 'wrong' type of children being born. Although the wrong sort of children could mean anything from those born illegitimately, to those born to the very poor or the Irish, the view that it was possible to categorise people scientifically and then make judgements on their relative worth, began to be formulated, encouraged by new ideas of human evolution.

Social Darwinism, as the name suggests, drew upon *On the Origins of Species* and *The Descent of Man* by Charles Darwin (1809–92).[156] Social Darwinists, such as Darwin's cousin, Francis Galton (1822–1911), took the theory of evolution through natural selection and attempted to apply it to the social world, seeing evolutionary mechanisms as the route to social progress. Galton inspired the 'human eugenics' movement, whose aim was to improve the 'human stock' through controlled breeding. Breeding better people and removing the 'weaker' elements of society could, Galton argued, accelerate social progress. Eugenic marriages could 'do providentially, quickly and kindly' what nature did 'blindly, slowly and ruthlessly'.[157]

In *Hereditary Genius* (1869) Galton set out his argument that 'eminent men are naturally superior and ... superior men are naturally eminent'.[158] Society's social hierarchy therefore reflected inborn differences in ability and worth, and consequently social welfare, for the weaker elements of society, was both detrimental to society and against the laws of nature. Galton established an anthropometric laboratory to measure fitness and which allowed the categorisation and measurement of human abilities. Such measurement later became a key part of eugenic thought and practice during the period 1901–1930 when Galton's ideas gained significant popularity.

While institutionalisation was seen as increasingly problematic for 'normal' young children in the twentieth century, thanks, in part to the influence of the eugenicists, thousands of so-called defective children were taken away from, or given up by, their

---

[153] It is estimated that in France in the 1990s, ten per cent of all babies available for adoption had Down's Syndrome and that 73 per cent of the population favoured the abortion of such babies. A.-C. Dumaret and D. Rosset, 'Relinquishment for Adoption of Babies with Down's Syndrome: Announcement of the Diagnosis to Parents and Institutional Practices of Maternity Staff, *Adoption and Fostering*, 25:2 (2001), 49–55.

[154] B. Conklin and L. Morgan, 'Babies, Bodies, and the Production of Personhood in North America and a Native Amazonian Society', *Ethos*, 24:4 (1996) 657–84, at pp. 657–58.

[155] For the first attempts in France to improve the lives of deaf, dumb and blind children in the second half of the eighteenth century, see D. Weiner, *The Citizen-Patient in Revolutionary and Imperial Paris* (Baltimore: Johns Hopkins University Press, 1993), ch. 8.

[156] C. Darwin, *On the Origins of Species* (London: John Murray, 1859); C. Darwin, *The Descent of Man* (London: John Murray, 1871).

[157] F. Galton, cited in D. Kevles, *In the Name of Eugenics* (New York: Knopf, 1985), p. 12.

[158] G. Miller, *Psychology: The Science of Mental Life* (Harmondsworth: Penguin, 1962), p. 155.

families and placed in institutions. Women deemed likely to produce such offspring were also incarcerated and in parts of the USA and Europe men, woman and children underwent involuntary sterilisation. Accompanying these events were implicit practices of withholding life-saving care from stigmatised newborn children or, as occurred in Europe during the Nazi regime, their explicit extermination. The next contribution looks at the ideas and practices of the eugenics movements in Britain and traces their continued influence on the care and treatment of children to this day.

Stigmatising and Removing Defective Children from Society: The Influence of Eugenic Thinking

Kieron Sheehy

At the start of the twentieth century, the terms feeble-mindedness, imbecile and idiots were in common usage regarding mentally defective children. In the late 1920s these categories were defined more precisely in terms of mental ratios (the ratio between chronological age and mental age) gained through tests scores – based partly on the anthropometric measurements set out by Francis Galton. Idiots were the lowest ranking group, then imbeciles and then the feeble-minded. It is against this background of measurement and stigmatisation that policies and practices for children, who today might be described as having learning difficulties, began to be developed.

In 1908, a national Eugenics Education Society was founded in Britain with branches in Birmingham, Cambridge, Manchester, Southampton, Liverpool and Glasgow. In America 'fitter families' competitions compared medical and psychiatric tests scores and prizes were awarded to the winning families.[159] Inevitably, the development of this ideology of genetic fitness also led to the stigmatisation of children and families who were deemed to be 'unfit' and the problem of what to do with these families became central to the eugenics movement. Galton had promoted involuntary sterilisation as an efficient means to reduce the burden of this group on society and this became keenly advocated by the British eugenics movement. The Eugenics Society and the National Association for the Care of the Feeble-Minded mounted a 'vociferous, nationwide campaign for legislation that would enact a framework for the ascertainment, certification and detainment of mental defectives'.[160] By sterilising the potential parents society might rid itself of defective infants.[161]

The Royal Commission on the Feeble-Minded of 1908 concluded that feeble-mindedness was primarily inherited and linked to degeneracy, criminality and promiscuity. The contribution of Sir James Crichton-Browne (1840–1938) to the Commission described the feeble-minded as 'our social rubbish [who] should be swept up and garnered and utilized as far as possible' – and prevented from reproducing.[162] However, the prevention of the birth of defective children was problematic. Feeble-minded adults were not always easy to identify. They were 'most dangerous' because

---

[159] Kevles, *In the Name of Eugenics*, pp. 61–62.

[160] D. Atkinson, *An Autobiographical Approach to Learning Disability Research* (Aldershot: Ashgate, 1997), p. 98.

[161] S. P. Davies, *Social Control of the Mentally Deficient* (New York: Thomas Y. Crowell Company, 1930), p. 104.

[162] T. Cole, *Apart or A Part? Integration and the Growth of British Special Education* (Milton Keynes: Open University Press, 1989), p. 44.

they 'lurked within the general population, posing as normal'.[163] But, unlike many other countries, the 1908 Commission did not see the compulsory sterilisation of feeble-minded defectives as a solution.[164] Rather, they saw residential institutions as an appropriate response for children whose families were genetically flawed, and economically and morally unfit. A strong drive to remove such children from society can be seen in the media of this period. Reporting on an unhygienic and overcrowded infants' school, the *British Medical Journal* noted: 'There is thus a double evil, the insanitary condition of these schools and the retention in them of mentally defective children'.[165] The stigmatising term 'evil' for defective infants and children mixing with their peers was part of an established popular discourse. *The News of the World* claimed that 'One very important thing is that the idiot child should not be allowed to play about or mix with other children who are healthy ... Confinement to an asylum is the most humane and kind treatment for idiots, beyond a doubt'. Not only was the idiot child 'unhealthy' but the cause of this disease was clearly indicated in 'the existence of some evil taint' in the parents of 'idiots and imbeciles and the feebleminded'.[166]

The 1913 Mental Deficiency Act charged local education authorities with the responsibility to identify and certify those children (aged seven to sixteen years) who were idiots, imbeciles, feeble-minded or 'moral defectives'. Each region of the country had a Mental Deficiency Committee and an Executive Officer who ran the process of certification and incarceration in colonies for Mental Defectives. The conditions were punitive and the standard of institutional care was poor both in Britain and the United States.[167] For example Elwyn school in Pennsylvania was noted for its high standards but nevertheless over two thirds of the children placed there died before they reached 20 years of age.[168]

The eugenic attitudes of the time were captured, and promoted, in the film *The Black Stork* (1916). (See Figure 13). It is based on a real case and features a Chicago surgeon, played by the surgeon himself, Harry Haiselden (1870–1919), and reflects his actual beliefs and practices. He advises a couple that, for eugenic reasons, they should not marry, but they do and consequently produce a defective infant. The mother then has a vision of the child's inevitable future: a criminal fathering yet more defectives. Horrified, she accepts the physician's advice and allows her baby to die. Propaganda such as this helped eugenics to become a worldwide way of thinking about the worth, treatment and removal of children and adults with learning difficulties. Many eugenicists even flirted with the idea of the 'lethal chamber' for ridding society of its unwanted.[169]

The drive to prevent the birth of defective children helped to make women's sexual

---

[163] Atkinson, *An Autobiographical Approach*, p. 99.

[164] In 1907, some states in the USA, for instance, introduced legislation that required or allowed involuntary sterilisation of defectives to remove the 'cancer of society'. P. R. Reilly, *The Surgical Solution: A History of Involuntary Sterilization in the United States* (Baltimore: Johns Hopkins University Press, 1991), p. 48. Between 1927 and 1957 approximately 60,000 Americans labelled either feeble-minded or insane underwent sterilisation at state institutions in the name of eugenics. 60 per cent of these were women and the majority were poor and white. A. Stubblefield, 'Beyond the Pale: Tainted Whiteness, Cognitive Disability, and Eugenic Sterilization', *Hypatia*, 22:2 (2007), 162–81.

[165] Anon., 'Insanity and Mental Defectiveness in Belfast', *The British Medical Journal*, 2:2487 (1908), p. 621.

[166] *News of the World*, 23 Sept. 1900, p. 9.

[167] S. Humphries and P. Gordon, *Out of Sight: The Experience of Disability 1900–1950* (Plymouth: Northcote House Publishers, 1992).

[168] W. D. White and W. Wolfensberger, 'The Evolution of Dehumanization in Our Institutions', *Mental Retardation*, 7 (1969), 5–9.

[169] D. Porter, '"Enemies of the Race": Biologism, Environmentalism, and Public Health in Edwardian England', *Victorian Studies*, 34:2 (1991), 159–78.

and reproductive behaviour a focus for regulation. Sex outside of marriage could result in a woman being diagnosed as a moral defective and in incarceration, which could lead to the most vulnerable being locked away for the rest of their lives. Illicit sexual behaviour could be seen, when mediated by gender, race and class, as almost synonymous with feeble-mindedness and such 'sexual offenders' were seen as a source of venereal disease and yet more degenerate children.[170] One victim of this viewpoint was Dorothy R. who 'waved at passing soldiers and blew them kisses'. With no reference to intellectual capacity in her assessment report, merely her moral sense, Dorothy was pronounced to be a feeble-minded moral defective. Once her sister had been prevailed upon to sign commitment papers she was incarcerated in 1917 aged nineteen.[171]

The concept of eugenically defective children quickly became entwined with class and race and this was reflected in the actions called for in order to prevent a swamping of the 'fit'.[172] In 1910 Winston Churchill (1874–1965) wrote:

> [The] unnatural and increasingly rapid growth of the feebleminded classes, coupled with a steady restriction amongst all the thrifty, energetic and superior stocks constitutes a race danger. I feel that the source from which the stream of madness is fed should be cut off and sealed up before another year has passed.[173]

The 1908 Commission, however, while recommending that the mentally deficient should be segregated rejected the idea, put forward by the Eugenics Education Society of using eugenics to ensure 'genetic purification'.[174] Other countries had fewer scruples and in Nazi Germany the idea of genetic, moral and mental defectiveness was taken to its radical extreme. By 1937 over 225,000 people had been subject to involuntary sterilisation in German territories alone.[175] Ultimately between 100,000 and 200,000 people designated as defective were shot, gassed or starved in asylums and hospitals in Nazi Germany.[176] The stigmatisation and sterilisation of those deemed defective was not limited to Germany, as pointed out in 1936 when the Nazi party produced a health publicity poster entitled, 'We do not stand alone', which featured the flags of the many nations who had eugenic sterilisation laws.

Eugenic beliefs did not disappear after the Second World War. Sterilisation for eugenic purposes remained in the USA until the 1970s, with the last carried out in 1981[177]

---

[170] W. Kline, *Building a Better Race: Gender, Sexuality, and Eugenics from the Turn of the Century to the Baby Boom* (Berkeley: University of California Press, 2001), pp. 28–29.

[171] J. Walmsley, 'Women and the Mental Deficiency Act of 1913: Citizenship, Sexuality and Regulation', *British Journal of Learning Disabilities*, 28:2 (2000), 65–70.

[172] R. M. Douglas, 'Anglo-Saxons and Attacotti: The Racialization of Irishness in Britain between the World Wars', *Ethnic and Racial Studies*, 25:1 (2002), 40–63.

[173] M. Gilbert, 'Churchill and Eugenics', The Churchill Centre and Museum (2009). Available online at http://www.winstonchurchill.org/support/the-churchill-centre/publications/finest-hour-online/594–churchill-and-eugenics (accessed 7 Jan. 2010).

[174] G. Grant, P. Goward, M. Richardson and P. L. Ramcharan, *Learning Disability: A Life Cycle Approach to Valuing People* (Milton Keynes: Open University Press, 2005), p. 113.

[175] Kevles, *In the Name of Eugenics*, p. 117. See also for a general introduction: P. Weindling, *Health, Race and German Politics between National Unificationand Nazism, 1870–1945* (Cambridge: Cambridge University Press, 1989); and P. Weindling and M. Turda (eds), *"Blood and Homeland": Eugenics and Racial Nationalism in Central and South-East Europe, 1900–1940* (Budapest: Central European Press, 2007).

[176] W. Wolfensberger, 'The Extermination of Handicapped People in World War II Germany', *Mental Retardation*, 19:1 (1981), 1–7; M. Burleigh, *Death and Deliverance: 'Euthanasia' in Germany c. 1900–1945* (Cambridge: Cambridge University Press, 1994).

[177] A. Stern, *Eugenic Nation: Faults and Frontiers of Better Breeding in Modern America* (Berkeley: University of California Press, 2005), p. 6.

and was also discussed in textbooks of British psychiatry in the 1960s.[178] The eugenic desire to prevent defectives being born remained evident in discussions of best medical practices. For example, in 1958 Ernest Watson raised the issue of the 'sterilization of mentally defective *children*, particularly girls' (my emphasis) and restates the eugenic argument that 'mental defectives produce mental defectives'.[179] He gives a case example in which 'unfortunately' a girl's IQ score was not low enough to allow involuntary sterilisation to occur legally. And if some children slipped through the net and were born defective, some commentators were still happy to suggest their complete and permanent removal from society. As late as 1952, the eighth edition of a *Textbook of Mental Deficiency* by British physician, Alfred Tredgold (1870–1952), contained the following quote:

> The 80,000 or more idiots and imbeciles in the country... are not only incapable of being employed to any economic advantage, but their care and support, whether in their own homes or in institutions, absorb a large amount of time, energy and money of the normal population which could be utilised to better purpose. Moreover, many of these defectives are utterly helpless, repulsive in appearance, and revolting in manners. Their existence is a perpetual source of sorrow and unhappiness to their parents, and those who live at home have a most disturbing influence upon other children and family life... In my opinion it would be an economical and humane procedure were their existence to be painlessly terminated.[180]

During the 1950s the terms 'subnormal' and 'remedial' became commonly used and there remained a category of children deemed uneducable and placed outside the education system. The large asylums and institutions were renamed 'mental handicap hospitals'. These dominated the lives of many 'educationally subnormal' children, who grew up and died within their walls. In 1951, at the age of five, Evelyn King was classified as such and sent to a large mental handicap hospital in the north of England:

> Sometimes I were just a bit frightened because they'd get right strict and funny with you, you know. Just had to keep your mouth shut. But we used to get punished and everything. And I remember as well, when we used to scrub floors, when we were naughty, if we were rude to the staff or anything like. We used to be scrubbing floors all day long. We couldn't go out anywhere. Right punish. We used to be locked inside our rooms, locked doors and the boys used to be in their pyjamas and the girls used to be in their night-dresses. And you used to scrub floors all day, and it wasn't very nice. Everyone looked fed up and browned off 'cos they couldn't do what they would like. And I used to be scared stiff. And I remember I couldn't use a knife and fork then. I can now, but I never used to. I used to use a spoon and if I spilt something, like tea ... Sometimes they would say, 'If you do this again, you won't see your mothers and fathers again'.[181]

Daryl Evans (1981) argues that through incarceration society treated these children as though they were dead, or 'ought to be'.[182]

Separation from families could also happen in infancy and the social procedures for how to separate newborn children from their mothers became well established in some hospitals. In 1947 the American paediatrician, Dr. Anderson Aldrich (b. 1917), published

---

[178] P. Hayes, *New Horizons in Psychiatry* (Harmondsworth: Penguin Books, 1964).

[179] E. H. Watson, 'Counselling Parents of Mentally Deficient Children: Report of a Round Table Discussion', *Pediatrics*, 22 (1958), 401–08.

[180] Quoted in Grant *et al.*, *Learning Disability*, pp. 113–14.

[181] Humphries and Gordon, *Out of Sight*, p. 89.

[182] D. Evans, 'Death and Mentally Retarded Persons', *Mid-American Review of Sociology*, 6:2 (1981), 44–60, at p. 46.

his 'successful technique' for taking 'newborn Mongols from the family'.[183] The first step is that the mother is deceived and told that their baby must remain away from her in the nursery for a few days, due to weakness. The physician then meets the father in a secret conference where he is told that 'immediate placement outside the family provides the only hope of preventing a long series of family difficulties'.[184] A clergyman might usefully be called upon to press home how important it is that the father accepts this solution. Once this has occurred then the physician and father together present the decision to the mother. The mother need not make a decision, merely accept the decision that has been made for her. 'This has the advantage of tending to prevent the natural feelings of guilt which might otherwise plague her after surrendering her child to an institution'.[185] Arrangements for the infant's institutionalisation could then be made immediately. A later description of successful separation techniques highlights the importance of developing the parents' awareness of the negative impact of the defective child on their 'family's social standing'. The social stigmatisation of the infant and their family could be used as an effective lever in gaining separation and avoiding an 'illogical... overprotection of the child'.[186]

In Britain, separated defective infants were placed in institutions under the Mental Deficiency Act, which allowed parents voluntarily to commit their children without a magistrate being involved.[187] However the commitment process itself was not necessarily smooth and there is evidence of long waiting lists to gain places within such institutions. In 1951 the Fountain Hospital in Tooting, south London rarely admitted young infants owing to a three-year waiting list of over 150 children.[188] So although recommendations for early institutionalisation were common, a lack of beds could delay the process. The outcomes for those infants who did gain a hospital place were mixed. In 1951, of the 29 babies admitted to the Fountain Hospital, nine were dead within a year. Brian Kirman, who was a physician at the hospital, noted how poor, overcrowded conditions contributed to these deaths when combined with the time-consuming nature of feeding the children and exposure to infections from the 50 other children on the ward.

Despite his sympathy, Kirman's opinion of these children's level of humanity seems to have had a eugenic underpinning, and he states that when they remained at home they became 'to some extent a family pet'.[189] During the 1970s this attitude could still be discerned. The 1970 *Encyclopaedia Britannica*'s description for Down's Syndrome used the cross reference heading 'Monster'[190] and a 1975 a survey of physicians found that 80 per cent would automatically recommended institutionalisation of 'severely and profoundly retarded children'.[191] Widespread *de facto* euthanasia was noted in special care nurseries[192] and, in 1975, withholding life-saving treatment from these

---

[183] C. A. Aldrich, 'Preventive Medicine and Mongolism', *American Journal of Mental Deficiency*, 52:2 (1947), 127–29.

[184] *Ibid.*, p. 129

[185] Watson, 'Counselling Parents of Mentally Deficient Children', p. 403.

[186] *Ibid.*, p. 404.

[187] B. H. Kirman, 'The Backward Baby', *The British Journal of Psychiatry*, 99:416 (1953), 531–41.

[188] *Ibid.*, p. 532.

[189] *Ibid.*, p 539.

[190] D. P. Mortimer, 'The New Eugenics and the Newborn: The Historical "Cousinage" of Eugenics and Infanticide', *Ethics and Medicine*, 19:3 (2003), 155–70.

[191] N. K. Kelly and F. Menolascino, 'Physicians' Awareness and Attitudes Toward the Retarded,' *Mental Retardation*, 13:6 (1975), 1–13, at p. 11.

[192] C. Duff and A. Campbell, 'Moral and Ethical Dilemmas in the Special-Care Nursery', *New England Journal of Medicine*, 289:17 (1973), 890–94.

children was reported as 'rapidly gaining status as good medical practice'.[193] In a famous American 'Baby Doe' case a child with Down's Syndrome was allowed to starve to death following the withholding of treatment.[194] There were similar legal cases in the 1970s and prosecution for fatally withholding 'ordinary medical care' from defective infants was rare.[195]

Today the process of gaining a separation of mother and baby has become less common, partly as consequence of prenatal screening. In the UK, from 1989 onwards the proportion of mothers choosing a termination of their pregnancy, following a screening diagnosis of Down's Syndrome, remained at around 90 per cent.[196] Some see this as carrying on the practices of a previous era, albeit cloaked in new technology. The actor, Lord Rix (b. 1924), a long-term campaigner for the rights of the disabled, claimed in a letter to *The Independent* that 'The ghost of the biologist Sir Francis Galton, who founded the eugenics movement in 1885, still stalks the corridors of many a teaching hospital'.[197]

Awareness of the influence of eugenic thinking remains important today as we gain increasing powers of differentiating between unborn children. For example one might discern the 'ghostly' influence in discussions concerning which foetuses be terminated. Professor Simon Baron-Cohen (b. 1958), an expert on autism has questioned whether it would be desirable if a prenatal test for autism was developed as this might lead some parents to abort such foetuses, even though some forms of autism are linked to valued skills, such as being good at maths or computing.[198] In defending one group of children, those with autism, he is making a link between a right to life and the possession of a talent or being able to perform particular functions in society. In the 1930s eugenic judgements of worth and fitness produced a similar argument. We have seen what this way of thinking created for infants judged to be at the bottom of this hierarchy: stigmatisation, segregation and sometimes being killed.

· ·

The British state today makes the adoption of healthy, 'normal' infants much harder and operates much stricter criteria on potential parents, but this has only been made possible because there are far fewer young babies to adopt. For those who are prepared to adopt older children or those with behavioural or learning difficulties, the measures are less restrictive. As the previous contribution suggested, however, as prenatal testing becomes more advanced, it is likely that even fewer children deemed defective will be born as parents abort or screen out problematic embryos before implantation.

The twentieth century has seen a revolution in women's control over reproduction

---

[193] J. A. Robertson, 'Involuntary Euthanasia of Defective Newborns', *Stanford Law Review*, 27:2 (1975), 213–69.

[194] G. J. Annas, 'The Baby Doe Regulations: Governmental Intervention in Neonatal Rescue Medicine', *American Journal of Public Health*, 74:6 (1984), 618–20.

[195] Evans, 'Death and Mentally Retarded Persons', p. 48.

[196] C. Mansfield, S. Hopfer, and T. M. Marteau, 'Termination Rates after Prenatal Diagnosis of Down Syndrome, Spina Bifida, Anencephaly, and Turner and Klinefelter Syndrome', *Prenatal Diagnosis*, 19:9 (1999), 808–12; J. K. Morris and E. Alberman, 'Trends in Down's Syndrome Live Births and Antenatal Diagnoses in England and Wales from 1989 to 2008: Analysis of Data', *British Medical Journal*, 339:b3794 (2009). Available online at http://www.bmj.com/cgi/content/abstract/339/oct26_3/b3794 (accessed 7 Jan. 2010).

[197] Lord Rix, 'Ghost of Eugenics stalks Down's babies'. Letter to *The Independent*, 24 May 2006, Available online http://www.independent.co.uk/opinion/letters/letters-choice-in-the-nhs-479440.html (accessed 7 Jan. 2010).

[198] S. Baron-Cohen, 'Is autism screening close to reality?' *The Guardian*, 12 Jan. 2009. Available online at http://www.guardian.co.uk/lifeandstyle/2009/jan/12/autism-screening-health (accessed 7 Jan. 2010).

and for the first time in the West, women need no longer bring children into the world if they fear they will be defective or if they are simply unwanted. The revolution has come about partly through the Pill. Contraceptive devices have been around for several centuries, but women have only been able to be in total control of their own fertility from the late 1960s. More importantly, in the context of this chapter, safe and legal abortion is another aspect of this revolution and a product of the same decade. It is to this issue that the chapter now turns. The extent to which abortion is a form of violence against children is extremely controversial and many forms of Christianity, including the Catholic Church and evangelical Christians, claim that abortion and infanticide are identical. In contrast, others argue that while a foetus has the potential to become a child and therefore a full social person, this potential is not always fulfilled, or indeed socially recognised, and therefore rigid distinctions must be made between foetus and child. Even among those with no religious convictions whether or not abortion is a form of violence against children is deeply contested. Some, as suggested above, fear that abortion might be used as a new form of eugenics while others point to a small, limited amount of evidence that suggests that the availability of abortion decreases infanticide and harm to children. It has also been claimed that abortion contributes more generally to the social good so that there are suggestions, in the USA at least, that legalised abortion has brought down crime rates as future criminals, from poor, marginalised backgrounds are more likely to be aborted than brought to term.[199]

Abortion, like infanticide, has been formally condemned from the Christian era onwards but, nevertheless, women have always tried to abort children and excuses have often been made for them.[200] The twentieth century saw the rise of a different justification for abortion, the right of a woman to control her own fertility, and, in consequence, debates over the extent to which the state (which has replaced the church as the guardian of morality) could intervene in the private life of individuals. Argument continues to this day but it is not perhaps surprising that the first country in Europe to legalise abortion was Soviet Russia in 1920 (although the policy was reversed by Stalin in 1936) as part of a radical overhaul of family and community life and the attempt to create a new society.[201] During the 1930s other countries, such as Poland, Turkey, Denmark, Sweden, Iceland and Mexico, lifted restrictions on abortion in particular circumstances such as rape, incest or threats to a mother's life or foetal deformation. Today only seven per cent of countries refuse to allow abortion on any grounds whatsoever, and 84 per cent allow it with restrictions (which may be interpreted liberally or very narrowly). Despite the many grey areas in law concerning abortion, the procedure is practised, legally or illegally, in all countries of the world.[202] 'Every year [abortion] is practiced by one woman out of every fourteen of reproductive age... With a level estimated at about 45 million per year ... it occurs over one-third as frequently as all births and just as frequently as deaths'.[203] Abortion may be controversial, but it is also

---

[199] D. Lester, 'Roe v. Wade was Followed by a Decrease in Neonatal Homicide', *Journal of the American Medical Association*, 267 (1992), 3027–28; S. Levitt and S. Dubner, *Freakonomics: A Rogue Economist Explores the Hidden Side of Everything* (New York: William Morrow/HarperCollins, 2005).

[200] On the practice of abortion in late eighteenth-century Rennes, see Hufton, *The Poor of Eighteenth-Century France*, p. 331.

[201] Abortion on demand was legalised again in 1955 and became one of the primary forms of birth control in the Soviet Union. Soviet women had on average five abortions in their lifetime. I. Hutter, 'Determinants of Abortion and Contraceptive Behavior in Russia', in A. M. Basu (ed.), *The Sociocultural and Political Aspects of Abortion* (Westport: Praeger, 2003), pp. 185–202.

[202] For the most up-to-date statistics on abortion laws worldwide see C. Francome and M. Vekeman, *Abortion, a Worldwide Perspective* (London: Middlesex University Press, 2007).

[203] J. C. Caldwell and P. Caldwell, 'Abortion in a Changing World', in A. N. Basu (ed.), *The Sociocultural and Political Aspects of Abortion*, p. 1.

ubiquitous, and rates of abortion show no signs of declining. The following contribution will discuss many of these issues through the lens of the history of abortion in England in the twentieth century.

Abortion in the Twentieth Century in England

Ellie Lee

Illegal abortion was available in backstreets throughout the country. Those who provided this service often had had midwifery, nursing or medical experience. Women were charged from £5 to £15 but sometimes as much as £80 (the value of money has to be multiplied by about 15 to allow for inflation since 1960). The abortion process was usually initiated either by directing a jet of fluid through the cervix, by the insertion of an object, such as a rubber catheter or by the puncturing of the foetal membranes with a thin instrument. Abortion was the usual outcome – the woman being told to go to the hospital only if pain or serious bleeding continued or if she began to feel ill. Heavy blood loss and infection were frequent complications but, in the majority of cases, did not threaten life. A significant minority developed chronic pelvic infection that could result in months of pain during intercourse, heavy painful periods, and subsequent infertility. A very few gynaecologists in private practice, sometimes in association with a psychiatrist, were prepared to terminate pregnancy virtually on request to prevent injury to mental health. These abortions were provided openly in registered nursing homes, but the fees of from £100 to £250 reflected the scarcity of this service and an element of 'danger money'; this was abortion only for the rich. The vast majority of gynaecologists were not willing to terminate pregnancy in the NHS or private practice except within their cautious interpretation of existing law.[204]

This description by retired gynaecologist David Paintin, of women's abortion 'choices' prior to the legalisation of abortion in Britain in 1967, paints a now almost forgotten picture. It is unimaginable to today's young women that for the most part their choices 50 years ago if they found themselves with an unwanted pregnancy would have been to have a baby they did not want, or risk infection and maybe much worse by visiting a clandestine abortionist (the only safe, legal alternative being for those who had enough money to pay for it). Today British women faced with an unwanted pregnancy can be almost certain they will be able to access a legal abortion (those whose pregnancies are not progressed beyond the first three or four months at least). It is fairly likely it will be available to them on the NHS. They can be pretty sure they will encounter an abortion service in which efforts have been made to provide evidence-based abortion care of a high medical standard. They will terminate their pregnancy either in an NHS hospital or an independent abortion clinic located, for most women, near or fairly near where they live. In 2008 almost 200,000 British women had safe, legal abortions.[205]

Many factors contribute to this changed situation. These include innovations in abortion procedures: for example the development of RU486 or 'medical abortion', a combination of hormones that induces miscarriage, and which can be used up to 63

---

[204] D. Paintin, 'A Medical View of Abortion in the 1960s', in E. Lee (ed.), *Abortion Law and Politics Today* (Basingstoke: Macmillan, 1998), pp. 12–13.
[205] Department of Health, 'Abortion statistics: England and Wales 2008', http://www.dh.gov.uk/en/ Publicationsandstatistics/Publications/PublicationsStatistics/DH_099285 (accessed 28 Aug. 2009).

days (nine weeks) gestation; the development of abortion services within and outside the NHS (the contribution of the independent abortion providers British Pregnancy Advisory Service and Marie Stopes clinics to the development of abortion provision and practice is very significant); and broader socio-cultural shifts that have made choosing to terminate a pregnancy more acceptable than in the past.[206] Central to all of this is the law, because without legal abortion, none of this would be possible.

One question that might be asked is why did it take so long for the law to change? Doctors knew full well decades before 1967 how to perform abortion safely.[207] Yet women were left to suffer the indignity and risk of illegal abortion. This suggests factors having little to do with medical safety were most important for law reform (and its tardy arrival). What were these factors?

Reading history backwards is always a mistake. With the abortion law the pitfall is imagining abortion law reform to be the product of an impulse to liberate women. Today the dominant understanding of the abortion issue sees it as a moral contest between 'women's choice' and 'foetal rights', in which the former tends to win out, yet both are quite recent social constructs. In so far as these claims formed part of the pre-1967 context, it was only in a very marginal way. As veteran campaigner for legal abortion Madeleine Simms has put it, 'Few people at that period thought of anything as unrealisable and extravagant as "A Woman's Right To Choose". That came many years later. People sometimes forget that abortion law reform preceded the Women's Movement'. Simms notes that there were 'visionaries' from the 1930s, for example Stella Browne (1880–1955), who 'arrived at the answer of "A Woman's Right to Choose" half a century ahead of her time', but 'Most of us took rather longer to arrive at this conclusion which commands overwhelming support today and hardly shocks anyone'.[208]

The tardiness of abortion law reform can be viewed in this light as by-product of the absence of wider acceptance that women's ability to control fertility is central to their social freedom (a wider acceptance that is arguably still partial and fragile). It was certainly the case that other kinds of social concerns motivated most abortion law reformers, and it was these which became more widely resonant in late 1960s.

One issue was that of 'handicap', as it was then called. The Thalidomide tragedy played an important part in increasing support for law reform, bringing to public view the problem faced by women who had been legally prescribed a drug that led to the birth of severely handicapped babies, but then left them with no option but illegal abortion when the effects of these drugs became apparent. In a context where more and more drugs were coming onto the market all of the time, abortion as a result, claims Simms, 'passed from being a subterranean and rather sordid criminal issue to being seen as a public health issue'.[209]

The sense of unfairness felt by those who saw the proper outcome of Thalidomide as access to legal abortion for women formed part of, perhaps, the most important wider sensibility impelling law reform; the post-war idea of 'social justice'. This was

---

[206] E. Lee, 'Young Women, Pregnancy and Abortion in Britain: a Discussion of Law in Practice', *International Journal of Law, Policy and the Family* 18:3 (2004), 283–304.

[207] E. Shorter, *Women's Bodies. A Social History of Women's Encounter with Health, Ill-Health and Medicine* (New Brunswick and London: Transaction, 1997). Ch. 8 provides a fascinating account of the history of abortion from traditional society to the mid-twentieth century, using documents and information mainly about western Europe.

[208] M. Simms, 'Abortion Law Reform in Britain in the 1960s: What Were the Issues Then?', in E. Lee (ed.), *Abortion Law and Politics Today* (Basingstoke: Macmillan, 1998), p. 5.

[209] *Ibid.*, p. 7.

discussed by Lord Horder writing a forward for a 1960 book entitled *Law for the Rich*.[210] He criticised, 'The anomaly that allows the well-to-do to get rid of an unwanted child before it is born, without danger to life and reputation, yet denies such relief to the poor'.[211] Lena Jeger (1915–2007) was a Labour MP and early parliamentary advocate of legal abortion, and her formulation of the problem was that, 'Abortion is like equal pay. The women who are best off get it'.[212] This concern with 'unfairness' also merged with the notion that it was the poor who in fact needed legal abortion *most*. They could be assisted to lead a better life, it was thought, were they able to prevent 'over large families', as one MP supportive of legal change put it. By the late 1960s 'family planning' came to be viewed as part of the solution to the problem of poverty and abortion was seen as especially important for the poor.[213] By the late 1960s legal abortion thus came to be viewed by many as a way of addressing harms to society and the issue moved as a result into the realm of public debate. The sensibility that connected legal abortion with 'social justice' helped facilitate legal abortion, although this must also be seen against a wider backdrop of the gap between the existing law and practice. Laws that make abortion illegal have always been routinely flouted in practice, but, by this point in twentieth century, this gap had arguably become cavernous.

Historian Edward Shorter points out that regardless of legal proscriptions, 'since the dawn of time women have been able to get rid of unwanted pregnancies, mainly through abortive drugs'.[214] What changes, he suggests, is degrees of desperation. When the only option was possibly effective but potentially very dangerous traditional drugs, as was the case in the middle ages, abortion was for the most desperate women. Moving into the late nineteenth and twentieth century, however, abortion became much safer (although still risky compared to today's standards). Surgical methods developed for use in obstetrics became incorporated into therapeutic (legal) abortion practice, and were diffused to the illegal practitioners (often midwives). There was a much better understanding of anatomy and of the need for aseptic conditions. As abortion became safer as a result, it was no longer for the strictly desperate; by the early twentieth century Shorter claims, on the basis of evidence from medical records and commentaries from doctors of the time like Berlin-based Max Hirsch, as many as one in four pregnancies ended in abortion.[215]

Women's propensity to abort pregnancies in the early twentieth century took place, however, in a context of very harsh laws. The main law governing abortion in modern times was introduced in 1861 as part of The Offences Against the Person Act. Formally keeping some possibility of abortion being considered legal by stating conditions under which abortion was *illegal* (thus *potentially* allowing medical professionals to practise abortion legally if they considered it necessary), this law set the harshest penalties ever introduced in the western world to punish abortionists and the women who sought abortion.[216]

Yet these laws prohibiting abortion did not even register in the consciousness of many women. Marie Stopes (1880–1958), the famous pioneer of birth control, noted that at her birth control clinic established in the 1930s she had many thousands of requests for abortion, from women who did not even know it was a criminal offence.

---

[210] A. Jenkins, *Law for the Rich* (London: Gollancz, 1960)

[211] Simms, 'Abortion Law Reform', p. 7.

[212] *Ibid.*, p. 7. See also K. Hindell and M. Simms, *Abortion Law Reformed* (London: Peter Owen, 1971).

[213] S. Sheldon, *Beyond Control, Medical Power and Abortion Law* (London: Pluto Press, 1997).

[214] Shorter, *Women's Bodies*, p. 177.

[215] *Ibid.*, p. 196.

[216] B. Brookes, *Abortion in England 1900–1967* (London: Croom Helm, 1998).

(See Figure 14). Historian Kate Fisher investigated women's experience of abortion in South Wales before the 1967 Act. One doctor working in the area wrote to Marie Stopes in 1937 that:

> We have had two requests for abortion this week and both seemed to think that the clinic existed for the purpose. The unlawful side of it had not struck them at all. One was a young woman who had recently re-married.... I think she intends to bring about an abortion by some means. The other said, 'surely you are going to do something for me'. I had to explain to her very plainly that we did not teach how to destroy life. She had douched with very hot lysol, taken salts, Beechams pills and female pills.[217]

Fisher used oral history methods to find out how women in South Wales perceived abortion at this time, and argues that women were, 'ignorant of the law regarding abortion', and that in working-class circles, 'there seems to have been very little condemnation of abortion, rather, an acceptance of its practical importance'.[218]

Abortion was, it appears, widely accepted by ordinary people, and for this reason prosecution when it was attempted was difficult. Abortionists were protected by community secrecy and popular support. As Simms notes for example, women from all over the country came to the funeral in 1939 of Dr. Daniel Powell from Tooting, south London. It was estimated he had aborted around 25,000 women and had thus been prepared to routinely flout the law and (successfully) defend himself against prosecution.[219]

It seems inevitable that, given this gap between highly restrictive laws and the relatively commonplace practice of abortion, something had to give. Prior to 1967 this 'giving' took the form of the opening up of 'legal loopholes' – provisions that made it more clear that professional doctors could practise abortion, if they considered it necessary, and not be prosecuted. One such loophole was created by the Bourne ruling in the 1930s, when Dr. Alec Bourne (1886–1974) deliberately provoked his own prosecution by aborting a fourteen-year-old girl raped by soldiers. His defence was that she was a mental wreck because of what had happened, and was therefore deserving of abortion. Through his acquittal of all charges, this case made it clear that there was legal abortion, and further it could be carried out for wider reasons other than risk to the mother's own life (namely her mental health).[220]

The law that eventually changed things altogether resulted from a Private Members Bill brought before Parliament by David Steel MP (b. 1938). Perhaps the most often ignored point about the 1967 Abortion Act that resulted is that it amends *but does not replace* the pre-existing law, the 1861 Offences Against the Person Act. This means abortion remains in Britain *de facto* a criminal offence. What the 1967 Act does is to provide a legal defence against its criminality for those doctors who authorise its performance or who practise abortion, where they believe this necessary on specified grounds:

> Subject to the provisions of this section, a person shall not be guilty of an offence under the law relating to abortion when a pregnancy is terminated by a registered medical practitioner if two registered medical practitioners are of the opinion formed in good faith –

---

[217] K. Fisher, 'Women's Experience of Abortion Before the 1967 Abortion Act: A Study of South Wales 1930–50', in Lee (ed.), *Abortion Law*, p. 27.
[218] *Ibid.*, pp. 27–28.
[219] Simms, 'Abortion Law Reform', p. 8.
[220] Sheldon, *Beyond Control*.

(a) that the pregnancy has not exceeded its twenty-fourth week and that the continuance of the pregnancy would involve risk, greater than if the pregnancy were terminated, of injury to the physical or mental health of the pregnant woman or any existing children of her family; or

(b) that the termination is necessary to prevent grave permanent injury to the physical or mental health of the pregnant woman; or

(c) that the continuance of the pregnancy would involve risk to the life of the pregnant woman, greater than if the pregnancy were terminated; or

(d) that there is substantial risk that if the child were born it would suffer from such physical or mental abnormalities as to be seriously handicapped.[221]

It is on this basis in part that it has been argued that it is profoundly wrong to see British abortion law reform as liberal legislation. In no sense does the liberal idea of individual 'rights over one's body' shape the law through its application to women and their bodies. Women (as well as abortionists who are not medical professionals) have *no* rights under this law. What this law does, however, by freeing doctors from the threat of prosecution where they believe 'in good faith' that an abortion should be performed, is create a legal loophole that is as wide as doctors want it to be.[222]

This abortion law is striking because it can be interpreted as both highly restrictive and highly facilitative of abortion. Potentially at least legal abortion could be provided to relatively small numbers of women, were it the case that doctors chose to form opinions 'in good faith' that risks posed by continued pregnancy to the health of women and their families should be defined narrowly. On the other hand, this law can be facilitative of access to abortion. Where abortion is viewed by medical professionals (at least those who opt to be involved in abortion provision) as preferable to the continuation of unwanted pregnancies, they can opt to make its provision on mental and physical health grounds commonplace. For example, doctors can define a 'threat to mental health' as the woman feeling stressed by the pregnancy and the prospect of unwanted motherhood.[223] The issue remains of how far into pregnancy women be aborted, but under British law (in contrast with most European laws) doctors can, if they choose to, also provide abortion up to a relatively late gestational stage. (The one amendment to law since 1967 has addressed this issue, since in 1990 Section 37 of the Human Fertilisation and Embryology Act specified abortion can be legally performed only up to 23 weeks and six days of a pregnancy, other than where the situations described in b), c) and d) above pertain, in which case no legal time limit applies).

What have been the effects of this law? It is unquestionable that since 1967 abortion has become very safe indeed in a medical sense. Serious health complications are negligible, minor ones rare. There have been no reports of 'backstreet abortions' for many years. The only discussion of illegally-sought abortion in recent years has focused on women who seek abortion at relatively late gestational stages and who cannot be provided with procedures legally in Britain, since the procedure would be performed after 24 weeks gestation were it to go ahead. It has been estimated that those who are prepared to offer women who seek late abortion a consultation in the first place (primarily doctors working for British Pregnancy Advisory Service) have turned about

---

[221] Abortion Act 1967 (c. 87). Available online at http://www.statutelaw.gov.uk/legResults.aspx?LegType=Al l+Primary&PageNumber=64&NavFrom=2&activeTextDocId=1181037 (accessed 28 Aug. 2009).

[222] J. Bridgeman, 'A Woman's Right to Choose?', in Lee, *Abortion Law and Politics Today*, pp. 76–94. See also E. Lee, *Abortion, Motherhood and Mental Health: The Medicalization of Reproduction in the U.S. and Britain* (New York: Transaction Publishers, 2003).

[223] Paintin, 'A Medical View of Abortion', p. 16.

100 such women away each year in recent years. The fortunes of these women are mostly unknown, although a small number do seek terminations abroad. The handful who have visited a clinic in Barcelona that will terminate pregnancies after 24 weeks, thus providing abortion that would be illegal in Britain, were at the centre of a flurry of media discussion in Britain in 2004, when something of a moral panic about late abortion was generated centring on this Spanish clinic.[224]

In the heat of this controversy (and the more general highly emotionalised discussion about late abortion that has emerged in recent years), it is easy to lose sight of some facts. The vast majority of abortions occur in early pregnancy with over 90 per cent performed before twelve weeks gestation, with the proportion dwindling as pregnancies proceed (to less than 1.5 per cent at 20 plus weeks). Late abortion is thus unpopular with women, but it is not the law that shapes this pattern of demand. Relatively few women terminate pregnancies late, not because the law discourages this, but because their own feelings about their pregnancies lead women to want abortion as early as possible. Evidence suggests that the small proportion of women who do seek late abortion include those who are young and inexperienced, abandoned by their partner and desperate, have been unable to get an abortion earlier, or have been affected by unexpected failure of usually very reliable hormonal contraception that normally leads to very light, infrequent periods.[225]

Most significant numerically and socially therefore is demand for abortion at early gestational stages, a demand that has increased almost every year over the past two decades. The abortion rate for England and Wales – abortions per 1,000 female residents aged sixteen to 45 – stood in 1976, 1986, 1991, 1996, 2000, and 2003 at 10.2, 13.0, 15.0, 16.0, 17.0, 17.5 respectively, with an increase in absolute numbers from 129,700 to 190,700 over this time. In 2008, 195,296 were performed and the age-standardised abortion rate was 18.2. In that year, 90 per cent of abortions were carried out at less than thirteen weeks gestation; 73 per cent were under ten weeks.[226] A set of socio-legal questions is raised by this growing popularity of abortion amongst women, which has emerged despite wider availability of contraception and in particular the advent of the contraceptive Pill. How might these statistics be explained?

Contraceptive failure is a part of it. This comprises 'method failure' (the Pill for example is 99 per cent effective but this means that even when used carefully, given almost four million British women use the Pill, many thousands of unplanned pregnancies will occur). Then there is 'user failure'. In real life, always using contraception optimally is difficult. Pill users forget to take it, and condoms stay in the packet. Perhaps most significant however is the changing social landscape regarding both sex and motherhood. Women are having their first child later than ever before, and are having fewer children than at any time in recent decades. Over the same time period these fertility trends have developed (from the early 1970s), the age of first sex has decreased, and a fairly widely accepted social practice has emerged in which sex is associated with pleasure (not procreation). Sex has also come to be considered a pleasure people can legitimately enjoy prior to marriage, which also happens later in life, if at all.[227]

---

[224] E. Lee, 'The Abortion Debate Today', in K. Horsey and H. Biggs (eds), *Human Fertilisation and Embryology: Reproducing Regulation* (London: Routledge-Cavendish, 2007).

[225] R. Ingham, E. Lee, S. J. Clements and N. Stone, 'Reasons for Second Trimester Abortion in England and Wales', *Reproductive Health Matters*, 16:31, Supplement 1 (2008), 18–29.

[226] Department of Health, 'Abortion statistics'.

[227] E. Lee, 'Women's Need for Abortion', in A. Glasier, K. Wellings and H. Critchley (eds), *Contraception and Contraceptive Use* (London: RCOG Press, 2005).

Added together, these trends generate a context in which many women are sexually active from around fifteen years of age, and at latest seventeen or eighteen, but do not start having children until well into their twenties, and then have few of them. During this time they expect, and are expected to, contribute fully to broader social life and the world of work. Is it any wonder that the abortion rate has increased? Perhaps the real surprise is that there are not *more* abortions. It is at least worth recognising (rather than bemoaning) the high degree of efficacy with which most women are regulating their fertility, given the context for sex and reproduction today. It is also worth asking whether, given all of this, a law that retains the assumption that abortion is a criminal act that should only be provided to women where two doctors agree their health at risk, is out of line with contemporary realities. It is arguable that abortion is now a fact of life for modern women in just the same way as contraception, and there should be laws that honestly reflect this reality.

· ·

As this chapter has shown, in a wide variety of different contexts and historical eras, there are, and always have been, pregnancies and children that are unwanted and that even when infanticide, abortion or abandonment are illegal or discouraged, this has had a limited effect on the numbers of unwanted children. What is equally clear is that abortion, infanticide and abandonment are placed in a special category of activity which is less concerned with the question of violence against the child and more with wider social issues such as gender relations, personhood and humanity. Increasingly such issues are now being debated in terms of children's rights. New understandings of children as rights-bearing citizens and social agents mean that children's rights, including the fundamental right to life, must be respected in all circumstances and that abandonment, exposure and infanticide are seen as unequivocal forms of violence against children. Yet this view remains contested, not just in the case of abortion but also in the case of neonatal infants and those with disabilities. A recent study of neonatal and premature babies examined the controversial question of whether premature babies are citizens with rights or in an ambiguous limbo.

On the face of it such issues may seem irrelevant or even absurd. Few would deny that a baby, once born, should be given every help to survive. Yet the question is not that simple and, as the authors of this study point out, 'Premature babies, born as early as 22 or 23 weeks gestation, are the same gestational age as the fetus that has no rights'.[228] Furthermore they argue that the right to life is not absolute for the prematurely born and that many neonatal units do not always treat those children born at 23 or 24 weeks. There is often a small period of time during which medical personnel and parents decide whether or not to give treatment or to withdraw any treatment given so far. This can range from allowing the baby to die by removing artificial ventilation to withholding fluids and nutrition. From a children's rights perspective, the authors argue that while some may see these premature babies as being in an anomalous state for whom the absolute right to life is, in fact, negotiable and which their carers may revoke, they should rather be seen as citizens with rights and an acknowledged personhood and individuality.

While the idea of violence against children, especially very young children, might occasion universal moral opprobrium, the reality, as this chapter has shown, is more complicated. Although violence has never been fully acceptable, approved of, or a normative way of dealing with unwanted children, it has always occurred and societies and individuals have always had means of disposing of inconvenient or unacceptable children. Not all these methods have been overtly violent but the vulnerability of the very young means they are

---

[228] Alderson *et al.*, 'Are Premature Babies Citizens with Rights?', p. 71.

particularly easy to condemn to death through neglect, passive infanticide, or active killing. Even today infants under one have a higher risk of being murdered than any other group of children and while forms of violence against the very young have changed, they show little sign of being eliminated entirely.[229]

---

[229] Around 37 newborn babies are killed every year. 'Although the risk of becoming a victim of homicide is exceptionally low among children as a whole, the reverse is true of infants below one year of age. In England and Wales infants under one year face around four times the average risk of becoming a victim of homicide'. F. Brookman and M. Maguire, *Reducing Homicide: Summary of a Review of the Possibilities* (London: Home Office, 2003), p. iii.

3. Physical Cruelty and Socialisation

Nigel Kennell, Henrietta Leyser, Laurence Brockliss, Anja Müller,
Jane Humphries, Heather Ellis and Stephen Cretney

In my research for "The WAVE Report" [Worldwide Alternatives to Violence] I came across over 100 examples [of child deaths caused by abuse] – Jean Titchener of Camberwell, whose mother used to burn her hands and feet with a lamp, and whose body was "just one mass of sores" (died 1946); Susan Yate, of King's Lynn, who died in hospital 3 days after she was found with a ruptured lung and multiple bruises from a savage beating (1955); Patrick Harvey of Birmingham, who was beaten to death by his mother with a 2-foot stick because he had soiled his trousers (1962); James Nunn, of Norfolk, whose father battered him, inflicting "horrifying injuries", because the 3-week old kept him awake at night (1973 – he got 2 years probation); Heidi Koseda of Hillingdon, who died of thirst and starvation, locked in a cupboard while her family carried on as normal outside. A post mortem found bits of nappy in her stomach, which she had eaten in a desperate attempt to keep alive (1985); Leanne White, who was beaten to death by her stepfather, who made her sleep on the floor. She suffered 107 external injuries and died of internal bleeding and repeated blows to the stomach (1992); Jacob Jenkinson who was smothered to death by his father (1999).

Deaths such as those above often led to Public Inquiries – I counted 24 in the 1970s, 25 in the 1980s and 22 in the 1990s – but no visible reduction in levels of child abuse.

> George Hosking, *A Tale of 10 Children*, Croyden Wave Trust Ltd. Available from
> http://www.wavetrust.org/index.htm?http://www.wavetrust.org/WAVE_Reports
> /A_Tale_of_10_Children.htm (accessed 16 Sept. 2009)

Generally ... the tawse [belt] in Scotland was given on the hands, often – contrary to the usual practice with the cane in England – in front of the class. And it was applied remarkably frequently: a 1977 survey by the Educational Institute of Scotland (the teachers' trade union) found that 36% of 12- to 15-year-old boys were belted at least once in 10 school days; 21% of these were strapped three or more times in the same period...

...In 1982 its monopoly manufacturer in Scotland, Lochgelly saddler John Dick, "whose family firm had been making the tawse in their Fife workshop since Victorian children were learning their three R's and being belted", went out of production.

> C. Farrell, *The Cane and the Tawse in Scottish Schools*. Available from http://www.corpun.com/
> scotland.htm (acessed 16 Sept. 2009)

He ...(Br X)... flogged me one time, I was working in the piggery. I used to be starving, the pigs used to get the Brothers' leftovers and one day there was lovely potatoes and I took some and I took a turnip. Br X caught me and he brought me up to the dormitory, he let down my trousers and he lashed me. He always wore a leather, around 18 inches ... (long)

... and it was all stitched with wax, his leather was very thin. It was about an inch and a half, others had leathers about 2 inches. He lashed me, he flogged me...

One lay member of staff ...X... she was cruel, she was absolutely cruel. There was one punishment she gave me that I will never forget it in my life. She used to say "hold your head up", she was very nasty. She got my hair and she tied it and she pulled my head back like that ... (demonstrated hair being tied to belt at back holding head up in fixed position) ... and she got a string and she tied it up. Oh the pain of it. So my head was up like that, held like that for a couple days, that is why I will never forget it. The nuns knew of it but they gave her a free hand.

> *The Commission to Inquire into Child Abuse. Confidential Committee Report.*
> Vol III, (Dublin: The Comission to Inquire into Child Abuse, 2009), pp. 59 and 142.

Just as western society in the Christian and modern era has always condemned baby killing and only ever accepted limited abortion, so it has always believed that children should not be gratuitously assaulted or starved by adults. On the other hand, western society has been much more ready until very recently to accept that physical chastisement, deprivation of food, incarceration and so on are perfectly legitimate tools in disciplining children and that thwarted adults can vent their fury on a child's body and spirit. The problem has only been acerbated by the fact that many, and eventually virtually all young children and adolescents, have lived part or most of their lives outside the family home as servants (high and low), apprentices or scholars.[1] Similarly many of the standard child-rearing customs of the pre-modern age cannot but seem barbaric and cruel to us today. Admittedly, the most painful rituals practised by some of our western ancestors seem to have had a short life: the Huns, for instance, who occupied much of eastern and central Europe in the first half of the fifth century CE, did not bequeath their custom of slashing the faces of male babies.[2] But for many centuries Europeans accepted as normal, and even promoted, a variety of practices which were arguably physically and psychologically harmful. The tight swaddling of babies in their first months of life was definitely established by the late Attic period and would last until the beginning of the nineteenth century.[3] The practice of taking infants away from their mothers shortly after birth and putting them out to nurse survived even longer, and in eighteenth-century France was practised by artisans as well as the rich.[4] In the sixteenth and seventeenth

---

[1] For children brought up in noble households in England, see N. Orme, *Medieval Children* (London: Yale University Press, 2001), pp. 313–16. See also Ch. 4, pp. 168–69. Rulers until the end of the sixteenth century would often demand that nobles deposited their offspring at court as security for good behaviour and could extract revenge if a noble stepped out of line. Lloyd deMause gives several gruesome, although unverified, examples. 'When Eustace de Breteuil, the husband of a natural daughter of Henry I, put out the eyes of the son of one of his vassals, the king allowed the enraged father to mutilate in the same way Eustace's daughter whom Henry held as hostage. Similarly, John Marshall gave up his son William to King Stephen, saying he "cared little if William were hanged, for he had the anvils and hammers with which to forge still better sons," and Francis 1, when taken prisoner by Charles V, exchanged his young sons for his own freedom, then promptly broke the bargain so that they were thrown in jail. Indeed, it was often hard to distinguish the practice of sending one's children to serve as pages or servants in another noble household from the use of children as hostages'. L. deMause (ed.), *The History of Childhood* (New York: Psychohistory Press, 1974), p. 33.

[2] The practice was presumably to emphasise their future role as warriors. The Huns also appear to have elongated the skulls of babies. See http://en.wikipedia.org/wiki/Huns (accessed 15 Sept. 2009). On the different conceptions around the world of what is violence or cruelty to children, see H. Montgomery, 'Children and Violence', in H. Montgomery, R. Burr and M. Woodhead (eds), *Changing Childhoods Local and Global* (Chichester: John Wiley, 2003), ch. 4; H. Montgomery, *An Introduction to Childhood. Anthropological Perspectives on Children's Lives* (Oxford: Wiley-Blackwell, 2009), ch. 6.

[3] M. Golden, *Children and Childhood in Classical Athens* (London: Johns Hopkins University Press, 1993), p. 17. There is no visual evidence of swaddling from fifth and fourth century Athens but the practice can be inferred.

[4] See below, fn. 71.

centuries, and probably in the late middle ages, children, just like adults, were constantly bled and purged as a prophylactic. In the Renaissance era, children of the well-to-do were never left to develop 'naturally': even teething had to be assisted, often by cutting a baby's gums with frequently fatal effects in an age which knew nothing of antisepsis.[5]

The present chapter explores the emergence of our modern belief that a harsh child-rearing regime embodies physical cruelty and neglect. It begins with an account of child-rearing practices in Ancient Sparta. We know surprisingly little about disciplining the young in classical Athens. It is quite clear that the children of citizens might be physically chastised at home or school. Plato (427–347 BCE) in the *Protagoras* has the eponymous hero of the dialogue, a famous teacher, say that disobedient children are treated 'as a bent and twisted piece of cord' and straightened ' with threats and blows'.[6] But in this and other of his writings, he never goes into details, and the practice is hardly mentioned by his contemporaries.[7] The one interesting incontestable fact about their upbringing is that male children could be punished by their *paidagogos*, the slave in charge of their socialisation. As someone who had to watch his back, the *paidagogos* may have been tempted to chastise misdemeanours committed in public rather than private, thereby encouraging the development of a citizen culture based on shame rather than absolute values.[8] Sparta, however, is a different story. By dint of the fact that its citizens were trained by the state rather than the family and that the regime seemed so foreign to contemporary Greeks, some account, albeit still limited, of its idiosyncratic child-rearing practices have survived in the Athenian sources. Moreover, since the Romans found Spartan 'exceptionalism' fascinating, there are numerous references to these practices in later sources, notably Pausanias (second century CE).[9]

Violence in the 'Upbringing' of Ancient Sparta

Nigel Kennell

Sparta was unique in the Greek world in having a standing army, consisting of its adult male citizens, who were trained for the purpose from childhood in a system often called the 'Upbringing' (*agoge*). Evaluating the role of violence in their training is a difficult task, because reliable evidence for Spartan social customs in the classical period (roughly 500–300 BCE) is extremely scanty. Classical Sparta produced no Herodotus, no Thucydides, indeed no writers at all. On the contrary, Thucydides himself complained in his history of the Peloponnesian War about Spartan secretiveness.[10] In the place of reliable information, ancient writers constructed an elaborate representation of the city as the Greek 'other', a state where most norms of society, as represented by Athens, were subverted or overturned. Philosophers, essayists, and biographers imagined a Sparta

---

[5] For a useful introduction, see J. Gélis, M. Laget and M.-F. Morel, *Entrer dans la vie: naissance et enfances dans la France traditionelle* (Paris: Gallimard, 1978).
[6] *Protagoras* 325D. See also *Laws* VII.808a, where Plato says boys need strict control because they are often difficult to deal with.
[7] Significantly, Xenophon (431–355 BCE) appears to find nothing exceptional in the fact that Cyrus, king of the Persians and Medes, was flogged at school: *Cyropaedia*, 1.iii.16–17.
[8] Golden, *Children and Childhood*, pp. 155 and 163.
[9] E.g. Pausianas, *Guide to Greece*, 3.16.10–11: on a variation of the whipping ritual at the temple of Artemis see below, p. 109.
[10] *Peloponnesian War* 5.68.2 and 5.74.3.

of utterly selfless citizen-warriors who shared most things, including their wives on occasion, in more or less complete harmony. In contrast to the raucous, individualistic, and litigious Athenians, Spartans were supposed to have been indoctrinated from early childhood in the communal ideals of their city – obedience, courage, and discipline. This process of self and external representation has been called the 'Spartan mirage', but it can also be termed the 'Spartan mirror', for each invented image of Sparta reflects the ideals, concerns, and prejudices of its originator in particular and the world around him in general.

Despite these difficulties, it is possible to identify certain genuine characteristics of the training system as it functioned at the time of Sparta's greatest influence. If childhood is defined juridically as the age before individuals enjoy full rights as citizens, then Spartan males had an extraordinarily long childhood, viewed from a modern perspective. Those male infants who had survived testing by the elders of their community and had not been tossed into the Kaiadas chasm underwent a lengthy process of acculturation beginning at age seven.[11] Paramount was the inculcation of a sense of group identity. Accordingly, they were enrolled into groups called 'companies' (*ilai*) and passed through three broadly-defined age grades: 'children' (*paides*), from seven to approximately fourteen years of age; 'youths' (*paidiskoi*), from fourteen to about twenty, when they first entered the army as subordinate soldiers; and 'young men' (*hebontes*), from age twenty to about 30, when they became full adult citizen soldiers (*Spartiatai*).

During the first two phases, the boys were subjected to a harsh training regimen. They were allowed only one piece of outer clothing, whatever the season or weather conditions; they were required to go without footwear and to make their beds by pulling up with their own hands the rushes growing along the banks of the Eurotas river, which flows just east of the city. Most notoriously, they were provided with inadequate sustenance so that they would be compelled to steal certain food items allowed by law to make up the difference. If caught, young Spartans were whipped for being careless thieves.[12]

The boys were under constant supervision, in preparation for life as Spartiate warriors. Within his 'company' each boy was to obey his leader, chosen from among the 'sharpest' of their number; during all his training, and indeed until he was 30, he was under the jurisdiction of a civic official called the 'child regulator' (*paidonomos*), who gathered the boys for exercise and punished infractions of the rules by means of his assistants, the 'whip bearers' (*mastigophoroi*); and every boy was always liable to chastisement by any adult at any time for failing to behave properly. There was a strict code of correct behaviour: each young Spartiate-in-training was expected to keep his hands in his robe while in public, to walk without talking, to keep his eyes always on the ground, and never to stare.[13]

While we know nothing of a young Spartan's daily activities, our sources do describe certain features that impressed themselves on the Greek imagination. In the fourth

---

[11] This was a local gorge into which criminals and prisoners were thrown. There is some dispute as to whether this was the place where unwanted infants were exposed.

[12] N. M. Kennell, *The Gymnasium of Virtue: Education and Culture in Ancient Sparta* (Chapel Hill: University of North Carolina Press, 1995), pp. 122–23; S. Hodkinson, *Property and Wealth in Classical Sparta* (London: Duckworth and the Classical Press of Wales, 2000), pp. 204–05.

[13] Girls were also trained outside the home to become good, healthy Spartan housewives through physical exercise: See P. Konstantinakos and M. Papapostoulou, 'Ancient Spartan "Agoge" and Socialization', unpublished paper given to the second annual conference of SSCiP (Society for the Study of Children in the Past), Stavanger, 28–30 Sept. 2008.

century BCE, Plato makes an allusion to 'hand-to-hand battles' among Spartan youths.[14] About 500 years later, under the Roman Empire, the Spartans held a regular fight between two teams of young Spartans on an artificial island surrounded by plane trees.[15] Kicking, biting, and eye gouging were commonplace. But we cannot know whether this battle at the Platanistas, as it was called, had any similarity to its distant ancestor mentioned by Plato, especially as the Spartans of the Roman period had systematically re-created a version of their traditional training system that conformed to contemporary expectations of Spartan uniqueness and ferocity.[16]

In fact, with one important exception, what we know of violence associated with classical Spartan training was between individuals and was confined to those in the eldest age grade, the *hebontes*. Bands of *hebontes* prowled the countryside by night armed with daggers and a licence to kill any agricultural slave (*heilotes*) they encountered, in a form of state terrorism aimed at removing potential sources of unrest, since the victims were often 'the bravest and the strongest' of the helots.[17] Xenophon, an Athenian writer of the fourth century BCE who is our most reliable source for Spartan institutions, states that the majority of *hebontes* were so jealous of the 300 who had been picked to join the elite fighting corps called the 'cavalrymen' (*hippeis*), even though they fought on foot, that they kept a keen watch over their every move in hopes of catching them acting improperly, with the two groups often coming to blows if they caught sight of each other.[18] Violence between individuals might go too far, however: at least one young Spartan was exiled for killing another boy with a sickle.[19]

Iron sickles had some importance in Spartan training, since they were awarded as prizes in contests at the sanctuary of the goddess Artemis Orthia. (See Figure 15). No specific details of these contests are known from the classical period, but their successors in the Roman age were competitions in singing, dancing, and hunting calls.[20] Since Spartans were renowned from their earliest history for choral singing and dancing, with the latter considered especially suitable for military training as it was conducive to marching in step, it is reasonable to assume that similar contests existed earlier as well.

The only violent contest known to have been held near the temple of Artemis was a *rite de passage* for *paidiskoi* 'graduating' into the *hebontes* grade. One team of youths tried to seize cheeses lying on top of the altar just east of the temple, while another fought them off with whips. Plato describes this ritual as 'certain snatchings amid many blows', while Xenophon explained it as showing young Spartans that 'after having suffered for a short time [they would] rejoice in being honoured for a long time'.[21] Such whipping rituals are known from other Greek cities, but the Spartan version was the most notable, especially in its much-changed Roman-era version.

Sparta's citizen training system had its roots in rituals and ceremonies that marked the transition from childhood to manhood, similar to those existing in other Greek cities and in many cultures around the world. The ritualised violence of the combats and the cheese-stealing contest can best be understood in this context. But the Spartans transformed their traditional practices into a coherent system designed to produce efficient citizen-warriors. In that, Sparta was a pioneer; not before the fourth century was

---

[14] *Laws*, 1.663b.
[15] Kennell, *Gymnasium of Virtue*, pp. 56–58.
[16] *Ibid.*, pp. 70–97.
[17] Plutarch, *Lycurgus* 28.4.
[18] *Constitution of the Lacedaemonians* 4.6.
[19] Xenophon, *Anabasis* 4.8.25.
[20] Kennell, *Gymnasium of Virtue*, pp. 48–69.
[21] *Laws* 1.663c; *Constitution of the Lacedaemonians* 2.9.

a similar institution founded elsewhere in Greece. Aristotle writing when the city's power had collapsed, commented that Spartans had been pre-eminent in war and athletics, not because they had trained their youth any differently from other Greeks, but that they had been the only ones to do so. When other cities started their own training, Sparta lost its position of leadership. His main criticism of the system, however, was directed against its reliance on brutality, which produced 'animalistic' men (*theriodeis*), who, like wolves and other beasts, were ill-equipped to face 'the noble risk'.[22]

Did this bias in the training of its citizens cause Sparta to be an unusually violent society, in Greek terms? The absence of information on Spartan daily life makes a definite answer impossible, but further evidence does not point that way. On the contrary, the violence the sources describe Spartans committing at home is on the whole state-organised. Most infamous was the clandestine massacre of 2,000 helots, who had provided the Spartans with the best service in war, on the grounds that such people would be more likely to lead a rebellion against their masters.[23] Despite such atrocities, Spartan failings in the eyes of other Greeks were not violence, but greed and duplicity. In fact, a high level of violence could be found in any Greek city, even Athens, whose internal history in the late fifth century was punctuated by periods of intense violence. Indeed, after enduring two *coups d'état*, defeat in the Peloponnesian War, and a vicious civil war in the thirteen years from 411 to 399 BCE, it is no wonder that some Athenian intellectuals looked to Sparta for a constitutional model.

· ·

While the Romans admired the toughness of a Spartan education, they made no attempt to imitate the city's child-rearing practices. The Roman Republic expected its citizens to serve in the army, but it also wanted them to be proficient administrators and judges, so placed an emphasis on a generalist education, which was continued in the changed conditions of the empire. The Romans also believed that the family was at the heart of the state and gave the head of the household, the *paterfamilias*, complete authority to oversee his children's upbringing. Nor was the childhood of the average Roman citizen particularly harsh, whatever powers of chastisement a father had in law. The Romans certainly treated their slaves extremely cruelly and arbitrarily, even to the extent of hiring private torturers to extort confessions. But their children seem to have been policed by words (*verba*) rather than blows (*verbera*). Corporal punishment, by dint of the fact it was used liberally on slaves, was considered dishonourable and servile. Nor could a Roman slave hit a young citizen.[24] Indeed, the children of Roman citizens may have suffered less violence at home than their Athenian predecessors. Parents who did step out of line and treat their children harshly suffered public condemnation. According to Seneca, when Tricho beat his son to death with a whip, the Roman people were so outraged that they nearly lynched him.[25]

The one place where the young Roman did encounter violence and where violence was condoned was in the classroom. Young citizens in the late Republic and early Empire were put to school about the age of seven. Once there, misbehaviour, inattention and ignorance brought a sharp reprimand, a reflection perhaps of the difficulties low status teachers had

---

[22] Aristotle, *Politics* 8.4.4 and 8.4.5. Aristotle believed that only men with a 'noble heart' would fight a good fight faced by a 'noble' danger (presumably one involving self-sacrifice).

[23] Thucydides 4.80.

[24] R. P. Saller, *Patriarchy, Property and Death in the Roman Family* (Cambridge: Cambridge University Press, 1994), ch. 6; R. P. Saller, 'Corporal Punishment, Authority and Obedience in the Roman Household', in B. Rawson (ed.), *Marriage, Divorce, and Children in Ancient Rome* (Oxford: Oxford University Press, 1996), ch. 7.

[25] Seneca, *De Clementia* 1.15.1.

in commanding respect from their social superiors. Most masters used a cane (*ferula*); some a taws (*scutica*); and boys could be struck on the hand or, more humiliatingly, on the bare buttocks, held down by their classmates in the so-called 'catomus' position, illustrated on a famous Pompeii fresco. Some teachers became a byword for brutality, notably Orbilius, to whose tender care the young Horace was entrusted.[26] Even in the classroom, however, the use of violence was not always condoned. Quintilian (*c.* 35–*c.* 100 CE), the most famous educationalist of antiquity, was a strident opponent:

> I disapprove of flogging, although it is the regular custom…, because in the first place it is a disgraceful form of punishment and fit only for slaves, and is in any case an insult, as you will realise if you imagine its infliction at a later age. Secondly if a boy is so insensible to instruction that reproof is useless, he will, like the worst type of slave, merely become hardened to blows.

Quintilian also felt that the fear and pain of corporal punishment led to unmanliness, thus breeding shame 'which unnerves and depresses the mind and leads the child to shun and loathe the light'. The right to beat also encouraged sadism. 'Children are helpless and easily victimised'. Therefore 'no one should be given unlimited power over them'.[27]

Whether the children of the Roman plebs (or from the beginning of the third century CE when citizenship came to be more broadly enjoyed, the offspring of the poor) were disciplined just as liberally in the home will probably never be known. But it is possible that in the late empire the position of all children deteriorated to some degree with the triumph of Christianity. The Christian church was heir to a Judaic tradition encapsulated in Solomon's *Book of Proverbs*, which stressed the value of corporal punishment for children of every class. 'He that spareth his rod hateth his son: but he that loveth him chasteneth him betimes'.[28] There is no suggestion in this and other similar verses in *Proverbs* that Solomon would have condoned arbitrary or unnecessary physical punishment, but it was certainly not deemed dishonourable or servile to suffer it. The Judaic-Christian emphasis on original sin probably only encouraged its use.

The change of heart among Rome's patrician class can be particularly seen in the writings of the church father, St Augustine of Hippo (350–430). Augustine himself does not seem to have been brought up harshly by his parents. He objected in his *Confessions* to the fact that they had not taken his side against a brutal teacher, but there is no hint in his autobiography that they had abused him in any way. Once converted to Christianity, however, he became a firm advocate of corporal punishment. The father who 'denies discipline is cruel… . When a father beats his son, he loves him'. In the eyes of God, there was no distinction between slave and free man. Everyone sins; everyone is in servitude; and children must be whipped to save them from damnation.[29]

Augustine's theological dominance over the medieval church is well known, so it is not surprising that his views on corporal punishment were the orthodoxy for the next 1,000 years. What effect this cultural shift had on day-to-day practice is more difficult to unravel. As in the pre-Christian era, there is very little information about how children were treated

---

[26] B. Rawson, *Children and Childhood in Roman Italy* (Oxford: Oxford University Press, 2003), pp. 175–77; G. Coulon, *L'Enfant en Gaule Romaine* (Paris: Éditions Errance, 2004), pp. 118–19; S. F, Bonner, *Education in Ancient Rome* (Berkeley: University of California Press, 1977), pp. 119–20, 141–42 and 144. Bonner (p. 144) suggests that harsh discipline in the classroom was also connected with the fact that the schools were private: parents would withhold the fees if their sons did not show signs of progress.

[27] Quintilian, *Institutiones oratoriae* 1.iii.13–17 (citations from Loeb edn, trans. H. E. Butler; London: William Heinemann, 1920).

[28] *Proverbs* xiii. 24.

[29] Augustine, *Confessions*, 1.9–10; Saller, *Patriarchy*, pp. 145–46.

in the home. The well-born were definitely physically chastised in the middle ages, in a way they were probably not in the Roman era. In 1449, even at the age of twenty, Elizabeth Paston, the daughter of Suffolk landowner, was frequently beaten by her mother, when she refused to marry the husband the latter had chosen.[30] But how representative such an incident was is anyone's guess. What we can say for certain is that corporal punishment was commonplace outside the family – in monasteries, convents and schools where young boys and some young girls were either permanently or on daily basis entrusted to the care of strangers.[31]

With the slow demise of the Roman empire in the west, schools of the Greek and Roman kind all but disappeared and learning retreated to the monasteries. In the twelfth century, however, they began to reappear, primarily offering the training in Latin grammar that was required by those destined for the secular clergy who wanted to attend the new universities.[32] Various types of evidence suggest that discipline was harsh, not least the fact that in England references to being beaten with a birch, the favoured instrument of punishment found their way into schoolboy songs:

> I would fain be a clerk,
> But yet it is strange work;
> The birchen twigs be so sharp
> It maketh me have a faint heart.[33]

So commonplace were beatings in English schools that the visual code for a grammar master in the fourteenth and fifteenth centuries was of a man seated on a chair holding a birch (sometimes with a book, sometimes without). (See Figure 16). Indeed, birching in England became a ritual. When degrees of Latin grammar were bestowed at the University of Cambridge, a boy was beaten as part of the ceremony.[34]

In that flagellation was an accepted penitential practice in the late middle ages, the readiness to use the birch on inattentive schoolboys was hardly surprising. But given the limited evidence for the use of corporal punishment in the home, we must be careful not to extrapolate too readily from a change in ideology to a change in practice with the coming of Christianity. Perhaps, especially for poor children, the gravest threat to their well-being came, as it always had, from accidents in and around the house. *Penitentials*, saints-lives, popular stories and legends and the records of coroners' courts (at the end of the middle ages), all tell of children, mostly toddlers, who come to a grim end by falling in the fire, scalding themselves with boiling water, or tipping into wells. In a world where animals and humans lived cheek to jowl, animals were a constant danger to the very young. Pigs were a particular threat 'wandering into houses through open doors, biting babies, or overturning their cradles'.[35] So too were other children who sometimes maimed and killed their friends

---

[30] N. Davis (ed.), *Paston Letters and Papers of the Fifteenth Century*, 3 vols (Oxford: Oxford University Press for the Early English Text Society, 2004–05), ii. 32.

[31] Monks and nuns may well have spared the well-born. St Eadberga, daughter of Edward the Confessor, was beaten by a nun, but the latter later apologised once she discovered the girl's royal blood: S. Crawford, *Childhood in Anglo-Saxon England* (Stroud: Sutton Publishing Ltd., 1999), p. 151.

[32] N. Orme, *Medieval Schools: From Roman Britain to Renaissance England* (London: Yale University Press, 2006). On the foundation and purpose of the first universities, see H. Ridder-Symoens (ed.), *A History of the University in Europe, vol. 1. Universities in the Middle Ages* (Cambridge: Cambridge University Press, 1992), chs 1 and 2.

[33] Beginning of a song recorded in the commonplace book of the London merchant Richard Hill in the early sixteenth century, with the refrain: 'Hay, hay, by this day, / What availeth it me though I say nay?' Discussed in Orme, *Medieval Children*, pp. 154–55.

[34] N. Orme, 'Violence in Medieval English Schools', paper given to the Oxford History of Childhood Workshop, 30 Oct. 2003.

[35] Orme, *Medieval Children*, ch. 3 (quotation from p. 99).

or siblings by mistake, while playing with weapons. From our modern perspective, many of these accidents to children bespeak parental neglect. The infant Lucy Senenok died on Christmas Day 1345 when she fell from her cradle into the fire. The fact that she had been left in the care of her three-year-old sister, while her parents went to church, and that the sister had inevitably wandered off to play, suggests to us that the parents had not got their priorities right.[36] But the demands of religion and work must have often meant that medieval parents could not keep as close a check on young children as 'best practice' demands today. The realities of medieval life meant that they balanced their responsibilities differently.

Yet if the medieval world drew the boundaries in a different manner from us, it never countenanced gratuitous neglect or cruelty out of spite or for personal gain, as is clear from literary sources that recount the comeuppance awaiting wicked step-wives and jealous mother-in-laws who kill or maltreat the young. The first ever children's tale printed in English, *The Friar and the Boy*, tells of a step-mother who tries to have her young step-son put into service and leaves him undernourished. He gets his own back when, in return for an act of charity, he is given a charm which makes her fart in public.[37] It is clear, too, that children knew when contemporary boundaries were being over-stepped, as a letter penned by a schoolboy to the margin of a book at the turn of the sixteenth century plainly reveals.

> Master Mullysworth, I would pray and beseech you that you would be my good master; for such matters as I learn that you would show it to me by fair means and punish me reasonably. Now you punish me overmuch, master, and, please you, I cannot abide this punishment. Here at first time, you did not punish me not half so much; then I did learn more by your fair means than I do now.[38]

More significantly, it needs to be realised that medieval culture was not monolithic or unchanging. Although Augustine's was the dominant voice or the one most heeded in the classroom, there were countervailing ones in the later middle ages as a new understanding of Christianity developed. Quintilian's perspicacity was shared by several late medieval clerics, even if few would have ever read his classical account of oratory before the Renaissance, and their point of departure lay in a new understanding of Christianity.

Corporal Punishment and the Two Christianities

Henrietta Leyser

> Every age and degree of understanding should have its proper measure of discipline. With regard to boys and adolescents, therefore, or those who cannot understand the seriousness of the penalty of excommunication, whenever such as these are delinquent, let them be subjected to terms by harsh beatings, that they may be cured.[39]

---

[36] H. Cunningham, *The Invention of Childhood* (London: BBC Books 2006), pp. 39–46; B. A. Hanawalt, 'Childrearing among the Lower Classes of Late Medieval England', *Journal of Interdisciplinary History*, viii (1977), 1–22, at pp. 16–17.
[37] Orme, *Medieval Children*, pp. 293–94.
[38] *Ibid.*, p. 338. The boy was in the care of a fellow of Magdalen College, Oxford, and probably a pupil at Magdalen College School, founded in 1480. The quotation is a modern English version of the original.
[39] Rule of St Benedict, c. 30, trans. L. J. Boyle, *St Benedict's Rule for Monasteries* (Collegeville.: St John's Abbey Press, 1948).

St Benedict's provision for the correction of children would not in his own day or indeed for many centuries to come, have caused the raising of a single eyebrow. Benedict (*c.* 480–*c.* 547) had set up his monastery as a 'school for the Lord's service' in which 'a certain strictness' was required both for 'the amendment of vice' and for 'the preservation of charity'.[40] Actual children needed beating, but so too might their recalcitrant elders. All, after all, were children of God so there would be times when the abbot would need to show to his monks 'the stern countenance of a master' and when he must be prepared to discipline them accordingly 'with stripes and other bodily punishments knowing that it is written "the fool is not corrected with words," and again "Beat your son with the rod and you will deliver his soul from death."'[41]

Even if St Benedict's words have a familiar ring – for it is only comparatively recently that the adage 'Spare the Rod and Spoil the Child' has fallen into disrepute – we should none the less pause to consider the ways in which Christianity as a new faith had added complexity to educational debates. As a religion of the book it placed a high value on the acquisition of literacy in ways which did nothing to impress the new barbarian rulers of St Benedict's day since it apparently involved the strap. 'Letters', said the Ostrogoths, 'are far removed from manliness... the man who is to show daring and be great in renown ought to be free from the timidity which teachers inspire and take his training in arms'.[42] If Prudentius (348–post 405 CE) is to be believed pagan hostility to Christian teaching had even on occasion led to a teacher's murder. The teacher, so Prudentius reported, 'was skilled in putting every word in short signs and following speech quickly with swift pricks on the wax'. His refusal to join pagan worship provoked action against him and provided his pupils for a pretext for revenge. 'Make the children a present of the man who used to flog them', said the teacher's persecutor.

> So he is stripped of his garments and his hands are tied behind his back and all the band are there, armed with their sharp styles. All the burning resentment they each vent now..... some throw their brittle tablets and break them against his face....others again launch at him the sharp iron pricks, the end with which by scratching strokes the wax is written upon, and the end with which the letters that have been cut are rubbed out...With the one the confessor of Christ is stabbed, with the other he is cut; the one end enters the soft flesh, the other splits the skin. Two hundred hands together have pierced him all over his body, and from all these wounds at once the blood is dripping.[43]

Prudentius's martyred school-teacher leads on the one hand back to Golgotha, to the jeering crowd who beat Christ about the head with a stick and reviled him (Mark 15.9); on the other, it points us forward to late medieval depictions of Christ as the Man of Sorrows, his body peppered with wounds. The route between these two is complex and needs exploring.

Our guide here is Mary Carruthers. Carruthers has illuminated the part played by violence in medieval school-teaching, in particular its mnemonic use, evident in Carruthers' words:

---

[40] *Ibid.*, Prologue.
[41] *Ibid.*, c. 2.
[42] Procopius, *Works English and Greek*, vol. 3, trans. H. E. Dewing (Cambridge: Harvard University Press, 1953), p. 19, quoted by P. Wormald, 'The Uses of Literacy in Anglo-Saxon England and its Neighbours', *Transactions of the Royal Historical Society*, 5th series: 27 (1977), 95–114, at p. 98.
[43] See Prudentius, *On the Crowns of Martyrs*, 9.5–60, trans. H. J. Thompson, *Prudentius* (Cambridge: Harvard University Press, 1953) vol. II, p. 225. Reproduced in Michael Maas, *Readings in Late Antiquity: A Sourcebook* (London and New York: Routledge, 2000), p. 56.

in the actual, pervasive brutality of ancient and medieval elementary pedagogy, precisely the time in a child's life at which the most important memory-work was done. One can speak of this violence as a neurosis of medieval pedagogy: perhaps it is, but many medieval people clearly saw it as necessary to imprint memories upon the brain, those all important, rote-retained 'habits' of their culture.[44]

The roots of this belief (as Carruthers reminds us) are linked to the fact that at all stages writing demanded considerable physical effort: in the first place the preparation of the vellum required stretching, scraping, puncturing; thereafter the writer's stylus inflicted further 'wounds'. Even now the ways in which knowledge can be stored in the brain rely on quite violent metaphors: we 'drum' essential information into students' heads; we expect certain levels of knowledge to be 'embedded' at the same time as being happy to 'root out' erroneous ideas. Such metaphors have long histories, stretching back to Plato and to Cicero and we can surmise that they played their part in the 'stern and harsh' teaching of Prudentius's school-teacher. But what gave them new force and particular poignancy in the history of western culture is their marriage with Christian imagery.

The opening chapter of the Gospel of St John has much here to answer for. The image of Christ as Word Incarnate exercised a powerful grip on the imagination of medieval Christians. Witness the exposition of Pierre Bersuire (*c.* 1289–1362):

> Christ is a sort of book written into the skin of a virgin... That book was spoken of in the deposition of the Father, written in the conception of the mother, exposited in the clarification of the nativity, corrected in the passion, erased in the flagellation, punctuated in the imprint of the wounds, adorned in the crucifixion, illuminated in the outpourings of blood, bound in the resurrection, and examined in the ascension.[45]

Allied with this is the notion that the heart of each Christian is also a book – hence the prayer of Gertrude of Helfta: 'Most merciful Lord, write your wounds in my heart with your precious blood, that I may read in them your suffering and your love alike'.[46]

Such ideas give the Christian a choice: should he offer up his own body for martyrdom or should he develop an empathetic awareness of Christ's own suffering? Broadly speaking, the shift from the one form of devotion to the other defines the difference between the spirituality of the early and the later middle ages, between the worlds of the Old and New Testament. The story of St Francis of Assisi (1183–1226), one of the foremost proponents of the new Christocentric piety is instructive here. His conversion had so horrified his father that 'he badgered, beat and bound him'; his mother on the other hand 'spoke to her son in gentle words'.[47] Some years later, Francis 'burned with the desire for holy martyrdom' but try as he might – and he made several journeys with this aim in mind – 'the Lord did not fulfil his desire, reserving for him the prerogative of a unique grace'.[48] The 'unique grace' was of course the stigmata –in other words, a radically new form of wounding.

---

[44] M. Carruthers, 'Reading with Attitude, Remembering the Book', in D. W. Frese and K. O'Brien O'Keeffe (eds) *The Book and the Body* (Indiana: University of Notre Dame Press, 1997), p. 33.

[45] P. Bersuire, *Repertorium Morale,* quoted by J. Gellrich, *The Idea of the Book in the Middle Ages: Language Theory, Mythology and Fiction* (Ithaca: Cornell University Press, 1985), p. 17.

[46] Gertrude of Helfta, *The Herald of God's Loving Kindness,* trans. A. Barratt (Kalamazoo: Cistercian Publications, 1991), p. 109.

[47] Thomas of Celano, *The Life of St Francis,* in vol. I of *Francis of Assisi: The Early Documents,* (eds) R. J. Armstrong, J. A. W. Hellmann and W. J. Short (New York, London and Manila: New City Press, 1999), p. 192.

[48] *Ibid.,* p. 231.

St Francis is not the only saint of the middle ages to have got on badly with his father. The same is true also of St Anselm of Canterbury (1033–1109). Both saints develop concepts of authority that use maternal imagery; their early experiences are of course likely to have been only part of the story. Both accept that men can 'mother'; for Anselm the supreme mother is Christ himself – 'Jesus, good Lord, are you not also a mother? Are you not that mother who, like a hen, collects her chickens under her wing?'[49] It follows from this that those in authority do not *control by fear*, indeed should not be fearsome, an idea that was to have much currency in the twelfth century particularly among the Cistercians:

> Here is a point for the ear of those superiors who wish always to inspire fear in their communities and rarely promote their welfare. 'Learn you who rule the earth [Ps. 2:10]. Learn that you must be mothers to those in your care, not masters; make an effort to arouse the response of love, not that of fear......Be gentle, avoid harshness, do not resort to blows, expose your breasts: let your bosoms expand with milk, not swell with passion....'.[50]

Fine rhetoric indeed. But in practice did such ideas have any influence as far as children were concerned? Just possibly they did; once again we must turn to Anselm, to the conversation he once had with an abbot about the boys in his cloister:

> [The abbot asked] ' What... is to be done with them? They are incorrigible ruffians. We never give over beating them day and night, and they only get worse and worse'. Anselm replied with astonishment: 'You never give over beating them? And what are they like when they grow up?' 'Stupid brutes' [said the abbot]. To which Anselm retorted, 'You have spent your energies in rearing them to no purpose; ...in God's name, I would have you tell me why you are so incensed against them. Are they not flesh and blood like you?... Now consider this. You wish to form them in good habits by blows and chastisement alone. Have you ever seen a goldsmith form his leaves of gold or silver into a beautiful figure by blows alone? I think not.... the weak soul which is still inexperienced in the service of God, needs milk – gentleness from others, kindness, compassion, cheerful encouragement [and] loving forbearance.[51]

The abbot in question, we are assured, 'promised emendment in the future'. How many others ever heard or heeded Anselm's teaching is quite another matter.

• •

From the beginning of the sixteenth century the information that has survived about child-rearing in Europe grows steadily more detailed. All over the continent, the next century and a half witnessed a great expansion in the number of schools and universities. Luther and the Protestant reformers wanted the laity as well as the clergy to be literate, so that ordinary people could read the Bible at home, and encouraged the foundation of elementary schools. Their Catholic opponents, who equally approved of the laity studying their catechism and appropriate devotional works, slowly followed suit. At the same time the explosion in the number of grammar schools and universities was fuelled by the ever growing demand for educated lawyers, administrators and bureaucrats, as Europe grew steadily wealthier and the power and reach of the state expanded to meet the cost of warfare in the age of

---

[49] *The Prayers and Meditations of St Anselm with the Proslogion,* trans. B. Ward (Harmondsworth: Penguin Books, 1973), p. 380.
[50] St. Bernard, Sermon 23 on the *Song of Songs,* quoted in C. W. Bynum, *Jesus as Mother: Studies in the Spirituality of the High Middle Ages* (Berkeley: University of California Press, 1982), p. 118.
[51] *The Life of St Anselm, Archbishop of Canterbury by Eadmer,* ed. R. W. Southern (Oxford: Oxford University Press, 1972), pp. 37–39.

gunpowder. Encouraged, too, by the belief of humanist educationalists, such as Erasmus, that nobility and gentility were inseparable from a knowledge of classical languages and literature, the lay elites no longer felt that only their sons destined for the church needed an institutionalised education.[52] The result, in a period which saw much more careful keeping of archives, was the inevitable survival of much more detailed information about schools and schooling: statutes, regulations, accounts, class registers, timetables, examinations, even record cards. And the pool of information becomes greater again from the beginning of the eighteenth century, as the state began to take an interest in elementary education (seeing its practical benefits for creating sober hard working subject-citizens) and many more schools for the poor were founded.[53]

The era of the Reformation and the Counter-Reformation, moreover, brought a novel interest in child-rearing *per se*. How parents brought up their children became crucially important, as the new confessional churches sought to ensure that the young became solid adherents of the true faith and lived a life pleasing to God. In the middle ages, the laity had been encouraged to express their Christian allegiance through continual and often colourful acts of formal piety, such as going on pilgrimages and mortification of flesh. From the second half of the sixteenth century, both Protestants and Catholics, if the latter did not totally disown traditional religiosity, placed a new emphasis on leading a Christ-like life, which entailed strict obedience to the ten commandments.[54] The upshot in this case was an ever-growing wave of childcare manuals in which parents were instructed how to raise their young, and a new literary genre – the spiritual and not-so spiritual diary and autobiography – in which men and women reflected on their moral progress and their success in raising godly offspring.[55] By the eighteenth century the fascination with children had grown to such an extent that they were visible everywhere – in court records, art, literature and so on – and not just on the periphery or in passive roles. Indeed, in a new period of economic growth, well-to-do children became visible for the first time as serious consumers, even to the extent of having their own literature.[56]

---

[52] The literature on the educational 'revolution' of the sixteenth and the first part of the seventeenth centuries is huge. For changing ideas about the value of education, see E. Garin, *L'Education de l'homme moderne 1400–1600*, French trans. (Paris: Fayard, 1968). For the expansion of educational provision in England and France in particular, see L. Stone, 'The Educational Revolution in England', *Past and Present* 28:1 (1964), 41–80; R. Chartier, D. Julia and M.-M. Compère, *L'Education en France du XVIe au XVIII siècle* (Paris: SEDES, 1976).

[53] The classic case is Prussia where there would be 11,000 village schoolteachers by 1800. The Prussian state, though, invested little money in the expansion of elementary education and left the task to local landowners and the church: see W. Neugebauer, *Absolutistischer Staat und Schulwirklichkeit in Brandenburg-Preussen* (Berlin: Walter de Gruyter, 1985).

[54] A good study of the change from the old to the new Christianity is J. Bossy, *Christianity in the West 1400–1700* (Oxford: Oxford University Press, 1985). A particularly sympathetic portrayal of late medieval religion is E. Duffy, *The Stripping of the Altars. Traditional Religion in England 1400–1580* (London: Yale University Press, 1992).

[55] For a good discussion of the growth of this literature in two parts of Europe, see A. Chevalier and C. Dornier (eds), *Le Récit d'enfance et ses modèles* (Caen: Presse Universitaire de Caen, 2003); R. Dekker, *Childhood, Memory and Autobiography in Holland from the Golden Age to Romanticism* (London: Macmillan, 1999). Before 1800, on the other hand, only a small number of Europeans wrote at length about their own childhood, and hardly any children are known to have kept a diary. Dekker has only discovered one in Holland, written by a ten-year-old in the late eighteenth century: see R. Dekker and A. Baggerman, 'Sensibilité et éducation d'un enfant à l'époque batave. Le journal intime de Otto van Eck', *Annales Historiques de la Révolution Française*, 326 (2001), 129–39, and A. Baggeman and R. Dekker, *Child of the Enlightenment. Revolutionary Europe Reflected in a Boyhood Diary* (Leiden: Brill, 2009), esp. ch. 2.

[56] This literature is now being extensively studied: *e.g.*, A. O'Malley, *The Making of the Modern Child: Children's Literature and Childhood in the Late Eighteenth Century* (London: Routledge, 2003). For the most famous account of children as consumers, see J. H. Plumb, 'The New World of Children in Eighteenth-Century England',

Yet if children were much more visible in the records in the early modern period, there is little reason to believe at first glance that their upbringing became any less harsh from out modern point of view. Although the state increasingly claimed a monopoly of force, and interpersonal violence seems to have been on the decline by the end of the seventeenth century, the forces of law and order continued to treat those that stepped out of line with great brutality. The eighteenth century was the age of Tyburn as well as the age of Enlightenment.[57] According to the much read English child-rearing manual of the first half of the seventeenth century written by the aptly named Dod and Cleaver, children had to have their stubbornness beaten out of them and good sense beaten in. Childcare manuals from the late Stuart age advocated a less harsh approach but they still supported for the most part corporal punishment. Children who failed to live up to expectations throughout the period could expect to be severely chastised. It was only in the second half of the eighteenth century that a growing body of European writers about child-rearing began to question the use of the rod.[58]

Many schoolmasters around the continent took the childcare pundits at their word and hit children not just for disobedience or inattention but for simply failing to learn. (See Figure 17). In the sixteenth century, out of all the city's grammar schools, the Paris collège de Montaigu was renowned for its austerity and discipline. This, though, according to the Benedictine Jacques de Breuil, in his 1612 guidebook of Parisian sites, only enhanced its reputation:

> [Here] the whip has never been spared on the slothful, uncommitted and wanton. And this has been so much the case that whenever a Parisian father or mother felt sorely tried by their vicious and incorrigible children, they were advised to send them to Montaigu in order that they be bent and softened beneath the whip of humility (*dessoubs la verge d'humilité*) and led back to the path of virtue from which they had been led away by bad company and too much liberty.[59]

Seventeenth-century schoolmasters equally forged a reputation as disciplinarians. The learned Dr Busby, headmaster of Westminster School from 1638–95, became a byword for his use of the birch: even in the early nineteenth century, his name was invoked by one of Nelson's childhood friends recalling the beatings they had endured in their Norfolk grammar school from the lash of 'Classic Jones'.[60] The birch, moreover, was used on adolescents not just young children. In England, where boys often went up to university in their early teens, they were frequently flogged by their tutors. At Oxford, under the 1638 Laudian statutes, the punishment could be inflicted on anyone under eighteen. At Cambridge, the victims included the young John Milton.[61]

Past and Present, 67:1 (1975), 64–93.

[57] See generally, M. Foucault, *Surveiller et punir. Naissance de la prison* (Paris: Gallimard, 1975). The book opens with the appalling treatment meted out to Damiens after he failed in his attempt to assassinate Louis XV of France in 1757. On interpersonal violence, see L. Stone, 'Interpersonal Violence in English Society 1300–1980', *Past and Present*, 101:1 (1983), 22–33.

[58] J. Dod and R. Cleaver, *A Godlie Forme of Householde Government…* (London: T. C. for T., 1614) [amended version of a text first published by Roger Carr in 1600]; also William Gouge, *Of Domesticall Duties, Eight Treatises…* 3rd edn (London: G. Miller for E. Brester, 1634). A less harsh punitive approach to child-rearing began to be promoted from 1673 with the appearance of Richard Allestree's, *The Lady's Calling*: A. Fletcher, *Growing Up in England. The Experience of Childhood 1600–1914* (London: Yale University Press, 2008), pp. 38–39. For eighteenth-century opposition to corporal punishment, see below, pp. 123–27 and 129–32.

[59] Jacques de Breuil, *Le théâtre des antiquitéz de Paris* (Paris: Pierre Chevalier, 1612), p. 676.

[60] R. Knight, *The Pursuit of Victory. The Life and Achievements of Horatio Nelson* (London: Allen Lane, 2005), p. 9. For the heavy use of corporal punishment generally in English schools, see K. Thomas, *Rule and Misrule in the Schools of Early Modern England* (Stenton Lecture, 1975; Reading: University of Reading, 1976), pp. 9–11.

[61] C. H. Firth, 'The Seventeenth-Century Undergraduate', *The Oriel Record* (1915–16), 285–86. In 1520 the

Well-to-do parents could be just as quick to espouse a tough regime and corporal punishment to harden and control their children. If the French nobility took their cue from their royal betters then young gentlemen across the Channel suffered a miserable time. Henri IV (b. 1552; king 1580–1610), initially heir to the kingdom of Navarre, was brought up to the age of seven in the mountains of Béarn: to ensure he became a proficient warrior, he was deliberately made to endure heat and cold, kept on a simple diet and frequently beaten. On the orders of his mother, 'he was whipped for a triviality and whipped vigorously. This continued during his adolescence, even … after he had begun his military apprenticeship'.[62] The trials and tribulations of Henri's son, Louis XIII (r. 1610–42), are known in peculiar detail thanks to a diary kept by his doctor, Jean Héroard. The young Louis was not deliberately toughened up but he was frequently beaten from the time he was weaned. In 1607, aged five to six he was whipped seven times in the course of the year by his female attendants and threatened with a whipping on a further three occasions.[63] His crimes included lying to his governess, not behaving properly at mass, and failing to take his hat off when a gentleman paid him a visit. In contrast, Louis XIV (b. 1638; r. 1642–1715), an apparently better behaved child, was whipped less often, and the Sun-King's son, the Grand Dauphin, not at all. There again, he was still struck repeatedly on the hand with a ruler for not learning his lessons.[64] It is evident, too, that cruel treatment was meted out to girls as well as boys. The ill-fated Lady Jane Grey (executed in 1553) was expected to be perfection in all things. If not she was continually taunted and threatened by her parents, who reinforced their displeasure 'with pinches, nippes and bobs, and some ways which I will not name for the honour I bear them, so without measure misordered, that I think myself in hell'. None the less, she considered it a great benefit that God had sent her 'so sharp and severe parents'.[65]

Admittedly, some affluent parents found it difficult to chastise their children. Others were content to deprive them of food or make them write out sermons that they failed to remember. But there can have been few who followed the early Tudor statesman, Sir Thomas More (1478–1535), in administering token punishments. Although More did whip his three children sometimes, he usually deployed a peacock's feather. 'Even this I wielded hesitantly and gently so that sorry welts might not disfigure your tender seats'.[66] Not that it should be thought that the well-to-do punished their children so immoderately in the early modern period that they caused them lasting physical harm. Beating a child to death in upper-class circles was extremely uncommon. This was an era in which the nobility were reared on the maxims of Castigilione's *Il Cortegiano* and a novel premium came to be placed on controlling one's temper and emotions. The most famous father to beat his son to death by mistake was the Russian Tzar, Peter the Great, who had only superficially imbibed the new European ethic.[67]

---

president of Magdalen College, Oxford, had been investigated by the college's visitor for using the birch too readily: L. W. B. Brockliss (ed.), *Magdalen College Oxford: A History* (Oxford: Magdalen College, 2008), p. 94.
[62] D. Lopez, 'L'Education du prince au XVIIe siècle: Regards sur l'enfance', in A. Defrance, D. Lopez and F. Ruggiu, *Regards sur l'enfance au XVIIe siècle: actes du colloque du centre de recherches sur le XVIIe siècle européen (1600–1700); Université Michel de Montaigne – Bordeaux III, 24–25 novembre* 2005 (Tübingen: Narr, 2007), pp. 70 and 92.
[63] *Journal de Jean Héroard sur l'enfance et la jeunesse de Louis XIII (1601–1628)*, ed. E. Soulié and E. de Barthélemy (Paris: Firmin Didot, 1868), pp. 239–301, *passim*.
[64] Lopez, 'L'Education', pp. 93–97.
[65] M. J. Tucker, 'The Child as Beginning and End: Fifteenth- and Sixteenth-Century English Childhood', in Lloyd deMause (ed.), *The History of Childhood* (New York: Psychohistory Press, 1974), pp. 247–48.
[66] Fletcher, *Growing up in England*, pp. 130–31; Cunningham, *Invention of Childhood*, p. 67; Tucker, 'The Child', pp. 248–49.
[67] N. Elias, *The Court Society*, trans. E. Jephcott (Oxford: Blackwell, 1983). For Castiglione and his popularity, see P. Burke, *The Fortunes of the Courtier: The European Reception of Castiglione's Cortegiano* (Cambridge: Polity Press, 1995).

Immoderate beaters, it can be suspected, were more common among the lower orders who were likely to come into contact with their offspring when tired, angry or under the influence of drink. This was certainly the view propounded in eighteenth-century literature of peasant patriarchs. The novelist Nicolas-Edme Rétif de la Bretonne (1734–1806) was brought up on a Burgundian farm. If the account of his paternal grandfather in *La Vie de mon Père* (1779) is any guide, the fathers of the poor at the turn of the eighteenth century were martinets using the rod pointedly to emphasise their authority over the most dutiful sons.[68] Admittedly, such texts were written for a well-to-do readership and may well have been intended to strengthen class prejudice rather than portray reality. None the less, there were enough real life 'horror' stories of neglectful and abusive parents to suggest that the portrait was not a literary fiction. And they were not all of abusive fathers. In London in 1734 a gin addict called Judith Dufour, who later claimed to have been out of her mind, took her two-year-old child into a field, stripped her naked and strangled her. She then sold the clothes for 1s 4d and spent the money on gin.[69]

Most children, however, even poor children, were unlikely to be permanently starved, maimed or killed by their families. The fact that many children experienced the death of one or both of their parents before they were grown up and frequently found themselves living with step-relatives does not seem to have generally led to unconventional ill-treatment. The evil step-mother certainly became a literary trope from the late seventeenth century with the emergence of the fairy tale as a new and popular literary genre, principally pioneered by the French writer, Charles Perrault (1628–1703), in his *Contes* of 1697. But though their narratives were drawn in some form from popular tales that had been circulating for centuries, it would be dangerous to assume that stories such as *Cinderella* reflected social reality.[70] Rather, the greatest danger to the well-being of all children in the early modern period was almost certainly when they were outside the care of their kin.

On the European continent throughout the early modern period, it was a commonplace for a large proportion of all infants born in towns to be put out to nurse in the countryside. For the next two years they were seldom or never seen by their parents. Most did not return, the victims of semi-starvation, neglect and disease. For children put out to nurse from a foundling hospital, transportation to the country was a virtual death sentence.[71] Children placed in the care of a surrogate father to learn a business or trade, or even serve at court, also sometimes found themselves at risk from malnutrition and severe punishments. Sir William Carew in the early 1520s took his son out of St Paul's school, London, and entrusted him to a friend at the French court, who promised to train him up as a page. But the friend once over the Channel reneged on the deal and made him his stable lad.[72] Again orphans or

---

[68] N.-E. Rétif de la Bretonne, *La Vie de mon père*, reprint edn (New York: George Olms Verlag, 1979), esp. pp. 28–30.

[69] http://www.oldbaileyonline.org/browse.jsp?id=t17340227–32–off1468&div=t17340227–32#highlight (accessed 14 Jul. 2009).

[70] E. Arnoul, 'Rôle et représentation de la belle-mère: Les enfants du premier lit face au remarriage du père', in in Defrance, Lopez and Ruggiu, *Regards sur l'enfance*, pp. 359–72. *Cinderella* was first put into print by Giambattista Basile in 1634 and exists in different forms around the world: the common theme, however, is of the ill-treated servant girl, not of a girl demeaned by her step-relations. For early views of the wicked step-mother, already a trope in Ancient Rome, see S. Dixon, *The Roman Mothers* (London: Croom Helm, 1988), pp. 155–59.

[71] The practice was particularly common in France: see T. G. H. Drake, 'The Wet-Nurse in France in the Eighteenth Century', *Bulletin of the History of Medicine*, 8 (1940), 934–48; and for a detailed study, M. Garden, *Lyons et les Lyonnais au XVIIIe siècle*, edn (Paris: Flammarion, 1975), pp. 59–84. Even children given to nurses who were closely supervised could suffer. The infant James VI of Scotland had a tipsy nurse. She fed him alcoholic milk which left him so weak he could not walk till he was six. See also Ch. 2, pp. 79–80.

[72] Orme, *Children*, pp. 316–17.

destitute children were the most likely to suffer abuse. Witness the graphic account of the maltreatment of an apprentice in George Crabbe's tale of the sadistic master, Peter Grimes, in his 1810 poem, *The Borough*:

> Pinn'd, beaten, cold, pinch'd, threatened, and abused –
> His efforts punish'd and his food refused, –
> Awake tormented, – soon aroused from sleep, –
> Struck if he wept, and yet compell'd to weep,
> The trembling boy dropp'd down and strove to pray,
> Received a blow, and trembling turn'd away,
> Or sobb'd and hid his piteous face; – while he,
> The savage master, grinn'd in horrid glee:
> He'd now the power he ever loved to show,
> A feeling being subject to his blow.[73]

And there were real life incarnations of Peter Grimes in eighteenth-century London. In the mid-eighteenth century Elizabeth Brownrigg, a midwife, received orphan girls as apprentices. Aided by her husband and son, the girls were whipped, starved, hung from hooks, cut and beaten. Despite protests from a girl who escaped, no action was taken by the London authorities, until a fourteen-year-old girl, Mary Clifford, died in their care. All three were tried at the Old Bailey, but the two men got off and only Brownrigg was hanged – in September 1767.[74] (See Figure 18).

The inadequacy of the magistrates' initial response was hardly surprising. Although cruelty to children technically fell within their province, there was a general belief that it was not their concern to pry too deeply into the domestic sphere. Only when the violence led to death was there likely to be an investigation. A study of 8,000 court protocols from one German village, Neckarhausen, between 1730 and 1870, revealed that no cases of child molestation by parents were brought to official attention. Neighbours did sometimes complain about the way parents were disciplining their children but there were no accusations of assault.[75]

Yet the fact that in the early modern period more and more children spent large parts of their lives outside the family home as servants and apprentices or simply in school (as day pupils or boarders) should not lead to the conclusion that growing up became increasingly hazardous as time wore on. There is undoubtedly much more evidence of physical abuse in the eighteenth century than hitherto, but this simply reflects the much greater wealth of material of all kinds that survives after 1700. Furthermore, it would be wrong to believe from the relative silence of judicial records that virtually any form of abuse was permitted in this era short of murder. In fact, there is good reason to believe that ordinary people as well as the cultivated had a clear idea of what was an acceptable and unacceptable use of violence in disciplining children inside and outside the home and had time honoured ways of expressing disapproval.[76] More importantly, the boundary between the acceptable and

---

[73] George Crabbe, *The Borough* (1810), Letter XXII, lines 79–89. For more on the harsh life of some apprentices, see Ch. 4, pp. 171–77.

[74] http://www.oldbaileyonline.org/browse.jsp?id=t17670909–1–off48&div=t17670909–1#highlight (accessed 14 Jul. 2009).

[75] D. Sabean, *Power in the Blood: Popular Culture and Village Discourse in Early Modern Germany* (Cambridge: Cambridge University Press, 1984), p. 201. Before the era of child welfare officers, complaints from neighbours was the only way the authorities were likely to ever learn about cases of unacceptable cruelty to children. Most instances of brutality to children lay beneath the official gaze: cf. the comments in B. Capp. *When Gossips Meet: Women, Family and Neighbourhood in Early Modern England* (Oxford: Oxford University Press, 2003), pp. 10 and 43.

[76] As in the middle ages, this was still a period where communities largely policed themselves and had

unacceptable seems to have changed across the period. In the sixteenth and early seventeenth centuries the best method of maintaining discipline in the classroom was the subject of serious discussion by those who supported an extension in educational provision. Their ruminations, which continued to be echoed in educational treatises in the eighteenth century, led them to define very carefully when corporal punishment could be used and how it was to be administered.[77] Their views were incorporated into the statutes and regulations of the new schools and were soon internalised by pupils and parents. In time, it can be assumed, they came to inform general assumptions about disciplining children. As a result, if violence and neglect were not eschewed in child-rearing in the period, their use was considerably refined.

Abusive Parenting: The Case of Jacques-Louis Ménétra

Laurence Brockliss

Jacques-Louis Ménétra was born in Paris on 13 July 1738 in the parish of Saint-Germain-L'Auxerrois, the only son of a master glazier. He was nursed at home but his mother died when he was two and he was then shipped off to his grandmother's. There he stayed until he was eleven when his father demanded him back in order not to have to pay any longer for his board and lodging and to put him to work. Throughout his teenage years he worked as his father's apprentice and in due course became a master glazier in his own right. He then embarked on the customary *tour de France* and spent several years perfecting his craft by working as a journeyman in different towns around the country. When he finally returned to Paris, he temporarily worked for another of the capital's master glaziers, one Vilmont, then married and set up his own business. In due course, Ménétra's own son followed him into the trade, although with the outbreak of the French Revolutionary Wars, he abandoned the profession for a life in the army. Ménétra himself continued to work as a master glazier until the mid-1790s when he sold the business and went to live with one of his daughters and her bureaucrat husband. He eventually died in 1812.

We know about Ménétra's personal history in considerable detail because he left a manuscript autobiography. This is a unique document because it is the only first person account of the life of an eighteenth-century French artisan hitherto discovered.[78] For the historian of childhood, the autobiography is doubly precious because the first half of the text, apparently written in Ménétra's mid-twenties, is devoted to his life before he married. What this reveals about the years he spent as his father's apprentice was that he was the constant victim of physical abuse. Ménétra's father was a bad-tempered

---

their own mechanisms for expressing disapproval, even if the state was becoming more intrusive: see Ch. 5, pp. 231–33. For one of the best accounts of community policing in the eighteenth century (though one that says little about disciplining children), see D. Garrioch, *Neighbourhood and Community in Paris 1740–1790* (Cambridge: Cambridge University Press, 1996).

[77] See below, pp. 123–27 and 129–32.

[78] Jacques-Louis Ménétra, *Journal de ma vie*, ed. D. Roche (Paris: Montalba, 1982). Working-class autobiographies are equally uncommon in other parts of Europe before the nineteenth century. There is one other eighteenth-century memoir of a French artisan's life but it is written in the third person: see N. Contat, *Anecdotes typographiques où l'on voit la description des coutumes, moeurs et usages singuliers des compagnons imprimeurs*, ed. G. Barber (Oxford: Oxford Bibliographical Society, 1980).

brute who frequently and arbitrarily whipped and assaulted his son, especially when he was drunk, and continually locked him out the house. On one occasion, while Ménétra was helping his father carry glass up a staircase by lighting his passage, he failed to do as he was asked and was kicked down the stairs for his pains with the result that he broke his arm. On another occasion, his leg was broken.[79] His father had married again, and while his step-mother was alive he received some protection. But when she too died, his father lost control completely. Ménétra responded to this treatment by taking evasive action as much as possible. When threatened he ran, once even in a fit of desperation signing up for the army. When he was nineteen, however, he finally turned. One evening Ménétra senior returned home drunk and began to maltreat his one daughter still at home. Ménétra went to her assistance, only to be attacked in turn. This time he defended himself, breaking off a shard of glass from a handy near-by sheet and threatening his father to do his worst. His father retaliated by rushing into the street screaming that his son was trying to assassinate him, a claim his daughter upheld. Faced with possible interrogation by the local police, Ménétra had little choice but to leave the city and lie low until his father had cooled down.[80]

Given the unique status of this autobiography, it is difficult to evaluate how typical a picture it paints of the formative years of an eighteenth-century artisan. The editor of the manuscript – Daniel Roche, France's leading living historian of the society and culture of the Ancien Regime – is confident that the image conveyed is broadly accurate. In respect of the harsh treatment suffered by the young Ménétra at the hands of his father, Roche has no doubt it was a commonplace: teenagers had to be toughened up to withstand the harsh realities of the pre-Revolutionary world; physical abuse was essential for successful acculturation.[81] In this regard in particular, however, there is reason to believe that Ménétra's experience was thankfully untypical. This is not to say that whippings and beatings were not a normal part of an early modern childhood in France or elsewhere. They clearly were, as every child, schoolboy and apprentice could have attested. And the rod was used from an early age and was no respecter of persons or gender. On the other hand, it must be emphasised that beating children in the early modern world was only socially acceptable as punishment for specific wrong-doing. It was never a good *per se*.

Children, it was assumed, were fallen creatures with an undeveloped rational capacity. Far less able than adults to control their desires, they were frequently likely to sin and had to be enticed into good behaviour. This did not mean, though, they had to be beaten into submission. From the turn of the sixteenth century, one group of Christian thinkers, the Renaissance humanists, more ready to see the potential for good in humanity, if it were only properly nurtured, than their medieval predecessors wedded to the pessimistic ideas of St Augustine, took up the views of the Roman orator, Quintilian, that children responded to kindness.[82] The leading exponent of this new educational philosophy was Desiderius Erasmus of Rotterdam (1466/69–1536). Erasmus's most influential treatise on child-rearing was his *De pueris statim ac liberaliter instituendis*, which was first published at Basel in 1529. This emphasised that the first act of the teacher was to make himself obeyed through love rather than fear. Means should be devised of making the teaching of Latin grammar enjoyable rather than a boring chore. Above all boys should be kept busy. Erasmus accepted that corporal punishment could be used as a last resort and he had no problem with the fact that

---

[79] *Journal de ma vie*, pp. 34 and 37.
[80] *Ibid.*, pp. 40 and 45. For a fuller discussion of victims fighting back, see Ch. 5, pp. 217–26.
[81] D. Roche, 'L'Autobiographie d'un homme du peuple', in Ménétra, *Journal*, pp. 9–26.
[82] For an introduction to humanist pedagogy, see Garin, fn. 52, above.

noble boys would find being chastised in public humiliating. Shame was part of the ritual. But he very much objected to its frequent use on the grounds it was counter-productive: unreasonable and violent punishments made children intractable, while also discouraging them from further effort.[83]

The ideas of the humanists were given formal shape in the disciplinary codes of the new colleges and grammar schools of the sixteenth and seventeenth centuries which taught the Latin and Greek humanities to adolescents bound for a career in the professions or the life of country gentleman. Although their Protestant and Catholic sponsors were less starry-eyed about man's potential than Erasmus and his friends, they saw the value of a pedagogical method where the emphasis was not on punishment but encouragement and competition: children could be made compliant if they were imaginatively taught. This new doctrine was particularly sustained in the many schools founded by the Jesuits, a new regular order established in 1540 to spearhead the Counter-Reformation. From the end of the sixteenth century the hundreds of Jesuit colleges operated according to the detailed rules laid down in the order's *Ratio Studiorum* (1591), which was the fruit of the Jesuits' teaching experience over the previous 40 years. In the late middle ages boys of all ages, abilities and attainment were taught in the same room and little attempt was made to hold the pupils' attention, with inevitable results. The Jesuits, committed to the Erasmian programme of maintaining discipline by love rather than fear, learnt to keep order by separating the boys into classes according to the level they had reached in their studies, by trying to ensure that the teacher moved up the school with his pupils, and by a constant round of classroom competitions, which pitted boy against boy and led to their weekly and annual ranking. They also believed that much bad behaviour could be nipped in the bud, if the children were carefully watched. An active surveillance was the key to obedience: hence their use of schoolboy monitors (*censores*) who could act as the teacher's eyes in a crowded classroom. Punishing a boy then was an admission of failure and in theory would be an uncommon occurrence. Much was expected from the well-timed cautionary word. If punishment were resorted to, then it should always fit the crime and boys should not be mocked or verbally abused. In preference, the obdurate were given lines, and only the worst malefactors were whipped. Moreover, to ensure that the punishment was administered calmly and coldly and without undue humiliation, the task was taken out of the hands of the teacher and given to the official school corrector, who was not a Jesuit and would punish in private.[84]

By the early seventeenth century, the humanists' thoughts on punishment had been adopted in the rearing of young aristocratic children as well, who were normally entrusted to private tutors rather than sent to school. The young Louis XIII might be threatened with a whipping for acts of petty disobedience, such as failing to get out of bed, but he was only ever actually punished for serious misdeeds, especially rudeness to superiors. Again he was seldom punished immediately but left to cool his heels overnight and whipped when he awoke, as he was on the morning of 10 May 1607, for not being nice to the formidable Reine Marguérite (his father's divorced first wife) the day before.[85] His younger brother Gaston was dealt with even more leniently. His

---

[83] D. Erasmus, *Declamatio de pueris statim ac liberaliter instituendis*, critical edn with French trans. by J. C. Margolin (Geneva: Droz, 1966), pp. 70–76. Erasmus was not the first Renaissance humanist to argue against corporal punishment. Guarino of Verona (1434–60) had argued in a similar vein: see W. H. Woodward, *Vittorino da Feltre and Other Humanist Educators* (Cambridge: Cambridge University Press, 1921), p. 163.

[84] *Ratio Studiorum*, bilingual Latin and French edn (Paris: Belin, 1997), esp. paragraphs 287 (*censor*), 288 (*corrector*) and 364 (forms of punishment). For a good introduction to Jesuit pedagogy, see F. de Dainville, *La Naissance de l'humanisme moderne*, vol. 1. *Les Jésuites et l'humanisme* (Paris: Beauchesne et fils, 1940).

[85] *Journal de Jean Héroard*, p. 265.

governor apparently attached rods to his belt but used them rarely, preferring to rebuke his charge by a sign of his eyes or reasoned argument.[86]

Inevitably, there was an absence of fit between the theory and classroom practice. The Jesuits and other Catholic teaching orders seem to have been able to keep within the spirit of the new pedagogy to a great extent. Even the Paris Collège de Montaigu appears to have been using the whip more sparingly from the turn of the eighteenth century.[87] Protestant teachers on the other hand appear to have had more difficulty, not because they were less committed to the new ideas on discipline but because they lacked the necessary resources. In England most of the grammar schools were small and poorly endowed: boys of different ages and attainments were taught together and not placed in separate classrooms, and schoolmasters were frequently lured to other posts so there was often no continuity.[88] An absence of fit in the classroom, however, did not stop the theory of creative discipline gaining widespread currency in wider society. The very fact that the writers of memoirs in the eighteenth century remembered and named teachers who had punished too readily would suggest that pupils had a clear idea of what was and was not acceptable in their minds.[89]

The sixteenth- and early seventeenth-century educationalists further felt that corporal chastisement of the young should cease once they had reached the age of reason. At all levels of early modern society, physical beatings were a punishment meted out by superiors to inferiors. It was not deemed proper therefore for guardians of the young to continue to beat their charges once they were deemed to be their moral equals. To beat an equal was an assault on his dignity, a parlous sin in a world obsessed with status. It was a wound keenly felt especially by the parvenu. When the 30-year-old, socially mobile Voltaire (1694–1778) was beaten up by the servants of the Duc de Rohan over a perceived affront in 1725, the poet, though no swordsman, felt so humiliated he challenged the Duke to a duel.[90] From the mid-teens, then, corporal punishment was supposed to stop, although the exact moment in an individual's life when he would cease to be subject to the rod would vary.[91] In the colleges of eighteenth-century France, the division came traditionally at the end of the second class (the penultimate of six), when boys had completed their study of Greek and Latin grammar but had not yet begun the final part of their humanities course, the study of rhetoric.[92] This meant that in the early seventeenth century, when the age range of pupils studying Latin

---

[86] M. Motley, *Becoming a French Aristocrat: The Education of the Court Nobility 1580–1715* (Princeton: Princeton University Press, 1990), p. 43.

[87] L. W. B. Brockliss, 'The Collège de Montaigu in the Seventeenth and Eighteenth Centuries', *History of Universities*, XXII/2 (2007), 116–19. On punishment generally in French schools in the early modern period, see J. de Viguerie, *L'Institution des enfants. L'Education en France 16e–18e siècle* (Paris: Calmann-Levy, 1978), pp. 242–51.

[88] Cf. the frequent turnover of the master and usher (the only two teachers) at Oxford's only grammar school in the sixteenth and seventeenth centuries: R. S. Stanier, *Magdalen School. A History of Magdalen College School, Oxford* (Oxford: Blackwell), pp. 233–34. Magdalen School consisted of one large room: see the engraving of 1828 in Brockliss, *Magdalen College*, p. 103.

[89] Guillaume Baston, *Mémoires de l'Abbé Baston, Chanoine de Rouen*, (eds) J. Loth and C. Verger (3 vols; Paris: A. Picard and *fils*, 1897–99), i. 116; L. M. La Revellière-Lépeaux, *Mémoires*, ed. O. La Revellière-Lépeaux (3 vols; E. Plon, Paris, 1873), i. 9.

[90] T. Besterman, *Voltaire* (London: Longmans, 1969), p. 106.

[91] The *Ratio Studiorum* recommended that older troublemakers should be expelled rather than beaten but laid down no age: *Ratio Studiorum*, paras. 289–92.

[92] In some French colleges by the end of the Ancien Régime corporal punishment had stopped altogether, as the young abbé Besnard discovered when he moved from a small school at Doué to the college run by the Oratorians (another teaching order at Angers): F.-Y. Besnard, *Souvenirs d'un nonagénaire*, ed. C. Port (Paris: H. Champion, 1880), pp. 25 and 203.

and Greek was wide, pupils as old as twenty might still have been beaten, but in the eighteenth century, there were few in the rhetoric class older than sixteen.[93]

These boundaries were well understood by contemporaries and breaches were frowned upon. Public punishment of the young was judged scandalous. When the principal of the college at Amiens had several boys whipped in the courtyard in 1785, passers-by were horrified.[94] Schoolmasters who were thought to be sadists could find themselves in court. At Avignon in 1759 the Frères des Ecoles chrétiennes (a teaching order which specialised in elementary education) had to appear before the archbishop's official to answer the accusation that one of their number had caused a pupil's death by kicking him in the belly.[95] At Eu in Picardy in 1788, a parent sued the school when his son was injured after being beaten by a master for playing a trick.[96] The pupils too were well aware of their rights. At the Jesuit college at Mauriac in the 1730s the future poet Jean-François Marmontel (1723–99) was summoned to the principal's study to be whipped for breaking into a local convent and pealing the bells. But Marmontel was in the rhetoric class and he refused to be punished. Instead, he returned to the classroom, locked the door and used his popularity to get his classmates to agree to stage a walk-out, supposedly so effective that the rhetoric class remained closed for the rest of the year.[97]

Ménétra's father therefore broke the rules in various ways. He punished his son arbitrarily, took no account of the degree of offence, still beat him in his late teens and washed the family's dirty linen in public. In fact, it is evident from the text that his behaviour was beyond the pale. Ménétra makes it quite clear that his father was a brute whose anger was coarsened by drink and whose cruelty was disliked by his mother's family. When Ménétra senior abuses his patriarchal position, Ménétra's maternal relatives have no qualms about coming to his assistance. Just as it was his grandmother who nursed him when his father broke his arm and his leg, so it was his maternal uncle, another glazier, who gave him a job when he returned to Paris after the incident with the shard of glass. The narrative, too, is satisfyingly shaped to allow Ménétra senior to eventually learn the error of his ways. When one of his father's journeymen marries his sister, the father retires and goes to live with the couple. There he is treated like a slave, thrown out the house and beaten up in his turn. Losing an eye in consequence, he ends up in the Hôtel-Dieu, the city's largest and most unsanitary poorhouse-cum-hospital. Inevitably the estranged son goes to visit his father and is reconciled, the latter begging Ménétra's pardon for his past actions.[98]

Ménétra's experiences as an adolescent primarily remind us that in an age when most adults did not consider beating children a crime, there were clear boundaries between the legitimate and illegitimate use of physical chastisement. These boundaries were redrawn and refined over time as educational pundits reflected more deeply on humanist pedagogical ideas, and state and church attempted to control and limit the exercise of interpersonal violence in the name of good order. Eighteenth-century

---

[93] W. Frijhoff and D. Julia, *Ecole et société dans la France d'ancien régime* (Paris: Armand Colin, 1975), pp. 60–61.

[94] C. Bailey, 'French Secondary Education 1763–90: The Secularization of Ex-Jesuit Colleges', *Transactions of the American Philosophical Society*, 68:6 (1978), 1–124, at p. 87. The Jesuits were expelled from France in 1762 and their colleges taken over by local committees who entrusted their care to other teaching orders or secular masters.

[95] Jean de Viguerie, *Une oeuvre d'éducation au XVIIe et XVIIIe siècles: La Doctrine Chrétienne en France et en Italie 1592–1792* (Paris: Editions de la nouvelle aurore, 1975), p. 652.

[96] Bailey, 'French Secondary Education', p. 87.

[97] Jean-François Marmontel, *Mémoires*, ed. J. Renwick (2 vols; Clermont-Ferrand: G. de Bussac, 1972), i. 12–17.

[98] Ménétra, *Journal de ma vie*, pp. 214 and 227–28.

sensibilities about hitting children were almost certainly more developed than those a century before. In the early modern era, however, corporal punishment always had a rationale and was culturally policed.

. . . .

The educational pundits of the sixteenth and seventeenth century were nearly all priests and clergymen, who shared a set of traditional theological assumptions about human nature and the necessity of Christ's sacrifice if mankind was to be redeemed. They accepted too that individuals if properly raised could perform virtuous acts. Where Catholics and Protestants divided was over the possibility of the individual's performing good acts that were meritorious in God's eyes and contributed to salvation. In the eighteenth century orthodox Christian clerics continued to publish influential educational treatises which promoted the humanist view on punishment. One of the most influential was the work published by Charles Rollin (1661–1741), a professor at the University of Paris, in 1728.[99] But from the middle of the century a growing number of books on child-rearing began to appear from the press which were written increasingly by members of the laity, especially doctors of medicine.

The new childcare gurus paid a novel attention to the early years of a child's life. As we have seen, the age-old practice of swaddling was a commonplace in the sixteenth and seventeenth centuries. So too was putting a child out to nurse, equally long practised by the rich but increasingly even practised by all but the poorest of the urban poor. The few medical practitioners (usually surgeons) who wrote about childcare pre-1700 took their cue from ancient writers, such as Soranos of Ephesus (fl. second century CE), and largely accepted these practices. They praised maternal breast-feeding but recognised social reality and offered guidance to the rich on how to choose a good nurse.[100] Their successors, however, who were normally learned physicians, took a very different tack. They lambasted restrictive swaddling as a danger to an infant's growth and strongly promoted the moral and physical benefits that would flow from maternal breast-feeding for both mother and child. They also wanted children, once weaned, to be dressed in loose fitting clothes (no tight stays and high-heeled shoes for little girls) and toughened up by a bland diet (no wine) and plenty of exercise. They were not averse to suggesting tips for improving a child's posture but their primary target was the plethora of traditional practices which they believed could permanently damage the growing child. While they argued that dentition could be surgically assisted by incising the gums, they generally believed that nature should be left to do her work. Intervention was needed only where a child, through no fault of its own, suffered from a physical imperfection. The eighteenth century saw a novel interest in straightening crooked limbs and feet and the development in particular of a successful operation to heal a harelip.[101]

Particular ire was reserved for the poorly chosen and inattentive nurse. The childcare manual of the Paris physician, Nicolas Andry de Boisregard (1652–1742), published in 1738, made her the cause of virtually every ill. On the one hand, such nurses infected the child

---

[99] C. Rollin, *De la manière d'enseigner et d'étudier les belles lettres* (4 vols; Paris: J. Estienne, 1726–8), iv. 462–91. The work was reprinted until the 1820s.

[100] *E.g.* Jacques Guillemeau (1550–1613), 'De la manière et gouvernement des enfans dès le commencement de leur naissance, in Jacques Guillemeau, *Oeuvres de la chirurgie* (Rouen: J. Viret, 1649), pp. 391–93; there is an encomium of maternal breast-feeding in the preface (pp. 387–89). The text appeared in an English trans in 1612. Soranos of Ephesus was the author of a gynaecological work: see *Soranos's Gynaecology*, Eng. trans. and intro. O. Temkin (Baltimore: Johns Hopkins University Press, 1991).

[101] For the development of the new paediatrics in one European state, see L. W. B. Brockliss and C. Jones, *The Medical World of Early Modern France* (Oxford: Oxford University Press, 1997), pp. 443–44, 448–51, 467–70, and 555–56.

with their poor morals and scarred the infant for life with superstitious stories. On the other, they left their charges pigeon-toed and rickety by tying them up too tightly 'as if they were packing up Goods to send abroad' and threatened their health by leaving them 'to soak in dirty clouts'. Affluent parents were encouraged to take their cue from the child-rearing practices of the peasantry and even the west African negro.

> ... In that country, they do not know what it is to swaddle their children... They leave Nature to act at full liberty in this respect, and as she understands her Business better than all the Midwives, Dressers and Nurses in the World, she manages those little Creatures so well, that you will not see crooked and lame Persons there, as you see in *France*.[102]

This sudden volte-face in advice on child-rearing can only be understood in the light of the medical profession's wider advocacy of therapeutic minimalism from the mid-eighteenth century, especially in France. The emergence of the new medical science of paediatrics was part of what medical historians call Neohippocratism, a movement that stressed working with rather than against nature in curing disease, purportedly based on the writings of Hippocrates rather than Galen, the historic prince of therapeutics.[103] According to the childcare writers themselves, the new science was also inspired by the appallingly high rate of eighteenth-century child mortality and the confidence that this was a man-made not a natural phenomenon that could be greatly improved.[104] It was then a movement closely associated with the wider drive for 'improvement', championed by the eighteenth-century Enlightenment: man's lot was not necessarily a vale of tears as Christians had always been taught; human beings could shape their environment for the better.[105]

It is in the context of this new childcare literature that the most notorious child-rearing manual of the eighteenth century should be placed: *Emile, ou l'éducation* (1762) by Jean-Jacques Rousseau (1712–78), frequently taken as the starting-point for our modern sensibility. Rousseau's book went much further in its critique of contemporary child-rearing practices than the medical manuals of his own day in that it famously inveighed against the existing methods of instructing the young, inside and outside the home, not just the treatment of babies. However, his views on swaddling and breast-feeding were cribbed from other authors, and his educational programme based on learning by doing was shaped by the new belief that a children's upbringing should be natural and bracing.[106]

However, the new childcare manuals were not the only influence on *Emile*. The work was also heavily indebted to the ideas of the late seventeenth-century English philosopher and medical practitioner, John Locke (1632–1704), who himself had written about education and

---

[102] Nicolas Andry de Beauregard, *Orthopaedia, or the Art of Correcting and Preventing of Deformities in Children*, English trans. (2 vols; London: printed for A. Millar, 1743), pp. 129 and 216–17.

[103] A. Cunningham and R. French (eds), *The Medical Enlightenment in the Eighteenth Century* (Cambridge: Cambridge University Press, 1990); Brockliss and Jones, *Medical World*, pp. 438–40.

[104] E.g., Jean-Charles Desessartz (1729–1811), *Traité de l'éducation corporelle des enfans en bas âge, ou réflexions pratiques sur les moyens de procurer une meilleure constitution aux citoyens* (Paris: J. Hérissant, 1760), esp. 'Discours préliminaire': Desessartz claimed only five per cent of babies sent out from Paris and London to be nursed survived. The mid-eighteenth century also saw a sustained campaign to promote smallpox inoculation, brought to Europe from the Ottoman empire in the 1720s, as a further way of reducing child mortality: see A. A. Rusnock, *Quantifying Health and Population in Eighteenth-Century England and France* (Cambridge: Cambridge University Press, 2002), chs. 2–4.

[105] Historians remain divided over whether the Enlightenment was the property of a small group of radical critics with a definite programme or a broadly dispersed reformist mood. Either way, it is accepted that it was only in the eighteenth century that some Europeans began to think seriously of permanent moral and material progress. The best study remains P. Gay, *The Enlightenment: An Interpretation* (2 vols; London: Wildwood House, 1973). The third part is called 'The Pursuit of Modernity'.

[106] Rousseau's account of infancy in Book 1 of *Emile* relies very heavily on Desessartz, which had appeared two years before.

queried the value of traditional pedagogical practice.[107] Locke and Rousseau were working within an heterodox Arian Christian tradition that was increasingly espoused by sections of the intelligentsia in the eighteenth century. They both rejected original sin and the Trinity, while Rousseau also believed man to be naturally good, and regarded Christ as an exemplar not a redeemer.[108] This led them to argue that the moral correctness of acting in accordance with the general good, if need be at the expense of our immediate gain, was not something that had to be drummed into a congenitally recalcitrant creature. It would be our automatic way of behaving, if we had been properly brought up.[109] As a result, though Rousseau was much more interested in the fashioning of a morally autonomous individual than Locke, they had a common dislike and distrust of corporal punishment that set them apart from even the most liberal of their orthodox Christian contemporaries. This was an opinion they shared with other deistic social critics, such as the early eighteenth-century English men of letters, the Whig moralists, Joseph Addison (1672–1719) and Richard Steele (1672–1729), authors of the run-away hit, the *Spectator* (1711–14).[110]

Children and Physical Cruelty – The Lockean and Rousseauvian Revolution

Anja Müller

Jean-Jacques Rousseau is commonly credited with raising the most fervent objections against child-beating as an educational means in the eighteenth century. His Emile outlines a 'negative education' encouraging the child to learn actively through trial and error (including bearing the consequences which may result from errors).[111] The goal of this education is the development of an individual, independent self. The educator's task is to provide selected environments, but not to form the child according to a certain pattern. Growth and development is the formula, not creation or perfectibility. Without a doubt, there is no room for physical punishment in such an educational concept, because it would be detrimental to the child's development of independence. Instead, the child would only learn to become cunning and hypocritical – and to get used to being guided by authorities.

The idea that physical punishment for children is 'tyrannical and injurious to the personality' of a child is no invention of Rousseau.[112] In the literary public sphere of

---

[107] John Locke, *Some Thoughts Concerning Education* (1693), (eds) J. W. and J. S. Yolton (Oxford: Clarendon Press, 2000).

[108] Arians were the followers of Arius (*c*. 250–336 CE) who denied that Christ was consubstantial with God. Rousseau espoused the radical Arianism of the Italian Socinus (1539–1604).

[109] The literature on Rousseau's psychological and moral theory is vast. A good introduction is E. H. Wright, *The Meaning of Rousseau* (London: Humphrey Milford for Oxford University Press, 1929).

[110] *The Spectator* was an instant success. It was reprinted many times as a book and translated into many European languages. Most *philosophes* were deists of some sort, although deism embraced a wide spectrum of opinion. J. Israel, *Radical Enlightenment. Philosophy and the Making of Modernity 1650–1750* (Oxford: Oxford University Press, 2001) is too ready to label many of them atheists.

[111] He believed for instance that children should not be mollycoddled but learn as a toddler to bear pain. 'I shall not take pains to prevent Emile hurting himself; far from it, I should be vexed if he never hurt himself'. *Emile*, English trans. (London: Dent, 1969), p. 41.

[112] S. T. McCloy, *The Humanitarian Movement in Eighteenth-Century France* (Lexington: University of Kentucky Press, 1957), p. 211.

eighteenth-century England, it was already a matter of some debate. Writers like Joseph Addison or Richard Steele, whose self-declared task to educate their contemporaries is manifest throughout their writings, greatly contributed to the popularisation of the issue. In 1711 and 1712, for instance, Addison's and Steele's *Spectator* included a sequence of articles on educational reform, that began with a scathing critique of corporal punishment in schools.[113] *The Spectator* no. 157 (30 Aug. 1711) contended that corporal punishment degraded children to animals who were mechanically conditioned through physical punishment and rewards as if they were entirely incapable of rational reflection. Against this practice, Mr Spectator held up his own vision of an education whose methods targeted the child's mind instead of the body. Cautioning his readers against whipping – for this punishment would only debase a child's mind by breaking virtues and spirit and fostering a hard and ferocious character – he proposed instead to transform learning entirely into a mental process: 'The Sense of Shame and Honour is enough to keep the World it self in Order without corporal Punishment'.[114]

The comparative levity of these punishments (shame and honour are said to be 'enough') cannot entirely obscure the fact that if the impressions of whipping are more than merely skin-deep, the same holds true for shame and honour which deeply ruffle a child's mind and soul. Mr Spectator was asking not for less but for more effective punishments. There again Addison and Steele were definitely heirs to the humanist tradition that placed a premium on kindness. This is exemplified in a letter, printed in a later issue of the periodical (*Spectator* no. 168, 12 Sept. 1711) by a fourteen-year-old schoolboy who says his love of learning is mainly inspired by his deep reverence for his teacher. The schoolboy's account of his broken-hearted older brother who craves to be restored to his teacher's benevolence illustrates beautifully how the tutor's power to educate should not lie in an externally applied instrument but should be a pervasive generative force.[115]

The maxims mentioned above correspond to the precepts outlined in Locke's *Some Thoughts concerning Education* (1693): '*Esteem* and *Disgrace* are, of all others, the most powerful incentives to the Mind, when once it is brought to relish them'.[116] Locke distinguishes between age-specific degrees of children's submission to their parents and tutors. Whereas the young child is to hold his parents in awe, the adolescent should be gradually admitted as an equal: 'So shall you have him your obedient Subject (as is fit) whilst he is a Child, and your affectionate Friend when he is a Man'.[117] Locke believes corporal punishment is only acceptable with young, very obstinate or rebellious children. He argues that 'Children are to be treated as rational Creatures' and that beating conversely foregrounds precisely the child's physical existence and sensations which ought to be subjected to the mind through education.[118]

To both Locke and the *Spectator*, physical punishment hence will only debase a child's character, rendering it either slavish and spiteful, or hypocritical. It will not promote judgement, reflection or moral insight – which are the essential goals when educating future free English citizens:

---

[113] The schools referred to in the following pages are largely grammar schools as well as the great boarding schools (*e.g.*, Eton, Winchester or Westminster) of the time.

[114] *The Spectator* (1711–14), ed. D. F. Bond (5 vols; Oxford: Clarendon Press, 1965), ii. 115.

[115] *Ibid.*, ii. 162.

[116] Locke, *Some Thoughts*, § 56 (p. 116). In the following two paragraphs, Locke elaborates further on these two principles.

[117] *Ibid.*, § 40 (p. 109).

[118] *Ibid.*, § 78 (pp. 138–40), § 54 (p. 115) and § 48 and 55 (pp. 112 and 115).

It is wholly to this dreadful Practice that we may attribute a certain Hardness and Ferocity which some Men, tho' liberally educated, carry about them in all their Behaviour. To be bred like a Gentleman, and punished like a Malefactor, must, as we see it does, produce that illiberal Sauciness which we see sometimes in Men of Letters.[119]

'Liberal education' is the contested key term, which the *Spectator* positions in a wider context that decidedly amalgamates the spheres of educational and political theory. Future citizens of a country boasting of its liberty need an education which meets the demands of an increasingly complex society.[120] This fusion of educational and political theory evokes Locke's *Second Treatise on Government*, where Locke revised the distribution of power relations in the traditional family-kingdom analogy. Limiting the extent and the duration of educational power relations between parents and children – while defining education as a parental duty – he uses these restrictions to qualify sovereign power which he considers to be largely the result of a mutual consent involving the subjects as active parts.[121] In *Some Thoughts*, Locke says with respect to corporal punishment: 'Such a sort of slavish Discipline makes a slavish Temper' and is therefore not 'fit to be used in the Education of those we would have wise, good, and ingenuous Men'.[122]

Although Locke does not entirely reject child-beating in education, he prepares the ground for the shifting opinions on child-beating that will later be radicalised by Rousseau. On one level he finds child-beating unacceptable on an emotional plane. In his view there is an affectionate bond between parents and children that should prevent parents from beating their children too violently and without any reason.[123] However, this does not explain intellectually his objection to corporal punishment. This rather stems from his psychological and political thought.

Firstly, by viewing the child as a *tabula rasa*, Locke removes the child from the religious and spiritual discourse of original sin and depravity. The idea of the *tabula rasa* has recently been criticised as a concept contrived by adults in order to project their desires on the child and to shape children according to the adults' wishes. Such an evaluation neglects the liberating implications of the *tabula rasa* that appear in our particular context: a child who is a blank paper, is also free from original depravities and therefore hardly offers a reason for excessive physical correction. As vice is no longer innate but rather results from a deficient upbringing, the responsibility lies with the parents rather than the child.

Secondly, Locke not only secularises the child by detaching it from original sin; by regarding children as potential future members of a political community, he also politicises the child. His educational theories and writings are inseparably intertwined with his political theories. In the *Second Treatise*, Locke says that even if children 'are not born in this full state of equality, they are born to it'; *i.e.*, the child's lack of understanding and judgement is only temporary. As a consequence, it is the duty of the parents to enable their children to achieve understanding and the control of their own wills.[124] Whereas the doctrine of original sin related children to the past (*i.e.*, the

---

[119] *Spectator*, ii. 116 (no. 157).

[120] Cf. *Spectator*, ii. 115 (no. 157).

[121] John Locke, *Two Treatises on Government* (1690), ed. P. Laslett (Cambridge: Cambridge University Press, 1988), esp. *Second Treatise*, §§ 67–76.

[122] Locke, *Some Thoughts*, §§ 50 and 52 (p. 113).

[123] Locke, *Second Treatise*, § 56.

[124] Ibid., § 65. The constitutive political and social framework of educational considerations also informs the letter by 'Philogamus' in *Spectator*, iv. 272–75 (no. 500, 3 Oct. 1712). This contributor sees children as a blessing, because they perpetuate the human species, the nation and Christian religion; *i.e.*, he values children

sin of Adam and Eve), the Lockean theory is oriented towards the future and implies a potential in the child for improving not only itself but also society and the state.[125] This view of the child is construed within a political framework of a state that is based on mutual contracts between the sovereign and the people. Whereas an absolute monarchy or a tyranny used physical punishment as a means to express the power of the sovereign that extended even to the subjects' bodies, Locke's contract theory asserts the individual's indelible rights over life, body and property. As a consequence and in analogy, a father's command over his children 'reaches not their life or property'.[126] Within such a framework, education must operate not on children's bodies but on their interior faculties, using habit formation and guilt or shame as internalised, more powerful and eventually more effective means of educating children's minds.

The link between educational and political theory takes us back to Rousseau, whose Emile is not supposed to remain solitary, either. After all, the education offered to Emile enables him to develop the freedom and independence which Rousseau presupposes for the individuals who form the *contrat social*. The differences between Locke's and Rousseau's educational concepts can hardly be denied. Locke's insistence on perfectibility and his aim to educate a future citizen is certainly incompatible with Rousseau's developmental approach which intends to educate a man, not a citizen. Nevertheless, each of the two not only objects to beating children, but also formulates a political theory of a social contract alongside his educational theory. Can we, therefore, relate the shift of opinion concerning the corporal punishment of children (or even concerning childhood in general) to the process of democratisation in western European societies? Or, more generally speaking, to the process of modernisation? An answer to these questions would, of course, require a project of its own. It does not seem implausible to suggest, on the other hand, that, by placing the child in a wider political context, the more radical eighteenth-century educational reformers discussed childhood within a framework that would sooner or later raise the issue not only of the rights of the adult into which a child is going to develop, but also of the rights of children themselves – and thus they paved the way for a rights-based argument against the beating of children.[127]

. . . .

Rousseau's *Emile* was a best-seller and in the following decades an avalanche of educational treatises cascaded from the press supporting, refining and attacking his ideas. In England alone 200 educational treatises were published between 1762 and 1800.[128] The new paediatrics

---

primarily for their relevance for mankind, state and church. Alluding to the analogy between kingdoms and families, Philogamus refers to the governmental structure of a monarchy only to break with its aristocratic implications when he declares that parents' most valuable gift for their children is not to secure an estate but to provide an egalitarian education for a professional trade – thus disparaging the aristocratic pattern of primogeniture.

[125] In a sequence of letters to the *Spectator* in 1712, Budgell proposes educational reforms that target the child first and foremost as a future citizen who should be initiated into a community as early as possible. He therefore deviates from Locke in acknowledging that school education may be a good training for the child's social skills – and in this respect, school education even surpasses the otherwise preferred method of home education by a tutor. Conversation, argumentation, rhetoric, discussion, and, especially, social networking are essential skills; even robbing an orchard can 'train [...] up a Youth insensibly to Caution, Secrecy and Circumspection, and fits him for Matters of greater Importance'. *Spectator*, iii. 133 (no. 313, 28 Feb. 1712).

[126] *Second Treatise*, § 65.

[127] For the eventual rights based argument, see below, pp. 147–51.

[128] R. Porter, *Enlightenment: Britain and the Creation of the Modern World* (London: Penguin, 2000), p. 343. On

was also reinforced by artists who painted touching scenes of upper-class mothers feeding their children, epitomised by a portrait of an anonymous woman by the Mâcon artist Jean-Laurent Mosnier (1743–1808), purportedly painted in the 1770s. (See Figure 19).[129] However, *Emile*, whatever the long-term significance of its insights into child psychology, did not dramatically upset the traditional pattern of child-rearing. Admittedly, by the end of the eighteenth century, far fewer French babies were being put out to nurse thanks to the efforts of the French revolutionaries instructing mothers to do their patriotic duty. Whereas perhaps only five per cent of Parisian mothers fed their own children in 1789, purportedly half were doing so in 1801/2. But that still left half who did not, and urban France continued to send infants out to the countryside to be nursed throughout the nineteenth century.[130] More importantly, the popularisation of *Emile* brought no immediate change to the way children were disciplined in the home. Some parents did attempt to bring up their offspring following Rousseauvian principles. But in most countries, his advice fell on deaf ears. In England especially his voice was all but drowned out by the stricture of evangelicals, like Hannah More (1745–1833), who believed as much as their puritan forebears that children were corrupt and that to spare the rod was to spoil the child.[131]

Indeed, it is difficult to decide how far the traditional pattern of child-rearing was profoundly altered even with the coming of industrialisation to large parts of western Europe. Rousseau had his heirs in the Romantic writers of the early nineteenth century, who valued imagination above reason and expressed their dissatisfaction with the constraints of the adult world by emphasising the specialness and creativity of childhood.[132] Yet, though the Romantics helped to establish a sentimental discourse about children and their needs that would survive until the present day, the age-old belief that the purpose of parenting was to mould the young into socialised adults was never driven underground. In France in the first half of the nineteenth century the children of the well-to-do seem to have been much more cosseted than in the past.[133] In Britain, on the other hand, the dominant form of parenting among the affluent was more confused, what Larkin would later describe as 'soppy stern'.[134]

Rousseau in France, see J. Bloch, *Rousseauism and Education in Eighteenth-Century France* (Oxford: Voltaire Foundation, 1995), esp. ch. 2.

[129] Portraits of breast-feeding mothers can be found from the early seventeenth century (*e.g.*, Pieter Franz de Grebber, *Moeder en kind*, 1622: Frans Hals Museum, Haarlem). But before the second half of the eighteenth century these are genre paintings, not studies of mothers of quality. The best study of family portraits in this period is K. Retford, *The Art of Domestic Life: Family Portraiture in Eighteenth-Century England* (London: Yale University Press, 2006).

[130] M. L. Jacobus, 'Incorruptible Milk: Breast-Feeding and the French Revolution', in S. E. Melzer and L. W. Rabine (eds), *Rebel Daughters. Women and the French Revolution* (Oxford: Oxford University Press, 1992), ch. 4; G. D. Sussman, *Selling Mother's Milk. The Wet-Nursing Business in France 1715–1914* (Urbana: University of Illinois Press, 1982), pp. 110–11 and 222. Breast-feeding on the eve of the Revolution was endorsed by the whole medical establishment: Marie Anel Le Rebours's, *Avis aux mères qui veulent nourrir leurs enfants* (1787) even carried a testimonial by the usually conservative Paris faculty of medicine.

[131] Fletcher, *Growing up in England*, pp. 8–10. The Dutch diarist, Otto van Eck (cited above in fn. 55) was brought up by Rousseauvians.

[132] The fullest statement is Wordsworth's *The Prelude* (written 1798 to 1805). Not all Romantics privileged childhood; others saw the antidote to modern life in peasants, gypsies and so on. To novelists and poets, like Rousseau, who rejected original sin, childhood was a peculiarly significant period of life, even if it was only the preliminary to adulthood; it was the key to adult contentment or unhappiness: see S. Matzner, 'Hunted by Paradise Lost: The Theme of Childhood in Eighteenth-Century Melancholy Writing', *Childhood in the Past*, 1 (2008), 12–35.

[133] M. Perrot (ed.), *A History of Private Life, vol. 4. From the Fires of Revolution to the Great* War (London: Belknap Press, 1990), pp. 208–11. The practice is critically appraised in Balzac's *Père Goriot* (1835).

[134] Philip Larkin, 'This Be the Verse', in P. Larkin, *High Windows* (London: Faber and Faber, 1974). Fletcher, *Growing up in England*, claims nothing really changes in parenting between 1600 and 1900. For similar views,

While it is hard to believe that Dickens's remorseless attack on harsh and unloving parents and guardians (particularly in *Dombey and Son*, where the children literally wither from lack of affection) did not have a profound influence on his huge middle-class readership, it remains the case that Victorian fathers could be martinets. Samuel Butler's autobiographical *Way of All Flesh* (begun in 1874 and published in 1903) purported to be an account of an authoritarian upbringing at the beginning of the nineteenth century, but Butler (d. 1902) had been born in 1835 and his own experience of being 'brought up by hand' by a clergyman father was in the very period that Dickens was in his prime.[135] The father in the novel, Theobald Pontifex, beats little Ernest at the least provocation, on one occasion thrashing the toddler (albeit in private) for failing after several warnings to pronounce 'come' properly.

> 'Very well, Ernest', said his father, catching him angrily by the shoulder, 'I have done my best to save you, but if you will have it so, you will,' and he lugged the little wretch, crying by anticipation out of the room. A few minutes more and we could hear screams coming from the dining-room, … and knew that poor Ernest was being beaten.
>
> 'I have sent him to bed,' said Theobald, as he returned to the drawing room, 'and now, Christina, I think we will have the servants in to prayers,' and he rang the bell for them, red-handed as he was.[136]

It must be remembered, too, that for all Dickens's popularity, there were other widely-read Victorian moralists, such as Charlotte Yonge (1823–1901), who continued to advocate a strict, though not loveless, form of parenting, one that included corporal punishment.[137]

Moreover, to the extent that a milder, child-orientated form of parenting did gain currency in nineteenth-century Britain and elsewhere, it was necessarily the preserve of affluent and relatively leisured middle-class households.[138] It had limited effect on working-class children, whose experience now became properly visible for the first time. In Britain they appear to have been relatively well-treated by their parents, but often sent out to work at an early age and frequently orphaned and left without family support, they were always much more vulnerable to arbitrary violence outside the home. Even with the establishment of the NSPCC in 1884 and the passage of the first Prevention of Cruelty to Children Act five years later, children left to the tender mercies of 'professional' carers could suffer appalling maltreatment. It is possible that the baby-farmer, Amelia Dyer, executed in 1896 had killed at least twelve infants of working mothers.[139] But British working-class children seem to have been comparatively fortunate. It is likely that children of the poor in some part of Europe

---

see also L. A. Pollock, *Forgotten Children: Parent-Child Relations from 1500 to 1900* (Cambridge: Cambridge University Press, 1983).

[135] *Dombey and Son* was published in 1848 and *David Copperfield* (where David is raised by the authoritarian Mr Murdstone) in 1849–50. 'Pip' was brought up by hand in *Great Expectations* (1860–1).

[136] Samuel Butler, *The Way of all Flesh*, introduction by R. Hoggart (Harmondsworth: Penguin, 1966), p. 125. Girls as well as boys could suffer from misguided authoritarianism. In 1855 a French governess called Celestine Doudet was found guilty, with their father's connivance, of torturing five English sisters and causing the death of one to stop them masturbating: see K. Hughes, *The Victorian Governess* (London: Hambledon Press, 1993), p. 135.

[137] See particularly *The Daisy Chain* (1856), which is an account of the godly upbringing of the large family of a provincial medical practitioner. Yonge later wrote a study of Hannah More.

[138] For a picture of a joyful Victorian childhood, see Molly Hughes, *A London Child of the 1870s*, original edn 1934 (London: Persephone Books, 2008). Hughes was the daughter of a stockbroker. She was beaten on one occasion by her father for crying to get what she wanted (p. 36) and her upbringing was heavily gendered, but she and her four brothers had a happy and carefree life.

[139] http://en.wikipedia.org/wili/Amelia_Dyer (accessed 15 Jul. 2009). On the growing concern for cruelty to children in the late Victorian era, see G. Behlmer, *Child Abuse and Moral Reform in England 1870–1908* (Stanford: Stanford University Press, 1982); L. Rose, *The Massacre of the Innocents: Infanticide in Britain 1800–1939* (London: Routledge, 1986). See also Ch. 2, pp. 85–86 and fn. 119.

were much more vulnerable. In Russia, where brutal child-rearing practices appear to have been commonplace before 1800, the intelligentsia was interacting much more positively with its offspring by the late nineteenth century. But the peasantry and the nascent working-class continued to favour the harsh parenting of the past. Two Russian Tzars – Ivan the Terrible and Peter the Great – had inadvertently killed their heirs in a fit of rage. In the 1870s there were still about 400 child murders a year.[140]

Childhood and Violence in Working-Class England 1800–1870

Jane Humphries

Early industrial Britain does not appear an auspicious environment for working-class children. The long eighteenth century linked back to a past in which some historians, notably Lloyd deMause, have argued that harsh treatment of children was standard.[141] If views of children were changing for some groups in society these had not yet percolated through the social structure to the working classes. Here there was no material revolution to prompt softer attitudes. Economic change was not accompanied by rapid increases in the real wages of working people and for many groups structural and cyclical unemployment put pressure on household incomes.[142] Even for those families who benefited from higher wages in the expanding sectors of the economy, a significant part of the wage premiums was eaten up by the higher costs of living in the new industrial centres. At the same time the late eighteenth and early nineteenth centuries saw Britain fighting what was a first full-scale national war and this imposed significant strains on manpower and on occasion food supplies. For many families these were times of economic and psychological strain, a context in which the abuse of children is understood to be more likely. Moreover although infant and child mortality remained high, falling age at marriage especially for women had pushed the birth rate to historically unprecedented levels. Families were large with children closely spaced.[143]

Was industrialisation a time of danger for working-class children and did their treatment relate to the economic changes of the era? To answer this question, over 600 working-class autobiographies have been consulted, as part of a larger project on children's experiences of industrialisation.[144] These memoirs almost all offer some

---

[140] P. P. Dunn, '"That Enemy is the Baby": Childhood in Imperial Russia', in deMause, *Childhood*, p. 394. All over Europe children were particularly likely to suffer from adult violence in the big cities. For the situation in one of late nineteenth-century Europe's capitals of culture, see L. Wolff, *Postcards from the End of the World. An Investigation into the Mind of Fin-de Siècle Vienna* (London: Collins, 1989).

[141] See Introduction, pp. 12–13.

[142] C. H. Feinstein, 'Pessimism Perpetuated: Real Wages and the Standard of Living in Britain During and After the Industrial Revolution', *Journal of Economic History*, 58:3, (1998), 625–58; R. C. Allen, 'Pessimism Preserved: Real Wages in the British Industrial Revolution', Oxford University, Department of Economics, Working Paper 314 (2007); G. Clark, 'The Condition of the Working Class in England, 1209–2003', *Journal of Political Economy*, 113:6, (2005), 1307–40; F. Cinnirella, 'Optimists or Pessimists? A Reconsideration of Nutritional Status in Britain, 1740–1865', *European Review of Economic History*, 12:3, (2008), 325–54.

[143] T. H. C. Stevenson, 'The Fertility of Various Social Classes in England and Wales from the Middle of the Nineteenth Century to 1911', *Journal of the Royal Statistical Society*, 83 (1920), 401–32.

[144] J. Humphries, *Childhood and Child Labour in the British Industrial Revolution* (Cambridge: Cambridge

comment on their authors' childhood. Here they have been read for what they have to say about violence against children: how common it was, where it took place, who the perpetrators were and who the likely victims. In this way it is hoped to piece together a picture of child abuse which casts light simultaneously on the times and the phenomena.

Violence was not ubiquitous in the lives of early industrial children. Many boys experienced happy childhoods and gentle handling, punctuated by an occasional rough encounter. But for a sad minority of boys, brutality was the norm. With the expected exception of sexual abuse the autobiographers appear to have had little shame in recalling abusive experiences, calming fears that violent encounters would be blocked out either by selective adult recall or anxieties about audience reaction. In assessing likely self-censorship it should be noted that a large proportion of the autobiographies were intended not for publication but to be read and passed on in the family. My own view is that the autobiographies probably provide a reliable indication of the pattern if not the extent of abuse. In particular the fact that the patterns detected in the historical record relate in a predictable way to family and environment reinforces confidence in the quality of the evidence. Not that the results of the survey are entirely without surprises for, as we shall see, both the settings and nature of many violent encounters are not perhaps what would have been expected.

Beginning then with the home, violence was not common in the family lives remembered by the British working-class autobiographers. It appears to have been less common than in continental European families in similar circumstances.[145] These relatively benign circumstances perhaps relate to the exceptionally precocious development in the British context of a male breadwinner family based on wage labour and long hours.[146] Fathers were away from home, detached from family life and until adolescence relatively uninterested in their offspring. Their obligations centred upon providing a family income and through their work linking their family to the economy. To the extent that they did so they were accorded reciprocal respect and obedience from their children. Their relationship was at arms' length, but the lack of immediacy and warmth was compensated for by the protection afforded children by separate spheres.

Where these distant and modulated relationships did not obtain, boys were vulnerable to domestic violence. Two different sets of circumstances left boys at risk. The first was if fathers retained a more traditional role in the family working from or even in the home and, more significantly still, directly undertaking the training of their sons. Fathers often chastised sons while trying to teach them or persuade them to work harder, the stress of the economic struggle taking its toll. On the other hand, working together created a closeness and mutual respect, which acted as a bulwark against anger and impatience. Fellowship generated other memories, which offset and drowned out the recollections of abuse. Sons were provided with some appreciation for the pressures under which their fathers operated, and this encouraged forgiveness of occasional violence. The second set of circumstances that exposed boys to danger was if fathers failed in their role as providers, especially if such failure was accompanied by wasting resources on drink. Stripped of the respect and obedience automatically

---

University Press, 2010).

[145] M. J. Maynes, *Taking the Hard Road: Life Course in French and German Workers Autobiographies in the Era of Industrialisation* (Chapel Hill: University of North Carolina Press, 1995). In France the bourgeois and working-class experience was very different.

[146] J. Humphries, 'Household Economy', in R. Floud and P. Johnson (eds), *The Cambridge Economic History of Modern Britain, vol. 1, Industrialisation, 1700–1860* (Cambridge: Cambridge University Press, 2004). J. Humphries, 'The First Industrial Nation and the First "Modern" Family', in T. Addabbo, M.-P. Arrizabalaga, C. Borderias and A. Owens (eds), *Gender, Households and Work: The Production of Wellbeing in Modern Europe* (Farnham: Ashgate, 2010).

accorded breadwinners and under economic stress, such fathers responded violently. The sons of unemployed, underemployed and alcoholic fathers were in the past, as in the present, particularly at risk.[147]

Child abuse by mothers, more common than abuse by fathers in modern contexts, appears rare in the autobiographies. It is possible that this is a historical construction, that the autobiographers' mothers were just as (relatively) violent as are mothers today but that their actions were re-categorised by their offspring. Of course, mothers' loss of temper was less threatening than fathers' was likely to be and boys often downplayed their mothers' beatings re-packaging them as 'smacks and wallops'. Sex-role standards and the sentimentalisation of family relationships played into the minimisation of mothers' cruelty; it was emasculating to have been beaten by a woman and it was unmotherly to have beaten one's sons. What might be understood as maternal cruelty today would not have been so perceived by the autobiographers of many years ago, and certainly not remembered as such in their memoirs.

None the less the relative lack of cruelty by mothers is intriguing. While acknowledging that it cannot provide a complete explanation, practitioners today link mothers' higher rates of abuse to their primary responsibility for childcare and the more time they spend with their children. But the dominance of mothers as carers was even more pronounced for the mothers of early industrial Britain and so cannot explain the differential. Perhaps the modern mother faces greater stress than her early industrial counterpart because of the ambiguity of her adult role, with the demands of maternity pulling in different directions from the aspirations for success in a career or even the need to fulfil the role of worker. Today time spent doing housework and childcare is commonly deprecated. Trapped in work, which contributes little to adult social identity, not surprisingly resentment can flare into violence. In contrast the homemaking and child-rearing roles of the early industrial mothers were celebrated. But it is easy to overdo this distinction. For the mothers in the sample also faced stress from economic and social conditions. Poverty, low wages and large numbers of children often prompted them to try to supplement their husbands' earnings creating strains familiar in modern two-earner time-poor households. Sometimes, too, mothers stretched in these ways did react violently especially if they thought their sons unhelpful and disobedient. But perhaps more important than simplified gender roles in explaining mothers' low-propensity to violence, was the nature and strength of the ties between mothers and sons. Sons were the most important secondary earners in the households of the industrial revolution, much more important that their mothers even in households without a male head. While it was quite common as the conventional wisdom on child labour asserts for parents to be paid for their children's work, the dominant form of payment appears to have been to the child himself. Moreover sons yielded up their earnings by and large not to their fathers but to their mothers. Thus the bond between mothers and sons was both economic and emotional and could operate to alienate the husband/father.

When children were chastised, the autobiographies suggest a division of labour between fathers and mothers that echoed the more general specialisation in their roles and probably strengthened the emotional ties between mothers and children. Fathers favoured corporal punishment while mothers resorted to remonstration and pleading, playing upon their children's emotional dependence. Moreover, and both reflecting and reinforcing the affective mandrel linking mothers and sons, when fathers played the disciplinarian, the 'hard cop' who delivered the pain, mothers followed up with kindness. They were the soft cops who extracted confessions, oversaw reconciliation

[147] J. E. Korbin, 'Child Maltreatment in Cross-Cultural Perspective: Vulnerable Children and Circumstances', in R. Gelles and J. Lancaster (eds), *Child Abuse and Neglect: Biosocial Dimensions* (Chicago: University of Chicago Press, 1987).

and promised redemption. Thus John Harris and his brother were disciplined by their father for some childish adventure that had gone dangerously wrong by being sent to bed without any supper. Then '... we heard the softest footfall on the chamber floor, and knew it was our mother stealing in to us with some thick slices of bread and butter. She could not bear to think of our going to sleep hungry'.[148]

Violence in the workplace was used to discipline and motivate children as Clark Nardinelli predicted in his study of early industrial child labour.[149] But alternative incentives were more common than he perhaps anticipated. Children's anxiety about retaining their positions and earning the highest wages possible underlines the importance of their contributions to their families and the ways in which economic responsibility had robbed them of a childhood. In particular the economic and emotional links between boys and their mothers ensured discipline and application. Moreover, violence seems to have been less widespread in factories and workshops where other mechanisms of control were developed and the presence of a large number of co-workers, some of whom were friends or relatives, afforded some protection. Symmetrically abuse appears to have been more common in less structured labour processes. In particular, isolation under the supervision of individual adults whose remuneration depended on their performance left many child workers at risk.

Parents often safeguarded children from violent and indeed debilitating workplaces withdrawing them if it seemed they could not stand the strain. Will Thorne for example eventually had to give up his work in a brickyard because his mother realised it was too hard. 'I remember her telling me that the 8s a week would be missed; some one would have to go short. But it was no use being slowly killed by such work as I was doing, and it was making me hump backed'.[150] Fellow workers too could be protective. Jesse Shervington, for example, was 'quite attached' to William Reynolds for whom he picked the big stones out of gravel.[151]

Children employed in more traditional jobs where they were cut off from other adults and subject to the temper of unrelated and often violent men were more vulnerable to abuse while at work. In agriculture, boys often lived and worked away from home in small isolated groups. In such settings neither parents nor caring adult co-workers could afford protection from a violent co-worker. Thus the children who were most vulnerable to long term abuse were those who had no recourse to protective adults or who could not be withdrawn from wretched situations because of poverty and a shortage of alternative jobs.[152] The children who were most likely to lack protectors either back at home or in their workplace were orphans and the fatherless, often placed at work by poor law officials whose main concern was to pass on the responsibility for the destitute.[153] But altogether the violence endured by children at the hands of co-

---

[148] John Harris, *My Autobiography* (London: Hamilton, Adams and Co., 1882), p. 18.

[149] C. Nardinelli, *Child Labor and the Industrial Revolution* (Bloomington: Indiana University Press, 1990).

[150] Will Thorne. *My Life's Battles*, with a foreword by the Rt. Hon. J. R. Clynes, MP (London: George Newnes Ltd., [1925]) p.19.

[151] Jesse Shervington, 'Autobiography of an Agricultural Labourer', copied in 1928 by H. P. Walker from the April, May, June 1899 issues of the *Baptist Banner*, MS. Hereford and Worcester Record Office, Worcester, p. 12.

[152] See Ch. 4, p. 194.

[153] S. Hindle, '"Waste" Children? Pauper Apprenticeship Under the Elizabethan Poor Laws, *c.* 1598–1697', in P. Lane, N. Raven and K. D. M. Snell (eds), *Women, Work and Wages in England, 1600–1850* (Woodbridge: Boydell, 2004). Recent work on the placement and treatment of parish apprentices has gone some way to rehabilitate both the poor law institutions and the individuals who represented them while recognising that Overseers and Guardians were under pressure to hold down the costs of maintaining destitute children, see K. Honeyman, *Child Workers in England, 1780–1820: Parish Apprentices and the Making of the Early Industrial Labour Force* (Aldershot: Ashgate, 2007).

workers and employers was of a second order of importance in comparison with the damage that they suffered as a result of early working and poor living conditions.

Schools appear to have been far and away the most common setting for violence against children in early industrial Britain, and this even though experience is charted through a selected sample (boys who grew into men who wrote autobiographies) that might be expected to have been bookish and receptive.[154] Perhaps this is not as surprising as might first be thought. Where large numbers of children were gathered together and presided over by a lone adult discipline could be expected to be a problem.

Violence in schools had a clear pattern, varying with the age and circumstances of the child. Dame schools, while sometimes remembered as Jonathan Rose notes, as educationally unrewarding, were nonetheless relatively benign environments for the young.[155] Joseph Gutteridge taught sewing and knitting as well as reading in his first school retained fond memories of his teacher's 'gentle placid features and her motherly kindness'. James Mullin followed a more strictly academic curriculum with his infant teacher, Miss Madden, whose 'formal appearance ... [had] ... all the conventionalities of the early Victorian period' but with 'a twinkle of genial humour in her dark eyes'.[156] Even when teachers in these first schools possessed the accoutrements of violence, they were often used for display rather than wielded with serious intent.

Relations were very different when boys grew older and were sent to National or British Schools or private local schools with male teachers. Many such institutions were conducted with what can only be viewed as astonishing levels of violence. 'School in those days were hard and detestable, playing truant was general. Thrashing in those days was cruel, bigger boys used to resent being laid on the desk and thrashed. It even now makes my blood boil when I think of it'.[157]

This graduation in violence is consistent with its interpretation as social control. Violence escalated, as boys grew older and increasingly unruly, exhibiting the high spirits and oppositional behaviour of adolescence. Schoolmasters unlike fathers and mothers and employers and co-workers often lacked alternative means to discipline their pupils. Individual schoolmasters rarely had sufficient market power that expulsion represented a significant cost to the boy or his family. Indeed all too often schoolmasters' themselves were desperate for customers, reliant as they were, through much of this period, on individuals' fees. New entrants to this particular market place faced few barriers to entry, with little training and few credentials thought necessary for the job of schoolmaster. Indeed the low status and poor circumstances of many schoolmasters, both in terms of their occupational and individual characteristics, stands out. Physical force was their only means to motivate children in an era when the returns on education were questionable and questioned and when masters had little training or inclination to make education intrinsically interesting.

---

[154] On the slow move towards compulsory education in Britain and other European states in the nineteenth century, see Ch. 4, pp. 199–205.

[155] J. Rose, *The Intellectual Life of the British Working Classes* (New Haven: Yale University Press, 2002). Dame schools were private institutions run by women that provided child-minding facilities and taught reading and, to a lesser extent, writing.

[156] Joseph Gutteridge, *The Autobiography of Joseph Gutteridge*, edited and with an introduction by V. E. Chancellor (London: Evelyn, Adams, and MacKay, 1969) p. 84; James Mullin, *The Story of a Toiler's Life*, edited by P. Maume (Dublin: University College Dublin Press, 2000) p. 12; see also [Charles Shaw], *When I Was a Child, by An Old Potter*, with an introduction by R. S. Watson (London: Methuen and Co., 1903).

[157] H. J. Ward, *My Early Recollections of Charing since 1868* (Rother Valley Press, Charing and District Local History Society, 2002), p. 11. For the development of British and National schools in the nineteenth century, see Ch. 4, pp. 199–205.

The interpretation of corporal punishment as the main if not only tool many masters had to ensure order in the classroom speaks also to the nature of the violence encountered. It was employed not necessarily as punishment for individual incapacity or misbehaviour but as more general social control. Hence its capricious nature with many of the boys not knowing why they were being punished or complaining that they themselves were not guilty of the crimes under indictment! This interpretation also speaks to the spectacle that punishment often involved, with idiosyncratic implements and ritual employed to terrorise the rest of the schoolroom.

· ·

Working-class children in England continued to be bruised and beaten in the classroom with the introduction of compulsory schooling in 1870. In a new democratic age, however, working-class parents appear to have been less ready to see their children punished at the hands of their 'superiors' and often complained to the authorities. The right to administer corporal punishment was seen as a prerogative of parents; teachers, especially pupil teachers who used the cane frequently were felt to be infringing on their province.[158] In this regard, working-class parents differed from middle-class ones who continued to accept that boys, if not girls, could be beaten at school, however unwilling many of them may have been to use corporal punishment in the home. Indeed, there is good reason to believe that well-to-do boys suffered physical chastisement at school much more than in the past, if only because so many more were boarding pupils with the growing popularity of the new public schools.[159] Historically, only a few elite schools, such as Eton and Winchester, had had a large boarding department. Most boys attending the old grammar schools had lived at home or taken lodgings in the town. However, the promoters of the new public schools, such as Rugby's Thomas Arnold (1795–1842), argued that boys needed to be taken out of their home environment completely if they were to gain the 'character' they would need to be a success in later life.[160] As boarders, boys were at school all the time and constantly faced by the threat of physical punishment. Beatings too were administered not just by teachers but by other boys through the prefectorial and fagging system. Most parents accepted this with equanimity.[161] So did the state. Except in the very rare cases where a boy was beaten to death (as at Eastbourne in 1860), teachers or their surrogates only found themselves in court for assault when they had administered punishment in an unnatural fashion. Thus, in 1910 a prefect at Magdalen College School, Oxford, seems to have only been pursued in law by the father of a young boy because he had beaten his son with an unusual implement.[162]

---

[158] See the chapter on corporal punishment in S. Pooley's pending Cambridge doctoral thesis on parenting in England 1860–1910.

[159] For the development, J. Chandos, *Boys Together: English Public Schools 1800–1864* (London: Hutchinson, 1984*)*; also Fletcher, *Growing Up*, ch. 13.

[160] For Arnold's views in particular, see M. McCrum, *Thomas Arnold, Headmaster: A Reassessment* (Oxford: Oxford University Press, 1989). Many of the new public schools were revivified old grammar schools.

[161] Middle-class boys who were not sent to public school tended to be depicted as sissies, afraid of being toughened up: *e.g.*, C. Bede, *The Adventures of Verdant Green*, originally published 1853–57 (Oxford: Oxford University Press, 1982), esp. pp. 6–7.

[162] Brockliss, *Magdalen College*, p. 550. For the Eastbourne case, see below, pp. 153–54

Corporal Punishment in the English Public School in the Nineteenth Century

Heather Ellis

The history of the English public schools in the nineteenth century is usually divided into two halves, an 'early' and 'later' period – before and after the 'reformation' brought about by the recommendations of the 1861 Clarendon Commission which reported on the state of education provided by England's nine leading public schools. So great is the difference perceived to be that historians often speak of 'pre-' and 'post-Clarendon' schools and use the date of the Commissioners' Report (1864) to structure the time-frame of their analyses.[163] While the improvements which took place were undoubtedly significant, in terms of financial efficiency, breadth of curriculum and living conditions, there is one aspect of school life which arguably became worse in the second half of the century – the practice of corporal punishment.[164]

Admittedly, some scholars have been keen to suggest that the Commissioners' Report marked an important watershed in this area as well.[165] Such a conclusion, however, is difficult to sustain. There is, first of all, little evidence to suggest that the Clarendon Commission was particularly concerned with corporal punishment; none at all that it was opposed on principle. An examination of the Commissioners' Report makes quite clear that their primary interest was in making the public schools more efficient, in broadening the narrowly classical curriculum and in giving the governing bodies the power to alter and reform their own statutes. Matters of internal discipline interested them only insofar as they contributed to the good running of the school; and corporal punishment was only one aspect of discipline which the Commissioners investigated. Their recommendations rarely refer to it directly and there is no mention of it in the 1868 Public Schools Act.

On the few occasions the Commissioners did mention corporal punishment in their Report, it is clear that they were primarily interested in regulating rather than

---

[163] See Chandos, *Boys Together*; C. Shrosbree, *Public Schools and Private Education: The Clarendon Commission 1861–64 and the Public Schools Acts* (Manchester: Manchester University Press, 1988). The Clarendon schools comprised the seven major boarding schools of Eton, Harrow, Winchester, Westminster, Rugby, Charterhouse and Shrewsbury and the two leading day schools, Merchant Taylors' and St Paul's. For the use of the terms 'early' and 'later' and 'pre-' and 'post-' in regard to the history of the English public school, see the reviews of Chandos's book by J. Halperin in *Victorian Studies*, 29:2 (Winter, 1986), 336; S. Rothblatt in the *American Journal of Education*, 94:1 (1985), 116–119, and J. A. Mangan in *Albion*, 17:1 (1985), 96–98; also. A. Bundgaard, *Muscle and Manliness: The Rise of Sport in American Boarding Schools* (Syracuse: Syracuse University Press, 2005), p. 27.

[164] For the view that the practice of corporal punishment in public schools remained largely unchanged, see J. A. Mangan, 'Bullies, Beatings, Battles and Bruises: "Great Days and Jolly Days" in One Mid-Victorian Public School', in M. Huggins and J. A. Mangan (eds), *Disreputable Pleasures: Less Virtuous Victorians at Play* (London: Routledge, 2004), pp. 3–34; J. Middleton, 'The Experience of Corporal Punishment in Schools, 1890–1940', *History of Education*, 37:2 (2008), 253–55.

[165] This view was first put forward by humanitarian writers in the late nineteenth and early twentieth centuries. Thus, H. S. Salt, *The Flogging Craze; A Statement of the Case Against Corporal Punishment* (London: G. Allen and Unwin, 1916), pp. 34–35, contrasted the present situation 'when the use of corporal punishment has been greatly restricted' in public schools with what he called 'the old flogging days'. For the influence of such arguments on more recent historians, see J. Roach, *Secondary Education in England, 1870–1902: Public Activity and Private Enterprise* (London: Routledge, 1991), p. 151.

opposing it *per se*. Their comments do, however, give us valuable information about where the boundary between the permissible and the impermissible lay at this time. Three issues appear of particular significance: who carried out the corporal punishment, how often it took place and what instrument was used. Thus, Eton was criticised for allegedly flogging boys 'five or six times a week', a number which, if true, rendered such punishment, 'much more frequent at Eton, in proportion to its numbers, than at other great schools'.[166] Charterhouse received even stronger censure for its regular policy of flogging boys who had committed three so-called 'ordinary faults' in a week. This practice, wrote the Commissioners, 'exists, so far as we are informed, in no other public school, and...appears to us undiscriminating and unduly severe. If this usage rests on any rule of the school', they declared, 'such rule ought in our opinion to be abrogated'.[167] Charterhouse was likewise criticised for allowing all its masters to flog pupils. This power, the Commissioners pronounced, 'should be strictly confined to the Head or Under Master or both'.[168] Similar concern was aroused in a couple of cases where senior boys were routinely allowed to administer lesser corporal punishments such as caning. In principle, the Commissioners had nothing against designated senior boys (usually prefects) being entrusted with such responsibilities as long as the system was carefully controlled. Once more, it is only what is considered abuse of the practice which is criticised. After hearing witnesses (including boys) from Westminster on the subject, they concluded that 'abuses of power may and sometimes do take place, and that undeserved or excessive punishments may be inflicted without the knowledge of the Masters, and without their interference'. 'To prevent such evils as far as possible ... proper regulations are required, and should be strictly and impartially enforced'.[169] In particular, boys should never be kicked and the right to punish should never be delegated to another boy who does not possess the requisite authority.[170]

From such comments, it is clear that the Commissioners were concerned only to prevent abuses. Their comments elsewhere reveal that they thought, when judiciously and correctly administered, corporal punishment was a necessary part of a school's system of discipline.[171] Their ideal in this respect was clearly Rugby where Arnold had been in charge from 1828 to 1842. There, flogging could only be administered by the headmaster and caning only by the masters and designated prefects or 'praepostors'. Moreover, such punishment was significantly less frequent at Rugby than at the other public schools covered by the inquiry. According to the Commissioners' findings, floggings occurred on average no more than eight times in a year and canings no more than five or six times in the course of a half year.[172] For the Commissioners, the key to an abuse-free system of corporal punishment was good relations between boys and masters, embodied in a carefully controlled monitorial system. While all the boarding schools investigated had historically developed such a system, in all, with the exception of Rugby, considerable problems had arisen in the way it was run. In the

---

[166] *Report of her Majesty's Commissioners Appointed to Inquire into the Revenues and Management of Certain Colleges and Schools, and the Studies Pursued and Instruction Given Therein* (London: George Edward Eyre and William Spottiswoode, 1864), p. 96. 'Flogging' refers to the practice of beating schoolboys usually with a birch rod.
[167] *Ibid.*, p. 182.
[168] *Ibid.*
[169] *Ibid.*, p. 162.
[170] *Ibid.*, p. 163.
[171] It should be pointed out that corporal punishment (along with a prefect-fagging system) was primarily a feature of boarding-school life. It took place significantly less often in private day schools such as Merchant Taylors' and St Paul's which were also investigated by the Clarendon Commission. See *Report* (1864), pp. 194 and 203.
[172] *Ibid.*, p. 257.

opinion of the Commissioners, this was directly connected with a tendency to permit extreme or unusual corporal punishment practices. Thus, in Westminster, as we have seen, boys other than prefects were found to be usurping the authority to physically chastise younger boys and using unlicensed methods. The problems of Charterhouse and Eton, in which masters were condemned for flogging boys too often, were explicitly related to the failings of their respective monitorial systems. In Charterhouse, as part of the fagging system, little boys were routinely treated as servants[173] and in Eton, the monitorial system had virtually disappeared.[174]

Rugby offered a striking contrast. Here, the Commissioners reported, there was a clear system of regulations (dating from Dr Arnold's time) which strictly limited the authority of praepostors:

> [T]hey are armed with power to set impositions [written tasks] to boys in all forms below the Sixth...and to inflict personal chastisement on any boy below the Fifth by not more than five or six strokes of a stick or cane applied to the shoulders. As the use of the fist is forbidden, they commonly carry canes when they are on duty...which they use on such occasion in the Master's presence and on the spot.[175]

'We are of opinion', the Commissioners concluded, 'that the monitorial power...could scarcely be guarded from excess or abuse with greater care than it is at Rugby'.[176] More important than all these official checks and balances, however, was the impressive moral tone of the school which had become noticeable ever since Dr Arnold's time. 'The moral and religious training of the boys at Rugby', they commented,

> is considered by the masters as the end of a Rugby education paramount to all others. The tutors aim at this in their intercourse with their pupils, and the Sixth Form are looked up to by the younger boys, though still in the character of boys, yet as the guardians of the School's good name.[177]

Moreover, the Commissioners felt that the positive effect which Rugby had had on other public schools since the days of Arnold had been enough to check excessive corporal punishment and reduce the need for physical chastisement generally. No particular intervention on their part was required. It was their impression that, within the system as a whole, 'corporal punishment has...greatly diminished; flogging which twenty or thirty years ago was resorted to as a matter of course for the most trifling offences, is now in general used sparingly, and applied only to serious ones'.[178] Indeed, far from the moral chaos of the 'unreformed' schools which historians like John Chandos encourage us to think of, the Commissioners generally found a system with which they were pleased and which had, without government assistance, already made substantial improvements.[179]

From this, then, we can see that the Clarendon Commissioners did not set out to reform a brutal and abusive system of public-school discipline. If there had been change for the better, it had been achieved through internal reform on the model of Rugby;

---

173 *Ibid.*, p. 182.
174 *Ibid.*, p. 94.
175 *Ibid.*, p. 257.
176 *Ibid.*, p. 258.
177 *Ibid.*, p. 259.
178 *Ibid.*, p. 44.
179 *Ibid.* 'On the general results of public-school education as an instrument for the training of character, we can speak with much confidence...We are satisfied, on the whole that it has been eminently successful, and that it has been greatly improved during the last 30 or 40 years, partly by causes of a general kind, partly by the personal influence and exertions of Dr. Arnold and other great schoolmasters'.

and corporal punishment, within accepted boundaries, continued to be recommended. By the end of the century, however, it is arguable, that there had been a change for the worse with government advisers and schoolmasters far less concerned about the negative effects of corporal punishment. What evidence we have suggests that physical chastisement, although more strictly regulated than before, actually increased in incidence in the so-called Clarendon schools; moreover, as these schools set the tone for the large numbers of private foundations established in the second half of the century, we should think in terms of a much larger number of boys receiving corporal punishment than in the early or mid-Victorian period.

Although there is no Commissioners' report comparable with that of 1864, a wide range of sources seems to confirm this picture. In his account of Eton in the second half of the nineteenth century under the government of Dr Hornby, Henry Stephens Salt declared that 'the Birch was in constant use'.[180] In the 1880s, at St James' School, a preparatory school for Eton, Winston Churchill wrote that 'Flogging with the birch in accordance with the Eton fashion was a great feature in its curriculum'. Two or three times a month, screaming boys were 'flogged until they bled freely'.[181] A French observer, writing in 1879, could barely 'conceive the perseverance with which English teachers cling to the old and degrading custom of corrections by the rod'.[182] By 1906, an expert commissioned by Parliament to compile a report on preparatory schools could write that the necessity of regular corporal punishment in the discipline of young boys was taken by him as 'an axiom'.[183]

In attempting to account for this hardening of attitudes, we must certainly attribute some importance to the fact that public schools remained bastions of conservatism throughout the second half of the nineteenth century. As calls grew, particularly from humanitarian groups, to abolish corporal punishment in other institutions such as prisons and in the armed forces, it is hardly surprising that public schools would seek to defend a traditional part of their system. As one French observer commented, 'The rod is one of those ancient English traditions which survive because they have survived'.[184]

However, we must go beyond mere force of tradition if we are to understand why the desire to minimise corporal punishment visible in the Commissioners' Report of 1864 did not continue to grow in the later decades of the nineteenth century. In particular, we need to look more closely at Britain's international position in this period and at the close association in the popular imagination between the public school and the British Empire.

In the 1870s, as is well known, Britain experienced an unprecedented wave of popular imperialism. This has been related convincingly by historians such as Bernard Porter to growing fears that Britain was falling behind her imperial rivals, America and Germany.[185] As the public schools were traditionally seen as the 'chief nurseries' of English statesmen',[186] their condition was believed to reflect the state of the Empire

[180] H. S. Salt, *Eton under Hornby: Some Reminiscences and Reflections* (London: A. C. Fifield, 1910), p. 109.
[181] W. Churchill, *A Roving Commission: My Early Life* (London: C. Scribner's Sons, 1941), p. 12.
[182] G. Compayré, *The History of Pedagogy*, trans. W. H. Payne (London: George Allen and Unwin Ltd., 1887), p. 202. It should be pointed out that the English-speaking world in general presented a stark contrast with continental Europe, particularly with France, Belgium and Holland, which had all taken steps to abolish corporal punishment in secondary education by the end of the nineteenth century: see below, pp. 146–47.
[183] *Special Reports on Educational Subjects vol. 6. Preparatory Schools for Boys: Their Place in English Secondary Education* (London: Wyman and Sons, 1900), p. 400.
[184] Quoted in W. M. Cooper, *A History of the Rod* (London: William Reese, 1910). p. 445.
[185] See *e.g.* B. Porter, *The Lion's Share: A Short History of British Imperialism 1850–2004* (Harlow: Pearson Longman, 2004).
[186] *Report* (1864), p. 56.

more broadly and analogies were frequently made between them. Thus, as fears began to grow about the fitness of Britain to compete with America and Germany, particularly in terms of the technological capacity required by the modern world, criticism of the public schools and their narrowly classical curriculum began to increase substantially. Such fears did play a role in the establishment of the Clarendon Commission in 1861 but became much more significant in the later decades of the century. As well as the curriculum, the general efficiency of public schools came in for regular attack. In an article in *Macmillan's Magazine* from 1905, Sir Charles Bruce declared public school education to be 'in a very bad way' and quite unable to play its important role in 'the imperial system'. Public schools must take account, he wrote, of 'the need of nations to keep abreast with others in their productive capacity'.[187] At such a time, 'there is special need', wrote Robert Gregory, Dean of St Paul's and a member of the 1886 Education Commission,[188] 'for what will strengthen the moral fibre of the boy, and by encouraging fortitude under the infliction of bodily pain, nurture true manliness and courage, without which no man can play well his part in life'.[189] In such an atmosphere, it is not at all inconceivable that public-school headmasters, in particular, felt under pressure to be seen to be improving discipline. A return to the rigorous corporal punishment of the early nineteenth century was hailed by a number of commentators as the best possible response to the perceived crisis in public-school education.[190]

A related factor which tended to increase the practice of corporal punishment was the rise of a cult of athleticism at the public schools in the latter half of the nineteenth century. This phenomenon has been well described by historians such as J. A. Mangan, who have linked it convincingly with the growing insecurities felt about Britain's imperial role and the need to improve the fitness of the future leaders of Empire.[191] As the athletic ideal privileged outdoor team sports above all else, it was naturally opposed to forms of punishment which detained boys behind after class, thus depriving them of free time. While detention was favoured by humanitarian activists, athletics enthusiasts thought traditional forms of corporal punishment far kinder and healthier for boys who should be outdoors, playing with each other and cultivating the qualities of hardiness and manliness. Hely Hutchinson Almond, Headmaster of Loretto School, near Edinburgh, declared that to deprive a boy of fresh air and exercise 'is as monstrous as to deprive him of sufficient food or sleep'.[192]

We should also place the increasing enthusiasm for flogging in public schools against the background of a more general reaction in favour of corporal punishment from the mid-1860s onwards. Henry Stephens Salt dated this tendency to the year 1863, when, following a spate of garrottings in London, one of which involved an M.P., a Security from Violence Act was passed which reinstituted flogging as a punishment for robbery with violence. Particularly in the 1880s and early 1890s, a number of private members' bills which advocated extending the use of flogging as a punishment for burglary, rape

---

[187] Sir Charles Bruce, 'Our Public Schools and the Empire', *Macmillan's Magazine*, n.s.1 (Nov. 1905–Oct. 1906), p. 76. It is noteworthy, in terms of the context in which these criticisms of public schools occurred, that the preceding article in the same issue of *Macmillan's Magazine* was entitled 'Has the British Soldier Deteriorated?' (written by Lt. General A. P. A. Pollock).

[188] The Education Commission of 1886 was charged with assessing the adequacy of the supply of schools established under the Education Act of 1870 that set up a national system of elementary education in England and Wales, and the Act's effectiveness in providing for the present and future needs of the new system.

[189] R. Gregory, 'Is Corporal Punishment Degrading?', *North American Review*, 153 (July December 1891), 701.

[190] See *e.g.*, 'Caning in Public Schools', *The Times* (8 Feb. 1910), p. 9; col. F.

[191] See *e.g.*, J. A. Mangan, *Athleticism in the Victorian and Edwardian Public School: The Emergence and Consolidation of an Educational Ideology* (Cambridge: Cambridge University Press, 1981), pp. 122–40, 179–206.

[192] H. H. Almond, 'Athletics and Education', *Macmillan's Magazine*, 43 (Nov. 1880–Apr. 1881), p. 291.

and a whole range of offences committed by juveniles received significant parliamentary and public support. The Vagrancy Act of 1898 and the Criminal Law Amendment Act of 1912 successfully extended the use of flogging as a punishment for a range of crimes including living off the immoral earnings of a prostitute. Writing in 1916, at the height of the First World War, Salt declared that in recent years 'the correspondence of the "yellow" Press have [sic] often teemed with letters demanding the lash as the sole adequate penalty for all sorts of evil-doers – hooligans [,] wife-beaters, dynamitards, train-wreckers, burglars, *etc.*'[193] Such a reaction was particularly associated with fears about Britain's imperial status – most obviously when flogging in Indian prisons (which had been abolished by Lord William Bentinck in 1834) was restored in 1864 as part of the official British response to the Indian Mutiny of 1857.[194]

A focus on the practice of corporal punishment in the English public schools raises important questions about the validity of the traditional tendency to separate the history of public schools in the nineteenth century into a pre- and post-Clarendon era. While there were undoubtedly important reforms in the latter half of the century, the continued (and increased) use of corporal punishment seriously undercuts the effectiveness of such a distinction. More broadly, it challenges the still popular tendency to present the history of the nineteenth century as a Whiggish narrative of social progress. While humanitarian calls for the reduction of corporal punishment perhaps made some headway in public schools in the early Victorian period, the Clarendon Commission of 1861 should in no way be seen as heralding a new period of humane punishments for public schoolboys. Rather, against a background of increasing anxiety about Britain's imperial position and the role of the public schools in educating future leaders of Empire, we see an increasingly unashamed defence of corporal punishment from government advisers and headmasters alike.

. . . .

Britain before the First World War was not peculiar in permitting boys at elementary and secondary school to be beaten. The only European countries where measures were taken to limit dramatically physical punishment in schools in the course of the nineteenth century were France, Belgium and Holland.[195] In France the first steps were taken in 1802 when Napoleon established the *lycées* as the new state-run secondary schools for elder boys (chiefly fifteen- to eighteen-year-olds) studying Latin, Greek, mathematics and philosophy. From their inception, the use of corporal punishment was banned. Instead, Napoleon put in place a military-style discipline where pupils (usually boarders) were subject to close surveillance and punished by being deprived of holidays and treats and even locked up for several days at a time in the school gaol. Beatings continued in French elementary schools and the private secondary colleges largely in the hands of the Catholic teaching orders. But when the provision of elementary education was in turn totally taken over by the state under the *Loix Ferry* of 1881 and 1882 (the system had gradually been laicised from the 1830s), the use of physical violence of any kind by teachers was banned from all government-financed educational institutions. This did not mean that teachers faced with large classes of unruly and unwilling children from poor backgrounds always obeyed the rules. It did mean, though, that those who struck their pupils frequently and arbitrarily

---

[193] Salt, *The Flogging Craze,* p. 19.
[194] *Ibid.,* pp. 20–1.
[195] Corporal punishment had been ended temporarily in the Austrian *lycées* in 1780/1 and Polish schools in 1783; there was also a Saxon school plan to end corporal punishment drawn up in 1773: see W. Clark, *Academic Charisma and the Origins of the Research University* (London: University of Chicago Press, 2006), p. 123.

were soon in trouble, all the more that working-class parents quickly learnt the law and complained to the authorities.[196]

The first European country after Holland and Belgium to follow in France's wake was Sweden where corporal punishment was banned from the state's secondary schools, the gymnasia, in 1928. Elsewhere, however, there was no significant change in the use of physical punishment in school (*i.e.*, no serious challenge to the Renaissance belief that its use was valid in the last resort, if administered calmly) until after the Second World War. Even then states moved slowly to abolish the practice in its schools. The new Federal Republic of Germany outlawed corporal punishment from educational institutions immediately, but in 1950s Britain the cane (which replaced the birch as the instrument of choice in the second half of the nineteenth century) continued to be liberally applied.[197] It was not until 1987, and after a long campaign by opponents, that its use was forbidden in state funded schools and only in 1999 that it was made illegal in the private system.[198]

By the 1980s, however, the tide of educated European and international opinion was fast running in favour of banning the physical chastisement of children altogether. Sweden was again at the vanguard. In the second half of the nineteenth and the first half of the twentieth centuries, there were a number of other state-controlled or state-supervised institutions, besides schools, where children were historically subject to a harsh disciplinary regime, notably orphanages and reformatories.[199] In 1960 Sweden led the way in outlawing the use of corporal punishment in childcare institutions completely; then in 1979 it banned caning and spanking in the home. In the following decade, the other Nordic countries followed suit, and by the turn of the twenty-first century most western European states had outlawed the practice. England still lags behind in that it has not banned physical chastisement in the home completely (smacking is deemed legal if it does not leave a permanent mark), but it is under pressure to do so. At the beginning of the new millennium, international, not just European, opinion moved decisively in favour of a blanket ban, and the United Nations targeted 2009 as the year by which it hoped that all forms of corporal punishment would have ended throughout the world.[200] As with so many international and national targets however, the deadline came and went without any meaningful worldwide ban.

It would not be wrong therefore to argue that our modern view of good parenting and

---

[196] J.-C. Caron, 'Maintenir l'ordre dans les collèges et les lycées: théories et pratiques disciplinaires dans l'enseignement secondaire français (1815–1870)', in J.-P. Bardet, J.-N. Luc, I. Robin-Romero and C. Rollet (eds), *Lorsque l'enfant grandit. Entre dépendance et autonomie* (Paris: Presses Universitatires Françaises, 2002), pp. 605–17; J. Krop, 'Punitions corporelles et actes de brutalité dans les écoles primaires publiques du département de la Seine', *Histoire de l'éducation*, 118 (2008), 109–32. For the general development of French education in the nineteenth and early twentieth centuries, see F. Lebrun, Marc Venard and J. Quéniart (eds), *Histoire générale de l'enseignement et de l'éducation en France* (4 vols; Paris: Labat, 1981), vol. 3.

[197] Private preparatory schools for nine to thirteen year-old-boys could be particularly harsh institutions: see A. Motion, *In the Blood: A Memoir of My Childhood* (London: Faber and Faber, 2006), *passim* (for life in a prep school in the early 1960s).

[198] For a general account, see M. Parker-Jenkins, *Sparing the Rod. Schools, Discipline and Children's Rights* (Stoke-on-Trent: Trentham, 1999). Paradoxically, in Britain, it was within the private system that the first moves to end corporal punishment were taken, though this was not the view popularised through children's books and television in the 1950s and early 1960s (especially the *Billy Bunter* series), nor in Lindsey Anderson's hard-hitting film, *If* (1968). For the debate, see P. Newell, *A Last Resort? Corporal Punishment in Schools* (Harmondsworth: Penguin, 1972).

[199] See Ch. 2, pp. 80–83 and 91–95.

[200] http://en.wikipedia.org/wiki/Image:Corporal_punishment_in_Europe.svg (accessed 5 Dec. 2008), esp. map; 'UN Secretary-General's Study on Violence against Children' (2006), p. 36: www.unviolencestudyorg (accessed 17 Sept. 2009). See also S. N. Hart with J. Durrant, P. Newell and F. C. Power, *Eliminating Corporal Punishment – The Way Forward to Constructive Child Discipline* (Paris: Unesco Publishing, 2005). Britain banned the use of corporal punishment in reformatory schools in the 1980s.

child-rearing that frowns on all forms of physical chastisement is only 30 years old, even if the debate over the rights and wrongs of corporal punishment goes back centuries and the voices condemning its use were gathering force from the beginning of the twentieth century. Such a dramatic and absolute revaluation of a practice that state and church had judged uncontroversial, if properly administered, for two millennia, can only be the result of a complex set of factors, to which we are arguably too close to unravel. Yet at the simplest – the political – level, the impulse for the revolution is easily fathomable. It is the result of a long-term campaign by a breed of childcare specialists unknown before the early twentieth century: child psychologists, educationalists and neurologists.

While medics replaced clerics as the predominant pedlars of child-rearing advice from the beginning of the eighteenth century, as we have seen, it was only in our modern era that this advice became scientised, that is to say based on purportedly objective observations and experiments. The first signs of a second new paediatrics and pedagogy can be found right at the beginning of the twentieth century with the work of figures, such as the American evolutionary psychologist, G. Stanley Hall (1844–1924), author of *Adolescence* (1904). But it was from the 1930s with the publication of the discoveries of the Swiss Jean Piaget (1896–1980) and his followers that child development became fully recognised as a serious academic endeavour. Today research into children's cognitive, physical and emotional development is an important and expensive part of any university's activities, one that occupies the attentions of the social as much as the medical scientist. And the predominant advice of the modern scientific expert is that physically punishing children is not just morally wrong but detrimental to their normal development and socialisation.[201]

From the beginning of the twentieth century, child development scientists and childcare experts have been quick to place their ideas before the wider public in magazines and popular childcare manuals where they found a receptive audience among a newly empowered, expanding and vocal political constituency, the female middle-classes. But it was only after 1946 that the market for their ideas exploded with the publication of the *Commonsense Book of Baby and Child Care* by Benjamin Spock (1903–98). In the Anglophone world for the next twenty years, there can have been few educated households uninfluenced directly or indirectly by his siren song of relaxed parenting. Spock's monopolisation of the genre rapidly declined from the mid-1960s and thereafter no single manual has commanded universal respect. Yet in some ways this has simply been result of the ever-expanding market which has allowed more and more childcare gurus to break into field. By the early 1980s the production of childcare manuals was an industry and the market was large enough for Britain and America to go separate ways. Towards the end of the twentieth century, authors such as Sheila Kitzinger (b. 1929) and Penelope Leach (b. 1937) were dominant on one side of the Atlantic; William and Martha Sears (b. 1940) on the other.[202]

However, the fact that child development was scientised in the course of the twentieth century and the scientists' theories marketed to the public only begins to explain the late twentieth-century revolution in child-rearing. After all, expert opinion on the best method of rearing a child was and is not monolithic. Once the monopoly of Dr Spock came to an end, the public was offered a smorgasbord of possible approaches: a normal child could be

---

[201] On the history of the science of child development, see E. D. Cahan, 'Child Development' and J. Kagan, 'Child Psychology', in P. Fass (ed.), *Encyclopedia of Children and Childhood. In History and Society* (3 vols; Indianapolis: Macmillan USA, 2004), i, pp. 152–56 and i, pp. 167–70.

[202] J. Mechling, 'Child-Rearing Advice Literature', in Fass, *Encyclopedia*, i, pp. 170–174; C. Hardyment, *Dream Babies: Childcare advice from John Locke to Gina Ford* (London: Frances Lincoln Publishers, 2007). One of the new gurus in Britain in the first decade of the twenty-first century is Gina Ford whose *The Contented Little Baby Book* and *From Contented Baby to Confident Child* first appeared in 1999 and 2000.

produced through diet, behavioural management, attachment parenting, and so on.[203] Even the Augustinian voice was not totally silenced. In 1981 the evangelical right in the United States published a childcare manual entitled *God, the Rod, and Your Children's Bod. The Art of Loving Correction for Christian Parents*. The scientification of childcare alone cannot explain the middle-class public's predominant preference over the last 30 years for the most gentle, child-centred options.[204]

It is here that we enter the realm of speculation. Given the timing of the change, especially outside Scandinavia, it is tempting to see the new sensibility as part of the post-war baby-boom generation's much wider rejection of tradition that was initially articulated in teenage rebellion in the 1960s and early 1970s but has come to mark their behaviour as adults too. In the main, better educated, wealthier and more mobile than their parents, middle-class baby-boomers were much freer than earlier generations to take their own decisions on child-rearing. Moreover, in general scornful of traditional Christian dogma and ethics and committed hedonists, they were hardly likely to follow earlier generations down the Augustinian road. But independence can breed anxiety and loneliness.[205] It is not surprising that many affluent middle-class mothers, unsure of how to proceed but keen to do their best by their children and raised to believe in the objectivity of the expert, fell easy prey to childcare gurus who preached a paediatrics of empathy; nor that they spent large sums of money on the many books, toys and games that were sold as essential child-rearing aids.[206] There can never have been a generation of children more agonised over than that born to the post-war baby-boomers. In many ways, they have been treated like precious china or fragile flowers, escorted to school, ferried from activity to activity, and never let out of the parental sight. In part, this must reflect the fact that most baby-boomers have had small families and often left parenting until their 30s. Children, it is argued, become more valued and cosseted, the fewer there are. Yet middle-class families were practising birth control in Europe from the early twentieth century, and no earlier generation of parents, including the baby-boomers' own, were so neurotically careful.[207]

Whatever the socio-cultural determinants underlying the revolution, there can be no doubt of one of its most profound consequence, the reconceptualisation of the child in law. Before the American and French revolutions in the late eighteenth century, it was accepted that human beings were equal before God. Only a few political theorists, notably John Locke, had drawn from this the conclusion that they should also be equal before the law. The existing social and economic inequalities were justified on the grounds that humans were also equally depraved and needed to be hierarchically organised if they were not to tear each

---

[203] Attachment parenting is favoured by the Sears. Parents are recommended to fall in with children's feeding and sleeping demands; many years of breast-feeding is promoted to improve bonding.

[204] The United States has not moved as far or as fast as most European countries towards outlawing harsh parenting, an indication of the power traditional Christianity has in many states.

[205] It can also lead to decisions potentially dangerous to wider society. In the 1990s many middle-class parents accepted the findings of one medical scientist who argued that the MMR vaccination could cause autism. The result is that the British population is far less protected against measles than a generation ago.

[206] Of course, the upsurge in 'learning-enhancement' toys sold by chains such as the Early Learning Centre (in the UK marketed to privately-run playschools as much as the middle-class home – state nurseries bought and buy from government-approved catalogues) was only the tip of the ice-berg: the growing commercialisation of childhood *tout court* was one of the leading consequences of post-war affluence: see A. Offer, *Challenges of Affluence: Self-Control and Well-Being* (Oxford: Oxford University Press, 2006).

[207] Cf. V. Zelizer, *Pricing the Priceless Child: The Changing Social Value of Children* (Princeton: Princeton University Press 1994). The role played by the size of families in determining patterns of childcare may explain the apparent indulgence of French middle-class parents in the nineteenth century (see above, p. 133). The French population remained relatively stable in the nineteenth century, while everywhere else in Europe it multiplied manifold.

other part and frustrate God's intention that we should obey (if necessary by force) divine law. The American and French revolutionaries for the first time asserted that all men were equal in civil society and had certain natural rights that could not be violated. Initially, men meant adult males, not women and children, but even in this limited form the doctrine of natural rights had an important impact on how nineteenth-century society was organised. In the context of punishment (of particular significance in this present chapter), it led to the abolition of the use of the lash on adult males in the armed forces and wider society. If men were equal before the law, then the poor and the rich must be punished in the same way: if flogging was dishonourable, it could no longer be used (as it had been historically) to control the lower orders. In most nineteenth century European states (Russia accepted) corporal punishment became the exclusive burden of children.[208]

The distinction now hinged on the equation of humanity with rationality. Children and women were not as rational as adult males and therefore did not enjoy the same natural rights. By the middle of the twentieth century, however, women too had successfully asserted that they had the same cognitive capacity as men (a claim enunciated as early as the 1790s by Mary Wollstonecraft) and won a place in the sun, leaving only children as inferior beings. And by then the equation was fast breaking down. In a post-Freudian world, it was difficult to argue that adults were rational, children only potentially so. The door was open to argue that all human beings had the same natural rights simply by dint of being human, and that children should not be treated differently. What has philosophically underpinned the move over the last 30 years to end corporal punishment in disciplining children is the novel belief that children should enjoy the same protection under the law as adults. Hence in the opinion of the United Kingdom's children's commissioners, pushing the British government, like other lobbyists, to make all forms of corporal punishment illegal in the twenty-first century, there can be no half-way house.

> Children have the same right as adults to respect for their human dignity and physical integrity and to equal protection under the law, in the home and everywhere else. There is no room for compromise, for attempting to define 'acceptable' smacking. This has been confirmed by United Nations and Council of Europe human rights monitoring mechanisms, and by the Westminster Parliamentary Joint Committee on Human Rights. The UK has been told repeatedly since 1995 that to comply with its human rights obligations, the reasonable punishment defence must be removed completely in all four countries of the UK.[209]

In the European context, the right of children to enjoy the immunities and advantages of adults has been implied from the promulgation of the European Convention on Human Rights in 1952. The nature of these rights, however, was only clearly articulated with the promulgation of the 1989 United Nations Convention on the Rights of the Child. Since

---

[208] Flogging was abolished in the British Army in 1868, though it could be administered for offences committed on campaign till 1881 and in military prisons till 1907. A. R. Skelley, *The Victorian Army at Home* (London: Croom Helm, 1967). Flogging was suspended in the navy in 1881 but not abolished and remained a theoretical punishment until 1939. Boy seamen were still caned in the first decade of the twentieth century: A. Carew, *The Lower Deck of the Royal Navy, 1900–1939: The Invergordon Mutiny in Perspective* (Manchester: Manchester University Press, 1981), ch. 2.

[209] Statement by the four UK Commissioners for Children and Young People on the physical punishment of children (Jan. 2006): see www.niccy.org/article.aspx?menuid=465 (accessed 17 Sept. 2009). For a general introduction, see J. M. Hawes, *The Children's Rights Movement: History of Advocacy and Protection* (Boston: Twayne Publishers, 1991), and specifically, P. Newell, *Children are People Too: The Case Against Physical Punishment* (London: Bedford Square Press, 1989). On the reasonable punishment defence, see below, pp. 153–54. Children's commissioners for the four constituent parts of the United Kingdom were first appointed at the beginning of the twenty-first century. Their existence emphasises the British government's professed new commitment to children's rights.

then the United Nations Committee established to oversee the Convention has continually called on states that are parties to it to prohibit corporal punishment and other forms of violence against children in their home and in institutions. 'To discipline or punish through physical harm is clearly a violation of the most basic of human rights. Research on corporal punishment has found it to be counterproductive and relatively ineffective, as well as dangerous and harmful to physical, psychological and social well being'.[210]

Embodying this principle in national law, on the other hand, has been a slow business, as is clear from what has been said above. In Europe's democratic polities the legislatures have had to take account of the more traditional views of the whole of the electorate, not just the more liberal baby-boomers. In England, too, where the pace has been particularly slow, legislators (many of whom are lawyers) have been constrained by the fact that the parental right to chastise has been a long-standing right under common law, which is always seen by the media as the bulwark of the people's liberty and not to be lightly tampered with.

Children, Cruelty and Corporal Punishment in Twentieth-Century England: The Legal Framework

Stephen Cretney

The law imperfectly reflects social facts. But the legal framework governing the relationship between parent and child, and between the family and the state, does throw some light on the 'official' perception of these matters. The civil law gives its own answers to some questions.[211] What, legally, is the relationship between parent and child? What authority does a parent have to take decisions on a child's behalf – for example, can the parent legally bind his child to an apprenticeship or take decisions about the child's employment, schooling, religious upbringing and so on?[212] In so far as a parent is entitled to exercise control over the child, what means is the parent entitled to use: can a father lock up his daughter to prevent her seeing someone of whom he disapproves? Can he beat his son or daughter in an attempt to discipline them? What are the obligations of a parent to maintenance – food, housing and so on – for the child? And what is to happen if the father and the mother disagree about their child's upbringing?

So the civil law is conceptually important. But, in the context of the relationship between child and family, it provides in reality only inadequate means for enforcing

---

[210] It was this committee which commissioned the report cited in fn. 200, above. The quotation comes from an UNESCO press release about the report: see www.canadiancrc.com/Child_Abuse/Supreme_Court_Case_Spanking.aspx (accessed 17 Sept. 2009). The key article of the United Nations Convention on the Rights of the Child regarding corporal punishment is, article 19.

[211] This expression is used here in contrast to the 'criminal law', concerned to secure the punishment of an offender and protect the public interest at the instance of the state. Although the distinction is clear in principle, the fact that the same act (*e.g.*, beating a child with force deemed excessive, as discussed below) may constitute both a crime and a civil wrong to the victim, has many difficult implications: see generally A. Ashworth, *Principles of Criminal Law*, 4th edn (Oxford: Oxford University Press, 2003), ch. 1.

[212] Until 1973 the parent, for these purposes, meant the father. However, if the child were illegitimate, it meant the mother: see generally, S. M. Cretney, *Family Law in the Twentieth Century* (Oxford: Oxford University Press, 2003), pt. iv.

legal rights. There are many reasons for this. One is that civil enforcement depends on there being someone directly interested who is able and willing to provide protection which the law theoretically offers. Sir William Blackstone (1723–80),[213] writing in the mid-eighteenth century, explained that whilst a father was legally obliged to provide maintenance for his children, the scope of this obligation was limited: the law 'ever watchful to promote industry' would not compel a father to maintain his idle and lazy children in ease and indolence, or provide them with anything beyond 'necessaries'. So the scope of the legal duty was much more restricted than might at first appear. And even if the father failed this undemanding obligation how was the child to compel him to do so? The law would not allow him to bring or defend a legal action in his own name, but only through a guardian or a 'next friend': the infant (like the married woman until 1882) was not regarded as a legal person. The result, according to Blackstone, was that, in practice, even the affluent were left to decide for themselves whether they would 'breed up their children to be ornaments or disgraces' to their families. It is not much use having a legal right if there are in practice no procedures whereby the right can be enforced.

For these reasons, what today is called public law – the law governing the relationship between public authorities – and the criminal law are of such great importance in the development of what we now call the 'rights' of the child. Thus Blackstone, only half ironically, claimed that the children of the 'poor and laborious part of the community' were in a favoured position compared with the middle and upper classes. This was (he claimed) because the Poor Law (created by Act of Parliament in 1601) would take destitute children out of the hands of their parents and place them 'in such manner as may render their abilities of the greatest advantage to the commonwealth'. And the guardians (as its local administrators were called) would then enforce the parent's obligation to maintain by getting an order from quarter sessions (the historic court of first instance) for the seizure and sale of his goods and chattels to recoup their expenditure on supporting the child.

The criminal law was the other formal sanction for the protection of the child. Wrongful killing and assault were offences whether the victim was a child or an adult. But getting a conviction depended, firstly, on someone being aware of the facts and deciding to institute a prosecution, and on the prosecutor then being able to prove the guilt of the defendant. In practice the 'veil of privacy' which society (supported by law) threw round the family meant that prosecutions were rare. Only in the late nineteenth century, with the foundation of the National Society for the Prevention of Cruelty to Children and the enactment of the Prevention of Cruelty to, and Protection of, Children Act in 1889, did it become accepted policy to seek to involve the criminal law in what in practice had previously been largely ignored.[214]

Concepts such as 'cruelty', ill-treatment and neglect can, however, only be interpreted in the light of contemporary understandings of the appropriate relationship between adults and children and knowledge about child psychology and development. The law governing the use of corporal punishment on children provides a salutary example of changing attitudes. The common law of England (although not as clearly structured as Roman Law and the modern legal systems directly influenced by it in formulating the scope of a parent's legal authority) allowed a child's father to use 'moderate and

---

[213] Vinerian Professor of the Laws of England in the University of Oxford and Judge of the Common Pleas and King's Bench: his *Commentaries on the Laws of England* (1765–9) were accepted as an authoritative statement when they appeared.

[214] For the limited attempt by Parliament in the eighteenth century to protect poor apprentices from abuse, see Ch. 4, pp. 176 and 189–90.

reasonable corporal punishment … for the purpose of correcting what is evil in him'.[215] And for a long time the statute book reinforced the view that corporal punishment was an effective way of achieving this end. Legislation not only allowed misbehaved children to be whipped but specifically provided that a child, committed to a so-called Industrial School because he was thought to be 'in moral danger', could be given twelve strokes of the birch for any 'serious and wilful' breach of the school rules.[216] And even if the law did not allow a court to order corporal punishment of a child delinquent, it seems that the father's unchallenged right to beat his child could often be manipulated to fill what was seen as a gap in the legal sanctions. In 1908 the Home Secretary refused to take any action in a case where a magistrate told the father that the law did not allow his fifteen-year-old son, convicted of indecent exposure, to be flogged and that the only alternative to a prison sentence would be for the father, within the court precincts, to exercise his parental right and administer twelve strokes of the birch to the boy. Then the boy would be set free provided that the gaoler reported that he had had a 'proper flogging'. It seems that the father did as he was told,[217] and it may be that this practice was not uncommon: in 1931 a Home Office official, arguing (unsuccessfully) for the removal of juvenile courts' powers to order whipping as the punishment for a juvenile delinquent, noted that if magistrates thought 'a child would be better for some corporal punishment it can, in most cases, secure that such a chastisement is given by the parent'.[218]

It is true that there were always some restrictions on the parent's powers. In 1860 a 'dull' teenager died as the result of a beating administered by an Eastbourne schoolmaster. The schoolmaster's defence against a charge of manslaughter was that he had acted lawfully: the boy's father had specifically authorised him to 'subdue the boy's obstinacy' by 'chastising him severely, and if necessary again and again' and even if the boy held out for hours. The Lord Chief Justice directed the jury that a parent could indeed lawfully delegate his authority to beat a child to a schoolmaster but that this authority was confined to what was 'moderate and reasonable'. This meant that punishment 'administered for the gratification of passion or rage', or punishment 'immoderate and excessive in its nature or degree, or… protracted beyond the child's power of endurance, or with an instrument unfitted for the purpose and calculated to produce danger to life or limb' would be unlawful. Hence, if the beating caused 'evil consequences to life or limb' the person inflicting it would be answerable to the law, and if death ensued it would be manslaughter.[219] The jury evidently thought this

---

[215] The authoritative statement of this position was given by Lord Chief Justice Cockburn in *R v. Hopley* (1860) 2 F and F 902: see below.

[216] Children's Act 1908, s. 71 (2). It is significant that such a provision could be retained in an Act described at the time and subsequently as a 'children's charter'. The 'industrial schools' were boarding schools run by the churches and charities that flourished *c*. 1890–*c*. 1930: children at risk were housed a long way from their home town and subjected to rigid discipline: see N. Sheldon, 'Socialising the Anti-Social: England's Industrial Schools', in L. W. B. Brockliss and N. Sheldon (eds) *Mass Education and the Limits of State-Building* (Basingstoke: Palgrave Macmillan, forthcoming).

[217] *Hansard's Parliamentary Debates* (4th series), vol. 194, col. 34 (under 12 Oct. 1908).

[218] The National Archive (Kew), HO45/14715, 'Memorandum on draft 1931 Children and Young Persons Bill'. It also appears that in a number of cases children were whipped by the police on the basis that the child's parents authorised the punishment. The court would then formally discharge the offender. By this time, 'informed opinion' as reflected by the officials in the Children's Department of the Home Office was opposed to state-inflicted corporal punishment, but the strength of opinion in the legislature (especially in the House of Lords) made it politically impossible to legislate for abolition.

[219] *R v Hopley* (1860) 2 F and F 202, Lord Chief Justice Cockburn. For the background to the case, see J. Middleton, 'Thomas Hopley and Mid-Victorian Attitudes to Corporal Punishment', *History of Education*,

particular beating had been excessive: the schoolmaster was convicted of manslaughter and sentenced to four years' penal servitude.

The principle that a parent could lawfully administer 'moderate and reasonable' punishment remained the governing principle of English law until the enactment of the Children Act in 2004. So powerful was the opinion (at any rate of those who counted) in favour of beating that every statute criminalising child cruelty specifically preserved the 'moderate and reasonable' defence,[220] thereby effectively leaving it to a jury (or the magistrates in cases in the lower courts) to assess what is 'reasonable' in a given context. For example, in 1998 a jury acquitted a man who had beaten and bruised his nine-year-old step-son on several occasions, evidently accepting the defence to a charge of assault that the punishment had been 'moderate and reasonable'.[221]

The twentieth century saw increasing criticism of the law's approach to the use of corporal punishment. The case of the reforming Metropolitan magistrate, William Clarke Hall (1866–1932), is significant.[222] At one time, prepared to accept arguments justifying judicially ordered corporeal punishment of children, study of the evidence convinced him that the case for abolition was overwhelming.[223] And the need to respond to the social upheavals associated with the Second World War (especially the evacuation of children from the major cities and the consequent separation from their families) led to greater recognition of the value of professional social work and medical skills in the observation and assessment of children's psychological and developmental needs. The emergence of recognised professions and of formalised training in dealing with children may have been a factor in the emergence of more 'progressive' attitudes, whilst the 1945 Labour Government was less reluctant than pre-War administrations to introduce 'welfareist' legislation. In 1948, the Criminal Justice Act removed the courts' powers to order that a child delinquent be whipped; and in the same year the Children Act created the legislative framework for an ambitious approach to the problems of the neglected and deprived child with much greater involvement of professional and trained social workers.[224]

None the less, there was still debate about the respective roles of social work and legal sanction in dealing with the delinquent, deprived and ill-treated child; and a cynic might argue that it required a well-publicised scandal to prompt government action in what was often a controversial field. Certainly, a succession of cases, starting with that of Denis O'Neill (killed by his foster parents in 1945), through those of Maria Colwell (killed by her step-father in 1973) and Jasmine Beckford (another killing by a step-father) in 1984, and concluding with that of Baby P (2008) prompted various, not always consistent, legislative responses. But none dealt specifically with the parental right to administer physical punishment, a topic which was still thought to be far too politically sensitive for government action.

The issue was however soon to cease being one for the United Kingdom alone; and eventually, the impact of the 1952 European Convention of Human Rights was decisive. The United Kingdom, whilst refraining from incorporating the Convention provisions

---

34:6 (2005), 599–616.

[220] Notably the consolidating Children and Young Persons Act 1933, s. 1 (7).

[221] See *A v. United Kingdom (Human Rights: Punishment of Child)* (1999), 27 EHRR [European Human Rights Reports], 611.

[222] Author of many books about the legal system's involvement with children; chairman of the Magistrates Association. See G. K. Behlmer, *Friends of the Family. The English Home and its Guardians, 1850–1940* (Stanford: Stanford University Press, 1998), p. 245.

[223] See W. C. Hall, *The State and the Child* (London: Headley Bros, 1917).

[224] 2,000 sentences of corporal punishment had been handed down in the year before the First World War, only 170 in the year before World War II: Cunningham, *Invention of Childhood*, p. 201.

until very recently into its own law, did in due course allow individuals to petition the Human Rights Court at Strasbourg on the ground that domestic law was incompatible with the rights guaranteed by the Convention. In the meantime, there had been much academic discussion about developing a concept of children's rights. The Strasbourg Court held that judicially ordered birching in the Isle of Man was incompatible with the provisions of the Convention, but the decision had a wider impact; and in 1987 corporal punishment in state schools was outlawed.[225] The most important decision was however that in *A v. United Kingdom (Human Rights: Punishment of Child)* in which the European Court of Human Rights held that in so far as English law permitted a jury to accept the defence of 'reasonable chastisement' on the facts before it, it failed to provide the required protection against inhuman and degrading punishment.[226] There was continued pressure through other international agencies, often invoking the 1989 United Nations Convention on the Rights of the Child. But the issue remained controversial: attempts to remove all specific defences based on the parental right to use corporal punishment were unsuccessful, but a provision included in the Children Act 2004 abolished the statutory defence, and confined the 'reasonable punishment' doctrine within narrow limits. It is evidently intended still to allow parents to resort to 'light smacks', but the legislation is in many respects unclear. What can be said with certainty is that the past 100 years have seen a huge change in attitudes to the physical punishment of children – at least in so far as these can be assessed by official policies and publicly expressed opinion.

· ·

The aim of legislators and lobbyists in outlawing the use of physical force in child-rearing was meant to issue in a new golden age where children would be nurtured through love rather than fear. It is incontestable, however, that many children in contemporary Europe continue to be 'brought up by hand', and a small number of the grossly abused pay the ultimate penalty. Despite the immense power and reach of the modern social-service state and the weight of educated public opinion, at least two (some sources say four) British children each week die from physical violence in the home.[227] It is only occasionally that the tragic histories of such children are placed in the public spotlight, but when they are the resultant, if understandable, hand-wringing that ensues unleashes a media frenzy which ends up demonising large sections of the adult population as potential or actual child abusers, the most popular target being welfare recipients. The response to the revelations at the trial of the parents of Baby P in 2008 has been par for the course.[228] The press has looked for scapegoats and a recent report in Britain's chief medical journal, the *Lancet*, has claimed that one out of ten British children today are the victims of abuse.[229]

---

[225] Subsequent legislation dealt with the position in other schools: see now Education Act 1996, ss 548–549.

[226] (1999), 27 EHRR 611. The facts are given in the 1998 jury case alluded to above.

[227] The upper figure, it must be said, suggests that late nineteenth-century Russia was not as benighted as some commentators have implied: see Introduction, fn. 1.

[228] For the case of Baby P, see Lord Laming, *The Protection of Children in England: A Progress Report* (London, HMSO, 2009).

[229] *The Sunday Times*, 16 Nov. 2008; p. 18; *The Times*, 20 Nov. 2008, p. 1. The situation in America is no different: cf. the panic created in 1997 among the well-to-do by the Louise Woodward case, which concerned a British nanny accused of killing a baby in Massachusetts. Could any nanny, especially a foreigner, be trusted? See http://en.wikipedia.org/wiki/Louis_Woodward_case (accessed 17 Jul. 2009). Much emphasis is placed in the media on feckless and inadequate parents. In many of the worst cases of parental brutality, sexual and physical abuse is combined, as in the appalling instance of the Austrian father, Joseph Fritzl, who kept his daughter locked up in cellar that came to public notice in Apr. 2008: see http://en.wikipedia.

As a result of such media hype, one might be forgiven for concluding that the recent revolution in establishment thinking about child-rearing has done little to reduce the incidence of harsh parenting, or perhaps merely uncovered the true level of the serious physical abuse of children that was always present in European society but largely hidden from view by more tolerant attitudes to the use of violence and the long held belief that the state had no right to intrude into family life. Before reaching this conclusion, however, three points should be borne in mind that counsel caution. First, in the course of the contemporary revolution, the goal posts have changed. The term child abuse has been stretched to include emotional and psychological, not just physical, abuse. Given our present-day understanding about the different ways in which a child's development can be permanently scarred (although not why a similar experience can harm one child but not another), the extension of the definition is legitimate. None the less, the much broader use of the term by modern researchers will inevitably lead to evidence of widespread abuse, if only because few children in the country have not at one time or another been spoken to too sharply, been deprived of a toy or been temporarily lost on a shopping expedition.

Secondly, the detection of abuse has itself become scientised and professionalised in the last 40 years, which has given tremendous power to experts – paediatricians and child psychologists in particular – who have a vested interest in demonstrating the validity and objectivity of their investigative techniques by uncovering abuse. This is not to deny the commitment and sensitivity of childcare professionals, nor the utility of their work. Child abusers go out of their way to hide or explain away the results of their actions, so the identification and description of the battered child syndrome by C. Henry Kempe and his team in the United States in the early 1960s was a crucial breakthrough in the state's campaign to identify and protect vulnerable children.[230] However, medical scientists, albeit well-intentioned, can make exaggerated claims about their ability to detect abuse. This seems to have occurred in Britain with the use of the anal dilation reflex test in cases of sexual abuse in the early 1990s.[231] It appears to have occurred as well in several cases involving multiple baby deaths, where dubious statistics were used to show that the only plausible explanation was that the mother had murdered her children.[232]

The dangers of over-confidence have been principally flagged in the claims of psychologists to be able to recover forgotten memories. One of the most problematic, if welcome, side-effects of the revolution in parenting has been the encouragement it has given to those abused in the past to speak out and no longer feel ashamed of their ordeal. Institutions and individuals *in loco parentis* have been particularly targeted, notably the children's homes run by the regular orders in the Republic of Ireland.[233] But even parents have been named

org/wiki/Fritzl_case (accessed 17 Jul. 2009).

[230] C. H. Kempe and R. E. Helfer, *The Battered Child*, 3rd edn (Chicago: University of Chicago Press, 1980). The syndrome was originally identified in 1962 in an article in the *Journal of the American Medical Association*, 181:1 (1962), 17–24. Kempe established that child abuse was usually the work of parents.

[231] See Introduction, p. 2, fn. 4.

[232] *Ibid.*, fn. 6. The most famous case involved a solicitor called Sally Clark, who was imprisoned for murdering two of her three children. By a bizarre twist, one leading paediatrician, Professor David Southall, accused the babies' father of being the real murderer after seeing him in a television documentary describe a nosebleed suffered by one of the dead infants: *The Guardian*, 15 Apr. 2005, p. 10.

[233] As a result, the Irish regular orders have been the subject of a nine-year judicial enquiry which was finally published in May 2009: see *The Commission to Inquire into Child Abuse. Confidential Committee Report* (5 vols; Dublin: Irish Government, 2009). At the end of 2009 Ireland was rocked by new revelations of clerical misconduct, this time concerning sexual abuse: see *Report by the Commission of Investigation Into the Catholic Archdiocese of Dublin* (December 2009). A number of searing accounts have been published of life in Irish children's homes: *e.g.*, K. O'Malley, *Childhood Interrupted. Growing Up under the Cruel Regime of the Sisters of Mercy* (London: Virago, 2005). Similar stories have begun to surface about orphanages in Northern Ireland

and shamed.[234] Some of the accusations, however, have definitely been malicious, while others, though true, have led to gross exaggerations in the press of institutional wrong-doing, as in the recent, ultimately unsubstantiated claim of murders committed in a Jersey children's home.[235] Psychologists have only fuelled the flames. Through their analysis of troubled adults, they have uncovered horrific stories of parental abuse that cannot be externally proven and are yet impossible to deny. The sceptical may suspect the reality of the psychologists' findings, but the apparent ubiquity of the abuse they uncover confirms the suspicion that abuse is everywhere and must be rooted out.[236]

Thirdly, it is a mark of a revolutionary moment that the revolutionaries fear that they have not carried people with them. Commitment to the new world view has to be total or it is judged opposition.[237] It is not surprising, therefore, that the handful of truly atrocious cases of neglect and abuse (which would have been considered an evil in any period of Europe's past) are seen as the tip of a horrendous and invisible iceberg, and parents who give their children an odd slap viewed as potential killers.

It would be unwise, in consequence, to believe that outside the enlightened middle-classes (and sometimes inside it – for revolutionaries always fear the fifth columnist) children in large numbers are being beaten up, starved and deprived of affection by feckless single mothers and abusive step-fathers. There are clear-cut and terrible cases of pathological behaviour, but we have no way of ascertaining whether proportionally more, fewer or the same number of children are being physically grossly maltreated.[238] It is probably best to assume that the very large majority of adults through the ages have always been conscientious and affectionate parents and carers, according to their own cultural beliefs, and that much of the child abuse – physical, emotional and psychological – that childcare professionals fear exists is primarily the reflection of historical and cultural diversity. There is an establishment norm in Britain and Europe promoted by the social-service state and the mainstream churches, which is increasingly enshrined in law. But it is not a form of parenting wholeheartedly subscribed to by the working-classes, ethnic minorities, or even sections of the middle-class who have come under the influence of evangelicalism.[239]

---

run by regulars: see F. Reilly, *Suffer the Little Children. The Harrowing True Story of a Girl's Brutal Convent Upbringing* (London: Orion, 2008).

[234] Most famously in Constance Briscoe's *Ugly* (London: Hodder and Stoughton, 2006), an autobiography of a black judge.

[235] The lengthy but inconclusive enquiry into allegations of child murder and abuse at the Jersey home at Haut de la Garenne ended with the chief police officer on the island stepping down: see http://news.bbc.co.uk/1/hi/world/europe/jersey/7724622.stm (accessed 17 Sept. 2009). On children, rather than adults, as informers about abuse, see Ch. 6, pp. 280–81.

[236] On the dangers of using analysis to recover childhood memories, see the partisan C. L. Whitfield, J. L. Silberg and P. J. Fink (eds), 'Misinformation Concerning Child Sexual Abuse and Adult Survivors', special issue of *Journal of Child Sexual Abuse*, 9: 3/4 (2001) [also as a book, Binghamton, NY: Haworth Press, 2002]. The ability of professionals, albeit unintentionally, to make children imagine that they have been abused was revealed in the United States in the 1980s with the cases of the McMartin preschool, California, and the Fells Acre Day Care Center, Mass.

[237] See the penetrating article on the French Jacobins by F. Furet, 'Augustin Cochin: la théorie du Jacobinisme' in F. Furet, *Penser la révolution Française* (Paris: Gallimard, 1978), ch. 3.

[238] Step-fathers are apparently 60 times more likely to kill very young children in their care than genetic fathers. These figures appear in a Canadian survey by M. Daly and M. Wilson, 'Some Differential Attributes of Lethal Assaults on Small Children by Stepfathers versus Genetic Fathers', *Ethology and Sociobiology*, 15 (1994), 207–17.

[239] At present the emphasis in Britain is on teaching correct parenting, especially through turning schools into all-purpose children's centres as part of the government's Sure Start programme. 'Sure Start is the Government's programme to deliver the best start in life for every child by bringing together early education, childcare, health and family support'. See www.decsf.gov.uk/everychildmatters/earlyyears/surestart/

The modern evangelical revival in Britain, which is a cross-cultural phenomenon, is a particular challenge to the new establishment orthodoxy. This became clear in 2005 when it was asserted in the court case concerning the cruelty inflicted on Child B that the young person had been physically harmed because he or she was thought to be bewitched. 'The Old Bailey heard that the Angola orphan… was beaten and cut to "beat the devil out of her"'. The fact that many evangelical churches in Britain and the United States believe in the reality of bewitchment and the need for exorcism immediately led the press and the police to conclude that yet another unspeakable horror had reared its head from the superstitious deep: physical abuse in the name of religion. But there was no evidence to substantiate the fear at the time and none has come to light in subsequent years. Child B's abuser aunt had attended a black evangelical church but been expelled two years before the child was harmed.[240]

It is necessary sometimes to stand back from the present 'child-centred' parenting practices and look at them through the critical eye of the outsider. Other parts of the world would find the behaviourist parenting advocated and practised by TV's 'Supernanny', where uncooperative young children have their toys taken away from them, unacceptably cruel.[241] Even such uncontentious practices as placing infants in their own rooms at night or feeding them to a set schedule seems unnaturally harsh to many other societies.[242] We are as guilty too as earlier civilisations in subjecting our young to painful procedures in the attempt to perfect the deficiencies of nature. We deplore the ancient Chinese habit of foot binding, but seldom see anything wrong with piercing the ears of young girls or subjecting teenagers to complex and lengthy orthodontistry or allowing them to undergo plastic surgery at an age when they are emotionally fragile.[243] It should be remembered, too, that the debate over physically punishing children is a long one. As we have seen in this chapter, writers on parenting and schooling have been querying its value since the beginning of the Christian era. We are living at a moment when for a complex, and as yet poorly understood, set of reasons the abolitionists occupy the high ground, but it would be dangerous, viewing the debate in the long term, to assume that the battle has been permanently won.

---

whatsurestartdoes (accessed 17 Sept. 2009). For American responses, see R. Chalk and P. A. King (eds), *Violence and Families. Assessing Prevention and Treatment Programmes* (Washington DC: National Academy Press, 1998), and N. D. Reppucci, P. A. Britner, and J. L. Woolard, *Preventing Child Abuse and Neglect through Parent Education* (Baltimore: Brookes Publishing Co., 1997). Some educationalists now feel that schooling at all levels in Britain is now placing too much emphasis on socialisation and well-being to the neglect of learning: see K. Ecclestone and D. Hayes, *The Dangerous Rise of Therapeutic Education* (Abingdon: Routledge, 2009).

[240] For a balanced and informative article on the Child B case, see *The Independent*, 18 Jul. 2005, pp. 34–36 (article by Paul Vallely). In Britain the fear continues to be stoked by media investigation into child witchcraft beliefs in Africa; *e.g.*, the powerful ITV1 documentary shown on 12 Nov. 2008, 'Saving Africa's Witch Children' (on the situation in a Nigerian province).

[241] See Introduction, fn. 59.

[242] J. E. Korbin, 'Introduction' in J. E. Korbin (ed.), *Child Abuse and Neglect: Cross Cultural Perspectives.* (Berkeley: University of California Press, 1981), p. 4.

[243] Purportedly 100,000 young children and teenagers in Germany have plastic surgery each year: www.lipo.com/health-articles/lifestyle-articles/germany-to-ban-cosmetic-surgery-on-children-20080429419 (accessed 17 Sept. 2009).

4. Child Exploitation

*Chrysanthi Gallou, Laurence Brockliss, John Cardwell,
Jane Humphries, Nicola Sheldon and Saul Becker*

More than 200 million children in the world today are involved in child labour, doing work that is damaging to his or her mental, physical and emotional development. Children work because their survival and that of their families depend on it. Child labour persists even where it has been declared illegal, and is frequently surrounded by a wall of silence, indifference, and apathy. But that wall is beginning to crumble. While the total elimination of child labour is a long-term goal in many countries, certain forms of child labour must be confronted immediately. Nearly three-quarters of working children are engaged in the worst forms of child labour, including trafficking, armed conflict, slavery, sexual exploitation and hazardous work. The effective abolition of child labour is one of the most urgent challenges of our time

International Labour Organisation, 'Child Labour' at http://www.ilo.org/global/Themes/Child_ Labour/lang--en/index.htm (accessed 10 Jan. 2010)

In 2001 [McDonald's] was fined £12,400 by British magistrates for illegally employing and over-working child labor in one of its London restaurants. This is thought to be one of the largest fines imposed on a company for breaking laws relating to child working conditions. In April 2007 in Perth, Western Australia, McDonald's pleaded guilty to five charges relating to the employment of children under 15 in one of its outlets and was fined AU$8,000

http://en.wikipedia.org/wiki/McDonald%27s (accessed 22 Sept. 2009)

"To help my dad out I dress him, take him to the toilet, keep him warm, listen for him in the night, give him medicines, watch him because when he smokes he drops his fags on the floor, he might set light to himself."

"It's horrible having to do that sort of thing for your dad. It's degrading and it was especially degrading for my dad losing control of himself, and then having to be washed and cleaned up by me.

"Dad will be really ill sometimes and sometimes I'll get pissed off about that. You just get so racked off... you just drop off to sleep and suddenly you hear him shouting for you. You never get two minutes on your own in this house, sometimes you think, 'Oh I've got to get some time by myself' and walk out, but I always come back"

Young carer's accounts of his life, published online by the Young Carers Research Group www.ycrg.org.uk (accessed 22 Sept. 2009)

There is, as Hugh Cunningham has argued, a tendency among some commentators to portray the story of child labour as a form of romance, a tale, very similar to that told by Lloyd deMause, where the story of childhood is one of movement from violence to protection, from brutality and indifference to love and care, and from exploitation in the factory to nurture in the schoolroom.[1] From the vantage point of the beginning of the twenty-first century, the decline in child labour in western Europe and North America is understood as one of the cornerstones of modernity. It is seen as a problem solved, an issue belonging to a cruel Dickensian past in which children were routinely sent up chimneys, worked until they dropped in factories, or were sent out on the streets to beg or steal. But is child labour a form of violence against children? This is not a straightforward question and discussions of child labour, like other issues concerning violence against children, revolve partly around definitions – how to draw lines between work, labour and exploitation – and partly around conceptualisations. Is childhood (or should it be?) a protected space in which children are spared the adult need to work? Or is childhood a preparation for life in which children must learn responsibility early on and where a child's income may be the only way of ensuring a family's survival? Are there 'good' forms of child labour, which exist under the watchful and caring eyes of parents, and abusive and violent forms that occur when children work outside the home? Is children's underemployment or idleness as bad a problem as their exploitation?

Today the phrase 'a child worker' tends to conjure up images of an urban child working in a factory, but this is unlikely to be how the majority of children worked, either now or in the past. In the contemporary developing world the majority of child labourers are poor, rural children, who give unpaid help on the family farm or who perform other unpaid domestic work, particularly minding children and doing household chores. Far less numerous (although more visible) are those who work in the informal economy, petty commodity trading, selling food or cleaning shoes or those who work in the formal sector, often producing goods for export in modern factories.[2] While there are no straightforward comparisons to be made, it is a reasonable to suppose that children in previous centuries carried out many of these same tasks and that child labourers were overwhelmingly rural based and worked on family lands, even though the urban factory child, now as then, has always received the most attention from reformers.[3]

There is a wealth of evidence to suggest that children have always worked and that children in poor and, particularly, rural communities have always been expected to contribute to the household at what might appear an extremely young early age. It is equally important to acknowledge that parents have usually understood the need for protection of children and themselves drew lines between labour and exploitation. Children's work was regulated by custom long before the Factory Acts and there were always boundaries which the overwhelming majority of parents and employers did not cross.

In recent years the International Labour Organisation (ILO) has drawn up the Convention Concerning the Prohibition and Immediate Action for the Elimination of the Worst Forms of Child Labour (Convention 182) which lists the most hazardous forms of child labour, while

---

[1] For deMauses's classic statement, see H. Cunningham, *The Children of the Poor: Representations of Childhood since the Seventeenth Century* (Oxford: Blackwell, 1991), pp. 8–9. See also J. Humphries, *Childhood and Child Labour in the British Indsutrial Revolution* (Cambridge: Cambridge University Press, 2010); deMause, 'The Evolution of Childhood', in L. deMause (ed.), *The History of Childhood* (New York: Psychohistory Press, 1974), p. 1. .

[2] J. Boyden, B. Ling and W. Myers, *What Works for Working Children* (Stockholm: Rädda Barnen, 1998).

[3] Jordanova claims that there were four types of economic activity undertaken by children in the past which contributed directly or indirectly to the family income: paid work; apprenticeships (which brought an indirect benefit to the families because they had one less child to feed and clothe); the care of younger children which freed up parents to undertake paid work; and working alongside parents and so increasing their productivity. L. Jordanova, 'Children in History: Concepts of Nature and Society', in G. Scarre (ed.), *Children, Parents and Politics* (Cambridge: Cambridge University Press, 1989), pp. 19–20.

acknowledging that for many children some form of work is a necessity and need not be inherently harmful.[4] Most pertinently, Convention 182 states that child exploitation differs from child work when 'by its nature or the circumstances in which it is carried out, it is likely to harm the health, safety or morals of children'.[5] Increasingly therefore both academics and policy makers are becoming more nuanced in their discussions of contemporary child labour. Few would now call for an outright ban but look instead at the impacts of particular forms of labour on the health and well-being of children. Such a stance is useful not only looking at child workers in the non-estern world today but also when looking at the expectations placed on children historically.

One final point when discussing children's work is the role of schooling and education. It is now taken as axiomatic that school is the right place for children to be and the labour market the wrong one but, as the previous chapter of this book has shown, some of the worst forms of violence against children occur within schools, and this situation finds parallels in children's accounts of schooling in some parts of the world today.[6] Furthermore, it can be argued that modern children's work has been transformed into education and that schoolwork is productive, economic work, with similar possibilities for exploitation. Ludmilla Jordanova writes that schooling is a form of labour so that 'children are not free to do as they please, and, although they do not receive payment for attending school, it certainly counts as "work" in one sense'.[7] Sociologist Jens Qvortrup has gone further, arguing that, in the west, where children's employment outside the home has a negligible impact on household economies, schooling is the real work of childhood. It is at school where children transform themselves into the next working generation and the future educated workforce and therefore their education is a form of production. He argues that if teaching is acknowledged as economically productive work, then the same logic must apply to learning.[8]

This chapter explores the reality of working children's lives in the past and examines the changing contours of the concept of child exploitation. It begins with an account of children at work in Mycenaean Greece (*c.* 1680–1050 BC). This piece shows that children in the late Bronze Age and even before were a central part of the workforce and, dependent on their age, class and gender, were expected to contribute to the family income as soon as they were able. What the sources are less able to tell us is whether this was seen at the time as exploitation or whether or not this work damaged children.

---

[4] The worst forms of child labour include all forms of slavery, prostitution and work in pornography and the use of children in illicit activities, especially drug production and trafficking.

[5] http://www.ilo.org/public/english/standards/relm/ilc/ilc87/com-chic.htm (accessed 14 Jun. 2009).

[6] M. Ramphele, 'Adolescents and Violence: "Adults are Cruel, They Just Beat, Beat, Beat!"', *Social Science and Medicine*, 45:8 (1997), 1189–1197.

[7] Jordanova, 'Children in History', p. 19.

[8] J. Qvortrup, 'School-work, Paid-work and the Changing Obligations of Childhood', in P. Mizen, C. Pole and A. Bolton (eds), *Hidden Hands: International Perspectives on Children's Work and Labour* (London: Routledge Falmer, 2001).

Children at Work in Mycenaean Greece (c. 1680–1050 BCE): A Brief Survey

Chrysanthi Gallou[9]

Children have formed an important constituent of the workforce in agricultural and pastoral Greek communities since antiquity.[10] Child labour in the prehistoric Aegean has started to receive a certain amount of scholarly treatment. In her discussion of metal objects in Neolithic and Early Bronze Age child burials (individuals aged five to fourteen), Christina Marangou has argued that the presence of specialist tools could indicate the age at which children started to be productive and attained a status connected with a craft passed down through their family.[11] Anne Ingvarsson-Sundström has suggested that in the Middle Bronze Age (2000–1700 BCE) children would also have been important contributors to the household and the community.[12] The deposition of tools made of bone, obsidian and stone, in child graves at Lerna and Asine could indicate children's labour tasks.[13] On the other hand, neither Marangou nor Ingvarsson-Sundström ruled out the possible ritual, amuletic or playful use of these objects. This present article surveys the evidence relating to child labour later in the Bronze Age, during the Mycenaean period.

In addition to archaeological remains, Mycenologists can turn to the evidence from administrative documents and iconographic representations, in trying to reconstruct Mycenaean society. Thus the study of the socio-economic role of children in the late Bronze Age can extract information from three categories of evidence:

a)   the Linear B administrative documents
b)   child burials and offerings
c)   iconographic depictions of children

One, however, should be aware of the limitations imposed on the interpretations of these sources. Thus although the decipherment of Linear B has provided unique insights into the Mycenaean world,[14] the documents record only those activities that were of concern to the palatial administrators. There is no mention of personal or domestic activities. Similarly, depictions on frescoes and the minor arts reflect an idealised reflection of the social and religious life of the elites. Although grave goods

---

[9] A shorter version of this study has been presented in the SSCIP International Conference 'Childhood in the Past – Recent Research. Socialisation, Learning and Play in the Past' (Stavanger, Sept. 2008), and many thanks are owed to the conference participants for their fruitful comments and discussions. I am most grateful to Professor W. G. Cavanagh, Dr M. Georgiadis and Dr M. Papapostolou for kindly reading and commenting on a draft of this paper.

[10] See, for example, M. Golden, *Children and Childhood in Classical Athens* (Baltimore: Johns Hopkins University Press, 1990), pp. 32–36.

[11] C. Marangou, 'Social Differentiation in the Early Bronze Age: Miniature Metal Vessels and Child Burials', *Journal of Mediterranean Archaeology*, 1 (1991), 211–25.

[12] A. Ingvarsson-Sundström, 'Children Lost and Found. A Bioarchaeological Study of Middle Helladic Children in Asine with a Comparison to Lerna' (Uppsala University: PhD thesis, 2003), p. 145.

[13] Ingvarsson-Sundström, 'Children Lost and Found', pp. 147–148.

[14] Cf. M. Ventris and J. Chadwick, *Documents in Mycenaean Greek*, 2nd edn (Cambridge: Cambridge University Press, 1973); Y. Duhoux and A. Morpurgo Davies, *A Companion to Linear B: Mycenaean Greek Texts and their World* (Leuven: Peeters Publishers, 2008).

may reveal clues about the tasks of children, obviously they should be interpreted with care. Moreover, the burial of a child was the responsibility of the family; therefore grave types and goods may reflect – to a major degree – the desires of the adult community. And, as if these limitations were not enough, the earlier archaeological bias against an archaeology of childhood has led to incomplete publication with few analyses of prehistoric children's skeletal remains. Given the greater vulnerability of child skeletons to complete decay, the collective character of Mycenaean burials and the exclusion – in several cases – of children from formal cemeteries, serious restrictions are imposed on a full understanding of the life and death circumstances of Mycenaean children.[15]

Michael Ventris and John Chadwick were the first to discuss the evidence for the listing of children on the Linear B personnel documents, dating to *c.* 1200 BCE.[16] The children recorded on approximately 200 tablets of the Pylos *Aa* and *Ab* and the Knossos *Ai, Ak* and *Am* series make up the bulk of those attested. Children are listed as members of units, recipients of rations and assisting in workshops of specialised adult workers.[17] They are differentiated by sex, namely *ko-wa* (girl) and *ko-wo* (boy).[18] Children are consistently documented along with women, with the exception of the Pylos *Ad* tablets in which boys accompany men who are inferred to be sons of various groups of women largely identifiable with those mentioned in series *Aa* and *Ab*.[19] It may have been that older boys are listed accompanying men for purpose of professional instruction as suggested by the reference *di.-*, probably an abbreviation for *di-da-ka-re* (to instruct), on the Knossos tablets.[20]

Girls predominate and are always listed before boys.[21] The total in numbers preserved, for example, in the Pylos *Aa* documents is 631 women, 376 girls and 261 boys. Those on the *Ad* series are considerably fewer: 370 women, 190 girls and 149 boys.[22] The shortfall of boys may be explained by the fact that when they reached a certain age grade, they were transferred to working groups of men, whereas daughters would have stayed with their mothers.[23] In this context, children are also differentiated – at Knossos only – by age grades, namely *me-wi-jo* (younger) or *me-zo* (older).[24] Unfortunately, it still remains obscure which age grades these epithets actually represented for the Mycenaeans.

[15] C. Gallou, 'More Than Little Perishers: Child Burials and the Living Society in Mycenaean Greece', *Ethnographisch-Archäologische Zeitschrift*, 45 (2004), 365–75.

[16] Ventris and Chadwick, *Documents*, pp. 155–68.

[17] B. Olsen, 'Women, Children and the Family in Late Aegean Bronze Age: Differences in Minoan and Mycenaean Constructions of Gender', *World Archaeology*, 29:3 (1998), 380–92 at p. 383.

[18] Ventris and Chadwick, *Documents*, pp. 155–68; Olsen, 'Women, Children and the Family', pp. 383–84. These and other italicised words are transliterations from the Mycenaean.

[19] J. Chadwick, *The Mycenaean World* (Cambridge: Cambridge University Press, 1976), p. 81.

[20] Ventris and Chadwick, *Documents*, p. 162; Olsen, 'Women, Children and the Family', pp. 383–84; M.-L. Nosch, 'Kinderarbeit in der Mykenische Palastzeit', in F. Blakolmer and H. D. Szemethy (eds), *Akten des 8. Österreichischen Archäologentages am Institut für Klassische Archäologie der Universität Wien vom 23. bis 25. April 1999, Wiener Forschungen zur Archäologie 4* (Wien: Phoibos Verlag, 2001), pp. 41–42.

[21] L. Dixon, 'Women, Children and Weaving', in P. Betancourt, V. Karageorghis, R. Laffineur and W.-D. Niemeier (eds), *Meletemata. Studies in Aegean Archaeology Presented to Malcolm H. Wiener as He Enters his 65th Year* (Liège: Annales d'Archéologie Égéenne de l'Université de Liège, 1999), p. 565; J. Killen. 'The Subjects of the *wanax*: Aspects of Mycenaean Social Structure', in S. Deger-Jalkotzy and I. S. Lemos (eds), *Ancient Greece: From the Mycenaean Palaces to the Age of Homer* (Edinburgh: Edinburgh University Press, 2006), p. 89.

[22] Ventris and Chadwick, *Documents*, p. 155.

[23] Chadwick, *The Mycenaean World*, p. 81; C. Shelmerdine and J. Bennet, 'Mycenaean States: Economy and Administration', in C. Shelmerdine (ed.), *The Cambridge Companion to the Aegean Bronze Age* (Cambridge: Cambridge University Press, 2008), p. 306.

[24] Ventris and Chadwick, *Documents*, pp. 162–63; Olsen 'Women, Children and the Family', pp. 383–84; Nosch, 'Kinderarbeit', pp. 39, 41.

The Pylos *Ab* series provides valuable information on the rations received by the children, namely wheat and figs. The amounts given are roughly proportional to the numbers of adults and children, and always the same. The basis of the calculation would appear to be a ration of 2T, now thought to be equivalent to 19.2 litres for each woman, with half that quantity for each child, regardless of sex.[25] The low status of these workers, including children, is reflected in the fact that they were merely supported with low food rations rather than wages or other benefits.[26] Interestingly, certain groups of children are listed with women identified either with an ethnic name, *e.g. Milesian* (PY Ad380), *Knidian* (PY Ad683) and *Kytheran* (PY Ad390), or as *do-e-ra, e.g.* PY Ae08, An 42. The ethnic epithets of the women may be taken to signify that their ancestors were foreigners.[27] The term *do-e-ra* has raised intense debate and scholarship tends to agree that it may denote a class of 'slaves' or 'servants'.[28] Although not necessarily slaves, these women and children appear to have been fully dependent on the palace.

Despite the problem of multiple possible interpretations, the Linear B documents, when combined with the archaeological evidence from child burials and iconographic depictions, can disclose important information about the economic activities in which Mycenaean children were involved. It appears that they were assigned demanding menial tasks such as cereal grinding and measuring, weaving, nursing and household responsibilities namely bath-pouring, serving and sweeping, as well as religious tasks.

The analysis of palm prints on clay tablets from Knossos show that they belonged to children aged eight to twelve who prepared (flattened) unbaked clay tablets for use by older scribes.[29] The children would presumably become scribes when they entered adulthood.[30] The deposition of tools in child burials has very often been interpreted as the provision of implements for the welfare of children in the underworld. For example, the discovery of stone pounders has been taken as a tool for crushing the child's food in the underworld, or the terracotta and steatite loom weights as toys or amulets.[31] On the other hand, it is worth noting that such artefacts included in child burials were of the same type as those recovered in adult burials. In the latter case, these objects have been associated with the occupation of their dead owners.[32] Moreover, such interpretations fail to explain why stone tools and other objects of similar function ever became standard offerings in infant and child burials. Thus, the character of the furnishings, namely a schist slab and a stone polisher from the burial of a twelve-year-old boy at Ayios Stephanos in Laconia,[33] may imply the child's cereal

---

[25] Ventris and Chadwick, *Documents*, pp. 157–58.

[26] T. Palaima, 'The Significance of Mycenaean Words Related to Meals, Meal Rituals and Food', in L. Hitchcock, R. Laffineur and J. Crowley (eds), *DAIS. The Aegean Feast. Proceedings of the 12th International Aegean Conference* (Liège: Annales d'Archéologie égéenne de l'Université de Liège, 2008), pp. 385–87; Shelmerdine and Bennet, 'Mycenaean States: Economy and Administration', p. 304.

[27] Shelmerdine and Bennet, 'Mycenaean States: Economy and Administration', p. 306.

[28] Chadwick, *The Mycenaean World*, p. 83; J.-C. Billigmeier and J. A. Turner, 'The Socio-Economic Roles of Women in Mycenaean Greece: A Brief Survey from Evidence of the Linear B Tablets', in H. Foley (ed.), *Reflections of Women in Antiquity* (New York: Gordon and Breach Science Publishers, 1981), pp. 8–9; Killen, 'The Subjects of the *wanax*', pp. 89–94.

[29] K.-E. Sjöquist and P. Åström, *Knossos: Keepers and Kneaders* (Göteborg: Paul Åströms Förlag, 1991), pp. 25–28, 30–33, fig. 30.

[30] Sjöquist and Åström, *Knossos*, p. 30.

[31] N. Polychronakou-Sgouritsa, 'Παιδικές ταφές στη Μυκηναϊκή Ελλάδα', *Archaeologikon Deltion*, 42A (1987), 13.

[32] Cf. S. A. Immerwahr, *The Athenian Agora XIII: The Neolithic and Bronze Ages* (Princeton: The American School of Classical Studies at Athens, 1971), p. 110.

[33] W. D. Taylour, 'Excavations at Ayios Stephanos', *Annual of the British School at Athens*, 67 (1972), 235–36;

grinding tasks during its short lifetime. This is further supported by the records of children (both boys and girls) as corn-grinders (*me-re-ti-ri-ja*, PY Aa62) and of boys as measurers of grain (*si-to-ko-wo*, PY An292) from Pylos.[34]

Children were active contributors in the Mycenaean textile industry, in particular in flax-working, carding, spinning, sewing and weaving as indicated by the recordings on a number of documents, *e.g.* PY Ad694 (boys as carders), PY Aa04 (boys and girls involved in spinning), PY Ad670 and Ad697+698 (boys as flax-workers), PY Ad684 (boys as weavers).[35] In all probability such tasks were also indicated in their grave offerings, terracotta and steatite spindle whorls and pins of ivory and bone.[36] Awls and pins could have been used for piercing and boring, and for scraping and incising soft materials such as cloth, leather or clay, as well as in basket weaving. A similar pattern of burial offerings for children has also been noted for the preceding Middle Helladic period.[37]

Linear B tablets indicate that household tasks such as nursing (PY Aa815, Aa717), bath-pouring (PY Ad676), serving (PY Ad690) and sweeping (PY Ad671) were also jobs performed by children.[38] It is also important to emphasise that certain of these tasks may have been more technical than they seem; for example, the 'bath-pourers' (*re-wo-to-ro-ko-wo*) might have been involved in some industrial process, such as the washing of wool for the perfumed oil and textile industries. If not listed in the tablets, the evidence for the performance of such tasks would have been silent in the archaeological record.

Another way in which children contributed to the household would have been the collection of food. Seashells sometimes pierced at one end have been associated with child burials. Various symbolic meanings have been attributed to this type of offering.[39] The symbolic and amuletic role of seashells may be suggested for the Shaft Grave Period (*c.* 1700–1550 BCE) through the find of a ritual vessel in the shape of a seashell associated with infant and female burials in Shaft Grave III at Mycenae.[40] This could indeed also be the case for the association of molluscs with burials belonging to infants

---

W. D. Taylour and R. Janko, *Ayios Stephanos. Excavations at a Bronze Age and Medieval Settlement in Southern Laconia* (London: The British School at Athens, 2008), p. 127.

[34] See also, Ventris and Chadwick, *Documents*, pp. 158, 166.

[35] Ventris and Chadwick, *Documents*, pp. 158–59, 161; Nosch, 'Kinderarbeit'.

[36] For other theories on the use of 'buttons', see K. Lewartowski, *Late Helladic Simple Graves. A Study of Mycenaean Burial Customs* (Oxford: Archaeopress, 2000), pp. 33–34, 48; for pins as possible symbols of female identity, see K. A. Kamp, 'Where Have All the Children Gone? The Archaeology of Childhood', *Journal of Archaeological Method and Theory*, 8 (2001), 1–34, at p. 18.

[37] Ingvarsson-Sundström, 'Children Lost and Found', pp. 147–48; G. Nordquist and A. Ingvarsson-Sundström, 'Live Hard, Die Young: Mortuary Remains of Middle and Early Late Helladic Children from the Argolid in Social Context', in A. Dakouri-Hild and S. Sherratt (eds), *Autochthon. Papers Presented to O. T. P. K. Dickinson on the Occasion of his Retirement* (Oxford: Archaeopress, 2005), pp. 168–74.

[38] Ventris and Chadwick, *Documents*, pp. 158–63.

[39] E. Vermeule, *Greece in the Bronze Age* (Chicago: University of Chicago Press, 1964), p. 300; Immerwahr, *The Athenian Agora*, pp. 109–10; Polychronakou-Sgouritsa, 'Παιδικές ταφές στη Μυκηναϊκή Ελλάδα'; G. Nordquist, 'Middle Helladic Burial Rites: Some Speculations', in R. Hagg and G. Nordquist (eds), *Celebrations of Death and Divinity in the Bronze Age Argolid. Proceedings of the Sixth International Symposium at the Swedish Institute at Athens* (Stockholm: Coronet Books, 1990), p. 40; C. Gates, 'Art for Children in Mycenaean Greece', in R. Laffineur and J. Crowley (eds), *Eikon. Aegean Bronze Age Iconography: Shaping a Methodology. Proceedings of the 4th International Aegean Conference, University of Tasmania, Hobart, 6–9 Apr. 1992* (Liège: Annales d'Archéologie égéenne de l'Université de Liège, 1992), p. 166; Lewartowski, *Late Helladic Simple Graves*, p. 43; Ingvarsson-Sundström, 'Children Lost and Found', pp. 149–50; Nordquist and Ingvarsson-Sundström, 'Live Hard, Die Young', p. 160.

[40] See K. Demakopoulou, *Troy, Mycenae, Tiryns, Orchomenos. A Hundred Years from the Death of Heinrich Schliemann*, Greek edn (Athens: Hellenic Ministry of Culture, 1990), pp. 276–78.

and children less than three-years-old. Without totally excluding these interpretations, ethnographic parallels may provide an alternative explanation for the association between seashells and children in later Mycenaean times. The presence of seashells may simply reflect the fact their collection was part of the food gathering duties of children living by the coast. Other duties would have been collecting vegetables and fruit and possibly hunting and trapping small animals and birds, tasks both entertaining for children and important for the household economy. Extrapolating examples from other historical periods and other cultures, further tasks that have left no traces in the archaeological record might have included fetching, transporting and pouring water, collecting plants, herbs and firewood, preparing food, and herding and tending to the animals as well as agricultural work, such as clearing stones from fields and breaking up clods of earth.[41]

Caring for younger children might have been another task.[42] Dixon has proposed that children referred to as 'older' in the weaving records, might have actually been employed to look after the 'younger' children when their mothers were at work.[43] However, there may be two problems with this hypothesis: a) as shown above grave goods may indicate children actually working as textile labourers, and b) it does not satisfactorily explain why children were allocated rations as wages by the palace since 'the arrangement of childcare for these people would have been a "private" matter'? One may also add Chadwick's observation that children listed in the tablets were weaned and aged three or over,[44] therefore able to contribute to more demanding tasks such as those of the Mycenaean textile industry.

Apart from the menial tasks, the few artistic representations on frescoes, jewellery and pottery may be taken to imply that girls, identified by cropped hair, calf-length skirts and immature breast development, would have served as acolytes in Mycenaean sanctuaries.[45] Such tasks could explain the deposition of ritual vessels in little girls' graves as, for example, the girl's burial in Koukounara tholos tomb 2.[46] The evidence from classical Athens offers a model for interpretation of this Mycenaean practice. At a certain age, apparently some time between eight and fourteen, young girls were called on to serve Artemis at Brauron for a period of time, during which they were educated in ritual customs, served the temple and were properly prepared to assume religious adult duties.[47]

Labour tasks were age dependent. The papillary line impressions from Knossos suggest that children as young as eight worked as tablet flatteners. One may also assume

[41] Cf. Golden, *Children and Childhood in Classical Athens*, pp. 32–36; M. Golden, 'Childhood in Ancient Greece', in J. Neils and J. H. Oakley (eds), *Coming of Age in Ancient Greece. Images of Childhood from the Classical Past* (New Haven: Yale University Press, 2003), p. 18; R. W. Park, 'Size Counts: The Miniature Archaeology of Childhood in Inuit Societies', *Antiquity*, 72:1, 276 (1998), 269–81 at pp. 274–75; Kamp, 'Where Have All the Children Gone?', pp. 14–16; Ingvarsson-Sundström, 'Children Lost and Found', pp. 144–45.

[42] Cf. Golden, *Children and Childhood in Classical Athens*, p. 33; Kamp, 'Where Have All the Children Gone?', p. 16.

[43] Dixon, 'Women, Children and Weaving', pp. 566–67.

[44] J. Chadwick, 'The Women of Pylos', in J.-P. Olivier and T. Palaima (eds) *Texts, Tablets and Scribes: Studies in Mycenaean Epigraphy and Economy offered to Emmett L. Bennett, Jr.* (Salamanca: Universidad de Salamanca, 1988), pp. 90–92.

[45] P. Rehak, 'Children's Work: Girls as Acolytes in Aegean Ritual and Cult', in A. Cohen and J. Rutter (eds), *Constructions of Childhood in Ancient Greece and Italy* (Princeton: American School of Classical Studies at Athens, 2007), pp. 205–25.

[46] S. Marinatos, 'Excavations at Pylos (in Greek)', *Praktika tes en Athenais Archaeologikes Hetaireias* (1958), 184–93, at p. 191.

[47] C. Sourvinou-Inwood, *Studies in Girls' Transitions. Aspects of the Arkteia and Age Representation in Attic Iconography* (Athens: Kardamitsa, 1988).

that children around three- to five-years-old would have been expected to perform simple household tasks, and from the age of five and over would have started to be productive and thereby attained a kind of status connected to the craft exercised by their parents.[48]

The analysis of the available evidence suggests that the prevailing socio-political conditions of the Mycenaean period would have determined the participation of children in labour activities. In an earlier study of Mycenaean childhood I have argued that the adult attitude towards the death of a child depended on the socio-political conditions prevailing at the time.[49] Thus, in transitional eras, such as the Early Mycenaean period (that is before the emergence of the palaces and the hierarchical administrative system) and after the collapse of the palatial administration, the lives of children were more valued. Fewer children meant fewer descendants for the family, thus fewer chances for claims over authority and succession to political power. This is why the death of children provided an occasion for competitive display expressed via the furnishing of child burials with valuable objects, such as gold suits and jewellery of precious materials. These are also the times when the graves provide no evidence for child specialised labour.

On the other hand, during the Late Helladic IIIA–B eras (fourteenth–thirteenth centuries BCE) the consolidation of the hierarchical political system, the greater improvement in prosperity and the unprecedented increase in agricultural and economic resources would have permitted, even necessitated, the participation of children in adult work. This also coincides with the period when children aged five years and over were buried in tholos and chamber tombs and received offerings comparable to those of adults.

Summarising, the archaeological evidence suggests that children formed an important constituent of the Late Bronze Age economy. From this brief discussion, it appears that the allocation of labour tasks to Mycenaean children was age-, gender- and class-dependent. Certainly, more systematic skeletal analyses[50] and the thorough publication of child burials will enlighten further our understanding of the role that children played in Mycenaean society and the Mycenaean economy.

. . . .

The evidence we have on Mycenaean children suggests that they worked at home or with their parents as part of the family economy, a pattern that appears fairly consistent throughout the pre-industrial era and indeed in traditional societies today.[51] Thus, among the

[48] See also Marangou, 'Social Differentiation in the Early Bronze Age', pp. 211–25; Ingvarsson-Sundström, 'Children Lost and Found', p. 144.

[49] Gallou, 'More Than Little Perishers', p. 368ff.

[50] As for example, J. L. Angel, 'Human Skeletons from Grave Circles at Mycenae', in G. E. Mylonas (ed.), Ο Ταφικός Κύκλος Β των Μυκηνών (Athens: Athens Archaeological Society, 1973), pp. 379–97; A. Papathanasiou, 'Prefecture of Lakonia. Sykia Molaon. Osteological Study', (in Greek), *Archaeologikon Deltion*, 54B1 (1999), 1009–11; P. J. P. McGeorge, 'Anthropological Approach to the Pylona Tombs: The Skeletal Remains', in E. Karantzali (ed.), *The Mycenaean Cemetery on Rhodes* (Oxford: Archaeopress, 2001), pp. 82–94; Nordquist and Ingvarsson-Sundström, 'Live Hard, Die Young', pp. 163–64; A. S. Bouwman, K. A. Brown, A. J. N. W. Prag and T. A. Brown, 'Kinship between Burials from Grave Circle B at Mycenae Revealed by Ancient DNA Typing', *Journal of Archaeological Science*, 35:9 (2008), 2580–84; E. Chilvers, A. S. Bouwman, K. A. Brown, R. G. Arnott, A. J. N. W. Prag and T. A. Brown, 'Ancient DNA in Human Bones from Neolithic and Bronze Age Sites in Greece and Crete', *Journal of Archaeological Science*, 35: 10 (2008), 2707–14.

[51] D. Lancy, J. Bock and S. Gaskins (eds), *The Anthropology of Learning in Childhood* (Lanham: Alta Mira Press, 2010).

Fulani of west Africa, to give but one example amongst many, by the age of four, girls are expected to be competent in tasks such as caring for their younger siblings, fetching water and firewood and water, and by six will be pounding grain, producing milk and butter and selling these alongside their mothers in the market.[52] As in traditional societies, so in the pre-industrial era it would seem that young children's contribution to the domestic economy was a normal and accepted part of daily life and was not generally regarded as exploitative (if indeed such a concept existed). Yet, it is also clear from the fuller documentation of child domestic labour which exists from the late middle ages, that adults could appreciate how the type of work should be suited to the child's age and strength.

Throughout the middle ages in England there are detailed accounts of children's work preserved in legal and other records, so there is evidence that, by the age of seven, many children were expected to undertake simple routine domestic tasks, such as gathering fruit and nuts, or shellfish from the seashore, or collecting firewood and water.[53] After this age, they became more specialised: boys started tending cattle and girls helping round the house.[54] This work is rarely commented on or discussed by contemporaries but by the late middle ages there are occasional cases hinting that distinctions between work and exploitation were well understood. In the late fifteenth century, for example, eight-year-old John Serle of Devon was ploughing for his step-father when he was gored by one of the oxen. The contemporary recorder noted that 'he was really too small' for the job,[55] thereby acknowledging that this sort of work was dangerous to someone of his size and that he should not have been undertaking it.

The later middle ages is an important period in that it saw the beginning of a long lasting custom in England and many other parts of Europe of sending older children away from home to work, either on a daily basis or as part of longer-term or even permanent arrangements. As ever, it is hard to see this pattern as intrinsically abusive although living away from home undoubtedly increases some children's vulnerability.[56] This custom arguably had its roots in the much earlier tradition of handing over boys (rarely girls) to monasteries, cathedrals and churches where they helped maintain the clergy. Boys were cheaper than adults and more likely to do as they were told: Orme notes that 'King Alfred, then trying to revive monasticism in England in the late ninth century, found it impossible to get recruits to be monks except for boys who had no choice in the matter'.[57] Although these boys were receiving an education and learning the liturgy, they were also working as domestic servants and field hands. The clergy also needed choristers and clerks or administrative assistants, and almonry boys (those who served as tonsured clerks) could enter the monasteries from the age of seven. Again, although they were educated and housed and fed, they were also expected to assist the monks and priests in the saying of mass and singing in the choir. In other cases boys and girls were brought to the monastery

[52] H. Montgomery, *An Introduction to Childhood: Anthropological Perspectives on Children's Lives* (Oxford: Wiley-Blackwell, 2008).

[53] N. Orme, *Medieval Children* (New Haven: Yale University Press, 2001), p. 308.

[54] This pattern is also observable in traditional societies today where ethnographers have shown a distinct division of labour emerging in middle childhood with boys looking after livestock while girls are kept closer to the homestead. D. Lancy, *The Anthropology of Childhood: Cherubs, Chattel, Changelings* (Cambridge: Cambridge University Press, 2008).

[55] Orme, *Medieval Children*, p. 308.

[56] Inevitably, deMause, 'The Evolution of Childhood', p. 32, sees living away from home as a sign of abandonment and lack of interest on the part of parents. He writes, 'up to about the eighteenth century, the average child of wealthy parents spent his earliest years in the home of a wet-nurse, returned home to the care of servants, and was sent out to service, apprenticeship, or school by age seven, so that the amount of time parents of means actually spent raising their children was minimal. The effects of these and other institutionalized abandonments by parents on the child have rarely been discussed'.

[57] Orme, *Medieval Children*, p. 223.

or nunnery by their parents as young children and pledged for the rest of their lives. By the end of the twelfth century this form of child oblation had fallen out of fashion and in 1234 the church declared that no one under the age of fourteen could become a permanent member of a religious order. It was recognised that boys who had no vocation might cause trouble in the future and also that with the growth in the numbers of urban schools, boys could be equally well educated outside the monastery and take up a religious life at a later age with an education already behind them.[58]

At the moment the habit of placing young children in the church was losing its allure, new opportunities for work outside the home opened up in royal or aristocratic households, where in the later middle ages boys from all ranks of life might be used as pages, attendants, grooms and kitchen boys. Orme describes the household of Henry Algernon Percy, earl of Northumberland in 1511 in which there were 27 boys or adolescents in a household of 160.

> The young people in the Percy family belonged to a hierarchy of ranks, with the earl's four children at the top of the tree. Beneath them came attendants from knightly or gentry families; carvers, sewers, cupbearers, henchmen, and young gentlemen as they were variously called. Some of these were paid for by their families to enjoy the benefits of serving in the earl's household. They totalled eleven. Further down, there were boys from lower orders of society. The chapel employed six 'children', and the working departments of the household had a boy each (also called a 'child') in the nursery, the wardrobe, the kitchen, the scullery, the stable, the coach-house, the bake-house, the butchery, the catery, and the armoury. The chamberlain of the household, the steward, and the 'arrasmender' who looked after the tapestries had a further boy apiece; thirteen working boys altogether. In return for their work, the boys received board, lodging and a wage reflecting their rank: £3 6s. 8d. a year for noble attendants, £1 5s. for chapel boys, and 13s. 4d. for working boys.[59]

We can see in this description a mixture of advancement and wage earning opportunities. Parents paid for their children to be part of the household where the family's tutor might teach them but they were also paying so that their children might earn money. Royal households provided similar opportunities for both education and work and while children may have worked long hours in uncomfortable circumstances, to talk about exploitation in these cases is problematic. These positions were highly sought after and represented considerable opportunities for children.[60]

While the church and the aristocracy provided work and support for children of higher ranks those lower down the social order in the late middle ages were regularly sent away as servants to less exalted households run by the neighbourhood gentry or the parish clergy. Children were popular because they were cheaper to hire, had no dependents and could be trained up into whatever capacity was needed.[61] Although the majority of medieval servants were boys and girls between the ages of twelve and fourteen, some children became servants at a much younger age. Orme gives the example of a seven-year-old girl, working as a servant in Kent in the late fifteenth century, who fell down a well when sent to fetch water.[62]

In the early modern period, this custom of sending out children, both boys and girls, to be live-in servants – both domestic and field – became commonplace. In northern Europe, not only the gentry and nobility but also tenant farmers and small-holders commonly employed one or two youngsters on a yearly or six-monthly basis. Alan Macfarlane argues

---

[58] Orme, *Medieval Children*, pp. 224–25; N. Orme, *From Childhood to Chivalry: The Education of the English Kings and Aristocracy 1066–1530* (London: Methuen, 1984), p. 62.

[59] Orme, *Medieval Children*, pp. 313–14.

[60] Similar positions were available in the households of great prelates, such as Wolsey, at the beginning of the sixteenth century, so to that extent churchmen, if not the church, continued to take in children.

[61] Orme, *Medieval Children*, p. 311.

[62] Orme, *Medieval Children*, pp. 308–09.

that between 1574–1821 60 per cent of the English population aged between fourteen and 25 were servants.[63] The reason for this, according to Ann Kussmaul, is to be found in the needs of the family farm. Year-on-year family farms required the services of three to four adults if they were to be productive. Most of the time, however, a farmer's children were too young to be much help, or too old: they had married and left home to set up their own farm. Having live-in unmarried adolescent servants who were hired on a short-term basis made economic sense. It also explains why live-in agricultural servants were not to be found in Mediterranean Europe where farms were worked by extended rather than nuclear families, or in Russia where the village land was continually redistributed among the families according to the size of their workforce.[64]

Sending children away as servants was also a way of defraying the cost of their upbringing and obtaining training and possible future patronage for them. The custom was especially useful for poorer rural households that farmed little or had no land themselves. Hugh Cunningham has noted that children were likely to be a net expense rather than a source of productive labour to their parents and, in agricultural families, children were rarely expected to do anything other than simple labouring tasks before the age of ten.

> Economists, many of them working on contemporary peasant societies, disagree about the 'value' of children, but in no possible scenario could there be anything but a net loss on the investment in the first six or seven years... Historians have rigorously guarded themselves against a romanticism of family life in the past with one exception that they still imagine a peasant family work unit in which all members contributed according to their age, strength and gender. In fact many children, unless there was a local industry, were frequently idle. Probably the labour input of the eldest child did not outweigh the costs of feeding, clothing and housing until it was fifteen, and the family as a whole might not be a net gainer from having children until the eighteenth year of the marriage.[65]

While adolescent children were away from home, moreover, they were being paid. Keith Wrightson claims that while there are accounts in the nineteenth and twentieth centuries of English servants sending money back to their families, there are none before this time.[66] Instead the child was expected to save his or her wages so that it would be possible to set up home later on.

Of course, children in northern Europe were not simply put into service in the countryside. All over Europe, in the course of the late middle ages, adolescents were engaged as live-in servants in the emerging towns and cities. And it was in the towns that service was most likely to be exploitative. In the countryside neighbours were frequently hiring each other's

---

[63] A. Macfarlane, *Marriage and Love in England: Modes of Reproduction, 1300–1840* (Oxford: Blackwell, 1986), p. 83.

[64] A. Kussmaul, *Servants in Husbandry in Early Modern England* (Cambridge: Cambridge University Press, 1981), p. 26. Adolescent living-in servants were to be found in serf as well as free European societies in the early modern period: see C. Kuklo, 'Le Modèle du life cycle servant a-t-il existé dans la Pologne préindustrielle', in J.-P. Bardet, J.-N. Luc, I. Robin-Romero and C. Rollet (eds), *Lorsque l'enfant grandit. Entre dépendence et autonomie* (Paris: Presse de l'Université de Paris-Sorbonne, 2003), pp. 717–32. For an overview, see the essays in A. Fauve-Chamoux and L. Fiavala (eds), *Le Phénomène de la domesticite en Europe, XVIe–XXe siècles* (Prague: Akademie ved Ceské Republiky, 1997). See also M. Rahikainen, *Centuries of Child Labour, European Experiences From the Seventeenth to the Twentieth Century* (Aldershot: Ashgate, 2004), ch. 2.

[65] H. Cunningham, *Children and Childhood in Western Society since 1500* (London: Longman, 1995), p. 84. For an opposing view, see Humphries, *Childhood*, ch. 9.

[66] K. Wrightson, *English Society, 1580–1680* (London: Unwin Hyman, 1982), p. 85. Kussmaul has found only one indirect suggestion that servants sent money home in her extensive work on sixteenth- and seventeenth-century servanthood. She writes that 'farm service gave the children of the poor a chance to save the wages they received in order to stock small farms or common land, or simply to furnish the cottage they would inhabit when they were married'. Kussmaul, *Servants in Husbandry*, p. 76.

children, and adolescent servants would regularly come into contact with other members of their family at work or church. When Joseph Mayett went into service on a farm at Quainton in Buckinghamshire aged twelve in 1783, his father was employed by the farmers as a labourer.[67] In towns, on the other hand, servants were often a long way from home and easy targets for sadists, bullies and sexual predators. That servant girls had difficulty hanging onto their honour in urban Europe was well-understood. In the eighteenth century, it became the stuff of fiction with Daniel Defoe's publication of *Moll Flanders*, a raucous tale of the trials and tribulations of a Colchester servant seduced by her master's son.[68]

In the urban context, however, living-in service was more clearly gendered. Girls were primarily taken on as domestic servants while boys became apprentices. This was a distinctive kind of service, based often on a written contract, as is explained in the following piece. The apprentice would serve his master for a stipulated and usually long period of time and receive no pay. The master would provide board and lodgings and teach his apprentice the craft.

Apprenticeship in Northwest Europe 1300–1850

Laurence Brockliss

Perrin Thierri, a merchant living in Blois, contracts that his son Perrin Thierri, who is about fifteen years old… will live and stay with Jehan de Mondidier, known as Pare, a merchant, banker [*changeur*] and burgher of Orléans… for three years from All Saints Day next, and agrees that the said son will serve the said Jehan… in all things licit and honest just as loyally as an apprenticed servant should serve his master. … As pledge of this, Perrin Thierri, the father, will pay the said Jehan twenty gold *réaux* [a Spanish coin]. … In return, the said Pare is expected to provide Perrin the son with drink, food, warmth, bed and lodgings and his footwear… and to teach him as far as he is able the knowledge and matter of his art [Notarial act, Orléans, 8 September 1437].[69]

The practice of formally handing over children to adults to learn a craft or trade goes back at least to Roman times. Besides scattered references to the phenomenon in classical literature, thirty contracts of apprenticeship involving both slaves and freeborn boys and girls have been found among the surviving documents of Roman rule in Egypt.[70]

---

[67] Kussmaul, *Servants in Husbandry*, pp. 85–93. In early modern England, living-in servants, even those working the fields, were to be distinguished from agricultural labourers, who were adult, lived at home and were paid by the day.

[68] Samuel Richardson's *Pamela or Virtue Rewarded* which appeared two decades later (1740) tackled the same theme (at great length) but was set in a Bedfordshire country house. The gentry were portrayed as just as untrustworthy. The hero of Smollett's *Humphrey Clinker* (1771) is the result of a union between a gentleman and a serving girl at Oxford. On the reality of the danger from predatory masters in France, see C. Fairchilds, *Domestic Enemies. Servants and their Masters in Old Regime France* (Baltimore: Johns Hopkins University Press, 1984).

[69] Cited in F. Michaud-Fréjaville, 'Bons et loyaux services: Les contrats d'apprentissage en Orléanais (1380–1480)', in *Les Entrées dans la vie, initiations et apprentissages: XII Congrès de la Société des historiens médiévistes de l'enseignement supérieur public* (Nancy: Presses Universitaires de Nancy, 1982), pp. 185–86.

[70] K. Bradley, *Discovering the Roman Family: Studies in Roman Social History* (Oxford: Oxford University Press, 1991), ch. 5; B. Rawson, *Children and Childhood in Roman Italy* (Oxford: Oxford University Press, 2003), pp. 182, 191–94, and 261–62.

In the relative chaos and economic disruption of the early middle ages the practice, if it continued to exist, disappears from the historical record. It only surfaces again in northern Europe at the end of the thirteenth century in a period of renewed economic growth and urbanisation.[71] Two centuries later formally apprenticing children to a wide variety of occupations by drawing up a signed indenture had become a commonplace and remained so until the end of the eighteenth century, parents frequently paying a hefty premium for the privilege of placing their offspring in high status trades. In most parts of northern Europe the rules governing apprenticeship were predominantly determined by the city guilds, so that the number of apprentices that a master might take and the number of years that an apprentice was expected to serve was the business of the individual trade. Apprentices might agree to serve for only a year or as many as twenty. In England, in contrast, under the Statute of Artificers of 1562, the apprenticeship system was brought under national law. Thereafter, all apprentices in urban trades had to contract for a seven-year term, which was already the longstanding custom in London. At the same time, in an attempt to discourage movement from the countryside, urban apprentices themselves had to be sons of townsmen.[72]

The proportion of early modern children who were formally apprenticed will never be accurately known, for no country in Europe kept a record of the number of indentures signed each year and many contracts were verbal.[73] In that most families were involved in agriculture, and apprenticeships in husbandry, if not unknown, were uncommon, it was definitely a minority. None the less, it was not just the sons of respectable tradesmen and artisans who would have found themselves under a master. Europe experienced two periods of demographic growth during the period: across the long sixteenth century and in the second half of the eighteenth. In neither case, however, did the economy grow quickly enough to absorb the rising population with the result that an increasing number of families became permanently or periodically destitute and their children dependent on charity. From the end of the sixteenth century, it became more and more common for pauper children dependent on institutionalised charity to be apprenticed to more menial trades as soon as they were judged to be of sufficient age. In England, the 1601 Act of Parliament, which established the national poor law, gave parish overseers the power not only to bind poor orphans and young vagrants but the offspring of parents 'overburthened with children'. Thereby the local community or the church ridded themselves of the cost of maintaining pauper children as soon as possible and salved their conscience by thinking that the objects of their benevolence would be taught to make an honest living. Prospective masters were bribed with a small premium or local ratepayers simply allocated a pauper apprentice on a rota system.[74]

---

[71] Orme, *Medieval Children*, pp. 311–13.

[72] O. J. Dunlop, *English Apprenticeship and Child Labour. A History* (London: T. Fisher Unwin, 1912), ch. 3. The statute in the seventeenth and eighteenth centuries was honoured in the breach; many English apprentices in the most prestigious trades and professions were the younger sons of lesser gentry: see C. Brooks, 'Apprenticeship, Social Mobility and the Middling Sort 1500–1800', in J. Barry and C. Brooks (eds), *The Middling Sort of People. Culture, Society and Politics in England 1550–1800* (London: Macmillan, 1994), pp. 61–68.

[73] N. Pellegrin, 'L'Apprentissage ou l'écriture de l'oralité. Quelques remarques introductoires', *Revue d'histoire moderne et contemporaine*, 40:3 (1993), 359–64. In England from 1709 a record exists of all indentures where a premium was paid, for thereafter premiums were taxed by the state: J. Lane, *Apprenticeship in England 1600–1914* (London: UCL Press, 1996), ch. 4. In sixteenth-century London supposedly ten per cent of the population were apprentices: see S. Rappaport, *Worlds Within Worlds. Structures of Life in Sixteenth-Century London* (Cambridge: Cambridge University Press, 1989), pp. 232–34.

[74] Lane, *Apprenticeship in England*, ch. 4; Dunlop, *English Apprenticeship*, ch. 16; I. Robin-Romero, '"Apprendre mestier et gaigner leur vie": La mise en métier des orphelins des hôpitaux de la Trinité et du Saint-Esprit au XVIIe siècle', in Bardet *et al.* (eds), *Lorsque l'enfant grandit*, pp. 657–72.

Apprenticing paupers also led to an increase in the number of girls being bound. Most crafts, apart from dressmaking, were virtually closed to girls until the end of the period, so few from modest or well-to-do families were apprenticed. In the Orléanais only 52 out of 821 contracts surveyed made between 1380 and 1490 concerned girls, and the number fell rapidly after 1440. In three English counties in the years 1710–60 non-pauper girls represented only three to six per cent of the total. Once it became the practice to bind paupers after 1600, girls must have formed a much larger percentage of the total, though their options were always narrow. 71.6 per cent of girls bound from the Parisian orphanage of La Trinité in the second half of the seventeenth century entered domestic service; a further 13.5 per cent were apprenticed to the needlework trade. In England, the opportunities for girls only opened up to a certain extent with the development of the first textile mills at the turn of the nineteenth century. Mill owners sought cheap and nimble operatives of either sex, and would take children of any background. In the years 1801–16 Benjamin Smart junior, owner of Emscote mill near Warwick took pauper apprentices from eleven Warwickshire and at least two Oxfordshire parishes. Most were girls, like the fourteen-year-old Phoebe Lancaster, an orphan from Stratford-upon-Avon, who was apprenticed for seven years with a premium of £4.14s. 6d. in 1805.[75]

The Statute of Artificers decreed that apprentices should be 24 at the end of their term, which meant that in England no-one should have been bound before they were seventeen. While guilds on the continent seldom laid down specific rules about age, the information provided in contracts and indentures suggests that children on average in France and the Netherlands were apprenticed a little younger than this. In the Orléanais in the fifteenth century they were fifteen-and-a-half; in Antwerp in the first half of the seventeenth century, just over fourteen-and-a-half (among orphans from the city hospital); and in Paris in the eighteenth century, the average age was just under sixteen. None the less, on the continent and in England, *pace* the statute, the range of ages revealed in contracts is so broad as to make the average of limited significance. When the information is broken down by trade, it becomes clear that the age of apprenticeship depended in part on the nature of the work. Physically strenuous trades, those that demanded care and a good eye, or those where apprentices were likely to be constantly dealing with customers, recruited boys in their late teens. In eighteenth-century Paris, for instance, most apprentices taken on by butchers, cloth merchants, engravers and makers of mirrors were eighteen; the average age of apprentice coopers was 23.5. More sedentary occupations or those with a premium on agility took quite young children. Chimney sweeps in England were frequently bound between the tender ages of seven and ten. Paupers also tended to be apprenticed relatively young. 80 per cent of the 290 pauper children apprenticed from Bedworth in Warwickshire in the eighteenth century whose age is known were thirteen or younger; 27 were nine or under. Orphans, whether supported by charity or not, were particularly likely to be bound at an early age. In the fifteenth-century Orléanais, one mite, Pierre Garrault, was only three years old when he was placed by his relatives with a vine-grower (*vigneron*) for fifteen years.[76]

---

[75] Michaud-Fréjaville, 'Bons et loyaux services', p. 183; Lane, *Apprenticeship in England*, pp. 40 and 176–77; I. K. Ben-Amos, 'Women Apprentices in Trade and Crafts of Early-Modern Bristol', *Continuity and Change*, 2:6 (1991), 227–53; Robin-Romero, '"Apprendre mestier et gaigner leur vie"', p. 667. K. D. M. Snell, *Annals of the Labouring Poor: Social Change and Agrarian England, 1660–1900* (Cambridge: Cambridge University Press, 1985), ch. 6. Girls who were apprenticed to domestic service should not be confused with the large numbers who became household servants; the latter were not formally contracted and were paid a wage: see above, pp. 169–71.

[76] Michaud-Fréjaville, 'Bons et loyaux services', p. 191; B. de Munck, *Technologies of Learning: Apprenticeship in*

All children and adolescents who entered an apprenticeship would have been used to work. Children would have helped in the home, around the farm or in their father's workshop from an early age, while the institutionalised would have been already introduced to the rigours of work discipline. Many parish orphans through the centuries would have had a similar, if perhaps not quite so heartless, experience as the eponymous hero of Charles Dickens's *Oliver Twist* (1838), who spent his young days in the workhouse picking hemp before he was apprenticed to the undertaker, Sowerberry. Children (mainly girls) in the Paris hospital of La Salpetrière (where 2,408 of its 5,000 inhabitants in 1701 were under sixteen) were expected to work throughout the day from the age of five, the routine punctuated with religious services. Young girls knitted garments for merchants; older girls earned their keep through embroidery and tapestry.[77] There can have been few apprentices, though, who did not find their new lives tougher than their old. Whatever their age, they were expected to work the same hours and to the same rhythm as adults. And the hours were long. Some contracts stipulated that the apprentice would work from dawn to sunset, irrespective of the time of year. The norm, however, was a fourteen-hour day, broken by three periods of half-an-hour for meals and rest. Only apprentices in trades where the need for natural light governed the length of the day would have enjoyed shorter hours. Apprentices in the most prestigious trades could fare the worst. William Lucas, an apothecary's apprentice in London in the eighteenth century noted that he and his fellows always worked a twelve-hour day (9 am–9 pm) but they also took turns at working a weekly shift from seven in the morning until eleven at night.[78]

Newcomers too would have had to get used to life at the bottom of the workshop ladder. Initially, apprentices whatever their social origins were given menial tasks and were ordered about by their workmates, unless there was a specific clause in their contract to the contrary. They would be expected to open and close the shop, sweep the floor, run errands and so on. According to Nicolas-Edme Restif de la Bretonne (1734–1806), who was a printer's apprentice in Auxerre in the early 1750s, he was even expected to be a go-between in his colleagues' affairs of the heart. Everything was done, he declared, to make him feel thoroughly alienated. 'I had to pander to all the needs, indeed every fantasy, of thirty-two workmen, the master, two women [his wife and daughter], my friend [fellow apprentice] and even the servant, who made me fetch the water in his place'.[79] New apprentices would also be the butt of jokes and forced to endure initiation ceremonies which were meant to make them feel foolish and understand their lowly position. Typical was the ceremony undergone by a young York printer, called Thomas, in 1713. He was forced to kneel, struck with a broadsword,

---

Antwerp Guilds from the Fifteenth Century to the End of the Ancien Régime (Turnhout: Brepols, 2007), pp. 171–81; S. Kaplan, ' L'Apprentissage au XVIIIe siècle: le cas de Paris', *Revue d'histoire moderne et contemporaine*, 40:1, 3 (1993), 436–76 at p. 452; Lane, *Apprenticeship in England*, pp. 13–18 and 129–30; Robin-Romero, '"Apprendre mestier et gaigner leur vie"', p. 659. Information about the ages of the apprentices is incomplete: many contracts and indentures do not give details.

[77] S. Beauvalet-Boutouyrie, 'Les Enfants de la Salpetrière au XVIIIe siècle', in Bardet *et al.* (eds), *Lorsque l'Enfant Grandit*, pp. 891–93. French hospitals in the pre-modern era were poor houses for the vagrants, the unemployed and the sick.

[78] W. Lucas, *A Quaker Journal: Being the Diary and Reminiscences of William Lucas of Hitchin (1804–1861) a Member of the Society of Friends* (London: Hutchinson and Co, 1934), p. 45.

[79] N.-E. Restif de la Bretonne, *Monsieur Nicolas, ou, le Coeur-Humain Dévoilé* [1794–97], 6 vols (Paris: Jean-Jacques Pauvert, 1959), i. 407. This book is a fictionalised account of Restif's life. For a much earlier complaint along similar lines, see the comments in the autobiography of the Elizabethan and Jacobean astrologer, Simon Forman, who was apprenticed to a hosier and grocer at Salisbury: *The Autobiography and Personal Diary of Dr Simon Forman, from AD 1552 to AD 1602*, ed. J. O. Halliwell (London: Richards, 1849), p. 6.

then had ale poured on his head, before being given the title of 'Earl of Fingall'.[80]

Such deliberate attempts to humiliate and belittle would have been all the more hard to bear because the apprentice was normally also living away from home. Just like the Orléans merchant and banker Jehan de Mondidier cited at the beginning of this section, the large majority of masters who took on an apprentice before 1700 contracted to give his charge board and lodging as well as teach the adolescent a trade or profession. Indeed, living away from home was so central a part of the concept of an apprenticeship in the period under a review that even sons who were destined to follow their fathers into the family workshop (probably the majority of apprentices) were usually sent out to learn the craft.[81] While the apprentice was in his master's home, the latter was completely *in loco parentis*. The master was expected to police the young person's morals and leisure and as much as possible keep him or her off the street, not just in working hours but in the evenings. Contracts sometimes stipulated that the master would ensure that his charge went to church and often laid down that the apprentice was not to gamble, frequent taverns or even play ball games. In England, where guilds, town councils and the state took a particularly close interest in the regulation of apprentices, their leisure activities, apparel and appearance (especially length of hair) were limited by by-laws and statutes: from 1692 they were specifically forbidden by Parliament to hunt.[82] And masters were given power to punish if apprentices stepped out of line: they could administer corporal punishment, gate them and withhold food.

It would appear that there were two factors governing the practice of boarding out an apprentice. Firstly, the practice taught the apprentice that he was leaving the world in which he had been raised and was entering a new society with its own rhythms, rules and mysteries, which would command his adult loyalties as much if not more than his nuclear family. Secondly, it was felt that the practice was the best way to inculcate work discipline. Only when fully immersed in a stranger's household could the apprentice be taught how to be an obedient and loyal worker. Parents were too indulgent. If left to their control outside working hours, they would undo all the good work of the master; even parents in the same trade could not be relied on to teach their children how to be submissive and reliable.[83] It was for this reason that the apprentice's life in the household was supposed to be hard; just as in the workshop, he was to expect no favours whatever his background. Restif 's confessor tells him that there is a spiritual value in his suffering, while his father insists that he accomplish base and servile acts. He must never refuse a request, and all will seem noble when properly considered. Above all, Restif must remember when asked to do something that offends him that 'my master represents my father and mother; heigh! Wouldn't I do that for them?'[84]

Admittedly, the life of an apprentice was not always closely regulated and dull. Sunday was a holiday and in Catholic countries there were frequent religious festivals when the apprentice was allowed out. Before the second half of the seventeenth century at any rate many played an active role in enforcing moral order in the wider urban community. In London for instance it was purportedly the city apprentices who regularly attacked the city's brothels on Shrove Tuesday.[85] There were also many masters

---

[80] J. Hunter (ed.), *The Life of Mr Thomas Gent: Printer, of York, Written by Himself* (London: T. Thorpe, 1832), p. 16.
[81] de Munck, *Technologies of Learning*, pp. 206–11.
[82] Lane, *Apprenticeship in England*, pp. 4–5.
[83] de Munck, *Technologies of Learning*, pp. 201–05.
[84] Restif de la Bretonne, *Monsieur Nicolas*, pp. 377–79 and 392–97.
[85] P. Griffiths, *Youth and Authority. Formative Experiences in England 1560–1640* (Oxford: Oxford University Press, 1996), pp. 147–69; Lane, *Apprenticeship in England*, p. 107; Dunlop, *English Apprenticeship*, pp. 190–93.

who treated their apprentices as one of the family or allowed them a great deal of freedom. In the 1780s the apprentice leather breeches-maker and future radical, Francis Place (1771–1854), seems to have roamed around London at will once the working day was over. Two decades later in Manchester, the apprentice surgeon-apothecary, Alexander Lesassier (1787–1839), was similarly indulged by his Quaker master, once the senior apprentice had left and he was no longer given irksome and demeaning tasks.[86] In some towns at the end of the period, an effort was made to improve the quality of an apprentice's life all round. In Birmingham in the early nineteenth century, apprentices were permitted to down tools at 5.30 pm on Mondays so that they could go to the theatre.[87]

Inevitably, however, there were many masters who treated their apprentices badly, forcing them to sleep in the shop and keeping them on meagre rations, although it is only in the eighteenth century that information about abuse becomes readily available when cases begin to appear in court records. Some trades by the end of the period were particularly notorious. Black and ragged chimney sweeps had attracted the attention of English philanthropists and legislators long before Charles Kingsley (1819–75) wrote *The Water Babies* (1863). Reluctant to ascend the narrow flues, which were the height of architectural fashion at the end of the eighteenth century, the boys were subject to frequent beatings; the cruellest masters were not unknown to encourage compliance by lighting fires in the grates. The result, as early as 1788, was Parliamentary intervention. In that year a law was passed, on the initiative of a concerned master sweep, David Poster, laying down a minimum age at which boys could be apprenticed (eight) and the earliest hour they could begin the day (7 am in winter, 5 am in summer). The apprentices were also to be 'thoroughly washed and cleaned from soot and Dirt at least once a week' and were to attend church on Sundays, while no master was to have more than six in his charge.[88]

Many children and adolescents were indentured to harsh and dangerous trades by their own parents, as the two poems entitled the 'The Chimney Sweeper', published in 1789 and 1794 by William Blake (1757–1827), remind us.[89] But it was inevitably paupers and orphans who were most at risk. Girls were always in danger of being sexually abused by masters or their sons while both boys and girls were victims of manslaughter. Elizabeth Robbins was apprenticed by her parish to the Coventry ribbon-weaver, Thomas Swift, in 1803. Seven years later, now aged sixteen, she starved to death after her poor diet was reduced further as a punishment for picking 'potato pairings off the muckhill' and stealing a loaf of bread. According to two other apprentices, Robbins was also beaten by her master, who threatened to kill her, had her ears pulled until they bled and had a candle stuffed in her mouth. She was also continually under surveillance, even when she went to the privy.[90] Crabbe's fictional master fisherman, *Peter Grimes* (from his poem, *The Borough*, of 1810), had many counterparts in reality.[91]

Griffiths suspects that 'apprentice' was a catchall term used by the authorities and not necessarily indicative of the composition of the Shrove Tuesday crowds. He also insists that the rioters did not have civic approval. For the role of adolescents in community policing, see below, Ch. 5, pp. 232–33.

[86] *The Autobiography of Francis Place (1771–1854)*, ed. M. Thrale (Cambridge: Cambridge University Press, 1972); L. Rosser, *The Most Beautiful Man in Existence. The Scandalous Life of Alexander Lesassier* (Philadelphia: University of Pennsylvania Press, 1999), pp. 16–17 (on the trials of a surgeon-apothecary's apprentice in Manchester).

[87] Lane, *Apprenticeship in England*, p. 111.

[88] *Ibid.*, pp. 129–30; Dunlop, *English Apprenticeship*, p. 264.

[89] 'A little black thing among the snow / Crying "'weep! 'weep!" in notes of woe. / Where are thy father and mother, say?" / "They are both gone up to the church to pray."': William Blake, *Selected Poems and Letters*, ed. J. Bronowski (Harmondsworth: Penguin Books, 1972), p. 47 (from *Songs of Experience*).

[90] Lane, *Apprenticeship in England*, pp. 220–22.

[91] See above, Ch. 3, p. 120–22. Other references to abusive masters are given in I. Pinchbeck and M. Hewitt,

Even apprentices who had good masters could suffer fatal accidents or become permanently disabled. Working in the mills was very dangerous, while in many trades the young were exposed to chemicals and substances that would lead to cancers and other injuries later in life.[92] From our modern perspective, it cannot but be felt that the younger live-in apprentices especially were denied a childhood, working long hours and allowed little exercise and time for play. Yet, it must be remembered that the practice made perfect sense to Augustinian Christians who saw children as fallen beings who had to be licked into shape as adolescents if they were not to behave as adults in a manner unacceptable to God. Like service more generally, the practice also (doubtless unintentionally) had a positive demographic consequence. In that the young were carefully policed until their early twenties, it helped to keep the illegitimacy rate low and the age of marriage for both men and women high. This in turn was a factor encouraging Europe's fairly slow population growth across the period 1350 to 1750, which ensured that the agrarian crises that hit the continent from time to time were less intense and relatively short compared with the devastating famines that appear to have affected pre-industrial societies in some other parts of the world.[93]

. . . .

The classic form of living-in craft apprenticeship described in the previous section began to decline in England from the beginning of the eighteenth century. By the end of the century apprentices were often not serving their entire seven years and were being contracted for shorter periods, making their period of service comparable to that of farm servants. In 1814 Parliament acknowledged that the system was falling into desuetude by abolishing the clauses relating to apprenticeship in the Statute of Artificers.[94] Thereafter only pauper children, the group most likely to suffer abuse or exploitation, continued to be placed as craft apprentices in large numbers. Often sent many miles from the parish in which they had been raised, it was hoped that they would never return to be a burden on the community.[95] Living-in service in the countryside also declined in England from the middle of the eighteenth century. By 1851, according to the census of that year, it only continued to flourish on pastoral farms in the north.[96]

The decline in formal apprenticeships can be directly attributed to the revolutionary changes that were occurring to England's manufacturing economy across the eighteenth and the first half of the nineteenth centuries. The guilds that had policed apprenticeships

---

Children in English Society (London: Routledge and Kegan Paul, 1969) pp. 246–47.

[92] Lane, *Apprenticeship in England*, pp. 44–54.

[93] Despite the surge in growth across the long sixteenth century mentioned above, the population probably only doubled across this period and may have been little higher in 1750 than it was before Europe was devastated by the Black Death in the 1340s. For Augustinian Christianity and theories of child-rearing, see above Ch. 3, pp. 111, 123–24, 133. Other factors affecting the pace of population growth included the continual return of the plague for more than three centuries after the Black Death and the readiness of some married couples in England and France to practise some form of family limitation.

[94] The issue of the decline of apprenticeship has been the subject of much discussion among historians. For a summary of this work, see Snell, *Annals of the Labouring Poor*, ch. 5. Snell points out that the decline of apprenticeships was very different in different parts of England and happened at different times so it is hard to make too many generalisations on this issue. Nevertheless there is evidence of a decline before the 1814 Act.

[95] Robert Blincoe at the age of seven was sent, along with 80 other children, to a mill near Nottingham, having been falsely promised roast beef and plum pudding. He had to work fourteen hours a day and was treated with appalling brutality. See p. 188 below.

[96] Kussmaul, *Servants in Husbandry*, pp. 127–28.

in the towns had more or less collapsed as a potent social and economic force by the end of the seventeenth century, having failed to adapt to new economic and social challenges.[97] Craft apprenticeships themselves were killed off by the more rapid economic changes of the Hanoverian age. Traditional apprenticeships with their long years of on-the-job training in all aspects of a craft did not sit well with a new industrial economy built on the division of labour and, in the textile industry in particular, factory production. There was, in the formalised system of craft apprentices, an 'inherent conservatism', as Heywood has pointed out, 'as each generation merely handed down what it knew from its own experience in a particular calling and region. It was doubtless appropriate to a relatively stable, agrarian society, but not to a more restless commercial and urbanized one'.[98] A more complex set of causes undermined living-in husbandry. The growing manufacturing economy offered adolescents in the countryside new opportunities of earning a wage outside the home, while the fast and continuous rise in population after 1750 provided a growing pool of adult labour that could be tapped. At the same time, recourse to adult labour became economically rational, as the enclosure of the midlands and the more general development of large farms changed the nature of farm work, and ratepayers began to subsidise the wages of agricultural labourers under the Speenhamland system.[99]

In other parts of Europe, where industrialisation occurred more slowly and took different forms, apprenticeship and living-in service survived longer. In France, where the population grew only slowly after 1800, and much industry remained workshop based, a long apprenticeship under a master continued to be prized in many specialist manufactures far into the nineteenth century. As late as the 1840s a director of a glass works in Lorraine could insist that an apprenticeship must be started early 'to avoid the risk of never acquiring the degree of dexterity which makes skilled workers'.[100] But even in France the nature of an apprenticeship had changed. Increasingly, it appears, children learnt in the family workshop and never underwent an apprenticeship. In addition, more and more apprentices lived at home. In 1845 there were 19,000 apprentices in Paris but only 10,000 boarded and lodged with the master. More importantly, only a fifth of the 19,000 now had formal contracts. It was perhaps for this reason that in 1851 the French government promulgated the country's first apprenticeship law, laying down the treatment an apprentice could expect and instituting a ten-hour day for those under fourteen. The 1851 law, however, did nothing to stop the disintegration of the traditional apprenticeship system. By 1898, when there were 602,000 adolescents in France under the age of eighteen working in industry or commerce, only 62,000 had contracts. The result was that apprentices had little security. At the same time, the changing nature of artisanal work in nineteenth-century France, as manufacturing became organised on the principle of the division of labour, meant that their work was often monotonous and repetitive as well as sometimes dangerous. It is unlikely that these quasi-apprentices were subjected to more abuse than in the past – though there are some tales in working-class autobiographies of horrific treatment – but they were certainly not protected by legislation.[101]

---

[97] For a summary of the debates on the decline of the craft guilds see S. R. Epstein, 'Craft Guilds', in J. Mokyr (ed.), *The Oxford Encyclopaedia of Economic History, vol. 2* (Oxford: Oxford University Press, 2003), pp. 35–39.
[98] C. Heywood, *A History of Childhood: Children and Childhood in the West from Medieval to Modern Times* (Cambridge: Polity Press, 2001), p. 160.
[99] Kussmaul, *Husbandry*, pp. 114–24. The Speenhamland system was developed in Berkshire in 1795 to counteract rural poverty. It allowed for a means-tested, sliding-scale of wage supplements to agricultural labourers so that the parish could top up their earnings.
[100] Quoted in Heywood, *A History of Childhood*, p. 138.
[101] C. Heywood, *Childhood in Nineteenth-Century France: Work, Health and Education Among the 'Classes Populaires'*, (Cambridge: Cambridge University Press, 1988), chs 4 and 5 and p. 248; M. Perrot, 'Worker Youth: From the Workshop to the Factory', in G. Levi and J.-C. Schmitt (eds), *A History of Young People in*

It seems fair to conclude, therefore, that the traditional craft apprenticeship died everywhere in industrialising Europe in the second half of the nineteenth century. Most children would still work but they would no longer be subjected to the trauma of a long separation from family and home.[102] In fact, in the nineteenth century, it was the sons of the rich who were most likely to spend long periods away from the family hearth as adolescents. For many this was because they were incarcerated in boarding schools where life could be extremely harsh.[103] For others it was because they were receiving in-house training for one of the professions. In most parts of Europe entry to the higher echelons of the traditional learned professions – church, law and medicine – had for many centuries required university study and a degree.[104] But the lowlier branches recruited through apprenticeship. Solicitors, notaries, surgeons and apothecaries had all learnt on the job in their teens after attending secondary schools for a few years. In most countries this ceased to be the case in the nineteenth century as all entrants to the legal and medical professions began to follow a common educational curriculum that required institutional study.[105] But there remained an ever-increasing number of new professions or occupations formerly never accorded the status, for which there was still little or no formal institutionalised education. In the course of the century careers in the civil and imperial service, surveying, accountancy, engineering, management and so on were elevated to a new status of respectability by the growth of the state and the economy. However, recruits received an old-fashioned training. Prospective entrants were taken into an office or shop and trained up for a career, frequently, in the case of the private professions, living with their employer.[106]

This was particularly the case in Britain (albeit somewhat paradoxically, given the early demise of craft apprenticeships there), where even entrants to the law were usually 'apprenticed' or 'articled' throughout the nineteenth century, and where medicine more slowly became a graduate profession.[107] Entrants to all branches of medicine in the first half of the nineteenth century combined apprenticeship with a formal medical education. After learning Latin to a respectable level in a local grammar school, tyro medics, like the

---

the West: Stormy Evolution to Modern Times (Cambridge: Harvard University Press, 1997), pp. 87–96. For the changing nature of artisanal work in nineteenth-century France, see W. H. Sewell, Jr., *Work and Revolution in France. The Language of Labor from the Old Regime to 1848* (Cambridge: Cambridge University Press, 1980). See also J.-L. Lenhof, 'L'Enfant et les mutations du travail industriel en France au XIXe siècle: Le regard des contemporains', in Bardet *et al.* (eds), *Lorsque l'enfant grandit*, pp. 733–50.

[102] More is said about children's work in the nineteenth century on pp. 185–92 below.

[103] See Ch. 3, pp. 141–46. It was not just English boys who were sent away for their secondary education. Good secondary schools were only found in the big cities, so boys all over the continent ended up living away from home while they gained a solid knowledge of the arts and sciences. The French *lycées* all had boarding establishments.

[104] In Protestant churches from the Reformation, clergy were expected to have a degree, although the Church of England was peculiar in merely demanding a degree in arts and not in theology. In Catholic states only the higher clergy needed a degree; parish priests were trained in seminaries. In most countries barristers and physicians had to have a professional degree.

[105] For developments in medicine see especially T. N. Bonner, *Becoming a Physician. Medical Education in Great Britain, France, Germany and the United States 1750–1945* (Oxford: Oxford University Press, 1995).

[106] For the situation in France in particular, see G. Geison (ed.), *Professions in the French State, 1700–1900* (Philadelphia: University of Pennsylvania Press, 1984).

[107] This reflected the fact that England operated under a common-law system, and law of any kind was an insignificant part of the Oxford and Cambridge curriculum before the second half of the nineteenth century. It was not until after the Second World War that barristers and solicitors were expected to have a law degree. On the entry requirements to different British professions in the nineteenth century, see L. W. B. Brockliss, 'The Professions and National Identity', in L. W. B. Brockliss and D. Eastwood (eds), *A Union of Multiple Identities. The British Isles, c. 1750–c. 1850* (Manchester, Manchester University Press, 1997), ch. 1; P. Corfield, *Power and the Professions in Britain 1700–1850* (London: Routledge, 1995), *passim*.

poet John Keats (1795–1821), would be indentured between the age of fourteen and sixteen to a surgeon or surgeon-apothecary with whom they lived. The apprenticeship would last from five to seven years and be followed by a period of study at Edinburgh or one of the London medical schools established in the previous century, where the young medic would supplement lectures with a few months walking the wards of a hospital. The affluent would then take a medical degree and be permitted to call themselves a physician, but most would make do with a diploma from the London Society of Apothecaries.[108]

Doubtless the life of most professional apprentices or pupils was relatively benign. Their social and economic status would have protected them from the abuses suffered by poorer apprentices in the past.[109] But there was one professional career in Britain where training on the job could be a nightmare for a sensitive adolescent (if a great adventure for the tough and gregarious). Virtually all continental countries trained military officers in specialist academies that had begun to be set up in the course of the eighteenth century so that young officers did not enter active service until their late teens.[110] Britain, in this regard too, lagged behind its competitors. Although academies were founded, beginning with the artillery school at Woolwich in the late 1790s, making attendance a formal requirement of entry to the military profession was a slow process.[111] The next contribution looks at the specific case of the system of training set up for young officers in the Royal Navy in the course of the long eighteenth century, an institution that continued to rely on quasi-apprentices until the eve of the First World War. Here young men were sent away at an early age, not just to an alien household, but to endure the rigours and dangers of life aboard ship. The future Edward VII (r. 1901–10) was sent to sea aged fourteen in 1855 and his son, George V (r. 1910–36) was sent away to train as naval cadet in 1877 aged twelve, exactly the same age that Lord Nelson (1758–1805) had joined the navy in 1770. The chief difference was that in the long naval peace after the ending of the French wars, the young officer recruits had little chance of being involved in a naval battle.

---

[108] From 1815, all medical practitioners in England were expected to obtain a testimonial of their expertise from the Society of Apothecaries, however they had trained. It was only with the establishment of an official medical register in 1858 that it became necessary for a licensed medical practitioner to have a medical degree or a qualification from one of the royal medical colleges of Britain and Ireland. See I. Loudon, *Medical Care and the General Practitioner 1700–1850* (Oxford: Clarendon Press, 1986), esp. chs 6–8; M. Ackroyd, L. W. B. Brockliss, M. Moss, K Retford and J. Stevenson, *Advancing with the Army: Medicine, the Professions and Social Mobility in the British Isles 1790–1850* (Oxford: Oxford University Press, 2007), ch. 3; L. W. B. Brockliss, J. Cardwell and M. Moss, *Nelson's Surgeon: William Beatty, Naval Medicine and the Battle of Trafalgar* (Oxford: Oxford University Press, 2005), pp. 20–22.

[109] Most professional apprentices came from the gentry or middle-classes. The premiums were too high for poorer parents unless their son found a patron. Keat's apprenticeship cost £210 for five years. £40 a year was a good wage. Doubtless many professional apprentices were still neglected: cf. the fictional account of a live-in pupillage in an architect's practice near Salisbury in Dickens's *Martin Chuzzlewit* (1844), where the eponymous hero is taken on by the less than assiduous, Pecksniff.

[110] In Prussia, boys entered the military academy aged twelve.

[111] H. Strachan, *Wellington's Legacy. The Reform of the British Army* (Manchester: Manchester University Press, 1984), pp. 132–33.

The Royal Navy's Commissioned Sea Officers 1700–1815

M. John Cardwell

There were several routes by which an eighteenth-century sea officer embarked upon his career. It is important in the following discussion to emphasise that there was no rigid correlation between social station and the Navy's official system of ranks and ratings, especially as they related to its prospective officers. The first steps for all entailed service upon the lower deck. Regulations stipulated that all aspirants to commissioned rank as lieutenant be twenty years of age, and have served at least six years at sea, including two years in the Navy rated either as midshipman or master's mate. During the late seventeenth century, the rating of midshipman comprised both experienced seamen known as senior petty officers as well as 'young gentlemen' seeking a commission. During the following century, the number of midshipmen who were young gentlemen, or junior officers serving their qualifying time before taking the oral examination for lieutenant, increased until they formed the great majority. Master's mates were assistants to the senior warrant officer responsible for a ship's navigation. Many mates sought to become masters themselves, but it was also common for candidates for a commission to serve some time as master's mate to improve their skills at sailing and navigation. No one could be rated midshipman or master's mate who had not served at sea for three years. An early start upon a naval career therefore was essential to complete the minimum qualifying periods for promotion to lieutenant.[112]

It is perhaps surprising for the modern observer to learn that the Admiralty exercised little formal control over the recruitment and training of its future officers. Most entered the Navy as protégés of a ship's captain, who possessed the power of appointing all but commissioned and warrant officers to the ship he commanded. Typically, they were the sons of relatives, fellow officers, or other connections whom he had agreed to launch upon a naval career. Patronage assisted the advancement of a naval career at all levels of its hierarchy, and it often facilitated the initial progression of well-connected prospective officers. Their names would be entered as ratings into the books of ships commanded by fathers, relatives or family friends several years before they eventually entered, often when they were still at school, accelerating their appointment to midshipman or master's mate when they finally joined. One of the most notorious examples of this practice involved Admiral Thomas Cochrane, Earl Dundonald (1775–1860), who was borne on the books of several of his uncle's ships until he went to sea at the late age of seventeen.[113] The most common method of entry for young gentlemen probably was as 'captain's servant'. Each captain could appoint four for every 100 men aboard his ship. Most were not servants, however, but the captain's protégés. Often a rating as able or ordinary seaman followed before these aspiring officers eventually completed their minimum service as midshipman or master's mate. In 1794, the Admiralty reformed this system by creating a new rating of 'Boy First Class or Volunteer' for the embryonic officer, who had to be at least eleven years of age. Later the minimum age was increased to thirteen for those whose fathers were not officers. Midshipmen and volunteers first class shared the officers' right to walk the quarterdeck.

---

[112] N. A. M. Rodger, *The Wooden World, An Anatomy of the Georgian Navy* (London: Collins, 1986), pp. 252–66; M. Lewis, *A Social History of the Navy 1793–1815* (London: Allen and Unwin, 1961), pp. 141–77.

[113] T. Cochrane, *The Autobiography of a Seaman*, vol. 1 (London: Richard Bentley, 1860), p. 46.

Regardless of how his career began, the typical sea officer first went to sea in boyhood or early adolescence. Most entered between the ages of eleven and thirteen, and some were below the age of ten. Initially, these 'youngsters' were customarily taken under the wing of the gunner, a senior warrant officer. Later they were quartered in the midshipmen's berth, on the orlop deck of a ship of the line, or on the lower deck of a frigate, where they messed, studied, and relaxed. (See Figure 20). They slept in hammocks slung across the middle of the deck. Since the pay of captain's servants was taken by that officer, and ratings' pay was modest, parents and guardians usually provided an allowance. Average sums over the long eighteenth century ranged from £20 to between £30–60 by its end, depending upon the sponsors' means.[114] Midshipmen ate the same victuals as the men, which could be augmented out of their own pockets. In addition, they provided their own uniform, bedding, books, and navigational instruments, which entailed some expense for their families.

The initial experience of the ruggedness of a life at sea could be a profound shock, above all for boys from affluent backgrounds. The ages and levels of maturity among the occupants of the midshipmen's berth varied considerably. Most midshipmen were between their mid-teens and early twenties. They often lived alongside some men who were ten or twenty years older: disappointed, sometimes disgruntled aspirants who had failed to achieve a lieutenant's commission. Former officers and observers frequently commented upon the exuberant, chaotic atmosphere of the midshipmen's berth. Pranks and bullying were common, especially against newcomers, and the younger or more unpopular inhabitants. Those who violated its code of conduct would be beaten by the rest. Naval surgeons constantly warned against widespread intemperance, to which its prospective officers were introduced at an early age. Eleven-year-old B. F. Coleridge wrote, 'Wine is no luxury to me, for I have two glasses at dinner every day and two at supper, which is my half allowance, I not liking grog'.[115] Disobedient and unruly midshipmen were punished in a number of ways, often by being sent to sit at the head of the mainmast for several hours. Corporeal punishment was also applied. 'Kissing the gunner's daughter' meant being bent over the barrel of a gun, and flogged by the gunner or one of his mates.[116]

There was no official system of education or training for officers. A Royal Naval Academy had been established at Portsmouth during the early 1730s, offering forty places at £70 to £80 per annum for the sons of the aristocracy and gentlemen aged between thirteen and sixteen. In 1773 fifteen free places were made available to the sons of officers. The curriculum included seamanship, navigation, gunnery, mathematics and physics. The school was poorly administered, however, and rarely full. It was unpopular with serving officers, who doubted the practical utility of a shore-based education. Only a small minority of officers ever passed through the academy in the eighteenth century, which was eventually restructured and renamed the Royal Naval College in 1806.[117]

The quantity and quality of education and professional training a boy or midshipman received depended very heavily upon the initiative of his captain. Admiralty regulations

---

[114] N. A. M. Rodger, *The Command of the Ocean: A Naval History of Britain 1649–1815* (London: Allen Lane, 2004), pp. 380–94.

[115] Lord Coleridge, *The Story of a Devonshire House* (London: T. Fisher Unwin, 1905), p. 93.

[116] B. Lavery, *Nelson's Navy: The Ships, Men and Organisation* (London: Conway Maritime, 1989), pp. 88–93.

[117] J. H. Thomas, 'Portsmouth Naval Academy: An Educational Experiment Examined', *Portsmouth Archives Review*, 3:1 (1978), 11–39; F. B. Sullivan 'The Royal Academy at Portsmouth, 1729–1806', *Mariner's Mirror*, 63:4 (1977), 311–26; H. W. Dickinson, 'The Portsmouth Naval Academy, 1733–1806', *Mariner's Mirror*, 89:1 (2003), 17–30.

from 1702 had included provision for ships to carry a schoolmaster, an inferior warrant officer, who received a midshipman's pay, and a £20 allowance if he returned a certificate from the captain confirming the favourable completion of his duties. There was no official syllabus, and instruction varied over time, although teaching the young gentlemen mathematics and navigation remained the schoolmaster's primary responsibility. The edition of the Navy regulations issued in 1731 also required tuition in basic literacy, which could be extended to the ship's other youth if ordered by the captain. After 1806, instruction for the young gentlemen was restricted to mathematics and navigation, and reading and writing for the others was abandoned, though they might learn navigation if the captain wished. Interestingly, schoolmasters were now directed to supervise the morals of their pupils, and report any behaviour which was unbecoming an officer and gentleman. There was never an obligation for a captain to take on a schoolmaster, however. The modest pay, poor living conditions (the schoolmaster lived among his pupils), and lack of any formal career structure or prospects, discouraged volunteers, and offered little incentive for those who had served from continuing. Consequently, there was a shortage of schoolmasters. In 1812, the inducement of increased pay was offered to chaplains who wished to double as schoolmasters, provided they passed the navigational qualifying examination. Some captains who took their pastoral duties to heart, such as Sir Edward Codrington (1770–1851), engaged a proficient mathematician as schoolmaster by offering an attractive salary, which was augmented by contributions from parents or occasionally from their own funds.[118] Navigation, especially by lunar calculation, demanded advanced mathematics. Given the young age of boys' entry, and the uneven opportunities to master these subjects aboard ship, they frequently interrupted their sea-going apprenticeships to attend specialist mathematical schools ashore for one or two years. This essential instruction was permitted without loss of a young gentleman's time afloat, by allowing him to be placed on the books of a non-seagoing ship.[119]

Conscientious captains ensured that their young gentlemen received a thorough practical course in seamanship and the fighting of their ships. Midshipmen on HMS *Amazon* during 1802 went through a vigorous six-day training programme, which included working with the rigging, handling sails, and exercises with small arms and the ship's guns.[120] Midshipmen were required to keep navigational logs recording their ship's positions, which might be inspected daily by conscientious captains such as William Cumby of the *Hyperion*.[121] Their formal duties varied according to age, experience, aptitude, and the type of ship they served upon. Senior midshipmen might be entrusted with a ship's watch, command of a boat in a cutting out operation, or the navigation of a prize into port. Service in the Navy's frigates provided excellent opportunities for ambitious officers to perfect their seamanship and fighting skills. These cruisers operated independently against enemy commerce and experienced frequent action. Although this system of practical professional training produced skilled and courageous seamen, the restricted general education and experience of some officers who exercised high command could at times limit their ability to meet their extensive strategic, political, diplomatic and administrative responsibilities. The problem was recognised by senior officers of intellect, education and culture, who advised their charges to broaden their horizons by the study of history, geography and literature.

[118] F. B. Sullivan, 'The Naval Schoolmaster during the Eighteenth Century and the Early Nineteenth Century', *Mariner's Mirror*, 62:4 (1976), 311–26.
[119] Rodger, *Command of the Ocean*, p. 382.
[120] A. Phillimore, *The Life of Admiral of the Fleet Sir William Parker*, vol. 1 (London: Harrison, 1876), p. 205.
[121] H. G. Thursfield (ed.), *Five Naval Journals, 1789–1817* (London: Navy Records Society, 1951), p. 342.

Many officers possessed well-developed scientific interests. Young men from privileged backgrounds, who aspired to high command and could afford to do so, were encouraged to read more widely, travel abroad, and learn foreign languages when the opportunity occurred during peacetime.[122]

A career at sea appealed to both parents and the boys themselves, explaining why the Navy never struggled to recruit officers. This was an era in which the younger sons of the propertied had to fend for themselves. The limited choice of respectable careers open to them, mainly in the law, the church or politics, required expensive education or training, some intellectual aptitude and application, or the right patronage to make a start and progress. An army career was also costly, entailing the initial investment in a commission, and an independent income to sustain life in a fashionable regiment. In contrast, for parents with limited resources the Navy provided an honourable career for their younger sons, which began at an early age and with little expense. Most young officers could survive on their pay if necessary. This principle applied not only to the younger sons of peers, but also to the many sea officers descended from the landed gentry or those engaged in the professions, business, or commerce. Life at sea was harsh, and the risks of death by illness, accident and enemy action were severe. On the other hand, the lottery of war offered tantalising prospects of promotion, wealth and glory for those who distinguished themselves in battle or were fortunate in capturing enemy merchantmen and warships. Prize money was a major incentive. Although few officers could expect the great rewards flowing from the most spectacular coups, such as the capture of two Spanish treasure ships in 1799, in which each of the four frigate captains received £40,730, the lieutenants £5,091 and the midshipmen £791, fresh hope rose with every dawn.[123] Tidy sums amounting to several years' pay or more, however, were accumulated by many officers especially during prolonged conflicts. It appears that many boys themselves were eager to join the Navy, attracted by its excitement and romance, and early independence of parents, tutors or schoolmasters. Some were undoubtedly coerced and quit if they did not take to it, but contemporary memoirs and correspondence repeatedly record youthful yearning for a life at sea.[124]

The social background of the Navy's sea officers was very diverse and limited sources render precise estimates difficult. A small minority was descended from the aristocracy, while the great majority were the sons of gentlemen. Approximately a quarter of those who served during 1793–1815 were themselves the sons of sea officers, and as the 'children of the service' were most favoured for advancement.[125] The Navy as a career was set apart by the opportunities it offered for social mobility through promotion by merit, especially by distinguished conduct during war. All who served the required time as midshipman or master's mate could take the examination for lieutenant, and if granted a commission, attain the status of officer and gentleman, provided that he possessed or acquired the necessary education and manners. Thus it was possible for some boys from the lower middle-class, or even below, who had entered the Navy alongside the privileged 'young gentlemen', but with no immediate aspirations or prospects, to work their way up to petty or warrant officer, and then achieve commissioned rank. Warrant officers, officers and artificers of the naval dockyards, and shipbuilders were well-placed to launch their sons upon successful careers as sea officers by securing them places as captain's servants. Some sea officers had transferred from the merchant service in search of advancement, such as the explorer, Captain James Cook

---

[122] Rodger, *Command of the Ocean*, pp. 386–7.
[123] Brockliss *et al.*, *Nelson's Surgeon*, p. 75.
[124] Rodger, *Wooden World*, pp. 252–58.
[125] Lewis, *A Social History of the Navy*, pp. 23–59

(1728–79), the son of a day labourer. Identifying the significant minority who profited from the relative openness of the Navy to improve their social standing is hindered by the paucity and complexity of surviving sources, and probably also by an inclination among some officers from humble backgrounds to conceal their origins. One analysis of candidates who passed for lieutenant between 1745 and 1757 suggests that only nine per cent were not gentlemen by birth.[126] The prestige of a naval career among the aristocracy and the gentry increased during the final decades of the eighteenth century, stimulated by George III's sending of his younger son Prince William Henry (later William IV, r. 1830–37) to sea in 1779 at the age of thirteen. Levels of education and politeness among officers rose accordingly. The king's instructions that his younger son receive no preferential treatment emphasised the unique status of the Royal Navy within eighteenth-century society. The sons of kings, nobles and gentlemen who went to sea at such an early age shared the harsh living conditions of seamen and learned their vital skills before earning the right to command. It was this extensive practical experience and pride in its seamanship which gave the Navy's sea officers such an advantage over their rivals.[127]

· ·

While adolescent boys from well-to-do British families left home for public school or a professional pupillage in the nineteenth century, what happened to poorer children?[128] The large majority of boys and girls might now live at home and no longer be placed out in service or a live-in apprenticeship, but they still had to make some sort of contribution to the family economy. The common view is that in the midlands and the north children flooded into the new factories and mills springing up in response to the demands of the industrial revolution, where they were thrust into soulless and repetitive jobs that required minimum strength and skill. In consequence, there is a widespread belief that industrialisation brought nothing but loss to the majority of Britain's children. Thanks to the labour hunger of the factories and the mills, it is maintained, many children in the first part of the nineteenth century entered the world of paid, organised employment at a much younger age than had been the case in the early modern period. Whereas in earlier centuries children had become apprentices or servants in their early teens, factory children in the first part of the nineteenth century could be in full-time employment by the age of ten with inevitable ill effects on their moral, intellectual and physical development. The child worker, as Jane Humphries emphasises, 'stands pitifully at the heart of contemporary perceptions of the British industrial revolution'.[129] The late E. P. Thompson went even further claiming that the 'exploitation of little children, on this scale and with this intensity, was one of the most shameful events in our history'.[130]

That there was a great expansion in the intensive use of the labour of pre-adolescent children in the industrial era cannot be gainsaid. In modern understanding, young children were certainly more exploited in the nineteenth century than they had been previously. None the less, the picture needs refining. Certainly factory children 'faced more regular

---

[126] Rodger, *Wooden World*, p. 266.

[127] Rodger, *Command of the Ocean*, pp. 388–94.

[128] Teenage girls from good families were also sent off to boarding schools but not in the same numbers: see A. Fletcher, *Growing Up in England: The Experience of Childhood, 1600–1914* (New Haven: Yale University Press, 2008); C. De Bellaigue, *Educating Women: Schooling and Identity in England and France 1800–1867* (Oxford: Oxford University Press, 2007).

[129] J. Humphries, *Child Labour in the Industrial Revolution: Causes, Consequences, Cures*. Available at http://www.history.ox.ac.uk/ecohist/synopses/1a_economic_business/child_labour.htm (accessed 1 Jul. 2009).

[130] E. P. Thompson, *The Making of the English Working Class* (London: Victor Gollancz, 1963), p. 349.

employment through the year, longer hours and a more sustained level of effort than their peers'.[131] However, the majority of pre-adolescent labourers in the nineteenth century were not employed in urban sweatshops or mills, for mechanisation did not occur uniformly across the manufacturing sector and initially developed only in specific parts of the manufacturing process. Rather, most small children in manufacturing employment worked at, or from, home in occupations such as knitting, lace-making, or straw plaiting.[132] The children of lace makers, for instance, were taught to handle bobbins from the age of four while at a similar age children of straw plaiters might be sorting straws and earning a regular wage at six or seven.

In this regard, the nineteenth century only saw a reinforcement of a trend already developing a century before. Helping around the house or farm did not always provide enough work to keep young children in the countryside occupied and in the late seventeenth and early eighteenth centuries, merchants began to take advantage of this reservoir of cheap labour, gradually pulling young children into manufacturing.[133] This sort of work far exceeded in time and intensity the household chores previously done by children but because it was hidden, it caused little comment.[134] Looking back on his childhood in 1760s Lancashire, George Crompton described being set to work in the domestic manufacture of cotton as soon as he was able to walk.

> My mother used to bat the cotton wool on a wire riddle. It was then put into a deep brown mug with a strong ley of soap suds. My mother then tucked up my petticoats about my waist, and put me into the tub to tread upon the cotton at the bottom. When a second riddleful was batted down I was lifted out and it was placed in the mug and I again trod it down. This process was continued until the mug became so full that I could no longer safely stand in it, when a chair was placed beside it and I held on by the back.[135]

Yet if it should never be forgotten that much of children's exploitative labour in the era of industrialisation was found in the domestic arena, it is certainly true that the most well documented and the most attention grabbing was to be found in the large towns and factories and mills of the north and midlands. As John Somerville writes in his account of the Industrial Revolution's impact on children, 'It was soon apparent that industrial technology can use unskilled labor, and lots of it. So, naturally, the mill owners thought of using children. Children could start tending the new machines immediately, without the apprenticeship training of the old crafts. As cheap as they were, they became more attractive laborers than their parents in the eyes of employers'.[136] Industrialisation, in undermining the corporative traditions of work encouraged the use of cheap child labour, which was unregulated by either parents or masters.[137] Steam power and machinery also removed the need for physical strength so that children could work the machinery as well as adult males

---

[131] Heywood, *A History of Childhood*, p. 129.

[132] Heywood, *A History of Childhood*, p. 123; H. Medick, 'The Proto-Industrial Family Economy: The Structural Function of Household and Family during the Transition from Peasant Society to Industrial Capitalism', *Social History*, 1:3 (1976), 291–315; Rahikainen, *Centuries of Child Labour*, pp. 70–78.

[133] Heywood, *A History of Childhood*, pp. 129–31.

[134] Medick, 'The Proto-Industrial Family Economy'; I. Pinchbeck, *Women Workers and the Industrial Revolution* (London: Routledge and Sons, 1930), p. 232.

[135] A. Davin, 'What is a Child?', in A. Fletcher and S. Hussey (eds), *Childhood in Question: Children, Parents and the State* (Manchester: Manchester University Press, 1999), p. 23.

[136] J. Somerville, *The Rise and Fall of Childhood* (Beverly Hills, Calif.: Sage Publications, 1982), p. 160.

[137] For a breakdown of the largest employers of children by manufacturing sector across Europe see Rahikainen, *Centuries of Child Labour*, p. 133. In England, Finland, France, Italy, Russia and Spain, the textile mills employed the most children, while the tobacco sector was the largest employer in Denmark. In Sweden and Norway, most children were employed in sawmills.

but could be employed at a much cheaper wage. Indeed the earliest spinning machinery of the late eighteenth century was specifically designed to be operated by children, although this had the effect of replacing women with children, not men. In 1799 40 per cent of Robert Owen's workforce at his mill in New Lanark, Scotland were under thirteen,[138] and in 1835, six per cent of all labourers in the textile factories were aged between eight and twelve, ten per cent between twelve and thirteen and 30 per cent between thirteen and eighteen.[139]

There are heart-rending accounts of child exploitation from those factories, used by campaigners eager to end the practice, which show the iniquity and moral degeneracy of child labour. One former child worker gave evidence to a parliamentary investigation in 1832 about his life in a factory where, aged eight, he had worked from six in the morning to eight at night. He told them that he was 'very much fatigued at night, when I left my work; so much so that I sometimes should have slept as I walked if I had not stumbled and started awake again; and so sick often that I could not eat, and what I did eat I vomited'.[140] According to E. P. Thompson, no matter how arduous work at home had been, that undertaken in the factories was of a demonstrably different and worse order, both in terms of the monotony of the tasks and the fact that children at home rarely had to work for set hours. Although parents in the eighteenth century may have been strict and hard taskmasters, children usually did their jobs 'interspersed with running messages, blackberrying, fuel gathering or play'.[141]

Work in the mills and factories tended to split along gender lines with girls carrying out more dexterous tasks and boys more physical ones. Although more boys than girls worked in the mines, in some areas of the country, girls also went underground. In 1842, an eight-year-old, called Sarah Gooder worked in a mine as a trapper – someone who controls the air vents. She told the Mine Commission of 1842 that:

> It does not tire me, but I have to trap without a light and I'm scared. I go at four and sometimes half past three in the morning and come out at five and half past [in the afternoon]. I never go to sleep. Sometimes I sing when I've light but not in the dark… I don't like being in the pit. I am very sleepy when I go sometimes in the morning… I would like to be at school far better.[142]

Such stories form the backbone of perceptions of child labour in the industrial revolution in Britain and elsewhere. Yet despite the badness of conditions in the factories, they were not necessarily typical of the experience of all child labourers, and the extent and nature of child exploitation has become a source of much debate. Hugh Cunningham has identified three distinct historiographies of child labour.[143] Firstly, those represented by E. P. Thompson and others, which follow the line of the reformers of the day, and point to the horror and brutality of children's lives in the mines or the mills. They tend to blame the owners or overseers or the rapacious demands of the capitalist system. In contrast, others have identified the continuities between factory work and home working, arguing that both can be exploitative and that parents can be as abusive as factory owners. They claim, furthermore, that only extreme accounts of child exploitation are ever given, which

[138] Heywood, *A History of Childhood*, p. 131.
[139] A. Stella, 'Introduction: A History of Exploited Children in Europe', in B. Sclemmer and P. Dresner (eds), *The Exploited Child* (London: Zed Books, 2000).
[140] Somerville, *The Rise and Fall of Childhood*, p. 162.
[141] Thompson, *The Making of the English Working Class*, p. 334
[142] Cunningham, *Invention of Childhood*, p. 159.
[143] H. Cunningham, 'Children's Changing Lives from 1800–2000', in J. Maybin and M. Woodhead (eds), *Childhoods in Context* (Chichester: Wiley, 2003), pp. 88–91. See also Rahikainen, *Centuries of Child Labour*, pp. 8–10.

are treated as if they were typical. Such stories often start with children 'as young as seven or eight' working in the factories, but this was relatively unusual. Most children did not enter textile making until they were between ten and twelve and, in iron and steel making until they were in their late teens. In the majority of cases, children worked as helpers and assistants to adults rather than replacing them or taking over their responsibilities.[144] There have also been doubts raised about the harshness of the conditions in the factories so that while they were very hard by modern standards, children were not necessarily ill-treated there and few were permanently harmed.[145]

A third group have taken a very different approach to child labour in this period, looking at it not in terms of whether or not it harmed children but in terms of family strategy. Clark Nardinelli analyses child labour in terms of the overall well-being of the family, not individuals.[146] Parents, he argues, make rational choices so that in the face of overwhelming poverty, a family may decide to send their children out to work, no matter how bad the conditions of labour. As economic conditions improve and the longer-term outcomes for children become better, it makes more sense to educate children in the hope of future success and better job prospects, thereby delaying the initial return. In term of child labour in the past, he argues, these decisions were inevitably affected not just by household economics but also by legislation, educational provision and new technologies. Nevertheless, he concludes that the most important factor was parental decision-making. Cunningham summarises this argument thus. 'And since the decision was a rational one - and since in this perspective people act rationally to maximise well-being - then it was not surprising that thousands or millions of families made the same decision about child labour at a similar stage of economic development'.[147]

Placing pauper children in factories and mills in the late eighteenth and the first part of the nineteenth centuries can be seen as an equally rational decision. Concern over idleness and drains on the parish trumped any fears there might have been about their exploitation. The mills offered children employment, an offer many parishes were only too happy to take up. When factories in the north and the midlands needed labour, London parishes began to send cartloads of children to them. An account of this was published in 1832, under the self-explanatory title, *A Memoir of Robert Blincoe, an Orphan Boy, sent from the Workhouse of St. Pancras, London, at Seven Years of Age, to Endure the Horrors of a Cotton-Mill, Through his Infancy and Youth, with a Minute Detail of his Sufferings, Being the First Memoir of this Kind Published.*[148] His story tells of being shipped from London to Nottingham in 1799, along with 80 others, and being set to work in a mill for fourteen hours a day where he was endured great hardships and abuse from the overseers.[149]

For many contemporary observers the use of child labour was defended as both necessary to ensure the smooth running of the economy and as a way of protecting jobs

---

[144] Heywood, *A History of Childhood*, p. 131.

[145] N. Smelser, *Social Change in the Industrial Revolution: An Application of Theory to the Lancashire Cotton Industry, 1770–1840* (London: Routledge and Paul, 1959).

[146] C. Nardinelli, *Child Labor in the Industrial Revolution* (Bloomington: Indiana University Press, 1990).

[147] H. Cunningham, 'The Decline of Child Labour: Labour Markets and Family Economies in Europe and North America since 1830', *Economic History Review*, 53:3 (2000), 409–28, at p. 414.

[148] Cunningham, *The Invention of Childhood*, p. 156. Workhouse children ceased to be apprenticed out from 1838. Thereafter the large majority stayed in the workhouse until they were sixteen – between 1834 and 1908 one out of three institutionalised paupers were under this age. Some were sent abroad to farms in the colonies: see above, Ch. 2, fn. 125.

[149] Throughout Europe, including Russia, poor children and orphans were regularly sent into the factories, rather than into foster homes, in order that they should work. Such workhouses were sometimes attached to orphanages. Children were on fixed contracts, could not leave before the age of 21 and were forcibly brought back if they ran away. Rahikainen, *Centuries of Child Labour*, pp. 24–32.

for both children and adults. Supporters of child labour argued that 'freedom of contract' was desirable in all forms of labour relations and campaigned against proposed reductions in the working hours of children, unless there was a corresponding reduction in wages, claiming it would damage Britain's competitiveness while also leading to unemployment.[150] Factory and mill owners themselves argued that the mechanisation of many of the tasks required less input and energy from the children who only had to work intermittently. What employers did not say, however, was that children were expected to concentrate for long periods of time and to work very long hours, even if their work did not involve great physical exertion (a rather dubious proposition anyway – as Colin Heywood notes, a piercer in a cotton mill in the 1830s was expected to work a thirteen-and-a-half hour day and mend up to 500 threads).[151]

That employers had to defend the use of child labour in the factories reflects the fact that its use from the beginning was contested. As we have seen, the eighteenth century was an era in which children and childhood were re-imagined and methods of child-rearing and training re-thought, and when child welfare was becoming a national as well as a parish issue. Childhood became a special moment that needed protecting and nurturing.[152] In consequence, the eighteenth century was also, the 'historical moment when child labour was no longer taken for granted, even if only by a limited number of people'.[153] By the end of the century, as the idea of the specialness of childhood gained greater currency within the elite, certain children became particularly visible as an affront to such a vision and concerns over the well-being of working children and their possible abuse began to attract political attention.[154]

The first Act of Parliament to protect chimney sweeps, the Act for the Better Regulation of Chimney Sweepers and their Apprentices of 1788, has already been mentioned.[155] Although the actual numbers of chimney sweeps was relatively small – in 1801 it was estimated that there were 500 apprentice sweeps working in London for 200 masters – they had great symbolic potential: their blackness suggesting stain, sin or slavery in opposition to a norm of purity and angelic innocence. Chimney boys were, in Ludmilla Jordanova's words,

> the quintessence of perverted childhood, a deviation from a norm established by nature. Attempts to reform their conditions permitted people to expound a philosophy of childhood in general, but without calling into question the social system which made child labour not only possible but also necessary for both those social groups who laboured and those for whom they laboured.[156]

[150] For a summary of these arguments see R. M. Hartwell, 'Children as Slaves', in R. M. Hartwell, *The Industrial Revolution and Economic Growth* (London: Methuen, 1971), pp. 390–408.
[151] Heywood, *A History of Childhood*, p. 132.
[152] See above Ch. 3, pp. 128–32. The most cited account of this new view of childhood remains J. H. Plumb 'The New World of Children in Eighteenth-Century England', *Past and Present*, 67:1 (1975), 64–93. Plumb's view has been heavily critiqued however on the grounds that he ignores the children of the poor and does not discuss child labour or apprenticeships: see L. Jordanova, 'New Worlds for Children in the Eighteenth Century: Problems of Historical Interpretation', *History of the Human Sciences*, 3:1 (1990), 69–83.
[153] Jordanova, 'Children in History', p. 20.
[154] In other countries, this moment may have come earlier. In Sweden, for instance, laws concerning the employment of children had been passed from 1686, when the herding of cattle by boys was banned. Admittedly, this law was introduced to counteract bestiality rather than child labour but none the less, the idea that certain jobs such as herding were men's work, rather than boys, was reinforced through this legislation. In 1736, six peasants were prosecuted for risking the lives of their sons by sending them off to herd. Rahikainen, *Centuries of Child Labour*, p. 61.
[155] See above, p. 176. For a fuller discussion, see G. L. Phillips, 'The Abolition of Climbing Boys', *American Journal of Economics and Sociology*, 9:4 (1950), 445–62.
[156] L. Jordanova, 'Conceptualizing Childhood in the Eighteenth Century: The Problem of Child Labour',

Nevertheless, without adequate enforcement, legislation had a limited effect on the boys' lives. Despite several Acts of Parliament introduced to protect them, in 1816 the Society for Superseding the Necessity of Climbing Boys could still report the following, particularly unpleasant, case.

> In the improvements made some years since by the Bank of England in Lothbury, a chimney belonging to a Mr Mildrum, a baker, was taken down; but before he began to bake, in order to see that the rest of the flue was clear, a boy was sent up; and after remaining some time, and not answering to the call of his master, another boy was ordered to descend from the top of the flue, and to meet him half way. But this being impracticable, they opened the brickwork in the lower part of the flue, and found the first mentioned boy dead. In the meantime, the boy in the upper part of the flue called out for relief, saying he was completely jammed in the rubbish, and was unable to extricate himself. Upon this a bricklayer was employed with the utmost expediency, but he succeeded only in obtaining a lifeless body. The bodies were sent to St Margaret's Church, Lothbury, and a Coroner's Inquest which sat upon them returned the verdict, Accidental Death.[157]

The elimination of child chimney sweeps took several more Acts of Parliament, including ones in 1834 and 1840. The last amendments were made in 1864, only a year after the publication of Charles Kingsley's *The Water Babies*.

In such legislation it is possible to see the beginning of attempts to improve working children's lives, although it is interesting to note that no reformers called for the abolition of chimney sweeping by boys, or the end of child labour generally, merely the alleviation of some of its worst effects.[158] There is a similar lack of zeal in the 1802 Health and Morals of Apprentices Act which applied to children in the textile mills; it limited their work to twelve hours a day, provided some education and set minimum standards of accommodation. It did not, however, call for the prohibition of pauper apprenticeships or child labour. Later Acts were more wide ranging and sought to establish much tighter limits on the categories of children allowed to work. The 1819 Cotton Mills and Factories Act forbade children under nine to work in cotton mills and limited children's working hours, while a second Act of 1825 limited the labour of children under sixteen to twelve hours and introduced meal breaks. The 1833 Mills and Factories Act covered all textile mills except silk and lace. It reduced the working-day of children younger than thirteen to eight hours and required that children under this age attended school for at least two hours a day on six days a week, and be given eight half-day holidays each year including all day off on Christmas Day and Good Friday. The Act also required its provisions to be executed, empowering inspectors to enter factories whenever they wished to in order to see how children were being looked after. The 1842 Mines and Collieries Act banned women and children under ten working in mines and provided for the appointment of inspectors of mines.

In the years following this Act several other pieces of legislation put forward offered further protections for children employed in industry. The 1847 Hours of Labour of Young Persons and Females in Factories Act (The Ten Hours Act) again covered the textile mills. It reduced the numbers of hours a week children between thirteen and eighteen and women were allowed to work – no more than ten hours a day and 58 hours in any one week (raised to 60 in 1850). The 1867 Factory Acts Extension Act prohibited children and women from

---

British Journal for Eighteenth-Century Studies, 10:2 (1987), 187–200, esp. pp. 194–95.

[157] Somerville, *The Rise and Fall of Childhood*, pp. 160–61.

[158] Jordanova, 'Conceptualizing Childhood', p. 197, notes the importance of social class in this new world for children; 'concepts associated with the child, despite their abstract nature, were not in fact applied to all children…the vast majority of eighteenth-century writings on children treated the middle class as a norm, the 'natural' group against which others could be measured'.

working on Sundays and extended the 1847 Act to all factories employing more than 50 people. In the same year the Workshop Regulation Act forbade children under eight from working in any handicraft industry while the Agricultural Gangs Act disallowed mixed sex gangs of workers and prohibited the employment of all children under the age of eight.[159]

Campaigners against child labour, such as Robert Owen (1771–1858), Lord Shaftesbury (1801–85), Michael Sadler (1780–1835) and Richard Oastler (1789–1861), focused on both the moral and physical vulnerabilities of children. Child labour was, in their terms, morally offensive, un-Christian and cruel to children. It separated children from families and exposed them to immorality.[160] It also damaged children physically, stunted their growth and imposed bodily hardships on them. The stories of these famous reformers are well known. Less acknowledged is the role that children themselves played. Hugh Cunningham calls the early 1830s 'a rare moment in the history of childhood when children can be seen to be aware of their place in history and engaged in political activity'.[161] In 1832 thousands walked from Leeds to York to agitate for the introduction of the Ten Hours Act, carrying banners asking 'Father, is it time?' Later that year hundreds of factory children marched to Manchester to meet their advocates and heroes, Michael Sadler and Richard Oastler.[162]

As other countries in Europe began to industrialise in their differing ways across the nineteenth century, there too young children began to play a novel and increasing role in the paid workforce as parents seized the opportunity to enlarge the family income.[163] And as in Britain humanitarian opponents of the development quickly voiced their objections and lobbied the state to intervene. By 1900 there were few European states that had not passed laws outlawing or controlling the use of the labour of pre-adolescent children. From 1841 France banned children younger than eight from working in factories or workshops using machinery and 'continuous fire', and limited the working hours of the under twelves in such places to eight. This was followed in 1874 with a blanket law that banned children under sixteen from working in most areas of manufacturing, while allowing children ten and over to work only in certain circumstances. More distant and less developed Sweden attempted to stop anyone under twelve working in a manufacturing industry as early as 1846, although a back-up ordinance had to be promulgated in 1881. Denmark and Norway imposed similar limitations in 1853 and 1892.[164]

---

[159] For full details of these Acts, see Cunningham, *The Children of the Poor*, ch. 7.

[160] Hartwell, 'Children as Slaves', pp. 398–99.

[161] Cunningham, *The Invention of Childhood*, p. 158.

[162] *Ibid.*, p. 158.

[163] It is very difficult to know the number of pre-teenage children employed in industry on the European continent in the nineteenth century. Individual examples abound, such as the eight- and eleven-year-old brothers Guillaumou from Carcassonne who were placed in a local wool spinning factory by their shoemaker father, described in T. Guillaumou, *Les Confessions d'un compagnon* (Paris, 1864), p. 22. But historians provide figures for the under fifteens or sixteens, not the under twelves. Thus 22.4 per cent of the workforce in the Belgian coal and coke industry was under fifteen in 1846, while in Alsace in the 1820s more than a third of the mill workers were under sixteen. According to the 1851 British census, only 3.5 per cent of children aged between five and nine were gainfully employed but 30 per cent from ten to fourteen: see E. Schrumpf, 'Child Labor in the West', in P. Fass (ed.), *Encyclopedia of Children and Childhood. In History and Society* (3 vols; Indianapolis: Macmillan USA, 2004), i, pp. 159–72; C. Heywood, 'European Industrialisation', in P. Fass, *Encyclopedia*, i, pp. 330–35; Cunningham, 'The Decline of Child Labour', p. 411; Rahikainen, *Centuries of Child Labour*, ch. 4; Heywood, *Childhood in Nineteenth-Century France*, p. 102. For a general overview of the French case, in addition to Heywood, *Childhood in Nineteenth-Century France*, chs 4–5, see B. Schlemmer, *L'Enfant exploité: oppression, mise en travail, prolétarisation* (Paris: Karthala/ORSTOM, 1996); and P. Pierrard, *Enfants et jeunes ouvriers en France XIXe–XXe siècles* (Paris: Editions ouvrières, 1987).

[164] Heywood, *Childhood in Nineteenth-Century France* chs 8–11, *passim*; L. S. Weissbach, *Child Labour Reform in Nineteenth-Century France. Assessing the Future Harvest* (London: Louisiana State University Press, 1989); B. Sandin, '"In the Large Factory Towns": Child Labour Legislation, Child Labour, and School Compulsion',

For many European children, however, the numerous child labour acts before the last quarter of the nineteenth century had little impact on their lives and they continued to work in often harsh conditions. Not only were the acts difficult to enforce – the early acts were usually backed up with an inadequate inspectorate – but many only dealt with factory children. As in Britain, they did not usually apply to pre-adolescent children working in the wider manufacturing sector, a group who formed an even larger proportion on the continent.[165] Moreover, throughout Europe until the last decades of the nineteenth century little attention was paid to children working in agriculture. (See Figure 21). Looking back in 1888, J. E. Thorold Rogers (1823–90) painted a dismal picture of the conditions under which young English farmhands had laboured a generation before: 'The work of the child in the fields, ill-fed, poorly educated, and exposed to the worst weather in the worst time of the year was to the full as physically injurious as premature labour in the heated atmosphere of the factory'.[166] It is the under-regulated and often harsh working conditions endured by children labouring outside the factory that the following contribution brings to life through the boyhood reminiscences of a Northamptonshire artisan.

The Rural Child Worker

Jane Humphries

William Arnold was born in Northamptonshire in a hamlet called Everdon about twelve miles southwest of Northampton on the next to last day of 1860. We know about his experiences because he told his story to a friend who jotted it down and had it privately printed in 1915, a copy surviving in Northamptonshire Record Office.[167] By any standards William's early life was one of poverty and exploitation. Few boys in the developing world today start work at such a young age, work such long hours in hazardous conditions and for such meagre rewards. Why did such levels of child exploitation occur in industrialising Britain?

Studying child labour through working-class memoirs has an important advantage. We can both view the children at work and follow them home, meet their families and survey their circumstances: essential if we are to probe the causes of child labour in terms of poverty, parental selfishness, low productivity, demographic pressures, social norms and technological changes.[168] William's father, Matthew, was 'a poor working man, a typical old-fashioned English village shoemaker … employed by [a middle-man] and did the work at home'.[169] Arnold senior made boots 'in the old way' sewing the

---

and E. Schrumpf, 'From Full-Time to Part-Time: Working Children in Norway from the Nineteenth to the Twentieth Century', both in N. de Coninck-Smith, B. Sandin and E. Schrumpf, *Industrious Childhood: Work and Childhood in the Nordic Countries 1850–1990* (Odense: Odense University Press, 1997). For a summary of European legislation, see Rahikainen, *Centuries of Child Labour*, pp. 150–54.

[165] See earlier comment about the continual buoyancy of artisanal industry in France, p. 178.

[166] Quoted in Hartwell, 'Children as Slaves', p. 396. On child agricultural workers in France, see Heywood, *Childhood in Nineteenth-Century France*, ch. 2.

[167] W. Arnold, *Recollections of William Arnold*, with a preface by H. Pickett and an introductory note by J. Saxton (Northampton: privately printed, 1915).

[168] Arnold, *Recollections*, p. 2.

[169] For an in-depth study of child labour based on working-class autobiography, see Humphries, *Childhood*.

soles to the uppers with waxed thread, his employer supplying him with the made-up uppers and the leather for the soles. By working hard he could make six pairs in a week whereas a very quick workman might manage seven. But few workmen ever made seven pairs of boots in a week because there was not enough demand. Matthew Arnold probably never in his life earned more than sixteen shillings in any one week. The exception was in harvest time when boots were laid aside and Arnold senior went reaping. Mrs. Arnold, as a shoemaker's wife, would have been counted as economically active by the 1861 census takers, who recorded the wives of men in selected occupations as active by dint of their husbands' work. But she would have been removed from counts of the active in later censuses when this procedure was reversed and would have been left out, even in retrospect, in the recalculation of activity rates made by the social researcher, Charles Booth (1840–1916), to ensure consistency with the 1881 definitions.[170] Nor would the April census have caught her reaping side-by-side with her husband. 'She was a woman of quite exceptional strength often spoken of as the strongest in the village... and with the sickle in her hand she could reap as well, and do as much, or more, than most men'.[171] In August and September by expending huge effort husband and wife could earn sufficient to pay off their debts and acquire some extra money to spend on clothing.

Yet despite his parents' industriousness, William's childhood was 'almost wholly a story of poverty and struggle...' Arnold depicted the ever-present proximity of want and destitution through an image that recurs in similar memoirs of the period: the metaphor of the wolf waiting just beyond the light to devour and destroy. 'Even the youthful escapades, the childish sports, and the buoyancy of health were shadowed by grim spectres, or haunted by the thought of the wolf that was always at the door'.[172] Extreme poverty was childishly experienced then, as now, in terms of hunger. William never had enough to eat. He was often reduced to picking up and eating the pieces of swede that had been rejected by grazing sheep. The collision between need and the law and the victory of the former produced the memorable moments of childhood when William and his siblings were woken in the middle of the night to feast on partridge and potatoes while next day 'all fur and feather' had been carefully disposed of.[173] William not only recalled his father's poaching, but also unusually in the canon of Victorian working-class autobiography, confessed to more flagrant violations of ownership rights. Sometimes, William was sad to recall, his father unable any longer to see his children hungry for days at a time came home in the night with a bushel of meal or sack of turnips that he had 'found' in a neighbouring barn or adjacent field.

If the census counts miss Mrs. Arnold's economic contributions, family historians leaping from structure to affection would overlook the importance in William's life of his grandparents and the ties that bound the generations of this poor family together. As eldest grandson William was drafted aged six to stay with grandfather when his wife was away 'monthly nursing' and used to sleep in the same room with him in case he might need assistance in the night. But although these ties cannot challenge the nucleated residential character of the Arnold household its structure eventually became extended. Despite the terrible poverty of the family 'as though their own boys and girls were not enough to keep', and this was a very large family of eventually

---

[170] See J. McKay 'Married Women and Work in Nineteenth Century Lancashire: The Evidence of the 1851 and 1861 Census Reports', *Local Population Studies*, 61 (1998), 25–37.

[171] Arnold, *Recollections*, p. 3.

[172] *Ibid.*, p. 5 (for both quotations).

[173] *Ibid.*, p. 3 and p. 4.

fourteen children, the fatherless boy of William's aunt was taken in when 'a mere babe'. According to Mrs. Arnold, 'It was only one more mouth to feed'.[174]

From this caring but over-stretched household, William was sent to work when he was six years and two months old. He recognises how harsh this might seem to his younger audience: 'Fancy that, only just over six years of age'. His first job, like that of many boys in similar circumstances, was scaring crows. Though an agricultural pursuit and organised within small-scale capitalism, it was no chocolate box activity of bucolic refinement. Only the dinner William received on Sundays along with eighteen pence as wages alleviated long days of cold and hungry boredom. 'The dinner they gave me made the Sunday the greatest and happiest day of the week'. Nor was William's working intermittent. His assignments varied with the agricultural year but were dovetailed together into continuous employment. When the barley was up, he had to mind a flock of sheep. Here the fearsome loneliness almost proved too much 'and in my despair I cried most of the time, and in desperation would shout as loud as I could 'Mother! Mother! Mother!' But mother could not hear me; she was at that time working in the hay field two miles away'.[175] After the sheep it was reaping along with his mother and father and then after the harvest minding about 40 pigs on their feeding ground. The pigs made William look back on the sheep with affection and the constant effort of trying when not yet seven to keep these 40 ornery and aggressive pigs together he described as 'pitiful work for a child'. After the harvest William went to ploughing. Here the pleasure of a 'smart and workmanlike' smock frock with frills in the front were offset by the brutality of having to carry heavy harness one and a half miles over eight stiles, back and forth, to the blacksmith for repair: the worst experience in all those long and hungry years.[176]

Aged just over seven William went to work in the boot trade. There was no room for children in his father's work, dependent as it was on deep-craft skill, but at this time an entirely new way of making shoes was being introduced called 'riveting'. Years later when the adult William came to tell his story, riveting had been relegated to the manufacture of cheap shoes but initially it was seen as a way of making all shoes cheaper. Instead of the soles being stitched to the uppers they were nailed. The nails were in actuality little rivets and iron lasts were used to blunt ('clinch') the rivets when they came through. The new method of shoemaking involved two separate tasks. The first was to set the upper to the last and fix the sole in its proper place. This was skilled work and needed a good eye. But the driving in of the rivets with a flat iron rasp was easier and it was soon discovered that boys could do this task quite as well and as quickly as men, so it was usual for each riveter to have a boy known as 'the sprigging boy'. Division of labour here as in many other nineteenth-century trades proved cheaper not only because of the classic specialisation cited by Adam Smith but because some tasks could be simplified down until children could be substituted for adults. When several shoemakers in Everdon branched into 'riveting', William became a sprigging boy working alongside them and by helping to produce a new cheaper, if inferior, quality boot reduced yet further the market for his father's product.

The twelve shillings that William earned when not yet eleven seemed an extraordinary amount to his family and was 'a wonderful help' to his mother as at that time 'there were five or six little ones to be kept'. But such prosperity was not permanent. Boot and shoemaking was seasonal, and periodic under-employment afflicted all branches of the trade, blighting both the skilled craft production of William's father and the de-skilled riveting. During slack times William did a variety of casual jobs: helping an old woman

---

[174] *Ibid.*, p. 12.
[175] *Ibid.*, p. 14.
[176] *Ibid.*, p. 19.

to hawk goods from a donkey, and working as a bricklayer's labourer. At times of peak labour demand in agriculture he forsook shoemaking to work at haymaking or bring in the harvest. He also used periods of slow demand to learn other shoemaking skills both from his father and from an uncle in Northampton. In a trade recession in his teens he was 'more pinched than any time in my life', living back at home with lots of brothers and sisters all younger than himself. But there were also periods of boom. The Franco-German war meant lots of work making boots for the French army. With the recovery of the trade and his own hard won mobility between types of production William eventually rose to earn 27 shillings a week, celebrating his first weekly wages of a sovereign with a pork pie and a pint of beer. Nor was this jubilation only William's. 'It was a great day for mother' he reported for she felt that the family could now at last escape the terrible pinch of poverty it had suffered for so long.[177]

William Arnold belonged to the last generation before compulsory schooling. Because of his early working, he attended school only very briefly, according to the introduction of his *Recollections* for only a week or two at a time and only about three months altogether. Whether or not this left him unable to read and write, among the illiterate twenty per cent of his generation, remains unclear but certainly he acknowledged that without help writing his memoirs would have been impossible.

William does not cover up his own shortcomings or those of his fellow workers. One theme of the memoir is the propensity of shoemakers to excessive drinking. William himself seems to have started drinking at a very young age, the habit inculcated along with the skills. Shoemakers' habitual drunkenness influenced the rhythms of work. Among early-industrial workers, Monday was often given over to nursing the hangover that inevitably followed the excesses of the weekend, a holiday ironically dubbed St. Monday. As late as the 1870s and 80s, St. Monday (and sometimes St. Tuesday too) continued to be celebrated. As a result all too often the high wages that shoemakers earned in good times were soon dissipated leaving them dependent on advances from their employers and likely to fall into debt.

William's own youthful recklessness and drinking he describes as characteristic of shoemakers. Less typical perhaps was his rehabilitation. Aged about eighteen he began to reflect on his future and regret the money he had wasted. He joined the Good Templars but although he kept his pledge for two years, he did not save and as a result relapsed and began to drink again.[178] But in his mid-twenties William had another attempt at reform, prompted this time by meeting a young woman but underpinned by a growing disgust with his way of life. He persuaded his uncle who was a Rechabite[179] to propose him for membership, and this time he persisted with the new course. As so often in Victorian working-class autobiography, courtship and marriage sealed a newfound steadiness. It is interesting to note that William's parents opposed his marriage despite its steadying influence. Perhaps they could not but regret the resulting loss of a financial support that had been so important over the previous decade. Mr. and Mrs. Arnold senior were eventually reconciled to the match and appear to have played active roles as grandparents of William's own growing brood of children. William continued to apply himself with industry and acumen to his trade

---

[177] *Ibid.*, p. 37.

[178] The International Order of Good Templars was founded in the USA in 1851 as a working-class organisation imitating freemasonry and advocating temperance. It spread to Britain in the 1860s. See, http://en.wikipedia.org/wiki/International_Organisation_of_Good_Templars (accessed 14 Sept. 2009).

[179] The Independent Order of Rechabites was a Friendly Society founded in 1835 as part of the Temperance Movement and set up to promote total abstinence. It transformed into a financial institution which still exists and still promotes abstinence, see http://en.wikipedia.org/wiki/Independent_Order_of_Rechabites (accessed 14 Sept. 2009).

eventually becoming, according to his amanuensis, one of the best known among the shoe manufacturers of Northampton.

During his lifetime the treatment and position of children changed so dramatically that William Arnold's story had the power to shock readers, even those only one generation removed from his experience as Arnold himself recognised. It is therefore possible to draw out from his story certain themes concerning the causes and consequences of child labour in the industrial revolution of the nineteenth century. One of the important points about William's first job was that it was in a sector that we often overlook in discussing children's work: agriculture. Only gang work in agriculture, which involved large-scale employment, often away from home, and organised in a nexus of purely commercial relations, attracted contemporary opprobrium and historians have generally followed contemporary accounts. But neither the traditional nature of the work nor the small-scale of capitalist relations within which it took place protected the six-year-old from hazardous labour, long hours and psychological and physical distress.

Secondly, William graduated from the farm sector to move into shoemaking. But he did so in an era when the trade was being transformed. The deep-craft skills and artisan home working of his father's day was being competed into oblivion not by the technological changes that often mesmerise historians, there were no new machines here, but by organisational shifts and new divisions of labour that made space for the unskilled and physically weak. Children were slotted into the new labour processes. As trade after trade in early industrial Britain went in this direction, new jobs for children appeared. And these were again outside the mills and mines on which the Royal Commissions turned their gaze.

Thirdly, although William's entry into shoemaking was through a de-skilled subdivided labour process, to make his way he needed to acquire some training. As the traditional institution of apprenticeship faded way William and many of his peers struggled to acquire skills sometimes reimbursing their teachers with unremunerated labour time without the protection of formal indentures.

Fourthly, William's parents were not the avaricious and uncaring adults that were at the root of child labour according to some contemporary accounts. Between William and his mother, in particular, there seems to have been a deep and abiding affection. Both parents worked hard. But the wages of the father, even supplemented by Mrs. Arnold's earnings, were inadequate to support his large family. The demographic pressures of the time filtered down to leave William needing to help support his many brothers and sisters. But of course in needing to work William himself contributed to the competitive pressures that weighed so heavily on his father's sector of the shoe trade and drove down the older man's employment and earnings. The unregulated labour market ground its way towards equilibrium characterised by low adult wages and large amounts of child labour.

Finally, in prompting William to work and extracting effort from him physical force occasionally featured. However, more important in this story, as in so many from this time and class, were positive inducements. Both the boys and their families valued their earnings: the importance of food as an inducement to the undernourished should not be overlooked. But perhaps the most important spur to industry for William and many of his peers was the responsibility that boys felt for their families and especially the love and regard they felt for their mothers.

By the end of the nineteenth century, the employment of children before their mid-teens had dramatically declined in nearly all European countries.[180] Technological developments made the employment of young children less useful, while the legal restraints, now backed up by a proper inspectorate, had begun to bite. In addition a rise in real wages meant that family economics were not as straitened as they had been and there was less need to send children out as wage labourers.[181] Obviously young children could still be forced into work. The children known to us from the studies of London life by Henry Mayhew (1812–87), from fiction, or the pioneering sociology of Charles Booth, suggest that child labour had not gone away in Britain and that many thousands of children continued to work, and sometimes work very hard, for their living. Equally many child workers still showed up in the census. In 1871 girls under the age of fifteen accounted for ten per cent of all domestic servants, and these girls had no formal protection.[182] None the less, the dark days of the first part of the nineteenth century had passed. In Britain, even life in the countryside seems to have improved. Comparing William Arnold's life with the 1890s world, albeit heavily romanticised, captured by Flora Thompson (1876–1947) in *Lark Rise to Candleford*, seems to suggest a chasm between them of centuries, not three decades. In Thompson's rural Oxfordshire, families are poor but while cash is hard to come by, food is plentiful and no one goes hungry.[183]

As a result the focus of the reformers' attentions shifted. Although children were still being exploited there was increasing recognition that this was occurring in the home as well as the factory, and in Britain newly formed groups such as the NSPCC and campaigners such as Lord Shaftesbury turned their attention to the family as a source of danger to children. Other reformers concentrated on the most extreme forms of child labour and exploitation, such as prostitution, and campaigns began to rescue girls not only from physical exploitation but also from moral corruption. The campaigns of W. T. Stead (1849–1912) and Josephine Butler (1828–1906) against child prostitution and 'white slavery' were typical of the moralistic and highly sensationalist crusades against this form of exploitation.[184]

Nevertheless, if the principle had been established in the final decades of the nineteenth century that children should not work before their early to mid teens, it was recognised that they still needed to be kept occupied. Alongside the drive to push children out of factories and workshops came the push to place them in schools. It was in these decades that all over Europe attendance at elementary school became compulsory for all children between the ages of about five to six and twelve to thirteen. Britain established a compulsory system in 1870 which required children to attend school until they were thirteen. In France, where an attempt had been made to set up a national system of elementary education as early as 1833, no one from 1882 could enter work in theory unless they could produce evidence of completing the school course satisfactorily. In the same year, Sweden made it obligatory to receive some form of tuition until the age of fourteen. Everything possible was done to dragoon the young into school, so much so that many historians have agreed with

---

[180] It did not, however, disappear entirely. In Spain, for instance, the children of agricultural day labourers still started work as soon as they were able (between the ages of six to nine for boys and nine to eleven for girls) collecting dung, ploughing, picking fruit, tending livestock *etc.* In Finland and Sweden, the children of a farmer's tenants and underlings were still expected to provide cheap, or even free, labour, on their parents' employer's farm. Rahikainen, *Centuries of Child Labour*, pp. 104–06 and 111.

[181] The leading advocate for the change being attributed to rising family income is C. Nardinelli. For an evaluation of the different factors, see Cunningham, 'Decline of Child Labour', and *Invention of Childhood*. See also Davin, 'What is a Child?', and Humphries, *Childhood*.

[182] Rahikainen, *Centuries of Child Labour*, pp. 181–83.

[183] F. Thompson, *Lark Rise to Candleford: A Trilogy* (London: Oxford University Press, 1945).

[184] W. T. Stead, 'Maiden Tribute of Modern Babylon', *Pall Mall Gazette*, 6 Jul. 1885, p. 2; J. Butler, *Personal Reminiscences of a Great Crusade* (London: Horace Marshall, 1910), p. 221

James Walvin that 'it was schooling, and not industrial or agricultural legislation, which effectively ended the nation's commitment to widespread child labour'.[185] Certainly, there was a dramatic turn around in school attendance. In the late 1830s, 80 per cent of Prussian children between six and fourteen appear to have been at school. But this was not the case in most parts of Europe. Even in 1881, the minister behind the French legislation, which came into force the following year, believed that 600,000 of his country's six to thirteen-year-olds were not attending school, while those who did were leaving when they were eleven and twelve.[186]

The next contribution examines the relationship between the rise of compulsory schooling and the decline in child labour in England. In the century and a quarter following the Reformation, a large number of schools for teaching the three 'Rs' were founded by charitable bequest, and others were maintained by the local parish incumbent. Many among the lower orders must have availed themselves of the opportunity to learn to read and write because, on the eve of the Civil War, approximately a third of the population was literate. A more concerted attempt to educate the poor was undertaken in the first part of the eighteenth century with the foundation of a network of so-called charity schools across the country under the patronage of the Society for the Propagation of Christian Knowledge (founded in 1699). These schools, however, appear to have had limited success – partly because there remained great hostility to giving the lower orders any form of education – although by 1800 65 per cent of adult males could read and write. It was only the panic caused by the French Revolution that led to a new campaign to get the poor into school at the turn of the nineteenth century. As part of this drive, Sunday schools were established all over country which taught reading as well as Christian doctrine, and two rival educational societies – the Church (run by Anglicans) and the National (run by dissenters), were set up. But the rapidly expanding population and the growth of paid labour for young children made it hard to make any headway. In Lancashire rates of literacy actually went down during the Industrial Revolution and as late as 1840 only two-thirds of the adult male population in England, the same proportion as in 1800, was literate. Thereafter, however, the situation began to improve, even if, in 1861, only 60 per cent of children under thirteen attended school for more than a 100 days per year. There was now a widespread acceptance among the elite that the poor needed to be given a basic education so that they would be good Christians, loyal and honest workers and law-abiding citizens who would use the vote (once they received it) properly. It was only a question of how a system of elementary education could best be organised. The churches lacked the funding to establish and support a complete network of schools throughout the country on their own, so it was inevitable that the state would finally step in to supplement church provision with rate-funded government schools, bring the societies' schools under a government umbrella, and demand compulsory attendance.[187] As will become clear, in England the connection between the ending of child labour and the coming of compulsory education for children under thirteen in the wake of the 1870 Education Act was complex. The existence initially of popular, rival schools outside the

---

[185] J. Walvin, *A Child's World: A Social History of English Childhood, 1800–1914* (Harmondsworth: Penguin Books, 1982), p. 33.

[186] K. A. Schleures, 'Enlightenment, Reform, Reaction: The Schooling Revolution in Prussia', *Central European History*, 12:4 (1979), 315–42; Heywood, *Childhood in Nineteenth-Century France*, p. 287.

[187] L. Stone, 'The Educational Revolution in England', *Past and Present*, 28:1 (1964), 41–80, esp. pp. 42–43; L. Stone 'Literacy and Education in England 1640–1900', *Past and Present*, 42:1 (1969), 69–139, esp. 112–13, 117, 119–20; M. Jones, *The Charity School Movement. A Study of Eighteenth-Century Puritanism in Action* (London: Frank Cass and Co., 1964); T. W. Lacqueur, *Religion and Respectability. Sunday Schools and Working-Class Culture 1780–1850* (London: Yale University Press, 1976); M. Sanderson, 'Literacy and Social Mobility in the Industrial Revolution,' *Past and Present*, 56:1 (1972), 75–103; F. Smith, *A History of English Elementary Education* (London: University of London Press, 1931).

embryonic state system, decentralisation (elementary schools were controlled by local boards and committees), the possibility of early leaving and part-time attendance, all meant that it was not until the start of the twentieth century, by which time illiteracy in the country had been virtually wiped out, that schooling had complete priority over the workplace.

What was the Effect of Compulsory Schooling on the Phenomenon of Working Children?

Nicola Sheldon

Recent historians of child labour have been critical of the connection traditionally made between the introduction of compulsory schooling and the decline of children's employment. The issue is still debated, but Peter Kirby claims that, by 1870, legislation plus changes in technology had more or less eliminated the demand for child labourers in paid work under the age of ten. It is argued that the labour market for ten- to fourteen-year-olds also contracted as technology in both industry and agriculture reduced the scope for children's unskilled work.[188] William Landes and Lewis Solmon concluded long ago that laws to enforce school attendance and lengthen the school career were passed only once the majority of parents were already sending their children to school – the law serving only to 'mop up' those who were slow to adopt the social norm of the rest.[189]

Opponents of child labour favoured compulsory education as it was easier to ensure children were in school than not at work. However, a child's registration at school did not guarantee attendance, nor did it prevent the child from working.[190] Children's work, whether formally waged or not, could and did continue alongside schooling, in the home and in casual and seasonal employment, particularly in agriculture.[191] None the less, compulsory schooling had a subtle and gradual impact on children's work because it entailed regularity, punctuality and, above all, careful monitoring of attendance, all of which restricted the flexibility which many working-class parents had enjoyed before 1880 to make use of their children's labour intermittently, on a casual basis or in the domestic economy.

Initially, compulsory schooling had little effect on children's work. The 1870 Act was not explicitly aimed at reducing child labour, although the link between education and labour had been established by the Factory Acts, which stipulated educational attendance as a requirement for permission to employ children.[192] Parents could in fact exploit the differences between the educational clauses of the Factory Acts and the 1870 and later Education Acts to enable their children to leave school earlier under the former.[193] Neither did compulsory elementary schooling reduce parents' perceived

---

[188] P. Kirby, *Child Labour in Britain, 1750–1870* (Basingstoke: Palgrave Macmillan, 2003), pp. 111–12.

[189] W. Landes and L. Solmon, 'Compulsory Schooling Legislation, An Economic Analysis of the Law and Societal Change in the Nineteenth Century,' *Journal of Economic History* 32:1 (1972), 54–91.

[190] A. C. O. Ellis, 'Influences on School Attendance in Victorian England,' *British Journal of Educational Studies*, 21: 3 (1973), 314–15.

[191] P. Horn, *The Victorian and Edwardian Schoolchild* (Gloucester: Alan Sutton Publishing, 1989), pp. 102–06.

[192] J. Lawson and H. Silver, *A Social History of Education in England* (London: Methuen, 1973), p. 274.

[193] Bradford School Board Attendance Committee Minutes (hereafter BradSBAC), letter to Education

(and actual) need for their children's earnings.[194] Simon Szreter has highlighted the critical importance of local child and female labour opportunities to decision-making over family size.[195] Decisions about a child's attendance at school were also closely related to the family's wage-earning capacity, balanced against the opportunity costs of schooling, which before 1891 included school fees. Delays in the provision of school places, the passing of by-laws and setting up systems for enforcement meant attendance did not increase significantly before 1880 in many towns and most rural areas. The requirements of the local labour market also tended to dictate the response of the new local authorities responsible for school attendance.

The starkest examples of this are to be seen in the textile areas of Lancashire and Yorkshire, where the rules were consistently bent to allow children to take up employment early or work half-time.[196] (See Figure 22). For many middle-class members of local attendance committees, it was a matter of necessary pragmatism and prudence (with regard to the poor rates at least), particularly in those places where male wages were relatively low compared with the earning potential of their wives and children. Absence from school was often 'negotiated' with parents and employers allowing the local authority gradually to tighten up the rules over time in relation to individual cases of truancy brought before them by attendance officers.[197] Employers tended to take a passive role; large employers might encourage school attendance, or maintain a factory school, but smaller enterprises tended to ignore the law unless 'reminded' by a letter from the attendance committee. Compulsory schooling was supported by the middle-classes as the answer to idleness of children on the streets rather than because children needed to be protected from early employment – in this respect the rights of parents to send their children to work as half-timers were accorded priority and of course this was to the employer's advantage too. In rural areas, antipathy amongst farmers towards schooling beyond the age of useful employment at ten or eleven was common, but they scarcely ever faced the magistrates' court for illegally employing children under age.

However, where the vigorous enforcement of compulsory attendance took place, it was bound to restrict parental rights over their children's labour. The initial impact was most forcefully seen in the capital, which had its own school board from 1870 and a posse of 'Board Visitors' to track down truants.[198] From 1876, all parts of the country were covered by attendance committees and provision of school places opened up the opportunity, if not the incentive, to parents to send their children to school. The 1880 Education Act compelled even the most reluctant (mainly rural) authorities to enact attendance laws and enforce them, though the effectiveness of the authorities varied greatly.[199] But the commitment of the Westminster Education Department to enforcing

Department 28.1.1880, BBT/13/2/20 (Bradford Local Studies Service, Central Library, Bradford, BD1 1NN).

[194] S. Horrell and J. Humphries, 'The Exploitation of Little Children: Children's Work and the Family Economy in the British Industrial Revolution,' *Explorations in Economic History* 38:3 (1995), 485–516, at p. 503; Ellis, 'Influences on School Attendance in Victorian England', p. 317; Humphries, *Childhood*.

[195] S. Szreter, *Fertility, Class and Gender in Britain, 1860–1940* (Cambridge: Cambridge University Press, 1996), pp. 488–502.

[196] J. Pressley, 'Childhood, Education and Labour: Moral Pressure and the End of the Half-Time System' (University of Lancaster: PhD thesis, 2000), p. 171; BradSBAC Minutes 16.7.1878, 13.1.1880, 19.6.1883, 16.10.1883.

[197] G. M. Belfiore, 'Family Strategies in 3 Essex Textile Towns 1860–1895: The Challenge of Compulsory Elementary Schooling' (Oxford University: DPhil thesis, 1986), p. 341.

[198] D. Rubinstein, *School Attendance in London 1870–1904: A Social History* (Hull: University of Hull Publications, 1969), ch. 6.

[199] P. Horn, *Education in Rural England 1800–1914* (London: Gill and Macmillan, 1978), p. 139.

compulsion rested not on a desire to restrict the paid work of children; it had much more to do with the need to ensure the loans and grants supplied were efficiently employed by filling public elementary schools every day they were open.[200] By contrast there were no such constraints on the many dame schools and 'adventure' schools which had been set up in many towns by private individuals to cater for the developing working-class market for elementary education. Typically, dame schools were small, taking mainly infants under five and providing a limited curriculum in the teacher's house for a small fee each week. Private adventure schools were larger enterprises, although often still located in a large house or rented premises and still charging a fee low enough for working-class families. In many towns, parents avoided the attentions of the local school attendance committee and its officers by patronising such schools, even if the fees were slightly higher than the local public elementary school. As they allowed for intermittent absences and late attendance when home needs were greatest, these schools were both accessible and flexible. After 1870, numbers attending such schools actually increased – parents may well have been getting the message that attendance at school was required, but they chose schools which were willing to meet the family's domestic and economic needs.[201] Despite the repeated moans of school boards and attendance committees, the Education Department took no action to close private working-class schools which competed for pupils with public elementary ones. The magistrates' courts were usually unwilling to convict parents for non-attendance when they could claim their children were pupils at a dame or private adventure school. Over time the economic position of such schools became tenuous, largely due to two factors: the privileged position of certified church and board (state-funded) elementary schools in being able to provide the certificate of attendance required for early leaving,[202] and the ending of fees in state elementary schools from 1891, which knocked the bottom out of the private school market.[203]

Flexibility continued to be available for parents and local authorities over the exemptions for early leaving from the age of ten or eleven. Although children were required to pass a specified standard before early exemption, the standard was often low, especially in those areas where child labour outside the domestic environment was common. This applied to areas with large factories and mills, to those with intensive cottage industries and to agricultural areas, where the farming interest was often the mainstay of the local attendance committee or school board. (See Figure 23). Pragmatism in general won out over local clergy and teacher concerns to obtain children's full attendance to age thirteen. Middle-class committee members knew that if they put up too many hurdles to early leaving, then parents and children would vote with their feet and truancy levels in the older year groups would get out of control.[204]

[200] Committee of Council on Education, 'Reports'. Parliamentary Papers (hereafter P.P.) 1878–79, XXIII, p. xiv.
[201] Oxford School Board (hereafter OSB) Annual Report 1874, OXFO 379 (Centre for Oxfordshire Studies, Westgate Library, Oxford, OX1 1DJ).
[202] Certificates were supplied when the school was able to prove that pupils had been in attendance for 250 sessions (half-days) for the past two years. This and their date of birth was accepted for the granting of the exemption certificate and their names and ages were entered in an 'exemption book' held by the local authority to show that their leaving was legal. Their parents could be prosecuted if they left without the exemption certificate – although the enforcement of this was variable. Children could also leave even earlier by means of passing an exam at the required standard but far fewer did this than those who simply waited for their thirteenth birthday.
[203] P. Gardner, *The Lost Elementary Schools of Victorian England* (London: Croom Helm, 1984), pp. 195–99, 206.
[204] Bradford School Board (hereafter BradSB) Triennial Reports 1889–91, BBT/13/3/6 (Bradford Local

In agricultural areas, the organisation of the school year was adjusted to allow children to participate in seasonal employment, the six-week break being moved according to the weather and ripening harvest in each locality. Committees in towns with fewer opportunities for early employment could afford to be scrupulous in their insistence that children pass the required standard in order to leave early for work – those in areas with a thriving child labour market were less likely to do so.[205] Indeed, there were a few authorities whose enthusiasm to restrict early leaving for work went beyond what was thought suitable by the Departmentof Education, as for instance in York, where they advised the attendance committee that their requirement children pass at Standard V in order to be given permission to work half-time was unrealistic and Standard IV should be allowed instead.[206] Many of the employers and some of the parents themselves were the ratepayers whose money went to fund the board schools, so that gave them a stronger interest in the effective use of the resources and buildings. As more money was invested in elementary schools, and their facilities improved, as well as the qualifications and numbers of teachers, acceptance by parents of the necessity, if not the concrete benefits, of schooling increased.[207]

Through the 1880s and 90s, pressure on local authorities grew in the wake of meticulous monitoring of attendance by the Education Department, as shown by the mass of statistics collected and reproduced in their Annual Reports. In order to receive grants and loans for buildings, a school had to be certified efficient by a school inspector, which meant keeping registers of attendance, ensuring punctuality and putting pupils forward for the annual examination. The lure of funding drew most of the rural Church schools to seek certification. The obligation to provide school places for the children of the locality also carried with it the suggestion that the authorities ought to ensure that the school places were regularly filled when the school was open. In the mid-1880s, civil servants in the Department were still responding to local queries about truanting children on an *ad hoc* basis, but their responses reflected a consistent policy 'line' on persistent absences, the need to prosecute and raise the standards and ages for early leaving.[208] In Bradford, for instance, where more than 8,000 children worked as half-timers from the age of ten, the by-laws had been drafted to require that children pass Standard V. In fact, this requirement was totally disregarded in the town and the local school board had even allowed schools to have blank certificates to fill in for those who wanted to go half-time.[209] The board was hoisted by its own petard when the Department insisted it apply its by-laws and only after special pleading did the Department allow them to lower the half-time requirement to Standard II. This was a temporary concession and the Bradford School Board was put under pressure in the following years to raise it to Standard III.[210] The impact of half-time working on school attendance is debatable but well into the twentieth-century Bradford continued to have one of the poorest elementary school attendance rates in England.[211]

Studies).

[205] OSB Reports 1889, 1899 (Centre for Oxfordshire Studies); York School Attendance Committee Minutes 13.2. 1882 (York City Archive, Exhibition Square, York YO1 7EN).

[206] The attainment and progress of elementary school pupils was tested under seven 'standards', the lowest covering a basic competence in the 3 Rs and the highest (Standard VII) reflecting the expected attainment of a fourteen-year-old.

[207] Rubinstein, *School Attendance*, p. 116.

[208] *E.g.* BradSBAC Minutes 24.2.1880, 8.1.1884, 3.2.1885.

[209] *Ibid.*, 16.10.1883.

[210] *Ibid.*, 24.2.1880, 8.1.1884; BradSB Triennial Reports 1889–91.

[211] Pressley, 'Childhood, Education and Labour', pp. 177–78; Board of Education Statistics of Public Education in England and Wales 1902–14, *e.g.* see P.P.1903 li (Cd.1476), table 17, pp. 386–89, P.P.1909 lxviii (Cd.4885),

Pressure on rural authorities increased in the late 1880s when the Department started to insist that they prosecute parents of truanting children. After the Education Act of 1891 offered extra funding to eliminate fees, the Department had even more cause to intervene in local enforcement of compulsory attendance. Some local authorities, such at the City of Oxford's, sought to establish both high academic standards for early leaving and to end the 'dunce's certificate' whereby early leaving was granted on the basis of a minimum attendance of 250 sessions (half-days) in the previous two years, without any evidence of educational achievement.[212] Over time, the claims of education *over* work were recognised as pre-eminent by the state at both national and local levels and the family's need for children's wages was relegated to second-place. That is not to say that it was ignored altogether, when family poverty pleaded the case for early leaving or time off, though often this was granted temporarily. The impact of the agricultural depression in the mid-1880s led rural local authorities to request a reduction in the (already low) leaving standard but, by this time, the Department was ready to refuse authorities the freedom to relax standards.[213] Increasingly absence was allowed only for specific purposes, where there were exceptional needs or for immediate family support.[214]

After 1892, there was a noticeable drop in the number of truancy cases in court, especially in urban areas, and many fewer of these cases concerned illegal working. Although children were still working outside school-time, their potential contribution to family income was necessarily much more limited than twenty years earlier. The impact on the family of compulsory schooling extended far beyond the effects it had on family incomes. The loss of flexibility to exploit seasonal and intermittent casual employments open to children was accompanied by a loss of control over children's time in the home as well. Working parents had previously relied on older children to look after babies and nurse their mother after a birth or in illness. Although a family could learn to manage without children's earnings due to compulsory schooling, family needs could interrupt a child's education on a regular basis, especially where a lone parent, usually the mother, was bringing up a family and working to support them. Local authorities were more sympathetic to these causes of absence than to what they often regarded as the more mercenary demands of families that children go into paid employment.[215] However, permission to take time off was often conditional on previous good attendance or a teacher's recommendation. Families with a record of truancy were marked out for punitive action, after warnings had failed to achieve an improvement.

Whereas truanting to work had declined, it was to some extent replaced by occasional truanting for what could be described as 'quality of life' reasons – to attend fairs and traditional festivals, for holidays with parents or even to watch football matches. Working-class community life had many interruptions and patterns of activity which did not fit into the rigidity of the school day or calendar. For most working-class children, the value of elementary schooling had to be weighed against the immediate

table 17, p. 300–21, P.P. 1914–16 li (Cd.8097), table 17 pp. 44–65.
[212] OSB Report 1899; Leicestershire County Council Register of Exemption from School Attendance 1912–20 shows fewer than one per cent of the thirteen-year-olds listed had passed the required standard: DE2144/270 (Leicestershire Record Office, Wigston Magna, Leicester, LE18 2AH).
[213] Bicester School Attendance Committee Minutes 7.11.1884 (Oxfordshire Record Office, Cowley, Oxford, OX4 2EX).
[214] Horn, *The Victorian and Edwardian Schoolchild*, pp. 118–9.
[215] A. Davin, *Growing up Poor: Home, School and Street in London 1870–1914* (London: Rivers Oram Press, 1996), pp. 105, 111.

needs of the family, whether in good times or bad, to take its pleasures whilst it could and pull together when there was no money to pay the bills. In mining villages, where all the lads left school for the pit, and the girls to 'help at home' before marrying, the demands of education had little to do with work or the day-to-day efforts to avoid poverty. Altofts Colliery School log book records the lonely battle of the schoolmaster to combat poor attendance over a 21 year period. His entry for October 19 1889 reads, 'The attendance this week has been most fluctuating and disappointing for the following reasons – Tuesday potato picking, Wednesday circus, Friday Volunteer funeral. Several children have been away more than half the week as this is extra to washing day'.[216]

By the end of the century, local authorities were much more willing to defend the inherent value of elementary education, fortified by the emerging rationale of 'national efficiency'. This was not specifically focused on the need for more literate and numerate workers, but centred on a more general concern about competition with other imperial powers. Sir John Gorst's publication of *Children of the Nation* in 1906 set out the case for the state's rights in the education and health of every child. Clergy, teachers and school board members, particularly in the metropolitan areas, put forward the arguments for the civilising and moral effects of elementary education, forming an increasingly vocal lobby on behalf of compulsory schooling.[217] In the first decade after 1870, the provision of places had taken priority over obtaining full attendance. The chief focus of attention had been the 'wastrel' children on the streets of urban areas, for whom only ragged schools had previously catered. Little concern existed in rural areas for enforcing full attendance, as there was perceived to be no problem of idle children there. From 1880, it was clear that the Department intended local authorities to enforce compulsory attendance, however reluctant they were to do so, including prodding them to take 'exemplary' prosecutions against parents of persistent truants.[218] The pressure of local ratepayers to see value for their money and the equal insistence of the Department that grants relate both to attendance and examinations reinforced the claims of the state that all working-class children attend school both regularly and punctually. And the simple process of investment in buildings, resources and staffing generated its own momentum towards social conformity by parents, so that it proved ever more difficult for them to resist the trend for sending their children to school every day, at least to the age when the rules allowed them to leave for work.

In many towns and cities, the demand for child labour was low by the 1880s when school attendance was being more or less consistently enforced. Children's employment was intermittent and casual, which meant that some work could be combined with school. This was especially the case in rural areas, and where domestic labour was needed in the home. The attentions of the local authority enforcing compulsory attendance necessarily interfered with parental rights over their children's time, whether wanted for paid labour or simply to help at home. The priority given to school attendance by the state did not stop parents bending the rules where they could or local authorities ignoring requirements for early leaving or a temporary absence where there were exceptional circumstances, for instance to meet the needs of sick parents who could not work, widows or deserted mothers. But such concessions became the exception not the rule during the 1890s. As the Education Department pressed local authorities, or as they took the initiative themselves, to enforce their by-laws and the Education

---

[216] Altofts Colliery School logbook 19.10.1889, WMD4/2 (West Yorkshire Archive Service, Wakefield WF1 2DE).
[217] Davin, *Growing up Poor*, pp. 210–11.
[218] Winslow Union School Attendance Committee Minutes 8.1.1890, G/6/6 (Centre for Buckinghamshire Studies, County Hall, Aylesbury, HP20 1UU).

Acts more consistently, the flexibility allowed to parents gradually disappeared, and so did the job opportunities.

Once school became the chief 'occupation' of the child, the balance of competitive interests in the use of the child's time was reversed – instead of school flexibly fitting round the work of the child, as had been the case before compulsory education, work opportunities had to fit around the demands of the school. Marginalised schooling had been transformed into marginalised working. Children's employment became focused on specialised areas, such as message or shop delivery, working as lather boys in barber shops, or newspaper-selling and street-trading, all low-paid urban employments which could be 'trimmed' to enable children to get into school on time – though this did not stop the objections of educationalists.[219]

Even in Lancashire, by the First World War the remaining bastion of half-time child labour, the employment market for children under fourteen was extremely localised.[220] Here child labour was institutionalised via the half-time system, and widespread, so the contest was inevitably drawn out, as so many parental and employer interests were involved. Jane Walsh describes how she first applied for millwork in 1917 in a Lancashire cotton town when she was twelve, but was 'so small and peaky-looking that nobody would take me'.[221] When she was thirteen however she found an employer and could leave school and so, in her own words, she 'came out into the world "educated", grown-up, a wage-earner'.[222] Other children, especially girls, remained heavily involved in domestic labour and the running of the house, so even if they did not accept waged work they were kept fully occupied within the domestic sphere, looking after younger siblings, washing, preparing breakfast for older brothers and sisters, shopping and going off to the pawnbroker.[223] But by 1918, the existence of half-time working for children from the age of twelve in the mills of Lancashire and West Yorkshire appeared both anomalous and exploitative to the rest of the country.[224] Despite a rearguard protest by the mill-workers, half-time leaving was ended with effect from 1921, closing the door on the formal child labour market for good.

. . . .

In mainland Europe, children continued to be employed in agriculture, although the numbers were falling. In Germany for instance, 390,600 children under fourteen still worked in agriculture in 1925, although this was down from 515,600 in 1907.[225] In Britain, too, the lack of able-bodied men during the First World War meant that, once again, farmers turned to boys to fill their places. The coming of universal schooling certainly did not put an end to children working, even if they were ultimately forced into school.

By the 1920s the worst excesses of the mills and factories had gone and the battles against overt exploitation had generally been won. By then there had been raging for several decades a new discussion over whether or not any form of work done by children was suitable.

---

[219] *Departmental Committee on the Employment of Children Act* (1903), P.P. 1910 XXVIII. Many witnesses wanted to end children's involvement in street trading despite recognising its value to poor families, *e.g.* F. Wilkinson, Director of Education for Bolton, p. 326, and A. Evans, Headmaster of a Liverpool elementary school, p. 306.

[220] M. Winstanley (ed.), *Working Children in Nineteenth-Century Lancashire* (Preston: Lancashire County Books, 1995), ch. 1.

[221] Davin, 'What is a Child?', p. 27.

[222] *Ibid.*

[223] E. Roberts, 'Learning and Living – Socialisation Outside School', *Oral History*, 3:2 (1975), 14–28.

[224] Pressley, 'Childhood, Education and Labour', p. 262.

[225] Rahikainen, *Centuries of Child Labour*, pp. 196–97.

According to Viviana Zelizer, in the United States the early twentieth century was the time when there was a shift in thinking about children. Their value was now measured in terms of sentimentality and the companionship they brought, not in terms of their economic value. The child, previously economically valuable, was now sentimentally priceless.[226] Yet there was still a reluctance to demonise child labour entirely and in North America disputes about child labour evolved not around its complete abolition but around how to distinguish between legitimate and illegitimate forms of work.[227] Even those like Raymond Fuller, Director of Research at the US National Child Labor Committee and a campaigner for child labour reforms, argued that 'Nothing could be further from the truth than the … widespread notion that child labor reform is predicated on the assumption that children should have no work'.[228] Others claimed that the 'dilemma for the city child seems to be either painful exhaustion and demoralizing work on the one hand, or futile idleness and its consequent immorality on the other'.[229] The author of this comment, William Noyes, was at pains to point out that he was in favour of some forms of child work because it solved the problem, discussed throughout the centuries, of what to do about children's idleness.

> [The] normal child is not averse to work; on the contrary he is bubbling over with energy which under normal conditions expends itself partly in play, partly in work. Children can work, under proper conditions children like to work. Enforced idleness either on city streets … is a horrible fate for child or adult, and children, we may well believe, are not idle because they want to be idle. They are idle because they are deprived of work, except under such conditions as make it over-wearisome, painful and demoralizing. Yet even so they submit to it, even embrace the opportunity to perform it. Enormous numbers of them quit school to take up work.[230]

His solution was to limit the hours and monotony of work but not to abolish work itself, which he saw as far more useful and educative than school. The answer to the problem was, in Fuller's terms, 'to establish children's work while abolish[ing] child labor'.[231]

This neat linguistic distinction proved much harder to translate into reality, leading to a situation in the United States where factory work was completely outlawed for children, while agricultural work was romanticised and categorised as work which was not only good for society but also for children themselves. A survey carried out in 1932 showed that the American public supported the employment of children in farms despite reports coming out in the 1920s which suggested that farm work could be hard and dangerous and that children were suffering as a result.[232] Again, the solution was not to ban all farm work but to differentiate between good and bad work, good work being carried out under parental direction with enough time for children to attend school.[233]

---

[226] V. Zelizer, *Pricing the Priceless Child: the Changing Social Value of Children* (New Haven: Yale University Press, 1985).

[227] Zelizer discusses one of these battles – the case of child actors – in some detail. These children were the subjects of several controversial legal battles in North America in 1910 and 1911. Discussions as to whether this was exploitation or work lay at the heart of such debates, given the long hours and relatively low wages children received, *Pricing the Priceless Child*, pp. 85–89.

[228] *Ibid.*, p. 74.

[229] W. Noyes, 'Idleness or Industrial Education?', *Annals of the American Academy of Political and Social Science* 27 (1906), 84–95, at p. 87.

[230] *Ibid.*, p. 88.

[231] Zelizer, *Pricing the Priceless Child*, p. 75

[232] In 1924 one inspector wrote: 'Everybody is against child labor but work on the farms... is not held to be child labor. The presumption that everything is well with the child in agriculture runs so strong that any inquiry …is held by some not only useless but also improper', Zelizer, *Pricing the Priceless Child*, p. 77.

[233] Farm work was exempted from child labour legislation across Europe, or the authorities turned a blind

In the United States, children were also still working in other industries, particularly selling newspapers or petty trading in the street. In the early years of the twentieth century these working boys (and they were rarely girls) were singled out for praise for being independent, small-scale entrepreneurs who turned a small profit, 'little merchants' rather than exploited children. Ridding the streets of such little merchants was seen as not only very difficult but also undesirable. However, there remained concern that these boys were too visible, too independent and exposed to the dangers and vices of the streets. The street, like the factory, gradually became seen as the 'wrong' place for children to be and once again distinctions between legitimate and illegitimate street working were drawn. Distributing newspapers was deemed legitimate because boys had no control over the distribution or pricing: they were working for others under strict rules; while vending in the streets, where children had independence was dismissed as illegitimate.[234]

By the 1930s the majority of children in America aged under fourteen were in school full-time rather than in work, although there remained some children who continued to combine both. The Fair Labor Standards Act of 1938 allowed children under fourteen to work for their parents in farms or in shops. They could also work as actors, newspaper distributors or on other people's farms, as long as they worked outside school hours. Socially there had been a bigger shift. Work, which had previously been done for the good of the family, was now seen as legitimate only if it was carried out for the good of the child, a form of education or training rather than 'real' work. 'The useful labor of the nineteenth century was replaced by educational work for the useless child. While child labor had served the household economy, child work would benefit primarily the child'.[235] Money too was transformed from something children and adolescents received as a wage to something they were given by parents in the form of pocket money, sometimes as a 'reward' for household chores, sometimes simply as a gift. Wages, like work, had become conceptualised as part of the adult world.

In the United Kingdom, the school leaving age has been progressively raised to fourteen in 1918, fifteen in 1944, and sixteen in 1972.[236] This has further reduced the possibility of adolescents or younger children working and contributing to their family income in any meaningful way. Social and cultural changes since the end of the Second World War have also meant that when young people do work both they and their parents regard their income as their own to dispose of rather than as a contribution to the family. Studies of household income have shown a progressive decline in contributions from children and young people. For example, in Merseyside, in the 1930s, those aged between fourteen and 21 contributed 24 per cent of the family's total income. Even in the 1950s working youngsters in the same area continued to hand over their entire wage packet to their mothers, receiving spending money in return. Today, working for the family economy is almost unheard of. In the 1990s only one per cent of young people between the ages of thirteen and eighteen claimed that they worked because it was 'essential for making ends meet for my family'.[237]

---

eye to the numbers of working children, see Rahikainen, *Centuries of Child Labour*, ch. 6.

[234] The idea of the child as entrepreneur elicited a much less ambivalent reaction in Europe, where it was more generally condemned, see Rahikainen, *Centuries of Child Labour*, pp. 169–76. From Henry Mayhew's depiction of the Little Watercress Girl published in 1851 to the 1928 film, *La petite marchande d'allumettes* (*The Little Match Girl*), made by Jean Renoir (1894–1979), the street was usually portrayed as a place where children came to harm and where they had no real place to be. While they might make their living on it, there was no possibility of social advancement and disappointment and death were the usual fate of these European child entrepreneurs.

[235] Zelizer, *Pricing the Priceless Child*, pp. 97–98.

[236] In 2007 the law was changed again so that by 2013 all children under the age of eighteen will have to be at school, in training or in an apprenticeship.

[237] Cunningham, 'The Decline of Child Labour', pp. 423–24.

Within the home also there have been great social and technological changes which have affected children's contributions to the family economy. Water no longer needs fetching or fires laying, food preparation does not take as long and bottling, pickling and other culinary skills are not expected of children, and pre-adolescent girls are no longer expected, or even legally allowed, to look after younger siblings. (See Figure 24). Shopping tends to be done by adults in their cars and children's role within the house is now much more limited so the child has become, in Viviana Zelizer's words 'a privileged guest who is thanked and praised for "helping out", rather than a collaborator who at a certain age is expected to assume his or her fair share of household duties'.[238]

At the beginning of the twenty-first century, child labour has become almost totally associated with the non-western world.[239] Thanks in part to successful campaigns by international agencies such as the ILO or UNICEF, the image now evoked by the words 'child labourer' is of a poor child locked in a sweatshop in Asia or on a cocoa farm in west Africa making goods for the western market, in conditions of near slavery. These campaigns reflect much of the imagery and rhetoric first used against the employment of children in nineteenth-century Europe, concentrating on sensational stories, first hand accounts and the grotesque situation of young children being exploited to provide useless products.[240] Indeed children who work in non-Western contexts are seen as an affront to 'civilised' values and 'a high incidence of child labour is considered a sign of underdevelopment'.[241] Looking again at the vignettes at the beginning of the chapter, it appears ludicrous to compare the situation of debt-bonded child labourers in India with teenagers working longer hours than they should in McDonalds in Surrey. Certainly it is very hard to see this as exploitation, even if it is an infringement of labour laws. Although the issue of child work and whether it is harmful *per se* is still debated within the UK,[242] there appears to be a consensus of sorts that children can do some forms of light work as long as it does not interfere with their schooling or their health. The NSPCC suggests that around one million children are now working illegally, and that 'Every day children's lives are put at risk by employers who don't realise there is a work permit system designed to protect children when at work'.[243] But this appears more to do with lack of correct paperwork than indicative of serious exploitation. And yet exploitation continues in Britain and other western countries, and not all children have the luxury of avoiding heavy work. This chapter ends with an account of the large group of British children, usually forgotten, who take on substantial and unpaid caring responsibilities within the home.

---

[238] Zelizer, *Pricing the Priceless Child*, p. 209.

[239] There are still reports of child labour on the fringes of Europe, or among illegal immigrants. In 1988, it was estimated that 90,000 children between the ages of eight to fourteen were illegally employed in southern Italy. The truth of this statistic is hard to verify, but it does suggest that child labour has not been completely eliminated, even in Europe. Rahikainen, *Centuries of Child Labour*, p. 206.

[240] See for instance *The Daily Telegraph* from Christmas Day 2007, 'British Patios Fuelling Indian Child Labour'. For a discussion about the veracity of many of the claims made about child workers see A. Berlan, 'Child Labour and Cocoa: Whose Voices Prevail?', *International Journal of Sociology and Social Policy*, 29:3 (2009), 141–51 and H. Montgomery, *Modern Babylon? Prostituting Children in Thailand* (Oxford: Berghahn, 2001).

[241] Olga Nieuwenhuys, 'The Paradox of Child Labor and Anthropology', *Annual Review of Anthropology*, 25 (1996), 237–51, at p. 237.

[242] See the contrasting views of P. Mizen, A. Bolton and C. Pole, 'School Age Workers: The Paid Employment of Children in Britain', *Work, Employment and Society*, 13:3 (1999), 423–38 and J. McKechnie, M. Lavalette and S. Hobbs, 'Child Employment Research in Britain', *Work Employment and Society*, 14:3 (2000), 573–80.

[243] NSPCC, *Child Employment Laws: Make the Legislation Work*. Available at http://www.nspcc.org.uk/whatwedo/mediacentre/pressreleases/2007_01_november_child_employment_laws_make_the_legislation_work_wdn52017.html (accessed 7 Jul. 2009).

Figure 1. Michelangelo Caravaggio, The Sacrifice of Isaac, *c. 1604. Perhaps the most famous Renaissance depiction of the Abraham and Isaac story. Abraham's murderous determination and Isaac's horror are palpable. A muscular angel points to the ram as a substitute, while the church in the background rising into the light seems to signal the new covenant of love. Caravaggio (1571–1610) is remembered today above all for his masterly use of light and shade to enhance the drama of his studies.*

Figure 2. Sacrifice of Iphigenia. This depiction of the sacrifice of Iphigenia on a Greek vase probably dates from the fifth century BCE. Iphigenia is superimposed upon a stag, who, according to one version of the myth, the goddess of the hunt, Artemis (far right) substitutes for the princess at the last minute. On the other hand, the artist may simply be reminding the viewer that Agamemnon had earlier angered the goddess by killing a deer in a sacred grove and boasting he was a better hunter than she. For revenge, Artemis stayed the wind and stopped Agamemnon's fleet from sailing to Troy. She would only restore the wind, if he sacrificed his daughter. The fact that the sacrificial knife is wielded by a man holding a spear suggests that it is Agamemnon not a priest who kills the girl.

Figure 3. The Croxton Play of the Sacrament. *This fifteenth-century play, which depicts Jews torturing the sacrament, was staged in Oxford in 2004 in a double bill with contemporary playwright, Steven Berkoff's* Ritual in Blood *(2001), which dramatises the conviction of the Jews for killing the child Hugh of Lincoln, and exposes the blood libel's socio-economic roots. The photograph is a still from the Oxford production, whose stylised staging was designed to highlight the theatrical nature of the miraculous events of the medieval play. The still depicts the bleeding Christ who appears in the consecrated wafer that the Jews have stabbed. Christ was played by a child actor, who wore a crown of thorns and red ribbons to symbolise the wounds of crucifixion. The image recalls medieval paintings associating Jewish sacrament-torture, violence against children, and representations of Christ as a crucified child. The kneeling Jews, who are wearing yellow gloves (yellow was the colour of perfidy) are converted by the apparition, and the Bishop (centre rear) stands ready to receive them into the Church.*

Figure 4. Felice Ficherelli, Abraham and Isaac, *c. 1650. One of the numerous depictions of the Abraham and Isaac story, this version has none of the terror and horror of the Caravaggio painted 50 years before. Isaac looks neither terrified nor resigned. He appears to be praying in a semi-ecstatic pose. The angel is not staying Abraham's hand, merely suggesting by his gestures that slaying his son is not what the Almighty intended. Ficherelli (1605–60) was a painter who worked primarily in Tuscany.*

Figure 5. Giuseppe Crespi, Massacre of the Innocents, *c. 1700. According to Matthew's gospel, when King Herod heard that the future 'king of the Jews' had been born in Judea, he ordered the destruction of all male children under the age of two so that he would have no potential rivals. Warned by an angel of the impending massacre, Mary, Joseph and the infant Jesus fled to Egypt. In Crespi's depiction of the story, some infants have already been killed by Herod's soldiers, some are being snatched from their mothers' arms, while a few are being rushed away. Crespi's composition takes the form of a macabre dance; even the horse on the plinth appears to be alive. Crespi (1665–1747) was a Bolognese painter who was patronised by the Tuscan court.*

Figure 6. Jacques-Louis David, La Mort de Bara, *c. 1793. Joseph Bara was a thirteen-year-old boy soldier in the army of the French Republic who was killed by royalist rebels in western France while looking after the horses of his platoon. He was quickly turned into a revolutionary hero, who was fêted all the more because he was using his wages to support a widowed mother. There were many depictions of Bara during and after the Revolution but David's was the most dramatic. Lying on the ground naked and androgynous, he represented martyred innocence. David (1748–1825) was the artist of the French Revolution par excellence who used his art in the 1790s to promote the regime.*

Figure 7. War memorial: Secondigny, France. The French lost some two million men during the First World War and the religious nature of the sacrifice was emphasised by the erection of memorials to the fallen within the parish church or churchyard. Here at Secondigny in the department of Deux-Sèvres in western France the memorial is just inside the church door. As on all French monuments the dead are described as 'children', and in this particular case the fallen are depicted as fresh-faced young men receiving the crown of glory for their sacrifice for France.

Figure 8. Princess Belle-Etoile *(1698) is a French literary fairy tale written by Madame d'Aulnoy (1650–1705). It tells the story of the lowly born Queen Blondine who was hated by her husband's mother. Her mother-in-law took Blondine's three children and replaced them in their cradles with three puppies. She then ordered a maid to kill them. The maid would not do this and instead set them adrift in a boat, where they were eventually rescued by a corsair. After many adventures, in true fairytale style, they were eventually reunited with their father.*

Figure 9."Title page woodcut of the execution and resuscitation of Anne Green in 1651 from News from the Dead. Or a true and exact narration of the miraculous deliverance of Anne Green, who being executed at Oxford afterwards revived. Written by a scholler in Oxford. R. Watkins, Oxford 1651*". Anne Green was a 22-year-old servant from Oxfordshire, who was probably seduced by the grandson of the house in which she was working. In 1650 she became pregnant but concealed the pregnancy and gave birth to a premature baby, whom she claimed was stillborn. She was convicted of the murder of her child and sentenced to hang on December 14, 1650. After she was cut down she was taken away for dissection but on opening her coffin, doctors found her still alive.*

A Declaration from *Oxford*, of *Anne Green*,

A young woman that was lately, and unjustly hanged in the Castle-yard; but since recovered, her neck set strait, and her eyes fixed orderly and firmly in her head again: With her Speech touching four Angels that appeared to her when she was dead; and their strange expressions, apparations, and passages that happened thereupon, the like never heard of before: Being a more full and perfect Relation of the great handiwork of God, to the said *Anne Green*, Servant to Sir *Tho. Read*, who being got with Child, and delivered of it in a house of Office, dead-born, received an unjust sentence to be hanged, and after half an hour, was cut down, and carried to the Colledge of Physicians, where all the learned Doctors and Chyrurgions met to anatomize her; but taking her out of the Coffin, and laying her on a Table, she began to stir; whereupon Dr. *Petty* & others, caused a warm bed to be prepared for her; and after 14. hours, she came to her self, uttering these words, *Behold Gods providence, in raising me from death to life*: With an excellent Prayer used by her morning, noon, and night, fit to be read in all Families, throughout *England, Ireland, Scotland,* and *Wales*: Whereunto is annexed another strange Wonder from *Ashburn* in *Darbishire*, shewing how a young Woman dying in Child-bed, was buried, and delivered of a young Son in the grave, the strange things that befell thereupon, at the taking her out again. *Licensed according to Order.*

Behold Gods Providence.

LONDON Printed by T. Clowes. 1651.

Figure 10. Foundling hospital barrel, Mâcon. These barrels or baskets allowed children to be placed anonymously in foundling institutions by their parents. A turning mechanism allowed a parent to place the child in a cradle on the outside wall, turn the wheel to take the infant inside and ring a bell to alert an attendant. Abandonment could thus be done anonymously although many parents left a token, such as a button or a piece of ribbon, in the baby's hand in order that they might be able to identify and reclaim the child later on, possibly when their circumstances improved. Wheels were often thought to confer a blessing on a child – there are cases in Italy of children being stuffed into the wheel so that they could be blessed, even at the cost of broken limbs.

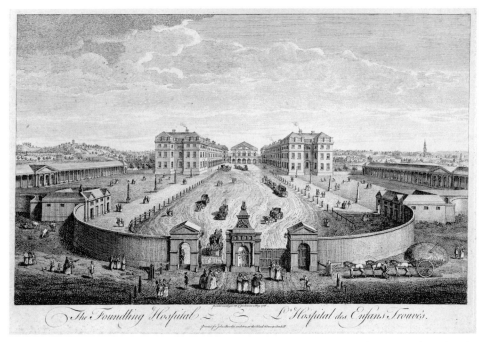

Figure 11. The Foundling Hospital, a bird's eye view, 1753, engraving by T. Bowles after L. P. Boitard. The London Foundling Hospital was established by Thomas Coram in 1741. For most of its history it took in only small groups of healthy infants and did so by ballot. Mothers had to draw a coloured ball from a bag; it they pulled out a white one, the child could be admitted, black meant they would not be admitted, but red meant they would be on the reserve list.

Figure 12. Poster from The US National Home Finding Society. This society was one of many set up in the USA to facilitate adoption. In the 1920s advertisements such as this appeared in newspapers ostensibly promoting the twin ideals of finding homes for homeless children and giving children to childless families. Other benefits of adoption include, in the words of this advert, filling the churches, exchanging immigrants for Americans and controlling births.

Figure 13. Advertising poster for the film 'The Black Stork Delivers A Baby', 1917. Chicago Surgeon Dr Harry J. Haiselden's film was designed to warn potential parents about the dangers of 'bad' breeding and the likelihood of producing defective babies. In the film he advocates allowing 'defective' newborns to die.

Figure 14. Nurse outside one of Marie Stopes's mobile birth control clinics, London, 1928. Marie Stopes set up the first family planning clinic in the UK in Holloway, north London in 1921 to offer advice and contraceptives to married women. It did not offer abortion, which was illegal, although many women appeared unaware of the law and the doctors and nurses were constantly requested to help women procure an abortion.

Figure 15. Temple of Artemis, Sparta. In Ancient Sparta the temple was the site of contests where boys would show off their skills in singing, dancing and making hunting calls. It was also the location of an important rite of passage where one group of boys would attempt to steal cheeses from an altar while another group beat them off with whips. Today very little of the temple survives.

Figure 16. Medieval schoolmaster with birch. In medieval iconography the schoolmaster was usually depicted with a birch or rod, both the symbol of his authority and his chief means of keeping order. Here a young clerk (he is beardless) is depicted seated with a birch in one hand and a scroll in the other. He looks out over the lawn of Magdalen College, Oxford's cloister, and was sculpted about 1480. It is generally assumed he represents the faculty of arts, as the statue is one of four purportedly depicting the four university faculties. However, he may well be the master of the newly founded Magdalen College School, which shared a site with the College.

Figure 17. Jan Steen, The Village School, *c. 1665. The Dutch genre artist, Steen (c. 1625–79) painted several school interiors. This one depicts the chaos of the elementary schoolroom in the pre-modern age which helps to understand the recourse to corporal punishment. The boy being hit with a wooden spoon (hard enough to make him cry) appears to have presented the teacher with some sums that he has done incorrectly. The teacher has crumpled up the paper and thrown it on the floor. The smaller children who are only learning to read are amused by his discomfiture but the older boy behind looks apprehensive, perhaps because he too has being doing sums and is waiting his turn.*

ELIZABETH BROWNRIGG.

Figure 18. Elizabeth Brownrigg flogging her servant Mary Clifford. Brownrigg recruited her domestic servants from the London Foundling Hospital and treated them to systematic abuse. Mary died as a result of multiple, cumulative injuries and infected wounds. Elizabeth Brownrigg was tried for Mary's murder, found guilty and hanged at Tyburn in September 1767. The case was notorious enough to make it into the Newgate Calendar ('The Malefactors' Bloody Register'), in 1774.

Figure 19. Jean-Laurent Mosnier, La jeune femme, *1770s. Mosnier (1743–1808) was a court painter who after the Revolution worked in London, Berlin and St Petersburg. This painting of a well-born mother breast-feeding her child illustrates the extent to which many high society women by the late eighteenth century had embraced the new child-centred paediatrics promoted by Rousseau and others. The good mother devoted her life to bringing up her children and shaping their minds and bodies; she did not have them put out to nurse or entrust them to a governess so that she could enjoy society life.*

Figure 20. Augustus Earle, Life in the Ocean Representing the Usual Occupations of the Young Officers in the Steerage of a British Frigate at Sea, *c. 1820–37. The image is a realistic depiction of the wide-ranging off-duty activities of midshipmen and other crew members in their mess below decks. It features figures shaving, chatting, writing, working upon mathematical and navigational calculations, sketching, playing the flute, drinking, grinding coffee and playing with a monkey. It was painted by the marine artist Augustus Earle some time during the 1820s or 1830s and exhibited at the Royal Academy in 1837.*

Figure 21. A group of Victorian farm workers during harvesting. While labour reformers campaigned for the abolition of factory work for children, those children working in agriculture were largely overlooked, even though their working conditions were sometimes miserable. By 1870 children were supposed to be in school until they were fourteen but many left by the age of eleven to help on farms to supplement their family's wages.

Figure 22. Children outside a school in Farnworth, Bolton, with 'half-timers' in the front in their working clothes, 1900. Although children were supposed to be in school full time, they were allowed to work as 'half-timers', so that they combined work with some sort of schooling. It was not until 1918 that the half-time system completely died out in the northern mill towns.

Figure 23. A boy 'piecer' in a spinning mill in Oldham, Lancashire about 1900. Piecing (joining threads during the spinning and winding process) was seen as a children's job. By this point legislation was in place to ensure that all children went to school. In the textile areas of Lancashire and Yorkshire, however, rules were consistently bent to allow children to take up employment early.

Figure 24. Girls and their younger siblings in the east end of London, 1950s. Until very recently, older girls would have been expected to look after younger children in the family and to help around the house. While this tradition has died out in the West, many children still provide informal care within the family, looking after parents and other relatives who are ill or disabled.

Figure 25. William Hogarth, 'First Stage of Cruelty', 1750/1. This is the first in a series of four engravings about the fall of Tom Nero, a parish boy, who ends on the gallows for killing his mistress. In the engraving, Tom is in the centre of the picture plunging an arrow into the anus of a dog. His eventual fate is depicted in the sketch on the wall beside him. In the series Hogarth wished to convey the message that permitting children to be cruel to animals only encouraged them to be violent when they were older.

Figure 26. George Cruikshank, 'Oliver plucks up spirit', 1837. In Dickens's novel Oliver Twist, *the eponymous hero, fresh from the workhouse, is apprenticed to an undertaker. Noah Claypole, an older boy in the service of the undertaker, proceeds to make Oliver's life a misery. When Claypole casts aspersions on Oliver's parentage, Oliver responds in time-honoured fashion: he thrashes his tormentor.*

Figure 27. William Hogarth, 'Hudibras and the Skimmington', before 1726. The engraving was one of a set done by Hogarth early in his life to illustrate a new edition of Samuel Butler's Hudibras, first published in the reign of Charles II. Hudibras is a satirical poem depicting the exploits of a greedy and dishonest Cromwellian colonel. In the engraving the colonel finds himself in the midst of an English charivari. The crowd (of all ages, not just the young) are making fun of a hen-pecked husband. The two figures on the horse represent the man and his wife. The man is seated behind his wife and appears to be holding a distaff. Hogarth emphasizes the cruelty of the skimmington ride by showing one of the younger participants swinging a cat (bottom left).

Figure 28. Johann Hulsmann, 'Streifzug von Soldaten', mid-seventeenth century. Hulsmann was a German artist who trained in Cologne. The etching depicts a detachment on the march and emphasises how much warfare in the first half of the seventeenth century was a 'family' affair. Women, children and even babes in arms were part of the retinue.

Figure 29. Anon., marauding soldiers, mid-seventeenth century. This etching of soldiers sacking a village during the Thirty Years War gives a good indication of the primary role of child soldiers at this time. As the boy stealing a chicken on the right of the picture demonstrates, children were used as scavengers to hunt for food.

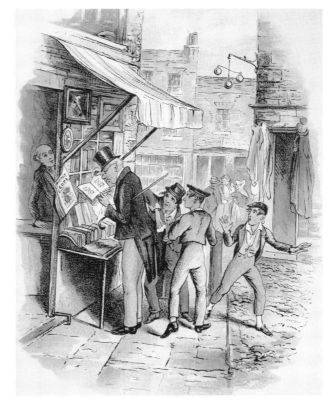

Figure 30. George Cruikshank, 'Oliver amazed at the Dodger's mode of "going to work"', 1837. When Oliver Twist arrives in London having run away from his master, he becomes part of a gang of masterless boys who thieve for Fagin in return for food and lodging. We now know that such gangs were rare in early nineteenth-century London and that most children who lived from crime worked on their own account. Dickens was nearer the mark when he had Fagin's gang working in small teams. In the engraving, the leading member of the gang, 'the Artful Dodger' is introducing Oliver to his future career by picking the pocket of a gentleman (Mr Brownlow) inspecting books.

Figure 31. The statue of Pavlik Morozov in Gerasimovka. The Soviet youngster who was purportedly murdered with his brother for denouncing his father to the authorities in 1932 became a hero of the Communist regime for his dedication to the cause. Numerous statues were erected in his honour, including the one depicted here in his home village. In the 1990s, however, with the collapse of the Soviet Union, most were pulled down or defaced.

Figure 32. Jewish children playing guards and inmates in the Lodz ghetto, early 1940s. Henryk Ross (b. Poland 1910–d. Israel 1991) was a photographer appointed by the Jewish Council in the Lodz ghetto in Poland to document the life of the inmates. He took thousands of photographs, including many of children playing, and before the ghetto was closed buried them all so that they would survive. What is clear from this photograph is how much pleasure children could get out of playing at 'being on top', even when their life was so constrained.

Figure 33. William Hatherell, 'I ought not to be born, ought I?', 1895. Thomas Hardy's Jude the Obscure *was initially published in serial form with illustrations by the British artist, William Hatherell (1855–98). In the novel, it is suggested that Father Times's decision to take his own life and that of his siblings is partly fired by his mother's over-readiness to confide in him about the family's poor circumstances. He is not given the chance to be a child free from adult worries.*

For Love, not Money: Children's Unpaid Care Work in Modern Britain

Saul Becker

Children speak out about their care work in the home:

Jimmy, aged sixteen

When I think about all those years I cared for my dad it makes me angry, not because I had to care for him – I wanted to care for him – but because I was left alone to cope with his illness for so long.

I wasn't just doing ordinary tasks like other kids might do around the house. I was having to cook for him, beg for money and food parcels so I could feed him, take him to the toilet, clean him up when he couldn't get to the toilet – because he couldn't get up the stairs towards the end.

No one should have to see their parents like that, when they lose all their bodily functions. I loved my dad and I couldn't bear to see him losing his dignity – getting more ill before my eyes. But because I loved him, I wanted to be with him. I wanted to look after him. I just wish someone could have helped me and that those who interfered in our lives and made them difficult could have left us alone.

All I ever wanted was to talk to someone and someone who could have warned me about my dad's fits, caused by his brain tumour.

It's too late for me now. My dad died and I'm no longer a 'young carer', but for all those other kids out there who are in the same situation I was, then something should be done to help them. Not take them away from their mum or dad, but to help them care without worrying, without being frightened.

Alison, aged eighteen

I've been caring for my mum for nine years now on my own. When my dad died suddenly my mum got ill and I had to look after her – prepare the meals, cook them, do all the housework, gardening. At first I hated it. I hated my mother because I resented having to do all those jobs – why did it have to happen to me?

I suppose I rebelled. But I shouldn't have been left to look after her on my own for so long. I know now I was rebelling but then I was just so scared. I didn't want to lose my mum as well.

Now I look upon her like any other mum – I never think of her as disabled and I don't mind as much doing all the jobs. I even love gardening now, in fact if anyone tried to help with my garden or tried to touch it I'd kill them!

And now I want to help others who are in my position. It's too late for me now – help should have come when I was a girl, but it didn't and now I don't want anyone coming in and interfering. I find it hard to express my feelings, but I really want to help – all those other young carers who might not be coping. I don't think there's much help for them at the moment and some of them are less fortunate than I was, but there should be help available.

I agreed to take part in this research because it's important everyone knows how we feel and how we've been ignored. Something has got to be done to help young carers.[244]

---

[244] Quoted in J. Aldridge and S. Becker, *Children Who Care: Inside the World of Young Carers* (Loughborough: Young Carers Research Group, 1993).

In Britain, as in almost every other country, unpaid care-giving within the family is rarely conceptualised or discussed as care *work*, rather it is referred to as *informal caring*. The understanding that care is given free of charge is at the heart of informal, as opposed to professional, caring relationships. Informal caregiving activities are often invisible, part of the private domain of the family, founded on love, duty, reciprocity, and an 'intergenerational contract', not monetary exchange.[245] Calling these activities care *work* is to politicise and make public the activities, financial and personal worth, and outcomes, that characterise unpaid caregiving. Everything that an unpaid carer does for another family member, if conducted by a non-family member (such as a nurse, social worker or personal assistant) would carry a monetary value and a charge. Carers UK has calculated that the annual cost of the hidden contribution by family carers is £87 billion, higher than the annual costs of all aspects of the National Health Service itself.[246]

While there is a high degree of acceptance and legitimacy in adults being involved in caregiving for other family members, we now also know that many children globally and in the UK are involved in unpaid care work within the home.[247] These children are generally referred to in the research literature and in UK social policy and social welfare legislation as 'young carers'. Young carers can be defined as children and young persons under eighteen who provide care, assistance or support to another family member. They carry out, often on a regular basis, significant or substantial caring tasks and assume a level of responsibility that would usually be associated with an adult. The person receiving care is often a parent but can be a sibling, grandparent or other relative who is disabled, has some chronic illness, mental health problem or other condition connected with a need for care, support or supervision.[248]

The 2001 Census showed that there are at least 175,000 children and young people aged under eighteen in the UK who can be classified as 'young carers'. Overall, across the UK, 2.1 per cent of *all* children have unpaid caring responsibilities towards other family members. Table 1 shows that 6,563 young carers in the UK are aged between five and seven, and that 940 of these provide at least 50 hours of care per week. Another 9,524 young carers are aged eight or nine, and 1,055 of these are providing 50 hours of care or more each week. In total, around 35,000 young carers are of primary school age and nearly 4,000 of these are caring for more than 50 hours per week. These are alarming figures because they show that many children are drawn into a caring role from a very young age and that many of these children will have to provide care work within the home for very long hours each week, with one in six young carers having to care for more than 20 hours per week and almost one in ten caring for more than 50 hours each week. Very young children who are involved in substantial and regular caring are those most likely to experience impaired psychosocial development and risks to their own health and safety and, it could be argued, are those at greatest vulnerability and risk of exploitation. [249]

---

[245] S. Becker, 'Informal Family Carers', in K. Wilson, G. Ruch, M. Lymbery and A. Cooper (eds), *Social Work: An Introduction to Contemporary Practice* (London: Pearson Longman, 2008), pp. 431–60.
[246] L. Buckner and S. Yeandle, *Valuing Carers – Calculating the Value of Unpaid Care* (London: Carers UK, 2007).
[247] S. Becker, 'Global Perspectives on Children as Caregivers: Research and Policy on "Young Carers" in the UK, Australia, the United States and sub-Saharan Africa', *Global Social Policy*, 7:1 (2007), 23–50.
[248] S. Becker, 'Young Carers', in M. Davies (ed.), *The Blackwell Encyclopedia of Social Work* (Oxford: Blackwell, 2000), p. 378.
[249] S. Becker and F. Becker, *Service Needs and Delivery Following the Onset of Caring Amongst Children and Young Adults: Evidenced Based Review* (Cheltenham: Commission for Rural Communities, 2008).

Child's age	1–19 hours	20–49 hours	50+ hours	Total number	Total %
0–4	0	0	0	0	0
5–7	5,015	608	940	6,563	4%
8–9	7,717	752	1,055	9,524	5%
10–11	16,120	1,433	1,615	19,168	11%
12–14	46,267	4,103	3,519	53,889	31%
15	21,024	2,282	1,494	24,800	14%
16–17	49,711	6,935	4,406	61,052	35%
All	145,854	16,113	13,029	174,996	100%
All as %	83%	9%	8%	100%	

Table 1. Number of children who are carers in the UK, by age and hours caring per week.[250]

However, the Census figures are likely to under-represent the true prevalence of children's involvement in unpaid care work because they rely on parents' self reporting their children's caring roles, and the data do not identify or adequately count children in certain circumstances, for example those who may be caring for parents who misuse alcohol or drugs or who have HIV/AIDS or those with a mental health problem. Up to 1.3 million children are affected by parental alcohol problems and there are around 360,000 children under sixteen in the UK who have parents who are problem drug users.[251] This is in addition to the estimated 2.5 million children in the UK who are affected by their parents' mental health problems.[252] Not all of these children, of course, will become young carers. Most will be 'affected' by their parent's conditions, many adversely, but only a small proportion will become caregivers to the degree captured in the definition offered above.[253] The great majority of children living in families where there is illness or disability do not become young carers. Reasons for this include the availability of other family members to care, good quality and reliable health and social care support and services, and adequate money to purchase alternative forms of care, to name but a few.[254]

So why do some children become unpaid caregivers in families where there is illness, disability or some other need for care, support or supervision? The 'trigger' in many of these cases is the nature of the condition itself, its intensity, duration and changing form, and how these are associated with a (changing) need for care. Other reasons include the fact that children are co-resident (they live in the same house as the person who needs help) and they have strong bonds of love and attachment with the person who needs their support. They are also immediately available (and flexible enough) to be able to provide care that is responsive to changing needs. There is some evidence too that certain children can be socialised into these caring roles from an early age.

---

[250] Becker, 'Informal Family Carers', p. 443.

[251] S. Gorin, *Understanding What Children Say: Children's Experiences of Domestic Violence, Parental Substance Misuse and Parental Health Problems* (London: National Children's Bureau for the Joseph Rowntree Foundation, 2004), p. 4.

[252] J. Tunnard, *Parental Mental Health Problems: Messages from Research, Policy and Practice* (Dartington: Research into Practice, 2004), p. 6.

[253] Becker, 'Young Carers', p. 378.

[254] S. Becker, J. Aldridge and C. Dearden, *Young Carers and Their Families* (Oxford: Blackwell, 1998); J. Aldridge and S. Becker, *Children Caring for Parents with Mental Illness: Perspectives of Young Carers, Parents and Professionals* (Bristol: The Policy Press, 2003).

Many children, however, are drawn into caring not through any informed choice but rather out of necessity. Their families lack affordable and good quality support services (which could prevent children from having to undertake care work in the first place), while most disabled parents receive no support in their parenting roles, so they often have to rely on their children for things that they would prefer to do themselves.[255]

Researchers, children's charities and carers' organisations in Britain have been instrumental in bringing knowledge and awareness of these hidden children to wider public attention, and to the notice of policy makers and professionals who work with vulnerable families and children, both in the UK and globally.[256] Many qualitative research studies have provided a uniform picture of the characteristics, experiences and needs of children who undertake unpaid care work within the family.[257] Additionally, three UK-wide surveys of young carers, carried out in 1995, 1997 and 2003, based on contacts with dedicated support projects, confirm the profile generated through qualitative studies.[258] The 1997 survey provides data on 2,303 young carers aged eighteen or under while the 2003 survey provides a profile of 6,178 young carers, the largest survey of its kind. The average age of young carers supported by the projects has remained constant across the surveys at just twelve years. Over half of the young carers are from lone parent families and most are caring for ill or disabled mothers. In the 2003 survey, 56 per cent were girls and 44 per cent were boys; sixteen per cent were from minority ethnic communities (virtually no change since 1997).

Half of the young carers in 2003 were caring for someone with a physical illness or disability; the other half were dealing with adults with mental health problems (29 per cent of young carers), learning difficulties (seventeen per cent) and sensory impairments (three per cent). One in ten children were caring for more than one person. The 2003 study also shows that while almost half of the young people in the cohort are caring for ten hours or less per week, a third of children care for between eleven and twenty hours per week and eighteen per cent care for more than twenty hours per week.

An additional question asked in 2003 concerned the number of years young people had been caring. Data were collected for 4,028 cases (66 per cent of the sample). 36 per cent had been caring for two years or less; 44 per cent for between three and five years; eighteen per cent for six to ten years and three per cent for over ten years. Given that all of the young carers were aged eighteen and under, and that the average age is just twelve, the findings suggest that unpaid care work will be a long-term commitment for many children, and can start at a very early age.

The nature of the care work undertaken by children ranges along a continuum from basic domestic duties to very intimate personal care. In 2003, most young carers (68 per cent), like many children who are not carers, do some level of domestic work within the home.[259] However, where young carers differ substantially from other children is in the extent and nature of the nursing and personal care work that they perform, the amount of time they spend on these caring tasks, and in the significance, and outcomes, of the adult-like responsibilities that they take on for other family members.[260]

---

[255] Becker et al., *Young Carers and Their Families*; M. Wates, *Supporting Disabled Adults in their Parenting Role* (York: Joseph Rowntree Foundation, 2002); Aldridge and Becker, *Children Caring for Parents with Mental Illness*; Becker and Becker, *Service Needs and Delivery*.

[256] Becker, 'Global Perspectives', pp. 23–50.

[257] See, for example, Aldridge and Becker, *Children Caring for Parents with Mental Illness* and R. Evans and S. Becker, *Children Caring for Parents with HIV and AIDS* (Bristol: The Policy Press, 2009).

[258] C. Dearden and S. Becker, *Young Carers: The Facts* (Sutton: Reed Business Publishing, 1995); C. Dearden and S. Becker, *Young Carers in the United Kingdom: A Profile* (London: Carers National Association, 1998); C. Dearden and S. Becker, *Young Carers in the UK: The 2004 Report* (London: Carers UK, 2004).

[259] Dearden and Becker, *Young Carers in the UK*.

[260] J. Warren, 'Young Carers: Conventional or Exaggerated Levels of Involvement in Domestic and Caring

48 per cent of young carers known to dedicated projects in 2003 were involved in general and nursing care work, which included organising and administering medication, injections, and lifting and moving parents.[261] 82 per cent of children provided emotional support and supervision, particularly to parents with severe and enduring mental health problems. One in five provided intimate or personal care work including helping parents with the toilet and bathing. A small proportion, about eleven per cent, also took on childcare responsibilities in addition to their caring roles for other family members. Around seven per cent were involved in other household responsibilities, including translating (where English is not the first language), dealing with professionals, the family's money management and so on (see Table 2).

	1995	1997	2003
Domestic work	65%	72%	68%
General care work	61%	57%	48%
Emotional support and supervision	25%	43%	82%
Intimate care work	23%	21%	18%
Childcare to siblings	11%	7%	11%
Other household responsibilities	10%	29%	7%

Table 2. The percentage of young carers performing various types of care work, 1995, 1997 and 2003.[262]

Much of the research literature on young carers, particularly qualitative studies, have given these children a 'voice' to express their experiences, needs and wants. The research evidence shows that many young carers can experience one or more of the following negative outcomes: restricted opportunities for social networking and for developing peer friendships; limited opportunities for taking part in leisure and other activities; poverty and social exclusion, health problems, emotional difficulties, educational problems, limited horizons and aspirations for the future; a sense of 'stigma by association', particularly where parents have mental health problems or misuse alcohol or drugs, or have AIDS/HIV; a lack of understanding from peers about their lives and circumstances; a fear of what professionals might do to the family if their circumstances are known; the keeping of 'silence' and secrets, again because of the fear of public hostility or punitive professional responses; and significant difficulties in making a successful transition from childhood to adulthood.[263] Research also suggests that some young carers can experience positive outcomes. These can include the development of children's knowledge, understanding, sense of responsibility, maturity, and a range of life, social and care-related skills; children and parents being brought closer together; children's anxieties, concerns and fears being reduced because they have some involvement in and control of the provision and management of care; and children feeling 'included'.[264]

Tasks?', *Children and Society*, 21:2 (2007), 136–46.

[261] Dearden and Becker, *Young Carers in the UK*.

[262] Dearden and Becker, *Young Carers: The Facts*; Dearden and Becker, *Young Carers in the United Kingdom*; Dearden and Becker, *Young Carers in the UK*.

[263] Becker and Becker, *Service Needs and Delivery*; F. Becker and S. Becker, *Young Adult Carers in the UK: Experiences, Needs and Services for Carers Aged 16–24* (London: The Princess Royal Trust for Carers, 2008).

[264] Aldridge and Becker, *Children Caring for Parents with Mental Illness*; C. Dearden and S. Becker, *Growing Up Caring: Vulnerability and Transition to Adulthood – Young Carers' Experiences* (Leicester: Youth Work Trust for the Joseph Rowntree Foundation, 2000); Becker and Becker, *Young Adult Carers in the UK*; Evans and Becker,

Not all young carers will experience physical, emotional, relationship or other psychosocial problems, and many do not experience difficulties in school or elsewhere. While just under a quarter of young carers in the 2003 national survey had educational problems, the majority appeared not to have such difficulties.[265] We cannot be certain at this stage why some young carers do not experience significant difficulties at school or elsewhere in their lives, nor can we be certain that for those who do, that it is their caregiving responsibilities that account for all problems encountered. Research, as yet, has been unable to isolate adequately 'caring' from other key factors that can impact on children's health, well-being and development, in particular factors such as low income, family poverty and other forms of disadvantage. Some have suggested that focusing on children's resilience may offer some explanation here.[266] A resilience perspective helps to explain individual differences in accessing and using support and in coping with stress and adversity. The concept of resilience emphasises people's strengths in coping with adversity and their agency in engaging with protective factors that may help reduce their vulnerability. Protective factors may be associated with personal attributes, family characteristics, or aspects of the wider community. It has been suggested that factors which build resilience among young carers include a good, loving, respectful and reciprocal relationship between parents and children, the capacity within the family and local community network to provide support to the family and children, and the provision of good quality health and social care support which meets the needs of the whole family, to name a few.[267]

In response to the growing research literature on young carers and the campaigning of carers and other organisations, young carers in Britain have been 'recognised' in social policy, legislation and professional practice from the mid-1990s onwards. Various pieces of UK legislation concerning carers, community care and children have provided young carers with a complex (and sometimes contradictory) safety net of 'rights' to assessments, services and support, and in some circumstances cash payments in lieu of social services.[268] However, research studies show that only a small proportion of young carers (around one in five of those surveyed) actually have had a formal assessment of their own needs and their ability to continue to provide care.[269] Moreover, it is estimated that only 35,000 young carers are actually in contact with dedicated young carers projects in Britain. This suggests that the majority of young carers identified in the 2001 Census, and the many more unidentified young carers of parents who misuse alcohol or drugs or who are in other 'stigmatising' situations, are unlikely to access any specialist support services or provision. We know very little about these hidden young carers, although if the average age of young carers is twelve, then there must be a great number of pre-adolescent children coping, or trying to cope in very challenging circumstances.

Young carers' experiences of unpaid care work, and the impacts on their health, well-being, psychosocial development and transition to adulthood, challenges common understandings of what 'childhood' is about in modern Britain. Because young carers

---

Children Caring for Parents with HIV and AIDS.

[265] Dearden and Becker, *Young Carers in the UK.*

[266] T. Newman, '"Young Carers" and Disabled Parents: Time for a Change of Direction?', *Disability and Society*, 17:6 (2009), 613–25; Evans and Becker, *Children Caring for Parents with HIV and AIDS.*

[267] Evans and Becker, *Children Caring for Parents with HIV and AIDS*; Aldridge and Becker, *Children Caring for Parents with Mental Illness.*

[268] See Aldridge and Becker, *Children Caring for Parents with Mental Illness*, pp. 175–98; J. Frank, *Making it Work: Good Practice with Young Carers and Their Families* (London: The Children's Society and The Princess Royal Trust for Carers, 2002); J. Frank and J. McLarnon, *Young Carers, Parents and Their Families: Key Principles of Practice* (London: The Children's Society, 2008).

[269] Dearden and Becker, *Young Carers in the UK.*

are involved in adult-like tasks which require maturity, responsibility and often a high degree of skill, expertise and competency (and which would, if undertaken by adults from outside the family, legitimately attract a fee or salary and specified conditions for work and safety), there is a question as to whether it is appropriate for children to be involved in significant or substantial care work at all, or whether there are appropriate ages at which children might be reasonably expected to take on these responsibilities. So, for example, at what age should children be allowed to meet a parent's needs for help with toileting or other personal assistance, or administer injections, or to carry parents up and down stairs? Could we define an age for these and other tasks or responsibilities? Even if it were possible to determine an 'appropriate' age, would it be desirable to do so?

The key issue here is that for healthy psychosocial development and transitions to 'adulthood', children should gradually increase their responsibilities both within, and outside, the home. Being responsible from an early age for care work, especially intimate and personal care – those labours which would usually be associated with (paid) adult social care work – can compromise a child's health, well-being and development and can lead to a number of negative outcomes that can affect children not only in their 'childhood', but also into later, adult, life.[270] This will be especially the case for very young carers – those children who have started caring at primary school age and who can expect to care for long periods of their 'childhood'. These children would be prohibited from most forms of employment under current guidance on the employment of children.[271] However, caregiving is not defined as employment even though it can be associated with harmful outcomes for children and young people.

In recognition of this, social policy in Britain, and those responsible for its implementation – social care, health and education professionals in particular – have developed policy and practice guidelines which emphasise the importance of taking into account the needs of the whole family (not just parents or children in isolation), and have developed services and responses which try to prevent children from taking on inappropriate caring responsibilities, or which try to reduce their current level of responsibilities.[272] New validated measures will enable policy makers and practitioners working with young carers to assess and identify the extent and nature of caregiving amongst children and both the positive and negative outcomes of caring on children.[273] These tools will also enable a better identification of those tasks and responsibilities which could be viewed as 'exploitative' and 'inappropriate' for children of particular ages, especially to protect the very youngest child carers. To date, children's unpaid caregiving responsibilities within the home, by being defined as 'caring', have hidden their importance and significance as care work. But to define these caring responsibilities as care work, and sometimes as exploitative unpaid care work, poses major challenges to how we understand, and then respond to, children's unpaid labour of love.

· ·

---

[270] J. Frank, C. Tatum and S. Tucker, *On Small Shoulders: Learning from the Experiences of Former Young Carers* (London: The Children's Society, 1999); Dearden and Becker, *Growing Up Caring*; Becker and Becker, *Young Adult Carers in the UK*.

[271] Department for Children, Schools and Families, *Guidance on the Employment of Children* (London: DCSF, 2009).

[272] J. Frank, *Making It Work*; Frank and McLarnon, *Young Carers, Parents and Their Families*.

[273] S. Joseph, S. Becker and F. Becker, *Manual for Measures of Caring Activities and Outcomes for Children and Young People* (London: The Princess Royal Trust for Carers, 2009); S. Joseph, S. Becker, F. Becker and S. Regel, 'Assessment of Caring and its Effects in Young People: Development of the Multidimensional Assessment of Caring Activities Checklist (MACA-YC18) and the Positive and Negative Outcomes of Caring Questionnaire (PANOC-YC20) for Young Carers', *Child: Care, Health and Development*, 35:4 (2009), 510–20.

Taking a long historical view, we can see that child labour in the West has changed significantly over the centuries and in many ways has come a full circle. Principally occurring in the ancient and early medieval world in the home, it then moved out for some five centuries into the farm, workshop and factory, and has now returned into the home again. Saul Becker's piece reminds us forcefully that the problem has not been eliminated and remains an issue, albeit an overlooked one, in today's society. Child carers may well represent the 'unfinished revolution' of child labour reforms. Child labour also remains a problem not just for British children but also for those children on whom the British market depends, in the clothes factories of Asia or the farms in Africa, producing goods for ever-expanding western markets. Globalisation means that it is now hard to ignore their plight or the fact that the west has not solved its own problem of child labour, simply outsourced it to poorer countries. We can see in many of the debates about the contemporary problems of child labour echoes of those that have existed throughout the centuries. What is the difference between work and exploitation? Are children exploited in the home or by their parents? Is earning a wage inherently corrupting to the child or is it something that is innately antithetical to childhood? Different eras have looked at these questions in different ways although it is hard to see any when exploitation as a form of violence against children was completely unknown, including our own. This possibility for violence and abuse is apparent in each of the periods discussed in this chapter; some may provide less evidence than others but as long as there are power differentials between adults and children, the possibility of exploitation, either physical or economic is always a possibility. Legislation may prevent some of the worst abuses but it does not eliminate them.

5. Violent Children, Youth Enforcers, and Juvenile Delinquents

Laurence Brockliss, Alexandra Shepard, Alan Ross, Heather Shore, Jüliane Fürst and Abigail Wills

> Jahmal Mason-Blair
> Had a very good calm flair.
> He was a good friend of mine.
> But killed by a boy who committed a crime.
> He always had a ball to his feet,
> He went past the defenders, with only the goalkeeper to beat.
> R.I.P., rest in paradise
> Killed by a flick knife

Anon. A pupil of Year 5, Kingsmead School, London. Kingmead Eyes, An Exhibition of Children's Photographs and Poems, Museum of Childhood, London, Autumn 2009

[A]ccording to a shocking poll commissioned by Barnardo's ... society casually condemns all children, with more than half the population (54%) thinking that British children are beginning to behave like animals. Research conducted by YouGov shows that the public holds a negative view of all children, despite the vast majority of children making positive contributions to their communities, attending school, taking part in activities and a significant number volunteering.

The findings show:

just under half (49%) of people agree that children are increasingly a danger to each other and adults

43% agree something has to be done to protect us from children

more than a third (35%) of people agree that nowadays it feels like the streets are infested with children

45% of public agree that people refer to children as feral because they behave this way

nearly half of people (49%) disagree with the statement that 'children who get into trouble are often misunderstood and in need of professional help'

'The shame of Britain's intolerance of children'. At http://www.barnardos.org.uk/news_and_events/media_centre/press_releases.htm?ref=42088 (accessed 17 Nov 2003)

As a country, we are rightly concerned to protect children from exploitation in other areas. We need to do the same in relation to violent extremism. As I speak, terrorists are methodically and intentionally targeting young people and children in this country. They are radicalising, indoctrinating and grooming young, vulnerable people to carry out acts of terrorism. This year, we have seen individuals as young as 15 and 16 implicated in terrorist-related activity.

Address to the Society of Editors by the Director General of the Security Service, Jonathan Evans, The Society of Editors' 'A Matter of Trust' conference, Radisson Edwardian Hotel, Manchester, November 5 2007; http://www.mi5.gov.uk/output/intelligence-counter-terrorism-and-trust.html (accessed 20 Mar. 2009)

In February 1993 a two-year-old toddler called James Bulger from Bootle near Liverpool was brutally murdered by two other young boys of ten years old, who had taken him away from a shopping centre. The abduction and murder was followed by a media-induced frenzy of abhorrence. How could two small children have ever perpetrated such an evil act? Although the murder was an exceptional event, it was taken as a figure of the state of the nation's children. Something was terribly wrong.[1] This belief was only confirmed over the coming years as the public was fed a continual series of stories about teenage murderers whose young and old victims' only crime was to be in the wrong place at the wrong time. Often they were simply waiting peaceably for that symbol of civic ordinariness, the bus.[2] The streets of the inner cities (even the suburbs) appeared to be controlled by young hooligans armed with knives and guns, who had no regard for the sanctity of human life. Behind the understandable bewilderment and hand ringing, there was also palpable anger, almost a cry for revenge. Children in the present day had never had it so good. No longer beaten, exploited and ignored, they were cosseted, educated and deferred to in a way that would have been inconceivable even a few decades before. And how had the ingrates responded to the creation of the first child-centred age? They had spat on their deliverers.

Lying behind this sense of betrayal was the equally deeply held belief that the situation was very different even a generation ago: violent children were deemed to be a new contemporary phenomenon. As the present chapter sets out to show, this is a mistaken belief. There is no intention here to play down the violence on the streets of Britain today: it is real enough. It is intended, however, to demonstrate that Europe's young in the past were not goody-two-shoes. By our standards, children until the turn of the twentieth century (and in some respects until even more recently) were frequently ill-used. It mattered little whether their parents and those *in loco parentis* kept within the boundaries of the permissible or loved them deeply (as most would have done). Yet children themselves were never angels. Gregory the Great deceived himself when he declared that the fair-haired young *Angli* displayed in the Roman slave market deserved a holier appellation.[3] In a pre-modern world where violence was a commonplace, the young could be just as violent as adults. Indeed, much of their aggression was licit. For most of history children have made an active contribution to Europe's ecology of violence by which order and hierarchy were traditionally maintained. They were never simply the victims of adult aggression.[4] Unsurprisingly, violence bred violence.

---

[1] http://en.wikipedia.org/wiki/Murder_of_James_Bulger (accessed 6 Apr. 2009); D. Jackson, *Destroying the Baby in Themselves: Why Did the Two Boys Kill James Bulger* (Nottingham: Mushroom, 1995). H. Davis and M. Bourhill, 'Crisis: The Demonization of Children and Young People', in P. Scraton (ed.), *'Childhood' in 'Crisis'?* (London: UCL Press, 1997); B. F. and J. Petley, 'Killing the Age of Innocence: Newspaper Reporting of the Death of James Bulger', in J. Pilcher and S. Wagg (eds), *Thatcher's Children?: Politics, Childhood and Society in the 1980s and 1990s* (London: Falmer Press, 1996); B. Goldson, 'The Demonization of Children: From the Symbolic to the Institutional', in P. Foley, J. Roche and S. Tucker (eds), *Children in Society: Contemporary Theory, Policy and Practice* (Basingstoke: Palgrove, 2001). S. Asquith, 'When Children Kill Children. The Search for Justice', *Childhood*, 3:1 (1996), 99–116; B. Morrison, *As If* (London: Granta Books, 1998).

[2] *E.g.*, the eighteen-year-old black teenager, Stephen Lawrence, murdered in south-east London in April 1993 only a few months after James Bulger: http://en.wikipedia.org/wiki/Stephen_Lawrence (accessed 5 Apr. 2009). For a recent study of the impact of the murder and the subsequent enquiry into police handling of the case, which found the Metropolitan Police guilty of 'institutionalised' racism, see S. Cottle, *The Racist Murder of Stephen Lawrence: Media Performance and Public Transformation* (Westport: Praeger, 2004)

[3] Venerable Bede, *Historia Ecclesiastica Gentis Anglorum*, bk. II, ch. I: see *Baedae Opera Historica*, vol. 1, (Cambridge: Harvard University Press, 1962), p. 200.

[4] It is now axiomatic within childhood studies that children are not passive victims but active agents: A. James, C. Jenks and A. Prout, *Theorizing Childhood* (Cambridge: Polity Press, 1998). Perhaps more pertinently there is also a greater understanding of the many roles they play in relation to violence, including those of perpetrator, colluder or enabler, as well as victim. For a summary of this literature see H. Montgomery, 'Children and Violence', in H. Montgomery, M. Woodhead and R. Burr (eds), *Changing Childhoods: Global*

The chapter begins with an account of the violence that children in the pre-modern era could show to adults. Children may have largely accepted the child-rearing culture in which they were raised (they knew no other) but they did not necessarily meekly submit to violence and exploitation. Presumably some children in the past, as is the case today, were much harder to control and discipline than others and kicked against the pricks. Parents and carers have always been aware that their charges have different temperaments, whether this has been attributed to demonic possession, the planetary conjunction that they were born under, environmental influences *à la* Locke, or, more recently, genetic make-up. More importantly, pre-modern children appear to have had a keen sense of justice; they were aware when adults crossed unwritten boundaries and frequently fought back if they thought their rights had been infringed. Before 1850 children seem to have little compunction about physically attacking and often harming quite badly those looking after their upbringing.

Understandably, little is known about the violence endured by parents once children were beyond infancy. Toddler temper tantrums, if frowned upon, were expected and socially acceptable, and could thus be reported. We saw in an earlier chapter that at the start of the seventeenth century the young Louis XIII, was whipped frequently for rudeness.[5] When he displayed precocious manly prowess, however, by attacking his nurse with a pike, he appears to have received no punishment at all. His doctor, Héroard, merely recorded the incident; his action was not seen as socially threatening.[6] Assaults by grown up children were a different matter. In a pre-modern Christian world that placed such an emphasis on 'honouring' one's father and mother, no adult was likely to admit publicly that he (or she) had been attacked by a teenage child. Equally children in later life were unlikely to own up to the fact. Among French autobiographies, for instance, we know of only one instance where a son admitted to turning on his father as a teenager. This was the Parisian Jacques-Louis Ménétra, whose assault on his abusive glazier father we have also already encountered.[7]

Where child on adult violence is most visible is in the pre-modern classroom. Teachers today are occasionally confronted with violent pupils, but before 1850 they periodically had to face full-scale riots. The rioters too were not the sons of peasants and artisans but the sons of the socially respectable, for the worst instances of violence occurred in the colleges and grammar schools. In early modern Europe there were two types of school: elementary schools where the sons of the poor learnt to read and write, and secondary schools, where the sons of the elite went to study Latin and Greek, and in some countries, the different parts of philosophy.[8] Children could be disruptive in the elementary schools – Ménétra recalls that he once locked the master of his Paris parish school in his room rather than suffer corporal punishment[9]– but it was in the secondary schools that the major rioting occurred. Often sparked off by the smallest of incidents, there can be no better illustration of the readiness of the pre-modern young to meet perceived injustice with physical force.

and Local (Chichester: John Wiley, 2003).

[5] See Ch. 3, pp. 119, 124–25.

[6] Jean Héroard, *Journal sur l'enfance et la jeunesse de Louis* XIII, ed. E. Soulié and E. de Barthélemy (2 vols; Paris: Firmin Didot, 1868), i. 241 (9 Jan. 1607). He was merely told to make peace and to promise 'de ne la battre plus'.

[7] See Ch. 3, p. 123.

[8] For a general introduction, see R. A. Houston, *Literacy in Early Modern Europe. Culture and Education 1500–1800* (London and New York: Longman, 1988), ch. 2.

[9] Jacques-Louis Ménétra, *Journal de ma vie*, ed. D. Roche (Paris: Albin Michel, 1982), p. 44.

Pupil Violence in the French Classroom 1600–1850

Laurence Brockliss

Most of France's 300 secondary schools during the Ancien Régime were in the hands of the regular orders, especially the Jesuits.[10] In early modern Europe, Jesuit education undoubtedly represented best practice: though discipline was strict, the Society had developed a sophisticated system of emulation in the form of continual tests and quizzes that encouraged attention and assiduity. None the less, the Jesuits' French schools were frequently disrupted by riots in the first half of the seventeenth century. Boys assaulted masters, organised mass strikes where pupils were physically intimidated from entering the school, and occasionally took up arms. The worst incident seems to have occurred at La Flèche in Touraine. La Flèche was the jewel in the Order's crown. Opened at the beginning of the seventeenth century as a school for the sons of nobles in particular, it boasted a number of famous alumni in its early years including Descartes. But its social cachet did not make its pupils any more compliant. At the time of the Lenten carnival in 1646 tension was running high because a number of older pupils in the higher classes had been publicly whipped. Boys living outside the college seem to have planned to get their own back by dressing one of their number as a girl and secretly infiltrating him into the building. Presumably, the aim was to discredit the Jesuits by informing the local authority that the fathers were harbouring a woman. But the plan backfired when the Jesuits discovered and unmasked the intruder and promptly incarcerated him. Infuriated by the failure of their plot, the *externes* sought weapons in the town (easy to do since many pupils wore swords outside school) and picketed all the entrances to the college over night. The next morning the mob broke into the college and prevented all the boarders from attending classes when the bell for lessons was tolled. At the point the Jesuits retaliated, armed their servants with muskets, and ordered them to clear the courtyard. Confronted with firepower, the rebels thought prudence the better part of valour and withdrew but not before one firebrand had been badly wounded. Less mindful of the danger than his colleagues, he charged the guns and received a ball in his thigh.[11]

Collective acts of violence seem to have subsided from the second half of the seventeenth century. Either boys came to accept less grudgingly the boring routine and discipline of the college as elite society more completely internalised the puritanical values of the Counter-Reformation and learnt self control, or eighteenth-century masters were better at tempering severity with mercy.[12] But French *collégiens* continued

---

[10] For an overview, see R. Chartier, M. M. Compère and D. Julia, *L'education en France du XVIe au XVIIIe siècle* (Paris: SEDES, 1976), chs 5–6. On the age of pupils in Jesuit colleges, see P. Ariès, *Centuries of Childhood* (Harmondsworth: Penguin, 1962), ch. 9. For pupils' ages and lengths of stay in the eighteenth-century college, see W. Frijhoff and D. Julia, *Ecole et société dans la France d'Ancien Régime* (Paris: Armand Colin, 1975).

[11] For this and other examples: Ariès, *Centuries of Childhood*, pp. 302–05; J. de Viguerie, *L'Institution des enfants. L'Education en France 16e–18e siècles* (Paris: Calmann-Lévy, 1978), pp. 246–47; J. de Viguerie, *Une oeuvre d'éducation sous l'Ancien Régime: Les pères de la Doctrine Chrétienne en France et en Italie, 1592–1792* (Paris: Editions de la Nouvelle Aurora, 1976), p. 508; L. W. B. Brockliss, 'Contenir et prévenir la violence. La discipline universitaire et scolaire sous l'Ancien Régime (XVII–XVIII siècles)', *Histoire de l'Education*, 118 (2008), 51–66.

[12] On the changing behavioural norms of seventeenth-century France, see esp. N. Elias, *The Court Society*, English trans (New York: Pantheon Books, 1983).

to be disruptive in various ways if they felt an injustice had been done. Petty acts of vandalism were commonplace, as at Nantes in 1788 where pupils in the third class at the college run by the Oratorians (another regular order) protested by throwing stones at the school's windows when they felt one of their peer group had been wrongly punished.[13] Those with more power, moreover, continued to organise strikes, doubtless in imitation of France's high courts, the parlements. We have encountered in an earlier chapter how the popular Jean François Marmontel persuaded his peers in the rhetoric class at the Jesuits' Mauriac college to boycott lessons in the 1730s.[14] Such strikes though were normally token gestures; boys were not usually intimidated by their peers and the strikes seldom got out of hand.[15]

Throughout the seventeenth and eighteenth centuries, there must also have been innumerable cases of individual insubordination in the French colleges that have gone unrecorded. Usually pupils who refused to accept chastisement would be expelled, thereby doubtless bringing dishonour on the miscreant's family.[16] But by the end of the Ancien Régime times were changing and there are signs that disobedient could live to fight another day, at least if they were socially prominent. In 1776 the young François-René, Vicomte de Chateaubriand (1768–1848), was sent as a boarder to the Breton collège de Dol. According to his memoirs, the future Romantic was a hardy rule breaker, who got hold of unexpiated classical texts and gained a sexual thrill from reading Massillon's denunciation of the passions under the bed clothes. On a trip to the countryside with his classmates, he was caught stealing birds' eggs and threatened with a whipping. On returning to school, he was sent to the *correcteur* but refused to accept the punishment. In his case, it was not a question of his age – he was still in a lower class – but of aristocratic *hauteur*: he did not wish to be dishonoured. Chateaubriand begged to be given extra homework or put on bread and water instead. The master refused; Chateaubriand kicked him in the shin; the master chased him round the room until a truce was called and the young blood agreed to go to the principal. Doubtless mindful of who Chateaubriand's father was and the possibility of losing fees, the principal graciously let the boy off, once he had acknowledged his fault.[17]

Widespread collective disruption came back to the French classroom in the first half of the nineteenth century. As we have seen, the Napoleonic regime abolished corporal punishment in the state-run *lycées* and colleges that replaced the secondary schools of the Ancien Régime.[18] The new schools, however, were run like military camps and the discipline was harsh. As fathers in elite households appear to have been adopting a more gentle approach to child rearing, there was a consequent disparity between home and school life that led to frequent mutinies. These, too, often had a political colour. The French elite in the era of the Restoration monarchy (1815–48) was divided between Catholics and secularists, and conservatives and liberals, and the boys frequently sided with forces opposed to the government of the day. In the 1820s, when the riots were

[13] Archives municipales de Nantes, GG 661, no pagination, report of 26 Feb.

[14] See above, Ch. 3, p. 126. The parlements had to register royal edicts before they could become law. On several occasions in the eighteenth century, they quarrelled with the crown and declared a strike when they did not get their way.

[15] For violence generally in the eighteenth-century classroom, see P. Marchard, 'La Violence dans les collèges du XVIIIe siècle', *Histoire de l'Education*, 118 (2008), 67–82.

[16] Cf. *Ratio Studiorum. Plan raisonné et institution des études dans la Compagnie de Jésus*, French–Latin edn (Belin: Paris, 1997), pp. 144–45. At the Caen Jesuit college, one or two pupils per class were expelled a year; see, *e.g.*, reports on students 1692: Bibliothèque Nationale, Paris, MS Latin 10991, f. 22.

[17] François-René-Auguste de Chateaubriand, *Mémoires de ma vie*, ed. J. M. Gautier (Geneva: Droz, 1976), pp. 80–84. Jean-Baptiste Massillon (1663–1742) was a great court preacher.

[18] See Ch. 3, p. 146.

particularly frequent, boarding pupils showed their dislike for the catholicising policies of Charles X (r. 1824–30) by ostentatiously subverting the religious services that they had to attend every day. The mutinies took a predictable form. Part of the school would be occupied at night (when it was difficult for the teachers to judge the extent of the disorder) and serious material damage would be done to the fabric in building barricades. But the pupils seldom had weapons (no longer so readily available as two centuries before) and rarely would harm be done to individuals, though masters were occasionally taken hostage. Similarly, though the sit-ins were frequently ended violently – the college authorities would call in the police, the national guard, and even troops of the line – there are no reports that mutineers were sabred or bayoneted. The *collégiens* were the governing class of the future and were not treated with the brutality accorded to striking artisans in the period. The perpetrators were always summarily expelled, but the punishment had limited effect: their cause was taken up by their families and powerful friends, and they were usually either readmitted or allowed to move to another school.[19]

Peace would finally be established in the French classroom only in the 1860s. Insurrections occurred at the prestigious Paris *lycée* Louis-le-Grand in 1869 and 1883, but they were the exceptional throw-backs to an earlier age.[20] Once established, that peace would last for a century, until it would be shattered again in 1968, when a new generation of politicised *lycéens* and *lycéennes* showed solidarity with the militant students and workers and ushered in a new cycle of disruption that is still with us. Apart from the recent agitation by some Muslim pupils over the right to wear the *foulard,* this has had little to do with discipline. The contemporary areas of conflict appear to be the curriculum and the examination system: in a democratic age, where the state's secondary schools are no longer monopolised by the elite, the quarrel is no longer over the *lycée* as a site of surveillance, but the *lycée* as the corner stone of equal opportunity and a platform for social mobility.[21]

There is no reason to suppose that the French experience in the pre-modern era was not mirrored in other countries. In fact, in Protestant England where there were no regular orders and no move towards state regulation of education before the end of the period under review, the secondary schools, whether run by lay or clerical schoolmasters, were probably more violent, and collective insubordination was similarly long-lasting. Riots with resultant damage to property if not persons were just as commonplace on this side of the Channel in the early nineteenth century, especially in the major public schools. Eton was particularly mutinous, the last riot occurring in 1832, which led to the flogging of 80 boys.[22] England and Scotland, too, were plagued

---

[19] J.-C. Caron, 'Révoltes collégiens, élites juvéniles et société post-Révolutionnaire (1815–48), *Histoire de l'Éducation,* 118 (2008), 83–107.

[20] The chief riots at Louis-le-Grand in the nineteenth century are listed in G. Dupont-Ferrier, *Du Collège de Clermont au Lycée Louis-le-Grand* (1563–1920): *la vie quotidienne d'un collège parisien pendant plus de trois cent cinquante ans* (3 vols; Paris: E. de Boccard, 1921–25), ii. 491–503. Until 1762 Louis-le-Grand (called after Louis XIV) was the Jesuits' Paris college.

[21] French *lycées* are more politicised than other European secondary schools because the most prestigious house *classes préparatoires,* where gifted pupils between the ages of eighteen and twenty study for the entrance exams of the *grandes écoles,* France's elite higher educational establishments that are the door to all the best jobs. A number of these elite schools were set up by Napoleon and have always had a higher status than the universities: see D. Julia *et al., Atlas de la Révolution Française. 2. L'Enseignement 1760–1815* (Paris: Editions de l'Ecole des Hautes Etudes en Sciences Sociales, 1987), pp. 64–70.

[22] Ariès, *Centuries of Childhood,* pp. 305–6; T. Card, *Eton Established. A History from 1440 to 1860* (London: John Murray, 2001), pp. 114–17; R. Cutance (ed.), *Winchester College. Sixth Century Essays* (Oxford: Oxford University Press, 1982), pp. 356–68, 362–65 and 368–72; P. M. Thornton, *Harrow School and its Surroundings* (London: William Allen, 1885), pp. 219–20.

by the widespread ritual of 'barring-out', which appears to have been seldom used in France. From at least the mid-sixteenth century, pupils in many schools north of the Trent would lock the master out and refuse to open the door until he agreed to grant an exceptional holiday or, over the Christmas period, not to punish malefactors.

'Barring-out' became a ritual colluded in by the teachers: the boys would draw up a petition (in much the same way as people would petition parliament) and the master would hand over a written reply. In Hull in 1662 the document was approved by the mayor and aldermen of the town. Usually, the worst that would happen would be that windows got broken. But 'barring out' sometimes became confrontational and violent. In Edinburgh in the late sixteenth century, where the kirk was attempting to abolish Christmas as a holiday, the boys would annually lock themselves in the high school, armed to the teeth. In 1595 when the authorities stormed the building, one of the officials was shot dead. Not surprisingly, puritanical officialdom took a dim view of the practice, and from the 1660s it was outlawed in many places. But the custom continued in village schools until the 1870 education act.[23]

Only thereafter did schools in Britain become relative havens of peace. And in Britain's case peace has survived. Secondary schools today may have many disruptive pupils, but they do not experience strikes and lock-outs. In modern Britain, school rebellion is the fantasy of artists, film-makers and song-writers. Even then it generally comes harmlessly packaged as fun. 1968 brought the British public Lindsay Anderson's *If*, which ends with the massacre of teachers and parents as they emerge from the chapel on Founder's Day. Eleven years later *Pink Floyd* went to the top of the charts with the protest song 'Another Brick in the Wall', purportedly a comment on their own school experiences.[24] Most British films about schoolchildren in revolt however have no political edge but are merely a good romp: witness the countless films of the derring-do of the terrible girls of St Trinian's.[25]

· ·

While pre-modern children might fight back and meet violence with violence, venting their spleen on their elders was probably a relatively uncommon occurrence. Where the violence was not ritualised – an example of the many instances in an only slowly changing hierarchical and agrarian society where tension was released by allowing the world to be turned upside down for a few days – it was sporadic and unpredictable, normally a response to a rag that failed or a peculiarly acute provocation.[26] This did not mean, though, that most children most of the time were pent-up volcanoes about to explode, for boys especially continually used up their anger and resentment on each other. Pre-modern society, by our own expectations, was not just violent towards children. While increasingly expressing a desire to stamp down on interpersonal violence and apparently succeeding by the eighteenth century to some degree, the early modern state and its ally the church continued to wink at many acts

---

[23] K. Thomas, *Rule and Misrule in the Schools of Early Modern England* (Stenton Lecture, 1975; Reading: University of Reading, 1976), pp. 21–31.

[24] For the background to the song and its effect on pupils, see: http://news.bbc.co.uk/1/hi/magazine/7021797. stm (accessed 30 Mar. 2009).

[25] The St Trinian's films (six to date) are based on the creation of the cartoonist Ronald Searle. The first film was made in 1954: see http://en.wikipedia.org/wiki/St_Trinian's_(film) (accessed 10 Nov. 2009). There was an attempt in 1968 to politicise school children in London but with limited success.

[26] There are instances where youths tested each other's fearlessness by daring one of their number to murder a random passer-by as in Munich in 1513: see N. Schindler, 'Guardians of Disorder. Rituals of Youthful Culture at the Dawn of the Modern Age', in G. Levi and J.-C. Schmitt (eds), *A History of Young People. Ancient and Medieval Rites of Passage*, trans. C. Naish (London: Belknapp Press, 1997), p. 275.

of aggression, especially by the upper orders: wife-beating, the physical abuse of servants and employees, duelling, and so on.[27] The state, too, by the public treatment meted out to offenders against its laws – whipping and branding beggars, hanging malefactors for trivial crimes, subjecting traitors to horrific punishments and exposing their quartered remains until they rotted away – not only reinforced the idea that violence was a legitimate form of redress but gave it a value as entertainment. Children before the nineteenth century were brought up in a world where violence (like death) was all around and not hidden from them.[28] Understandably, teenagers, not just young boys, mimicked adult behaviour in their own relations and chose to settle their peer group quarrels by violence.

As with violence towards adults, peer-group violence has left a limited historical record. That for teenagers, regardless of social background, fighting was a part of everyday life is evident once again from the information that has survived about boys at secondary school and university students. On the continent, only a small proportion of those in secondary and higher education boarded. If they did not live at home, they resided in private lodgings in town even in their early teens, and were regularly free from direct adult authority.[29] In Ancien Régime France it also proved impossible to stop the majority sporting swords despite the flurry of edicts banning the practice – hence the ease with which the *externes* of La Flèche armed themselves in 1646.[30] The result was that the fights were often lethal, and thereby came to the attention of the local magistrate and the college or university authorities.

In the first half of the seventeenth century, French *collégiens* were continually fighting formal duels. At Aix in the same year as the riot at La Flèche, the Jesuits lost three of their pupils in this manner.

> One of our pupils, a nobleman from Sisteron and a metaphysician [philosophy student] was killed in a duel without having the opportunity to show any sign of contrition. There were four of them who fought, two of whom were not students. It was nine o'clock in the morning, and they had spent the night together in the Carthusians' barn, in order to be able to fight more conveniently afterwards. A few months before, another pupil in the third class had been killed in the same way by a surgeon and had died just as un-Christian a death.[31]

Similar misguided acts of bravery continued in the second half of the seventeenth century but largely died out in the reign of Louis XIV as duelling no longer found favour at court.[32] However, mock duels were fought by schoolboys until the end of the Ancien Régime, if Chateaubriand's childhood experiences were typical. Having already gained a reputation as a street thug in Saint Malo before he went to college, he was soon orchestrating fights and taking part. While at the college at Rennes in the early 1780s, frequent fights were held in the local Benedictine gardens. 'We used a mathematical compass at the end of a cane,

---

[27] On declining rates of homicide in eighteenth-century England, see L. Stone, 'Interpersonal Violence in English Society, 1300–1980', *Past and Present*, 101:1 (1983), 22–33.

[28] The death penalty was intentionally carried out in public as a violent and horrifying spectacle: see esp. M. Foucault, *Surveiller et punir. Naissance de la prison* (Paris: Gallimard, 1975), pt. 1.

[29] The Jesuits did organise some sort of surveillance of *externes* at their Mauriac college: see Marmontel, *Mémoires*, i. 9–10.

[30] Thirteen edicts were issued against bearing arms at Bordeaux, 1636–1740; twelve at Toulouse 1603–1739: R. Chartier *et al. Education en France*, pp. 283–4. Many other towns issued similar edicts; *e.g.*, Dijon 1675; Bourges 1680; Paris 1681; and Rennes, 1767: Ariès, *Centuries of Childhood*, p. 303; Brockliss, 'Contenir et prévenir la violence', p. 62, fn. 30; Bibliothèque Nationale MS français 21735, fs 105–38.

[31] Cited in Ariès, *Centuries of Childhood* , p. 307 (from the Aix college 'Annales').

[32] It was under attack from the late sixteenth century: see F. Billacois, *Le Duel dans la société française des XVIe–XVIIe siècles: Essai de psychosociologie historique* (Paris: EHESS, 1986). The edicts against duelling do not seem to have specifically been extended to universities: see a 1615 pamphlet by one Maran: Bibliothèque Nationale MS français 9948, f. 189ff.

or we wrestled more or less dangerously according to the gravity of the challenge'.[33] Girls could be equally pugnacious. On one occasion at Angers in the eighteenth century, the girls of the local Ursuline convent finally cracked under the continual taunts of the boys of the neighbouring Oratorian college. They called them out and gave the juvenile male chauvinists a sound thrashing.[34]

Yet if formal bouts of honour became less murderous as time went on, there were plenty of unpremeditated clashes with fellow scholars and other youth that could end in disaster, as the elder boys, mainly law students, took advantage of the new leisure facilities of the eighteenth century and took to frequenting billiard halls, bars and coffee houses. The small university town of Cahors played host to numerous brawls in the first half of the eighteenth century. In February 1720 a student died during a quarrel in a tavern involving logicians and theology students; in 1728 another was murdered after an all night student pub crawl; while in 1737 a bar tender was stabbed by a drunken scholar who was condemned to death in his absence.[35] Students who felt their group honour was at stake were quick to anger. In Paris in 1557 after a Breton student had been killed by monk from Saint-Germain-des-Prés, the students of the capital's university stormed the abbey and then rampaged through the city: 200 troops had to be brought in to clear their barricades. In 1740 at Toulouse a full scale riot broke out after a student was ejected from the theatre for whistling at a performance and annoying the attending magistrates. According to contemporary estimates 1,500 students paraded on the streets, carrying swords and firearms. When the magistrates appeared on the scene backed up by troops, the students threw stones, and when a number were arrested, they declared a strike and organised another *manifestation* for the following day.[36]

That adolescence in early modern France was a constant round of fisticuffs is confirmed by the one autobiography of an artisan which has so far been discovered in this period. Jacques-Louis Ménétra in his late teens escaped the clutches of his father and went on an extended *tour de France* to perfect his trade, as did other journeymen. Wherever he went he was involved in fights, often over his making advances to local girls.[37] What early modern French memoirs, court records and the archives of educational institutions do not reveal so clearly is the extent to which more mundane and muted forms of child on child violence existed, especially what we today would disown as bullying.[38] Such intimidation, it can be presumed, must have been commonplace. By our definition of the term, most children in the early modern era were bullied in some fashion by adults. As it is now generally accepted that bullying begets bullying, it seems plausible to conclude that early modern children would have bullied others as soon as they had the power, or, if lacking in strength and status, that they would have imposed their limited authority on animals, as Hogarth's *First Stage of Cruelty* (1750/1) so graphically reminds us.[39] (See Figure 25).

---

[33] Chateaubriand, *Mémoires de ma vie*, p. 94.

[34] J. Maillard, *L'Oratoire à Angers aux XVIIe et XVIIIe siècles* (Paris: Klincksieck, 1975), p. 77.

[35] P. Ferté, *L'Université de Cahors au XVIIIe siècle (1700–51): Le coma universitaire au Siècle des Lumières* (Toulouse: Fournie, 1974), pp. 209–21.

[36] J. B. L. Crévier, *Histoire de l'Université de Paris depuis son origine jusqu'en l'année 1600* (7 vols; Paris: Desaint & Saillant, 1761), vi. 29–49; F. Dumas, 'Une émeute d'étudiants à Toulouse en 1740', *Revue des Pyrénées*, 19 (1907), 29–43. Town-gown riots, it should be said, were much more murderous in the late middle ages: see H. Rashdall, *The Universities of Europe in the Middle Ages*, ed. F. M. Powicke and A. B. Emden, vol. 1 (Oxford: Oxford University Press, 1936), pp. 294–95 and 334–36 (on the riots of 1200 and 1229).

[37] *E.g.* Ménétra, *Journal de ma vie*, p. 65.

[38] Bullying only became a major concern in Britain in the 1990s; for a call for it to be moved up the agenda, see D. Tattum and D. Lane (eds), *Bullying in Schools* (Stoke-on-Trent: Trentham, 1989). Earlier interest had been taken in Scandinavia: see D. Olweus, *Bullying at School: What We Know and What We Can Do* (Oxford: Blackwell, 1993).

[39] William Hogarth (1697–1764) was one of the first to take issue with the way human beings – children and adults – treated other living creatures. For an idea of what children did to animals in early modern England,

Certainly there is evidence that well-to-do youths in early modern France bullied their social inferiors. In 1725, for instance, three students of Cahors university were indicted for seeking revenge on a group of servant girls, washing clothes in the Lot, who repulsed their advances. They dragged them by the hair, tore their clothes, pitched them and their washing into the river, and would have raped one of the girls 'had she not been promptly saved'.[40] However, the French educational records are silent about seniors imposing their will on or gratuitously beating up juniors of the same social class. Presumably this reflects the fact that in the early modern era this abuse of power was not seen as reprehensible. Rather it was perceived as a part of growing up and arguably served as a useful safety valve. Licit bullying or intimidation allowed older boys (and girls) to exercise a form of adult authority while still legally children. It gave them the power to assist adults in initiating the young into a hierarchical, authoritarian and hard-knocks society, arguably thereby making their own subject status easier to cope with. This becomes clear, if we turn the focus of attention to the public schools and universities of England. Here from the second quarter of the nineteenth century bullying became for the first time a subject of concern. Yet while some forms of bullying were declared a moral evil, others, in our modern understanding of the term, were given official sanction and seen as legitimate instruments of socialisation.[41]

Bullying in English Schools and Universities

Laurence Brockliss

Thomas Hughes's *Tom Brown's Schooldays* (1857) is a novel about life at Rugby school in the mid-1830s, which devotes many of its early pages to the bullying of younger boys by a wealthy and indolent fifth former called Flashman. Tom Brown enters Rugby aged eleven. Flashman and his cronies expect younger boys to fag for them at will and strike and verbally abuse any who fail to provide the level of service and respect to which they feel entitled. On one occasion this leads to the eponymous hero being badly injured. Every Saturday the boys of School House are given a shilling as pocket money but on the eve of the Derby Flashman commandeers the lump sum before it is divided to be the pool for a lottery. The boys of the house line up in the hall to draw a ticket and the eponymous hero of the novel pulls the favourite. Flashman immediately demands that Brown sell him the ticket for 5 shillings or face the consequences. Brown refuses and Flashman gets the crowd on his side by accusing the younger boy of ingratitude. He and his friends who have taken the trouble of organising the lottery draw blanks, but a pip-squeak in the lower fourth walks off with the best ticket. Flashman takes his revenge.

---

see K. Thomas, *Man and the Natural World* (Harmondsworth: Penguin, 1984), pp. 147–48. For the growing compassion for animals in early modern England, *ibid.*, ch. 4, *passim*.

[40] Ferté, *Cahors*, pp. 212–13.

[41] For earlier uses of the term 'bully', see OED, *sub verbo*. The campaign to end cruelty to animals had begun a little earlier. The RSPCA was founded in the 1820s. For an early pamphlet, see Sarah Trimmer, *Fabulous histories designed for the instruction of children respecting their treatment of animals* (1786), which was published until the early twentieth century.

"Very well, then, let's roast him, " cried Flashman, and catches hold of Tom by the collar: one or two boys hesitate, but the rest join in. ... Tom is dragged along struggling. His shoulders are pushed against the mantle piece, and he is held by main force before the fire, Flashman drawing his trousers tight by way of extra torture... "Will you sell now for ten shillings?" says one boy who is relenting.

Tom only answers by groans and struggles.

"I say, Flashey, he has had enough," says the same boy, dropping the arm he holds.

"No, no, another turn'll do it," answers Flashman. But poor Tom is done already, turns deadly pale, and his head falls forward on his breast. ...[42]

Hughes had been at Rugby himself in the late 1830s and there is no reason to doubt the authenticity of the incident. Indeed, it is quite clear from the many surviving reminiscences of old boys of the major public schools of England in the late eighteenth and first part of the nineteenth century that roasting and other equally arbitrary, bizarre and painful punishments were a commonplace.[43] Until the middle of the nineteenth century, it would appear that the schools were run, not by the teachers who were too few or too incompetent, but by the elder boys who were given licence to treat the younger boys as virtual slaves. Unsupervised fagging existed in all the big schools, and as in any slave society, whether a junior boy was well-treated or brutalised by his 'master' was a matter of luck. Schools were societies, too, where even the moment of entry was marked with pain and humiliation, for every new boy was initiated into the club by some barbarous ritual dreamt up by his fellow pupils.[44]

What was notable about *Tom Brown's Schooldays* was that it graphically and for the first time in a novel depicted a shift that was happening in British educational thought. At the turn of the eighteenth century the sadism of schoolboys would not have been an issue. By the middle of the nineteenth century, the behaviour of the Flashmans of this world was no longer thought acceptable in liberal circles, and older boys who used their age and power to coerce youngsters were now being called 'bullies'.[45] Hughes's account of Tom's roasting is a crucifixion scene. On the other hand Hughes's novel emphasises that the shift was not total. He finds nothing wrong in fagging *per se*, nor in the fact that boys in the sixth form can cuff or thrash their juniors when they fail to complete the tasks that they have been given quickly or adequately. Tom Brown may have been ill-treated by bullies (and this was wrong) but he is also a bad fag who is deservedly 'licked' for spoiling a good pair of candlesticks.[46] Nor did Hughes expect the bullied to 'tell' on their tormentors. This was against the school and the Victorian manly code. The bullied had to stick up for themselves. In *Oliver Twist*, Oliver gains the strength to run-away from the undertaker to whom he has been apprenticed by first asserting his manhood through worsting his tormentor, the older and bigger Noah Claypole, in a fight. (See Figure 26). So Tom and his friend East escape the clutches of Flashman by finding the courage to set upon him and beating him up.[47] '[H]e never laid a finger on them again'. But Flashman is only expelled when he gets drunk once

---

[42] Thomas Hughes, *Tom Brown's Schooldays* (Oxford: Oxford University Press, 2008), pp. 183–84.

[43] For a late eighteenth-century reference to roasting at Rugby, see W. L. Collins, *The Public Schools* (Edinburgh: William Blackwood and Sons, 1867), p. 359.

[44] J. Chandos, *Boys Together. English Public Schools 1800–1864* (Oxford: Oxford University Press, 1984), chs 4 and 5.

[45] The term was used frequently in the novel. The boys themselves were complaining. Milnes Gaskell, sent to Eton at the age of thirteen during the reign of John 'Flogger' Keate (1773–1852), was bullied immediately and wrote daily letters to his mother complaining: Card, *Eton Established*, pp. 123–25.

[46] Hughes, *Tom Brown's Schooldays*, pp. 195–98.

[47] The novel is a *Bildungsroman* in which Tom finally learns Christian responsibility through mentoring the fragile new boy, Arthur.

too often and has to be carried back to Rugby in a litter.[48] We are a long way from our modern official views on bullying.[49]

In both respects Hughes's was prescient. The leading opponent of the reign of schoolboy terror in the English public school was Thomas Arnold, the headmaster of Rugby when both Hughes and the fictional Tom attended the school. Arnold dreamt of turning Rugby into a new type of school that taught a gentler form of manliness consistent with Christian charity. He found it difficult to end the moral evils that he found at the school, however, as *Tom Brown's Schooldays* reveals, and in the end was thwarted. Instead, he and other liberal heads were forced to tame the system of misrule rather than abolish it. In the second half of the nineteenth century, discipline outside of the public-school classroom continued to be largely left in the hands of the elder boys and the juniors continued to labour as fags. But the appointment of carefully selected prefects and better oversight by the headmaster removed much of the arbitrariness of the system, if not its brutality.[50] Middle-class parents who began to send their sons to the public-schools in droves seem to have accepted the compromise, and the practice was adopted throughout the system.[51] The right of prefects to cane younger boys was still broadly accepted on the eve of the First World War, despite frequent reports of abuse of the rod.[52] And elder boys continued to be given the power to beat younger ones until the recent past. The caning given in the school gymnasium to the rebellious fifth formers by the head prefect in *If* still touched a chord with many young men straight out of public school in 1968.[53]

The history of bullying in English schools before the late eighteenth century, however, is a closed book. How early even the fagging system developed in the leading public schools is unknown: the word 'fag' to mean a schoolboy servant can only be traced to 1768.[54] The school 'fag' though does bear some resemblance to the late sixteenth

---

[48] *Ibid.*, pp. 190–94. In the recent film of *Tom Brown's Schooldays* (2005; directed by Dave Moore), Tom fights Flashman on his own and the fight is based on Tom's pugilistic encounter with the Slogger at the end of the novel (pt. ii, ch. 5). Flashman is also sent down for impregnating a servant girl: there is no sex in the novel.

[49] The public's views may be different. In a very different society admittedly – an American prison – fighting back, even murdering a bully, is seen positively in the extremely popular film *The Shawshank Redemption* (1994; dir. Frank Darabont). There remains, too, an ambivalence towards bullying itself; how otherwise could George MacDonald Fraser have written a series of best sellers about the fictional military exploits of the adult Flashman, still the unrepentant cad and a bully.

[50] Thomas Arnold, 'The Discipline of Public Schools', in T. Arnold *Miscellaneous Works* (London: B. Fellowes, 1845), p. 361ff. For Arnold at Rugby, see M. McCrum, *Thomas Arnold. Headmaster. A Reassessment* (Oxford: Oxford University Press, 1989). Bullying (in the Victorian sense) still continued, of course: cf. the travails under which Thomas Field (1855–1936), later Warden of Radley, laboured at King's College Canterbury; in the late 1860s: he claimed to have been scorched; see H. S. Goodrich, *Thomas Field DD* (London: SPCK, 1937), pp. 15–16.

[51] Had the system not been reformed, the public school network could not have been expanded. In the mid-nineteenth century, the schools were seen as too rough for retiring souls: see Cuthbert Bede's gentle satire of boys who feared fagging and mothers who did not dare loose the umbilical cord in *The Adventures of Mr Verdant Green, An Oxford Undergraduate* (Oxford: Oxford University Press, 1982), pp. 6–7 (first published 1853–57).

[52] For a particularly famous case at Winchester in 1872 which was taken up by the national press, see P. Gwyn, 'The "Tunding Row". George Ridding and the Belief in "Boy-Government"', in Custance (ed.), *Winchester College* , ch. 13. There were limits to parental tolerance: see Ch. 3, p. 140.

[53] Author's memory of a conversation at the time with the former head of school of Dulwich College (where prefects could not beat boys in the 1960s).

[54] OED, letter 'F', p. 19. Fagging, though not always called such, was definitely present in the leading public schools in the eighteenth century but possibly dated from much earlier; at Westminster juniors were serving seniors by 1666 and the service was described as onerous: see A. K. Cook, *About Winchester College* (London: Macmillan, 1917), ch. 6; Card, *Eton Established*, pp. 102 and 180.

and seventeenth-century 'servitor' in Oxford and Cambridge colleges, so it is possible that the two forms of exploitation developed in tandem. Servitors in the early modern English universities were undergraduates who lacked the wherewithal to finance their studies and paid for their board and lodging in an Oxbridge college by performing menial tasks for a rich commoner or foundationer. Servitors were normally of a lower social status than their young masters and of much the same age. In this respect, they were not like fags. But they were completely under their patron's thumb. He paid for their battels and determined how much they could eat and drink, and he appears to have had the right to chastise them: the college's regulations usually applied only to foundationers. As with fags, then, servitors could be easily bullied in the nineteenth-century sense of the term if their student master did not use his power mercifully. Indeed, they were in a worse position than a fag. A fag master could not throw a boy out of a school, although he could make his life a misery. A servitor's survival as a scholar depended totally on the whim of his young lord.[55]

It is in the universities, too, that we must search for the first signs of initiation ceremonies in English educational institutions. In the early seventeenth century, if not before, many colleges at Oxford and Cambridge welcomed newcomers with a 'salting'. This is best described in the autobiography of the antiquarian Anthony Wood (1632–95), who went up to Merton College, Oxford, at the age of fifteen, in 1647. Around Candlemas each year it was the custom in the college for all freshmen (his word) to give an amusing speech in the hall to the assembled undergraduates. After dinner on the chosen evening, once the fellows had left, the new students were told to take off their gown and bands and make themselves 'look like a scoundrel'.

> This done, they were conducted each after the other to the high table [where the head of house and the college officers would dine], and there made to stand on a forme placed thereon; from whence they were to speak their speech with an audible voice to the company.

What happened next depended on how well they had managed this difficult task.

> [I]f well done, the person that spoke it was to have a cup of cawdle and no salted drinks; if indifferently, some cawdle and some salted drink; but if dull, nothing was given to him but salted drink or salt put in college beere.

Finally, having been helped down from his perch, he was admitted to the 'fraternity' after taking an oath full of gobbledegook administered by the college cook. Needless to say, Wood's speech went down well and he was given a 'good dish of cawdle'.[56] This, however, was not Wood's only initiation ceremony. A few months before he had participated in another of a similar nature. The new students were made to sit on a form in the middle of the hall, and one by one come up to the 'declaiming desk' and narrate 'some pretty apothegme, or make a jest or bull, or speake some eloquent nonsense, to make the company laugh'. This time there was no reward for success, but the dull were 'tucked', punished by an elder student drawing a sharp finger nail from their lower lip to their chin, so it left a mark.[57]

---

[55] Except for their presence which is recorded in the matriculation registers of Oxford and Cambridge, little is known about servitors. The only servitor to leave an autobiography (in MS) was the magus Simon Forman (1552–1611) who came up to Magdalen in 1573 but he has little to say about his time at the University.

[56] *The Life and Times of Anthony Wood, Antiquary of Oxford, 1632–1695, Described by Himself*, ed. A. Clark (5 vols; Oxford: Oxford History Society, 1891–1900), i. 138–40; he provides an extract from the speech. Saltings also occurred at Brasenose and Balliol colleges (*ibid.*, p. 141fn.) and at Christ's Cambridge where Milton presided over a similar initiation ceremony in 1628: A. Beer, *Milton: Poet, Pamphleteer and Patriot* (Bloomsbury: London, 2008), pp. 41–44. The speeches were supposed to be 'salacious'.

[57] Wood, *Life and Times*, i. 133–34. Dullards at saltings were also tucked.

A salting served both as a rite of passage and as a way of putting a newcomer in his place. At least one new undergraduate at a different college refused to undergo the ritual. This was Anthony Ashley Cooper (1621–83), later the first earl of Shaftesbury, who had gone up to Exeter College, Oxford, in 1637, aged sixteen. At Exeter it would seem that there was no forfeit. New students were simply summoned to stand by the fire in hall and then forced to drink a 'beer-glass of water and salt'. Shaftesbury obviously considered the ritual demeaning and conspired with his fellow freshmen to resist. When called upon by the son of the earl of Pembroke to advance to the fire, he promptly boxed him on the ear, at which his fellow initiands launched themselves on the other seniors present and cleared the hall. However, the seniors called up reinforcements from the college's graduate community, and Shaftesbury's party had to barricade themselves in a ground floor room in the quad, where they again proved their superior valour.

> They [the seniors] pressing at the door, some of the stoutest and strongest of our freshmen, giant-like boys, opened the doors, let in as many as they pleased, and shut the door by main strength against the rest; those they let in they fell upon, and had beaten very severely, but that my authority with them stopped them, some of them being considerable enough to make terms for us, which they did.

The upshot of the riot, according to Shaftesbury, was that the head of house, Dr Prideaux, 'always favourable to youth offending out of courage', pardoned the freshmen for their temerity, then banned the initiation ritual.[58] John Prideaux (1578–1650) had puritan leanings, and puritans thought all traditions and customs that could provoke unseemly disorder the spawn of the devil. The good doctor presumably took advantage of the mutiny to rid the college of a practice that could too easily become an excuse for misrule. Whether such rituals disappeared from Oxford and Cambridge colleges altogether during the Interregnum when puritans ruled the roost is impossible to say, but thereafter accounts of tucking and salting freshmen as a matter of course cease, and initiation ceremonies retreated to the public schools.[59]

Collective bullying, however, certainly did not disappear from the old universities. In the second half of the nineteenth century it was normal for students whose dress or lifestyle was judged to be transgressional to be intimidated and even physically abused. The Magdalen history tutor, C. R. L. Fletcher (1857–1934), a stalwart member of the boat club as well as a scholar, recalled an incident of 1880 where 'Mr X … a large, fat, flabby creature who scented himself profusely, and would perhaps later have been called an "aesthete"', was carried 'an unresisting parcel, half-dead with fright' and ducked under the college pump. The mob then ran back and plundered his room.[60] As late as 1932 a later generation of Magdalen boat-club hearties broke into the room of a 'pale-faced young man whose Oscar Wilde propensities were secretly deplored', smashed his piano to pieces, then threw his suits on a bonfire.[61] In neither case did the college authorities evince much concern. Peer-group ragging of the unpopular was considered an acceptable form of acculturation.

Today, of course, individuality is prized and collective bullying, like any other act of student on student violence, is deemed beyond the pale. None the less, some traces

---

[58] W. D. Christie, *A Life of Anthony Ashley Cooper, First Earl of Shaftesbury* (London: Macmillan, 1871), pp. 14–18.

[59] Saltings were still being held at Tom Brown's Rugby in the 1830s where new boys had to please their seniors with a song or 'drink a mug of salt and water': Hughes, *Tom Brown's Schooldays*, p. 120; Chandos, *Boys Together*, pp. 80–82; in *Tom Brown's Schooldays* the ceremony is depicted as being less barbaric than it was.

[60] Magdalen College Archives, MC:F31/MS1/1, pp. 51–53.

[61] A. Hegarty, 'The Tutorial Takeover, 1928–1968', in L. W. B. Brockliss (ed.), *Magdalen College. A History* (Oxford: Magdalen College, 2008), pp. 669–73, for various examples of undergraduate rowdyism.

of the misrule of the past still survive in the modern British army, and even in the modern British university.[62] Student sporting societies in particular frequently insist that new members are initiated, often in the most bizarre and potentially dangerous ways. In 2008 a video emerged from the University of Gloucestershire showing students 'putting plastic bags on their heads, lining up against a wall and then following someone dressed as a Nazi'. This very public revelation of student high jinks immediately caused an outcry in the press and a demand from the National Union of Students that all initiation ceremonies be banned, albeit that the participants were (presumably) willing victims. More sensibly, the students union of the University of Warwick decided that all such ceremonies would be called in future 'adoptions' and sports clubs had to provide details of the ritual in advance.[63]

It is also the case that it has proved extremely difficult to eradicate the Flashmans from the school precincts of modern Britain altogether, despite the media, teachers and pupils joining together over the past twenty years to tackle the problem. The bullied are still frequently left to fight their own wars. It is often said that girls use much subtler ways of bullying their peers than boys, notably by ostracism, so that their victimisation of the vulnerable misfit is particularly hard to police. The new digital technology, moreover, has opened up new ways of making the lives of picked-upon children a misery. On the one hand, now that digital images can be instantaneously transmitted around the world, older children in Britain and elsewhere have taken to filming assaults so that the sufferings and humiliation of the bullied can be passed to friends and continually revisited. But 'happy slapping' as the phenomenon has been called is usually only a piece of fun, if not so amusing for the victim. More sinister is cyber-bullying where children are constantly sent digital text messages intended to hurt or embarrass. A recent survey of middle school children in the southern United States discovered that ten per cent had been cyber-bullied in the previous month while more than seventeen per cent claimed to have been cyber-bullied at least once in their life. Arguably bullying is not disappearing from western culture, merely taking new forms.[64]

. . . .

Much more work needs to be done about the way adults in the past have used older children to socialise their juniors by violence and intimidation, especially in schools and universities. It is evident that initiation ceremonies in particular have never been a purely English phenomenon. In early seventeenth-century Italy, where students were divided into nations, freshmen had to undergo the right of *spupillazione*: on arrival, they were forced to

---

[62] Bullying in the army, which appears to have led to suicides among trainees, has been the subject of much recent comment: see J. K. Wither, 'Battling Bullying in the British Army, 1987–2004', *The Journal of Power Institutions in Post Soviet Societies*, 1 (2004); electronic text available on http://www.pipss.org/index46.html (accessed 26 Mar. 2009).

[63] *The Coventry Telegraph*, 3 Oct. 2008, p. 7. The BBC was given a copy of the Gloucester initiation ceremony: for a moving image with voice-over, see http://news.bbc.co.uk/1/hi/uk/7647721.stm (accessed 26 Mar. 2009). The question of whether someone who volunteers to be a victim is bullied was debated in *Tom Brown's Schooldays*. The head of School House gives the boys a coming-up lecture on the evils of bullying, but the fifth formers traditionally toss the juniors in a sheet on the first night back and go hunting for victims. When one of their number reminds them that they would be ignoring the head boy's homily, they ask for volunteers: Tom and East agree to be sacrificed: Hughes, *Tom Brown's Schooldays*, pp. 123 and 130–34.

[64] http://en.wikipedia.org/wiki/Happy_slapping#United_Kingdom (accessed 15 Dec. 2009); S. Hinduja and J. Patchin, *Bullying Beyond the Schoolyard: Preventing and Responding to Cyberbullying* (Thousand Oaks: Corwin Press, 2009).

provide older students with presents and a meal or face having their scholar's cloak (the identity of their new status) stolen and their lodgings ransacked.[65] Two centuries later in France, new boys at the small school in Villers-Côterets attended by Alexander Dumas *père* (1802–70) from 1811 were 'baptised' with urine.[66] But we know little about when and how the university and school authorities seriously began to counter this and other kinds of bullying, nor whether or not the compromise promoted in the English public schools found favour in other parts of Europe.

Adults in the past, however, have not just used older children to police youngsters. Adolescents were also used more widely as local community enforcers. When much of Europe in the early middle ages was little more than a congeries of tribes and clans, it was the youth who were entrusted with maintaining the community's authority and independence vis-à-vis outsiders. In Ireland, for instance, they were sent out to rustle cattle and fêted on their return.[67] By the early modern period, with the slow emergence of regional states, youth in the countryside continued to be allowed to uphold the honour and reputation of their community in annual fights and football matches against neighbouring villages and parishes. Moreover, from the fifteenth century – and probably much earlier – they were also given a prominent role in maintaining community norms against transgressive adults through the organisation of various intimidatory rituals, known as charivaris, skimmington rides, nightwalking, rough music, and so on. In the Anglo-American world the phenomenon only began to be studied seriously in the 1970s after the appearance of a pioneering article on France written by Natalie Zeman Davis in 1971. Since then our knowledge of the phenomenon has been greatly extended. All over rural and small-town Europe, it is clear, youth played a key part in extracting fines from those who married outside the community, policing the sexual behaviour of women, mocking cuckolded husbands and so on. But it was also generally the case that adolescents were not supposed to be enforcers on their own. In most regions of Europe, they were part of mixed-aged and sometimes mixed-gender societies with names implying authority, as in south-east France where they were called *royaumes* or *abbayes*.[68]

In Europe's towns and cities, on the other hand, the enforcement role permitted to youth was less ritualised and not always so closely supervised. Early modern cities were complex social entities: they were not really one community or even a series of parish communities, but a number of self-conscious religious, occupational and familial interest groups whose status in the hierarchy was unclear or contested. In the cities youths were frequently employed to uphold the rights and claims of the group, not the town as a whole. Quarrelling guilds would often encourage their younger members to settle their differences by violence. So too would quarrelling families. This could sometimes lead to anarchy, if the overarching authority was weak and the families were socially prominent, as Shakespeare's *Romeo and Juliet* written in the early 1590s makes plain. The rivalry between the houses of Montagu and Capulet is a 'plague' on the city of Verona because their junior representatives are allowed to assert the honour of their respective families in the streets. There was always the

[65] P. Grendler, *The Universities of the Italian Renaissance* (London: Johns Hopkins University Press, 2002), pp. 503–05. 'Nations' were regional associations of students and had been commonplace in Europe's medieval universities.

[66] Alexander Dumas, *Mes Mémoires*, preface by Alain Decaux (Paris: Plon, 1986), pp. 105–06.

[67] K. McCome, 'Werewolves, Cyclops, Diberge and Fianna: Juvenile Delinquency in Early Ireland', *Cambridge Medieval Celtic Studies*, 12 (1986), 1–22; N. Patterson, *Cattle Lords and Clansmen: The Social Structure of Early Ireland*, 2nd edn (London: University of Notre Dame Press, 1994).

[68] The literature is now vast: *e.g.*, N. Z. Davis, 'The Reasons of Misrule: Youth Groups and Charivaris in Sixteenth-Century France', *Past and Present*, 150:1 (1971), 41–75; E. P. Thompson, ' "Rough Music": le charivari anglais', *Annales e.s.c.*, xvii (1972), 285–312; Schindler, 'Guardians of Disorder', pp. 240–82; J.Y. Champeley, 'Les Organisations de la jeunesse à l'époque moderne', in J.-P. Bardet, J.-N. Luc, I. Robin-Romero and C. Rollet (eds), *Lorsque l'enfant grandit. Entre dependence et autonomie* (Paris: Presse de l'Université de Paris-Sorbonne, 2003), pp. 765–78.

possibility, too, that youthful enforcers might temporarily make cause with their opponents against their elders if they had common grievances, or act independently, so stoking fires which their seniors would have preferred extinguished. In the sixteenth century youth had often been to the fore in the iconoclasm and physical violence sponsored by reformers and counter-reformers. Once unleashed, youth was difficult to rein in. The university of Paris prided itself on being a bastion of Catholicism and its students had been continually caught up in the communal violence of the French wars of religion. It is not surprising, then, that it took Paris students a while to recognise that a new order had been issued in with the promulgation of the Edict of Nantes in 1598 granting Protestants religious and civil rights. As late as September 1605 a placard appeared on the gates of the abbey of Saint-Victor in Paris calling on Catholic students at the university to assemble with clubs and arms after dinner to attack the city's Huguenots.[69]

University cities could be particularly difficult to police. University students had an array of fiscal and judicial privileges which set them apart from other inhabitants and inevitably caused jealousies. Where, as at Oxford and Cambridge, the university had full powers of policing the student body and the right to interfere in the business of ordinary citizens, if they were thought to be aiding or abetting student misbehaviour, the possibility of conflict was greatly enhanced.[70] Giving youth a share in community policing made a sense as a rite of passage to adulthood but outside the village youthful enforcers were hard to control.

Student Violence in Early Modern Cambridge

Alexandra Shepard

The prevalence of quotidian interpersonal violence in early modern society meant that children and youths routinely experienced physical correction as part of their socialisation. This ranged from ear-boxing to public whipping, with rituals of chastisement designed as much to humiliate and subordinate as to inflict pain. In a culture in which regulatory violence was widely dispersed, routinely exercised by every household head and in a range of institutional settings, as well as by the more formal mechanisms of judicial administration, the right to administer blows was a central component of adult masculinity.[71] This was reinforced by and further reflected in an honour code that condoned interpersonal violence as a means of avenging insults and, as contemporaries put it, 'proving manhood'.[72]

---

[69] M. Pattison, *Isaac Casaubon* (Oxford: Oxford University Press, 1892). p. 211. Only one Huguenot was killed. Paris was always a Catholic university and students had been involved in communal violence in the second half of the sixteenth century.

[70] Oxford and Cambridge's privileges vis-à-vis the local community were particularly extensive. Cases concerning the students of the two universities, even if they related to outside parties, were heard in the vice-chancellor's court. Essentially, Oxford and Cambridge were each governed by two independent corporations. For Oxford, see Rashdall, *Universities of Europe*, vol. 2, ch. 3.

[71] S. D. Amussen, 'Punishment, Discipline and Power: The Social Meanings of Violence in Early Modern England', *Journal of British Studies*, 34 (1995), 1–34. See also S. D. Amussen, '"The Part of a Christian Man": The Cultural Politics of Manhood in Early Modern England', in S. D. Amussen and M. Kishlansky (eds), *Political Culture and Cultural Politics in Early Modern England: Essays Presented to David Underdown* (Manchester: Manchester University Press, 1995), pp. 213–34.

[72] See, *e.g.*, J. Swetnam, *The Schoole of the Noble and Worthy Science of Defence* (London: N. Okes, 1617), pp. 41–42. See also J. M. Beattie, 'Violence and Society in Early-Modern England', in A. N. Doob and E. L. Greenspan

Ritualised violence by groups of young men was therefore often implicitly condoned, if not licensed, and served as more than a simple 'safety valve' enabling them to let off steam. As Keith Thomas has argued, violent rites of inversion often reaffirmed normative hierarchies, while Natalie Zemon Davis has demonstrated the ways in which youthful misrule was harnessed to the regulation of norms and boundaries, functioning as 'the raucous voice of communal conscience'.[73] Yet, as Davis also observed, the violent rituals of charivari and carnival were not void of social or political criticism, and did not always confirm the social and political order. Davis's concern was with fissures along class lines, but, besides being an expression of shared communal interests or codes of masculinity, youthful violence was often also a product of conflict between youth and age. Paul Griffiths, for example, has questioned the degree to which the youthful disruption at Shrovetide was condoned by the early modern authorities, and the line between tacit approval and strategic tolerance of youthful violence was thin.[74] The rituals of group violence served as initiation rites not only into forms of adult masculinity, therefore, but were also designed to confer belonging in a rebellious fraternal culture that defined itself in opposition to age and that pursued counter-codes of male prowess rooted in excess rather than order.[75]

A variety of interests and identities, then, both converged and diverged in the rituals of youthful violence, related to tensions and alliances shaped by age, class and gender. A case study that well illustrates these points is provided by the rites of violence performed by young men in early modern Cambridge. Disciplinary violence was as central to the socialisation of scholars by the university as it was to household discipline in the town and beyond. Public beatings were regularly staged (usually in college halls, and, occasionally, in the streets of the town) to punish insubordinate students deemed 'non-adultus', or under the age of eighteen.[76] By contrast, it was through access to the use of violence that young men claimed and were socialised into manhood. The presence of the university distorted further the preponderance of youths in the town, but it also amplified class conflict and territorial disputes along town-gown lines which offset the considerable potential for age-related divisions.[77] Young men were therefore socialised into vertical alliances with their elders in town-gown conflict, affording them a share in regulatory violence and an opportunity to prove themselves as men. Yet many of these rituals were also appropriated by groups of male youths in a more rebellious culture of misrule. There was sufficient overlap between these different impulses that the latter generally received a degree of tolerance if not tacit approval. Tellingly, the university authorities found the violence of its charges most threatening when it

---

(eds), *Perspectives in Criminal Law* (Aurora: Canada Law Book, 1985), pp. 36–60; E. A. Foyster, *Manhood in Early Modern England: Honour, Sex and Marriage* (London: Longman, 1999), pp. 177–81; A. Shepard, *Meanings of Manhood in Early Modern England* (Oxford: Oxford University Press, 2003), ch. 5.

[73] Thomas, 'Rule and Misrule'; Davis, '*Reasons of Misrule*', esp. pp. 55–56. See also S. R. Smith, 'The London Apprentices as Seventeenth-Century Adolescents', in P. Slack (ed.), *Rebellion, Popular Protest and the Social Order in Early Modern England* (Cambridge: Cambridge University Press, 1984), ch. 11.

[74] P. Griffiths, *Youth and Authority: Formative Experiences in England, 1560–1640* (Oxford: Oxford University Press, 1996), pp. 111–75. In early seventeenth-century London, it was commonplace for apprentices to invade the city's brothels at Shrovetide and catch worthy citizens *in flagrante*. The city authorities were not amused.

[75] Shepard, *Meanings of Manhood*, ch. 4.

[76] For examples, see Shepard, *Meanings of Manhood*, pp. 135–36.

[77] V. Morgan with C. Brooke, *A History of the University of Cambridge, vol. II: 1546–1750* (Cambridge: Cambridge University Press, 2004), ch. 7; A. Shepard, 'Contesting Communities? "Town" and "Gown" in Cambridge, c. 1560–1640', in A. Shepard and P. Withington (eds), *Communities in Early Modern England: Networks, Place, Rhetoric* (Manchester: Manchester University Press, 2000), pp. 216–34.

involved fraternisation with youths from the town, and they went to considerable lengths to prevent town-gown interaction. Student misrule therefore functioned as much as an expression of elite status, serving both to demonstrate that university men were above the rules and to stake out privileged claims to the exercise of power.

The most vivid example of young men being drawn in to the disputes of their elders, expressed in ritual violence, is provided by the actions of the university's proctor's watch. Proctors were charged with ensuring the proper conduct of members of the university in the public spaces of the town and at formal academic exercises. Their policing duties included regular night watches that were ostensibly designed to impose the curfew that restricted students to their colleges after 8 pm in the winter and 9 pm in the summer, and to police the university regulations forbidding townspeople from 'entertaining scholars', particularly when this involved drink, gambling and sex. Notwithstanding, proctors appear to have enlisted weighty membership from amongst the student body for their night watches, thereby legitimising nocturnal activity serving a regulative agenda. Their activities were referred to by the university authorities as 'jetting' – a kind of vaunting parade – and condoned as such. The proctor's watch therefore frequently comprised bands of heavily armed young men strutting around the streets of Cambridge adopting aggressive gestures of territorial possession. This inevitably exacerbated town-gown animosity, and sometimes resulted in the creation rather than prevention of violent disorder.

Territorial rivalries clearly took precedent above the maintenance of order in 1559, for example, when it was proposed that the town and university watches combine during Sturbridge Fair – the annual trading fair that brought a tide of people to Cambridge. In response to the proposal that every town and village in Cambridgeshire and the Isle of Ely should double their night watches during the fair, the mayor and vice-chancellor of town and university agreed to join forces. The mayor subsequently complained that the proctor's watch had ignored this order, and, comprising 'a greate company of men to the nombre of Threscore & more', had instead 'beatt the Quenes watche verye sore', robbing them of their harnesses and sending them home. Further orders were issued from the Lord Chief Justice and the local Justice of the Peace and Member of Parliament for Cambridgeshire, Roger, Lord North (who was also a prominent patron of the town) that the watches should 'lovinglie joine togither' against the threat posed by 'Sturdye Vacabonds & masterles men' flocking to Cambridge. However, town-gown tensions escalated further when scholars beat the men of the town watch with clubs and hurled stones on their heads. According to this set of complaints, the order to combine watches had unleashed an unchecked attack against the townsmen by scholars acting under the authority of the university.[78] This was apparently deemed less serious by the central authorities than the dangers of 'masterless men', whose lack of social status denied them the opportunity (unlike students) of exploiting any ambiguity between order and disorder.

The membership of the town watch remains unclear, and so it is impossible to discern whether it also enlisted the brawn of young men allied to its interests (or merely looking for an opportunity to participate in such rites of violence). There is evidence, however, that young townsmen could be as easily rallied as the university's charges. This is suggested by another incident connected with Sturbridge Fair in 1591. At the centre of this dispute was Richard Parish, a retainer of Lord North and constable of Chesterton (a parish on the outskirts of Cambridge), who was arrested to answer charges of 'outragiouse violences' against scholars during Sturbridge Fair. The scene of his arrest

---

[78] C. H. Cooper and J. W. Cooper, *Annals of Cambridge* (5 vols; Cambridge: Warwick and Cambridge University Press, 1842–1908), ii, pp. 154–57.

– resisted by Parish and 'his fellowes' – saw the instant mobilisation of the proctor's watch and many scholars with clubs and drawn swords, clanking and 'glistering' threateningly. Their various companies numbered over 500, if Lord North's account of the clash is to be believed. This was the culmination of an episode that had begun with Parish preventing a group of scholars from crossing the river at Chesterton in order to get to the fair. As the conflict escalated, Parish stabbed one of them with a dagger and then cried for help – which appeal was presently met by an armed crowd appearing on the river bank who stopped the students from alighting owing to Parish's warnings that they would spoil the booths in the fair. On being apprehended by university officers, Parish escaped arrest by appealing to the apprentices at the fair, claiming that 'he had bene sometyme an apprentise and [was] now in the hands of Scholars to be wronged by them, unlesse he might be releived by there meanes' – which relief involved considerable violence according to the vice-chancellor's complaint to the Privy Council regarding the episode.[79] Just as the university had willing participants with weapons to hand to defend its honour, so Parish was able to appeal to the honour of apprentices in order to enlist their violent intervention that was readily forthcoming.

Such details survive in this case because of Lord North's involvement which gave it more serious political import, but the readiness of young men on both sides to become involved suggest that such reactions were not unusual. William Austin, for example, who was a Cambridge merchant, responded to the proctor's order that he return home late one night by raising a 'tumult and hurly burly' with the assistance of a 'great number' armed with clubs, many of whom were Austin's household servants – described in the proctor's complaint as 'most notoriously quarrelling and disorderly fellowes'.[80] The youths involved appear to have treated such violent conflict as a collective test of honour, and were quick to rise to the challenge. Such rivalries were not always played out along town-gown lines – as suggested by the extent of inter-collegiate violence that also occurred – but the territorial and political conflicts between the town corporation and the university provided a potent incentive to violent exchange, to which the bravado of male youth was readily harnessed.

Although in many such cases young men were admitted to – and sometimes central to – the regulative rituals of their seniors, they were also adept at appropriating such rituals for their own, often more rebellious, ends. This is particularly clear from the ways in which students masqueraded as the proctor's watch in pursuit of a more disorderly agenda. The university authorities were well aware that the regulative authority of the proctors was illegitimately claimed, and drew up measures against unlicensed 'night jetters' whose company included 'divers unfit and unstayed persons' carrying guns, cross-bows, and stone-bows as well as clubs and swords. Such orders were issued in conjunction with complaints against student drunkenness and hunting expeditions.[81] Nocturnal activities of dissolute students included smashing windows and beating up any suspicious characters they encountered. Much of this behaviour was not very different in character from the activities of the proctor's watch. In one violent exchange, for example, the watch responded to townsmen's verbal abuse and stone-throwing by breaking open their doors, smashing their windows, and boxing their servants' ears, ostensibly in order to disarm them and confine them to their households in observation of the curfew.[82] When students mimicked such actions without the legitimising presence of the proctor – and even more so when town lads parodied his watch – the main

---

[79] Cooper, *Annals*, ii, pp. 494–508.
[80] Cambridge University Library, Cambridge University Archive, (CUA), V.C.Ct.III.32, no. 52.
[81] Cooper, *Annals*, iii, pp. 25–6.
[82] CUA, V.C.Ct.III.17, no. 99.

offence was the misappropriation of the university's regulative authority, rather than the violence *per se*. Many of the violent rituals that they performed served as role play, allowing young men to experiment with disciplinary violence as protagonists rather than recipients.

Also woven into male youth culture (although not exclusive to it) were violent practices that were further removed from the regulative agenda or character of official violence and that were more explicitly disorderly, if not openly rebellious. The 'riots' that sometimes broke out between students at plays or disputations in violent expressions of college rivalries fall into this category, as does the violence that often accompanied football matches (which, as a result, were banned by the university from taking place between students of different colleges).[83] No less disruptive was the ungoverned destruction of property by bands of young men, such as during the 'night disorders' following a drinking spree which ended with students tearing apart a townsman's work stall and pulling up the poles that supported it.[84] Such collective exploits were fuelled less by the need to display male prowess to older men than by the desire for peer recognition. The resulting fraternal bonds often transcended town-gown rivalries. This is clear, for example, from a complaint about a group of scholars who broke into an alehouse and pulled up the poles surrounding a neighbouring close as part of a nightwalking episode, who were joined in their exploits by a baker's son 'in a schollers gowne'.[85] It is also evident from the considerable efforts of the university authorities to limit fraternisation between students and young men from the town who none the less established extensive networks facilitating a male youth culture of excess.[86]

All these modes of violence into which young men were drawn – regulative, imitative, and subversive – shaded into each other and involved many of the same actions and rituals. The wide dispersal of regulatory violence beyond officers of the state, as well as the pervasive links between violence and masculinity, meant that young men were easily drawn into violent conflict as participants (rather than victims) well before they reached other points of entry into socially recognised adulthood. In addition, proving the ability to defend one's ground – with blows if necessary – was a vital part of gaining recognition amongst one's peers, and was integral to male youth culture. Enjoying relatively elite status that placed them in a 'fast stream' to adulthood, students of the university were better placed than most young men to take advantage of the blurred boundaries between regulative, imitative and subversive violence.[87]

It is clear that throughout the sixteenth and early seventeenth centuries, at the very least, the gestures of regulatory violence were routinely adopted to signal students' social superiority – whether through the ritual beating of college servants that was licensed as part of Christmas misrule, or through the actions of the proctor's watch.[88] Just as the crown failed to outlaw duelling amongst the gentry and aristocracy, so

---

[83] For riots at plays, see A. H. Nelson (ed.), *Records of Early English Drama: Cambridge* (2 vols; Toronto: University of Toronto Press. 1989), i. 359, 358, 407, 424–86. For violence during disputations, see, *e.g.*, CUA, V.C.Ct.II.3, fos 95–97. For football related violence, see, *e.g.*, CUA, Comm.Ct.I.18, fo. 80; V.C.Ct.III.24, fo. 91. For university regulations against it, see Cooper, *Annals*, ii. 382.

[84] CUA, V.C.Ct.II.14, no. 88.

[85] CUA, V.C.Ct.III.14, no. 92. See also P. Griffiths, 'Meanings of Nightwalking in Early Modern England', *Seventeenth Century*, 13:2 (1998), 212–38.

[86] Shepard, 'Contesting Communities?', pp. 227–28; Shepard, *Meanings of Manhood*, pp. 111–13.

[87] K. Thomas, 'Age and Authority in Early Modern England', *Proceedings of the British Academy*, 62 (1976), 205–48 (esp. p. 213).

[88] For the rites of violence accompanying Christmas misrule, see Shepard, *Meanings of Manhood*, pp. 99–100.

the university's emphasis on modest decorum had limited impact on the violent imperatives underpinning male honour.[89] If there was a gradual shift towards restraint and politeness as the markers of gentility over a 'long' eighteenth century, this was nonetheless accompanied by the violent excesses of libertine behaviour that signalled status by flouting the rules.[90] Violence was therefore intrinsic to expressions of status by young gentlemen, either asserting their privileged access to the regulative violence associated with adulthood and elite power, or to demonstrate that they were above normative codes of conduct. Yet the strong links between violence and male youth culture was far from an exclusively elite phenomenon. This is clear from both the readily mobilised young men from the town to add weight to town-gown conflict and also the solidarities of age that sometimes transcended town-gown divisions in the fraternal bonds forged by participation in the rituals of violent excess. The strong links between violence and manhood persisted throughout the social scale, profoundly influencing the ways in which male youths sought social recognition both amongst themselves and in the adult world.[91]

Early modern rites of violence drew young men into webs of authority, allowing them to experiment with and participate in the rituals of regulation and territorial possession that were such important facets of adult masculinity. While providing an opportunity for male youths to prove their manhood to and earn respect from their elders, violence none the less also gave them the means to resist the constraints imposed by adult male authority. That there was sufficient overlap between the violent gestures and rituals intrinsic to both modes is suggested by the extent of tolerance the latter received – often condoned as mere 'sport', especially when pursued by social elites. The successful manipulation of such rites of violence as proof of manhood smoothed the rite of passage for male youths from being objects of disciplinary violence to exercising its force as its protagonists.

· ·

In some parts of Europe, such as Germany and Switzerland, moral policing societies survived into the nineteenth century. Indeed, it was then that a number (in imitation of developments in national politics) began to adopt constitutions.[92] By and large, though, these societies were fast disappearing by the beginning of the eighteenth century, especially in England where the London authorities were already losing patience with youth who took the law into its own hands before the Civil War. Admittedly, the most famous depiction of a charivari in England was drawn by Hogarth in the 1740s. (See Figure 27). But the engraving was one of a set to illustrate a new edition of *Hudibras*, a satirical poem by Samuel Butler (1612–80), which had first appeared in the reign of Charles II. It is unlikely that the London artist had actually witnessed a skimmington ride in the capital. Fifty years later he would have

---

[89] M. Peltonen, *The Duel in Early Modern England: Civility, Politeness and Honour* (Cambridge: Cambridge University Press, 2003); R. Manning, *Swordsmen: The Martial Ethos in the Three Kingdoms* (Oxford: Oxford University Press, 2003), chs 5–7.

[90] Beattie, 'Violence and Society'; R. Shoemaker, *The London Mob: Violence and Disorder in Eighteenth-Century England* (London: Hambledon Press, 2004); A. Bryson, *From Courtesy to Civility: Changing Codes of Conduct in Early Modern England* (Oxford: Clarendon Press, 1998), ch. 7. See also K. B. Brown, 'Gentlemen and Thugs in Seventeenth-Century Britain', *History Today*, 40:10 (1990), 27–32.

[91] For similar observations relating to different contexts, see A. Davies, 'Youth Gangs, Masculinity and Violence in Late Victorian Manchester and Salford', *Journal of Social History*, 32:2 (1998), 349–69; N. Schindler, *Rebellion, Community and Custom in Early Modern Germany* (Cambridge: Cambridge University Press, 2002).

[92] Schindler, 'Guardians of Disorder', pp. 252 and 254.

been hard pressed to see one even in the provinces: the custom was virtually moribund.[93] Thomas Hardy describes a rough music in The *Mayor of Casterbridge*, a novel purporting to portray life in early nineteenth-century Dorchester, albeit published in 1886. However the author makes clear that the townspeople are reviving a dying tradition when they decide to organise a charivari to punish Mrs Farfrae for apparently reneging on her first love.

'I say, what a good foundation for a skimmity-ride', said Nance.
'True', said Mrs. Cuxsom, reflecting. "'Tis as good a ground for a skimmity-ride as ever I knowed; and it ought not to be wasted. The last one seen in Casterbridge must have been ten years ago, if a day'[94]

It is not difficult to see why youth societies disappeared. In the late middle ages both church and state may have welcomed the charivari when the moral health of the individual and the community were thought to be one and the same and when the secular arm had little local authority. In the post-Reformation world the societies seemed anomalous.[95] So too, given the chance of a breakdown of law and order, did the tradition of allowing adolescents the right to assert group interests. From the mid-seventeenth century, it was less and less acceptable for youth to be used by warring factions in the cities as a way of solving quarrels (or keeping them alive). The group violence that youth continued to get involved in was now usually looked on askance, if it was still difficult to control. Then from the early nineteenth century, all capital cities began to be professionally policed. The role of youth as enforcers became redundant.[96]

Where it has survived until the present day in Europe is in moments of political turmoil and social breakdown. Revolutionary regimes, uncertain of the loyalty of the adult population, have been quick to use adolescents to cajole adults into compliance. Witness the role of the communist party's youth wing, the Komsomol, in 'facilitating' forced collectivisation in the Soviet Union in the early 1930s.[97] Underground groups in the post-war era, too, who aim to weaken or overthrow the existing order by force have frequently enlisted children into their ranks as *agents provocateurs*. During the long-lasting 'Troubles' in Northern Ireland in the final third of the twentieth century, both Loyalists and Republicans were more than happy to put stone-throwing children in the front line of riots and demonstrations in order to spike the containment measures adopted by the police and armed forces.[98] In Britain today, there are fears that radical Islamicists, who have declared holy war against the decadent west, are grooming young Muslim boys to be teenage terrorists.[99]

---

[93] Cf. above fn. 90.
[94] Thomas Hardy, *The Mayor of Casterbridge* (London: Macmillan, 1968), pp. 259, 277–79.
[95] Sin was now much more a personal affair, epitomised in the Counter-Reformation church by the replacement of public confession by the confessional box: see J. Bossy, 'The Social History of Confession in the Age of Reformation'. *Transactions of the Royal Historical Society*, 5th series: 25 (1975), 21–38.
[96] Remnants of the tradition lingered in rural France until the second half of the twentieth century: see D. Fabre, '"Doing Youth" in the Village', in Levi and Schmitt (eds), *A History of Young People*, pp. 58–60.
[97] O. Figes, *The Whisperers. Private Life in Stalin's Russia* (New York: Metropolitan Books, 2007), pp. 77–81. The Nazis, on the other hand, did not use youth in this way: our thanks to Nicholas Stargardt for this information.
[98] E. Cairns, *Caught in the Crossfire: Children and the Northern Ireland Conflict* (Belfast: Appletree, 1987), ch. 2; E. Cairns, *Children and Political Violence* (Oxford: Blackwell, 1996), ch. 4, surveys the literature on children as political activists in the recent past in several countries.
[99] *The Independent*, 28 Mar. 2009. In December 2009 a leaked memo revealed that police in the Birmingham area were fearful that Muslim children as young as four were being groomed as terrorists: see http://www.dailymail.co.uk/news/article-123520/Terror-grooming-watch-nurseries-police-fear-children-young-FOUR-radicalised.html (accessed 15 Dec. 2009). In the developing world children have been and are used as enforcers by both Muslim political groups and their opponents. During the Iranian revolution, bands of young militants

The growing intolerance of youthful enforcers from the mid-seventeenth century meant that their exploits increasingly came to be looked on as crimes. When caught, even those from well-to-do families were subjected to the process, if not the rigours, of the law. Indeed, in the minds of the adults who represented the ever lengthening arm of the state, adolescent violence in defence of community or group interests came to be barely distinguishable from the activities of an initially entirely separate group of the young: 'masterless' children and adolescents. For the latter who lived outside adult control altogether, violence and intimidation was not a convivial pastime but a way of life. Living on the fringes of society, they largely survived by thieving and begging.

Children forced to fend for themselves or to seek refuge in the society of adult beggars must have been a relatively common phenomenon from the late middle ages onwards.[100] Given the continual return of the plague in the three centuries following the arrival of the Black Death, not to mention the mortality peaks caused by other, often equally virulent, epidemic diseases, there would have been many uncared for orphans. The problem must have been particularly acute in northern Europe where the nuclear family was the dominant household formation and contact with wider kin not necessarily strong. Before the era of the Reformation and Counter-Reformation masterless children were generally tolerated. At the turn of the sixteenth century the young Felix Platter of Basel was able to survive for many years as part of a wandering band of schoolboys who went from town to town living on their wits.[101] From the mid-sixteenth century, however, as the number of masterless men and women swelled with the growing agrarian distress that was consequent to the rising population, state and civic authorities took fright. In England through the Elizabethan poor law, every effort was made to keep the masterless and unemployed in their villages. In most parts of the continent, the destitute were rounded up and institutionalised in workhouses or orphanages (often called hospitals) where they were taught, none too gently, to be good hardworking Christians.[102]

However, there were always some adults, and children, who escaped the net, especially in time of prolonged war when accompanying famine and disease led to an increase in civilian mortality rates and the forces of law and order collapsed. The Thirty Years' War, Europe's last great religious conflict, that ravaged the Holy Roman Empire from 1618 to 1648 inevitably increased the number of orphan children adrift in the towns, surviving the best they good. Although the young were not the sacrificial victims that some contemporary witnesses claimed – children were deliberately used as figures of innocence to emphasises

---

called 'The Patrol of God's Avengers' acted as the street wing of the 'Office for the Propagation of Virtues and the Prevention of Sins'. In modern India the Hindu nationalist party, the VHP, has a youth wing, the Bajrang Dal boys, who act as political storm troopers: see E. Fernandes, *Holy Warriors. A Journey into the Heart of Indian Fundamentalism* (London: Portobello Books, 2007), pp. 282–83. Children have been particularly used in the Palestinian *Intifada*. The use of children as moral policemen was also endorsed in Mao's China. See K. Wells, 'Children and International Politics', in H. Montgomery and M. Kellett (eds), *Children and Young People's Worlds: Developing Frameworks for Integrated Practice* (Bristol: The Policy Press, 2009).

[100] In the late middle ages, some masterless children must also have attached themselves to the bands of young knights wandering around Europe in search of adventure and a wife while waiting to enter their inheritance on their father's death: G. Duby, *The Chivalrous Society*, trans. C. Postan (London: Arnold, 1977), ch. 7.

[101] Thomas Platter, *Autobiographie*, French trans., ed. M. Helmer (Paris: Armand Colin, 1964), pp. 30–49. Platter's experience was not a happy one for he was continually bullied by his elder cousin who was supposed to look after him.

[102] For an introduction, see J.-P. Gutton, *La Société et les pauvres en Europe (XVIe–XVIIIe siècles)* (Paris: Presses Universitaires de France, 1974). For a recent study of the debate over the poor in France, see T. McHugh, *Hospital Politics in Seventeenth-Century France. The Crown, Urban Elites and the Poor* (Aldershot: Ashgate, 2007), ch. 1.

the cruelty of invading forces[103] – many were displaced. Some children too ended up in the rag-tag, ill disciplined armies that criss-crossed central Europe during the endless conflict, thereby gaining a novel licence to prey on society, though they never seem to have been as feral and violent as adult soldiers.

Masterless Children during the Thirty Years' War

Alan Ross

The increased interest in what German historiography has labelled *Selbstzeugnisse* ('Ego-documents') has brought to light a whole range of eyewitness accounts of the Thirty Years' War. Among these sources are ten relatively detailed autobiographies of men who lived through the war as children. A large number of chronicles also mention children in passing and give the reader some idea of what the living conditions of children were judged to be like by the war-time communities they lived in. These documents allow us to get a close-up, 'micro-historical' view of events in the immediate vicinity of the writer. If the texts are, however, examined in the context of other literature of the time, it is also possible to retrace the themes and literary *topoi* that are very likely to have acted as models for the description of violence we find in 'ego-documents'. In the 'ego-document' literature, events might have been recorded for personal remembrance only and for that reason a high degree of credibility can be afforded to these sources; yet, as writers did not live in a literary vacuum, they made references to themes which we know from literature were meant for public consumption. While the 'ego-documents' allow for a comprehensive revaluation of children's relationship to violence, it is necessary to keep the recurrence of certain common themes in mind.[104]

Throughout the duration of the conflict, both towns and rural communities made efforts to provide for uncared for children, at least for those whose parents were known to have been members of the community. The Franconian chroniclers, the Dötschel brothers, mention that during the worst years of the war illegitimately born children were given eight god-parents instead of the usual three to ensure they would have someone to support them.[105] In Würzburg, though it already had an orphanage in the Juliusspital, a second orphanage was founded in 1636 specifically to care for children

---

[103] Two slain and dismembered children were used by Protestant propagandists in an allegorical print which extolled Gustavus Adolf as the saviour of the Christian church and of the long-suffering German population: see W. Harms, M. Schilling and A. Wang (eds), *Deutsche illustrierte Flügblatter des 16. und 17. Jahrhunderts. Die Sammlung der Herzog August Bibliothek in Wolfenbüttel* (Munich: Kraus International Publications, 1980), vol. ii, pp. 456–57.

[104] As there is insufficient space here to describe in any depth the genre of eyewitness accounts of the war, readers are recommended to refer to G. Mortimer, *Eyewitness Accounts of the Thirty Years' War 1618–1648* (London and New York: Palgrave, 2002), and G. Mortimer, 'Models of Writing in Eyewitness Personal Accounts of the Thirty Years' War', *Daphnis*, 29 (2000), 609–47. On *topoi* of violence in writing about the Thirty Years' War, see R. G. Asch, ' "Wo der soldat hinkömbt, da ist alles sein": Military Violence and Atrocities in the Thirty Years War Re-examined', *German History*, 18 (2000), 291–309, at p. 293.

[105] Andreas Dötschel (1607–1638) and Georg Dötschel (1618–1680) were stepbrothers from Mitwitz/Franconia. The account for 1606–1624 was written in retrospect, for 1624–1679 contemporaneously. See R. Hambrecht, '"Das Papier ist mein Acker..." Ein Notizbuch des 17. Jahrhunderts von Handwerker-Bauern aus dem nordwestlichen Oberfranken', *Jahrbuch der Coburger Landesstiftung*, 29 (1984), 317–450, at pp. 361–62.

orphaned as a result of the war. In Erfurt, a private entrepreneur, ostensibly out of charity, established a 'Spinnstube' in which orphans were housed and put to work spinning. His business apparently flourished, but he still asked for further funds from the council to maintain his 'orphanage'.[106] However, despite these efforts, both towns and rural communities were faced with great numbers of unsupervised children, a development historians generally agree triggered the wave of foundations of orphanages in Germany from the 1640s onwards.[107] Town councils across Germany discussed how to deal with a growing number of child vagrants, a problem that is also evident from the surviving eyewitness accounts of the period.[108] The chronicle of Münchingen mentions that on 19 September 1634 a child beggar (*armer Bettelbub*) was found dead in a barn, and on 29 June 1635 an 'unknown half-grown girl' (*halbgewachsenes fremdes Mädchen*) was found dead in Jörg Scheyhing's stables.[109] Johann Georg Oberacker tells of how he and his companion stumbled across a little girl, alone in a forest, while travelling through Bavaria in the late 1640s.[110]

How were these unsupervised children affected by violence? Life on the margins in early modern Europe was certainly highly precarious. Unfortunately, very few eyewitness accounts comment on the lives of children who were unsupervised. Although Johann Georg Oberacker, mentioned above, had himself been an itinerant child, his account leaves blank the periods during which he was not in 'honourable' employment, and one can only guess at how he supported himself during these periods, which lasted at times up to half a year.[111] Court records and council minutes from various areas in Germany show that towns and cities certainly did have a problem with children's gangs.[112] Odd references to children begging and poaching are, however, the only references to children on the margins that individual memoirs contain. Though we do hear of fights among children and in one instance of a child stealing an apple in a churchyard, the children mentioned here are never from outside the community, and the violence described completely in par with the way children played during the period.[113]

While the memoir literature is therefore not very informative about children's involvement in violence in marginal society, children in the military feature very prominently. As Geoffrey Parker has suggested, it could often appear to be safer to be within an army than outside of it, and the sources examined testify to the attraction the army, and the manifold opportunities it offered for earning a living, exerted on people of all ages, including children and adolescents.[114] Armies offered extensive employment

---

[106] H. Raschke, 'Aus einer Abrechnung des Erfurter Waisenhauses für das Jahr 1684', *Mitteilungen des Vereins für die Geschichte und Altertumskunde von Erfurt*, 64 (2003), pp. 97–121, at p. 98.

[107] J. N. Neumann, 'Der Waisenhausstreit', in U. Sträter, and J. N. Neumann, *Waisenhäuser in der Frühen Neuzeit* (Tübingen: Niemayer Verlag, 2003), pp. 169–70.

[108] H. Bräuer and E. Schlenkrich, *Armut und Armutsbekämpfung: schriftliche und bildliche Quellen bis um 1800 aus Chemnitz, Dresden, Freiberg, Leipzig und Zwickau; ein sachthematisches Inventar* (Leipzig: Leipziger Universitätsverlag, 2002).

[109] NN (Münchingen), minister of Münchingen in Franconia. Hoffmann, 'Aus den Schreckensjahren des Leonberger Amts nach der Nördlinger Schlacht', *Württembergische Vierteljahreshefte für Landesgeschichte*, N. F. 21 (1912), 167–70.

[110] H. Teichert (ed.), 'Aus der Chronik der Familie Gruner, Ittlingen. Ein Schicksal aus dem Dreißigjährigen Krieg', *Kraichgau*, 1 (1968), 106–10.

[111] Teichert, 'Aus der Chronik der Familie Gruner', p. 107.

[112] F.-A. Lassota, 'Formen der Armut im späten Mittelalter und zu Beginn der Neuzeit. Untersuchungen vornehmlich an Kölner Quellen des 14. bis 17. Jahrhunderts', Ph. D. dissertation, Freiburg/ Breisgau, 1993, pp. 208 and 298.

[113] Hoffmann, 'Aus den Schreckensjahren des Leonberger Amts', p. 169.

[114] G. Parker, *The Thirty Years' War*, 2nd edn (London: Routledge, 1997), p. 200.

opportunities to children. Whenever the mercenary Hagendorf was issued a horse a boy (*Junge*), who would also perform other services such as assisting in the gathering of loot, was commissioned to look after the animal.[115] These young members of the military have also found their way into art. In an etching by Johann Hulsmann (active 1632–1646), a young boy carrying baggage is shown accompanying two mounted soldiers, another on foot, two women on horseback and an elderly one on foot. In an etching by an anonymous artist, a young, elaborately dressed boy – without doubt a member of the marauding troops shown in the background – is seen running away with a chicken during the looting of a village.[116] (See Figures 28 and 29).

A section in Segers's account of the war suggests that young people were sometimes forced into the military. He describes how in 1638 he ran away from school, partly because

> through quarterings and the passing through of a large number of different troops the frequency with which school was held had declined to the extent that no-one wanted to stay or come to it anymore. So I left home (...) around the month of July 1638 with the agreement of my cousin, *out of fear that I also, like others, might be led away by the soldiers* [my italics].[117]

Interestingly, Segers does not run away suddenly and in panic. Though he is not accompanied by an adult, his flight is sanctioned by Segers's guardian, his cousin, suggesting that Segers's fear of being taken away by the soldiers was taken seriously by adults in the community. The monk Bozenhart mentions another instance of children being abducted by soldiers:

> On December 8th, 9th and 10th Altringer camped at Leipheim with three regiments. But Gustav Horn, as I have heard, was seen at Erbach and its surroundings, with some 14,000 troops. They followed each other across the Danube and Yler and finally crossed into Bavaria. This time, thank God, we were spared and did not suffer any great harm. On the Danube's other shore there was however such looting, pillaging and ransacking between the 11th and 18th of December, that no-one could stay at home, and if a man or woman was found they were terribly maltreated, beaten and tortured. They especially brutally had their way with the women, of whom many were led away, including *many girls aged only seven* [my italics]; to summarise: the soldiers behaved in such an evil and destructive fashion that one can barely live in this area any longer.[118]

What were the young girls mentioned here led away for? From the context described, can we really expect something as harmless as to act as childminders or the like? Bozenhart does not comment further on this, but he clearly wrote in a way meant to suggest or at least to leave open the question of whether these girls were subjected to rape, quite possibly followed by forced prostitution, as older girls and women were.

[115] Hagendorf, dates unknown, wrote his account of the war contemporaneously and made a fair copy in 1648. J. Peters, *Ein Söldnerleben im Dreißigjährigen Krieg. Eine Quelle zur Sozialgeschichte* (Berlin: Akademie Verlag, 1993), pp. 146–47, 163.

[116] Johann Hulsmann, 'Streifzug von Soldaten', etching, Staatliche Graphische Sammlung, Munich, Inv.-Nr.113961 D; reproduced in H. Langer, *The Thirty Years' War*, Eng. trans. (Poole: Blandford Press, 1980), fig. 80, p. 86. Unknown artist, Staatsbibliothek zu Berlin – Preussischer Kulturbesitz Handschriftenabteilung, Einblattdruck YA 2344 kl.

[117] Simon Segers (1623–1684) from Insterburg. G. Sommerfeldt, 'Die Reisebeschreibung eines Altmärkers, Simon Segers aus Tangermünde, um das Jahr 1664', *Thüringisch-Sächsische Zeitschrift für Geschichte und Kunst*, 4 (1914), 30–40, here pp. 32–33.

[118] P. L. Brunner, 'Schicksale des Klosters Elchingen und seiner Umgebung in der Zeit des dreissigjährigen Krieges (1629–1645). Aus dem Tagebuche des P. Johannes Bozenhart', *Zeitschrift des historischen Veriens für Schwaben und Neuburg*, 3 (1876), 157–283, here p. 182.

Oberacker on the other hand tells of how he entered the Imperial army voluntarily by first providing 'various services' for one of its officers during a period of cease-fire, and then, as the troops moved on, joined them, and claims to have eventually become the regiment's piper. Regardless of whether he actually reached this position, his claim to have followed a regiment for a period of four years as a child is itself plausible.

Just how many children there were in the military at the time cannot be said. A supplication by the village of Langenau near Ulm of 1630 complaining about the costs of quartering troops suggests that their numbers were substantial. 368 horsemen were accompanied by '600 horses, 66 women, 78 girls, 307 boys (*Reiterjungen*), 94 children and a large number of dogs'.[119] The differentiation between 'boys' and 'children' suggests that the latter were part of the baggage train without any specified duties. Soldiers' families travelled with the regiment, as Hagendorf's account testifies. Friese also gives a detailed portrait of the family of the soldier who led them out of Magdeburg, and recounts how his mother looked after their young child while the soldier and his wife re-entered the city to gather loot.[120]

The accounts which mention abductions of children might remind the reader of the recent phenomenon of child soldiers in Africa. With many African countries plagued by civil war, anti-government resistance groups and, at times, the government forces themselves have resorted to recruiting children, most notably in Northern Uganda, Liberia, Côte d'Ivoire and the Democratic Republic of Congo. In Northern Uganda, the Lord's Resistance Army's bloody programme of recruitment of children and young adolescents has led to a widely publicised wave of children fleeing their home villages and heading for the greater safety of bigger towns.[121] Similarly, if the abduction of young girls described above is taken as an example of children being forced into prostitution, it is sadly very easy to find corresponding examples from African civil conflicts.[122]

Given the relative wealth of information we have about children in the armies of Africa today, it is very tempting to take the comparison further, and to speculate about other issues, such as the problems involved in reintegrating children into rural society who are known to have been in the military. However, the degree to which the role of children in the military in the Thirty Years' War and in present day Africa can be compared is very limited. The following example, taken from Bozenhart's account, illustrates this very well. The writer first describes how his monastery was stormed by Imperial cavalry. During the storming of the monastery, all the violence is carried out by the troops themselves – there is no mention of the *Buben* of whom we are about to hear much more. When given orders by an officer, the soldiers leave the monastery in a matter of hours, whereupon the troops' entourage immediately descends upon the monastery:

---

[119] G. Zillhardt, *Der Dreissigjährige Krieg in zeitgenössischer Darstellung. Hans Heberle's 'Zeytregister' (1618–1672). Aufzeichungen aus dem Ulmer Territorium* (Ulm and Stuttgart: Kommissionsverlag Kohlhammer, 1975), p. 21.

[120] Peters, *Ein Söldnerleben*, pp. 170 and 175; F. Friese, 'Historischer Extract aus einem Manuscripto, welches Herr Daniel Frisius, Cancell. Secret. zu Altenburg von seinen Fatis hinter sich gelassen, Und von dem Autore dieser historischen Fragen, seinen Untergebnen zur Vergnuegung, wie auch dem unparteyischen Leser zu dienstlicher Nachricht, hier abgedruckt worden', in *Leichte Historische Fragen: in welchen Vor die zarte und galante Jugend die Profan-Historie von den Käysern nicht nur vorgetragen, sondern auch mit Biblischen Exempeln und Sprüchen erläutert, und durch heraus gezogene Sätze in der Oratorie nützlich angewendet wird* (Leipzig: Groschuff, 1703), pp. 27–327, 381–423, at p. 319.

[121] Christian Aid press release 11/ 03/ 03, downloadable at http://www.christianaid.org.uk/news/features/ 0311uganda.htm

[122] G. Machel, *Impact of Armed Conflict on Children. United Nations Report* (New York: United Nations, 1996), pp. 91–102; see also the various contributors to J. Boyden and J. de Berry (eds), *Children and Youth on the Front Line: Ethnography, Armed Conflict and Displacement* (Oxford: Berghahn, 2004).

When the horsemen had quit with a good load of booty, about 900 or rather 1,000 sick stormed in, and set up quarters everywhere together with scores of whores and boys (*mit Huren und Buben allenthalb*), but mostly in the convent and even in the church itself. At once all rooms were full of whores and boys, who took out all the beds, all the sheets and didn't leave a farthing in the chapel, and took all the gowns with them or tore them to shreds so that they were rendered useless, and took all carpets, all cloth, and indeed all paintings and all the decoration of the altar were torn to pieces and destroyed, and in the end such a stench was left it took us day and night to clean up after them.[123]

We must not be confused here by the impression of chaos given by the author – what Bozenhart is in fact describing in some detail is a clear division of labour within the armies of the Thirty Years' War. While violence was committed by combatants, their 'work' was followed by the collection of booty, without which no army of the war would have been able to sustain itself in the field, by the non-combatants. Though Bozenhart does mention the soldiers also collecting booty themselves, various sources, among them most explicitly the Hagendorf diary, attest to the relationship of interdependence between combatants and the non-combatants who assisted them, in Hagendorf's case his 'boy' and his wife.[124]

There will of course have been exceptions to this, as an account of a German traveller who stayed in besieged Paris during the Frondes in 1649 suggests.[125] Melchior Pastorius describes how one of his acquaintances attempted to leave the town through a town gate on his way to St Germain. When having already passed two guards, the third guard, 'a boy of eleven to twelve years of age' demanded to know where he was going and who he was and, when he did not reply, 'shot him dead on the spot'.[126] It cannot be said how a boy of this age came to be on duty at the gate, whether he was in training to become an officer or through some other circumstance. While during such a protracted and bitter conflict as the Thirty Years' War similar occurrences would have been very likely, they were certainly exceptional. There is no evidence of children being drafted into armies as combatants in any way similar to what we see in the armed conflicts of Africa. We therefore do not find children in the Thirty Years' War involved directly in the same kind of gruesome violence as we see in Africa today, a fact that can to some degree be explained by the comparative ease with which present-day automatic weapons can be wielded by the inexperienced and young.

Children in the army could however be considered to be a great nuisance, and, as a further section of Bozenhart's chronicle attests, could suffer extreme repercussions as a result:

The Imperial troops are so angry with the Ulm troops that, when they recently came across 26 soldier-boys, like they had done many times before near Leyben, they took the horses off them and shot them dead three days later in front of the town gate and threw their bodies into the Danube, and they have repeated this process already several times.[127]

The extent to which children were subjected to and were likely to commit violence during the Thirty Years' War presents itself in the following way in the contemporary literature. Children who were part of households were not more likely to suffer violence than civilian adults. However, especially during the years of greatest demographic crisis in the 1630s, it was not uncommon for a child to become orphaned. With this came

[123] Brunner, 'Schicksale des Klosters Elchingen', pp. 197–98.
[124] Peters, *Ein Söldnerleben*, pp. 142–47.
[125] The French civil wars, 1648–1653.
[126] A. R. Schmitt, *Des Melchior Adam Pastorius von 1670 bis 1696 Bürgermeisters der Reichsstadt Windsheim Leben und Reisebeschreibungen von ihm selbst erzählt...* (Munich: Delp, 1968), p. 113.
[127] Brunner, 'Schicksale des Klosters Elchingen', p. 207.

the greater likelihood of displacement, vagrancy and a life on the margins of civic or rural society or in the 'baggage-train' of an army. In these settings, the likelihood of children being subjected to violence was certainly much higher. On the other hand, we have no evidence of children being deployed as combatants. Although their role within the armies of the day was an integral one and certainly aroused the wrath of civilians, these children cannot be considered to have been 'child-soldiers' in the modern sense.

· ·

As Europe's population stagnated during the century following the end of the Thirty Years' War, it is likely that the existing mechanisms for dealing with orphaned and homeless children left to fend for themselves were largely sufficient, except in the few fast-growing cities, such as London. After 1750, however, the population started growing again quickly everywhere and has continued to do so. The result, as in the sixteenth century, was increasing poverty and social dislocation. In most countries before 1850 per capita income failed to keep pace with the expanding population, while thereafter the increased wealth brought sooner or later by industrialisation was very unevenly distributed. Healthcare, too, scarcely improved before the twentieth century, apart from the introduction of vaccination against smallpox. Children were particularly vulnerable to the *Zeitgeist*. Orphaned, abandoned, or simply ordered out of the house to earn a crust by indigent parents, the streets of Europe's big cities teemed with children who were the visible detritus of Europe's 'Hard Times'.

Many marginalised and masterless children survived on casual employment. The affluent always wanted parcels carried or water drawn from the parish pump (Paris still had no water on tap in 1850). The more resourceful created permanent jobs for themselves and in the first part of the nineteenth century could be found working as shoe-blacks, newspaper boys, road sweepers and so on from an early age. In 1842, across the Atlantic in New York, the abolitionist and philanthropist, Lydia Maria Child (1802–80), found an urchin selling papers, with a bundle under his arm 'more big as he could carry', who was only about four.[128] Some street children even tried to live respectably, such as the two orphan flower sellers depicted in the famous sketches of the London poor by Henry Mayhew (1812–87), published first in the *Morning Chronicle* in the late 1840s. One was fifteen, the other eleven. Irish by background and Catholic by confession, they and their brother, a costermonger's boy, had looked after themselves since their mother had died seven years before. They had a room in a house near Drury Lane, which they sub-rented from an Irish couple (who lived in a recess). The elder girl prided herself on her independence. On her mother's death, she had taken control. 'I've got myself, and my brother and sister a bit of bread ever since, and never had any help but from the neighbours. I never troubled the parish'. Neither girl 'ever missed mass on a Sunday'.[129]

A large number of uncared for children however – indeed perhaps most – must have eventually ended up at odds with society rather than finding a precarious niche within it. In France in the second half of the eighteenth century, it was calculated that nearly two million children were without support (a seventh perhaps of the total).[130] At best they were beggars

---

[128] V. DiGiralomo, 'Crying the News. Children, Street Work and the American Press, 1830–1920s', (Princeton University: Ph.D. thesis, 1997), p. 33.

[129] *Mayhew's Characters*, ed. P. Quennell (London: Spring Books, n.d.), pp. 87–90. Mayhew has been accused of creating 'types', so the portrait may be coloured: see G. Himmelfarb, 'Mayhew's Poor: A Problem of Identity', *Victorian Studies*, 14 (1970–71), 307–20.

[130] Figures either now or in the past for those today we would call 'street children' are notoriously hard to come by and depend very much on definition. For an account of the creation of the numbers of street children in modern Brazil, see T. Hecht, *At Home in the Street: Street Children of Northeast Brazil.* (Cambridge:

– some operating in packs under an adult controller but others working on their own and scarcely able to look after themselves. Gervaise and Anne Séranges, apprehended by the *maréchaussée* (France's roving mounted police force) in the Puy-de-Dôme, were two and six, and too young to answer questions. At worst the girls became prostitutes or the boys petty and not so petty criminals. Girls as young as eight were taken in by the Aix-en-Provence *maison de pureté*; at Riom the *dépôt de mendicité* held street walkers who were syphilitic before they had even menstruated. Toulouse, Lyons and Paris were all plagued by bands of child thieves, usually orphans and often scarcely into their teens. In the French capital, one gang was so notorious, it had its own sobriquet: the *bande de Raffia*. Made up of boys from eleven to eighteen, it specialised in stealing chickens and rabbits from the suburbs, then selling them in the centre of the city. One of their number also 'knew how to cut noiselessly through the grills that covered watchmakers windows' and pilfer watches. Children were also heavily involved in the contraband trade. The French finance minister towards the end of the American war of Independence, Jacques Necker (1732–1804), suggested there were a staggering 6,600 children hauled before the French courts for smuggling salt (a state monopoly).[131]

Paris only had 600,000 inhabitants at the end of the century, although it would grow by a further 60 per cent by 1850. London, on the other hand, was Europe's largest city and had a population of nearly a million by 1800. 50 years later its size had more than doubled. In 1837, the year that Charles Dickens, ever a friend to the downtrodden child after his own early experiences in the blacking factory, began to publish *Oliver Twist* in *Bentley's Miscellany*, London must have had more children living by their wits on the streets than anywhere else in the world. Dickens was not the first by any mean to bring the problem of masterless children and their criminal activities to the public's attention. In fact, Europeans had been worrying on and off about child criminals since the sixteenth century, from the moment some aspect of youthful behaviour began to be labelled anti-social, and for the previous 25 years it had been a particular English fixation. Nor, as modern research has shown did Dickens provide an accurate representation of juvenile delinquency: child gangs were uncommon in the first half of the nineteenth century, and the eponymous hero was hardly a plausible street child.[132] Rather his novel was important because it helped to disseminate and shape a more reflective attitude towards children caught up in crime. This had its roots in Romantic views of childhood as special and different from adulthood but was also fired by more utilitarian fears of the potential threat of the poor to middle-class well-being. Just as the early nineteenth century witnessed a growing concern for child chimney sweeps and factory children, so reformers in the British elite were anxious that child criminals should not be confused with or become hardened adult villains.[133]

Cambridge University Press, 1998), For some modern estimates, see below fns 207 and 208.

[131] O. Hufton, *The Poor of Eighteenth-Century France 1750–1789* (Oxford: Oxford University Press, 1974), pp. 108–12, 241, 268–69, 287–88, 306–16. In eighteenth-century France, the *dépôts de mendicité* contained vagrants and beggars; the *hopitaux générales* (which had performed this function in the seventeenth century) chiefly held the elderly sick. Prostitutes were only rounded up if they were diseased. Some were offered the chance to redeem themselves in houses run by the Catholic church.

[132] For a recent account of child criminals in Dickens's day, see H. Shore, *Artful Dodgers: Youth and Crime in Early Nineteenth Century London* (Woodbridge: Boydell Press, 1999).

[133] On child labour reforms, see Ch. 4, pp. 189–92, and M. Flegel, *Conceptualizing Cruelty to Children in Nineteenth-Century England. Literature, Representation and the NSPCC* (Farnham: Ashgate, 2009).

Juvenile Delinquents in Early Nineteenth-Century London

Heather Shore

By the end of the Napoleonic wars in 1815 there was a widespread belief in the increase of juvenile crime in London.[134] Whether there was more juvenile crime in the nineteenth century than before or since is a moot point and one which has less bearing than the question of how juvenile crime was perceived by contemporaries, and on which 'facts' and 'stories' they based their understandings. However, what we do know is that this apparent 'rise' was not peculiar to London. There *were* concerns about juvenile crime in places other than London. The industrial/urban conurbations of Manchester, Birmingham and Liverpool provoked similar sentiments. Arguably, in this period, a number of factors, such as population rise, urbanisation, poverty, and demobilisation inter-reacted, leading to something of a 'moral panic' about such crime. London, though, had long been the organising focus for both debate, and legislative enactment concerned with crime.[135] As a result, in the case of law and order issues, London remained a major focus. Thus, the metropolis was thought to be home to a criminal class of juvenile offenders, bred in the particular circumstances produced by urban life.

Whilst concern had been expressed about delinquent youth in previous centuries it was only from the 1810s that consistent representations and inquiries started to appear.[136] Why it happened at this time is the subject of some broad debate amongst historians of delinquency. However, in London, as well as perhaps other urban centres, the convergence of the public and the private sectors in many matters of domestic policy was surely important. Initiatives in the metropolis focused on a range of causes. Juvenile crime was perhaps such a key focus, because it combined a range of themes of early nineteenth-century philanthropy: the children of the poor, the state of the penal system, and the disorderly streets. Moreover, by 'rescuing' London's delinquent children, it would mean that future generations of criminals could be diverted.[137]

As a result, private initiatives set up to deal with juvenile crimes, such as the Marine Society (1756), the Philanthropic Society (1788), the Refuge for the Destitute – not exclusively for juveniles but strongly involved with the rescue and reform of the young (1804) – and private individuals – such as Mary Carpenter (1807–77), Sydney Turner (1814–79), and Matthew Davenport Hill (1792–1872) – mirrored the ideological leanings of parliamentary penal policy.[138] Individuals involved in the voluntary sector became enmeshed in the public machinery of juvenile justice. Parliamentary committees and commissions did not consist solely of government officials, magistrates and constables,

---

[134] For discussion of the juvenile crime debate in this period see P. King, 'The Rise of Juvenile Delinquency in England, 1780–1840', *Past and Present*, 160:1 (1998), 116–66; Shore, *Artful Dodgers*, particularly appendix 2.

[135] The best guide to nineteenth-century juvenile justice legislation is to be found in L. Radzinowicz and R. Hood, *A History of English Criminal Law: vol. 5, The Emergence of Penal Policy in Victorian and Edwardian England* (London: Stevens, 1986), pp. 133–70.

[136] See P. Griffiths, 'Juvenile Delinquency in Time', in P. Cox and H. Shore, *Becoming Delinquent: British and European Youth, 1650–1950* (Aldershot: Ashgate, 2002), pp. 25–43.

[137] See H. Cunningham, *The Children of the Poor: Representations of Childhood Since the Seventeenth Century* (Oxford: Blackwell, 1991), and on popular and elite fears, see G. Pearson, *Hooligan: A History of Respectable Fears* (London: Macmillan, 1983).

[138] For discussion of the philanthropic response to juveniles, see I. Pinchbeck and M. Hewitt, *Children in English Society, II: From the Eighteenth Century to the Children's Act 1948* (London: Routledge and Kegan Paul, 1973).

but also took evidence from the voluntary sector. In many ways, it was from these people that the penal professionals of the later nineteenth century were descended. These commentators and activists promoted a more child-centred approach to juvenile criminals. Though early modern policy makers and welfare practitioners had not been unaware of the specific needs of children, truly separate institutions for youngsters, both at the level of trial and punishment, were an innovation of the nineteenth century. The Juvenile Offenders Act of 1847 allowed children under the age of fourteen to be tried summarily before two magistrates, thus making the process of trial for children quicker and removing it from the public glare of the higher courts (the age limit was raised to sixteen in 1850). Then, between 1854 and 1857, a series of Reformatory and Industrial School Acts replaced prison with specific juvenile institutions. These acts represent the culmination and codification of both public and private initiatives, which from the late eighteenth century increasingly corresponded.

It seems that a number of factors influenced the way in which policy makers imagined and understood the 'problem' of juvenile crime. According to an influential report from 1816 the main causes were:

The improper conduct of parents
The want of education
The want of suitable employment
The violation of the Sabbath, and habits of gambling in the public-streets
The severity of the criminal code
The defective state of the police
The existing system of prison discipline.[139]

These 'causes', particularly the first four, became a mantra for the majority of commentators, whatever their background or interests. In debates over the following years about the emergence of summary trial for juveniles, and the establishment of the industrial and reformatory schools, these causes fluctuated little. Although contemporary reports commented on the 'swarms of ragged children' infesting the metropolis, the investigations of social and penal reformers were heavily influenced by what might be called a 'hard-core' of juvenile offenders. These were youths, overwhelmingly boys, who were found in London at Newgate and Coldbath Fields prisons, in the houses of correction at Tothill Fields and Clerkenwell, and in the courts of the Old Bailey and Westminster. Discussion of juvenile offenders in other parts of the country did occur – the factory increasingly became the focus as a site of disorder and delinquency, while the work of the Reverend John Clay (1796–1858) with prisoners in Preston in the 1840s was referred to frequently. Significantly, however, the parliamentary debate was coloured by an understanding of metropolitan delinquency. Thus, in the early nineteenth century, juvenile crime in a London setting tended to dominate the construction of the young offender.

This was further consolidated by prevalent stereotypes of London pickpockets and thieves. For example, the most famous interviews with criminals in the nineteenth century are those conducted by John Binny (active mid-nineteenth century) in volume IV of Henry Mayhew's, *London Labour and the London Poor*, published in 1861–62 and titled *Those That Will Not Work, comprising Prostitutes, Thieves, Swindlers and Beggars, by several contributors*. Binny had been influenced by Mayhew himself, who in 1850 had published in the *Morning Chronicle* an oral history of a young delinquent that was later used in *London Labour*. Mayhew's skills as an interviewer of nineteenth-century street

---

[139] *Report of the Committee for Investigating the causes of the Alarming Increase of Juvenile Delinquency in the Metropolis* (London: J. F. Dove, 1816), pp. 10–11.

types were unparalleled, and are of value both in terms of social history and in revealing the ways in which the model of the juvenile criminal was constructed. Interviewing a fifteen-year-old pickpocket in a London lodging-house, Mayhew's physical description of the boy's tools of the trade is almost uncomfortably intimate:

> He was a slim, agile lad, with a sharp but not vulgar expression, and small features. His hands were of a singular delicacy and beauty. His fingers were very long, and no lady's could have been more taper. A burglar told me that with such a hand he ought to have made his fortune.[140]

The characteristics implicit in the work on delinquents by both Mayhew and Binny continued a tradition of describing the juvenile offender in a particular mode. He was male, often of small stature, and sharp-witted. Like Dickens's Artful Dodger he often had the manner of a small adult, a boy-man, a combination of innocence and experience, of immaturity and mature masculinity which seems to have both disturbed and attracted reformers and investigators.[141] One of these was William Augustus Miles, a confused and sometimes controversial figure, who interviewed delinquents in the 1830s as part of the investigations of the Victorian reformer, Edwin Chadwick (1800–90), into the constabulary.[142] For Miles and many of his contemporaries, the archetypal juvenile offender was a pickpocket, or an aspiring one. Juvenile criminals were understood to be working their way through a model of criminal progression. From scrumping apples from orchards, to shoplifting from stalls and generalised petty thieving, according to this view, a boy aspired to the more skilful occupation of picking-pockets. (See Figure 30).

Why was this characterisation so important and central to the ways in which Victorian juvenile offenders have been mythologised? Firstly the pickpocket suggested a level of skill and thus training. For the social commentators of the early nineteenth century this opened a frightening vista of an organised sub-culture in which adult agents trained the children of the street into crime. Secondly, there was progression beyond picking pockets: the most skilful thieves became burglars. The most admired of these boy-men, pickpocket-burglars were described as being members of the 'swell mob', a loose, and probably semi-mythological, group of prosperous thieves who dressed stylishly, lived in the best parts of town and cruised the streets of London with their girls on their arms, flaunting their success in the hierarchies of the criminal underworld.[143] Indeed, whilst commentators might have talked generally about ragged children and poor urchins, in the pamphlets and reports the emphasis was placed on a particular representation of the young offender that closely reflected fears about the criminal classes, the street and the underworld. It was a characterisation that was implicitly, and often explicitly, gendered. Although the proportion of female to male juvenile offenders was low, many girls were tried summarily or through other informal methods. The model of the juvenile criminal that appears in nineteenth-century texts was determinedly male; the female played a peripheral role, and was remarked upon more often as being a source of sexual corruption.

So what was the reality for juvenile offenders in the nineteenth century? Youths

---

[140] *The Morning Chronicle*, 29 Jan. 1850, Letter XX.
[141] H. Shore, 'The Trouble with Boys: Gender and the "Invention" of the Juvenile Offender in the Early Nineteenth Century', in M. Arnot and C. Urborne (eds), *Gender and Crime in Modern Europe* (London: UCL Press 1999), pp. 75–92.
[142] For a discussion of Miles's role in Chadwick's investigations see D. Philips and R. Storch, *Policing Provincial England, 1829–1856: The Politics of Reform* (Leicester: Leicester University Press, 1999), ch. 6, pp. 111–35.
[143] Shore, *Artful Dodgers*, pp. 44–45.

who fitted the popular caricatures of the 'swell mob' could certainly be found, but most children were drawn into crime through poverty and debilitating backgrounds. To some extent the activities engaged in by delinquent children were the actions of unruly teenagers influenced by peers and the need for adolescent excitement, and have been described on the streets of seventeenth-century Norwich and twentieth-century Manchester, as much as nineteenth-century London.[144] But most were criminals by necessity, and they worked on their own or in small groups: more organised gangs of youth delinquents are uncommon in this period. There were occasional references to gangs of young men and boys, yet these are few and far between. For example, in 1817 the constable of St. Giles and St. George's, Bloomsbury, complained about the gangs of young boys who could be found gambling in the streets.[145] Similarly the year before, the magistrate William Fielding described the 'enormous associations in the Metropolis that went by the name of the "Cutter lads"'.[146] The 'swell-mob' was also a popular caricature, as we have seen. However, these references to gangs and to the 'swell mob' were often vague. How far these represented a real gang presence is doubtful.

The most typical experience for juvenile offenders in this period was to spend some time, perhaps a year or more, committing fairly minor crime, petty theft and vagrancy, for which they would occasionally be brought in front of the magistrate, and if found guilty receive a fine, a whipping, or more likely a short spell in the house of correction, or in London, Bridewell. If this did not divert them, sooner or later they would be indicted for a felonious crime, larceny, pick-pocketing or theft from a dwelling-house (often in their capacity as domestic servants), for which they would appear at a higher court: in London this would be Clerkenwell, the Old Bailey, or Westminster. From there, having already spent time in prison on remand, they would be acquitted, or if found guilty, sentenced to a spell in the house of correction, or to transportation, or to death.

Of course there were a number of other routes by which children could be incorporated into the criminal justice system. We have to remember the co-existence of the public justice system with its trials and model institutions – such as Parkhurst prison on the Isle of Wight, opened for boys in 1838 and much criticised by contemporary reformers such as Mary Carpenter – with the private initiatives that continued to take in both children who had actually committed crime, and those it was felt were in danger of becoming delinquent. These were the children that Mary Carpenter designated as the 'perishing' in her 1851 text, *Reformatory Schools for the Children of the Perishing and Dangerous Classes, and for Juvenile Offenders*.

Ultimately, I would argue that the early nineteenth century was a crucial period in the 'making' of the juvenile delinquent. Whilst certainly there are strong continuities with early modern attitudes to and more formal strategies of dealing with disorderly youth, it was in this period that language, legislation, as well as criminal justice structures converged. As a result, in a period when the social lives of the poor came under considerable scrutiny, the children of the poor became a key cypher in the need to understand and control crime and disorder.

. . . .

---

[144] Griffiths, *Youth and Authority*; Davies, 'Youth Gangs'.

[145] *Select Committee on the State of the Police of the Metropolis*, 1817, viii, pp. 360–1, evidence of Samuel Furzon.

[146] *Select Committee on the State of the Police of the Metropolis*, 1816, i, p. 129; Shore, *Artful Dodgers*, p. 45.

For the first two-thirds of the nineteenth century Europe's masterless and homeless children were treated with the same ineffectual brutality as in an earlier age: if apprehended, they were incarcerated in austere conditions but for the most part were allowed to roam free. So too were poor children put on the streets to earn some sort of living by hard-pressed parents and relatives. Even in Britain, where all outdoor relief was theoretically abolished from 1834, women and children were not usually forced into the workhouse.[147] Efforts to address the problem more positively or show child criminals in a more sympathetic light were met with conservative suspicion. In 1839–40 *Bentley's Miscellany* followed *Oliver Twist* with the even more popular, *Jack Sheppard*, by W. Harrison Ainsworth (1805–84). Ainsworth's romanticised story of an early eighteenth-century petty thief, hanged at 21, who had been notorious in his own day for his astonishing gaol breaks, was quickly transferred to the stage. There were eight versions being played in London theatres while the serial was still running. The young in the 1840s and 50s seemed to have been particularly drawn to such iconic anti-heroes as Sheppard and Dick Turpin (immortalised in Ainsworth's *Rookwood* in 1834) and lapped up cheap abridged versions of these and other 'Newgate' novels. Conservatives were appalled and thought their authors were encouraging vice.[148]

In western Europe towards the end of the century, however, the state and the burgeoning voluntary sector began to approach the problem of street children more humanely. Thanks to the initiative taken by figures such as Dr Barnardo (1845–1905) in Britain real efforts were made to clear the streets of homeless or neglected children living off their wits. The orphaned, abandoned, abused and delinquent were still institutionalised but now in much greater numbers, under much better conditions and for a much longer time (until they were in their early teens and judged old enough to work outside).[149] At the same time, the introduction of universal elementary education across western Europe from the 1870s ensured that poor children generally (homeless or not) were off the streets and out of trouble for large parts of the day, while the growth in the towns and cities of Sunday schools, boys' clubs and youth movements primarily run by the churches, unions and political parties, offered novel opportunities for many poor children to spend their leisure hours more profitably.[150] As a result, the street children of Dickens's day became a thing of the past. This is not to say that young children were no longer to be seen on the streets. In an age when motorised transport was still in its infancy they still commanded the lanes and side streets of working-class districts. But now the street was a site of children's play and their activities offered little danger to adults beyond the odd broken window.

Yet, despite these developments, in Britain at least, adults still felt threatened by the feral young on the eve of the First World War. This was largely because the great drive to tame the working-class young, epitomised by the founding of the Boys' Brigade (1883) and later the Boy Scouts (1908), had limited success. Even in the mid-1920s only half of Oxford's young males were in a youth organisation. Many sons of the poor refused to join or lacked

---

[147] M. E. Rose, *The Relief of Poverty, 1834–1914* (London: Macmillan, 1986), esp. p. 53 (amounts spent on indoor and outdoor relief).

[148] J. Springhall, *Youth, Popular Culture and Moral Panics. Penny Gaffs to Gangster Raps* (London: Macmillan, 1998), ch. 1.

[149] G. Wagner, *Barnardo* (London: Weidenfeld and Nicholson, 1979); L. Murdoch, *Imagined Orphans: Poor Families, Child Welfare and Contested Citizenship in London* (New Brunswick, NJ: Rutgers University Press, 2006). One of the most interesting but little known institutions for neglected children established in the late nineteenth century was the boarding industrial school, deliberately sited in isolated areas. Set up by a range of charities and churches, these schools contained 24,000 children in 1900: see N. Sheldon, 'Socialising the Anti-Social: England's Industrial Schools', in L. W. B. Brockliss and N. Sheldon (eds), *Mass Education and the Limits of State Building, c. 1870–c. 1930* (Basingstoke: Palgrave Macmillan, forthcoming).

[150] On the boys' movements, see J. Springhall, *Youth, Empire and Society: British Youth Movements, 1883–1940* (London: Croom Helm, 1977).

the means to become members, while those who took the plunge were frequently expelled for misbehaviour. When the organisations paraded around town in neat array, emphasising that the streets were now in the possession of respectable youth, the sturdily disrespectable responded with jeers and taunts. As a result, middle-class do-gooders were convinced that the resistance to their overtures reflected a deep-rooted and dangerous subversiveness.[151] This belief was only enhanced by new views about adolescence at the turn of the twentieth century, which were enunciated most stridently by the American psychologist, G. Stanley Hall (1844–1914) in a work published in 1904. Hall famously claimed of adolescence that: 'every step of the upward way is strewn with wreckage of body, mind, and morals. There is not only arrest, but perversion, at every stage, and hoodlumism, juvenile crime, and secret vice'.[152] Adolescence was now seen as a special time in a child's development, when all children, not just working-class boys, were likely to be disruptive and potential criminals.[153]

In Britain as well, there was a particular fear which continued throughout the post-war era that unsupervised adolescents would form gangs and terrorise the local neighbourhood, especially in the 1930s when teenage cinemagoers were subjected to a relentless diet of Hollywood gangster movies.[154] Some writers of fiction gently mocked this new panic. The first of many *William* books by Richmal Crompton (1890–1969) came out in 1922. Their hero was an unsupervised, albeit middle-class, boy on the edge of adolescence, who had his own gang 'The Outlaws'. But William and his friends were scarcely hooligans. Though they regularly clashed with a rival gang, 'the Hubert Laneites', they spent most of their time trying with no success to right wrong and succour distress: they were dysfunctional knights errant.[155] Other authors, though, fed the alarm, none more so than Graham Greene who in 1938 published *Brighton Rock*, an underworld thriller about the live and death of a teenage gang leader, Pinkie Brown.[156]

Eastern Europe, on the other hand, was very different from the west. Far poorer and less industrially developed street-children remained a fact of life long into the twentieth century. The writer, Maxim Gorky (1868–1936), was just one of many Russians who grew up on the streets in the late nineteenth century. Brought up by his drunken grandfather in Novgorod, he was thrown out of the house aged nine and forced to fend for himself in the industrial towns along the Volga. His experiences in the 1880s were harrowing.[157] Later generations of Russian children, too, fared no better. The breakdown of society that followed the 1917 Revolution created unprecedented numbers of orphaned and lost children, whose fate was movingly depicted in a 1922 film made for the newly formed Save the Children Fund, called *Famine – The Russian Famine Of 1921*.[158] So too did the Second World War in which the Soviet Union lost at least twenty million dead. Even children with parents were to all intents and

---

[151] J. Gillis, 'The Evolution of Juvenile Delinquency in England, 1890–1914', *Past and Present*, 67:1 (1975), 96–126 (specifically on youth crime and youth movements in Oxford).

[152] G. S. Hall. *Adolescence: Its Psychology and its Relations to Physiology, Anthropology, Sociology, Sex, Crime, Religion, ad Education* (New York: Appleton, 1904), p. xiv.

[153] H. Chudacoff, 'Adolescence and Youth', in P. S. Fass (ed.), *Encyclopedia of Children and Childhood. In History and Society* (3 vols; Indianapolis: Macmillan USA, 2004), i, pp. 15–20; On Britain in particular, see J. Springhall, *Coming of Age: Adolescence in Britain, 1860–1960* (Dublin: Gill and Macmillan, 1986).

[154] Springhall, *Youth*, ch. 4.

[155] http://en.wikipedia.org/wiki/Just_William (accessed 2 Apr. 2009).

[156] It was made into a film in 1947.

[157] His experience of working in a bakery fourteen hours a day is recorded in his story *Twenty-Six Men and a Girl* (1899). Gorky's life to the age of nine is depicted in *My Childhood* (1913).

[158] *Save the Children* was set up after the First World War to bring succour to children in need in the defeated nations. See H. Montgomery, 'Socialising the Enemy Child', in G. Lillehammer (ed.), *Socialisation: Archaeological and Historical Approaches* (Stavanger: University of Stavanger Press, 2010).

purposes abandoned in the years of reconstruction that followed. Simply to survive and fulfil the government's economic plan, both parents were forced to work long hours and left children to their own devices. Many ended up in violent gangs for mutual support.[159]

Juvenile Delinquents in the Post-War Soviet Union

Juliane Fürst

In April 1953 a document from the Poltava Party committee informed Ukrainian officials in Kiev of the discovery and unravelling of a criminal teenage gang that, according to the author, had 'terrorised the town of Poltava for a considerable period of time'. Only the night before they had robbed seventeen people threatening them with pistols and knives. In the scuffle that broke out during their capture they killed one policeman and wounded another gravely. Their leader, Viktor Sil'nichii, who, at eighteen, was by far the oldest member of the gang, dramatically committed suicide when police burst into his flat.

It became apparent that the majority of those involved in the highly organised and strictly hierarchical group were offspring of very respectable parents and attended the local secondary school. Sil'nichii was the son of the head of the Department for Party, Komsomol and Trade Union Organisations at the local party committee – a position that carried quite some prestige and influence. The father of fifteen-year-old I. Turlo was the head of the regional agency for transport. This position entitled him to possess a pistol, which was frequently used by his son in his criminal endeavours. It was from this pistol that Sil'nichii fired the shots that killed both the policeman Shveits and himself. Another five members of the gang had less illustrious parents, but came from solid families with either one or both parents in employment. They attended school regularly and had hitherto not come to the attention of the authorities. Yet at least two of them had no fathers and one came from a household whose members had to rely on a single state pension for their living. The gang also included four teenagers, who neither studied nor worked. In the coded language of Soviet documents this meant that these youngsters had fallen through the tight net of Soviet control, which left little room for voluntary or involuntary unemployment and idleness. They were akin to street children – outside the controls and privileges of the social system and largely left to fend for themselves. Their refusal to participate in the Soviet system in the proper manner also gave them a whiff of anti-Sovietness. In the eyes of the authorities they were condemned before they even committed a crime.[160]

Is this just a tale of a few teenagers having gone off the rails in a small town in Soviet Ukraine? Is this little more than an unfortunate incident, which took place in a society that prided itself on the eradication of crime and the creation of a new man devoted to the service of the collective? Or does this story give us a glimpse into the hidden world of Soviet juvenile delinquency – childhoods that were not filled with Stalinist happiness – and societal problems, which had implications far beyond the

---

[159] The most recent study of Russian childhood in the twentieth century is C. Kelly, *Children's World: Growing up in Russia, 1890–1991* (New Haven.: Yale University Press, 2007).

[160] TsDAHOU (Tsentralnyi Derzhavnyi Arkhiv Hromadskykh Organisatsii Ukraini / Central State Archive of Civil Organisation of Ukraine, Kiev) f. 1, op. 24, d. 2818, l. 240–43.

loss of life and property? The bare facts, as reported by the Poltava Party committee, certainly refer to a number of features that were characteristic of Soviet post-war juvenile delinquency and the way in which late Stalinist society made sense of and responded to the phenomenon of criminal children.

Approximately half of the members of the Poltava gang came from poor or disadvantaged backgrounds and were likely to have had material motives for their crimes. The fact that hunger, displacement and material deprivation had a direct correlation to juvenile delinquency is borne out by the statistics of the Soviet prosecution organs, which show a remarkable rise in the number of convicted youngsters under sixteen, during and in the immediate aftermath of the war. While in 1940 only 20,881 young offenders faced charges, in 1942 40,006 children under sixteen were convicted of crimes. The number of children picked up by the police and charged by the courts rose steadily during the war, peaking in 1944, when 77,970 youngsters between twelve and fifteen were charged. In 1948, with living conditions improving, the number fell below pre-war level and continued to decline until 1955.[161] The vast majority of crimes by children consisted of some form of theft. In 1944, a secret report by Lavrenti Beria (1899–1953) to the members of the Defence Council put the number of thefts and robberies at roughly 58,000 out of a total of just under 65,000 crimes committed by youth.[162] In 1947, Stalin was informed that 90 per cent of crimes committed by minors (twelve to seventeen-year-olds) were of a material nature.[163]

The examples provided by the Soviet prosecution organs demonstrate that most incidences of theft were of small-scale nature and hardly surpassed what was needed for subsistence. In terms of perpetrators, the largest group of young offenders consisted of those who neither worked nor studied (making up close to a third of all those charged in 1944), followed by homeless children, who represented just over a tenth of all offenders. Both categories were, to a certain extent, results of the chaos and destruction of war. While parentless and homeless children – classified as *besprizornye* (without home) in Soviet terminology – reflected the loss of civilian and military life, children, who neither worked nor studied, indicated the break-down of much of Soviet control in those years. A lack of teachers, absence of parents and disorganisation of those Soviet institutions, which were charged with child supervision, such as the pioneer and the Komsomol organisations or the trade unions, all contributed to the fact that more and more children roamed the streets on their own.[164] These youngsters, who, if parental control was judged to be virtually absent, were called *beznadzornye* (without supervision) in official Soviet jargon, often had close contact with networks of homeless children and the adult criminal underworld. Many *besprizornye* and *beznadzornye* preferred life on the street to that in a dysfunctional family or in a Soviet institution. While *beznadzornye* tended to stay in their local area, many orphans and children, who had left home permanently, embarked on long and extended train journeys across the Soviet Union. Stations and markets were their favourite places to hang out, reassemble into groups and gather food.[165]

---

[161] GARF (Gosudarstvennyi Arkhiv Rossiskoi Federatsii / State Archive of the Russian Federation, Moscow) R-f. 8131, op. 37, d. 4774, l.8–9; R-f. 8131, op. 29, d. 501, l. 117–118; R-f. 8131, op. 29, d. 506, l. 135; RGASPI (Rossiskii Gosudarstvennyi Arkhiv Sotsialno-Politicheskoi Istorii / Russian State Archive of Socio-Political History, Moscow) M-f. 1, op. 8, d. 236, l. 238; RGASPI f. 1, op. 7, d. 35, l. 10; GARF 9401, op. 2. d. 93; GARF R-f. 8131, op. 32, d. 1892, l. 83; GARF R-f. 8131, op. 32, d. 4556, l. 40.

[162] GARF R-f. 9401, op. 2, d 93, l. 374.

[163] *Ibid.*, op. 2, d. 199, l. 178.

[164] RGASPI M-f. 1, op. 7, d. 69, l. 26–28; TsDAHOU f. 1, op. 24, d. 2993, l. 116.

[165] J. Fürst, 'Homeless and Vagrant Children and the Reconstruction of Soviet Society', *The Slavonic and Eastern European Review*, 86:2 (2008), 232–58.

They were hardly a new phenomenon to the Russian and Soviet urban landscape. Revolution and Civil War had pushed thousands of children onto the street in previous decades.[166] Every major town had child collection points in an attempt to overcome the persistent problem of homeless waifs. Fuelled by famine and post-war displacement the number of children passing through these points, which served as a kind of temporary detention centre, peaked in 1947 with roughly 360,000 children collected by the police and other agencies.[167] Likely to commit petty thefts for a living and vulnerable to arrests because of their ragged appearance, these homeless and neglected children made up a large segment of post-war juvenile offenders. A 1948 report estimated that 40 per cent of all juvenile crime in the Soviet Union was committed by children classified as *besprizornye* and *beznadzornye*.[168] The homeless waifs' own popular culture demonstrates how they considered themselves victims of poverty and destitution. Their songs, often handed down from previous generations of street children, focus on the transformation of innocent orphans into petty thieves and ultimately into professional criminals.[169]

Thus, while the criminal youth gang in Poltava operated at a time when overall crime was on the decline, some of their members fit the typical profile of offenders in the war and immediate post-war years. Even though living conditions improved remarkably for the country after the good harvest of 1947, which ended the years of extreme hunger and poverty, many families continued to struggle to make a daily living. Single parent families were still the norm rather than the exception. Reconstruction had not succeeded in eradicating the traces of war. Poltava in Ukraine was a place likely to have borne the scars of the recent conflict as late as 1953. It is telling that, while in the Soviet Union overall 40 per cent of crimes were estimated to have been committed by homeless or neglected children, a Ukrainian document of the previous year puts the number for the republic at 69 per cent, indicating that material problems remained of significant importance in this region.[170] Similarly, a secret NKVD report of 1945 reported more *besprizornye* and *beznadzornye* to have been arrested in Ukraine than in any other location including the cities of Moscow and Leningrad.[171]

The family histories of other juvenile offenders point to another factor that was more prominent among those who had lived through occupation. Far worse than having a dead father, who was a hero of the war, was to have parents accused of collaboration and imprisoned as traitors. The stigma of being the child of a 'non-Soviet person' appears again and again in police and prosecution reports. The child murderer of a seven-year-old schoolgirl, bludgeoned to death for her coat and a sandwich, was revealed to have a father accused of collaboration. Without a male breadwinner, his family was destitute. The taint of treason meant that official financial support was not forthcoming. Family and neighbours shunned the social outcasts.[172]

None the less, poverty and other consequences of war alone cannot account for the events in Poltava or for similar crimes committed by minors all over the Soviet Union. After all some of the prominent members of the gang had been children of well-to-do, even privileged, parents. The fact that not only socially disadvantaged children turned to a life of loitering and criminal activity is already visible in the

---

[166] A. Ball, *And Now My Soul is Hardened: Abandoned Children in Soviet Russia, 1918–1930* (Berkeley: University of California Press, 1994), pp. 44–60.
[167] GARF R-f. 8131, op. 32, d. 1893, l. 39.
[168] *Ibid.*, op. 37, d. 4774, l. 8.
[169] For the 1920s see Ball, *And Now My Soul is Hardened*, p. 50.
[170] TsDAHOU f. 7, op. 5, d. 391, l. 111.
[171] RGASPI M-f. 1, op. 7, d. 128, l. 1.
[172] TsDAHOU f. 7, op. 2, d. 116, l. 174.

statistics concerning the social make-up of children picked up by police as so-called *beznadzornye*. Right after the war the group of 'neither studying nor working' made up the largest percentage, yet regular pupils followed closely.[173] By 1951 84.1 per cent of all children that went through the busy Odessa reception room had parents, who were in regular employment and integrated into normal Soviet life. Overall, it seems that, as the immediate consequences of war receded, street children and juvenile offenders became smaller in numbers, but more determined. 72 per cent of the Odessa sample were repeat offenders and adhered to the strict codex of street life rather than Soviet norms.[174] Offences became more likely to be group offences and, subsistence theft was replaced by more large-scale and organised operations. At the same time the percentage of 'normal' children involved in crime rose.[175] The authorities noted with concern that even Komsomol members, supposedly the ideological elite among youth, were frequently found among those sentenced for criminal deeds.[176]

The fact that these unlikely offenders operated almost exclusively in gangs and organisations indicates the importance of the collective as a factor motivating criminal activity. The clandestine and forbidden nature of crime provided a strong sense of identity to groups of youngsters, who hungered for adventure and a feeling of belonging. While this sentiment was nothing new to either the Soviet Union or the post-war period, it was none the less strengthened by the circumstances of time and place. The Soviet Union actively promoted the idea of the perfect collective as one of the prerequisites of achieving communism. Successful and strong collectives pervaded official propaganda. Soviet children grew up with wonderful groups of friends inhabiting their books and imaginary worlds: Pavel Korchagin, Timur and his group and the brave members of *Molodaia Gvardiia* (Young Guard).[177] The latter group, a Komsomol underground organisation in the Donbass during the German occupation, was made famous through a celebrated novel by Alexandr Fadeev and a blockbuster film. Young people's response to this story of heroism, sacrifice and undying loyalty indicates how quickly the officially endorsed sentiment of collectivity could be perverted and resurface in a criminal context. The group was imitated by children and youngsters all over the country.

Most of the formations secretly set up by youngsters were harmless childish games, disliked by the authority because they challenged the monopoly of the Komsomol, but remaining firmly within the legal framework. Some, however, used their newly found collectivism to commit petty theft or other small crimes. Instead of turning their energies against the fascist invader, they directed their desire to rebel against the law and order of the state they lived in. Just like their underground models they liked to carry weapons. In a school raid, which took place after one such group was discovered, the authorities found seventeen flick knives, four rifles, three Finnish knives, three boxes full of ammunition and one dagger.[178] Eric Naiman has pointed out that the communal nature of gang-related crime was very troubling to the Bolshevik authorities, who saw 'in the event ... a distorted reflection of [their] own desire'.[179]

Most gangs did not need any direct inspiration. The desire to belong and find a

---

[173] RGASPI f. 17, op. 126, d. 28, l. 217.

[174] TsDAHOU f. 1, op. 24, d. 2993, l. 105.

[175] *Ibid.* f. 1, op. 24, d. 2993, l. 116.

[176] See for example GARF R-f. 8131, op. 29, l. 147.

[177] Pavel Korchagin was the hero of the celebrated novel *How the Steel was Tempered* by Nikolai Ostrovskii. Timur was the child hero of *Timur and his Friends* by Arkadii Gaidar.

[178] TsDAHOU f. 1, op. 23, d. 5039, l. 256.

[179] E. Naiman, *Sex in Public: The Incarnation of Early Soviet Ideology* (Princeton: Princeton University Press, 1994), p. 272.

collective identity was both an integral part of growing up and a logical consequence of a society that stressed communality. Official collectives, however, were only one side of life in the Soviet Union. A strong and long-established underground world operated according to its own rules, spoke its own jargon and provided an alternative society to that ruled by Soviet norms and laws. This other world had a huge fascination for children. In post-war Moscow the legend of a group of robbers, who called themselves Black Cat (*Chernaia Koshka*) enjoyed huge popularity among children, who replayed the group's supposed adventures. (In all likelihood the group never existed).[180] The Jazz musician Aleksei Kozlov also testifies to the allure of the criminal world to the children of his courtyard: 'The image of thieves evoked not just fear, but also a certain feeling of admiration. A thief displayed not just contempt for risk and fox-like skills, he also lived under strict laws, which unlike the state laws, could not be broken under any circumstances'.[181]

Youth gangs aspired to belong to this world with its whiff of adventure, its unabashed celebration of masculinity and its rebellious nature. Vagabond children came into contact with the adult criminal world by sharing the same spaces – trains, markets and streets – and often adopted their culture and way of life as a survival strategy. The alliance between the waifs and the criminal underground was likely to have existed already in Tsarist times. It is certainly well-documented in the 1920s and has been shown to continue to exist even in modern-day Russia, where rapid capitalisation and the break-down of social structures has led to a new flood of children living on the street.[182] However, it was not only street children, but ordinary youth gangs who sought to imitate the world of adult thieves. They smoked cigarettes, dressed in the fashion of the underground and adopted the jargon of thieves, which was incomprehensible to outsiders. Tattoos, found on the bodies of young convicts, demonstrated their desire to become like the grown-up thieves.[183] Stealing, robbing and mugging were part of the process of belonging to this world, which was so much more adventurous than the ordinary lives of Soviet citizen.

The prosecuting organs were very well aware of the influence of the adult criminal world on impressionable youngsters keen for a piece of adventure. They noted the gradual disenfranchisement of these children from the norms and conventions of Soviet life, who, after repeated truancies, quit school just to submit to the authority of the underground of thieves.[184] In particular they worried about Oliver Twist style groups of young bandits, led and organised by an adult criminal. In 1951, at least five such groups were unravelled in the Moscow region (this excludes the actual city of Moscow). Often adult criminals would look out for psychologically vulnerable youngsters, who were in need of a community. In 1946, in Kiev a group was arrested that had been formed by a 25–year-old former conscript by the name of Pavlenko. In the youth club of the central telegraph office he sought the friendship of the fifteen year-old Barkhaevyi, whose father and brother had been arrested during the purges; the sixteen-year-old Bobrovenskii, who had been excluded from his secondary school and whose mother was a lowly paid waitress, while his father was still in the Red Army; the sixteen-year-old Zinkevich, who had neither work nor a school to attend and his

---

[180]   E. Zubkova, *Poslevoennoe obshchestvo: Politika i Povsednevnost 1945–1953 gg* (Moscow: Rosspen, 1999), p. 90.

[181]   A. Kozlov, *Kosel na sakse – i tak vsiu zhizn'* (Moscow: Vagrius, 1998), pp. 55–56.

[182]   Ball, *And Now My Soul is Hardened*, pp. 71–72; S. Stephenson, 'Searching for Home: Russian Street Youth and the Criminal Community', paper presented at the Annual Conference of the British Association of Slavonic and Eastern European Studies, Cambridge, Apr. 2005.

[183]   *Russian Criminal Tattoo Encyclopaedia* (Göttingen: Steidl/Fuel, 2003), pp. 119, 142, 188, 189, 271, 287.

[184]   GARF R-f. 8131, op. 29, d. 506, l. 146.

twin, who worked as a smith, but was marked as a former *Ostarbeiter*;[185] and the sixteen-year-old Belan, whose mother was out of work and whose father was in the Red Army. All youngsters were thus scarred by traumatic experiences and in material need. They agreed to commit muggings and robbery for Pavlenko and obtained a pistol from a well-to do acquaintance. After a spree of six armed robberies in eight days they were arrested.[186]

While these youngsters were predominantly poor, the prominence of privileged children in quite a number of similar cases, as evident in the case from Poltava, highlights another fact about late Stalinist society. Boredom and arrogance were ripe among the children of the *nomenklatura*, who turned the privilege of their homes into a base for criminal activity. Often they turned the very status symbols of their fathers – their official pistols – into the instruments of crime, indicating that theft and robbery represented a personal rebellion against the over-conformism of their parental home. In 1945 the Central Committee of the Communist Party called out sixteen party members from the Ivanovo region, whose children were discovered to have been connected to the criminal world. Among other things these children had organised several groups of thieves, who usually specialised in the robbery of flats and houses. Their parents ranged from well-known artists to members of the local party elite.[187]

Another feature of the Poltava incident was the use of violence. Threats to use knives or pistols were typical for gangs, which specialised in muggings. Yet violence could go further. In Poltava members of the gang killed a policeman. Their leader turned violence against himself – he committed suicide. While most crime committed by minors of all age groups was not violent, the use of brutal force by youngsters and even children was not unheard of. In 1945 the number of minors under sixteen charged with murder peaked at 870. Even if one assumes that roughly three children were charged jointly for one murder case, this still leaves almost one murder per day committed by children, who were hardly old enough to be out of school. The immediate post-war years in particular show a rash of cases, where children murdered other children for very small rewards. In Omsk a gang of children, none of them more than fourteen-years-old, had systematically killed smaller children for their shoes and clothing. Horrified employees of the local cinema found thirteen little corpses behind their building.[188] In Kiev two twelve-year-olds bludgeoned a seven-year-old girl to death with a stone in order to obtain her coat and boots. The prosecutor was shocked that the two boys ate her sandwich at the place of the murder and sold her shoes in order to buy sweets.[189] In other places, too, children were murdered for items that aroused the envy of other children. Trophy items brought back from Germany such as bicycles and cigarette lighters became the instigators of murderous desire in places throughout the Soviet Union.[190] Undoubtedly, part of the explanation for such casual use of violence can be found in the general high levels of brutality pervading Soviet society at the time. It was not only war and destruction, but also the preceding campaign for collectivisation and the 1930s purges that shaped children's understanding of the role and place of violence in society. The ubiquity of weapons, which were either left over from the war or owned by Soviet officials, contributed to the high levels of serious crime. Knives,

---

[185] Labourer of Eastern European origin working in Nazi Germany either by force or voluntary enlistment. Not all Ostarbeiter were forced labour.
[186] TsDAHOU f. 1, op. 23, d. 3655, l. 25–26.
[187] RGASPI f. 1, op. 122, d. 103, l. 14–16.
[188] GARF R-f. 8131, op. 37, d. 3522, l. 4–6.
[189] TsDAHOU f. 7, op. 2, d. 116, l. 156–57.
[190] *Ibid*. f. 7, op. 2, d. 116, l. 174; TsDAVO f. 288, op. 9, d. 463, l. 3.

pistols and even grenades were status symbols coveted even by children and youngsters, who were not involved in any criminal activity.[191] The casual use of violence also included the perpetration of sexual crime. Group rapes committed by minors were no rarity in the Soviet Union. The famous case of the Chubarov alley, when in 1924 a group of young workers raped a girl in a dark Leningrad park, indicates that such violence was not new to the post-war Soviet Union.[192] None the less, instances of mass rape by army soldiers, sexual violence perpetrated in Partisan units and the precarious position of women relegated to a worthless demographic majority all contributed to the surprisingly high numbers of instances of sexual assault. Children and youngsters re-enacted the norms and practices transmitted to them from the adult world. In Kiev a 23-year-old factory worker was raped by a group of children between twelve and fourteen, who had been playing war when the victim and a friend walked past. The spectacle was watched by a group of two dozen youngsters who viciously beat up a passer-by, on his trying to intervene.[193] The collective conquering of a woman strengthened the sense of solidarity so important to these units of young criminals. Typically the incidents happened on or around public holidays in an alcohol-fuelled mood. The public mood of collectivism and parading was continued in a more sinister fashion. In the Amur region young students of a factory school (aged fourteen to sixteen) raped a fourteen-year-old girl after a public dance. The perpetrators and spectators, who watched and cheered the gang rape, numbered up to 30 youngsters – all younger than sixteen years of age.[194]

While crimes by children could be as horrific as those perpetrated by their adult contemporaries, punishment for child offenders also hardly differed to that meted out to mature criminals. In 1935 Stalin lowered the age of criminal responsibility to twelve. The Soviet justice system revoked its commitment to a separate policy for young offenders.[195] The decline of a pedagogical approach towards child offenders, dominant in the 1920s and early 1930s, is demonstrated by a letter from Molotov to Stalin, in which he proposed not only the incarceration of all criminal, homeless and vagabond children, but also demanded that serious child offenders should be shot.[196] The campaign against juvenile delinquency resulted in an increase in arrests of young offenders in the mid-1930s. The juvenile prison population was boosted again with the introduction of strict labour laws in 1941 and the draconian anti-theft and misappropriation decrees of 1947. Special labour camps for underage offenders were created alongside the regular GULAG system. Here juvenile criminals lived alongside repeat *besprizornye* and *beznadzornye* and homeless children, who had not been accepted by either an orphanage or boarding schools under factory supervision.[197]

---

[191] See for example A. Zhigulin, *Chernye Kamni: Dopolnennoe Izdanie* (Moscow: Kul'tura, 1996), p. 16. V. Kirilenko, 'Po sledam velikogo Alkhemika', in *O Tar'kovskom: Vospominaniia v dvukh knigakh* (Moscow: Dedalus, 2002), p. 273. On accidents and killings caused by playing with weapons, see TsDAHOU f. 7, op. 5, d. 303, l. 37; TsDAVO f. 228, op. 9, d. 452, l. 3. For a knifing in a pioneer camp: TsDAHOU f. 1, op. 24, d. 2993, l. 118.

[192] On the collectivity of the perpetrators as seen by the public and the authorities and experienced by the forty young offenders, see Naiman, *Sex in Public*, pp. 250–88.

[193] TsDAHOU f. 7, op. 5, d. 391, l. 34.

[194] GARF R-f. 8131, op. 29, d. 506, l. 147.

[195] P. Solomon, *Soviet Criminal Justice under Stalin* (Cambridge: Cambridge University Press, 1996), pp. 198, 201–03.

[196] O. Khlevniuk, *The History of the GULAG; From Collectivisation to the Great Terror* (New Haven: Yale University Press, 2006), p. 133.

[197] Between 1943 and 1947 roughly 90,000 homeless children were sent to child labour colonies: GARF R-f. 9312, op. 1, d. 18, l. 1; f. 9401, op. 2, d. 171, l. 228. In 1944 the child labour colonies had a capacity of 20,300

Even though some separate instructions existed for the arrest, interrogation, transport and detainment of children, life as a juvenile prisoner differed little from that of an adult *zek* (Gulag inmate).[198] Indeed, since many young offenders remained in the youth labour camps after they had turned seventeen, since the camps relied on a reservoir of support staff made up of adult criminals and since, despite rules to the contrary, minors ended up again and again in adult camps, young offenders were drawn even deeper into the criminal underground world, admiration of which had often caused their decline into delinquency in the first place. Camps were schools of criminal behaviour, codes and rituals. Memoirs of political prisoners testify that youngsters tended to drift towards the thieves and other hardened criminals becoming their 'slaves', 'jesters', 'prostitutes' and sometimes even their 'contract killers'.[199] Crime and violence were daily features among juveniles both in regular and child labour camps. Guards overstepped regulations, subjecting their young charges to beatings and abuse. Prisoner prefects established regimes of corruption and terror. Inmates organised killings of brigade leaders or other prisoners.[200] Mass riots against the camp authorities were also no rarity and usually involved severe violence, which often resulted in the death of some inmates and guards.[201] In a mass revolt in Ukraine youth prisoners attacked their brigadiers and resisted all attempts to restore order. The 70 rebels burnt the camp furniture, ripped the windows out of their frame and destroyed other items such as musical instruments. Out of the debris of their violent rampage they constructed barricades, behind which they retreated into the upper floors and held even the police at bay for several hours. When a local battalion of soldiers was called in for help, the children started to take apart the roof construction and bombard the soldiers with burning wood. Nineteen soldiers, six policemen and fifteen inmates had to be hospitalised.[202]

Most of the camps were located in far-away republics and isolated places of the Russian east and north. Communication with the centre was limited allowing the camps to develop their own norms and codes. Living and working conditions were hard and made harder by camp administrations that were more often than not corrupt and under pressure to turn the camps into viable production sites rather than educational establishments.[203] Juvenile criminals were isolated from what constituted Soviet society not only physically, but also mentally. While much rhetoric was devoted to the topic of re-education (*pereobrazovanie* – literally trans-education) and the integrative powers of Soviet society, the reality of young Soviet criminals was more determined by a discourse and practice of exclusion and separation. While in the 1920s young homeless children were still considered 'the country's flowers', who could be nurtured and cultivated into model Soviet citizens at the 'vanguard of cultural change', the trend in the later Stalinist years pointed to a strict dichotomy between saved Soviet children and criminal non-Soviet children.[204]

Indeed, criminal children became non-children. They could not exist in a society that was heavily dominated by narratives of salvation and success stories of happy

---

places. In 1955 this had rise to 36,950 available spaces: GARF R-f. 9412, op. 1, d. 35, l. 35–36; GARF R-f. 9401, op. 1a, d. 545, l. 102–03, published in S. Vilenskii *et al.* (eds) *Deti GULAGa* (Moscow: Mezhdunarodnyi Fond Demokratiia, 2002), pp. 515–16.

[198] A. Applebaum, *GULAG: A History of the Soviet Camps* (London: Allen Lane, 2003), pp. 302–06.

[199] *Ibid.*, pp. 304–05.

[200] GARF f. 9412, op. 12, d. 210, Tom 1.

[201] *Ibid*, f. 9412, op. 2, d. 210, Tom 1; RGASPI f. 1, op. 7, d. 129, l. 3; Applebaum (2003), p. 304.

[202] TsDAHOU f. 1, op. 24, d. 4299, l. 178–79.

[203] See for example GARF R-f. 9412, op. 1, d. 62; R-f. 9412, op. 12, d. 210, Tom I and II.

[204] On early Bolshevik ideas of saving children see L. Kirschenbaum, *Small Comrades: Revolutionizing Childhood in Soviet Russia, 1917–1932* (London: Routledge, 2001), pp. 1–2; Ball, *And Now My Soul is Hardened*, p. xiii.

childhoods, which heralded the near coming of a communist order. In Bolshevik ideology the new generation was to be the test case of a new society. The happy childhoods of Soviet children were supposed to show up the capitalist states and prove the superiority of the socialist system. Stalin turned childhood into a cult, which cleverly supported his own cult of personality. 'Thank you, comrade Stalin, for our happy childhoods' became a slogan that every child knew – and believed in most sincerely. The cult established Stalin as a kind and thoughtful father figure, the incarnation of the Soviet state itself, which handed out paternal care as well as admonition – however only to those, who participated in the happy Soviet family. Childhoods had to be happy for a larger purpose, not for the sake of happiness as such. Children were rescued from the darkness of ignorance and poverty in order to build socialism. The propaganda of the Great Fatherland War rested heavily on the image of helpless Soviet children suffering from the brutality of the fascist invader. Children were portrayed as the symbols of the achievements of the Soviet state – its progressiveness, its innocence and its earnestness. Saving Soviet children guaranteed the survival of the nation and the system.

Obsessed with constant progress, the Soviet system had no place for non-conforming children. Rehabilitation of children in the midst of society, tolerance towards weakness and acknowledgement of poverty would all do significant damage to the carefully constructed belief system that a Soviet childhood was the happiest of all possible childhoods. Non-conformist, disturbed children were not only a disturbance, but also a threat to the self-identity of a whole regime. This fact was borne out in the frequent association of juvenile crime with other menacing phenomena, which challenged Soviet norms. In the early 1920s the myth surrounding the life and death by suicide of the poet Evgenii Esenin was made responsible for hooliganism, while in the post-war period western cultural influence was identified as leading Soviet youth onto a path towards a life of crime.[205] A parallel world, as it existed among the *besprizornye* and young thieves and criminals, in which other laws ruled and other customs dominated, belied the Soviet idea that a new society had been successfully created. It reminded the authorities that their rule was constantly challenged by new and existing counter-cultures, whose existence could not be eradicated even among the youngest and most malleable. The 'fight' against vagabonding and juvenile delinquency had to result in the 'liquidation' (*likvidatsiia*) of these phenomena.

The vocabulary of officials when speaking about waifs, homelessness and youth crime betrays that the emphasis was on an aggressive campaign against child evil. Homeless youth were 'flushed out' from their hideouts in stations and trains in 'raids' that not only linguistically, but also in reality, resembled animal hunts. These abnormal children had to be separated from normal society, which was not even allowed to learn about the existence of these reminders of failure. Officially war-damaged or unruly children did not exist, could not be discussed or even be acknowledged – not in the press and not among medics, psychologists, pedagogues or any other profession. Under Stalin, homeless and delinquent children only show up as objects of police attention. Excluded from official discourse, physical removal and liquidation was the next logical step. They were removed from 'healthy' society and put in the underbelly of the Soviet system, where they mingled with the other outcasts of Soviet life. The child hell of the child labour camps was the direct consequence of Soviet visions of a child utopia.

· ·

---

[205] On Esenin see Naiman, *Sex in Public*, p. 257; on western influence see among others A. Sakharov, *Die Persönlichkeit des Täters und die Ursachen der Kriminaliät in der UdSSR* (Berlin: Staatsverlag, 1961), p. 64.

Street-children did not return to plague the cities of western Europe in the aftermath of the Second World War, despite the horrors of its closing stages. Society never fell apart to the same extent and American aid quickly kick-started reconstruction. By the 1960s they had all but disappeared from the whole of the continent as both east and west invested heavily in improving the conditions of the poor. A raised school-leaving age, better housing and health provision, child allowances, much greater state intrusion in parenting, and less austere and regimented care-homes all helped to ensure that few children, whatever their social background, were denied the chance of a childhood. Many children, of course, continued and continue to be raised in poverty, but they were far less likely to be orphaned, abandoned, or simply thrown out of the home.[206] Homeless children in their late teens were not unknown, and appear more visible at the dawn of the twenty-first century, but their numbers were and are small in comparison with an earlier age.[207] In the second half of the twentieth century, street-children primarily became the problem of the fast-growing cities of the developing world and attracted media attention because they were exotic.[208]

Yet, though youth was better looked after than ever before and most parents, whatever their social background, joined the schools and the churches in preaching the virtues of respect for persons and property, juvenile delinquency did not disappear, as the social reformers assumed. Indeed, its history in Britain since the end of the war suggests it got steadily worse. In the 1950s and 60s, there is certainly reason to believe that the bullying and ragging that had long gone on behind the closed doors of the country's leading educational establishments became much less vicious. Oxford students continued to celebrate raucously by drinking heavily, lighting bonfires and removing the college's lavatory seats, when a first eight won its blades on the river. But they no longer engaged in the collective bullying of odd-balls as they had as late as the 1930s.[209] Less privileged youth, however, soon slipped back into old ways. After an initial fall following the war, indictments for juvenile delinquency began to rise again in the course of the 1950s and have continued to rise ever since, albeit with periodic lulls. From the late 1960s, moreover, the indicted were not necessarily the disadvantaged. This was the decade in which British youth of all classes began to assert a separate identity vis-à-vis adults, primarily expressed in dress and music, and even claim a

---

[206] Problems did remain, of course. In recent years, particular attention has been drawn to children who are forced to care for adults at home: see Ch. 4, pp. 209–15. The definition of child poverty is determined by the overall standard of living: it is therefore a relative notion. At present, one-third of British children live in poverty.

[207] In 1848 purportedly 30,000 children were living on the streets of London. Today, there are about 130,000 children recognised to be homeless in the UK but they live in hostels or other accommodation provided by local authorities and charities, not on the street. Children who sleep rough are to be found in the UK and in other west European countries but no one knows the exact number. A recent figure for Germany suggests the problem may be worse than supposed. There, it is said, 20,000 children, three per cent of whom are under fourteen, sleep on the streets each night: see www.guardian.co.uk/society/2009/mar/08/homeless-children-britain (accessed 15 Dec. 2009); http://en.wikipedia.org/wiki/Street_children (accessed 15 Dec. 2009); www.earthtimes.org/articles/show/191615,growing-number-of-street-children-in-germany-report-says.html (accessed 15 Dec. 2009).

[208] H. Montgomery and T. Hall, 'Home and Away: "Childhood", "Youth" and Young People', *Anthropology Today*, 16:3 (2000), 13–16. Worldwide there are supposedly 100 to 150 million children who are literally homeless, including one million in Russia. A number of films have been made of non-European street children by western cineastes since the Second World War: *e.g.*, in 1950 *Los Olividados*, directed by Luis Buñuel (about Mexico City); and more recently *City of God* (2002), directed by Fernando Meirelles and Kátia Lund (about Rio de Janeiro); and the most famous, *Slumdog Millionaire* (2008), directed by Danny Boyle (about Mumbai).

[209] Brockliss, *Magdalen College: A History*, pp. 667–73. Traditional inter-collegiate rivalry however did continue: the students of Trinity and Balliol colleges in the 1950s and 60s were continually mounting raids on each other's premises, and the results were frequently reported in the press: see C. Hopkins, *Trinity. 450 Years of an Oxford College Community* (Oxford: Oxford University Press, 2005), pp. 419–21.

superior wisdom.[210] University students went further and placed themselves at the forefront of movements of political protest to change the world. As a result middle-class adolescents, probably for the first time in their history, found themselves in the dock facing charges of criminal damage, trespass and assault, following demonstrations and sit-ins.

In the third quarter of the twentieth century juvenile delinquency amounted to little more than vandalism, petty crime and minor affray. The clashes between mods and rockers on Brighton beach in the mid-1960s made such a stir because violent adolescent invasions of a public space were almost unheard of.[211] In the two decades following the war, teenage gangs and violent teenage crime were seen as a peculiarly American peril, associated with the much more volatile and ethnically-mixed society across the Atlantic. Leonard Bernstein's hit musical, *West Side Story*, which was originally staged on Broadway in 1957, was inspired by the contemporary Chicano turf wars in New York. When it transferred to the West End a year later for a long run, the clashes of the Jets and the Sharks were as alien (and entertaining) to the London audience as the lethal spats between the adolescent Montagues and Capulets of Shakespeare's *Romeo and Juliet*, on which the show's plot was based.[212] Gangs of child thieves were even less of a concern. The Artful Dodger was a figure from the country's dark Victorian past who no longer engendered unease. When Lionel Bart's ever popular musical, *Oliver!*, premiered in London in 1960, Dickens's knowing young blackguard was transformed into a cheeky cockney chappy with a heart of gold.[213]

The student demonstrations and sit-ins of the late 1960s and 70s were equally non-violent in the main: in Britain at least. It was only in the big anti-Vietnam protests in London, which were off campus and not student demonstrations at all (most of the protestors were adults), that violence really flared.[214] But from the late 1970s, as the ethnic mix of the population became increasingly diverse, youth unemployment soared, and recreational drugs, virtually unknown before the mid-1960s, were tried at an ever earlier age, older teenagers became involved in much more serious offences. In the inner cities, they began to form into American-type gangs, based on race or ethnicity, and became an important part of the criminal economy as muggers, car thieves and drug-traffickers. By the 1990s the gangs were armed to the teeth and appeared to be taking over the streets. Youths joined them in search of protection and status, and were quick to punish those who failed to give them 'respect'. A new phenomenon, teen on teen killings began to hit the news, and in

---

[210] The new arrogance of Britain's young was encapsulated in John Lennon's famous remark in an interview with the London *Evening Standard* in the spring of 1966 that the Beatles were more popular than Jesus. When news of the assertion reached the USA four months later, Christians in the southern United States protested by burning Beatles records and other items.

[211] S. Cohen, *Folk Devils and Moral Panics. The Creation of the Mods and Rockers* (St Albans: Paladin, 1973). Cohen memorably cites an apoplectic magistrate who demonised the youth who came before him, as 'long-haired, mentally unstable, petty little hoodlums … sawdust Caesars who can only find courage like rats, hunting in packs', p. 88.

[212] http://en.wikipedia.org/wiki/West_Side_Story (accessed 5 Apr. 2009). Violent adult gangs, on the other hand, certainly existed: witness the Krays in the east end of London. See G. Sparrow, *Gang-Warfare: A Probe into the Changing Pattern of British Crime* (London: Feature Books, 1968).

[213] http://en.wikipedia.org/wiki/Oliver! (accessed 5 Apr. 2009). The film of the show released in 1968 also enjoyed great success. Interestingly, a film about the life of Jack Sheppard, *Where's Jack* (directed by James Clavell), released the following year, bombed. Perhaps thieves in their early twenties caused more unease, especially when the ending suggested Sheppard may have escaped justice: Springhall, *Youth*, p. 168.

[214] Britain's university students never claimed to be intent on bringing down the state to change the world like their continental counterparts in 1968. The militancy of French students has been traced to a peculiar feeling of impotency: fêted from the end of the war as the builders of a new patriotic and communal France, they found that even at the end of the 1960s power was still in the hands of the old guard who had experienced defeat and/or occupation: see R. I. Jobs, *Riding the New Wave. Youth and the Rejuvenation of France after the Second World War* (Stanford, Calif.: Stanford University Press, 2007).

parts of London and Manchester in the early years of the new millennium almost weekly occurrences.[215]

The unexpected resurgence of juvenile delinquency led to a long and acrimonious debate within the establishment which has lasted until the present. Social psychologists, social workers, jurists and politicians clashed over the causes and what was to be done. Initially in the 1950s and 1960s most would have concurred with the Jets in *West Side Story* who proudly declared that they were 'psychologically disturbed' and 'sociologically sick'.[216] Less convinced than their Soviet counterparts that they had built utopia, liberal Britons, like their American cousins, were ready to admit that juvenile delinquency might have its roots in the limitations and stresses of the post-war social order. As the level of violence grew, however, tolerance began to wear thin, and large parts of the media, claiming to speak for the voiceless 'people', demanded tough action. Politicians on both left and right, mindful of the fears and votes of an ageing population, unsurprisingly bowed to the pressure, especially as the muggers and murderers seemed to get steadily younger and younger. Today, the wheel has come full circle. Kindness and understanding are out. The call once again is for the streets to be won back from the delinquents by intensive policing, and the young to be subject to the kind of discipline as they grow up that will keep them on the straight and narrow.

Juvenile Crime in Post-war Britain

Abigail Wills

In the context of this volume, the issue of juvenile crime raises two notable questions: how 'violent' or delinquent children have been dealt with historically, and how far such children's misbehaviour can itself be seen as a response to 'violence' – literally and metaphorically – visited upon them by the adult world. By the early 1950s, intensive discussion of the latter question had been underway for at least a century in Britain. The mid-nineteenth century had seen social reformers such as Mary Carpenter and Sydney Turner put forward the idea that criminal behaviour in children was the result not of innate evil, but rather of parental inadequacy and social disadvantage.[217] This belief was at the heart of the gradual moves towards separate legal and custodial provision for unruly children, most notably the establishment in the 1850s of a network of Reformatory and Industrial Schools which aimed to 'reclaim' children from the corrupting environment of the slums.

This distinct system of juvenile justice was further extended in the early decades of the twentieth century. The 1908 Children Act established separate juvenile courts, which were to deal with almost all cases concerning individuals under seventeen years of age. The residential reform system was consolidated through the replacement of Reformatory and Industrial Schools with Home Office 'Approved Schools' in 1933, and

---

[215] For a recent overview of the situation, see the recent report by the Centre for Social Justice, 'Dying to Belong: An In-depth Review of Street Gangs in Britain', published in Feb. 2009: http://www.centreforsocialjustice. org.uk/client/downloads/DyingtoBelongFullReport.pdf (accessed 5 Apr. 2009). For a detailed study, see P. Walsh, *Gang War: The Inside Story of the Manchester Gangs* (Lytham: Milo, 2003).

[216] In the song 'Gee, Officer Krupke'.

[217] M. Carpenter, *Reformatory Schools for the Children of the Perishing and Dangerous Classes and for Juvenile Offenders* (London: C. Gilpin, 1851); S. Turner, *Report on the System and Arrangements of 'La colonie agricole' at Mettray* (London: J. Hatchard and Sons, 1846).

the introduction in 1908 of Borstals for older, more hardened delinquents. Both systems were underpinned by the conviction that poverty and criminality had similar origins, and that all disadvantaged children, whether they were delinquent or merely unruly, could be restored to full and productive citizenship through a disciplined programme of trade training, religious instruction and physical education.[218]

Earlier ideas about the structural causes of juvenile delinquency were also supplemented in this period by a concern with its psychological dimensions. The psychologist Cyril Burt set the mould for such approaches in his *The Young Delinquent*, published in 1925, in which he argued that juvenile crime was primarily 'a mental symptom with a mental origin'.[219] In this understanding, poor upbringing resulted in emotional imbalance, which could in turn find expression in criminal behaviour. This focus on mental disturbance led to the growing scientisation of the study of delinquency during the interwar period. Scholars within new university departments of criminology, psychology and sociology sought to establish a clinical typology of deviance through the detailed statistical analysis of the family backgrounds and psychological characteristics of delinquents.[220] In 1931, an 'Institute for the Scientific Study of Delinquency' was set up with the aim of developing what it saw as no less than a 'new branch of science'.[221]

By the end of the Second World War, then, the juvenile justice system in Britain had arguably 'come of age': there was a generalised confidence that both the origins of and the solutions to juvenile delinquency were within reach. The rise in juvenile crime that had taken place during the war was seen as evidence of the dual structural and emotional origins of the problem. As the magistrate John Watson put it in 1950, 'those who appear in juvenile courts are largely victims of conditions in their earlier years' – most notably, he believed, the 'happenings in wartime which tended to break up families and disrupt homes'.[222] There was a cross-party political consensus that juvenile delinquents should be treated – at one level at least – as part of a broader constituency of 'wretched little children who have been deprived for one reason or another of a normal home life'.[223] Faith in this interpretation was further strengthened in the early 1950s, when rates of juvenile crime began to decrease from their wartime high and thus appeared to confirm the key importance of poverty in causing delinquency. The criminologist Max Grünhut (1893–1964), for example, optimistically attributed the drop to 'the return to normality of the economic life of the nation', arguing that with the end of rationing and the rise of prosperity, there was a reduced temptation to 'steal scarce goods known to be in high demand'.[224]

---

[218] For an overview of the development of the juvenile justice system in Britain over the nineteenth and twentieth centuries, see J. Hyland, *Yesterday's Answers: Development and Decline of Schools for Young Offenders* (London: Whiting and Birch, 1993); V. Bailey, *Delinquency and Citizenship: Reclaiming the Young Offender 1914–1948* (Oxford: Clarendon Press, 1987); Shore, *Artful Dodgers*; L. Mahood, *Policing Gender, Class and Family: Britain, 1840–1940* (London: UCL Press, 1995).

[219] C. L. Burt, *The Young Delinquent* (London: UCL Press, 1925), p. 4.

[220] See for example L. E. Grimberg, *Emotion and Delinquency: a Clinical Study of Five Hundred Criminals in the Making* (London: K. Paul, Trench and Trubner, 1928); L. Le Mesurier, *Boys in Trouble: A Study of Adolescent Crime and its Treatment* (London: J. Murray, 1939); W. Norwood East, *The Adolescent Criminal: A Medico-Sociological Study of 4,000 Male Adolescents* (London: J. and A. Churchill, 1942).

[221] *British Journal of Delinquency: The Official Organ of the Institute for the Study and Treatment of Delinquency*, 1 (Jul. 1950), 3.

[222] J. A. F. Watson, *The Child and the Magistrate* (London: J. Cape, 1950), p. 32.

[223] *House of Commons Standing Committees. Official report: Children Bill (Lords)*, Session 1947–1948, vol. III, col. 81.

[224] M. Grünhut, *Juvenile Offenders Before the Courts* (Oxford: Clarendon Press, 1956), pp. 132–33.

However, the move towards prosperity rapidly brought new problems. As early as 1951, the president of the Approved Schools Headmasters' Association argued that 'a considerable section of the working population of this country has become infected with a cynical and selfish materialism which has lowered moral standards and exercised a disastrous influence on family life'.[225] By the mid-1950s, juvenile crime figures had again begun to rise precipitously, raising grave fears about the impact of mass consumption on the moral health of the nation. There was a new sense in which, as A. C. Brownjohn noted in 1959, 'we shall need to look for [the causes of crime] not in starvation and destitution but in that very prosperity which we thought would reduce crime'.[226] Affluence was seen as undermining 'traditional' standards. The general secretary of the National Union of Teachers, Sir Ronald Gould (1913–2008), captured the national mood in worrying that 'the values of truth, honesty, courtesy, kindness to others and a sense of duty [...] were being threatened by materialism and some of the values put over by the mass media'.[227]

Such fears were sustained by the emergence of highly visible and challenging youth subcultures, most notably the Teddy Boys. The latter began as loosely-constituted groups of working-class London adolescents adopting a distinctive 'Edwardian' style of clothing. The style rapidly spread, and came to be associated with gang violence and intimidation on a nationwide scale. By the mid-1950s, the Teddy Boys had become, in Stanley Cohen's famous phrase, the first 'folk devils' of the post-war era.[228] Portrayed as a national menace by the media, they became emblematic of the belief that affluence was producing a terrifying epidemic of youth lawlessness. New American cultural influences were held up for particular censure, especially horror comics and rock'n'roll which were thought – on both sides of the Atlantic – to be fuelling the crime wave. The American psychologist Hilde Mosse, speaking in England at the invitation of the Comics Campaign Council, echoed a widespread belief in her statement that 'violence among children of the vicious kind [...] was not known before the advent of the horror comic'.[229]

As a result of this generalised panic about youth, the decade saw calls for a return to harsher, more retributive penalties for juvenile delinquents. Chief among these was a demand for the return of judicial corporal punishment, which had been abolished in 1948. Conservative Party conferences in the late 1950s were particularly vocal on the matter: the Home Secretary, Rab Butler (1902–82), noted wearily in 1958 that 'I am to answer 28 bloodthirsty resolutions at [...] Blackpool. It is with the greatest difficulty that we have chosen one of the 28 which is at least moderate'.[230] Although birching was not reintroduced, the sense that new methods were required to meet an unprecedented problem was more widely shared, as was Butler's assurance that it was necessary to deal with juvenile crime 'with whatever methods may be thought best and however strong the methods may have to be'.[231] Chief among these methods were

---

[225] 'The Annual General Meeting and Conference, Ilfracombe, May, 1951. The New President, N. Mattock: President's Address', *Approved Schools Gazette* (Jun. 1951), p. 82.

[226] A. C. Brownjohn, 'Advertising and Delinquency', *Approved Schools Gazette* (Sept. 1959), p. 219.

[227] R. F. Spence, 'Popular Culture and Personal Responsibility', *Approved Schools Gazette* (Nov. 1960), p. 339.

[228] Cohen, *Folk Devils*.

[229] 'Horror comics in the US', *The Times*, 20 Jun. 1955, p. 6. See also M. Barker, *A Haunt of Fears: The Strange History of the British Horror Comics Campaign* (London: Pluto Press, 1984).

[230] Quoted in A. E. Bottoms and S. Stevenson, '"What Went Wrong?" Criminal Justice Policy in England and Wales 1945–70', in D. Downes (ed.), *Unravelling Criminal Justice: Eleven British Studies* (Basingstoke: Macmillan Press, 1992), p. 11.

[231] 'Mr Butler wins the day on criminal reform', *The Times*, 10 Oct. 1958, p. 12.

detention centres, provided for under the 1948 Criminal Justice Act and in rising use over the 1950s. These involved three- to six-month sentences of 'brisk activity under strict discipline and supervision, with a minimum physical amenity'.[232] At the other end of the scale, attendance centres were set up during the later part of the decade in order to deprive children of Saturday leisure time.[233] The prevailing ethos of the 1950s thus involved a sense that, notwithstanding the social and psychological causes of crime, many delinquent children had been 'spoilt' by affluence and needed, in the words of one Approved School headmaster, to be 'taught to work, to respond at once, taught to fit in and taught to become anti-self'.[234]

The 1960s saw an intensification of some of the fears of the previous decade. The era saw the rise of increasingly self-confident and visible youth cultures, epitomised by the fashion and music of 'swinging London'. There was also a relaxation in the strict moral codes that had characterised the previous decade, and a raft of new 'permissive' legislation on issues such as abortion, censorship and divorce.[235] To many, the continuing rise in levels of youth crime was inextricably linked to these social changes: there was a feeling that it was the 'permissive and materialistic society which produces our problem children [...]'[236] Relaxations in the laws and social sanctions relating to sexual behaviour were believed to have led to an increasing amorality, and to a situation where, as the psychiatrist J. A. Krawiecki put it, 'respectable people are seen to take sides with the wrong side of the law, in leading demonstrations against the police, defending homosexuality, pornography, [...] making good intellectual excuses for immorality and corruption'.[237]

However, there were also a number of contrary tendencies developing in the understanding and treatment of juvenile crime at the time. Most notable among these involved a new awareness that deprivation, both relative and absolute, continued to be a problem even in the so-called affluent society. Studies such as Richard Titmuss's *Income Distribution and Social Change*, published in 1962, stressed the continuing existence of significant class inequalities in wealth and opportunity.[238] Drawing on insights from American scholars working on 'subcultural theory', sociologists such as David Downes and Peter Willmott noted the key importance of such inequalities in the aetiology of delinquency. For them, groups such as the Teddy Boys had come into being partly as a protest against their subordinate position within the affluent society.[239]

As a consequence of such new understandings, the 1960s saw a move towards more lenient, 'childcare' principles in dealing with young offenders. Use of custodial sentences decreased; institutional regimes became less severe. There was a new sense that young people in trouble with the law should become active partners in their own rehabilitation, that they 'must not in any way lose their self-respect or identity and

[232] 'New treatment for young offenders', *The Times*, 18 Aug. 1952, p. 2.
[233] Home Office, *The Sentence of the Court: A Handbook for Courts on the Treatment of Offenders* (London: HMSO, 1964), p. 7.
[234] C. Cook, 'President's Address', *Approved Schools Gazette* (Jul. 1952), p. 86.
[235] See A. Marwick, *The Sixties: Cultural Revolution in Britain, France, Italy and the United States, c. 1958–1974* (Oxford: Oxford University Press, 1998). For an account of changing ideas and practices in juvenile justice in the post-war period, see A. Wills, 'Delinquency, Masculinity and Citizenship in England 1950–1970', *Past and Present*, 187:1 (2005), 157–85.
[236] Association of Headmasters, Headmistresses and Matrons of Approved Schools, 'Approved Schools 1969: A Study of Development', *Technical Sub-Committee*; no. 9 (1969), p. 21.
[237] J. A. Krawiecki, 'Our Society – Permissive or Impotent?', *Approved Schools Gazette* (Dec. 1969), p. 385.
[238] R. M. Titmuss, *Income Distribution and Social Change: A Study in Criticism* (London: Allen and Unwin, 1962).
[239] D. Downes, *The Delinquent Solution* (London: Routledge and Kegan Paul, 1966), pp. 123–34; P. Willmott, *Adolescent Boys of East London* (London: Routledge and Kegan Paul, 1966), pp. 160–61. See also Springhall, *Coming of Age*.

they must be encouraged always to make full use of their personality potential'.[240] Relatedly, practices of reform became increasingly sensitive to the class contexts under which they operated. As Willmott noted, 'the staff of residential establishments need to recognise and as far as possible respect the mores and values of the local community, even when they differ from their own'.[241] In professional and administrative terms, the period saw a shift from legal to social work principles within juvenile justice: the 1969 Children and Young Persons Act significantly reduced the sentencing powers of juvenile courts, transferring decision-making responsibility to the new Social Services departments.[242]

At one level, this increased leniency resulted in a backlash. The 1970s and 1980s have been argued by many historians to have been a period of reactionism in juvenile justice – a return to a conception of crime as a matter of personal responsibility rather than social circumstance. The highly liberal provisions of the 1969 Act were rejected by the incoming Conservative administration. The use of custody for young offenders increased significantly through the 1970s, culminating in the introduction of new military-style 'short sharp shock' regimes within detention centres in the early years of the Thatcher government.[243]

However, the period also saw a political commitment to what has been referred to as 'bifurcation': the use of 'tough' measures on confirmed criminals was to go hand in hand with initiatives seeking to divert less hardened cases away from the criminal justice system altogether.[244] Most notable among these were the use of cautioning for first-time offenders, and the establishment of 'Intermediate Treatment' – solutions often involving 'recreational, educational or cultural activities' which did not involve long-term removal from the home environment.[245]

Nevertheless, by the 1980s, the tenor of political rhetoric on juvenile criminality had arguably undergone a quantum shift towards retribution. By the mid-1990s, there existed an overwhelming political consensus in favour of 'tough' measures, in spite of the fall in rates of juvenile crime that had taken place since the mid-1980s.[246] The extent of the new retributive tone was epitomised by political statements made in the aftermath of the James Bulger murder case of 1993, when John Major famously argued that society should 'condemn a little more and understand a little less'.[247] Amongst the consequences of such pronouncements was a near-doubling of the use of child custody over the decade.[248] The new Labour government's criminal justice policy continued in

---

[240] B. P. Soper, 'The Complexity of Residential Child Care. Report of the Address Given at a Recent South-East Area Meeting of Housemasters by Mrs P. J. Ozanne, Assistant Children's Officer for Surrey', *Approved Schools Gazette* (Jul. 1967), p. 172.

[241] 'Summary of Talk by Peter Willmott, Institute of Community Studies, at the Approved Schools Conference, in Dec. 1967', *Approved Schools Gazette* (Feb. 1968), p. 547.

[242] *Children and Young Persons Act* (London: HMSO, 1969).

[243] L. Gelsthorpe and A. Morris, 'Juvenile Justice 1945–1992', in M. Maguire (ed.), *The Oxford Handbook of Criminology* (Oxford: Clarendon Press, 1994), pp. 965–80; Bottoms and Stevenson, '"What Went Wrong?", pp. 36–37.

[244] Quoted in Gelsthorpe and Morris, 'Juvenile Justice 1945–1992', pp. 970–71.

[245] 'Minister suggests rock climbing and sailing as 'treatment' for children in trouble with law', *The Times*, 3 Jan. 1972, p. 2. See also P. Beresford and S. Croft, *Intermediate Treatment: Radical Alternative, Palliative or Extension of Social Control?* (London: Battersea Community Action, 1982).

[246] D. Haydon and P. Scraton, '"Condemn a Little More, Understand a Little Less": The Political Context and Rights Implications of the Domestic and European Rulings in the Venables-Thompson Case', *Journal of Law and Society*, 27:3 (2000), 416–48, at p. 426; M. J. Allen and S. Cooper, 'Howard's Way: a Farewell to Freedom?', *The Modern Law Review*, 58:3 (1995), 364–89, at p. 368.

[247] *Mail on Sunday*, 21 Feb. 1993, p. 1.

[248] Youth Justice Board, *Strategy for the Secure Estate for Children and Young People* (London: YJB, 2005), p. 8.

much the same vein. In 1998, the longstanding presumption that a child under fourteen was *'doli incapax'* – incapable of telling right from wrong – was abolished by the new Crime and Disorder Act.[249] In 2004, Tony Blair pledged to end what he described as the '1960s liberal social consensus on law and order', which he argued had involved the granting of 'freedom without responsibility'.[250] The keystone of his government's 'zero tolerance' approach involved the introduction of punitive 'anti-social behaviour orders', which imposed more or less serious restrictions on the freedom of movement and association of young people deemed to be causing a social nuisance.

The history of juvenile crime in the post-war decades in Britain is thus one which is crucially interlinked with developments in social thinking on questions of youth, class, psychology and morality. As a result, the sharp rise in levels of juvenile crime that took place between the 1950s and the 1980s is problematic to interpret. Rising crime figures are hard to disentangle from the complex of social and political fears that attached to them. As Peter King has noted in relation to the nineteenth century, juvenile delinquents have particular significance as 'powerful representatives of the shape of the future and as potential mirrors of the broader state of social order'.[251] Ultimately, it is arguably the symbolic weight attached to child criminality, rather than its historical reality, that has determined how it has been treated. The idea of the post-war period as one of unprecedented criminality among the young should thus be treated with caution.

On the other hand, as the commentators of the 1960s pointed out, affluence had social casualties, and did not spell the end of either social deprivation or parental inadequacy. It is likely that rising juvenile crime levels were in part a reflection of this. Indeed, the immediate post-war decades witnessed a degree of consensus that children's misbehaviour was in part a result of their poor treatment by the adult world, and that responses to it should be framed accordingly. Since the 1970s, however, political 'tough talking' on the subject of crime has altered this situation beyond recognition. With a renewed focus on the personal responsibility of children for their crimes, the longstanding separation – both philosophical and practical – between adult and juvenile justice provision has been diminished; the uniquely vulnerable position of children as compared to adults is no longer a *prima facie* determinant of their treatment by the justice system. As a result, 'reformative' child custodial provision is no longer the political priority that it once was; penal reform charities have been vocal in denouncing the brutality and indignity experienced by many children within the system today.[252] There is perhaps an irony here, given the consensus of earlier eras that children's misbehaviour should be seen in part as a response to the 'violence' of the adult world.

• •

This chapter has demonstrated that the physically violent child, especially the physically violent adolescent, is not a new phenomenon but one with a long past. Demonstrably from

[249] S. Bandalli, 'Abolition of the Presumption of *Doli Incapax* and the Criminalisation of Children', *Howard Journal of Criminal Justice*, 37:2 (1998), 114–23.
[250] T. Blair, 'A New Consensus on Law and Order', 19 Jul. 2004. Availalble online at http://news.bbc.co.uk/1/hi/uk_politics/3907651.stm (accessed 10 Jan. 2010).
[251] King, 'Rise of Juvenile Delinquency', p. 157.
[252] See B. Goldson, *Vulnerable Inside: Children in Secure and Penal Settings* (London: Children's Society, 2002); Children's Rights Alliance for England, *Rethinking Child Imprisonment: A Report on Young Offender Institutions* (London: Children's Rights Office, 2002); Lord Carlile of Berriew and the Howard League for Penal Reform, *An Independent Inquiry by Lord Carlile of Berriew QC into Physical Restraint, Solitary Confinement and Forcible Strip Searching of Children in Prisons, Secure Training Centres and Local Authority Secure Children's Homes* (London: Howard League for Penal Reform, 2006).

the fifteenth century – and probably long before – children have assaulted adults and each other, frequently with lethal results. James Bulger's abductors were very young but child murderers have not been absent from the historical record. Sometimes children have used violence to assert their own or their community's rights; sometimes they have used force simply to impose their will on others and bring them under their power. The difference between the past and the present has been the degree to which the violence perpetrated by children has been viewed as licit or seen as problematical. For Augustinian Christians of the sixteenth and seventeenth centuries, a child's propensity to be violent was quite understandable, and if used to uphold the normative social order was often condoned, even when adults were targeted. It was only in the eighteenth century with the development of a more optimistic view of children's nature and an increasing insistence that the state should have the monopoly of violence that the use of physical force by the young came under serious scrutiny. Even then, a way was eventually discovered in the English public schools of licensing violence, not just through physical sports but through devolving disciplinary powers to prefects.

It is a moot point how much children's violence in the past has been a coping mechanism. Subject themselves to forms of control and labour which to us seem brutal and exploitative, it is plausible that their recourse to violence was more than just mimicry of adult behaviour. Arguably, violence was a necessary, often unconscious, release from the pressures of being a child in a harsher age. If this were so, then child, especially teenage, delinquency in the present day may be less mindless than it appears on the surface. Of course, in our modern child-centred society, this violence seems to make no sense. To contemporary adults, youth (girls as well as boys, since aggressive behaviour is no longer gendered) appears at best puzzling, at worst ungrateful. It may be, though, that the destruction that youth frequently wreak on each other and on private and civic property is perfectly understandable. What those who despair of the behaviour of the young may care to ponder is the extent to which our own world contains new forms of violence and neglect that may not be considered such but may be the key to the conundrum.

In the course of a generation the traditional forms of disciplining children have undergone a revolution. Children are no longer caned or hit at school; most parents administer nothing stronger than a gentle slap; even the horror stories of life in orphanages and hostels seem to be a thing of the past. And for those who have not learned or cannot learn the art of gentle parenting, the state stands ready at the gate to fold its protective arm around all but a tiny minority of the unlucky victims of out-dated child-rearing practices. But to be raised in a child-centred environment at home and school counts for little if the world into which many children will graduate in their mid to late teens offers none of the opportunities that they have been told in their early years to expect. There is a profound tension in early twenty-first century Britain between the values promoted in schools – the inherent importance of every human soul, the emphasis on individual well-being, the right to fulfil one's potential, the right to happiness, and so on – and the reality of the adult world. The bases of material and spiritual contentment, being well-housed, clothed and fed, and being able to exercise real choice, depend on having the qualifications and personality to land a lucrative and enjoyable job. For most youngsters in Britain this is an impossible idyll, especially for teenagers from poor families and certain ethnic minorities. For the perennial losers in modern society – a growing number in the fall-out from the present economic crisis which is destined to see the cushion provided by government spending deflate significantly – the destruction of persons and property is an understandable way of asserting the crushed self.[253]

---

[253] Some educationalists are beginning to query the value of the well-being culture promoted in schools, suggesting that it is disempowering rather than empowering the next generation. So much attention is placed on maintaining the pupils and students' self-esteem that less and less learning takes place: see K. Ecclestone and D. Hayes, *The Dangerous Rise of Therapeutic Education* (London: Routledge, 2009).

6. Coping Strategies and Exit Routes

Catriona Kelly, George Rousseau, Lyndal Roper,
Nicholas Stargardt, Josephine McDonagh and Rosemary Peacocke

ChildLine was launched in 1986

ChildLine has counselled nearly two million children and young people

The main problems children contacted us about last year (April 2007 to March 2008) were: bullying (18 per cent of calls); family issues (13 per cent); physical abuse (10 per cent); sexual abuse (6 per cent); facts of life (6 per cent) and concern for others (5%)

Last year **ChildLine** counselled around 176,000 children and young people

www.nspc.org.uk/whatwedo/aboutChildLine/FactsFigures/factsandfigures_wd,
(accessed 29 Jun. 2009)

11% of children (1 in 9) in the UK run away from home or are forced to leave, and stay away overnight, on one or more occasion before the age of 16. It is estimated that 100,000 young people run away each year in the UK.

12% of young people said experience or the threat of physical abuse or violence, emotional abuse or emotional neglect, domestic violence, sexual abuse or being scared was the reason they ran away.

More than a quarter (30%) of young people who run away overnight had first done so before the age of 13. 10% had run away before their 11th birthday.

Girls are more likely to run away than boys, with 12% of girls and 8% of boys reporting they have run away overnight. Disabled children or children with learning disabilities are 20% more likely 'than average' to run away.

NSPCC, *Young runaways: Key child protection statistics*. Available online at
http://www.nspcc.org.uk/Inform/research/statistics/young_runaways_statistics_wda48741.html,
(accessed 21 Jan. 2010)

An 18-year-old bride-to-be has become the 14th young person to commit suicide in Bridgend and the surrounding area in the past year [2007–2008]. Friends said that Angeline Fuller, who described herself as a Goth, had a history of depression and had made two previous suicide attempts. Paramedics were called to the flat that she shared with her boyfriend in Nantymoel, Bridgend, early on Monday morning [5 Feb. 2008]. Her fiancé Joel Williams, 21, said that she had recently become engaged and she had "everything to live for". He had left her downstairs with friends while he went to bed. Later he went to look for her but found his bedroom door had been locked. By the time he managed to open it, she was dead, hanged from the banister.

'Further Teenage Suicide in Bridgend' posted on http://www.clinicallypsyched.com/teenage-
suicide-bridgend-wales-angelina-fuller.html (accessed 8 Jul. 2009)

In the last chapter we saw how the young have not simply been the victims of heavy-handed and, in our terms, abusive treatment from those in authority but have been continual agents of violence themselves. In the late medieval and early modern eras, children accepted what we would consider ill-treatment if it were just by the norms of their day, but they did not tamely submit when harassed indiscriminately by their peers or unfairly punished, especially by those *in loco parentis*. Nor did the orphaned and abandoned lie down in the gutter to die, or meekly allow themselves to be institutionalised. In a violent culture with a strong sense of honour, unhappy children met violence with violence and destitute children preyed on the better off. Such behaviour was seldom condoned by adults but it was encouraged by parental readiness to use children to police the behaviour of younger siblings, and the wider community's deployment of teenage boys as community enforcers. Children were active participants in society's ecology of violence. The abnormally abused, the outcast and the peculiarly sensitive could not but deduce that violence was the default response to boundary-breaking, while the young more generally quickly learnt to endure being 'brought up by hand', secure in the knowledge that they would soon be empowered to be petty tyrants themselves.

Even in the violent culture of pre-modern society, however, not every disgruntled child and adolescent had the space to fight back. Some were too vulnerable and isolated to assert their sense of justice with their fists or profit from the licence to intimidate or abuse others. Many, like Raphaël in *La Peau de Chagrin* by Honoré de Balzac (1799–1850) must have been simply too cowed by an authoritarian father or father-substitute to react against perceived tyranny.[1] After 1850, moreover, it is clear that the alienated young found it more and more difficult to use violence as a response, except in periods of virtual anarchy or where their grievances were shared by adults (as on the factory floor).[2] By then there were few socially acceptable ways of physically expressing discontent, since most forms of adolescent aggression (verbal, gesticulatory or physical) were all demonised. In consequence, children of all ages, just like any other subordinate group in society, have always had to develop alternative, less confrontational ways of coping with their lot.

One strategy has been to take advantage of the fact that power in the adult world has usually been organised hierarchically. Fathers, teachers, lords of the manor, employers and so on may have been, and still are to some degree, gods in their immediate world. But they in turn have been subject in some way to a higher authority even when the state was relatively powerless. The aggrieved have nearly always been able to complain over the head of their tormentor, however difficult this may have been. The early modern English peasant realised this only too well. When the earl of Shrewsbury tried to impose much higher rents on his tenants in Glossopdale in the reign of Elizabeth I, the farmers did not pick up their pitchforks and storm their lord's castle. Instead, they petitioned the queen in London, who fearful of rural unrest in a country with no standing army, took the side of the peasants and ordered the earl to reduce his demands.[3] Admittedly, until recently children and adolescents were unlikely to receive such a generous hearing. In the pre-modern world paternal authority was seen as the keystone of law and order and was not to be lightly challenged by outsiders. Indeed, in the classical era it would have been impossible for a minor to have protested

---

[1] H. Balzac, *La Peau de Chagrin*, original edn 1831 (Paris: Flammarion, 1971), pp. 128–30. According to Raphaël he only had one recourse: 'J'exhalais mon malheur en mélodies'; he hummed Mozart and Beethoven.
[2] In late nineteenth century France, for instance, teenage workers played a prominent role in the often violent strikes that affected French industry: see M. Perrot, 'Worker Youth. From the Workshop to the Factory', in G. Levi and J.-C. Schmitt, *Stormy Evolution to Modern Times. A History of Young People in the West* (London: Belknap Press, 1997), pp. 97–99.
[3] S. E. Kershaw, 'Power and Duty in the Elizabethan Aristocracy: George, Earl of Shrewsbury, the Glossopdale Dispute and the Council', in G. W. Bernard (ed.), *The Tudor Nobility* (Manchester: Manchester University Press, 1992).

against the treatment of a parent or one *in loco parentis*.[4] None the less, in the Christian centuries, it has always been recognised that authority could be abused and that the young might need protection from outsiders: long before the appearance of the social worker and the child protection officer, the parish priest (or in Calvinist societies the consistory) kept, with the help of neighbours, a weather eye on cruelty to the young.[5]

In early modern England apprentices were thought to be particularly at risk, and guilds permitted boys and girls as well as their fathers to complain against harsh treatment.[6] By the eighteenth century, when guilds were on the decline, formal complaints were usually dealt with at the local quarter sessions. In the thirteen year periods 1757–63 and 1773–80, the Coventry court tried some 50 cases involving misbehaviour or neglect by the city's masters, and many were brought by the apprentices themselves. In nearly half the master was accused of running away and leaving his apprentice in the lurch, but ten were indicted on charges of cruelty and two on sexual abuse, including William Burgess, a substantial ribbon merchant, who was charged by his apprentice George Farmer of making 'Sodomitical' advances.[7] By the eighteenth century, too, the most vulnerable and poorer apprentices who dared to denounce their master were even protected by statute law. In 1747 Parliament passed an act giving those whose premium was less than £5 (and thus unlikely to have influential relatives) the right to complain to two local justices of the peace concerning 'any Misusage, Refusal of Necessary Provision, Cruelty or Ill-Treatment'. If the charge was proved, then the apprentice would be discharged.[8]

Of course, only a small number of badly treated youngsters in the past can ever have taken their cause to an outside authority. In a patriarchal society, only a very strange child was likely to denounce their parents for causing physical harm. Equally, the victims of peer-group bullying in or out of the classroom can seldom have complained to adults. Children today learn at an early age from other children that telling tales is an unforgivable sin, and before the last decades of the twentieth century this was a viewpoint largely endorsed by adults. Thomas Hughes led the fight against bullying in England's public schools in the mid-nineteenth century but he unequivocally attacked snitching in *Tom Brown's Schooldays*, as we saw in the previous chapter.[9] Even apprentices in England must have seldom availed themselves of their right to complain, given that masters brought before the courts were often exonerated or let off with a fine even in the most heinous cases. In 1764 a farmer, Henry Timbrell, was accused of maiming and castrating his two apprentices, eight- and twelve-years-old, 'in the hope of selling them as singers to the Opera'. Found guilty, he was fined 13s 4d for each offence and given two years in prison.[10]

It was probably only at times when adult society was fractured that the young felt truly empowered to complain. In the normal course of events, it can be assumed that only the most egregious cases of physical abuse received sympathetic attention from higher authority. At moments of social tension, on the other hand, when adults suspected scores of heretics, witches or traitors to be lurking in their midst, it became much more possible for the young to seek revenge for their woes or simply curry favour with the powerful by denouncing adults as religious or political deviants. This presumably explains the notorious events

---

[4] We are indebted to the Oxford classical historian Al Moreno for this information.
[5] As in George Crabbes's early nineteenth-century poem, *Peter Grimes*, where the community acts as a chorus denouncing Peter's inhumanity to his apprentices and ultimately bringing him before the mayor: *The Borough,* Letter XXII, ls 95–101 and 154–55.
[6] O. J. Dunlop, *English Apprenticeship and Child Labour: A History* (London: T. Fisher Unwin, 1912), p. 174.
[7] J. Lane, *Apprenticeship in England 1600–1914* (London: UCL Press, 1996), p. 216.
[8] *Ibid.*, pp. 4–5. For apprenticing the poor see Ch. 4, pp. 171–77.
[9] See Ch. 5, p. 227.
[10] Lane, *English Apprenticeship*, pp. 223–34.

at Salem in 1692 when, in a colonial society peculiarly nervous about witchcraft, teenage servant girls *en masse* started accusing their masters and mistresses of being in league with the devil.[11] Even then, though, youngsters did not normally indict their own parents or substitute parents but transferred their vengeance to innocent third parties. This appears to have been what happened in a Württemberg village at about the same date (1683) when a thirteen-year-old servant girl, Anna Catharina Weissenbühler, acting as a nanny in her cousin's household, claimed that the wife of one Gall Baum had forcibly initiated her into witchcraft. The witchcraft panic was largely over in Europe by then but it still resonated in rural communities. Motherless and abandoned by her father, Anna had been passed around her relatives where she had received little food and less love. Forced to look after her cousin's baby, she seems to have fantasised about killing it, and assuaged her feelings of guilt and her understandable bitterness by denouncing a neighbour.[12]

There is no sign that church and state actively encouraged such denunciations and children who accused adults of 'political incorrectness' were usually met with suspicion and hostility, at least at first.[13] It was not until the early years of Stalinist Russia that children were actively encouraged to denounce their elders for crimes against the state. All revolutionary states in Europe since 1789 have been suspicious of the loyalty of their adult citizens who have been brought up under the values of the old regime. Such revolutionary states, too, have been very aware that the survival of the new order depended on winning the hearts and minds of the next generation, primarily through schooling.[14] But the communist regime of the early 1930s was the first to suggest that it was young people's patriotic duty to inform on any adult, even a parent, who seemed lukewarm. In the era of forced collectivisation a child's denunciation of an adult for political crimes was not swept under the carpet or dealt with reluctantly but greedily seized upon. Not that the policy heralded a collapse in family solidarity. There appear to have been few verifiable examples of child denouncers in the early 1930s and the regime soon had second thoughts about encouraging the practice. As the Stalinist era wore on, the importance of the family as a unit was once again emphasised as the key to social stability. The idea that children might report their parents because of ill-treatment made sense; the thought that they might turn them in for a few ill-chosen words soon seemed monstrous, even to committed communists.

Pavel Morozov: Soviet Hero

Catriona Kelly

In September 1932, during the campaign to collectivise agriculture in the Soviet Union, two young boys, aged nine and thirteen, were found dead in woodland near the village of Gerasimovka, on the borders of the Urals Province and western Siberia. Both had

---

[11] For two recent accounts of the Salem witch hunt, see L. D. Cragg, *The Salem Witch Crisis* (London: Praeger, 1992); L. M. Carlson, *A Fever in Salem: A New Interpretation of the New England Witch Trials* (Chicago: Dee, 1999).

[12] D. W. Sabean, *Power in the Blood* (Cambridge: Cambridge University Press, 1984), ch. 3. For a discussion of the young's participation in the witchcraft craze from a different perspective, see below, pp. 292–97.

[13] Anna-Catharina's accusations were dismissed and she was sent to live with a schoolmaster who was ordered to socialise her.

[14] E.g., R. R. Palmer, *The Improvement of Humanity: Education and the French Revolution* (Princeton: Princeton University Press, 1985).

repeated stab wounds, and their bodies were scattered with cranberries, the result of a foraging expedition that had taken them into the forest. A murder investigation began soon after the bodies were found, under the direction of the local inspector of police, with assistance from an auxiliary. At first, the conclusion was that the killings had been the result of a local feud. Once the reports had reached the district centre 40 kilometres away, however, the case began turning political. The authorities concluded that the boys, Pavel and Fyodor Morozov, had been slaughtered by members of their own extended family, acting as the instruments of a 'kulak plot': a conspiracy by the so-called 'wealthy peasants' who opposed collectivisation. The two boys, it was declared, had been fervent child activists, members of the Young Pioneer organisation (the junior wing of the Communist Youth Movement).[15]

By the time the case reached *Pioneer Pravda*, the organisation's official newspaper, new layers had been added. A story published in the newspaper on 15 October 1932 presented the elder boy, Pavel, as a quite exceptional figure, a hero so committed to the Communist cause that he had even been prepared to denounce his own father to the authorities when he found out that the latter was providing peasants exiled as kulaks with false identity papers. (See Figure 31). At his father's trial, Pavel (or 'Pavlik', to use the affectionate diminutive that was now preferred) had stood up and declared: 'Uncle judge, I am acting not as a son, but as a Pioneer!' In the words of the paper, the boy had 'placed the interests of the Party and the working class above his personal interests', acting thereby as a model not only to children, but also to their elders, in a society that was supposed to be based on rational collectivism.[16]

At the time when it was first reported, the case of Pavlik Morozov was not unique. Other stories published earlier had acclaimed children who stood up to adults at the cost of their lives, or who called their parents into line, up to the level of appeal to the authorities. For example, on 19 April 1930, a schoolboy wrote to the newspaper *Red Kurgan*, 'I consider it disgraceful to rely any longer on the financial support of my idle drone of a father, who is shoring up religion, and impeding the development of socialist construction, and I therefore rupture any connections with my father, an obscurantist and a village priest, the disseminator of lies and deceit to the population'.[17] This was

---

[15] The first report was by Titov [no first name, patronymic, or initials given, but probably the police inspector investigating the case], 'Kulatskaya banda ubila pionera Morozova', *Tavdinskii rabochii*, 17 Sept. 1932, p. 1 (published in *Smena* section of the newspaper), and this was followed by other reports in *Tavdinskii rabochii* on 18, 20 and 21 Sept. 1932. After backstage discussion in the Party Committee in the district centre of the area where the Morozov boys lived, Tavda, and the Children's Bureau of the Sverdlovsk Regional Committee of the Komsomol (the documents related to which are preserved in the Centre for Documents of Public Organisations in Sverdlovsk Province, Ekaterinburg), the case was later reported in the newspaper of the Sverdlovsk organisation of the Young Pioneers, *Vzory kommuny* (on 23 Sept. 1932) and in the Sverdlovsk Komsomol paper *Na smenu!* (on 24 Sept. 1932). On 2 Oct. 1932, the first report appeared in a metropolitan (or to use the Soviet term, 'central') newspaper – *Pionerskaya pravda*, the official organ of the Young Pioneer organisation. The central Pioneer press then reported regularly on the case and provided detailed accounts of the trial of the alleged murderers, as did the local papers. For a more detailed account of the chain of transmission, see C. Kelly, *Comrade Pavlik: The Rise and Fall of a Soviet Boy Hero* (London: Granta Books, 2006), ch. 4.

[16] *Pionerskaya pravda*, 15 Oct. 1932, p. 3.

[17] See Kelly, *Comrade Pavlik*, ch. 4. Quoted in A. Bazarov, *Durelom, ili gospoda kolkhozniki* (2 vols; Kurgan: Izd. Zauralye, 1997), i. 133. In the early 1930s, the official gazette of the Leningrad city administration, *Vestnik Leningradskogo oblispolkoma i Leningradskogo soveta*, regularly carried small ads from individuals officially severing links with members of their family, usually their fathers. See, for example, 'I, Chvyrov, V. I., living in the town of Lyubash, Bannyi pereulok, 3, hereby reject my father, citizen Chvyrov, I. M., living in the village of Zapolye, Starorusskii raion'. *Vestnik Leningradskogo oblispolkoma i Leningradskogo soveta*, no. 4 (1931), p. 3. Such advertisements were, obviously, more likely to be placed by adults, but a gesture of this kind might also be exacted from teenagers – for instance, when someone attempted to proceed to tertiary or even

not the first case of a child activist allegedly murdered by counter-revolutionary forces either. Already in 1930, *Pioneer Pravda* had reported on the case of Grisha Akopyan, a Pioneer activist slaughtered in the North Caucasus by criminal kulaks.[18] The Pavlik Morozov case put the two different motifs of civic virtue together: the fearless denouncer and the martyred activist. It also represented a notable case of the 'darkness into light' trope characteristic of early Soviet culture: the person from a 'backward' social milieu who had progressed to heroic action.[19] The combination had an inalienable power. Though the legend of Pavlik was repeatedly rewritten, and though it lost some of its force during the Second World War (at which point heroes who remained silent despite torture and execution became more popular than those who told what they knew despite risking murder), it was dethroned only after the Soviet Union collapsed.[20]

In its early years, the legend stood for licensed strife between the old and the young. Pavlik, and other child activists, symbolised the part played by youthful energy and unprejudiced new values in transforming backward Russia into the world-leading Soviet Union.[21] Such children had abandoned the old patriarchal family and inscribed themselves in the new family of the state: not for nothing was the title used by Pavlik to the judge at his father's trial 'Uncle'.

Among commentators who did not subscribe to Soviet orthodoxy, the legend of Pavlik Morozov was more often taken to exemplify all that was bad about the Soviet Union, or the 'totalitarian system' more generally. The boy's denunciation of his father represented the violent incursion of the state into the family as well as the capacity of political conflict to tear families apart. This was the way that the story was widely interpreted not just by foreigners, but – during the late Soviet period – by Soviet citizens as well. In a debunking study written secretly in the 1970s and early 1980s, the journalist and writer Yury Druzhnikov attacked the moral iniquity of Pavlik's cult, and argued that it was founded on a lie: the real Pavel Morozov had been no Pioneer and no hero, but a dirty and probably feeble-minded lout who had denounced his father for squalid family reasons (the Morozov parents were at loggerheads).[22] Thus the myth was rewritten, but the denunciation motif was left to stand.

The question of whether Pavel Morozov really did denounce his father remains open. A denunciation text in the secret police file on the murders is highly suspect. Transcribed here as a piece of oral narrative, it also appears in another secret police document as a written text (clearly, it cannot have been both).[23] There was no coverage of Trofim Morozov's trial around the time that this is supposed to have happened (November 1931), though the sensational denunciation of father by son ought to have attracted widespread press interest. And in 1932, the novel *Hitler Boy Quex* by Alois Schenzinger (1886–1962) had provided a fictional, Fascist example of the young boy

---

secondary education.

[18] See Kelly, *Comrade Pavlik*, ch. 4.

[19] See, I. Halfin, *From Darkness to Light: Class, Consciousness and Salvation in Revolutionary Russia* (Pittsburgh: University of Pittsburgh Press, 2000).

[20] See further Kelly, *Comrade Pavlik*, chs 5, 6, and 7.

[21] On the ideological role of youth and on generational identity and conflict in the Soviet Union, see E. Omelchenko, *Molodezh – otkrytyi vopros* (Ulyanovsk: Simbirskaya kniga, 2004), ch. 1; J. Fürst, 'Prisoners of the Soviet Self? – Political Youth Opposition in Late Stalinism', *Europe-Asia Studies*, 54:3 (2002), 353–75, and the contributions by A. Krylova and C. Kelly in S. Lovell (ed.), *Generations in Europe* (Basingstoke: Palgrave, 2007).

[22] Y. Druzhnikov, *Donoschik 001: Voznesenie Pavlika Morozova* (Moscow: Moskovskii rabochii, 1995).

[23] The secret police case file (TsA FSB H7825), to which I had access when writing *Comrade Pavlik*, is preserved in the Central Archive of the Federal Security Service, Moscow. Kelly, *Comrade Pavlik*, ch. 3, is a detailed discussion of the documents in the file and the problems of deducing evidence from them.

who denounces his (Communist) father for political reasons. Was Pavlik's denunciation invented in order to furnish a Soviet example of the same heroic act, or were both texts responses to an established tradition of competing Communist and Fascist youth martyrs, as expressed also in the reworking of the German Communist ballad 'The Little Trumpeter' (rendered into Russian as 'The Little Drummer Boy') as the Fascist 'Horst Wessel Song'?[24]

By extension, one might wonder how many of the other accounts of political denunciations by children in the early Soviet press can in fact be authenticated. Most recollections, even by writers who are in every other way thoroughly anti-Soviet, suggest that such denunciations were rare to non-existent.[25] Even if they admired Pavlik, children continued to think that 'telling on' anyone was wrong, and the idea of 'telling on' a member of your own family was too dreadful to contemplate. The most plausible-sounding cases often stemmed from pre-existing family conflict – something not peculiar to the Soviet system.[26] Back in the 1870s, the future writer Vasily Rozanov (1856–1919) and his siblings dreamed of denouncing their mother, whom they loathed, to the authorities, so that they would not have to see her again.[27] Generational conflict does not necessarily have to be artificially stimulated by ideology: children may seek to have their parents punished without propaganda to direct their thoughts.

But the force of Pavlik Morozov's legend did not depend on whether or not it was true – as is indicated by the constantly modulating details in official versions of the boy's biography. The boy represented an ideal. Yet at this level, too, he proved troubling. Even early Soviet commentators found the idea of a child making an independent civic denunciation against his father implausible or threatening. Later versions of Pavlik's story, unlike the first newspaper reports, sought to defuse Pavlik's action by motivating it by family causes as well. Thus, the first full-length biography of the boy, by the provincial journalist Pavel Solomein (1933), represented Pavlik's father as a brutal thug, who had even tossed a pan of hot fat over the boy in one of his violent rages.[28] To mute the scary social force of the boy's attack on the family, Pavlik's denunciation began, in versions of his story published from the mid-1930s, to be made indirectly: to a local teacher or secret police agent, who confirmed that the boy was right to pass on the information, and who acted as mediator for its passage to the public eye.[29] Thus the Soviet establishment sought to manage a father-destroying hero in changed circumstances, when the family had begun to be perceived as an essential 'social cell', an instrument of Communist rectitude and of Stalinist discipline.[30] Pavlik's rebellion against the family was now seen as an act of solidarity with family values – of an ideal kind, such as had been betrayed by his biological father, a man not worthy to be his father in a spiritual sense.

Remoulded like this, Pavlik's reasons for denunciation were made to seem more respectable. Once the boy had become the victim of family abuse, his action seemed more readily comprehensible, more sympathetic. Denunciation from within the family can be tolerated when the child's own safety seems in question. This tolerance is not

[24] See Kelly, *Comrade Pavlik*, ch. 4.
[25] Examples include the Soviet Russian 'displaced persons' interviewed for the post-war collection edited by N. K. Novak-Deker, *Soviet Youth: Twelve Komsomol Histories* (Munich: Institute for the Study of the USSR, 1959).
[26] See Kelly, *Comrade Pavlik*, ch. 5.
[27] V. Rozanov, *Opavshie listya* (Moscow: no publisher given, 1913), p. 236.
[28] P. Solomein, *V kulatskom gnezde* (Sverdlovsk: Uralkniga, 1933).
[29] *E.g.* A. Yakovlev, *Pioner Pavlik Morozov: Povest* (Moscow: Detskaya literatura, 1936).
[30] This shift in attitudes to the family is described in detail in chs 2–3 and 9–10 of C. Kelly, *Children's World: Growing Up in Russia, 1890–1991* (New Haven: Yale University Press, 2007).

politically or morally problematic. Consequently, in a more conservative Soviet era, the figure of the child denouncer came to symbolise not so much children's accession to political or legal power, as the ways in which this was tamed. It is no coincidence that the most famous exponent of the strategy in the Soviet Union was also a murder victim, suggesting the fearful fate of those who unsettle the generational power hierarchy.

Is it possible that my own unhappiness with the idea of a child denouncing its parents has led me to play down the exemplary force of Pavlik's narrative and the likelihood that he 'really did' behave in that way? Cases like Pavlik's do come up in oral history, not just in propaganda. In summer 2004, an elderly woman brought up in Pskov province recalled a schoolmate of hers who had denounced his father and uncle early in 1932 to the authorities for having murdered the chairman of the village soviet.[31] The two men had vowed revenge on the chairman when he confiscated a valuable horse and appropriated it for his own private use; they killed him, tied stones to his belt, and threw him in the local lake. When the chairman came up in the nets during the spring fishing, the boy piped up: '"My uncle killed him [...] my uncle Matvei done it, and there was blood on our gates, me mam wiped off the blood with soot from the stove."'[32] The boy concerned was only eight. Perhaps, then, it was not Pavlik Morozov, but his forgotten brother Fyodor, who was the source of the denunciation, exultantly pouring out what he knew for the sheer joy of being heard and having no idea of the consequence of his actions?

Whichever way, such a denunciation may have been made without a sense of political or even social resonance. Children who lived through the terrible years of the Russian Revolution and Civil War often survived, it seems, through a pervasive sense of unreality and detachment. In his memoir, 'Through the Eyes of My Generation', the poet Konstantin Simonov (1915–79) remembers his emotions when he stumbled on a house search being carried out in his uncle and aunt's apartment – not outrage or fear, but overwhelming surprise.[33] Children who fought in the Russian Civil War – as fairly large numbers did – recalled afterwards that guilt or concern were far from their thoughts. 'I used to shoot at a condemned man with no sense of pity at all and in fact with a huge sense of curiosity,' a man caught up in the war as a late teenager remembered.[34] In similar vein, a woman brought up in Leningrad in the 1930s has recalled the gloating sensation with which she listened to a conversation between her

---

[31] It is extremely unlikely that this woman's testimony was influenced, even retrospectively, by the legend about Pavlik Morozov; the twenty interviews that were carried out in rural areas during 2004 and 2005 as part of our Leverhulme-sponsored oral history project (see following fn.) revealed a remarkably low level of awareness, among informants who grew up in the 1920s, 1930s, and 1940s, of propaganda texts, including even those connected with the Lenin and Stalin cult for children, which – unlike the story of Pavlik – were published in school textbooks (the Pavlik story was set for 'extra-curricular reading').

[32] Woman, b. 1920, Pskov province, recorded Aug. 2004, Karelia. Interview carried out in a settlement in Leningrad province for the Leverhulme project, 'Childhood in Russia, 1890–1991: A Social and Cultural History', interviewers Ekaterina Melnikova and Oksana Filicheva, code Oxf/Lev V-04 PF4A, p. 22. For further details of the interviewing project, see www.mod-langs.ox.ac.uk/russian/childhood; www.ehrc.ox.ac.uk/lifehistory.

[33] K. Simonov, 'Glazami cheloveka moego pokoleniya', *Znamya*, 8 (1988), p. 12.

[34] L. I. Petrusheva (ed.), *Deti russkoi emigratsii* (Moscow: Terra, 1997), p. 401 (anon. man b. 1902). To be sure, this man also recollected being overcome with a severe reaction in the aftermath: 'But then, after the execution was over, I'd be filled with nervous trembling and a dim sense of being in the wrong. Much later, I came to a full spiritual understanding of the dreadful sin that I'd committed so cold-bloodedly and with such curiosity. I understood what I'd done and I was horrified. Now I only feel deep and immutable repentance when I remember all this. I can't even stand to see anyone else in pain; I'm a total realist, but I turn away like a sentimental schoolgirl when I see blood, even a scratch' (*ibid.*).

mother and her uncle, just released from prison, exulting in the man's accounts of the tortures that he had undergone.[35] Perhaps the horror provoked by Pavlik's denunciation is partly to do with children's capacity to exult in violence, if only at the level of imagination (developmentally, the age group eight to fourteen is the key stage for genres such as horror stories and 'sadistic verses').[36] Arguably, this capacity generates unease in adults who would prefer not to remember that they themselves once felt like this – and who, of course, are now the possible targets of the child's unpredictable hostility.

· ·

The Soviets may have felt more comfortable with the thought that children who denounced their parents to the authorities did so because of ill-treatment rather than for political reasons. Yet, it is unlikely that the Russian, more than any other European, state in the years following the Second World War made this any easier to do. The management of 'children at risk' is an area of social life where the importance of intervention by the representatives of state power and by childcare professionals has come to be seen as far more essential than ever before in the last 60 years. But it is only since the promulgation of the United Nations' Convention of the Rights of the Child in 1989 that European states have seriously begun to think not only about how children might be protected from abuse and exploitation but also how they might be empowered and enabled to participate more fully in decisions made about them. Indeed, in Britain even in the 1980s one of the most important initiatives came from outside government with the foundation of ChildLine in 1986.

ChildLine was set up after a survey of child abuse conducted by a BBC TV consumer rights programme, *That's Life!*, presented by Esther Rantzen. The resultant BBC questionnaire, filled in by 3,000 adults, revealed that children in the era of the Welfare State were suffering as much as they had ever done from adult violence. This finding encouraged Rantzen, with the help of childcare professionals from both the statutory and voluntary sectors, to establish a free telephone helpline manned by volunteers where children could seek advice anonymously. On the night the helpline was launched 50,000 children tried to make contact. In the following years ChildLine, operating as a service of the NSPCC, quickly became a national institution, offering a vital point of contact outside the home for distressed and stressed children. Providing advice on all manner of worries from physical and sexual abuse to exam nerves, twenty years on it deals daily with 2,500 calls.[37]

In important respects ChildLine's success cannot be divorced from wider changes in British and western culture. Whistle-blowing, which was formerly thought 'bad form', is now widely approved of, while people under 40, thanks to the new emphasis on individual well-being, self-fulfilment and the right to respect promoted in schools and in the media, are much more ready than hitherto, indeed are often eager, to unburden themselves to strangers. The most recent developments in communications technology have only accelerated the trend.[38] None the less, the degree to which this new culture has really

---

[35] Interview carried out by Catriona Kelly in Oxford, 2003, code CKQ-Ox-03 PF6B, p. 12.

[36] On 'sadistic verses', see M. Lurye, 'Sadistic Verse as a Genre of Russian Urban Folklore: Typical and Specific Features, Child and Adult Audiences', *Forum for Anthropology and Culture*, 5 (forthcoming, 2010).

[37] For an account of ChildLine's activities, see the timeline of the charity's work since 1986 on www.nspcc.org.uk/whatwedo/aboutChildLine/childline_history (accessed 29 Jun. 2009). Similar services have been set up in a number of other countries with historic ties with the UK, notably Ireland, India and South Africa.

[38] The result has been the division of Britain into two cultures epitomised by the different response of the young and the old to the death of Diana, Princess of Wales, in 1997. The new and old Britain are effectively portrayed in the film, *The Queen* (2006). For the new emphasis on well-being in education, see below, pp. 313–14.

empowered children and adolescents to complain of their lot should not be exaggerated. Children may have a much greater ability to make their complaints heard: adult outsiders do listen. But the testimony of children continues to excite unease. In myth, a child's voice may be associated with verity unveiled – as in the folk tale of the 'Emperor's New Clothes', where only a child is courageous, or foolish, enough to state the obvious. But in practice, paediatricians, child psychiatrists and lawyers continue to wrestle over the question of the weight that should be assigned to children's testimony, suggesting that these are witnesses who readily fantasise, provide questioners with what they want to hear, who cannot tell the difference between truth and falsehood – who are, in sum, not to be relied on.[39] It is also the case that an organisation such as ChildLine, through its guarantee of anonymity, protects the perpetrators of child abuse as much as the victims. In Britain today, children are encouraged to report victimisation to strangers and seek advice, but they are asked to do so decently on the telephone without dishonouring their tormentors. They may not protest against violence too vehemently: their access to the power of the denunciatory word must not be too free.[40]

Given that even in the present appealing to outsiders is fraught with uncertainty, it is scarcely surprising that over the centuries an alternative strategy for dealing with unacceptable levels of physical abuse and deprivation has been to run away. Putting as much distance as possible between the victim and the victimiser is on the surface both the simplest and the most sensible response. We know very little about youngsters who ran away from their parents in the past. But the number must have been large. At present in Britain, despite all the outside support available for the unhappy child, 100,000 under sixteen-year-olds spend one night or more away from home without parental permission. And many never return.[41] Admittedly, this is a much more hypersensitive age and children in the past would have suffered rebukes and punishments more stoically. But there is no reason to suspect that children suffering perceived abuse in former centuries would have never deserted the family hearth.[42] Jacques-Louis Ménétra, the Parisian apprentice glazier encountered on several occasions in this book, certainly did. Faced with a brutal father, he ran away twice. On the first occasion, he decamped to live with a relative (doubtless a common strategy); on another, he signed on with the army.[43]

Moreover, it is quite clear that children in the past ran away all the time from the workplace or service only to discover that they faced a more uncertain future on the streets, frequently descending into vagrancy or prostitution.[44] In eighteenth-century England court records and newspaper advertisements reveal that apprentices were always absconding, apparently particularly in the early hours of Sunday morning when the family was asleep. Some were clearly truculent and unmanageable by nature but most felt that they could no longer endure what they considered unacceptable ill-treatment. Typical was William Hutton, apprenticed to his uncle, a Nottingham stocking-maker. Having been starved, poorly clothed and continually subjected to his aunt's ire, the seventeen-year-old departed for Birmingham

---

[39] See, for example, A. Melinder, G. S. Goodman, D. E. Eilertsen and S. Magnussen, 'Beliefs about Child Witnesses: A Survey of Professionals', *Psychology, Crime and Law*, 10:4 (2004), 347–65; see also L. Hoyano and C. Keenan. *Child Abuse: Law and Policy Across Boundaries* (Oxford: Oxford University Press, 2007), chs 8–9.

[40] The editors would like to thank Catriona Kelly for offering these words of caution about the extent of children's empowerment in the early twenty-first century.

[41] www.childrensociety.org.uk/resources/documents/Policy/Stepping_Up_The_Future_For_Young_ Runaways (accessed 29 Jun. 2009), p. 13.

[42] Some felt compelled to run away from normal homes. The sixteenth-century mystic, Teresa of Avila (1515–82), slipped out of her house at the age of seven with her brother to seek martyrdom among the Moors.

[43] Jacques-Louis Ménétra, *Journal de ma vie*, ed. D. Roche (Paris: Albin Michel, 1982), p. 37.

[44] Anna Catharina Weissenbuhler ran away from service in her brother's household before she ended up as a nanny to her cousin: see above, p. 275.

one day in 1741 with a loaf, his Bible, assorted clothing and 2 shillings in cash.[45] But it was not just the relatively poor who took to their heels. Children from good families, too, were no more ready to knuckle down and submit if they felt aggrieved. Boarding school pupils frequently ran away. An early example was Robert Buck who absconded from a school in Clitheroe about 1280, no longer able to take the beatings of a sadistic master. Usually, like Buck, the scholars had good cause, but sometimes they ran simply because they had too high a sense of their own dignity. John and Edmund Isham were fourteen and twelve respectively when sent by their father, a prominent Northamptonshire gentleman, to Rugby School in 1700. After initially flourishing in their studies, they began to slacken three years later and were suitably admonished for their laziness. Although seemingly only caned on the hand, they took umbrage at the punishment and absconded. They had gone five miles before they were caught and brought back.[46]

If running away was a common recourse of those who found themselves poorly treated by surrogate fathers, it is hard not to believe that many children also flew the family nest. Children living under the authority of a step-parent or guardian, of whom there would have been many in the nuclear households of pre-modern northern Europe, must have frequently left home in protest. Although we must be careful not to take the many European folk tales of evil stepmothers and wicked uncles too literally, there must have been many homes where children found the replacement parent a poor substitute, even if they were properly fed. Otherwise the creation and dissemination of tales such as *Cinderella, Hansel and Gretel* and its English variant, *Babes in the Wood*, do not make sense.[47]

Understandably, running away was no more acceptable in the pre-modern world than telling tales. It was an equally visible affront to patriarchy that was not to be lightly dismissed. Like slaves, absconding apprentices were hunted down and captured, masters frequently helping each other in the task: in 1789, the very year of the French Revolution, Sheffield employers founded a permanent society to track down the renegades.[48] As English theatre audiences from the early seventeenth century were continually told in the popular drama of 'Dick Whittington' (and still learn today), the best road that a runaway servant could take, however ill-treated, was the road back to his abandoned master. Repentance not rebellion was the path to future riches.[49]

---

[45] Lane, *Apprenticeship*, pp. 180 and 201–06. See also P. Griffiths, *Youth and Authority: Formative Experiences in England 1560–1640* (Oxford: Clarendon, 1996), pp. 333–34. In Antwerp in the first half of the seventeenth century apparently nearly twenty per cent of apprentices absconded: see B. de Munck, *Technologies of Learning: Apprenticeships in Antwerp Guilds from the Fifteenth to the End of the Ancien Regime* (Turnhout: Brepols, 2007), p. 190.

[46] M. T. Clanchy, *From Memory to Written Record. England 1066–1307*, 2nd edn (Oxford: Blackwell, 1993), p. 225; A. Fletcher, *Growing Up in England. The Experience of Childhood 1600–1914* (London: Yale University Press, 2008), pp. 169–70. A century later Nelson's future chaplain, Alexander Scott, ran away from school rather than take a flogging: M. and A. Gatty, *Recollections of the Life of the Rev. A. J. Scott, D. D., Lord Nelson's Chaplain* (London: Saunders and Otley, 1842), p. 9. In an earlier period, children had also absconded from monasteries when they had been cloistered at an early age: F. D. Logan, *Runaway Religious in Medieval England, c. 1240–1540*, Cambridge Studies in Medieval Life and Thought; 4th Ser., 32 (Cambridge: Cambridge University Press, 1996).

[47] *Babes in the Wood* was first told in print in a ballad of 1595. It is purportedly based on an actual event in Norfolk. None of the three tales, of course, involve runaways.

[48] Dunlop, *English Apprenticeship*, p. 144.

[49] Richard Whittington, Lord Mayor of London (d. 1423), was the third son of a Gloucestershire knight. The legend that Dick was an orphan servant boy who ran away from his cruel master but returned, became rich and married his master's daughter appears to have been first played in 1605: T. Keightley, *Tales and Popular Fictions, Their Resemblance and Transmission from Country to Country* (London: Wittaker and Co., 1834), pp. 241–86.

Attitudes presumably softened in the second half of the nineteenth century as the new interest in London's poor emphasised the fate that could await many runaways who were not found and returned. But there seems to have been limited interest in runaways *per se*. Their cases seldom sparked the interest of the famous campaigning novelists of Victorian England. Indeed, if the great literature of the century is any guide, then the child runaway was virtually absent from the Victorian age. Runaways can certainly be found in nineteenth-century fiction, but seldom the children who ended up roaming the streets of London looking for food and shelter.

Child Runaways in Nineteenth-Century Fiction

George Rousseau

Considering that the English novel after Defoe developed in part as an imaginative forum for describing family life and that no one would dispute that many youngsters ran away from home in the late Georgian and Victorian eras, one would expect dozens of runaways in the great nineteenth-century novel. Yet the reality is that there are few. No one has made a statistical count; but in the approximately 100 canonical British novels of the century, written by native Britons, only a few runaways can be found. Even in Dickens's prolific novels, where abundant numbers might be expected, only a few exist. Oliver Twist is the best-known example, and he is a parish orphan, someone whose status on the surface would make him an unlikely hero for a family drama.

If we pause on *Oliver Twist* (1837–38), we can understand how Dickens accommodated the orphan's history to his readers' interests. Less masterful novelists than Dickens would have turned boys like Oliver into artificial, flat stereotypes.[50] Only Dickens's masterful understanding can render Oliver's story attractive to readers expecting realism of a high order; this achievement, coupled to Dickens's unique sense of the injustice orphans suffer, permitted him to rescue runaways for serious fiction in a way they had not been before. Dickens knew that orphans are among the most mistreated, neglected, and despised of children. Oliver Twist is one such orphaned lad, but in the story – as everyone knows – unlike other boys Oliver has not allowed the bitterness surrounding him to tarnish the goodness of his spirit. He is honest to a fault, even accepting he is morally obliged to request a forbidden 'more' for his supper having drawn the short straw. He earns the loathing of the men in charge of the workhouse where he resides. They do everything within their power to send him away, even down to willingly paying a man to take Oliver off their hands. So little Oliver, no more than ten-years-old, finds himself working for the local undertaker. Mr. Sowerberry seems a kindly man, apart from the ferocious nature of his wife. Yet when it comes down to deciding whether to do right by the boy or obeying his wife, he fails immeasurably. Oliver is left with no choice but to turn his thoughts and feet toward London society, where perhaps he might find a kind soul. With butchered and bleeding feet, Oliver finally drags himself on the last

---

[50] The fullest analysis is found in B. Hochman and I. Wachs, *Dickens: The Orphan Condition* (Madison and London: Fairleigh Dickinson University Press; Associated University Presses, 1999). For the background leading up to Dickens's social milieu, see J. Robins, *The Lost Children: Children in Ireland, 1700–1900: A Study of Charity* (Dublin: Institute of Public Administration, 1980).

legs of his 70–mile journey to London, Victorian fiction's most memorable runaway.[51]

Elsewhere in Dickens, David Copperfield briefly runs away but few other characters in his fiction do, causing the modern reader to wonder why this is when the historical reality was so prevalent. Pip tries to abscond in *Great Expectations* (1860–61), but never does, and by blurting out 'this way for the runaway convicts' interestingly suggests that he sees his own escape plan as a criminal act. Elsewhere in canonical Victorian fiction, Charlotte Brontë's Jane Eyre – the heroine of the book of the same name (1847) – can be said to have to run away when she lands on St John Rivers's doorstep, but she is already an adult rather than a child. Brontë (1816–55) constructs a world in which the characters feel so locked up – so perpetually incarcerated – that the reader somehow expects they will escape: the fact is that they do not. Emily Brontë (1818–48) has Cathy run away when she flees, albeit temporarily, to Thrushcross Grange in *Wuthering Heights* (1847). And in Charlotte Brontë's *Villette* (1853) a few children try to escape from the school. But these are minor episodes without any of the stirring motion of Oliver's great escape to London.

Readers of the *Mill on the Floss* (1878) by George Eliot (1819–80) remember that young Maggie Tulliver runs away to the gypsies when feeling disaffected and alienated in the Dodson family; she cannot fit their mould, behave suitably, or rival the standards of behaviour displayed by the pale and pretty Lucy Deane. But her flight turns out to be doomed: no sooner have the gypsies taken her in than she discovers she has no place. She is too clever by far, even eccentric by their norms; and her intellect causes her to behave in a manner they consider 'wilful'. George Eliot seems altogether uninterested in runaways as literary possibilities, and in another work – *The Spanish Gypsy*, her longest poem written a decade earlier – where one might expect all sorts of runaways to appear, none do. Elsewhere in the broad map of canonical Victorian fiction even Dickens's strangely named Abel Magwitch in *Great Expectations* only runs away belatedly from his Australian exile. One might expect this social misfit and convicted criminal to have abundant opportunity to abscond but he seems not to: runaways do not easily fit into the plot schemes of Victorian novels even if the social reality of the epoch reveals a very different state of affairs.[52]

The absence of young runaways in realistic Victorian novels, however, does not mean that they were absent from nineteenth-century fiction. In the first place, they can be found in fables, fairy tales and other fabulous literary forms where they were already well established. In fairy tales and ballads, orphaned children forever flee the 'wicked witch', their parents (if they have parents) having surrendered them, willingly or not, to this force of evil. Fairy tales and ballads identified runaways as favourite characters because they were so useful for demonstrating, especially to child readers, the forces of evil and good.[53] Secondly, runaways were to be found in what may be called 'exotic' tales: exciting adventures for readers in search of vicarious experience. Again, the appearance

---

[51] Roman Polanski's recent film *Oliver Twist* (2005) casts this scene as the most moving one in the film, suggesting the psychological importance he attached to his protagonist's orphan status. Polanski has built on a recent filmic genre of orphan runaways, in which the psychological drama is pre-eminent. See, for example, Harry Harris's and Nadine Trintignant's *Fugueuses* ('Runaways', 1995), in which a sullen teenage orphan, Johnny Miles, is wrongfully accused of stealing from his foster parents. He runs away from home and forms a bond with another youthful runaway – a leopard who has escaped from a nearby wild-animal compound. The film was adapted from Victor Canning's novel, *The Runaways* (1975).

[52] As an aside, contemporary Australian novelist Michael Noonan (1921–2000) makes rather more of the runaway theme in his reconstruction of Magwitch's life: *Magwitch* (1982).

[53] See D. Purkiss, *Troublesome Things: A History of Fairies and Fairy Tales* (London: Allen Lane, 2000). For a trans-historical view of the genre and its relation to evil and good see D. Purkiss, *The Witch in History: Early Modern and Twentieth-Century Representations* (London: Routledge, 1996).

of runaways in this genre had a long pedigree. Even in ancient literature – Homer and Aesop to Ovid – the runaway was an exotic object and the cause of wonder. And the first English writers of action novels had been quick to see the subject's potential. One version, already evident in the seventeenth century was the runaway princess, fleeing from evil forces – including parents – among her aristocratic enslavers, a version that continues to be used in contemporary film.[54] From the eighteenth century, the vicarious element increased, especially in unrealistic tales and fables about runaways; and by the time the mystery thriller developed in the nineteenth century (with Wilkie Collins, 1824–89), the runaway had become a stock feature of the genre.[55]

The subject was further aired in sentimental literature, which on its development in the Enlightenment had also tapped into the runaway as a stereotypical figure of adventure. For example, few English comedies of the late eighteenth century attracted as much attention as Hannah Cowley's sentimental comedy, *The Runaway* (1776), the last theatrical work David Garrick (1717–79) supervised, in which the runaway heroine was played by the popular actress Sarah Siddons (1755–1831).[56] Cowley (1743–1809) was thought to be something of a 'natural untutored genius' in her time. Her heroine Emily, a fugitive from a distasteful marriage, takes refuge in the Hargraves's household and is unscrupulously lured away from this retreat because her charms threaten to seduce young Hargraves from his promised marriage with a wealthy old maid. Emily is not orphaned, nor does she flee any evil other than her imprisoning marriage. Her husband does not strike her, nor is he violent in any way. Garrick even expurgated Emily's references to the destruction that would be done to her land upon her flight. The *Runaway*'s heroine delighted its audiences by her portrayal of sentimental love rather than as a fugitive. A century later this sentimental strain was still enchanting the readers of sketches of rural life. The chapters about runaways in *Our Village* (1832) by Mary Russell Mitford (1787–1855) were typical of a genre that blossomed all century.[57] The innocent village variety was not limited to adolescent male runaways looking for work as well as adventure, but was often generalised in the literature to both sexes in flight from life's broader disappointments.

Whereas this grass-rooted theme seems to have fit into minor domestic fiction and short stories published in magazines, the great novelists eschewed it. Admittedly, there was one serious British novelist in the period under review who did consistently make use of the runaway theme but he was not reared in Britain. This was the ex-merchant seaman and Polish born Joseph Conrad (1857–1924), who began to publish only right at the end of the Victorian era. Significantly Conrad's novels were mainly set, not in the standard nuclear family, but among communities of expatriates, often sailors, in exotic locations. Conrad demonstrated the potential of the theme in his *Bildungsroman* of 1899, *Lord Jim*. Jim is a young man with a vivid, romantic imagination who decides to become a sailor after reading sea stories, 'a course of light holiday literature'. He is neither orphaned nor in flight from violence, but rather loves picturing himself as a hero. As a mate on a passenger ship, he misses his chance when it comes in a great

---

[54] In *Roman Holiday* (1952) Audrey Hepburn plays the runaway, orphan princess who escapes from her palace to fall in love with an ordinary newspaper reporter (Gregory Peck). It was not incidental that the film was released during the year of the accession of Queen Elizabeth II.

[55] It has continued among mystery thrillers to the present time; see, for example, C. Watson, *Runaway* (London: Hale, 1986).

[56] For the theatrical background, see 'Hopkins Diary', cited in C. B. Hogan *et al.* (eds), *The London Stage*, part 5, vol. I, entry for Feb. 1776, Drury Lane, 'The Runaway'.

[57] See M. R. Mitford, *Our Village: Sketches of Rural Character and Scenery* (London: Whittaker, Treacher and Co., 1832), vol. 5, 'The Runaway', pp. 151–63.

storm. Convinced against his better judgement by the other officers that the ship is doomed and its cargo of Muslim pilgrims of no consequence, he joins his fellow white men when they abandon the vessel to save their own lives. The subsequent action of the novel – Jim retreats from civilisation to the Malayan jungle where he works to rebuild his self-respect – confirms the 'runaway impulse' of Conrad's fiction. This was particularly on display in one of his last novels, *Victory* (1915), where all the characters, both good and bad, are in some way on the run from the life that had been waiting them in Europe.

Serious nineteenth-century continental novelists, too, did not shrink from writing about runaways, which emphasises that we are dealing with a particular English 'absence'. In Germany, for instance, Theodor Fontane (1819–98) captured the runaway type in *Grete Minde* (1880), the strange story of a runaway girl trapped in the turbulent religious and social prejudices of seventeenth-century Sweden. Born of a noble Lutheran father and his second wife, a Spanish Catholic, Grete is abused by her anti-Catholic older half-brother while her father is living; when he dies, she is dealt with even more violently. Orphaned and maltreated, she flees to the home of an uncle with the help of a local boy who has grown accustomed to protecting her. Later, unwed and pregnant, she flees yet again: this time back to her home town, where she is tragically ill-received. Fontane presents her as a perpetual fugitive, and places her in a realistic narrative tradition capable of demonstrating the raw misery of the runaway. But she has none of Oliver Twist's good luck in Dickens. In contrast, Fontane captures the tragic dimension in the runaway and pushes it to limits the plot is capable of absorbing.[58]

English-language writers across the Atlantic also deployed the theme to good effect. In a society built on slavery and indentured imported labour, young runaways were a commonplace in the eighteenth-century colonies. Indeed, in some ways every white American was a runaway or the descendant of one. And some, like the legendary Dick Whittington, made good.[59] The most famous representative of the new independent America, Benjamin Franklin (1706–90), whose successful escape from poverty every young American was taught to admire and imitate, was himself a runaway. Franklin at the age of twelve had been apprenticed as a printer to his brother, the sole 'Founding Father' to have been indentured. But his brother frequently maltreated him and Franklin fled his master before his term was complete. In later years, he built a financial empire selling newspapers that not only promoted the goods of a slave economy but also ran advertisements of slaves for sale and notices about runaways. Franklin's life typified the paradox of colonial American: slavery and freedom. It also highlighted the paradox of a world where running away could be both good and bad, a sign of independence and initiative, and a sign of rebellion. There is no evidence that Franklin's early history caused him any scruples of conscience in helping to track down fugitive slaves.[60]

---

[58] Perhaps this limit is what appealed to the script writers about the Austrian full-length film of *Grete Minde* (1977). Other examples include Gottfried Keller's *Romeo und Juliet auf dem dorfer* (1850), which influenced various librettists, and, a generation earlier, Annetta von Droste-Hülshoff's *Juden Buche* (1820), translated into English as *The Jew's Beech*.

[59] A large secondary literature exists on slave runaways, child and adult, especially in the American colonies prior to the American Revolution. See, for example, B. G. Smith and R. Wojtowicz, *Blacks Who Stole Themselves: Advertisements for Runaways in the Pennsylvania Gazette, 1728–1790* (Philadelphia: University of Pennsylvania Press, 1989); see also the website: 'Virginia Runaways', http://people.uvawise.edu/runaways/biblio.html (accessed 11 Jan. 2010).

[60] D. Waldstreicher, *Runaway America: Benjamin Franklin, Slavery, and the American Revolution,* (New York: Hill and Wang, 2004). Also, D. Waldstreicher, 'Reading the Runaways: Self-Fashioning, Print Culture, and Confidence in Slavery in the Eighteenth-Century Mid-Atlantic,' *William and Mary Quarterly*, 56:2 (1999), 243–72.

It was perhaps the contrasting attitudes to the black and white runaways in the independent United States that attracted the interest of writers in the subject. Runaway slaves were the stuff of American fiction long before Mark Twain (1835–1910) made it a stock feature of his masterpiece, *The Adventures of Huckleberry Finn* (1885).[61] While travelling down the Mississippi, through Missouri and Arkansas, with a runaway slave (Jim), Huck – an adolescent boy – is forced to decide for himself what genuinely matters. Set in the decade 1835–45, before the Civil War, Twain's picaresque novel centres on a boy's loss of innocence and the runaway slave's struggle for freedom. In his fiction Twain embraced the American twin values of rugged individualism and freedom of speech; and by writing in the American vernacular, he helped to create a distinctively American literary tradition. But his real aim in *Huck Finn* is to explore the theme of childhood through the crucibles of racism and slavery, intellectual and moral education, and the hypocrisy of 'civilised' society. He appears to have decided he could not achieve the first of these (racism) without depicting the slave specifically as a runaway, a black man freed from his shackles and able to meet the white boy on equal human terms.

The interest of American novelists with runaways, moreover, did not end with the abolition of slavery and the partial resolution of the old tensions. It even found its way into the family novel, *Ethan Frome* (1911) by Edith Wharton (1862–1937), if in an unexpected form. Here, in this novella's engrossing drama, Wharton constructed her least characteristic and most celebrated book. Set in a stagnating New England village appropriately called Starkfield, it is the story of a husband and wife – Ethan and Zeena – who need an extra hand around the house due to Zeena's debilitated body and constant illness. Mattie, the young woman who joins them, is a beautiful, spirited person. She and Ethan fall in love, to the dismay of Zeena, prompting Ethan to fantasise plots of escape to remote places. Eventually Ethan decides to run away to the Wild West with Mattie, but his felt commitment to Zeena prevents him. After a good deal of further exploration about the possibility of running away, Ethan decides against it and hatches a suicide pact with Mattie. They decide to kill themselves in an accident that goes amok and leaves them badly wounded instead.[62]

Running away, this time in the guise of desertion, was also an important theme of American war literature in the period before and after the First World War in a way that was not mirrored in Britain, though in some of this literature it is unclear whether the actors are child soldiers or adults. In two such canonical works as *The Red Badge of Courage* (1895) by Stephen Crane (1871–1900) and *A Farewell to Arms* (1929) by Ernest Hemmingway (1899–1961) the fighting boys can be defined either way. In the former, Henry is preoccupied about whether or not to run when the time comes to fight; in Hemingway, American Lieutenant Frederic Henry jumps to escape German spies. Crane probes the relation of the military runaway to his potential heroism. After the second war skirmish, his soldier hero flees from battle owing to cowardice. Crane's story shows Henry rationalising and justifying. Henry's running is '... not a fault, a shameful thing; it was an act obedient to a law'. Crane's text appeals to nature to justify his protagonist's

---

[61] Like Twain, earlier literature also displayed interracial runaways, as when a white and black girl run away from a southern farm to make the difficult journey north to freedom in Jennifer Armstrong's *Steal Away* (1855).
[62] Carson McCullers's *Member of the Wedding* (1945) is a latter-day version of the Wharton story, especially in a war mode. Frankie, the heroine, dreams of running away to become famous flying aeroplanes and winning gold medals for bravery, and much of the plot concerns itself with her plans for a great escape that come to nothing. McCullers's theme of escape and flight as inherent in the human condition is captured when Frankie's friend Bernice extemporises: 'We all of us are somehow caught. We are born this way or that way and we don't know why. But we are caught anyhow', edn. (New York: Houghton-Mifflin, 2004), p. 119.

flight, as when Henry throws a rock at a squirrel and it runs away. Henry's claim that flight should be executed with 'dignity' – as if cowards are less cowardly because they run in dignity – is also suspect. The story's contours contain further rationalisations of escape, none of which obliterate the cowardice. These war novelists rarely condone flight, even when the circumstances are so dire that sure death awaits their characters. Their moral world of necessitated staying is a long way from Dickens's.[63]

We began with great Victorian canonical novels as containers for runaways on the premise that these literary artefacts might be repositories for them. Close examination revealed the opposite: they contain few runaways and when found are always orphaned and/or in flight to pursue the dream of a better world. Violence – domestic, external, physical, violence at home versus violence in the workplace of the young – enters the runaway's decision in only a few cases. One reason for this absence of runaways must lie in the realism and subject matter of the great nineteenth-century British novel. The canonical novelists wrote primarily about middle-class families: their courtships, marriages, family arrangements and children. However dysfunctional some of these families were (one thinks of the loveless atmosphere of the Dombey household), running away was not a normal middle-class child's reaction to hardship and neglect, if presumably not unknown. Moreover, the runaway, given his or her probable fate, was of sorely limited utility to these novelists. Runaways (orphaned or otherwise) are of little use to the narrators of massive fictions whose protagonists – our putative runaways – will be studied especially for their moral and psychological development. Without parents or guardians to supervise this growth there can be little moral education, or *Bildung*, as the Victorian commentators influenced by the Germans liked to refer to the new novel in the aftermath of Dickens.[64] In brief, the massive novels of the nineteenth century had little time for homeless heroes and heroines.

Furthermore, the world had moved on from the 1830s, when Dickens wrote *Oliver Twist*, the great exception. It is instructive here to close on *Tess of the D'Urbervilles* (1891) by Thomas Hardy (1840–1928), another canonical Victorian novel that makes the point in brief. Here the main figures are neither children nor runaways: they are abandoned adults forced to flee, escaping from rueful domestic situations, searching for gainful employment, and roaming the countryside for cheap accommodation. Angel Clare, the minister's son who has fallen in love with Tess, departs for faraway South America, and – most poignantly among the characters – Tess herself is constantly seen to be in flight from one location to another, running from distress, shame, and outright abuse until she commits the murder for which she will be hanged. Hardy's tale of seduction, abuse and execution for murder has no space for a child protagonist on whom to peg these social dislocations. Nor would an outright runaway – like Oliver Twist – among any of the major figures, even if this had been Tess herself, have served Hardy's purpose as it did Dickens two generations earlier in the very different world of the 1830s.[65]

The differences are historical and representational. By 1891 Dickens had been dead

---

[63] While Dickens and his contemporaries were spinning their plots, medical doctors sought to understand the runaway in terms of the newly emerging category of psychological pathology; several articles on runaways appeared in *The Journal of Psychological Medicine: A Quarterly Review of Diseases of the Nervous System, Medical Jurisprudence, and Anthropology*, which started in 1848.

[64] The standard treatment of the Victorian *Bildungsroman* is found in J. H. Buckley, *Season of Youth: The Bildungsroman from Dickens to Golding* (Cambridge: Harvard University Press, 1974). For the long view, see F. Moretti, *The Way of the World: The Bildungsroman in European Culture* (London: Verso, 1987). Also useful for its emphasis on the abandoned child is J. A. Kushigian, *Reconstructing Childhood: Strategies of Reading for Culture and Gender in the Spanish American Bildungsroman* (Lewisburg and London: Bucknell University Press; Associated University Presses, 2003).

[65] See F. R. Southerington, *Hardy's Vision of Man* (London: Chatto and Windus, 1971).

for over two decades. Even his last major works – *Our Mutual Friend* (1865), *The Mystery of Edwin Drood* (1870) – could not have contained a plot like that of *Oliver Twist*: so much had changed in the world about him. A child runaway, like Oliver, who falls in with all manner of criminal types was no longer capable of satisfying the sophisticated palates of late Victorian readers. The new claims of social mobility had usurped the stark, old realities of unmitigated poverty. Besides, the passage of diverse child labour laws over a half-century, especially pertaining to child workers and the protections given them, had made the charcoal-nightmare conditions of Oliver's existence virtually obsolete.[66] The nineteenth-century British *fin-de-siècle* held out hope for children – especially the children of violence – compared to the bleaker decade of the 1830s when the Houses of Parliament were accidentally burnt down and the New Poor Law was grinding its way through the legislative process. Hardy, in contrast, wrote in the 1890s in the atmosphere of a secure colonial British Empire steeped in global glory as its Queen basked in her Victoria Jubilee (1887). His audiences no longer craved the economic realism of an *Oliver Twist* but subtle psychological nuance deliverable in adult characters like Tess. By the 1890s Oliver had been cast into the realms of nostalgia.[67]

. . . .

Late Victorian optimism of course was a false dawn: large numbers of children were still reared in a brutal environment. Arguably, what discouraged most hapless youngsters from absconding at the end as well as at the beginning of the nineteenth century, especially those raised in appalling conditions in London, was that there was no obvious Mecca to which they could run.[68] Indeed, it is possible that running away became much more attractive and imaginable in the twentieth century, as opportunities for casual work multiplied for both sexes, everyone became more mobile, and children's horizons expanded through education, television and, from the 1990s, the new digital technology. As has already been pointed out, children who have grown up in the west in the last 40 years have also had a far keener sense of entitlement and a lower tolerance threshold than their forebears. It is not surprising, then, that runaway youngsters remain a problem that shows no sign of diminishing. However, running away remains a strategy fraught with danger, even at the beginning of the present century. It is suggested that between a fifth and a quarter of the 100,000 children in Britain who run away each year put themselves at risk. A recent survey has revealed that sixteen per cent of runaways end up sleeping rough, twelve per cent have to beg or steal to survive and seven per cent are hurt or harmed in some way.[69]

Modern writers, unlike their nineteenth-century predecessors, claim the gamut of human experience for their subject and are often more interested in a character's thoughts than his or her social interactions. Inevitably, now much more is known about the size of the problem

---

[66] Sarah Wise has recently shown that the world of Oliver Twist was even grimmer than has been thought; see S. Wise, *The Italian Boy: Murder and Grave-Robbery in 1830s London* (London: Jonathan Cape, 2004). For Oliver's pauper conditions as runaway see P. Hollis, *The Pauper Press: A Study in Working-Class Radicalism of the 1830s*, Oxford Historical Monographs (London: Oxford University Press, 1970).

[67] Oliver's life on the run in London of course was not absolutely true to life. There were few child gangs in the early nineteenth century: see Ch. 5, p. 247.

[68] The optimism was not, it must be said, shared by all novelists. Two late Victorians in particular tried to convey to readers the poverty that many London children continued to endure: see George Gissing (1857–1903), *The Nether World* (1889), and Arthur Morrison (1865–1945), *A Child of the Jago. A Novel Set in the London Slums of 1890* (1896).

[69] www.childrensociety.org.uk/resources/documents/Policy/Stepping_Up_The_Future_For_Young_Runaways (accessed 30 Jun. 2009), p. 13. One of the most important recent studies of the problem is E. Smeaton, *Living on the Edge: The Experience of Detached Young Runaways* (London: The Children's Society, 2005).

and the kind of life a runaway leads, the runaway can be found in serious as well as escapist fiction. Two Anglophone novelists in particular have mined the theme to powerful effect. Jacqueline Wilson's *Dustbin Baby* (2001) is the story of a girl who runs away from a foster home after a row. Wilson (b. 1945), one of Britain's leading authors of teenage fiction, uses the theme as a device to explore the deep deficiencies in our present system of dealing with the many children placed in the care of local authorities.[70] William Trevor's *Felicia's Journey* (1994) focuses much more closely on the dangers that can await the penniless runaway and is also a disturbing *Bildungsroman*, a sinister version of *Huckleberry Finn*. Trevor (b. 1928), a master narrator of the plight of the isolated, lonely and unloved of all ages, tells the story of an ironically named young Irish girl who slips out of her Dublin home early one morning and takes the ferry to England in search of her boyfriend, only to end up facing the perils and uncertainties of life on the London streets. Having been befriended and abused in turns, Felicia is completely down-and-out at the end of the novel. She knows there is no way back and that her life's journey is purposeless. None the less the experience has not been totally negative. She is now a woman 'no longer a child, no longer a girl', and there remains a glimmer of hope. 'There will be cities, and the streets of other cities, and other roads. ... There will be charity and shelter and mercy and disdain; and always, and everywhere, the chance that separates the living from the dead'.[71]

Today in Britain few youngsters can be unaware of the dangers of running away. In a risk averse age, its inadvisability is continually emphasised and advertised by childcare agencies and charities.[72] Whether children in an earlier age were equally alive to the misery of living on the streets or the physical harm that they would there be exposed to is harder to judge. After all the gap between the standard of living of the domiciled poor and vagrants was not large in the pre-modern world, and a half-starved or brutally beaten youngster must have thought that sleeping under a hedge and begging for food was scarcely a step down. Many too in rural areas may have really believed the streets of London were paved with gold: the big city still retains its lure in the present. There again in pre-modern England the young must have known something of the dangers. Under the old Elizabethan Poor Law tramps and vagabonds, if apprehended in a parish in which they had no right of settlement, were sent back to their parish of origin. Every rural child must have encountered one or two poor creatures who had left their native village in hope only to be ignominiously returned as a whipped and branded pauper.[73] Even if youngsters in the past took no heed of the potential dangers of running away, many must have been deterred by the fate that would await them if caught and returned. At the very least apprentices could expect to serve a further term commensurate with the period for which they had been absent.[74] The prudent or the timid therefore had to find another strategy to cope with perceived ill-treatment.

One doubtless satisfying way through the ages of settling scores with limited risk of exposure to adult wrath has been for the put-upon to get their own back by secretly displaying disrespect and in some way hurting, chastising or simply thumbing their noses at their persecutor. This has been an obvious strategy because it has been one that adults have continually fostered themselves by periodically allowing the customary hierarchical relationship between adult and child to be reversed. As we saw in the last chapter, past

---

[70] A BBC film was made of the book in 2008. April, the heroine, was abandoned in a dustbin by her mother; hence the book's title.

[71] William Trevor, *Felicia's Journey* (Harmondsworth: Viking, 1994), pp. 212–13.

[72] E.g., http://www.childline.org.uk/Info/HomeFamilies/Pages/HomelessnessRunaway.aspx (accessed 30 Jun. 2009).

[73] P. Slack, 'Poverty and Politics in Salisbury 1597–1666', in P. Clark and P. Slack (eds), *Crisis and Order in English Towns, 1500–1700: Essays in Urban History* (London: Routledge and Kegan Paul, 1972), p. 165.

[74] In England this was confirmed by Act of Parliament in 1766: Dunlop, *English Apprenticeship*, p. 193.

societies recognised the cathartic potential of giving older youngsters a role in policing the wider community or younger children. But past societies too understood the need to let the young mock the system, if only to reinforce it, just as the rich and privileged allowed social distinctions to be subverted in Carnival.[75] In Europe's courts, cathedrals and colleges, Christmas rituals where the world was turned upside down were commonplace until about 1600. For a few days rulers and ruled would exchange places,[76] possibly in acknowledgement of the potential that lay in the young embodied in the Christ child. Barring-out, the custom of boys taking over the grammar schools of early modern England at a certain time of the year, was another example of licensed anarchy.[77] And even today, if formal rituals of this kind have long since gone, teachers in some schools still subject themselves to ridicule in staff pantomimes or allow their charges to amuse themselves on the last days of term.

Understandably, little is known about the ways in which the downtrodden in the past empowered themselves in private. It is clear, however, that when the young turned their world upside down without adult connivance, their behaviour could be vicious and very pointed, as an incident related in the memoirs of an eighteenth-century Parisian printer, Nicolas Contat, reveals. Contat in the 1730s had been an ill-treated apprentice in the workshop of a printer called Jacques Vincent. Kept awake at night by howling alley cats, he and his fellow apprentice decided to give the master and mistress a taste of their suffering. His companion was a good mimic and one night crawled across the roof and howled like a cat outside the couple's bedroom. After several nights of discomfort, the printer's wife ordered the apprentice to get rid of the cats. This they gleefully did, bludgeoning to death as many as they could and trapping others stunned in sacks. For good measure the two apprentices then staged a mock trial of the half-dead cats before the assembled workshop, pronounced them guilty and strung them up on an improvised gallows. When the mistress discovered the scene, she was horrified but had no redress, despite fearing justly that her own pampered cat was among the deceased. In contrast, the apprentices and the journeymen in the workshop were overjoyed at the pain the spectacle had caused and the scene was re-enacted in play over subsequent days. In their eyes, revenge had been suitably exacted without reprisals. The fate of the mistress's cat sent out a strong warning that the master and his wife should mend their ways. Moreover, through the mock trial, justice had been formally done against the master and mistress by aping the practice of the French courts, where a dummy would be hanged in the place of an offender who had not been apprehended.[78]

It is unlikely though that many youngsters could have acted out such a perfectly choreographed act of revenge in their leisure time. Most would have accidentally dropped or purloined a treasured possession to get their own back, just as today the disgruntled school student will break a teacher's car windows, rip down a display or write offensive slogans on the blackboard.[79] Some may simply have taken delight or found relief for their woes in

---

[75] See Ch. 5, pp. 226–38. The seminal account of the significance of carnival is M. Bahktin, *Rabelais and His World*, trans. H. Iswolsky (Cambridge: MIT Press, 1968).

[76] W. C. Mellor, *The Boy Bishop and Other Essays on Forgotten Customs and Beliefs of the Past* (London, 1923). For the custom in Magdalen College, Oxford, see L. W. B. Brockliss (ed.), *Magdalen College: A History* (Oxford: Magdalen College, 2008), pp. 83 and 208–09.

[77] See Ch. 5, p. 223.

[78] N. Contat, *Anecdotes typographiques où l'on voit la description des coutumes, moeurs et usages singuliers des compagnons imprimeurs*, ed. G. Barber (Oxford: Oxford Bibliographical Society, 1980). pp. 51–53. The incident is analysed (famously) in R. Darton, 'Workers Revolt: The Great Cat Massacre on the Rue de Saint-Séverin', in R. Darton, *The Great Cat Massacre and Other Episodes in French Cultural History* (Harmondsworth: Penguin, 1985), pp. 79–104. See also the comments in M. Sonenscher, *Work and Wages: Natural Law, Politics and the Eighteenth-Century French Trades* (Cambridge: Cambridge University Press, 1989), pp. 11–21.

[79] Servants and apprentices were always being accused of stealing. Runaways frequently took off with money: Lane, *Apprenticeship*, p. 192. Given the stiff penalties for theft, of course, 'cheating' the master or

playing with ideas and images that they knew adults considered transgressive. Children in seventeenth-century Germany were well aware that what really alarmed contemporaries was witchcraft. Witches were outsiders like themselves but outsiders with the power. They therefore mimicked what they knew of witchcraft lore in much the same way as children now may deliberately provoke liberal-minded parents and teachers by acting out gun-fights, violent robberies and murders.[80] Indeed, in a world that accepted the omnipresence of the supernatural and the possibility of capturing and harnessing the powers of angels and other spirits, it is quite possible that German children thought that in imitating witchcraft rituals they were indeed witches.[81] If so, then such play for the powerless was intended not just to irritate but empower. What was really going on in the mind of the child witch, however, must be a matter for surmise, for early modern witch play can only be glimpsed through the often extorted testimonies of terrified youngsters who ended up in court for their temerity.

Child Witches in Seventeenth-Century Germany[82]

Lyndal Roper

In 1628 Hans Merckler, an orphan aged twelve, was tried for witchcraft. He had forced two much younger boys, aged six and eight, to put a milk-bucket on a dung heap, place the Devil in the bucket, a board over the bucket and a chair on top. Then, perched on the chair, each was made to forswear God, Mary and the saints, while the other boy knelt. Merckler wanted, the witnesses said, to establish 'a witches' school'. In place of the prayers and catechisms children had to learn by heart, everyone was to learn the nonsense verse the Devil had taught him, starting 'Lyrum larum spoon game, old women eat a lot'.

This may look like a version of king-of-the-castle, nothing but a child's game. But this was not how the authorities saw it, and when the other boys' parents testified against him, Merckler soon found himself taken to the nearby town of Karlstadt where he was put through a criminal interrogation, and eventually, brought to the capital of the prince-bishopric of Würzburg, the town of Würzburg, where one of the largest witch hunts ever seen in western Europe was reaching its climax.[83] Things looked grim for young Merckler, who seemed to be in league with the Devil and could well have found himself executed for witchcraft. Yet he was lucky. By 1629 he was denying the

---

mistress would require cunning.

[80] Since the Second World War British schools have done their best to outlaw 'gun-play' of any kind on the grounds that it legitimises violence. For the orthodoxy and an alternative viewpoint, see P. Holland, *We Don't Play with Guns Here: War, Weapons and Superhero Play in the Early Years* (Buckingham: Open University Press, 2003).

[81] For the broad belief in the presence of active spirits in the terrestrial world, see S. Wilson, *The Magical Universe. Everyday Ritual and Magic in Pre-Modern Europe* (London: Hambledon, 2000).

[82] A longer version of this article and one written later can be found in T. M. Saley (ed.), *Ad Historiam Humanam: Ein Gedenkbuch für Hans-Christoph Ruhblack* (Tübingen: Bibliotheca Academica, 2005).

[83] Staatsarchiv Würzburg (hereafter cited as SAW), Historischer Saal (hereafter cited as Hist Saal) VII 25/377, f. 50r ff, 18 Jun. 1627: first the schoolmaster was informed, then witness statements were taken locally, then the case moved to Retzbach and from there to Karlstadt, the district administrative centre, and finally to the territory's capital.

whole story, and he wisely asked to be transferred to a different school, that of the Jesuits. Six months later, he was returned to his guardian who was admonished to raise him well and take him to school and church.[84]

Other children in the prince-bishopric of Würzburg at around the same period were not so fortunate. Valtin Winter claimed that his parents had seduced him into witchcraft: the resulting trial ended in the execution, first of his father, and then of himself.[85] In the summer of 1628, fear erupted in the Juliusspital, a huge hospital established by the Counter-Reformation Bishop of Würzburg, Julius Echter, which had a school attached to it; and a mass panic resulted in which scores of people met their deaths, many of them children. Probably over 1,200 people died during the witch-hunt in this large Catholic territory, and it was in its final stages that children and priests found themselves accused. In all we know that at least 40 children died during the last two years of the panic in the city of Würzburg, about the same number as the total of clerics who also perished during this phase of the witch-hunting there. Not until 1629 was the panic, which had begun in 1590, and proceeded in waves, finally over.[86]

It was unusual for groups of children to be suspected during witch hunts in this way, though it was certainly not unknown. The most notorious case was that in Lutheran Mora, in Sweden in 1669–70; but there were others, including a small outbreak in 1683–4 in Calw (south Germany), and another in 1723 involving 30 children in Augsburg. Such episodes were deeply shocking to contemporaries. For Gottlieb Spitzel, who included the case in his *The Power of Darkness Broken* in 1687, such dreadful events were certain proof of the Devil's activity in the world and should be a warning to all parents. Yet for the witchcraft sceptic Balthasar Bekker, writing in 1691, the Mora debacle, with its involvement of children, was proof that witchcraft was nonsense. And it was axiomatic to Georg Hauber in his vast sceptical compendium on magic published in the late 1730s and early 1740s that the Swedish case had been a shocking miscarriage of justice: he included an illustration as well as a detailed account of the story. Interestingly, he omitted any reference to the Augsburg case which had concluded a few years before, though he did include other cases from Augsburg in the book.[87]

---

[84] He was also financially well off, with assets of over 1,000 gulden and farms and fields. SAW Hist Saal VII 25/377, f. 52r ff, 19 Jun 1627; f. 73r/v, 22 Jan. 1628. However, some of the children who were executed also came from prosperous and elite families.

[85] SAW Hist Saal VII 25/377, f. 70 ff, 22 Jan. 1628.

[86] On the Würzburg trials, E. Weiß, 'Die Hexenprozesse im Hochstift Würzburg', in P. Kolb and E.-G. Krenig, *Unterfränkische Geschichte. Band 3: Vom Beginn des konfessionellen Zeitalters bis zum Ende des Dreißigjährigen Krieges* (Würzburg: Echter, 1995), pp. 327–62; C. Beyer, *"Hexen-Leut, so zu Würzburg gerichtet". Der Umgang mit Sprache und Wirklichkeit in Inquisitionsprozessen wegen Hexerei*, Euröpäische Hochschulschriften, I, Deutsche Sprache und Literatur 948 (Frankfurt: P. Lang, 1986), and F. Merzbacher, *Die Hexenprozesse in Franken*, 2nd edn (Munich: Beck, 1970). On children in witch-trials in Würzburg, see R. Walinski-Kiel, 'The Devil's Children: Child Witch-Hunts in Early Modern Germany', *Continuity and Change*, 11:2 (1996), 171–91; and H. Weber, *Kinderhexenprozesse* (Frankfurt: Insel Verlag, 1991), pp. 261–67. On child witches, see in particular R. Beck, 'Das Spiel mit dem Teufel. Freisinger Kinderhexenprozesse 1715–1723', *Historische Anthropologie*, 10:3 (2002), 374–415; and W. Behringer, `Kinderhexenprozesse. Zur Rolle von Kindern in der Geschichte der Hexenverfolgung', *Zeitschrift für historische Forschung*, 16 (1989), 31–47; R. Walz, `Kinder in Hexenprozessen. Die Grafschaft Lippe 1654–1663', in J. Scheffler, G. Schwerhoff and G. Wilbertz (eds), *Hexenverfolgung und Regionalgeschichte: die Grafschaft Lippe im Vergleich*, Studien zur Regionalgeschichte 4 (Bielefeld: Verlag für Regionalgeschichte, 1994); H. Sebald, *Der Hexenjunge. Fallstudie eines Inquisitionsprozesse* (Marburg: Diagonal-Verlag, 1992); and H. Weber, `Von der verführten Kinder Zauberei'. *Hexenprozesse gegen Kinder im alten Württemberg* (Stuttgart: Jan Thorbecke Verlag, 1996).

[87] G. Spitzel, *Die Gebrochne Macht der Finsternuss/oder Zerstoerte Teuflische Bunds- und Buhl-Freundschafft mit den menschen...*(Augsburg: Gotlieb Göbel, 1687); Weber, *Kinderhexenprozesse*, p. 283: Bekker mocked the children's testimony about sex. They reported that the Devil would withdraw into a private room with the children he

Individual children were occasionally accused of witchcraft or became caught up in trials. Children's allegations were taken seriously in court because witchcraft was a *crimen exceptum*, a crime so serious that the normal rules of evidence could be suspended. Witches, it was believed, harmed young children and infants in particular; and this meant that children's stories often became part of witchcraft testimony. Children might become entangled in witch trials as suspects when their parents named them, under torture, as their accomplices; or they might, in the frenzied atmosphere of witch-hunting, give evidence against their parents, often under compulsion.[88] Since only fellow witches could see the Devil in league with an accused individual, when children gave testimony about witchcraft itself (as opposed to statements about what harm had been caused by witches) they readily became suspected. It was believed that witchcraft travelled in the blood, and that witches offered their children to Satan, and so the children of convicted witches were likely to be witches too. On the whole, authorities did take account of the youth of offenders and their punishment was milder; but there were also occasions, like Valtin Winter's, where youth offered no protection.[89]

Cases of witchcraft concerning children are amongst the most shocking documents of the European witch-hunt. They certainly betray a very different sensibility towards children, who, contemporaries believed, might be agents of the Devil. But they can also tell us something about children themselves. Difficult as such sources are, we can also use the records of the trials to offer a rare window onto the imaginative worlds of children, revealed in their games and in what they said about the Devil. Witchcraft cases always raised the question of imagination and fantasy, and even the author of the most infamous witch-hunting treatise, the *Malleus maleficarum* of 1486, dealt with the issue of the nature of illusion in its opening chapters.[90] Authorities were only too well aware that children might confess to things that were not true and they themselves worried about reality and illusion in such cases – after all, the Devil was the master of illusion. Thus, for contemporaries as well, child witches raised the question of the limits of fantasy, which is also why they offer some of the few glimpses we have onto children's play.

Why did Merckler want to set up a witches' school? So far as I know, the idea of a school occurs nowhere in writing about the Devil and witches, and was Merckler's own invention. With it, Merckler took the idea of the Sabbath convention of witches

---

wanted to have sex with – Bekker poked fun at this Devil who retained such a sense of propriety. Eberhard David Hauber, *Bibliotheca, Acta et Scripta Magica* (3 vols: Lemgo: Johannes Heinrich Meyer, 1738–1745), vol. 2, Stück 30 (1742).

[88] On children denouncing their elders in witchcraft investigations, see above, pp. 274–75.

[89] Another reason children sometimes became embroiled in witchcraft cases was because youngsters and adolescents were the most likely groups in the population to suffer from possession, when the Devil was thought to enter the body of the sufferer and cause them terrible torments. Possessions were directly linked to the witch-craze because they dramatised the power of the Devil so luridly and because a witch might cause someone to become possessed. Clergymen like the Lutheran Gottlieb Spitzel became fascinated, like many, by such a case, when he desperately attempted to free a young woman called Regina Schiller from the power of the Devil: she suffered from possession for over a decade. Where Catholic priests could perform exorcism, commanding the Devil to leave, Lutherans like Spitzel could use only prayer. Spitzel and other Augsburg Lutheran clergy became pastorally involved in a series of high-profile possession cases, all of which concerned adolescents and young adults. A Pietist, Spitzel was deeply interested in education and child psychology, and this concern explains why he should have found the Swedish case of the child witches so compelling that he included it in his book. See L. Roper, *Witch Craze. Terror and Fantasy in Baroque Germany* (London: Yale University Press, 2004).

[90] H. Kramer and J. Sprenger, *The Malleus Maleficarum* [sic], tr. and ed. Rev. Montague Summers, edn. (New York: Dover, 1971), pp. 3 ff, part 1, qu. 1; and see qu. 2 on fascination and perception.

and transposed it to the environment he knew, the school. This was a compensatory inversion of school life: it is no accident that his victims were younger children, who were to be trained not to become pious apprentices and servants, but to be the Devil's minions. What do we make of the perilous tower of bucket and plank on the dung-heap? His extravagant ritual of renouncing God and the Virgin was not unique: Anna Reuss, aged twelve, also stood on a dung heap and denied Jesus, and afterwards she rode on a cat to the Sabbath. She claimed her mother made her do it.[91] Dung-heaps, then as now, were probably irresistible to children, and when Merckler staged his blasphemous renunciation of Christianity on the dung-heap, he desecrated the holy with excrement. The nonsense prayer the children were to be compelled to recite suggests what children may have felt about the stultifying rote learning that typified Counter-Reformation school education. Valtin Winter, the young boy executed for witchcraft, taught other children a blasphemous prayer he said he learnt from his father about cats. So too in Augsburg, rumours about witchcraft circulated in the orphanage, where two girls whose mother had been executed for witchcraft some years before knew a 'witches' prayer', which concerned 'white patches, blue patches'.[92] What Merckler meant by his ditty about spoons and old women is hard to know, but the rhyme does suggest a revulsion for old women and their appetites: they were the most frequent victims of the witch hunt. By the time he was interrogated at Würzburg, he could tell the authorities another rhyme he had chanted: 'Here I stand on the dung, and deny Lord Jesus Christ' – another of the children, Anna Reuss, recited the same ditty.[93] All these cases indicate how important rhythmic chants, verses and mock prayers were in children's play.

Above all, beatings figure repeatedly in what many children said about witches and the Devil, and suggest what a terrifying prospect they were in children's imaginations. Sometimes thrashings are mentioned in the context of explaining why someone had recourse to the Devil. Merckler saw the Devil standing by the house door one day while his mistress was beating him. One young student aged seventeen claimed the Devil had given him a special string and parchment charm which he could stuff down his trousers to prevent the pain of the rod. Here, witchcraft seems to be a kind of compensation fantasy, a way of coping with the routine violence of school discipline. Just as beating featured prominently in children's accounts of school routine, so also it was used, ironically enough, to force children to confess. Hans Philip Schuh, aged thirteen, was given 46 strokes and a further 77 strokes during interrogation in Würzburg: this brutal treatment eventually led him to confess to taking part in witchcraft at school; other children were beaten by their parents and masters during the eighteenth-century witch panic in Augsburg to make them confess, one child so severely that his finger was almost severed.[94]

In Merckler's case, rumours and talk about children's games had clearly been circulating for some time before the case reached court, and the case reveals a good deal about children's social interactions. What is interesting about this particular case is that the stories emerged not from the adult world, because a parent had been suspected of

[91] SAW Hist Saal VII 25/377, f. 71v, 22 Jan. 1628.
[92] Stadtarchiv Augsburg, (hereafter cited as StadtAA), Urgichten, The text of the prayer can be found in the third interrogation of Maria Fleck (1685, qu. 113). It was repeated four years later in the interrogation of Anna Juditha Wagner, who had learnt it in the orphanage where Fleck's daughters were placed after their mother's execution. StadtAA, Anna Juditha Wagner 1689, qu. 57: testimony 24 Dec. 1689.
[93] SAW Hist Saal VII 25/377, fs 71v, 73r, 22 Jan. 1628, 'Hier stehe ich auf dem Mist vnd verlaugn den H. Jesus Christ'.
[94] SAW Hist Saal VII 25/377, fs 107–18, 26 Oct. 1628; on the Augsburg case, see Roper, *Witchcraze*, ch. 9.

witchcraft, but from the world of the children themselves. The witches' school was a kind of anti-society, where Merckler could lord it over the kneeling younger boys, just as the older children probably lorded it over him. Indeed, even in the institutional confines of the Juliusspital in Würzburg, where a fevered emotionality was fostered by the fact that children suspected of witchcraft were housed there, making others more likely to give lurid confessions, the idea of the diabolic was not simply imposed from without. Rather, these children had been talking about and playing with the idea of the Devil before the trial began. They knew each other because the Hospital housed an orphanage, and over thirty schoolchildren there were suspected of witchcraft in 1628. The panic was also triggered by three children who suffered from possession and who began to blame others for their plight and to talk about the Devil. The way the rumours and stories spread amongst the children reflects the importance of their social networks: once Merckler was in prison in Würzburg, he recited the same rhyme as Anna Reuss, while another child confessed he taught Valtin Winter a prayer about witches and cats when both children were in prison. The children came from the same schools and many mentioned a 24-year-old woman who was also in the Hospital and was burnt as a witch; interestingly, boys and girls mentioned each other and knew each others' names.[95]

Because children made the witch fantasy their own, they also tended to get it wrong. Witches generally saw the Devil as a man dressed in sombre black, occasionally green, but Merckler was adamant that he had been red, a striking colour that has nothing of the strict inversion of religious imagery implied by black. Merckler insisted that only he could see the Devil, and that he saw him in the presence of others – this too was unusual, because encounters with the Devil were usually secret, taking place when the individual was alone: here, the Devil has something of the character of an imaginary friend. Children made statements which were simply ridiculous, like the child who said the Devil came down the chimney on a donkey, or they got basic facts twisted: instead of whipping up fearsome storms, one child simply learnt to make rain.[96] Merckler had sprinkled water on one boy's hand in an attempt to baptise him in the Devil's name – this was a standard demonology, except that Merckler managed only a hand, not the head.[97] Valtin Winter was said to have gone about boasting he could make people 'lame and blind': normally, witches claimed only to harm or kill. The concrete nature of his boast suggests that he had mixed up fairytales with ideas about witches. Children's sense of play and fascination with dirt and insects is also reflected in what they confessed: Niclas Dornhauser of Alleshausen allegedly claimed he could conjure plagues of mice; Anna Krug aged eight and a half said her mistress taught her how to make fleas: you poke a thorn into a cherry pip and out they crawl; while Valtin Winter said his parents and sisters knew how to make fleas out of black wax.[98] The possibilities of magic to disrupt adult society were intensely fascinating to children.

But the issue over which their testimony was most likely to diverge from the standard

---

[95] See Weiß, 'Die Hexenprozesse im Hochstift Würzburg', pp. 350–52; Weber, *Kinderhexenprozesse*, pp. 283–4. Boys and girls may also have mentioned each other because the judges were interested in sex between them; but the statements mention similar details, and it is clear that boys and girls knew what the others were confessing. School also featured in the case of another young girl, Regina Groninger, who was accused of witchcraft in Augsburg in 1702, and had become caught up in a trial when she brought sandwiches of excrement to school, horrifying her schoolmates. A loner, she does not seem to have involved other children in her diabolic fantasies or to have tried to recruit other children to the Devil: Roper, *Witch Craze*, pp. 204–07.

[96] Roper, *Witch Craze*, p. 221; SAW Hist Saal VII 25/3777, f. 70r, 22 Jan. 1628.

[97] Witches famously flew into cellars and stole the wine, but Merckler got this detail slightly wrong too, and confessed to flying into his own cellar: SAW Hist Saal VII 25/377, f. 73v, 22 Jan. 1628

[98] Roper, *Witch Craze*, p. 232; SAW Hist Saal VII 25/377, f. 43v, 31 Mar. 1627; f. 75r, 22 Jan. 1628.

adult confession was sex. Sex with the Devil was the key admission in most women's confessions to witchcraft, and the story of how the Devil had seduced her formed part of most stories women told. Men who confessed to witchcraft also confessed to diabolic sex, but in their case, the Devil usually took the shape of real women they knew: few men confessed to sodomitical intercourse with a male devil. Young and adolescent children's confessions to sex with the Devil are thus occasionally very revealing, because they lack adults' pre-formed words and narrative structures to talk about sex. Even when their confessions were standard, they could fail to persuade: so Veit Karg, a truant from the Jesuit College at Ingolstadt, came up with a story that was so moralistic and formulaic about sex with a diabolic prostitute in a tavern that the judges at Augsburg apparently did not believe it – this did not prevent his execution for witchcraft however.[99] Valtin Winter claimed only that he had 'lived in indiscipline' with his girl lover four times, while Hans Philip Schuh said that he had intercourse with a young girl, her 'shame' being 'warm': the standard narrative of sex with the Devil was that his seed was very cold and that intercourse was painful.[100] He had shoved 'his thing in hers'. Other children who confessed during the Juliusspital panic also admitted to kisses, and to 'committing shame' with each other and flying out to Sabbaths: they did not confess to sex with the Devil, or with other adults like carers or teachers, but only with each other. Like men accused of witchcraft, the boys named not the Devil but real girls as their sexual partners, and instead of claiming that the Devil came in the form of a girl, these children described sexual fondlings between real children. So Anna Marielein Fischer, a girl named by many of the other children in the Juliusspital case, said that there was a bed on which they all lay with their lovers at the Sabbath, which had been prepared on the Klessberg to which they flew: conventional witches dispensed with beds at their nocturnal revels, but Anna Marielein seems to have been struggling with how to explain sleeping together without beds.[101] Regina Groninger from Augsburg, aged twelve, in a confession which was highly idiosyncratic, claimed that the Devil came to her in the shape of a mysterious black man who 'lies on her whole body, and thus presses on her in such a way that her (if you will excuse the expression) shit goes out of her body'; he 'put something pointed like a spindle in the front part of her body..., from which she felt great pains, but she did not feel that anything was left behind in her body, and when he had to do with her thus, it lasted a quarter of an hour'.[102] The precision of her description and her avoidance of any of the diabolic clichés that other children knew to use suggest this account comes from a real and deeply traumatic sexual experience. Again, sexual and excremental themes merge in stories about the Devil, a characteristic of children's witchcraft narratives.

Children were beaten at school, at work and at home. They played on dung heaps, imagined themselves wielding magical powers over fleas and confessed to sexual fumblings with one another – and freely looted the repertoire of rhymes and tales they knew about witches, Jesus, the Devil and fairytales to give shape to their games. But it was the authorities who interrogated them who tried to find a coherent and consistent diabolic structure in the slipping kaleidoscopes of their violent adventures.

· ·

---

[99] StadtAA, Urgichten, 31 May 1680.
[100] SAW Hist Saal VII 25/377, f. 70r, 22 Jan. 1628; fs 107–18, 26 Oct. 1628.
[101] SAW Hist Saal VII 25/377, f. 92v, 12 Aug. 1628.
[102] StadtAA, Urgichten, Regina Groninger, 1st interrogation, 17 May 1702, qu. 4; and see also, on this case, Roper, *Witchcraze*, p. 204 ff.

There is good reason to believe that adults have always been alarmed by children's activities that they did not control, even if the witch games must be unique in the violent reaction that they caused. Boisterous, unsupervised children's games have continually annoyed adults because they often led to damage to persons and property. Unruly ball games played by the young irritated late sixteenth- and early seventeenth-century Londoners as much as they appear to worry today's head-teachers.[103] Today, too, some adults evince concern even about the most unthreatening games when they are accompanied with a repertoire of actions and chants that are the children's private property. On one level, these actions and chants carry no threat to adults. The many examples of playground chants that have been collected in Britain from the mid-nineteenth century suggest that they owe much of their inspiration to the poetry taught in the elementary school, especially the nonsense rhymes of Edward Lear.[104] They are simply evidence of children, especially girls (for boys have a limited repertoire of chants), delighting in mangling language.[105] On another level, however, they are more significant. At the very least, they have served and serve an educational purpose. For the last 150 years they have been part of the way that British children have taught each other about the possibilities, pleasures and pitfalls of adult life: hence their changing content as the social and cultural reality of the adult world alters. More importantly, the chants recorded in the British playground today, just like those of Germany's witch children 300 years ago, have a subversive edge, provoking adult suspicion. Through their unseemly, irreverent and nonsensical content, they seem to outsiders to make fun of adult behaviour, promote values that the adult world affects to scorn, or provide a jaundiced commentary on the life of their elders. In their chants, modern British children arguably find a means of putting two fingers up at the adult world, while recognising that it is a world that they must eventually enter.[106]

It would be completely wrong, though, to conclude from this that there is always an element in children's play that is confrontational or purgative. Just as playground chants are principally educational, so too is children's play. Much of that play is imitative. Children experience and learn about adult roles through their spontaneous and imaginative games, whether played at home, outdoors or at school.[107] At the same time, as has been recently argued by Donna Lanclos in her study of Northern Ireland, children do not directly mimic the adult world but exaggerate and burlesque the crises and conflicts that they encounter

---

[103] Griffiths, *Youth*, pp. 138–40. For an idea of the sheer variety of recorded games played in the past, see A. B. Gomme, *The Traditional Games of England, Scotland and Ireland: with tunes, singing-rhymes, and methods of playing according to the variants extant and recorded in different parts of the kingdom* (2 vols; London: David Nutt, 1894–1898).

[104] They are though the children's creation and should not be confused with classic nursery rhymes. Although many nursery rhymes began as satirical adult verse – 'Old Mother Hubbard' for instance may be Cardinal Wolsey and the bare cupboard the Catholic church – since their publication in the course of the nineteenth century (and sometimes before) their text has been stabilised by adults in a way that teaches basic moral lessons about the values of good housekeeping, hard work ('See-Saw Marjorie Daw'), family limitation ('There was an old woman who lived in a shoe') and so on. Nursery rhymes are printed tales that adults teach children, a vital difference. For a recent survey of the origin of nursery rhymes, see A. Jack, *Pop Goes the Weasel. The Secret Meanings of Nursery Rhymes* (London: Allen Lane, 2009).

[105] For the fullest collection, see I. and P. and Opie, *The Lore and Language of Schoolchildren* (Oxford: Clarendon Press, 1967).

[106] For a discussion of the scatological and sexual content of many contemporary chants, see 'Playground Rhymes', *The Sunday Times Magazine*, 21 May 2005, pp. 27–30. Subversive rhymes do not appear in the Opies' collection. Believing children to be naturally good, they excluded obscene ones.

[107] For an introduction, see H. Montgomery, *An Introduction to Childhood. Anthropological Perspectives on Children's Lives* (Oxford: Wiley-Blackwell, 2009), pp. 141–54. P. Barnes and M.-J. Kehily, 'Play and the Cultures of Childhood', in M.-J. Kehily and J. Swann (eds) *Children's Cultural Worlds* (Chichester: Wiley, 2003).

and dramatise them in order to prevent themselves becoming upset. In Lanclos's opinion children in the playground are learning about the identities – cultural, gender and generational – that they will later take on. They are not getting back at adults. On the other hand, she does recognise that for some Ulster children playground play was more than an education. For those caught up in the Troubles, it could be cathartic. Peculiarly aggressive or spoiling behaviour on the part of boys, for instance, may well have been a response to the mayhem brought into a child's home when a released paramilitary returned to the domestic hearth.[108]

It is evident, furthermore, that when children collectively are living through abnormal times, their games may be a coping mechanism. The games will not just reflect the peculiar and often exciting adult world around them but may be structured in a way that gives comfort to their fears. In war time when all children are potential victims – parents may be absent or killed; their homes may be destroyed; they may end up miles away living with strangers – such games become particularly pertinent. All children want to believe that they are on the winning side and will be safe. As the case of children in Germany during the Second World War poignantly demonstrates, so great is the young's need to reconstitute normality when their life is turned upside down that they will begin to identify positively with their oppressors and conquerors, imitating through play the behaviour of those who now monopolise power and authority over them, even when their new 'guardians' are bent on their destruction.

The War Games of Children in Nazi Germany

Nicholas Stargardt

Throughout the Second World War, children played war games. From her boarding school in Krumbach, twelve-year-old Rosemarie wrote to her father in his artillery battery on the Rhine, revelling in her deeds in battle during the first winter of the war. On one occasion the girls trounced the boys who had tried to imprison them in a wall of tables and chairs while they were all left unsupervised in the school gym. Detlef, her younger brother, was also able to convey some of the excitement of his battles to his enlisted father during that first winter, as the ten-year-old described how his side had retaken their position under 'murderous fire'. His side had used sticks as hand grenades, but the enemy had thrown stones. Then Detlef had led the charge, his 'sabre' raised, putting the enemy temporarily to flight. As battle resumed, Detlef's side attacked once more and withstood a fierce counter-attack: 'None of us cried out and we won,' he wrote triumphantly to his father.[109]

Just as younger children had envied their elder brothers' Hitler Youth uniforms, and their tassles and braid of rank before the war, so now they lusted after the trophies and accoutrements they had collected in the war. Eight year-old Christoph wrote to his older brother Werner begging him to send home a French 'Käppi' and epaulettes so that he could kit himself out properly as the 'General'. 'Please, get hold of them for me as

---

[108] D. M. Lanclos, *At Play in Belfast: Children's Folklore and Identities in Northern Ireland* (New Brunswick: Rutgers University Press, 2003).

[109] H. Lange and B. Burkard (eds), *Abends wenn wir essen fehlt uns immer einer: Kinder schreiben an die Väter 1939–1945* (Hamburg: Rowohlt, 2000), pp. 45–46 and pp. 97–98.

quickly as possible,' he urged, 'I am waiting for them already'.[110] Werner obliged and soon Christoph's younger sister – who acted the Red Cross nurse – could report back that he looked very fine in his uniform, even though he still lacked a cap. By March 1942, Christoph, now aged ten, related to Werner how their boys from Eiersdorf had triumphed 'in the war against Rengersdorf'.[111]

Desperate as Christoph was to bring his war games up-to-date, he was continuing a fine old tradition of the boys of one village taking on those of another, which goes back hundreds of years in Europe. In the cities, boys' street gangs drew both their membership and their territory from the immediate neighbourhood.[112] For Erwin Müller in Vienna, it was the kids who lived across the water course near the brewery who provided the most regular and fearsome opponents. Throwing stones at one another, the boys protected their heads by keeping a considerable distance, imagining themselves in a static war of position, and using the sequence of water courses as successive defensive lines.[113]

There was nothing very new about this.[114] Jürgen Schlumbohm has shown that similar battles were being waged in Aachen in 1757 and Cologne in 1810. Everywhere in these fighting and beating games, the lead was taken by the older boys. It would seem that such games have taken place as long as children have played in unsupervised groups.[115] Only the roles which the children competed for altered over time. As we have seen in the previous contribution, the Augsburg children were investigated for witchcraft for their playful uses of the figures of Jesus and Mary and the host. The Cologne children wanted to be the 'king' or the 'robber captain'. By the interwar period, German and Austrian children were playing *Räuber und Gendarmes*, cops and robbers.

Adding the accoutrements of the war, like Christoph's 'Käppi', may have changed little in the children's appreciation of the game they were playing. By 1943, the Wehrmacht was bogged down on the eastern front. Seven-year-old Andreas coveted a Commissar's red star which his father, an officer, had sent back from the Eastern front. He may not have known exactly how it was acquired but he did guess that he carried a valuable or dangerous secret: his mother warned him to hide it from his new nanny. Nastasia was a fourteen- or fifteen-year-old Ukrainian girl who had been sent to Germany along with millions of other forced labourers. To boys like Andreas, these slave nannies arrived Mary Poppins-like at their front doors, clad in their head scarves and padded steppe jackets. He quickly developed a warmer and more intimate relationship with her than he had with his rather strict and distant mother. But Andreas

---

[110] Achiv der Akademie der Künste, Berlin, Kempowski Archiv (hereafter KA) 3936, Marianne Walter (née Marx), b. 1922, MS letters from her younger brother, Christoph, and sister, Regina, b. 1932 and 1933 to Werner, their elder brother by thirteen years, *c.* 1940–44, second, undated letter.

[111] *Ibid.*, Christoph to Werner, 20 Mar. 1942.

[112] H. Lessing and M. Liebel, *Wilde Cliquen. Szenen einer anderen Arbeiterjugendbewegung* (Bernsheim: Pädogogisher-Extra-Buchverlag, 1981); R. Sieder and H. Safrian, 'Gassenkinder – Strassenkämpfer: zur politischen Sozialisation einer Arbeitergeneration in Wien 1900 bis 1938', in L. Niethammer (ed.), *Wir kriegen jetzt andere Zeiten: auf der Suche nach der Erfahrung des Volkes in nachfaschistischen Ländern* (Berlin: Dietz, 1985), pp. 117–51.

[113] Dokumentation lebensgeschichtlicher Aufzeichnungen, Institut für Wirtschafts- und Sozialgeschichte, University of Vienna (hereafter DLA), Müller, pp. 6–8.

[114] E. Rosenhaft, *Beating the Fascists? The German Communists and Political Violence, 1929–1933* (Cambridge: Cambridge University Press, 1983; Lessing and Liebel, *Wilde Cliquen.*

[115] As Jürgen Schlumbohm points out, the upper classes were the first to withdraw their children from the wild freedom of the streets at the turn of the eighteenth century, in a sense setting the precedent for the wholesale withdrawal of the middle-classes from the streets into private recreational spaces in the last third of the nineteenth century. J. Schlumbohm, *Kinderstuben: Wie Kinder zu Bauern, Bürgern, Aristokraten wurden 1700–1850* (Munich: DTV, 1983), p. 222.

would have had no understanding of how her tale might have begun, amid forced round-ups carried out by the village head-men or being hunted down by troops with dogs in the woods after the village had been burned down in an anti-partisan action. Although German officers and men routinely wrote home to their wives about such things, they equally routinely warned them not to tell the children. Andreas spent most of his time playing with toy soldiers, invariably Germans against Russians. As if to make the game fully authentic, one day when he was playing at war with Nastasia he unexpectedly burst out with one Russian phrase he knew, '*Rukij werkh*', 'hands up!' Only as a middle-aged man did he begin to grasp her shock. To the boy, the lapse into Germans versus Bolshevik 'sub-humans' was just a game, and, on his part, she probably returned just as quickly to being his closest confidante, Nastasia, as a slave nanny in the old American South would have done for a white boy in similar circumstances.[116]

Play is as natural to children as talk is to adults. As the behaviour of children who cannot play reminds us, at its most essential play is an expression of fantasy. Play is creative in itself, and even destructive games satisfy some urge to appropriate space and objects and subjugate them to the will and whim of children. For elaborate games to continue they also have to be secure from outside interruption, which is one of the reasons that kids who belonged to a gang liked hanging out together in their own territory, under the canal bridges in the Berlin neighbourhood of Kreuzberg, or on the staircases and backyards of the Warsaw ghetto. Being outside adult control of course meant that it was the children who would determine how long the game lasted and how violent it became. Anything which is historically specific about children's games in central Europe during the Second World War is only evident against the backdrop of these more general characteristics of children's playing.[117]

Many games remained unaltered by this war. Growing up in the poor mining community of Grünbach in Lower Austria, Karl Kalisch had access to very few toys. So he and his friends collected shards of broken glass for their colours, or dug out the spent bullets after a military exercise to use as 'beer bottles' when they played shop. They shied stones at the burnt out bulbs the electricians gave them.[118] Throughout the Greater German Reich, boys cut out the pictures of soldiers on discarded packs of cigarettes.[119] And they collected and traded cigarette cards in school yards throughout Germany in a mania which gripped boys far more than girls. Perhaps the most striking thing about these activities is how little the first years of the war had altered children's behaviour. Children's games, in all their repetitive familiarity, turn out to be one of those truly resilient social activities.

When eight-year-old Christoph had begged his older brother Werner to send him a French 'Käppi', he had been adding a dash of contemporary colour and a frisson of power to an age-old game. The conquered went on playing similar games too. Amid much face-slapping, Polish boys in occupied Warsaw soon started to act the 'Gestapo', while Jewish children played at being Germans and Russians or Germans and partisans.

But, for the conquered, bringing the old games up-to-date often meant playing with humiliations and threats which might really happen to them or their families. In the Jewish ghetto in Vilna, children also began to play with a literal reality. There was only one main gate in and out of the ghetto, and each evening the Jewish police searched

---

[116] A. Mendel, *Zwangsarbeit im Kinderzimmer: Ostarbeiterinnen in deutschen Familien von 1939 bis 1945: Gespräche mit Polinnen und Deutschen* (Frankfurt: Dippa, 1994), pp. 182–84.

[117] KA 3024, Otto Peters, p. 56.

[118] DLA, Karl Kalisch, b. 1931, (MS) 'Kindheit und Jugend im Bergarbeiterdorf Grünbach', pp. 12–14.

[119] Kalisch, p. 16; KA 3936, Christoph to Werner, letter cited in fn. 111, above.

the Jewish workers as they returned from the workshops on the Lithuanian side of town for smuggled food. We know from the diary of a fourteen-year-old boy that the head of the Jewish gate guards, Meir Levas, had proved himself capable of personally flogging a small boy for smuggling flour and potatoes into the ghetto, but for all that children often lingered near the gate in the hope of getting something. They also played at what they saw. Children enacted 'Going through the gate', one survivor recalled:

> Two main characters were selected; Levas, the hated head of the Jewish gate guards, and Franz Murer, one of the most murderous Gestapo men. The rest of the children played the Jewish workers who tried to smuggle some food into the starving ghetto and the guards who attempted to find the contraband. While the Jewish gate guards search everyone 'Murer' comes, which propels the Jewish police to intensify its brutality and, at the same time, precipitates a tumult and panic among the 'workers'. They try desperately to toss away the small food packages, but 'Murer' finds some with the incriminating evidence and the 'workers' are put aside and later are whipped by the police.[120]

The two biggest boys got to play Franz Murer and Meir Levas, leaving it to the smaller ones to take the role of the adult Jewish workers, who, in reality, would often have included their own older brothers, sisters, aunts, uncles and parents. (See Figure 32). Like the adults they were playing, they were powerless to protect themselves from the blows rained upon them, in this case by the bigger, stronger children.[121] As in the war games of Christoph and Detlef, power still resided in the uniform. But the choice of role models was a stark one, as fear and detestation mingled with envy and longing. Where Detlef and Christoph wanted to be just like their fathers and elder brothers in France, for these children being like their elders promised only fear and suffering.

For ten months from September 1943 until July 1944, several thousand Jews from the Theresienstadt ghetto were kept in a special section of Auschwitz-Birkenau known as the 'family camp', just in case the SS were to open the camp to inspection by the International Red Cross. To the great envy of inmates in other sections of Birkenau, this so-called 'family camp' had special blocks for children and the inmates were allowed to keep their hair and the clothes they had come in. The children played organised games and sang, even performing a full-length musical loosely based on Walt Disney's *Snow White*. One of the Czech kindergarten teachers in the family camp also noticed the games the younger children played when they thought no one was watching. They played 'Camp elder and Block elder', 'Roll call' and 'Hats off'. They played the sick who were beaten for fainting during roll call, and they played the doctor who took their food away and refused to help them if they had nothing to give him in return.

The 'family camp' in Birkenau was a rectangular barbed-wire enclosure situated within sight of the three crematoria. Their chimneys belched out three and four metre high flames when in constant use. Whereas the adults attempted to ignore their proximity to the gas chambers, the children drew them directly into the fabric of their daily lives. The older ones played games with death, daring each other to run up to the electric fence and touch it with their finger tips, knowing the high voltage current was usually – but not always – switched off during the day time.[122] One day one of their

[120] G. Eisen, *Children and Play in the Holocaust: Games Among the Shadows* (Amherst: University of Massachusetts Press, 1988), p. 77: based on account of Tzvia Kuretzka.

[121] Children with power will frequently try to allocate to themselves the best roles in games. In interwar Russia where children played versions of 'cops' and 'robbers' with a contemporary resonance ('Reds and Whites' and 'Search and Requisition'), children of party members would demand to play the 'goodies': see O. Figes, *The Whisperers: Private Life in Stalin's Russia* (New York: Metropolitan Books, 2007), pp. 24–25 and 31–33.

[122] Yad Vashem Archive, Jerusalem, 0.3 1202, Bacon, interview with Chaim Mass, Jerusalem, 23 Feb. 1959, p. 17, and Dokumentation des österreichischen Widerstandes, Vienna, 13243, interview with Ben-David Gershon,

teachers came upon the younger children playing 'Gas chamber' outside their block. They had dug a hole and were throwing in one stone after the other. These were to be the people who were going into the crematorium and the children mimicked their cries. In one way, their game broke down here. Whereas in their normal games of 'Roll call', the little children may have had to submit to beatings for 'fainting', here no one jumped into the hole which was the gas chamber. They had to use stones instead. But this did not stop their curiosity. When the teacher came over to watch them, they even asked her how to make the chimney.[123] Here too the children may have instinctively sought to master the thing itself within the one space over which they had complete control – playing.

Games in concentration camps did not protect children from the reality around them by preserving an ideal world of make-believe. On the contrary, they reshaped their games to incorporate that reality. In so doing they drew the most extreme conclusion from the key lessons defeat and occupation taught all children. The first thing that defeated children witnessed was the sudden impotence of the adults they had grown up thinking were all-powerful. Power and success, the strivings of ambition and envy, were suddenly incorporated in their enemies. In some cases, children could imagine themselves as partisan fighters or members of one of the underground armies of the Resistance. But complete defeat and capitulation left few positive role models. During the war years, conquered children had not just feared and hated their enemies. They had also profoundly envied them, often preferring to imagine themselves in the position of their enemies rather than their parents, their elder brothers and their sisters.

As the Third Reich crumbled in the rubble of Berlin during the last days of April and the first days of May 1945, German children began to express the dilemmas of their new predicament in their games. Before they had even emerged from their Berlin cellars, children started playing at being Russian soldiers. Waving make-believe pistols, they relieved each other of imaginary watches, crying, 'Uhri, uhri' to mimic the Red Army looters. As they assimilated the real and terrifying power of their enemies and masters into their games, these Berlin children were also enacting their own impotence and envy.

Yet, the very fact of children's play leaves a degree of openness and ambiguity about the meaning of their games: what does it mean for children to consciously enact such scenarios? When Emmanuel Ringelblum overheard an eight-year-old Jewish boy in the Warsaw ghetto screaming, 'I want to steal, I want to rob, I want to eat, I want to be a German,' he was hearing the voice of pure desperation and rage.[124] But to play at robbing, stealing and being German was somehow different from this starving child's scream. Children knew it was a game, the one scenario that they could truly control, however powerless they might be in other respects. And for this reason children generally played such games when they did not think that anyone else would interfere with them. And then there were things they did not play at altogether – German children might enact Russian plunder but not rape; the gas chamber game needed stones for a role which could not be performed even by the smaller children who were

---

Jerusalem, 17 Nov. 1964, p. 49. H. Hoffmann-Fischel, report for Yad Vashem, reprinted in Inge Deutschkron, *Denn ihrer war die Hölle: Kinder in Gettos und Lagern* (Cologne: Verlag Wissenschaft und Politik, 1985), p. 51.

[123] H. Hoffmann-Fischel, report for Yad Vashem, p. 51. 'Einmal spielten sie auch "Gaskammer". Sie machten eine Grube, in die sie ein Steinchen nach dem anderen schoben. Das sollten die Menschen sein, die ins Krematorium kamen, und sie ahmten ihre Schreie nach. Mich zogen sie zu Rate, ich sollte ihnen zeigen, wie man den Kamin aufstellen müsse'.

[124] J. Sloan (ed.), *Notes from the Warsaw Ghetto: The Journal of Emmanuel Ringelblum* (New York and London: Schocken Books, 1958), p. 39.

routinely dragooned into the roles where they were punished or beaten. To perform one's own powerlessness is to attempt to master one's own destruction, but this had its limits: they could not play at their own death. Even so, the ambiguity of such play was that it also naturalised a world in which children were killed. In making this world their own, children could not help expressing utterly contradictory feelings, fear entwined with envy of their enemies, love rent by pity and hatred of their own families.

· ·

Even finding solace in peer group games has not been available for all neglected, abused or worried children who have had no other way of fighting back. This has been obviously denied to the handful of children who have been permanently and deliberately isolated by their parents or guardians, and whose sorry existence was briefly touched on in Chapter 3.[125] But there have always been other unhappy youngsters who have been detached from their peers by circumstance, particularly 'only ones' brought up on distant farmsteads with none but adults and animals for company. More importantly, many abused children must have been totally or partly excluded from the chants and games of their peers because in some way they were deemed not to fit the norm. As we know today, the psychological effect of being ignored by one's peers is profound even among children who come from loving homes. The effect on the self-esteem of children from troubled backgrounds through the ages, on their discovery that the marks of parental neglect (under-nourishment, ragged clothing, open wounds and so on) were the very stigmas that prevented them from relating with their peers, must have been totally crushing.

Solitary and sensitive children, abused and unabused, would have often dealt with their loneliness by escaping into a private fantasy world. An obvious recourse for those unable to find contentment in the universe that they are forced to inhabit is to build another one which can be personally controlled. In the pre-modern world when children's horizons were limited and their world, in most cases, strongly influenced by the church, Bible stories and saints' legends must have provided the material for solitary play as much as the folk tales told on dark nights. The numerous child visionaries through the ages may not have been the victims of adult abuse, but they were often children who had had their lives upset by warfare, such as Joan of Arc (c. 1412–31), or who had been forced to cope with poverty, disease or disability, which set them apart from their peers in some way, such as Bernadette of Lourdes (1844–79).[126] Since the end of the nineteenth century, the lonely or solitary child has had a much expanded repertoire of alternative universes to wander in. The ever-growing genre of children's literature, the emergence after the First World War of the children's comic and the cartoon, and the rapid development of children's television from the 1950s have been grist to the imagination of the solitary, as much as they have offered fresh material for children's games.[127] The appearance of the digital game at the end of the twentieth century and the

---

[125] See Ch. 3, p. 138.

[126] Joan of Arc's voices have been interpreted in various ways by her biographers; for the most recent study, see L. J. Taylor, *The Virgin Warrior: The Life and Death of Joan of Arc* (London: Yale, 2009). For a good analysis of the environment in which Bernadette was raised, see R. Harris, *Lourdes. Body and Spirit in the Secular Age* (London: Allen Lane, 1999), pt. 1. For works on other child visionaries, see *ibid.*, p. 380, fn. Protestant children did not have visions of the Virgin but Blake in *Songs of Innocence* imagines 'little Tom Dacre' being reconciled to his lot as a chimney sweep after being afforded a vision of a green paradise by an angel. 'And the Angel told Tom, if he'd be a good boy / He'd have God for his father and never want joy': 'The Chimney Sweeper', in *Songs of Innocence* (1789), ed. G. Keynes (Oxford: Oxford University Press, 1970).

[127] Many children's books actively encourage fantasy play. Their heroes are children who are bed-ridden, bored or forced to live away from home and who are distracted from their real world by entering another. C. S. Lewis's, *The Lion, the Witch and the Wardrobe* (1950) is a classic of the genre, as is Philippa Pearce's, *Tom's*

growing opportunities for players to customise the action has taken the possibilities of solitary fantasy play one stage further. Children can now make virtual friends and enemies and can ignore their peer group altogether if they wish, much to the despair of educationalists who fear we are breeding a generation of 'loners'.[128]

Yet what of the few especially fragile children for whom the burden of their hurt has been too painful to be released through any form of coping mechanism? As in the present, these children can have had only one way out. Presumably, they blamed themselves for their predicament and turned their anger inwards. Understandably, we have limited information about children who self-harmed or committed suicide before the modern era. But there is evidence to suggest that they were not unknown in England. Of the 13,968 cases of suicide recorded in the central law court of King's Bench, in the period 1485–1710, 38 per cent of the victims were under 21 and 17.5 per cent under fifteen.[129] But in the pre-modern era the information remained largely hidden in court records and was seldom openly discussed. Suicide was a great sin abhorred by the church – God's creatures did not have the right to end their own lives – and the suicide of the young was felt to be particularly outrageous.[130] The ending of Shakespeare's *Romeo and Juliet* would have shocked the audience when the play was first performed in the 1590s, if its scandalous conclusion quickly helped to make it popular. So unimaginable was the act in real life to good Catholics, even in the eighteenth century, that a suicide in Toulouse of a 29-year-old young man in 1761 (still living at home and a minor under Roman law) led to the arraignment of his father on a charge of murder. The Calas family were Protestants in a period when Calvinism was illegal in France. As it was rumoured that the young man, Marc-Antoine, was about to convert to Catholicism, it was assumed by the Catholic authorities of the city that his father had killed him in fury at his decision, and had then tried to make the murder look like suicide. Calas *père* was tried, found guilty and broken on the wheel, causing Voltaire to take up his pen in the family's defence and spend the last period of his life waging war on religious intolerance.[131]

It was only towards the end of the eighteenth century that the taboo surrounding suicide at any age began to be lifted. With the dawn of the Romantic era, a more tolerant attitude was championed by the literary and artistic avant-garde who had lost their Christian faith

---

Midnight Garden (1958). A beautiful filmic evocation of a lonely child's fantasy life is Guillermo del Toro's *El laberinto del fauno* (*Pan's Labyrinth*) (2006). This is the story of a young Spanish girl forced to live with her mother and brutal stepfather in a temporary army camp in the Pyrenees at the end of the Spanish Civil War.

[128] Adults, too, can now escape from the real world and create a virtual life for themselves using 'Second Life'. Some adults choose to live in a fantasy world of childhood. The late 'King of Pop', Michael Jackson (d. 15 Jun. 2009), raised by a stern father and denied a conventional childhood by being a child star, was obsessed with James Barrie's *Peter Pan* (1904), the story of a child who never grew up. His Californian home was called 'NeverLand' and filled with children and things to delight them, see *The Sunday Times: News Review*, 5 Jul. 2009, pp. 2–3, 'Jackson's Peter Pan Obsession'.

[129] T. Murphy, '"Woful Childe of Parents Rage": Suicide of Children and Adolescents in Early Modern England, 1507–1701', *Sixteenth-Century Journal*, 17:3 (1986), 257–70. Murphy attributes the high proportion of teenage suicides to the loneliness many youngsters felt when sent out of the home to be servants and apprentices. He also suggests that the children saw taking their own lives as an act of revenge: cruel and unkind masters could no longer profit from their labour.

[130] A MS in medieval French recounting 'Les miracles de la glorieuse vierge' tells how the Virgin Mary appeared in order to dissuade a young girl who had given birth to her uncle's bastard from committing suicide. The girl, though, had already murdered the child and three earlier babies she had had by her uncle: the Virgin had made no attempt to stop infanticide. The editors are indebted for this information to Dr Sophie Oosterwijk of the University of St Andrews. For a general account of suicide in the Middle Ages, see A. Murray, *Suicide in the Middle Ages* (2 vols.; Oxford: Oxford University Press, 1998).

[131] D. Bien, *The Calas Affair. Persecution, Toleration and Heresy in Eighteenth-Century Toulouse* (Princeton: Princeton University Press, 1960). For Voltaire's role, see R. Pomeau, *Voltaire en son temps, vol iv. Ecraser l'infâme. 1759–1770* (Oxford: Voltaire Foundation, 1994), ch. 9.

and frequently found life burdensome and pointless.[132] In 1774 the pain that could lead a young adult male out in the world to kill himself was explored for the first time in the new genre of the novel, when Johann Wolfgang von Goethe (1749–1832) published *The Sorrows of the Young Werther*, an instant best-seller on the theme of unobtainable love. Other 'suicide' novels followed. In 1830–31 two appeared in France in consecutive years. In *Le Rouge et le Noir* by Stendhal (1783–1842) Julien Sorel allows himself to be executed on the guillotine as a better option than continuing the mucky life of pole-climbing in Restoration France, while the unrequited lover, Raphaël, in Balzac's *La Peau de chagrin* seeks a slow death through a life of relentless debauchery.[133] Thereafter suicide became a literary commonplace, especially on the stage, where a series of depressed tragic heroes brought the drama to an end with a gun shot.[134] It was inevitable therefore that a writer would eventually present his audience with a juvenile suicide. The first to do so was Henrik Ibsen (1828–1906) in his 1884 drama of middle-class hypocrisy, *The Wild Duck*, where the fourteen-year-old Hedwig kills herself in despair at the loss of her father's love. Audiences disliked the play but seem to have been unperturbed by the child's suicide, doubtless because the text leaves open the possibility that her death was accidental.[135] Eleven years later, when Hardy narrated the suicide of a younger child in *Jude the Obscure* (1895–96), the public reaction was much more critical. But in the ensuing years the world had changed. In the context of the popularisation of Darwinism, the rise of feminism and widespread concern that the urban and industrial poor were virtually a separate, degenerating species, suicide had become scientised and was now a 'hot' medical and media issue. Hardy's novel worried his readers because it was a novel about working-class life that explored current middle-class fears: the self-murder of a child was just one element among many that raised the critics' ire.

Child Suicide in *Jude the Obscure*

Josephine McDonagh

The unremitting desolation of Thomas Hardy's last and grimmest novel, *Jude the Obscure* comes to a climax with the suicide of Jude's son, the 'too reflective' Little Father Time aged nine, and his murder of two younger half-siblings. The three corpses were found, two hanging on a coat peg on the back of the door, by Sue Brideshead, the mother of the younger children, together with the poignant, and famously misspelt suicide note: 'Done because we are too menny'.[136] In this short essay I will consider some of

---

[132] English romantics glorified the suicide of the seventeen-year-old poet, Thomas Chatterton, in 1770 – Wordsworth's 'marvellous boy'. In fact, Chatterton died unwittingly from an overdose of arsenic and opium. See *Oxford Dictionary of National Biography*, sub nom.

[133] Raphaël sees the thought of suicide as a commonplace among young adult males: Balzac, *La Peau de Chagrin*, p. 203. 'Ecoute … j'ai comme tous les jeunes gens médité sur les suicides. Qui de nous, à trente ans, ne s'est pas tué deux ou trois fois?'

[134] At the turn of the twentieth century all but one of Chekhov's five-act plays ended with a suicide (male and female).

[135] M. L. Meyer, *Ibsen. A Biography* (Harmondsworth: Pelican Books, 1974), pp. 383–94. Hedvig is an isolated, vulnerable child who constructs an emotional life around a crippled wild duck that she keeps in the attic (a pretend forest). Audiences may also have been reconciled to her fate from the fact that she was usually played by a mature woman.

[136] Thomas Hardy, *Jude the Obscure*, ed., N. Page (New York: Norton, 1999), pp. 262 and 264.

the reasons why Hardy's already renowned pessimism should have manifested itself in this gruesome and shocking manner.

The interest in suicide in *Jude the Obscure* reflects a preoccupation with suicide in late nineteenth-century English culture. Many commentators considered the nation to be in the grip of an epidemic of suicide.[137] While the primary concern was with adult suicide, there was also a strong belief that child suicide was on the rise. The novel draws on contemporary beliefs about suicide, based on ideas about the hereditary nature of mental disorders, the decline of marriage as an institution fitted to modern sexual relations, the changing roles of men and women, the stresses of education, and the dispossession and alienation that were the result of demographic and socio-economic trends. The depiction of the child suicide in *Jude the Obscure* thus weaves together various explanations for suicide that were circulating in contemporary society, as well as evoking a layer of more ancient associations that such acts had accumulated over time.

Jude the Obscure was published at a time in which the novel's capacity to portray realistically – or 'naturalistically' – aspects of life considered unsuitable for literary representation, was a subject of intense debate. Hardy was often compared with the French writer, Emile Zola (1840–1902), whose novels had caused controversy across Europe for their graphic depiction of social problems, such as alcoholism and prostitution, often based on documentary evidence of real cases.[138] In England, the scandalous nature of Zola's naturalism had been highlighted in 1888 and 1889, when the publisher of English translations, Vizitelly, was tried, and imprisoned for obscenity.[139] Against the backdrop of heightened concern for the ethics of novelistic representation, *Jude the Obscure* provoked considerable controversy. W. W. How (1823–97), Bishop of Wakefield wrote in protest to the *Yorkshire Post* that he had been 'so disgusted with its insolence and indecency that I threw it into the fire'. Retrospectively Hardy claimed that he 'was mildly sceptical of the literal truth of the bishop's story;' but 'remembering that Shelley, Milton and many others … had undergone the same sort of indignity at the hands of bigotry and intolerance' was, perhaps, flattered by the lofty associations of the Bishop's act.[140] With this in mind, it is perhaps surprising that the child suicide and sibling murders are not the main causes of offence, but figure merely as elements in a much longer list of passages of concern to reviewers. The adumbration of 'revolting' incidents by W. D. Howells (1858–1916) is typical in that it lurches from the seemingly trivial – 'Arabella's [Jude's legal wife and the mother of Father Time] dimple-making' – to the more shocking and grave – 'the boy suicide and homicide'.[141] Many critics singled out the episode early in the novel in which Arabella tosses a pig's scrotum at Jude, as a way of attracting his attention. Throughout the early responses it is Hardy's frank – the term often used is 'coarse' – representation of sexual relations, rather than incidents of childhood violence, that critics attack. In particular readers were offended by his delineation of female characters with a higher degree of sexual agency than would be typical, or acceptable, in most Victorian fiction. For these readers, the child suicide and homicides are to be seen as the inevitable outcome and the symbol of the

---

[137] On the history of suicide see O. Anderson, *Suicide in Victorian and Edwardian England* (Oxford: Clarendon Press, 1987). On the *fin-de-siècle* suicide craze, see J. Stokes, *In the Nineties* (New York: Harvester Wheatsheaf, 1989), ch. 5.

[138] L. R. Furst, *Naturalism* (London: Methuen, 1978).

[139] See C. Dekker, *The Victorian Conscience* (New York: Twayne, 1952).

[140] W. W. How, letter to the *Yorkshire Post* (9 Jun. 1896); F. E. Hardy, *The Life of Thomas Hardy, 1840–1928* (London: Macmillan, 1962): both reprinted in Hardy, *Jude the Obscure*, pp. 390 and 340.

[141] W. D. Howells in *Harper's Weekly* (7 Dec. 1895), reprinted in Hardy, *Jude the Obscure*, p. 378.

moral mayhem that is the result of the decline of marriage, growing promiscuity, and the breakdown of traditional gender roles.

This view is most clearly represented by Margaret Oliphant (1825–97), the author of an essay entitled 'The Anti-Marriage League', published in the literary journal, *Blackwood's Edinburgh Magazine*. This was the most vituperative response to the novel. The infant deaths are 'Mr Hardy's solution of the great insoluble question of what is to be the fate of children in such circumstances', referring to the kinds of sexual permissiveness described in the novel. She highlights the vulgarity of Arabella ('she is a human pig, like the beast whom in a horrible scene she and her husband kill'), and the perversity of the 'fantastic Susan [Jude's cousin and lover], … holding him on the tiptoe of expectation, with a pretended reserve which is almost more indecent still'.[142] But the real cause for concern is the 'passivity' of Jude, whom she sees as manipulated 'like a puppet' by two unstable and omnipotent women. The decline of masculine authority and the emergence of new kinds of femininity were considered by many to be part of the general decline of civilised standards that characterised the culture of the *fin-de-siècle*. This was described by Max Nordau (1849–1923) in his influential work *Degeneration* (1893, English trans. 1895) as an age of sexual freedoms, intellectual pessimism, avant-garde artistic experimentation, and political radicalism, all of which were symptoms of a civilisation in decline. Sue Brideshead was recognisable as an example of the New Woman, one of the *dramatis personae* of the degenerate *fin-de-siècle*: in his 'postscript' to the 1912 edition, Hardy described her as 'the woman of the feminist movement – the slight pale "bachelor" girl – the intellectualised, emancipated bundle of nerves that modern conditions were producing mainly in cities as yet'.[143] While the emergence of this 'type' in literature by both men and women writers reflected the existence of politically active feminists at the end of the century, inevitably literary representations tended to exaggerate certain characteristics in relation to the anxieties that such women provoked. In the main, these focused on women's sexual and reproductive lives: their resistance to marriage, their homosexual tendencies, and above all, their control of fertility.[144] During the 1890s, contraception was more widely practised than in past decades, and now was underpinned by emerging beliefs in eugenics, which brought a new and compelling scientific rationale for the regulation of population.[145] The auto-destruction of the children in the novel, therefore, could be read as a particularly graphic consequence of the New Woman's refusal of maternity, an instance of deferred contraception in a climate of unnatural feminine power.

This view is supported by the fact that in the novel, Father Time's act is seen to have been provoked by Sue's too frank discussion with him of the causes of the family's poverty and homelessness. Sue's Malthusian view – that their 'adversity and suffering' are at some level caused by having too many children – is repeated by the boy, who expresses the view that 'whenever children be born that are not wanted they should be killed directly, before their souls come to 'em, and not allowed to grow big and walk about!',[146] and is reiterated in the suicide note. As if to underline this, the first published version of the novel in 1895, serialised in bowdlerised form in *Harper's*, accompanies the episode leading up to the deaths with an illustration of a stern-faced

[142] Margaret Oliphant in *Blackwood's Edinburgh Magazine* (Jan. 1896), reprinted in Hardy, *Jude the Obscure*, pp. 380 and 383.
[143] Hardy, *Jude the Obscure*, p. 8.
[144] S. Ledger, *The New Woman* (Manchester: Manchester University Press, 1996).
[145] A. Richardson, *Love and Eugenics in the Late Nineteenth Century: Rational Reproduction and the New Woman* (Oxford: Oxford University Press, 2003). See also Ch. 2, p. 88–95
[146] Hardy, *Jude the Obscure*, p. 262.

Sue and a small boy (much smaller and more vulnerable-looking than his fictional age would suggest) walking through the streets of Christminster (Oxford), watched by two hostile shopkeepers. (See Figure 33). The illustration bears the caption, '"I ought not to be born, ought I?" said the boy'. Indeed, in the novel, Sue also considers herself to be to blame; and, as if to underline her culpability as an agent of child death, on the day of the children's burial she gives premature birth to her new child, who immediately dies also. The idea that Sue is responsible for the children's deaths is repeated by many commentators on the novel, most famously by the novelist D. H. Lawrence (1885–1930), writing some years later, who dwells on Sue's pathological femininity as the cause of the young deaths. For Lawrence the children's self-destruction is directly caused by a maternal spirit that both depends on the children for its existence, but also sees the children as a threat:

> [Father Time] feels, as any child will feel, as many children feel today, that they are really anachronisms, accidents, fatal accidents, unreal, false notes in their mothers' lives, that, according to her, they have no being: that, if they have being then she has not. So he takes way all the children. And then Sue ceases to be. ....[147]

Lawrence generalises from Sue's dysfunctional maternal spirit, to all mother-child relations. This view of women, as controlling and antagonistic towards their children, is expressed frequently in Lawrence's work, and while idiosyncratic for the extreme terms in which it is expressed, nevertheless has wider currency in the early decades of the twentieth century and beyond. In Freudian psychoanalysis, for instance, fantasies about the mother's ambivalence towards her children are a key component of an infant's psychic development. According to Freud (1865–1939), memories of the mother's perceived aggression towards her child are important factors in adult psychological disorders.

Although critics often take an unsympathetic view of Sue, Hardy's text ultimately insists that the causes of the tragic suicide and homicide are much more various and undecidable than this. In the novel, Sue's self-accusations are an aspect of her overwrought nature, rather than a statement of truth. The text provides different explanations for the deaths, including not only maternal deviance and marital breakdown, but also the family's social exclusion and homelessness, evolutionary forces, the child's mental disorder and modern pessimism, all of which were topical issues at the time. As noted above, Hardy's novel was read by an audience that was fascinated by suicide. Newspapers reported multiple instances of suicide, some of which, according to John Stokes, may well have been fabricated, answering a growing taste for self destruction among the reading public.[148] From the late 1870s, magazines and periodicals were full of discussions of what seemed to be a new and distinctively modern outbreak of world-weariness, expressed in ever increasing instances of self-destruction. This often had a literary aspect to it. A debate sparked by W. H. Mallock (1849–1923) in an article entitled 'Is Life Worth Living?' published in September 1877 in the magazine, *Nineteenth Century*, for instance, blamed current attitudes on the work of agnostic writers such as George Eliot.[149] Suicide is a recurrent theme in literary texts of the 1880s and 1890s – in the *Suicide Club* of Robert Louis Stevenson (1850–94) and *Dorian Gray* by Oscar Wilde (1854–1900), for instance – as well as in philosophical and sociological

---

[147] D. H. Lawrence, *Phoenix: the Posthumous Papers of D. H. Lawrence*, ed. E. D. McDonald (London: Heinemann, 1935), p. 508.
[148] Stokes, *In the Nineties*, p. 141.
[149] B. T. Gates, *Victorian Suicide: Mad Crimes and Sad Histories* (Princeton: Princeton University Press, 1988), p. 152.

texts, many of which were translated into English from continental sources. *Studies on Pessimism* (1891) by Arthur Schopenhauer (1788–1860) which included his essay 'On Suicide', *Suicide* (1897) by Emile Durkheim (1858–1917), and Henry Morselli's *Suicide: An Essay on Comparative Moral Statistics* (1881), all had wide influence, and helped to produce a prevailing sense that modern society was 'suicidal'. The general tenor of these accounts was to propose that suicide was no longer an act of individual choice with serious moral consequences, but was now driven by a universal will that was a greater force than that of any particular individual, and to whose power all were subject: suicide was thus the paradoxical reaction to a loss of individual agency in the modern world, a distinctively modern response to irregular and unstable conditions. This view chimed not only with philosophical ideas, taken in the main from Schopenhauer (despite Schopenhauer's own disapproval of suicide, as an ill-judged and futile attempt to assert individual will), but also with post-Darwinian ideas about the inexorable and tragic force of evolution. The child's suicide in *Jude the Obscure*, therefore, can be seen as a sign of the times, an expression of a *fin-de-siècle Zeitgeist*. A doctor is reported in the novel as having expressed the opinion that: 'there are such boys springing up amongst us – boys of a sort unknown in the last generation – the outcome of new views of life. They seem to see all its terrors before they are old enough to have staying power to resist them. ...it is the beginning of the coming universal wish not to live'.[150]

That it is a doctor that gives this analysis is significant, because by the late 1800s suicide has become a medical problem. Morselli's work of moral statistics was highly influential in this regard. Using statistical evidence, Morselli, himself a medical man, sought to prove that the increase in suicide was a pan-European urban phenomenon, a mental disease provoked by the environmental conditions of city living, and which struck individuals in whom a proclivity for self-destruction had been inherited from previous generations of diseased individuals. This combination of environmental and hereditary factors provided the dominant explanation for all mental disorders in this period, conditions that in turn were diagnosed as the symptoms of the too-civilised culture turned degenerate.[151] For Morselli, suicide is an evolutionary mechanism, a means of ridding the species of its weaker and infirm members. He writes, it is 'an effect of the struggle for existence, and of human selection, which works according to the laws of evolution among civilised people'.[152] These ideas were repeated in works by English authors, many of them medical men too, such as the W. Wyn Westcot, the deputy coroner for central Middlesex, whose *Suicide: Its History, Literature, Jurisprudence, Causation and Prevention* was published in 1885, and S. A. K. Strahan, doctor and barrister, in *Suicide and Insanity: A Physiological and Sociological Study* (1893). These works typically conjoined Morselli's social statistics with accounts of hereditary mental disorders gleaned from prominent and influential English medical experts on mental dysfunctions, such as Henry Maudsley (1835–1918) and Sir James Crichton-Brown (1840–1938), the author of ground-breaking works on child development, whose personal friendship with Hardy has been interestingly explored by Sally Shuttleworth.[153]

---

[150] Hardy, *Jude the Obscure*, p. 264. Cf. S. Shuttleworth, '"Done Because We Are Too Menny": Little Father Time and Child Suicide in Late-Victorian Culture', in P. Mallett (ed.), *Thomas Hardy: Texts and Contexts* (London: Palgrave, 2002), p. 147.

[151] For the medical origins of late nineteenth-century theories of degeneration, see D. Pick, *Faces of Degeneration: A European Disorder* (Cambridge: Cambridge University Press, 1989).

[152] H. Morselli, *Suicide: An Essay on Comparative Moral Statistics*, the original expressly revised and abridged by the author for the English version (London: C. Kegan Paul, 1881), p. 354.

[153] For Hardy's associations with doctors and especially child mental health experts, such as Crichton-Brown, see Shuttleworth, 'Done Because We Are Too Menny'.

As Shuttleworth shows, Father Time's suicide is almost literally a text book case: that his act was provoked by his family's outcast situation is emphasised over and over again, as is its hereditary origins. Suicide is in his blood: a family history of suicides is woven into the early chapters of the novel: Jude's mother (Father Time's grandmother) had drowned herself, Jude's own boyish attempt to drown himself is thwarted, and towards the end of the novel, Jude claims to be committing suicide by visiting Sue in a storm. There is insanity in Jude's family: we are told of an ancestor who went mad when her husband was hanged for stealing their child's coffin. And finally, the fact that Jude and Sue are first cousins and their relationship was, as a consequence, incestuous would be, according to Maudsley, a further contributing cause of his and his children's, mental ill health. The novel follows closely the psychological literature on child psychological development, carefully presenting the aetiology of disordered childhood as described by the medical literature of the day.

The suicide of children is not the principal concern of much of the medical literature, but nevertheless all the works express the concern that it is a growing problem. 'Monstrous and unnatural as the event seems at so tender an age,' writes Maudsley in *The Pathology of Mind* (1895), 'suicide is an occasional result of melancholy in young children'. Maudsley's suggestion that suicide in children is the result of a 'sudden impulse springing out of the sad mood of the moment and most trifling motive' bears no real comparison with the seriously considered logic of Father Time. Nevertheless, the conclusion that this 'constitutional indifference to life and the ready impulse to end it betray a distinct neuropathic inheritance' is clearly repeated in Hardy's insistence on the hereditary nature of the child's condition.[154] Other writers lay more emphasis on the environmental factors causing suicide in children, identifying the stresses imposed by education as a primary factor. Crichton-Brown's work on the detrimental effects of education on the nervous system was highly influential in suggesting that newly available systems of education may have had a deleterious effect on the mental health of the nation's young.[155] Strahan concurs: 'there is no doubt', he writes 'that much of this self-destruction among children has education either for its true or its exciting cause'. And while he agrees that there must be an underlying and inherited weakness within the child ('The healthy organism,' by contrast, 'is marvellously tolerant of abuse') none the less sees the present education system as introducing mental problems that will in turn be inherited by future generations.

> The worshippers of this Moloch seem to forget, if they are not ignorant of the fact, that the injury done by this system is cumulative, and transmissible from generation to generation. To increase the strain to just short of the breaking point is to take up an untenable position, for what one generation can just bear without apparent injury two or three successive generations cannot.[156]

As Shuttleworth points out, Father Time's suicide reflects on his father's failed 'educational desires'.[157]

Hardy's appropriation of contemporary medical and scientific literature contributes to the novel's powerful psychological realism. Yet, it is striking that, despite its strict

[154] H. Maudsley, *The Pathology of Mind: A Study of the Distempers, Deformities and Disorders* (London: Macmillan, 1895), p. 381.
[155] See for instance J. Crichton-Brown, 'Education and the Nervous System', in M. Morris (ed.), *The Book of Health* (London: Cassell, 1892–95).
[156] S. A. K. Strahan, *Suicide and Insanity: A Physiological and Sociological Study* (London: Swan Sonnenschein, 1893), p. 175.
[157] Shuttleworth, 'Done Because We Are Too Menny', pp. 140–41.

adherence to scientific facts and theories, early reviewers found the suicide of Little Father Time the most troubling, and least convincing episode, in the whole novel. This was the moment at which many commentators felt that the structure of the novel, and the fabric of its realism, broke down. It was a moment of 'pure farce', wrote Margaret Oliphant; or, according to the anonymous reviewer in the *Illustrated London News*, an instance of 'grim mockery'.[158] Rather than seeing the deaths as the climax of realistic representation, many readers instead found them a structural flaw, the point which exceeded the limits of psychological realism. In the *Illustrated London News*, it was felt that 'the tragedy of the children strains [the reader's] belief to snapping point'. Even the sexologist, Havelock Ellis (1859–1939), whose review of the novel was generally appreciative, expressed puzzlement regarding the episode, seeing in it an excess of realist detail: 'whatever failure of nervous energy may be present in the Fawley family', he writes, 'it is clear that Mr Hardy was not proposing to himself a study of gross pathological degenerescence, a study of the hereditary evolution of criminality. If that were so, the story would lose the wide human significance ...' The child deaths, therefore, present a paradoxical moment in the text, at which realism exceeds itself, the point at which its capacity to convince collapses.[159]

To conclude: based on contemporary psychological and scientific works, the death of Father Time presents a persuasive case study of juvenile suicide. However, the suicide also, paradoxically, presents problems for the form of the novel, which is brought to a breaking point precisely around its representation. The suicide encapsulates the nihilism that is at the heart of this novel but, as such, it also represents the impossibility of representing the traumatic experience of modernity in the conventional forms of realism.

· ·

Although attacked at the time, Hardy's account of the pressures that can lead to a child's suicide even in a loving if dysfunctional family continues to attract the attention of psychologists today, a reminder that much of our present clinical understanding of self-harming was developed over a century ago. In an essay entitled '*Jude the Obscure, A Pathway to Suicide*' published in 1989, child psychologists Eleanor C. Guetzloe and Ralph M. Cline use the novel as a case study of continuing relevance to their own society. Using a contemporary analytical vocabulary that jars somewhat with the late nineteenth-century literary text, they argue that Jude has 'a suicidal career', marked by his 'multiple problems' which include a propensity to alcoholism, depression, marital breakdown and sexual deviancy. While theories of the hereditary origins of mental disorder in their late Victorian form are now discredited, Guetzloe and Cline nevertheless point out that a history of suicide in the family continues to operate in late twentieth-century psychology as a 'significant risk factor associated with youth suicide'. 'Mental health professionals', they write, 'suggest that children may adopt as a model the self-destructive behaviour and attitudes of their parents and other family members' including 'the actual suicidal act'. The novel, too, they continue,

---

[158] Hardy, *Jude the Obscure*, p. 383; unsigned review in *Illustrated London News*, 11 Jan. 1896, reprinted in R. G. Cox (ed.), *Thomas Hardy: The Critical Heritage* (London: Routledge, 1995), p. 275. Some later critics have concurred. A. Alvarez (himself the author of a notable work on suicide in 1971 – *The Savage God*) described the episode as 'dangerously close to being laughable': see his '*Jude the Obscure*: Afterword', in G. Clarke (ed.), *Thomas Hardy: Critical Assessment, vol. iv. A Twentieth Century Overview* (East Sussex: Helm Information, 1993), p. 209.

[159] H. Havelock Ellis, 'Concerning Jude the Obscure', *The Savoy: An Illustrated Monthly*, Oct. (1896), 35–51, at p. 42; reprinted in Cox, *Thomas Hardy*, p. 307.

portrays other factors that are still considered chief among causes of child suicide today: 'previous suicidal behaviour; depression and other psychiatric disorders; substance abuse; loss of a parent through death, divorce or separation; family disorganization; physical or psychological abuse; isolation; and knowledge of suicide'.[160] Moreover, the authors emphasise, the exacerbating environmental factors that Hardy depicts – homelessness, separation of children from one or other parent, hunger and poverty, and the stresses of education – persist today as social problems that are held to be factors contributing to suicide in children.[161]

However, if our understanding of child suicide and self-harming has perhaps not greatly developed since Hardy's era, we are now properly informed of the magnitude of the problem and committed to dealing with it. Until the end of the Second World War the British state was primarily concerned with children's physical health. The incoming Labour Government shifted the emphasis to identifying and counselling children with psychological problems and this has remained the priority ever since.[162] Our children's state of mind is now at the top of the national agenda. Since the turn of the new century engendering emotional well-being (or more specifically helping children to develop a series of positive psychological states) has become an important part of the school curriculum leading to the Department of Education and Skills temporarily being rechristened the Department of Children, Families and Schools in recognition of schooling's wider remit.[163] Indeed, Geoff Mulgan, former adviser to British Prime Minister Gordon Brown's strategy unit, has recently claimed 'that well-being would come to be as important in the goals of national governments as military prowess was in the nineteenth century'.[164]

What is surprising is that despite countless initiatives by both the state and the voluntary sector, the ever-improving standard of living since the 1950s, and the new culture of parenting and schooling with kindness, there remain a large number of desperate children in Britain who attempt to self-harm.[165] There can be few adults who do not know of at least one adolescent (and teenage males between fifteen and nineteen and young adult males are most at risk) who has tried or succeeded in committing suicide. Whether self-harming is a greater problem today than it was in Hardy's time will never be known but there are reasons not to dismiss the possibility out of hand.[166] Arguably, in earlier centuries all but

---

[160] E. C. Guetzloe and R. M. Cline, 'A Pathway to Suicide', in S. M. Deats and L. T. Lenker (eds), *Youth Suicide Prevention: Lessons from Literature* (New York: Plenum Press, 1989), pp. 126, 129, and 133.

[161] The editors are indebted to Josephine McDonagh for the details of the Guetzloe and Cline article.

[162] The leading historian of this change of emphasis and its foundations in the interwar period is Harry Hendrick, see H. Hendrick, *Child Welfare in England 1872–1989* (London: Routledge, 1994).

[163] These psychological states are identified as stoicism, optimism, altruism, being in the moment, emotional literacy or managing and expressing one's emotions and those of others constructively, and self-esteem. Whether emotional well-being should be responsibility of the school and whether the inculcation of a set of psychological states is a form of brainwashing has already sparked a lively debate. For a positive endorsement of the new priority see F. A. Huppert, N. Baylis and B. Keverne (eds), *The Science of Well Being* (Oxford: Oxford University Press, 2005). The pluses and minuses of trying to control children's emotional well-being is at present the subject of a research project being undertaken by Professor K. Ecclestone of the University of Birmingham. For an opening statement, see K. Ecclestone and D. Hayes, *The Dangerous Rise of Therapeutic Education* (London: Routledge, 2009).

[164] K. Ecclestone, 'Changing the Subject: Interdisciplinary Perspectives on Emotional Well-Being and Social Justice', unpublished ESRC seminar series working paper, Jul. 2008, p. 1.

[165] The depth of contemporary unease can be measured by the fact that, in recent years, child well-being has attracted the attention of voluntary bodies and institutions not specifically associated with child health. In Sept. 2004, for instance, the Globe Theatre in London (dedicated to staging Shakespeare in an authentic setting) devoted a week to the problem of self-harming children, using *Romeo and Juliet* and other plays to raise awareness.

[166] Between 1970 and 1990 the number of male suicides in the fifteen- to nineteen-year-old range went up by

the loneliest, most miserable and most closely policed children could put up with extremely high levels of what we would deem physical abuse and exploitation because they lived in a culture where self-harm was decried and violence of all kinds was perfectly acceptable. Furthermore, as we saw in the last chapter, the young were the perpetrators and not just the victims in this ecology of violence.[167] In our modern child-centred society, physical abuse may be much less but it is likely that it is much more keenly felt, while the taboo against suicide has largely disappeared. Moreover, the emphasis in school on the individual's specialness, self-fulfilment and right to happiness can breed stress and self-doubt, as can the demands placed on children by competitive consumerism in the post-industrial age and the images of bodily comeliness and ideal relationships promoted in the media.[168] Children were formerly taught that they were imperfect, fallen creatures who should learn to accept the station into which they were born. Now they are offered often-conflicting visions of perfection that they are urged to reach out for and that they see their peers enjoying. The more open, mobile, pluralistic and interconnected modern capitalist democracy becomes, the greater the chance that many children, especially adolescents, will feel unhappy, anxious and inadequate, even though living in loving homes, and that some children, especially the brutalised, neglected and insecure, will find life so unbearable that they resort to self-harm.[169]

Self Harm – The Curse of Modern Britain

Rosemary Peacocke

In 1716 William Fleetwood said in one of his sermons on the case of 'self murther', 'If there be any room for Charity, it is, that though all we see is wrong, yet we may not see all that truly is in the condition of these poor people...'[170] The same is true today, particularly in the case of juvenile suicides.

In England and Wales general hospitals see 25,000 cases of self-harm or attempted suicide per year. Although figures on self-harm have fluctuated since the 1960s, it appears that between 1989 and 1992 the rates of deliberate self-harm in the United Kingdom were among the highest in Europe.[171] There are a variety of reasons why young people should be behaving in this way but there is no doubt that a lack of self-

---

70 per cent; the figure for the equivalent female cohort decreased slightly. No suicides of children under ten were recorded between 1970 and 1998, and the suicide rate of ten- to fourteen-year-olds remained unchanged, having fallen from the level recorded in the 1940s: see G. M. Clure, 'Suicide in Children and Adolescents in England and Wales, 1970–1998', *British Journal of Psychiatry*, 178 (2001), 469–74.

[167] See Ch. 5, pp. 217–19.

[168] For a good introduction to the problems of consumerism, see A. Offer, *The Challenge of Affluence: Self-Control and Well-Being in the United State and Britain since 1950* (Oxford: Oxford University Press, 2006).

[169] The statistics given below do not reveal the full extent of the problem for they do not include the very many teenagers suffering from eating disorders. Anorexia in particular is clearly a form of self-harming, even if the victim does not see it as such. Although presumably linked in some way with the media's valorisation of thinness, it also reflects a desire to avoid growing up and entering the competitive, sexually charged adult world.

[170] W. Fleetwood, *The Relative Duties of Parents and Children, Husbands and Wives, Masters and Servants. Practical Discourses with Three Sermons upon the Case of Self Murther* (London: John Hooke, 1716), 3rd sermon, p. 62.

[171] Mental Health Foundation, *Statistics on Mental Health*. Available online at http://www.mentalhealth.org.uk/information/mental-health-overview/statistics (accessed 14 Jan. 2010). The rate is not uniform across the country. There is a big difference in the suicide rate of eleven- to seventeen-year-olds between England and Wales. In England in 2003 the rate was 0.3 per 100,000, in Wales 2.2: see http://wales.gov.uk/caec/cabinetstatements/2006/word/170206–child-suicide-e.rtf (accessed 8 Jul. 2009).

esteem and a sense of hopelessness are a common theme. In 2003 ChildLine reported that 759 children and young people had phoned to say that they had attempted or were thinking of committing suicide and a further 1,475 calls were about depression in children. The children gave the reasons for their despair as bullying, sexual and physical abuse, bereavement and exam stress.[172]

It is interesting to compare the children's self diagnosis with the psychological and emotional states that typically precede suicide in chronological order. These are intolerable pressure, a depressed attitude, initial attempts at adjustment and coping, accumulated frustrations, appearance of the idea of suicide, attempts to adjust through self destructive means, environmental responses to destructiveness, a resulting confirmation of the child's pessimistic view of life and the idea that suicide is the only solution, and a continuing accumulation of new frustrations leading to the ultimate act of self destruction.[173] One common thread runs through both lists: there is no one to listen, and therefore no-one to understand.

Poverty is a key factor which must be considered in the lives of young people at risk. The United Kingdom has one of the highest rates of child poverty in Europe, for one in five children in England and Wales live on benefits and this must affect a child not just nutritionally but in their life chances, health and education.[174] It is a false perception that childhood is a carefree happy time for all children. The cries for help from children are often for trivial reasons in our eyes – 'I didn't get a present'; 'you did not come to see me at the school concert'; 'you love my sister more than me'. These are not trivial to the child: poverty in the family affects not just the child but the parent's attitudes and self-esteem. Violence can become a way of life where poverty and other pressures on the adult lead to depression, and the child suffers accordingly.

The recourse to self-harming in the present day may also be fuelled by the omnipresence of surrogate violence. Even if we live in a world where real violence is not tolerated as it was in the past, children are constantly bombarded with fictive examples and images of violent behaviour. This begins in the early years in singing and listening to nursery rhymes, which are frequently concerned with serious brutal harm and death ('Rock a Bye Baby'; 'Goosey, Goosey Gander'; 'Humpty Dumpty'; 'Who killed Cock Robin'; and so on). As children grow up these concepts are reinforced by TV and videos. Many cartoons are extremely violent but at the end the cartoon character gets up and walk away. The ludic quality of so much of this fictive violence may lead children to believe that pain and death are not serious and in the case of death not fatal. Young and adolescent children who attempt suicide may not see this as a final act, or possibly do not intend that it should be. The exposure of young people to violence on television has been considerable, in the context of television drama decreasing the child's emotional response to the experience of real life aggression.[175] There is the added problem today, too, of media-induced copy-cat suicides. Modern communications ensure that teenagers know what is happening to their role models and encourage them to emulate their heroes. In 1986 Yukiko Okada, an eighteen-year-old Japanese pop idol, committed suicide after an argument with her lover and in the following three weeks 33 young people in Japan followed her example.[176]

---

172 For ChildLine, see above, pp. 272 and 280–81.
173 I. Orbach, *Children Who Don't Want to Live* (San Francisco: Jossey Bass, 1998).
174 H. Montgomery, 'Children, Young People and Poverty', in H. Montgomery and M. Kellett (eds), *Children and Young People's Worlds: Developing Frameworks for Integrated Practice* (Bristol: The Policy Press, 2009).
175 M. H. Thomas, R. W. Horton, E. C. Lippincott and R. S. Drabman, 'Desentitization to the Portrayals of Real-life Aggression as a Function of Exposure to Television Violence', *Journal of Personality and Social Psychology*, 35:6 (1977), 450–58.
176 http://en.wikipedia.org/wiki/yukiko_okada (accessed 10 Jul. 2009). The cluster of suicides in the Bridgend

There are other possible factors to consider about the extent of child suicide and self-harm in the present. Parents are the most important influence on a young child's life and the pattern for most families in the immediate post-war era was for the mother to be at home and the father to be out at work. But it is now the case that many children have both parents working or come from a single parent home and come back from school to an empty house. There are obvious links here between parental absence and obesity, where the children snack on junk food. Obese children are more likely to experience psychological and psychiatric problems than non-obese children.[177] The role of parenting is crucial, and support is often needed but not always available. Doctors have said that children as young as three are being taught to smoke by their parents, and since the use of cannabis is much more common now, this early smoking is significant. Cannabis has a much more serious effect on children, particularly if they are disturbed in some way, and often leads to schizophrenia. Many children who are suicidal have smoked cannabis.[178]

The British psychiatrist and psychoanalyst, John Bowlby, claimed that depression in adults and children has its base in early childhood. Between the ages of two to four forms of depression are accompanied by sadness, and from five to six years, when an image of self is being formed, there is apparent negative self-esteem. At school age the depression begins to change into sorrowful moods which are no longer transitory. As in so many parts of the child's development early diagnosis is very important, and in this case it is the task of the educator to identify through observation where and when a child needs treatment. It is unrealistic to expect a parent to recognise symptoms of this type with no knowledge of normal child development or comparison with other children.[179]

Sometimes suicide messages can be observed in early play. From my own observation, I have witnessed a seven-year-old, who felt rejected, who would bury her dolls in the sandpit, and a twelve-year-old who played death games with cruel experiments on living things. Careful observation and listening are clearly essential if we are to help these troubled children. But it is not enough to observe and diagnose need in a young child; it is also necessary to know what it is to be pre-disposed to live a happy life. Michael Argyle's work in this field was focused on adults but the issues he identifies are relevant, for the most part, for children of all ages. The markers he highlighted were these: the ability to like oneself (high self-esteem); the ability to feel in control of one's life; optimism-extroversion; involvement in relationships; and involvement in community projects.[180] Meaningful activity and religious and spiritual pursuits also appear to improve people's potential for happiness.[181]

The first four issues are seen in their opposing negative sense when looking at suicidal children. Poor self-esteem, the lack of control over one's life, pessimism and a lonely

area of Wales in 2007–2008 had nothing to do with the death of a media celebrity but was attributed to the new technology. Seven of the fourteen victims (aged seventeen to 27) knew each other, and experts believed 'that the death may have been copycat suicides triggered by tributes on social networking sites': http://www.clinicallypsyched.com/teenage-suicide-brigend-wales-angeline-fuller.html (accessed 8 Jul. 2009).

[177] National Obesity Forum, Mar. 2008. J. Arehart-Treichel, 'Problems Common in Obese Youngsters', *Psychiatric News*, 39:19 (2004), 33. Available online at http://pn.psychiatryonline.org/content/39/19/33.full (accessed 10 Jan. 2010).

[178] A. L. Beautrais, P. R Joyce and R. T. Mulder, 'Cannabis Abuse and Serious Suicide Attempts' *Addiction*, 94:8 (1999), 1155–64.

[179] J. Bowlby, *Attachment and Loss*, Vol. III. *Sadness and Depression* (Harmondsworth: Penguin, Hogarth Press and the Institute of Psychoanalysis, 1985).

[180] M. Argyle, *The Social Psychology of Everyday Life* (London: Routledge, 1992).

[181] Argyle's account has clearly influenced the present child well-being agenda: see above, p. 280–81 and 313–14.

existence describe the sad life of these young people. It is possible, even with very young children, to turn these negative qualities into their positive counterpart, if they are identified early enough. In nursery school, children can be made to feel in control of their lives by giving them simple choices in the daily programme. The sadness of young children can be turned into a happier aspect by praise at simple successes, and the introduction of beauty and delight in the natural world can transform the attitude of the child. Every child needs positive involvement in relationships, and this must come first from an adult who can give the support and care that the child needs to take the first steps when s/he is ready to make friends with children of the same age.[182]

The 2003 British Government report *Every Child Matters* is an overview of the reforms proposed for the children's services in the United Kingdom after the Victoria Climbié inquiry.[183] It makes many organisational proposals for all the services but throughout there is great stress on listening to the child. This implies the existence of someone prepared and willing to listen and who will find the time to listen – whether it is a teacher, parent, social worker, health visitor or other friendly adult.

· ·

It is rare to get a real insight into the mind of a suicidal person but the poem that closes both this chapter and the book provides one.[184] The poem was a piece of work handed in to an English teacher shortly before the author committed suicide. It is the story of a boy who had found his own route to happiness before he started school and then had his coping strategy pulled from under him. We know nothing about the boy's home life, his state of mental and physical health, or where and when he killed himself.[185] But his poignant leaving note reminds us that all historical actors are individuals and that a child's reaction to abuse, exploitation, trauma, ill health or simple loneliness is ultimately subjective. This book has dealt specifically with the aspects of child-rearing in the past that we would consider today violent and exploitative and has shown how the boundaries between acceptable and unacceptable behaviour have shifted over time. The degree to which children have found this violence bearable or unendurable, it has been argued, has been largely determined by the cultural norms of their own day. Children for the most part will have only felt hurt, neglected and estranged when the boundaries have been overstepped. Even pain is a historical construct.[186] Yet in all ages there will have been peculiarly imaginative, sensitive, frail or intellectually weak children for whom the boundaries were too loosely drawn, who must have found coping always difficult and their situation bewildering; Dickens spoke up for all such children through the characters of the gangly simpleton, Smike, in *Nicholas Nickleby* (1839), and the child of the circus, Sissy Jupe, in *Hard Times* (1854).[187] How

---

[182] On the potential of the British nursery school, see S. Isaacs, *The Educational Value of the Nursery School* (London: Nursery School Association of Great Britain and Northern Ireland, 1954). The redemptive power of nature to transform the alienated child was famously depicted in the 1970 Ken Loach film, *Kes*, about a bullied boy's encounter with a kestrel in a dour northern mining community.

[183] For the Climbié case, see Lord Laming, *The Victoria Climbié Inquiry* (London: HMSO, 2003). This report was the starting-point for the new emphasis on emotional well-being in British schools.

[184] Child suicides do not necessarily leave notes, though their feelings in the days leading up to the act are today sometimes recoverable through internet messages. For an example, see *The Times*, 29 Jan. 2005, p. 31 (on the state of mind of a fourteen-year-old French girl).

[185] The poem was received anonymously many years ago by Rosemary Peacocke.

[186] R. Rey, *History of Pain* (Paris: La Découverte, 1993), esp. intro.

[187] Smike is abused more than the other boys at the appalling Doodleboys Hall because he is stupid and penniless, while Sissy is dismissed as ignorant by Gradgrind and M'Choakumchild because she has an imaginative not a numerical understanding of the world.

all unhappy children react too is both culturally conditioned and very personal. When children have agency, their behaviour cannot be totally predicted. Like all human beings, they are complex, vulnerable and never really fathomable. It is the poet, not the historian or the anthropologist, who best expresses the irreducible and indomitable 'I' that is at the heart of us all.

He always
He always wanted to explain things but no-one cared
So he drew.
Sometimes he would draw and it wasn't anything,
He wanted to carve it in stone or write it in the sky.
He would lie out on the grass and look up in the sky and it would be only the sky and
    the things inside him that needed saying
And it was after that that he drew the picture
It was a beautiful picture. He kept it under his pillow and would let no one see it.
And he would look at it every night and think about it.
And when it was dark and his eyes were closed he could see it still.
And it was all of him and he loved it.
When he started school he brought it with him
Not to show anyone, but just to have it with him like a friend.
It was funny at school.
He sat in a square brown desk like all the other square brown desks and he thought it
    would be red.
And his room was a square brown room, like all the other rooms.
And it was tight and close. And stiff.
He hated to hold the pencil and the chalk, with his arm stiff and his feet flat on the
    floor, stiff, with the teacher watching and watching.
The teacher came and spoke to him.
She told him to wear a tie like all the other boys.
He said he didn't like them and she said it didn't matter.
After that they drew. And he drew all yellow and it was the way he felt about morning.
    And it was beautiful.
The teacher came and smiled at him. 'What's this?' she said.
'Why don't you draw something like Keith's drawing?
Isn't it beautiful?'
After that his mother brought him a tie and he always drew aeroplanes and rocket ships
    like everyone else.
And he threw the old picture away.
And when he lay alone looking at the sky, it was big and blue, and all of everything, but
    he wasn't anymore.
He was square and brown inside and his hands were stiff
And he was like everyone else. All the things inside him that needed saying didn't need
    it anymore.
It had stopped pushing. It was crushed.
Stiff.
Like everything else.

Index